INTERNATIONAL ECONOMICS

THE IRWIN SERIES IN ECONOMICS

Consulting Editor
LLOYD G. REYNOLDS
Yale University

AMES *Soviet Economic Processes*

ANDERSON, GITLOW, & DIAMOND (eds.) *General Economics: A Book of Readings* rev. ed.

BALASSA *The Theory of Economic Integration*

BEAL & WICKERSHAM *The Practice of Collective Bargaining* 3d ed.

BLAUG *Economic Theory in Retrospect* rev. ed.

BORNSTEIN (ed.) *Comparative Economic Systems: Models and Cases*

BORNSTEIN & FUSFELD (eds.) *The Soviet Economy: A Book of Readings* rev. ed.

BUCHANAN *The Public Finances* rev. ed.

CARTTER *Theory of Wages and Employment*

CARTTER & MARSHALL *Labor Economics: Wages, Employment, and Trade Unionism*

DAVIDSON, SMITH, & WILEY *Economics: An Analytical Approach* rev. ed.

DAVIS, HUGHES, & MCDOUGALL *American Economic History: The Development of a National Economy* rev. ed.

DOLL, RHODES, & WEST *Economics of Agricultural Production, Markets, and Policy*

DRUMMOND *The Canadian Economy: Organization and Development*

DUE *Government Finance: Economics of the Public Sector* 4th ed.

DUE & CLOWER *Intermediate Economic Analysis* 5th ed.

FELLNER *Probability and Profit: A Study of Economic Behavior along Bayesian Lines*

FERGUSON *Microeconomic Theory*

INTERNATIONAL ECONOMICS

CHARLES P. KINDLEBERGER, PH.D.

PROFESSOR OF ECONOMICS
MASSACHUSETTS INSTITUTE OF TECHNOLOGY

Fourth Edition · 1968

RICHARD D. IRWIN, INC.

Homewood, Illinois

FOURTH EDITION

First Printing, March, 1968
Second Printing, September, 1968
Third Printing, December, 1968

Library of Congress Catalog Card No. 67–30239

PRINTED IN THE UNITED STATES OF AMERICA

PREFACE

The fourth edition has been reorganized in response to a modest but perceptible demand from instructors. The earlier arbitrary organization based on the balance of payments is now discarded, and the book is divided fundamentally into halves, of three parts each, corresponding to a semester of international trade and one of international monetary problems. This means that the balance-of-payments chapter, which used to be something of a stumbling block for some students, has been relegated from pride of place as Chapter 2 to a position in the rear ranks. Other changes are the addition of explicit chapters on trade theory and commercial policy for less developed countries, and one on economic integration; the elimination of the separate chapter on exchange control; and the telescoping of material on disequilibrium. The result in my judgement is a more orderly, logical, and readily comprehended treatment. The instructor limited to a one-semester course will be guided by his own interests and requirements. My own suggestion, for what it may be worth, is that such a semester include fourteen chapters, and in particular Chapters 2, 3, 4, 7, 8, 11, 12, 15, 16, 17, 18, 23, 24, and 27.

The gains from this reorganization have been partly compromised by the intrusion of an idiosyncratic bias in the treatment of balance-of-payments equilibrium and international financial intermediation— "personal piffle," to use a phrase of Paul Samuelson, which he believes should be rigorously excluded from works like this. The major task throughout, however, is to incorporate the advances in the theory of international trade and finance to the extent that I am able to comprehend them. The amount of purely institutional description of such agencies as the International Fund and Bank has been reduced in the interest of more analysis.

The level of treatment remains high but nonmathematical, except for the appendices on the Marshall-Lerner condition and the foreign-trade multiplier, prepared, for this edition, by Professor Miltiades Chacholiades. This is not so much the result of adroit marketing as of limited capacity. But while recognizing that advanced students must go forward and work in abstract formulations, I am persuaded that the visual approach through geometry, related to historical and institutional discussion, retains an important place. It enables the general student to

vii

obtain a mastery of the subject at a respectable level, and constructs a base from which the specialized student can penetrate the subtleties.

My thanks are due to a long list of correspondents who have pointed out errors, raised questions, and debated interpretations through the third and earlier editions. The list is too long to detail. Most are instructors; some intrepid souls were students. Like all textbook writers, I applaud them for their valuable contribution. I am grateful to Professors Pranab Bardhan and John H. Williamson, with whom I taught international trade and international monetary theory, respectively, at M.I.T. in the academic year 1966–67. Many of their ideas are incorporated in this revision. Dr. Scott Pardee, Foreign Manager, Federal Reserve Bank of New York, generously commented on Chapters 23 to 27 in painstaking detail, and provided a number of concrete suggestions for improvement, almost all of which were eagerly adopted. Barry Friedman performed faithfully as a research assistant. Miss Deirdre Evans worked cheerily and competently with the typewriter, the scissors, and the paste.

C. P. KINDLEBERGER

Massachusetts Institute of Technology
September, 1967

P.S.   The devaluation of the pound on November 18, 1967, and the imposition of controls on direct investment by the United States in January 1968 caught this work between galleys and page proof. The first event is taken into account only by changing the foreign-exchange rate of the pound from $2.80 to $2.40 in all examples. The second is unhappily altogether ignored.

January, 1968   C.P.K.

TABLE OF CONTENTS

PART II. COMMERCIAL POLICY

PART III. INTERNATIONAL RESOURCE ALLOCATION: TAXATION AND MIGRATION

ments of the Host Country. The Exploitation of Less Developed Countries. The International Corporation. Efficiency and Citizenship. Harmonization of National Policies. Summary.

PART VI. BALANCE-OF-PAYMENTS EQUILIBRIUM AND INTERNATIONAL MONETARY ARRANGEMENTS

APPENDIXES

INDEXES

LIST OF ILLUSTRATIONS

xvi · *LIST OF ILLUSTRATIONS*

LIST OF TABLES

Chapter
1

THE STUDY OF INTER-
NATIONAL ECONOMICS

International Trade and Economics

The student approaching international economics for the first time may well ask why it is a separate branch of economics. Money and banking, labor economics, and price theory are all reasonably distinct parts of the subject. International trade, however, seems to be merely general economics applied in a particular context. Why not treat the allocation and exchange parts under microeconomics and the monetary and income parts under macroeconomics, and have done with it?

This is a legitimate question, and it can be answered in a number of ways. International trade is treated as a distinct subject because of tradition, because of the urgent and important problems presented by international economic questions in the real world, because it follows different laws from domestic trade, and because its study illuminates and enriches our understanding of economics as a whole.

The International Trade Tradition

In today's world of rapid intellectual change, many students will find tradition a not very compelling reason for studying international trade. It may be satisfactory to segregate international trade in the history of economic thought and learn what Adam Smith, Ricardo, Mill, and Marshall thought about it. But if Bertil Ohlin, the modern Swedish economist, proved that there is no intrinsic difference between interregional and international trade, why not include international with interregional economics?

The separation of international trade as a subject, however, is not based solely on theoretical discussions of the topic. Facts and figures are needed to convert economics from political philosophy into a social science. Data were originally available from two sources: from the separate markets of towns and villages and from the information collected by the king's custom. The market data could not be added up to get a complete picture because not all markets were covered. By aggregating the information collected at the separate ports of entry, however, one could form an overall picture of foreign trade, correct except for errors due to smuggling. Foreign-trade statistics were thus the first source of material for empirical investigation into economics. And the study of the relations between economic entities must start at the level of the nation, the only unit for which we have adequate data.

International Economic Problems

But there are more, and more significant, reasons for studying international economics as a separate subject. Its details may not differ in kind, but they certainly differ in degree. Problems of money and banking, wages, and prices—to use the three separate branches of economics with which we began our comparison—are more difficult of solution in an international than in a national context.

In money and banking, the more difficult character of international problems is self-evident. Foreign exchange crises are chronic in some countries such as Argentina, India, and Turkey, and sporadic in others such as Britain. After almost 10 years of balance-of-payments surpluses, the countries of Europe began to experience alternating surpluses and deficits after about 1963. In the United States, there is some doubt as to what is the right balance-of-payments concept to use, and even, in the writer's opinion, there is doubt whether the country has the persistent deficit it is widely believed to labor under. These problems testify to the unsettled character of international payments as contrasted with those within a country.

Interregional wage difficulties arise, but are of a different order of magnitude from those in international trade. Textile workers in New England, for example, are strong advocates of higher wages for textile workers in the Carolinas and other areas of southern competition. Union settlements in the steel industry now include no regional wage differentials for the same job categories. The Teamsters Union aims for a single scale of rates for truck drivers across the country. But these examples are rare within the United States. For the most part, local industry is not particularly conscious of, or interested in, the return to competitors in other parts of the country. In international trade, on the other hand, we continually hear about the competition of "pauper labor" in foreign countries.

Interregional problems of price arise with more frequency. Farmers want parity; and city dwellers worry about the high cost of living. In periods of emergency, price controls are imposed to alter the operations of the price system. Internationally, however, the price seems seldom to be right. Underdeveloped countries complain about the low returns on the primary products which they sell and demand "fair and equitable" prices, whether for Brazilian coffee, Chilean copper, Malayan rubber and tin, and so on. One can have the interesting picture of underdeveloped countries worrying about their declining terms of trade—the relation between the prices at which they sell, and those at which they buy—at the same time that developed countries, especially Britain, regard the terms of trade at which they deal as seriously adverse.

This is not a conclusive demonstration. There is, however, something of a presumption that economic problems are different, and more difficult of solution, when they run between countries than when they lie within the jurisdiction of a single government.

Those international problems are pressing, as well as difficult of solution. Moreover, they have a way of changing. In the 1920's, the important problem was how to transfer German reparations to the Allies and Allied war debts to the United States. In the 1930's the major problem was employment; its international aspect was how to prevent one country from exporting its unemployment to others. After World War II, the international problem changed again—from reconstruction in Europe and the Far East in the late 1940's, to the expansion of trade and the restoration of convertibility in the 1950's, to a diverse array in the late 1960's: deficits in the balance of payments of the United States, which have replaced the dollar shortage of the postwar period up through 1957; international economic integration in Europe, with or without Britain, and among the developing countries of various regions in Central America, Latin America, the Middle East, East Africa, and so on; trade between the developed and the less developed world, including the barriers to trade which have been lowered among the developed countries, but remain embarassingly high on imports from the less developed countries which the developed world is committed to assist; and the transformation of the present international monetary system, which many economists, financiers, and politicians find unsatisfactory in one or another respect, into something which will occasion less concern.

Interregional versus International Trade

What distinction between interregional trade and international trade can account for the differences in the character and intensity of the economic problems which arise in them? Why does international trade follow different laws of behavior from those of domestic trade?

Here it is possible to collect a number of different answers, no one

of which necessarily implies a denial of the others. The classical economists found the difference in the behavior of the factors of production—land, labor, and capital. A few people appear to believe that the
difference lies in the fact of different moneys and monetary systems.
Modern liberal economists, using the word "liberal" in a special sense,
believe that the crux of the matter is interference by the state. Political
theory would ascribe the difference to national solidarity.

It is important, however, to underline one aspect of interregional
and international trade which distinguishes them both from the rest of
economics. In these subjects space becomes important. General equilibrium theory normally appears to operate as if a national economy were
located at a single point in space and as if national economies were
separate points close beside one another. Goods and services then move
in costless fashion. In interregional and international trade this is shown
not to be so. For many purposes the assumption of costless transfer is
borrowed from general equilibrium theory. But for others, it is explicitly laid aside. In Chapter 6 we discuss the effects of space on prices, the
movement of goods, and the location of industry.

Factor Mobility

In differentiating international from domestic trade, the classical
economists stressed the behavior of the factors of production. Labor and
capital were mobile within a country, they believed, but not internationally. Even land was mobile within a country, if we mean occupationally
rather than physically. The same land, for example, could be used
alternatively for growing wheat or raising dairy cattle, which gave it a
restricted mobility.

The importance of this intranational mobility of the factors of
production was that returns to factors tended to equality within, but not
between, countries. The wages of Frenchmen of a given training and
skill were expected to be more or less equal; but this level of wages bore
no necessary relation to those of comparable Germans or Italians, Eng-
lishmen or Australians. If a weaver received higher wages in Lyons than
in Paris, Parisian weavers would migrate to Lyons in sufficient numbers
to bring down wages there and raise them in Paris, until equality had
been restored. But no such forces are at work between Lyons and Milan,
Dresden, Manchester, or New Bedford. The wages of weavers in these
cities are independently determined and can fluctuate without affecting
one another. The same equality of return within a country, but inequality internationally, was believed to be true of land and capital.

Today it is thought that this distinction of the classical economists has been made too rigorously. There is some mobility of factors internationally: immigration has been important for the United States and is currently of great significance to the economic life of Australia, Argentina, and Israel, to name but a few examples. Emigration has been a factor in the economic life of many European countries, but perhaps outstandingly of Ireland, now Eire, and Italy. Perhaps the most interesting aspect of migration in the postwar period, however, has been the mass movement, affecting as many as 4 million workers from the Mediterranean countries of Portugal, Spain, southern Italy, Greece, and Turkey northward across the mountains especially to France, Germany, and Switzerland. The movement slowed down in 1966 as recession slowed down European growth, but it did not reverse itself very far. There is even a sense in which it is now possible to think of a European market for labor.

There is also some considerable degree of immobility within countries. The example used of Paris and Lyons is particularly unapt because the French do not typically move about. Migration within the United States takes place on a broad scale under the influence of major forces such as war. The invasion of Ohio, Michigan, and Illinois by the South in and immediately following World War I was paralleled by a similar movement to California and Texas in World War II. But movement on this scale is not normal.

It may be accurate to say that there is a difference of degree in factor mobility interregionally and internationally and that in the usual case people will migrate within their own country more readily than they will emigrate abroad. Identity of language, customs, and tradition cannot be assumed between parts of the same country, but they are more likely than between countries.

Capital is also more mobile within than between countries. It is not, however, completely mobile within countries; and regional differences in interest rates do exist. At the same time, it is not completely immobile between countries. We shall see in Part V what happens when capital moves from country to country.

To the extent that there are differences in factor mobility and equality of factor returns, internationally as compared with interregionally, international trade will follow different laws. If there is a shift in demand from New England pure woolens to southern synthetic woolen compounds, capital and labor will move from New England to the South. If, however, there is a shift in demand from French to Italian silk, no such movement of capital and labor to Italy takes place. Some other adjustment mechanism is needed.

Different Moneys

To the man in the street the principal difference between domestic and international trade is that the latter involves the use of different moneys. A dollar is accepted in California and in Maine. But the Swiss franc, which is the coin of the realm in Basel, must be converted into French francs or German Deutschemarks before it can be used to buy goods in Strasbourg in France or Freiburg in Germany, each but a few miles away.

With a little more sophistication, however, it is evident that the important fact is not the different moneys so much as the possibility of change in their relative value. When Switzerland, Belgium, and France belonged to the Latin Monetary Union and all three francs were convertible into each other on a one-for-one basis, an individual would be almost indifferent whether he held one franc or another, unless he were on the verge of making a purchase. For actual buying, it was necessary to have the unit acceptable to the seller; but if exchange rates were fixed, currencies convertible, and both were expected to remain so, one currency was as good as another.

This aspect of international trade is evidently linked to the mobility of capital. One of the reasons capital moves freely in the United States is that a dollar is a dollar from Florida to Minnesota (although not necessarily in purchasing power from 1932 to 1968). There are other reasons for the internal mobility of capital, such as the existence of a single law covering creditor and debtor, which makes debts more readily collectible, but the elimination of all currency risks and uncertainty is an outstanding one. If the exchange rate may move, the mobility of capital is likely to be affected. In some cases, capital movements will be increased: the prospect of appreciation of the German mark against the British pound attracts British capital. But the risk of a change in the value of foreign currencies on balance tends to make people keep their capital at home. On the other hand, after a long period of stable exchange rates, capital becomes more venturesome in moving over the world, and international mobility approaches that which obtains within countries.

If all currencies of the world were on the gold standard at fixed and unchanging rates, then, as we shall see in greater detail later, exchange rates would be fixed. On this showing, it is the fact that different countries follow different foreign exchange policies, rather than the existence of different national moneys, which distinguishes international from domestic trade.

Different National Policies

Foreign exchange, however, is only one of a number of areas in which countries can pursue separate ways. Closely associated with the exchange value of a currency is its internal value, which may be affected by policies in the field of money and banking, government debt management, federal expenditure, and taxation. Tariff policy, action with respect to quotas, subsidies, and other controls of trade are also adopted by governments to interfere with the course of trade between nations.

This is not to assert that governments do not interfere in the economic life of regions. They do. The difference, however, is that for the most part this interference is based on general principles affecting individuals, and the geographic incidence of the effects is a matter of accident. In international trade, however, the liberal economist tells us, national policy is undertaken in order to achieve a geographic effect.

We may illustrate what we mean by the example of progressive taxation. If we tax incomes progressively within a country by legislating proportionately higher taxes on higher incomes, regional results will follow. The richer regions will pay a higher proportion of the yield of the tax, and poorer regions a lesser. But this is quite different from levying taxes by regions. The poorer man in the rich region pays only the same tax as a man of equal income in the poorer region, under the first of these two methods. If regions were taxed, on the other hand, he might pay more, the same amount, or less, depending upon how the burden of the tax was shared within regions. In international trade, independent national policies affect the separate national units as such, whereas within a country national policies affect the various regions incidentally in the course of legislating about individuals.

The liberal economist of a somewhat earlier day had the answer to this. If all national policies in the field of international economic relations were identical, then differences of incidence would be comparable to those which follow in a region. Governmental policy should be one of noninterference in the working of certain tried and true measures or rules of thumb, handed down by tradition. These measures were the gold standard, the small and balanced budget, and free trade. The policy of laissez-faire or noninterference applied only to trade. Positive measures were called for in the monetary and fiscal areas. If these rules were obeyed, the state would not interfere, and trade would be conducted only among firms and consumers whose nationality did not matter.

There would be no reason to think of the French market for wheat, since there would be no need to distinguish between French consumers and those of any other national group.

Separate Markets

Apart from purposeful state interference, however, national markets are frequently separate. On occasion, the reason for this separation will be interference by the state for national reasons. The British drive on the left. The French drive on the right. These traffic regulations are decreed by governments for national traffic safety. Since it is safer to sit close to the side of the car which passes the stream of traffic coming in the opposite direction, the British use right-hand drive cars, the French left-hand. To export automobiles to foreign markets requires a variety of design changes which slow down the assembly line, raise costs, and separate markets to some extent.

But markets are also separated by language, custom, usage, habit, taste, and a host of other causes of difference. Standards differ. Some goods are designed in inches, feet, pounds, and short tons; some in metric measurements. Even within the nonmetric system, the Americans reckon oil in barrels per day, the British in short tons per year. Export and import trade must get outside of the culture of the domestic market to become acquainted with different goods, described in different words, using differing measurements, bought and sold on different terms, for different currency units.

Politically Different Units

These cultural distinctions between markets, important in the absence of different national measures, have led political scientists to take a look at the nature of countries. This brings us to perhaps the most significant distinction of all. A country organizes itself into a political unit, when it does so successfully, because its citizens and subjects have a sense of cohesion or belonging together. There may be more or less power applied from the top to repress deviations from the national pattern of behavior. But there must be some centripetal force, or the country falls to pieces. The point was emphasized by Ortega y Gasset in *Invertebrate Spain,* explaining how the centrifugal forces of regional antagonism, class warfare, and individual distrust shook the weak central government in the 1930's and led to the Civil War.

There may be regional pride. This is particularly noteworthy among Texans, Californians, and inhabitants of smaller areas in the United States. But if a country is flourishing, particularism is a subject for humor and sentiment rather than decision and action. Individuals belong to various groups of differing coverage—family, town, church, lodge, political party, profession, college, state, and region; but their primary loyalty runs to the nation, and every other geographical loyalty is secondary.

This cohesion of the national group helps to explain national differences in tastes and custom, which are dividers of national markets. It also explains the fact of national economic policies. Government has a responsibility to the national group, which transcends its responsibility, in the liberal formulas, to the nationals of other countries or to a world code. In the 19th century this was true to a lesser extent than it is today, with the increase of national sentiment and the breakdown of the old international community. It has frequently been said that members of the *haute bourgeoisie*—upper middle class—of widely different countries were closer spiritually to each other a hundred years ago than they were to the working class of their own community. Under these circumstances, an international code was possible. It would not be today. The difference between interregional and international trade is that trade between regions is trade among the same group, whereas trade between countries runs between different cohesive units. Friedrich List a hundred years ago expressed it: "Domestic trade is among us; international trade is between us and them."

This is one way of stating the difference, and a way which is suggestive of the links which run between international economics and international politics. But there are other ways, more positive and more hopeful. The task of international economics is to find, if it can, a basis for economic relationships which will be satisfactory among the various components of a peaceful world. This statement may be said to apply within the North Atlantic community of developed nations, to extend to relations between developed and developing nations in the West, or to embrace East and West, developed and developing countries alike, as one chooses.

National Economic Life

The view of international economics as relating to the economic relations between national units of more or less internal political cohesion should not altogether neglect the valuable insights afforded into the changing character of the individual units themselves. This takes us back, in part, to the initial view that we have data for national units but not for constituent regions. But the point has more significance.

This is a world in which national independence has had a new lift in the years since World War II. Along with the political independence has grown a demand for economic self-reliance and self-esteem, expressed largely in plans and hopes for economic development. Increasing production, capital formation, and consumption are being sought in national units. A study of international trade has some purpose in enabling us to understand what is taking place, how development has occurred in other cases, and how other countries of the world are likely to be affected by the economic changes now burgeoning.

The interest of the United States in economic development is not confined to its indirect concern in the growing younger countries of the world. The developmental process extends to the final stages of decline and decay. In some quarters it may be regarded as indecent to contemplate the possibility of this country's ceasing to be the richest and most powerful nation in the world. But other countries have had to adjust their thinking in this regard. In particular, Britain has had to face an adjustment in its world economic and political position. It is unlikely that the laws of social, political, and economic development, which carry over into a stage of decline, will be set aside in the case of our country. The theory of international trade has lessons to offer on how a country makes the best adjustment to its position in the world.

Widening the Economic and Political Unit

At the same time as political and economic nationalism is growing in Africa, Asia, Latin America, and the Middle East, the old answers in terms of national interest have lost much of their validity in Europe and North America. While France holds out to some degree, the smaller countries of Europe, and to a considerable extent Italy and Germany, find national boundaries too confining. With the disintegration of the economic ties of the British Commonwealth, Britain feels the need to enter a wider economic entity. The United States, Canada, and Western Europe all cooperate in the economic partnership of the Organization for Economic Cooperation and Development and lowered tariffs in the Kennedy Round of 1967. Increasingly international corporations which used to produce entirely in one country have extended their horizons to the world as a whole and constructed facilities in Europe, Japan, and the underdeveloped countries. Civil servants of international bodies, cooperating national governmental officials and economically linked business executives may forge new common elements in a new international community.

In a world of rising nationalism, rising internationalism or both, international economics is an important tool of understanding and negotiation.

Scheme of the Book

The previous editions of this book have been organized on an explicitly arbitrary basis which patterned itself after the balance of payments, which was discussed along with the foreign exchange market and the adjustment process, immediately following this introductory chapter. Increasingly, however, this has proved to be too arbitrary, and the present edition produces a substantial alteration.

The book deals first with microeconomic aspects of international economics—the pure theory of trade and the theory of commercial policy, and then with macroeconomic policy—the adjustment mechanism, the movement of capital, the balance of payments, and the international monetary system. There is some slight expositional inconvenience, in that one must discuss, say, the balance-of-payments aspects of tariffs before the adjustment process has been dealt with. But this inconvenience is far less important than the gain in logical form. Part I which follows deals with the pure theory of trade, and the effects on it of changes in technology, economic development, and transport costs. Part II covers commercial policy. Part III treats two special problems which are not usually covered in books on international economics, but which are of increasing importance: international taxation and labor migration. This completes the first or microeconomic half of the book. The second, dealing with macroeconomic questions is also divided into three parts, Part IV on the adjustment process, Part V on capital movements, and Part VI on the balance of payments and international monetary arrangements.

Summary

International economics, which is a traditional branch of the discipline, has a more solid basis for separate study than tradition. It differs from domestic or interregional trade in degree. Factor mobility is greater between regions than between countries; and equalization of factor prices is therefore greater. National markets also differ more widely than regional markets on grounds of tastes, customs, habits. But international trade can also be distinguished in kind from domestic trade. It runs between different political units, each with a sovereign government responsible for the well-being of the unit. This accounts for differences in national economic policies—in monetary, exchange, trade, wage, and similar areas.

Interregional and international trade are both concerned with problems of overcoming space. The relative abundance of records on the trade of nations, as contrasted with that of regions, makes the former a better subject for the study of the growth and decay of complex economic, political, and social entities.

BIBLIOGRAPHICAL NOTE

Additional reading is provided in separate chapters on an annotated basis, to distinguish between treatments of the same material on different levels, both less and more difficult, to point the student in the direction of deeper treatments of portions of it, and to provide references for particular points made in the text (since there are no footnotes). These are grouped separately under "Texts," "Treatises, Etc.," and "Points." Since economists are concerned especially with price, particular attention is paid to paperback editions which the student may want to add to his library.

The five textbooks most frequently referred to by name of the author, will consist in:

Delbert A. Snider, *Introduction to International Economics* (4th ed.; Homewood, Ill.: Richard D. Irwin, Inc., 1967), which is less difficult than this book.

Leland B. Yeager, *International Monetary Relations* (New York: Harper & Row, Publishers, 1966), which is about of the same degree of difficulty as this book but with emphasis on the financial portion of the material.

M. O. Clement, R. L. Pfister, and K. J. Rothwell, *Theoretical Issues in International Economics* (Boston: Houghton Mifflin Co., 1967), which pursues relatively few subjects in some depth.

Murray C. Kemp, *The Pure Theory of International Trade* (Englewood Cliffs, N.J.: Prentice-Hall, Inc., 1964), which operates at a high and mathematical level of abstraction.

Jaroslav Vanek, *International Trade Theory and Economy Policy* (Homewood, Ill.: Richard D. Irwin, Inc., 1962), also fairly advanced.

Under "Treatises" will be found repeated references to a few books which the student may want to consider adding to his or her personal library (if he or she proposes to go more deeply into international economics), and which no college or university library should be without. These include:

American Economic Association, *Readings in the Theory of International Trade* (Homewood, Ill.: Richard D. Irwin, Inc. [formerly Philadelphia: The Blakiston Co.], 1949).

American Economic Association, *Readings in International Economics* (Homewood, Ill.: Richard D. Irwin, Inc., 1967). These two volumes are collections of outstanding articles from the periodical literature.

Richard E. Caves, *Trade and Economic Structure* (Cambridge, Mass.: Harvard University Press, 1960).

G. Haberler, *The Theory of International Trade* (London: Macmillan & Co., Ltd., 1937).

Harry G. Johnson, *International Trade and Economic Growth* (London: George Allen & Unwin, Ltd., 1958).

J. E. Meade, *The Theory of International Economic Policy,* Vol. I, *The Balance of Payments* (New York: Oxford University Press, Inc., 1951).

J. E. Meade, *A Geometry of International Trade* (London: George Allen
& Unwin, Ltd., 1952).

J. E. Meade, *The Theory of International Economic Policy*, Vol. II, *Trade
and Welfare* (New York: Oxford University Press, Inc., 1955).

J. Viner, *Studies in the Theory of International Trade* (New York:
Harper & Bros., 1937).

Other articles in the major professional journals will be referred to by
abbreviations as follows:

> *AER—American Economic Review*
> *EIF—Essays on International Finance* (Princeton)
> *EJ—Economic Journal* (London)
> *Econ—Economica* (London)
> *JPE—Journal of Political Economy*
> *MS—The Manchester School*
> *OEP—Oxford Economic Papers*
> *QJE—Quarterly Journal of Economics*
> *RES—Review of Economic Studies* (London)
> *RE & S—Review of Economics and Statistics*
> *SP—Staff Papers* (of the International Monetary Fund)

The Princeton International Finance Section has made a major contribution to the literature in international economics in recent years, under the
editorship of Fritz Machlup, with *Essays on International Finance, Studies in
International Finance,* and *Special Papers in International Economics.* Summa-
ries of articles in the field are contained in the *Journal of Economic Abstracts*
published by the American Economic Association, which gathers précis of
articles from journals all over the world by subject matter and uses International
Economics as a category.

We may note here, since there is no better or more appropriate situation
for it in this book, a series of articles summarizing and reviewing the theory of
international trade—as has apparently become fashionable in recent years. These
include:

Lloyd A. Metzler, "The Theory of International Trade," in H. S. Ellis
(ed.), *A Survey of Contemporary Economics* (Philadelphia: The Blakiston Co., 1948).

Norman S. Buchanan, "International Finance," in B. F. Haley (ed.), *A
Survey of Contemporary Economics,* Vol. II (Homewood, Ill.: Richard
D. Irwin, Inc., 1952).

Gottfried Haberler, "A Survey of International Trade Theory," Princeton
Special Papers in International Economics, No. 1, July, 1961.

J. Bhagwati, "The Pure Theory of International Trade," *EJ,* March, 1964.

W. M. Corden, "Recent Developments in the Theory of International
Trade," Princeton *Special Papers in International Economics,* No. 7,
March, 1965.

John S. Chipman, "A Survey of the Theory of International Trade,"
Econometrica, July, 1965; October, 1965; and January, 1966—abstract
and difficult.

Since many courses require term papers on international economic problems, it may be useful to list the major international sources of statistical and other material. Domestic statistical yearbooks, annual economic reports (of the President or the Chancellor of the Exchequer), monthly and annual trade and financial statistics, etc., must of course be consulted for some problems.

The two major sources for current data are: International Monetary Fund (IMF), *International Financial Statistics* (monthly), which is organized by countries; and United Nations (UN), *Monthly Bulletin of Statistics* (monthly), where data for a wide number of countries are gathered by function.

For detailed international trade data, the UN's *Direction of World Trade* (monthly) and its *Yearbook of International Trade Statistics* may be consulted.

In addition to these statistics, the United Nations publishes a series of useful annual reports and in some instances quarterly bulletins of analysis from its headquarters in New York and its regional commissions for Europe, Latin America, Asia, and the Far East and Africa. Particularly outstanding are the annual *Economic Survey of Europe in 196–* and the *World Economic Report.*

The Bank for International Settlements has published an *Annual Report* on international financial questions since 1931.

The contracting parties to the General Agreement on Tariffs and Trade (GATT) put out an annual report entitled *International Trade,* followed by the appropriate year since 1952.

A highly useful reference book for the interpretation of statistics of international economic significance is R. G. D. Allen and J. S. Ely (eds.), *International Trade Statistics* (New York: John Wiley & Sons, Inc., 1953).

The two outstanding sources of information on world economic questions, of course, are *The New York Times* and *The Economist* (London weekly). It has frequently been remarked that the United States badly lacks the equivalent of the latter, an informed weekly magazine of opinion on international economic and political questions; but, like the weather, nobody has successfully done anything about it.

Finally student and teacher alike should bear in mind the flood of useful and stimulating material which flows, at least in the United States, from the legislative process. Hearings before committees of the Congress, reports commissioned by these same bodies, information (or propaganda) from the Executive Branch, from lobbies, including such representative bodies as the U.S. Chamber of Commerce and the AFL–CIO and such disinterested groups as the Committee on Economic Development and the League of Women Voters—much in the way of fact and opinion can be gleaned from a variety of sources when legislation is before the Congress. Particularly useful are the compendia and hearings before the Joint Economic Committee of the Congress of the United States on international aspects of the U.S. economy. This material is rich in nuggets of fact and opinion, but difficult to find one's way through.

SUGGESTED READING

TREATISES, ETC.

The major work on the subject is B. Ohlin's *Interregional and International Trade* (Cambridge, Mass.: Harvard University Press, 1933; rev. ed.,

1967). This pioneering study advances the proposition that international trade differs but little from interregional as it attempts a complete revision of the theory of international trade.

Lionel Robbins, *Economic Planning and International Order* (London: Macmillan & Co., Ltd., 1937), is representative of the view that the difficulties in international trade come from state interference.

Marina von Neumann Whitman, "International and Interregional Payments Adjustment: A Synthetic View," Princeton *Studies in International Finance,* No. 19 (1967), explores anew the differences between monetary adjustment between and within economies, and presents a useful summary of the literature.

See also Haberler, chap. i; and Viner, Appendix A.

PART I

The Theory of International Trade

THE PURE THEORY OF
INTERNATIONAL TRADE:
SUPPLY

In Part I we start off directly with the theory of international trade. This is the so-called pure theory, which is concerned with basic questions of production and exchange at the barter level, without the intervention of money and monetary problems, and without— though they could be brought into the analysis—international movements of capital or income transfers. The issue is what goods a country will export and import, and at what relative prices, or terms of trade. In Part II we come to interferences with trade, and their removal on a universal or discriminatory basis. The questions posed by national moneys, their exchange one for another, and balance-of-payments adjustment, are left for much later in the book. In the four chapters starting with Chapter 2, we spend half our time, and two chapters, on the classical and neoclassical answer to the question of what goods are traded and at what terms of trade. More complicated answers which derive from more varied assumptions are set forth in the three chapters which follow.

Law of Comparative Advantage

The classical economists asked what goods would be traded between two countries, because they thought the answer for trade between countries was different from that for trade within a country. Within a country, a region produces the goods it can make cheaper than other regions. The value of a commodity within a country, moreover, is determined by its labor content. If the product of a certain industry can be sold for more than the value of the labor it contains, additional labor will transfer into that industry from other occupations. Supply will expand until the price is brought down to the value of the labor it contained. Similarly, if a commodity sells for less than the worth of its labor, labor will move into other lines until the gap is closed. The tendency of wages toward equality within a country results in prices of

19

goods equal to their labor such as to equalize the return to labor in all occupations and regions. If wages are higher in Ohio than in Massachusetts, labor will migrate to Ohio. This will lower wages in Ohio and raise them in Massachusetts, and the movement will continue until the return to labor is equated in the two regions. After labor has spread itself among several regions to equalize wages, these regions will produce and sell to each other what each region can make the cheapest. Its advantage in such commodities over other regions will be absolute, and the theory of trade applicable to regions of a country, is the theory of absolute advantage.

The labor theory of value valid in trade within a country cannot be applied between nations, classical economists thought since factors of production are immobile internationally. If wages are higher in the United States than in Britain, they stay higher, for migration cannot take place on a scale sufficient to eliminate discrepancies. Under these circumstances, the classical economists asked, what will the United States sell to Britain and Britain to America?

Let us assume two countries and two commodities. If each country can produce one good cheaper, i.e., with less labor, than it can be produced in the other, as in the case of domestic trade, each will have an advantage in the production of one commodity and a disadvantage in the production of the other. Each country will then be anxious to export the commodity in which it has an advantage and import the commodity in which it has a disadvantage. The position is suggested in the following table, where wheat can be produced more cheaply in the United States and cloth more cheaply in Britain. The United States has an absolute advantage in wheat and an absolute disadvantage in cloth. It will export wheat and import cloth, which, with the numerical values given, may be assumed to exchange one for the other at something like the rate of one yard of cloth for one bushel of wheat:

PRODUCTION OF ONE MAN IN ONE WEEK

Product	In United States	In United Kingdom
Wheat	6 bushels	2 bushels
Cloth	2 yards	6 yards

But suppose that the labor content of both wheat and cloth is less in the United States than in Britain. Suppose that instead of merely 2 yards of cloth per week a man in the United States can produce 10. The position is then as follows:

PRODUCTION OF ONE MAN IN ONE WEEK

Product	In United States	In United Kingdom
Wheat..............	6 bushels	2 bushels
Cloth...............	10 yards	6 yards

It is evident that labor is more efficient in the United States than in the United Kingdom, and wages in the United States will be higher on that account. But migration by assumption will not take place to equalize wage rates.

Trade cannot now follow the decree of absolute advantage, and a new principle is needed to take its place. This was developed by David Ricardo, more than 150 years ago, in the law of comparative advantage. Ricardo observed that in cases similar to ours, while the United States had an absolute advantage over Britain in both wheat and cloth, it had a greater advantage in wheat than in cloth. He concluded that a country would export the product in which it had the greater advantage, or a comparative advantage, and import the commodity in which its advantage was less, or in which it had a comparative disadvantage. In this example the United States would export wheat and import cloth, even though it could produce cloth more efficiently than Britain.

The reasoning underlying this conclusion may be demonstrated arithmetically. Without international trade, wheat and cloth would exchange for one another at their respective labor contents, which would differ in the two countries. In the United States, 6 bushels of wheat, or one week's labor, would buy 10 yards of cloth. In Britain, by the same token, 6 bushels of wheat—three weeks' labor in the less productive country—would buy 18 yards of cloth. If the United States could get more than 10 yards of cloth for 6 bushels of wheat, or more than 1⅔rds yards per bushel, or anything up to the 3 yards per bushel, which is the price in Britain without trade, it will pay the United States to do so. Conversely, if Britain can get anything more than ⅓ a bushel of wheat per yard of cloth, and something nearer the United States no-trade price of ⁶⁄₁₀ths of a bushel, it pays Britain to trade.

The price ratios should be quoted the same way for comparison. At any price of cloth cheaper than 10 yards for 6 bushels and approaching 18 yards for 6 bushels, it would pay the United States to stop producing cloth at home and to buy it abroad by trading wheat for it. Or at any price of wheat higher than 6 for 10, it pays the United States to sell wheat abroad where it can get a higher return rather than to sell it at home. And conversely for Britain. Trade raises the price of wheat and lowers the price of cloth in the United States; it raises the price of cloth and lowers the price of wheat in Britain. Both countries can gain from specialization and exchange.

On the basis of this type of demonstration, the classical economists concluded that international trade does not require offsetting absolute advantages but is possible where a comparative advantage exists. It goes without saying, but must be said, as it is frequently forgotten, that a comparative advantage is always and by definition accompanied by a comparative disadvantage.

Production Possibilities Curves

The labor theory of value on which this analysis rested was subsequently rejected as invalid. The tendency for the return to labor to be equal throughout a country was seen by observation to be weak and faltering. Labor is not homogeneous. If there is an increase in the demand for barrels, the wages of coopers will rise above those of smiths, with whom they are not interchangeable. It became recognized that there is not one great class of labor with a single wage but a series of noncompeting groups between which the tendency to equalization of wages, at least in the short run, is weak or nonexistent.

A more fundamental objection, however, which would apply even if labor were homogeneous and commanded one price in a perfectly competitive market, is that goods are not produced by labor alone but by various combinations of all the factors of production: land, labor, and capital. To compare the labor content of two commodities—say, gasoline and textiles, or meat and shoes—gives an erroneous view of relative values. Gasoline production requires far more capital per unit of labor than textiles, and meat output more land than shoes. Variable proportions of factors in the production of different commodities make it impossible to use the labor theory of value, however qualified.

An escape from this impasse has been provided by Professor Haberler in the theory of opportunity costs. The cost of wheat in the long run is how much cloth a country has to give up to get additional units of wheat. It makes little difference whether the factors which leave the production of cloth are all suited to the output of wheat or not. The question is simply how much of one commodity must be given up to get more of the other.

The notion of opportunity costs is illustrated in international trade theory with production possibilities or transformation curves. Instead of saying that a week's labor will produce either 6 bushels of wheat or 10 yards of cloth, one says that all the factors of production can produce either 6 bushels of wheat or 10 yards of cloth per some appropriate unit of time, or some intermediate combination of them. In Figure 2.1, where the vertical axis represents wheat and the horizontal axis cloth, the U.S. curve means that the resources of the United States, in the absence of foreign trade, can be used to produce entirely wheat, in which case 6 bushels (per capita per week) can be produced, 10 yards of cloth, or some appropriate intermediate combination, such as 3 bushels of wheat and 5 yards of cloth. The production possibilities curve cannot tell what will in fact be produced. More information is needed for this purpose, on the side of demand. It merely sets out what the possibilities are.

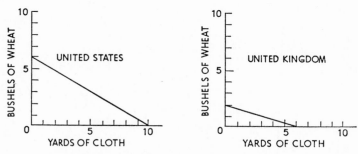

FIG. 2.1.   Production Possibilities Curves, Constant Opportunity Costs

Constant Costs

A straight-line production possibilities curve, such as those in Figure 2.1, indicates constant opportunity costs. At the limits in the United States, all resources can produce either 6 bushels of wheat or 10 yards of cloth. Moreover for any resources shifted out of cloth into wheat or vice versa, 10 units of cloth must be given up to get 6 units of wheat, or the other way round. Six bushels of wheat for 10 yards of cloth is the marginal rate of transformation in production whether all or only a small proportion of total resources are shifted.

A straight-line possibilities curve represents more than constant costs. The slope of the straight line can be taken as a price. Wheat and cloth will exchange in this economy for 6:10. Any higher price for cloth—say, 7:10—will shift resources out of wheat into cloth. The supply of wheat will decline, that of cloth increase, until the price ratio of 6:10 is restored. Any lower price for cloth will similarly shift resources in the other direction until the 6:10 ratio is reestablished.

Let us now take a look at what happens when trade opens up between the United States and Britain. Figure 2.2 shows the two production possibilities curves superimposed upon each other and blown up to the same scale. Instead of showing the two curves of the wheat/cloth scale with wheat at 6 and cloth at 10 and 18 in the two countries, respectively, the scales are enlarged and equated at the cloth end. Without trade, 60 yards of cloth will exchange for 36 bushels of wheat in the United States. In Britain, 60 yards of cloth will exchange for only 20 bushels of wheat.

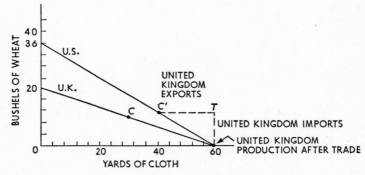

FIG. 2.2. International Trade under Constant Opportunity Costs, 1

Assume that demand conditions were such that before trade the United Kingdom has been consuming 10 bushels of wheat and 30 yards of cloth (at point C on Figure 2.2) on its production possibilities and price line. With a price different from 60:20 made possible by trade, the United Kingdom would be able to reach a higher level of consumption. If it could trade at the U.S. price, for example, it could move from point C to C′ where it could consume 12 of wheat and 40 of cloth—a clear gain of both cloth and wheat. It could do this, it may be observed, if it produced only cloth and exchanged 20 of its total output of 60 for 12 bushels of wheat of the United States. Its production is indicated by the arrow in Figure 2.2, consumption by C′, and exports and imports by the dotted lines converging at T. The horizontal dotted line represents exports of cloth, which, subtracted from total production, leave the amount consumed domestically. The vertical dotted line represents wheat imports. The ratio at which exports and imports exchange for each other—i.e., the slope of the hypotenuse of the right-angle triangle formed by them—is the price line of the United States. In this case the United States has not benefited from foreign trade, exchanging wheat for cloth at 6:10 before and after trade. Production has changed. Twelve additional bushels of wheat are produced and 20 yards less of cloth.

The price after trade may be the same as the price before trade for one of the parties. It cannot be the same for both. The new price may, however, land somewhere between the two prices before trade. It may, for example, settle at 60 yards of cloth for 28 bushels of wheat, as indicated in Figure 2.3. In this case, both parties will gain. The United

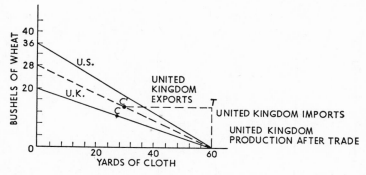

FIG. 2.3.   International Trade under Constant Opportunity Costs, 2

Kingdom will not gain as much as in the previous example, but the United States will share the gains from foreign trade. To demonstrate the fact of the U.S. gain diagrammatically, it is necessary to shift the wheat and cloth axes, or to quote both prices with a common point on the wheat axis, in order to show the U.S. production possibilities curve lying inside the British. It is clear enough without an additional diagram, however, that if the United States can trade wheat for cloth at 60 cloth for 28 wheat instead of 60 cloth for 36 wheat, the country has gained in trade. It can take the gain by increasing its consumption of wheat (giving less wheat for the same amount of cloth), or of cloth (giving the same amount of wheat for more cloth), or, in lesser degree, both. But, so long as it can obtain from trade a higher price for wheat in terms of cloth, it gains.

Under conditions of constant opportunity costs, with straight-line production possibilities curves, specialization in production after trade is likely to be complete. Before trade took place, a country produced some of one good and some of another. To maximize the gain from trading at a higher price, however, it is desirable to sell as much as possible, consonant with the satisfaction of domestic demand for the export article. Thus production will move from a central point on the curve before trade (Fig. 2.2) to one of the limits. It does not pay the United Kingdom, for example, to produce any wheat with resources which can produce either 6 yards of cloth or only 2 bushels of wheat, if the price at which it trades is anything more than 2 bushels of wheat for 6 yards of cloth.

Increasing Opportunity Costs

Our production possibilities curves thus far have been those in which opportunity costs were constant and the ratio between commodity costs equal to price. But the notion that all resources can equally well

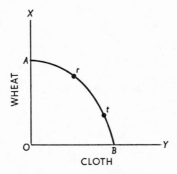

FIG. 2.4*a*. Production Possibilities under Increasing Opportunity Costs

FIG. 2.4*b*. Production with Increasing Opportunity Costs

produce either of two commodities involves an assumption as extreme as the discarded labor theory of value. If all resources are not equally at home in the production of wheat or cloth, but some, such as land and out-of-doors men, are better at wheat, and others, such as spindles, looms, and city folk, are better at cloth, we may have a situation of increasing costs. Some resources may be equally adaptable to wheat or cloth production, but not all are.

The production possibilities curve, under increasing costs, is concave to the origin at *O*. In Figure 2.4*a*, for example, where a production possibilities curve *A–B* is shown, wheat and cloth are fairly substitutable for one another between points *r* and *t* on the curve. To the left of *r*, however, one can get only a small increase in wheat by giving up cloth, primarily because the resources taken out of the production of cloth are not suitable for the production of wheat. Possibly there will be no land with which to combine the labor previously in the textile industry. Similarly, to the right of *t*, a country can get only a little bit more of cloth by giving up a relatively large amount of wheat.

Under increasing costs, the production possibilities curve is not identical with a price curve, as in the case of constant costs. The price at which wheat will exchange for cloth cannot be determined by the production possibilities curve by itself, but can be found only with the assistance of data on demand. The complex of problems presented by demand will be taken up later in the following chapter. At the moment, however, it may be noted that price is indicated by a straight line between the *X* and *Y* axes, the slope of which represents the ratio at which cloth will exchange for wheat, and that production, under a transformation curve representing increasing costs, will take place at the point on the curve tangent to the price in the market. In Figure 2.4*b*, production will take place at *r*, on the production possibilities curve, *AB*, whenever the price is *p–p*. At *r*, production will consist of *O–W* units of wheat and *O–C* units of cloth. If the economy produced cloth and wheat at point *m* on the production possibilities curve, the price *p–p* could not be sustained. At this price there would be too much wheat in relation to cloth or too little cloth in relation to wheat. The unsold quantity of wheat and the unsatisfied demand for cloth would require a change in price to maintain production at *m*.

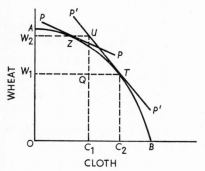

FIG. 2.5. International Trade under Increasing Opportunity Costs

If demand keeps the price at *p–p*, however, it will be possible to earn a higher return in cloth than in wheat, and resources will shift out of wheat into cloth, moving production from *m* toward *r*. This shift of resources will continue until, given the price *p–p* and the production possibilities curve *A–B*, an optimum allocation of resources is reached at point *r*. At this point, the marginal rate of transformation in production will be equal to the marginal rate of transformation through trade.

Foreign trade will take place under increasing costs in broadly the same way as under constant costs, except that complete specialization of a country in a single commodity is not so likely. Figure 2.5 shows such a case. Before trade the United Kingdom price of wheat in terms of cloth is $p-p$, with production at Z. Omitting several steps discussed in the next chapter, by which the price ratio between wheat and cloth after trade is determined, the opening up of trade is assumed to raise the price of cloth in terms of wheat to $p'-p'$. Here $p'-p'$ is a higher price for cloth than $p-p$ (and a lower one for wheat) because more wheat is obtained for a given amount of cloth.

It now pays the United Kingdom to shift resources from the production of wheat into cloth, moving the point of production from Z to T, and exchanging cloth for wheat in foreign trade. The higher the price for cloth, the more resources should be taken out of wheat and put into cloth. Production will settle at that point where the new price is tangent to the production-possibilities curve, i.e., where the price line is equal to the marginal rate of transformation in production.

Exactly how much cloth is exchanged for wheat is again indeterminate with the analytical tools we have developed. Consumption will take place somewhere along the price line, $p'-p'$, to the left of T,—say at U. Let us assume that demand conditions yield the consumption point U. The United Kingdom will then produce $O-C_2$ of cloth and $O-W_1$ of wheat at point T; export C_1-C_2 of cloth and import W_1-W_2 of wheat; and consume $O-W_2$ of wheat and $O-C_1$ of cloth. The quantities C_1-C_2 and W_1-W_2 are equal to $Q-T$ and $Q-U$, which by simple geometry, are exchangeable for one another at the price ratio $p'-p'$. Through trade, Britain will have been enabled to consume more wheat and cloth than it could produce for itself with its own production possibilities.

The failure of specialization to become complete, of course, is due to decreasing returns. As factors less suited for the production of cloth are drawn into that industry, per-yard production costs rise. As factors less suited for production of wheat are drawn from the farms, per-bushel costs of wheat fall. The opposite occurs in the United States. The cost ratios between the two countries may well be equalized before either country specializes in a single product.

Deprived of the labor theory of value and expressed in terms of opportunity costs, the law of comparative advantage is still valid. In a two-good world if one country is more efficient in producing both goods than another country, it profits by concentrating on the product in which it has a greater or comparative advantage and buying the good in which it has a comparative disadvantage. The basic criterion is that with trade it gets a higher price for its specialty or pays a lower price for the commodity in which it is relatively not so productive.

The law of comparative advantage has general validity. Billy Rose, a well-known New York character of a generation ago, was a theatrical impresario and a world champion typist. Despite his championship it paid him to employ a secretary. While he had an absolute advantage over his secretary in typing, his advantage in this activity was narrow compared to that in his other occupation. It therefore paid him and his secretary to specialize.

More generally speaking, if the price of X in terms of Y is lower abroad than at home, it will pay a country to shift resources out of X and into Y, trading Y for X until the prices of X and Y (abstracting from transport costs) are equal at home and abroad. But in these terms the law of comparative costs comes closer to being a law of comparative prices. This would be the case if there were nothing economists could say further about it.

In answer to the question put by the classical economists, the law of comparative costs says that a country exports those products which are comparatively cheap in price at home, and imports those which are comparatively expensive. But economics can say more than this.

Factor Proportions

If international trade is based on differences in comparative costs, the curious student will proceed to the next question: What makes for differences in comparative costs? Why do the transformation curves of various countries differ?

The answer given to this question by the Swedish economist, Bertil Ohlin, is twofold: Different goods, he stated, require different factor inputs; and different countries have different factor endowments. If wheat is technologically best produced with lots of land relative to labor and capital, countries which have an abundance of land will be able to produce wheat cheaply. This is why Australia, Argentina, Canada, Minnesota, and the Ukraine export wheat. On the other hand, if cloth requires much labor relative to capital and land, countries which have an abundance of labor—Hong Kong, Japan, India—will have a comparative advantage in cloth manufacture and be able to export it.

In Appendix A we show how transformation curves are derived from production functions for commodities. It is noted there that there may be some ambiguity about the technological factor proportions involved in producing a given commodity. Where these factor proportions are technically unalterable, we can agree that one commodity is more labor intensive than another. Oil refining is more capital intensive than cabinetmaking, and hydroelectric power generation unambiguously requires land, in the form of specialized waterpower sites. But in the production of many commodities, there is a range within which one factor can be substituted for another. Eggs can be produced by chickens roaming the range, using land, or cooped up in batteries of nests, in which capital substitutes for land and labor. It is impossible to say that one of these commodities is more capital intensive or labor intensive than another until we know more about the possibilities of factor substitution and the factor availabilities.

The factor endowments explanation of trade further rests on the assumption that each country has the same technological possibilities of producing a given good, i.e., that the production functions are the same in both countries. This assumption will be modified in Chapter 4 where we explore the existence of trade based on technological differences between countries.

Again there is considerable difficulty in defining what a factor is for the purpose of using this explanation. For one thing, to define factors broadly as land, labor, and capital, is to overlook the point that these factors are not homogeneous for many purposes but divided into noncompeting groups. It is not enough to have land to raise sheep, but one must have grazing land; nor can minerals be produced by land in general, but only by certain ore-bearing types. Many natural resources are so-called specific factors, limited to one or a few countries. If one defines factors narrowly, and makes separate factors out of noncompeting groups or specific factors, it turns out that much trade is based on absolute advantage, the existence of a factor in one country but not in its trading partner. One can keep the explanation of comparative advantage developed by Ohlin from the insights of his teacher, Eli Heckscher, and overlook noncompeting groups and specific factors, or define factors narrowly, and have to give up their broad explanation of why prices differ before trade.

Related to noncompeting groups of labor is the question whether one can, in fact, separate capital from labor, particularly when some industries are intensive of skilled labor, which takes education, or capital, to produce.

Another difficulty is that it is hard to separate goods from factors, especially when one recognizes that much of world trade is in intermediate goods, goods sought not for final consumption but for use in making other goods. It is not necessary to import copper, lacking copper mines, if one can import copper ore. Britain could produce cotton cloth, without growing cotton, by dint of importing the fiber. But this means that the Heckscher-Ohlin account of comparative advantage should be linked not with commodities, so much as with activities. Mining copper ore must be done in countries with ore deposits, but refining copper can be done anywhere in the world that the abundant capital, skilled labor and copper ore can be combined. The fact that Japan imports iron ore from Australia and coal from the United States, suggests that trade in intermediate goods has reduced the importance of specific factors as an explanation of comparative advantage.

Despite the difficulty of deciding how broadly or narrowly to define factors, and whether to relate factors to commodities or economic activities, most economists regard the Heckscher-Ohlin explanation of trade as broadly true. The United States is thought to be well endowed with capital and to export capital intensive goods. Foreign countries are more favorably situated with respect to labor and sell labor intensive products to the United States. A study by Professor Leontief, however, greatly disturbed the serenity in which these conclusions were held by purporting to demonstrate statistically that the labor content of U.S. exports was higher than that of this country's imports, and that the capital content of imports exceeded that of exports. These findings are still being debated. The debate has been highly useful in producing a thorough examination of the underlying basis of the Ohlin doctrine. For the purpose of what follows in this book, the Leontief claim is taken as not proven and the Ohlin explanation of U.S. trade, modified for technology as in Chapter 4, as presumptively true.

Trade and Factor Efficiency

What about trade between two countries with the same factor proportions and different factor efficiencies (and, what we have yet to discuss, the same tastes)? Suppose we have two countries, Britain and Japan, with the same proportions of land, labor, and capital, but with these factors of production more efficient in Britain than in Japan. Let us assume that labor is not more efficient in Britain than in Japan because it is combined with more capital and land; it merely works harder in every industry. And British land is richer, let us assume, than Japanese; and British machinery more highly developed. Can trade take place then?

The answer is "No." Japanese factors of production will receive less income than British because of their reduced effectiveness in production; but this will not help trade, because all factors receive proportionately less. The production possibilities curves of the two countries will resemble those set forth in Figure 2.6, showing the Japanese capable of producing less than the British. But if tastes are the same in the two countries, the prices of wheat in terms of cloth and cloth in terms of wheat—to restrict ourselves to our two familiar commodities—will be

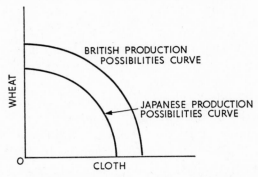

FIG. 2.6. Different Real Costs; Identical Comparative Costs

the same. When the Japanese production possibilities curve is adjusted to a common point with the British, as must be done following the technique of this chapter, it will be seen that the shape of the two curves is identical. This clinches the point that trade is impossible.

It follows from this that it is not the efficiency of factors as a whole which creates a basis for trade but the existence of factor differences, or of differences in factor efficiency which are not the same for all commodities and which are not offset by differences in tastes. If Japanese people were more efficient in cloth, because they had a predilection for city life, and less efficient in agriculture, the basis for a difference in relative prices and for trade would exist.

The fact is, of course, that Japan and Britain have roughly the same factor proportions, and do trade a lot. This is because the real world does not conform to our two-country, two-commodity model. Two countries with identical shapes of their production possibilities curves can both trade with third countries, though not with each other; and in a multicommodity world, two countries with roughly the same factor proportions will find a number of commodities which they can profitably exchange directly.

Equalization of Factor Prices

Trade takes place when relative prices differ between countries, and continues until these relative differences—aside from transportation costs—have been eliminated. In the absence of transportation costs, in fact, trade would equalize relative commodity prices. In a more roundabout way, it may be noted further, trade tends to bring about the equalization of factor prices.

The export of products of the abundant factor increases the demand for its services and makes them relatively less abundant. The import of products embodying large amounts of scarce factors makes those factors less scarce in the domestic market. Exports will raise the price of the abundant and cheap factor; imports will reduce the return to the scarce and expensive factor. For example, the export of farm products from the United States raises the income of agricultural land, and hence its value, while the import of precision instruments reduces the scarcity and hence the return to the type of skilled labor employed in this field.

Under certain limited conditions, this tendency toward factor-price equalization will be carried to the point where factor prices are fully equalized. The assumptions are highly restrictive. There must be as many or more commodities than factors; broadly similar tastes; identical production functions of a simple character, different as between the two commodities and each providing a limited degree of factor substitution; no transport costs or other barriers to trade to inhibit full commodity price equalization; perfect competition; and something of every commodity produced and consumed in every country after trade. Appendix B contains a formal proof of the proposition with two commodities and two factors. But while full factor-price equalization may be an intellectual curiosity rather than a significant proposition for the real world, the tendency toward factor-price equalization is much more meaningful. Trade tends to raise the price of the abundant factor and weaken the price of the scarce factor, and where trade is based on differences in factor endowments, this repercussion of trade on factor prices is vastly important, politically as well as economically.

Increasing Returns

All this has been described in terms of constant and decreasing returns. Economic theorists, moreover, object to discussion of increasing returns because where economies are internal to the firm the assumption is not consistent with the assumption of perfect competition. With competition, increasing returns to the firm would quickly lead to its expansion, until one firm took over an industry, the country, or the world. Economies external to the firm are accepted as legitimate but thought not to be very extensive.

But increasing returns based on internal economies have always played a role in discussion of international trade theory and policy, usually in connection with the infant industry argument for a tariff. This can be justified in one of two ways: as a reflection of a long-run cost curve which falls i.e., moves down and to the right historically, even though at any point in time it is sloping upward; and more recently, as discovered by the theorists, through "learning by doing." In both cases, and where the economies are external to the firm, diagrammatic representation of increasing returns must be undertaken with care, since the path toward lower costs is irreversible.

Increasing returns may be diagrammed in several ways. In Figure 2.7*a* the production possibilities curve *AQB* is convex to the origin and shows decreasing costs of automobiles in terms of agricultural machinery and of agricultural machinery in terms of automobiles, starting from

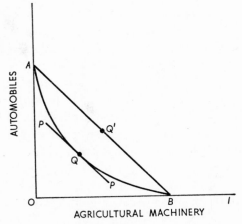

FIG. 2.7*a.*   Increasing Returns, Two Commodities

the position *Q* where the price of automobiles in terms of agricultural machinery is given as *p–p*. If the increasing returns are due to internal economies, *Q* is an unstable equilibrium which cannot exist under competitive conditions. Any slight disturbance, increasing the price of automobiles in terms of agricultural machinery, i.e., flattening the *p–p* line, will make producers shift out of agricultural machinery into automobiles. They will, however, be unable to find a new equilibrium position until they have shifted all their resources and arrive at *A*. If originally the price of agricultural machinery had risen, i.e., if the *p–p* line had become steeper, there would have been a pull toward *B* which would have to continue until *B* was reached.

Figure 2.7*b* shows a position where there are increasing returns in one commodity, but decreasing returns in the other. The production possibilities curve *A–B* between primary products and manufactures starts out from primary production concave to the origin, suggesting increasing opportunity costs, or diminishing returns, between the two classes of goods. With production in this range, the country finds that it pays to specialize on primary products, to produce at P and to trade $P–T$ of primary products for $T–C$ of manufactures. But if production of manufactures could be expanded beyond an inflection point say, x, the zone of increasing returns would be reached which would carry production all the way to complete specialization in manufactures. Manufactures would now be exchanged for primary production, instead of the other way round, and at C' the country would be better off than at C.

In Figure 2.7c, the problem is not so much decreasing opportunity

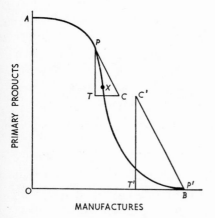

FIG. 2.7b.   Decreasing Opportunity Costs, One Sector

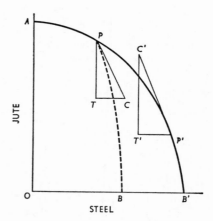

FIG. 2.7c.   Decreasing Opportunity Costs, One Commodity

costs as the departure of private from social costs. One form this departure can take is that of economies external to the firm. The production possibilities curve $A–B'$ represents the social transformation curve between jute and steel, but entrepreneurs, given market prices of factors of production which, let us say, exaggerate the real costs of making steel, operate as if the production possibilities curve were $A–P–B$. Under these circumstances they will produce at P, trade $P–T$ of jute for $T–C$ of steel, and consume at C, which is below the social transformation curve. If there were some way to equate private to social costs, the production point would move to P', the country would export $T'–P'$ of steel and import $C'–T'$ of jute to end up much better off.

Under increasing costs there is no reason for relative prices in two countries with roughly the same sort of resources and comparable tastes to differ sufficiently to disclose comparative advantages which will lead to trade. And yet it is known that trade takes place among industrial countries with roughly the same factor proportions, such as Britain, Germany, Japan, and the United States, and that between countries with different factor proportions some trade takes place in like, but not quite identical, goods. Twenty-five percent of Britain's imports consist of finished manufactured goods, and 33 percent of the imports of the United States. This trade is of the sort based on specialization which springs from increasing returns.

While increasing returns may be inadmissible in the short run as largely incompatible with static equilibrium, their long-run historical validity makes Figure 2.7a an important explanation of the rise of trade. Differences in comparative costs come about not only because of differences in factor endowments but also through specialization in different commodities. To a degree the choice of whether the United States or Britain specializes in one kind of an automobile or another, or this tractor or that, may be determined by historical accident. The fact is that, with each specialized, a basis for trade exists, since each can produce one good cheaper than the other.

When increasing returns are due to internal economies of scale, Figure 2.7a represents the position only momentarily as the country in question is poised between specialization in automobiles or agricultural machinery. After a choice has been made, capital committed, and capacity built, the production possibilities curve will no longer be convex to the origin but will resemble the more normal curves in previous diagrams.

The other two diagrams, Figures 2.7b and 2.7c illustrate standard arguments for tariffs. This fact will merely be noted here, since tariffs will not be addressed until Chapter 7. To take Figure 2.7b, if a tariff on manufactures can raise the price in terms of primary products sufficient to push output beyond x, the country can realize the external economies, and trade in the other direction. Or if a tariff on steel (or possibly an export tax on jute combined with a subsidy on steel) can move entrepreneurs from the transformation curve A–B to A–B', the welfare of the country in Figure 2.7c can be improved.

Summary

The basis for trade, so far as supply is concerned, is found in differences in comparative costs. One country may be more efficient than another, as measured by factor inputs per unit of output, in the production of every possible commodity; but so long as it is not equally more efficient in every commodity, a basis for trade exists. It will pay the country to produce more of those goods in which it is relatively more efficient and to export these in return for goods in which its absolute advantage is least.

Differences in comparative costs arise because of the fact that different countries have different factor endowments and because different commodities are best produced with a predominance of one or another factor. Trade arises out of differences in relative factor prices but assists in narrowing them.

Differences in factor endowments explain that a large portion of total trade which is represented by economic interchange between the temperate zones and the tropics, between densely populated industrial communities and sparsely settled agricultural lands in the temperate zone, not to mention mining communities, and other countries with specialized resources. But trade may also flourish between countries with similar factor endowments, particularly industrial areas, owing to differences in comparative costs produced by historically increasing returns.

Comparative costs thus furnish the basic ingredient of the answer to the classical question: What commodities will a country buy and sell in international trade? It is not the whole answer, since we have been concentrating on supply to the complete neglect of demand. But the subject of demand, as we shall see in the next chapter, can appropriately be covered in providing the answer to the second classical question: At what price will these goods be traded?

SUGGESTED READING

See Suggested Reading for Chapter 3, and Appendices A and B.

THE PURE THEORY OF INTERNATIONAL TRADE: DEMAND

The Law of Reciprocal Demand

There is a temptation to say that the law of comparative costs determines what commodities will be bought and sold in foreign trade, while the law of reciprocal demand sets the prices at which they will be traded. Some economic literature comes close to stating this. And many students learn the theory of foreign trade with some such generalization. But it is not quite true. In general equilibrium theory, of course, both demand and supply together determine the quantities of goods bought and sold and their prices. In a famous analogy Alfred Marshall compared demand and supply to the upper and lower blades of a pair of scissors, neither of which can be said to do the cutting alone. For ease of exposition, however, we may follow the development of classical theory for a distance and approach something like an analytical separation of supply and demand.

Let us go back to our simple example of wheat and cloth produced in a man-week in the United States and Britain:

PRODUCTION OF ONE MAN IN ONE WEEK

	In United States	In United Kingdom
Wheat...........	6 bushels	2 bushels
Cloth...........	10 yards	6 yards

Before trade, wheat and cloth will exchange at 6 : 10 in the United States and 6 : 18 in the United Kingdom. These will be the limits beyond which the price after trade will not settle. Britain will be unwilling to pay more for 6 bushels of wheat than 18 yards of cloth; the United States to accept less than 10 yards for the same amount of wheat. The United States is indifferent to foreign trade at 6 : 10; it makes no difference whether it exports wheat for cloth or produces both at home. But

38

at this price, when it gets all the gain, Britain will be eager to trade. Conversely, Britain will be indifferent to trade, and the United States eager for it, at 6:18. Where, then, will the price settle?

There may be a tendency for the lazy theorist to split the difference and suggest 6 bushels of wheat for 14 yards of cloth. This was the method we used, arbitrarily, in the last chapter. But the technique cannot be defended. John Stuart Mill found the answer to the difficulty. More information is needed to settle on a price. In addition to production costs, there must be data on demand. What counts is the strength of the U.S. demand for wheat and cloth and the reciprocal strength of British demand for the same products. The price at which foreign trade will take place is determined by what Mill called the "law of reciprocal demand."

The nature of the interacting demands can be illustrated by the device of stationing an auctioneer in mid-Atlantic. He has the task of finding a price to apply in both countries, where the exports of wheat which the United States is willing to ship against imports of cloth will match the exports of cloth which Britain is willing to sell for wheat. Too high a price for cloth in terms of wheat will call forth offers of cloth from Britain and demands for wheat, but inadequate offers of wheat or calls for cloth. Conversely, too high a price for wheat in terms of cloth will burden the auctioneer with unsought wheat from the United States and more bids than offers for cloth.

If the two countries are of unequal size, the reciprocal aspect of demand may not come into play at all. The price ratio of the larger country will prevail, and the smaller country can sell as much cloth or wheat to the other as it chooses at the established given price. This is the importance of being unimportant. The small country can reap large gains from trade. Guatemala, which cannot dream of manufacturing cash registers for years to come, can buy them at the U.S. price and sell coffee at the price determined by Brazil and the United States. The case of trading at the price ratio existing in the larger country before trade, which is one limit of profitable trade, may be more frequent than the classical economists have suspected. But where demand and supply in one country or the other are not so large as to overwhelm demand and supply in the other, the law of reciprocal demand comes into play to settle price.

Marshall-Edgeworth Offer Curves

The theory behind Mill's law of reciprocal demand has been portrayed graphically by Edgeworth and then by Marshall with so-called offer curves. These start out with a somewhat different geometrical perspective than production possibilities curves. In Figure 3.1*a* we show a price ratio between *X* and *Y,* which is the same as the production possibilities curve with constant costs. As a production possibilities curve, we are concerned with the increase in the production of one good as the other's production is decreased, i.e., in the absolute values of the curve. As a price, however, we are interested merely in the quantity of *X* which has the same value as a quantity of *Y,* i.e., in the slope of the line. In this case the negative slope, that is, the downward slope from left to right, has no significance, and we can draw the line *X* with a positive slope from the origin (*O*). In Figure 3.1*b* the price ratio between *X* and *Y* can be extended any distance to show what quantity of *X* will be exchanged for what quantity of *Y.*

The offer curve of a country, i.e., the amount of wheat it is willing

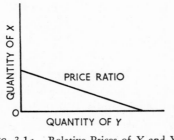

FIG. 3.1*a*.   Relative Prices of *X* and *Y*

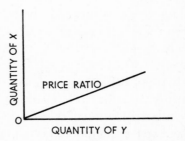

FIG. 3.1*b*.   Relative Prices of *X* and *Y*

to offer for cloth, may start out like this price curve. In any event, the price line is a limit beyond which the offer curve cannot go. This has already been stated and is obvious enough; no country will export products for less in the way of imports than it can produce in import-competing goods at home. For a small amount of imports, moreover, a country may be indifferent whether it produces at home or buys at the same price in foreign trade, so that the offer curve, shown in Figure 3.2 may follow for a distance the price line in the absence of trade, shown in Figure 3.1*b*.

Beyond this distance, however, the offer curve moves away from the price line. Figure 3.2 portrays the British offer curve, *O–B,* which shows the amounts of cloth Britain will offer at various prices for given amounts of wheat. Line *a* is the ratio at which cloth and wheat exchange in the absence of trade (6 bushels against 18 yards). The offer curve can be regarded as a supply curve in international trade, representing various amounts of cloth which Britain is willing to exchange against specified amounts of wheat. Or it can be regarded as a demand curve (of a special sort), indicating given amounts of wheat which Britain is interested in acquiring for specified amounts of cloth. The offer curve is derived by ascertaining the amount of cloth which Britain wants to exchange for wheat, or wheat which it wants to acquire against cloth, at various prices for the two commodities, one in terms of the other. The prices are represented by rays from the origin. The offer curve connects up the amounts which Britain wants to trade at various prices, and includes the straight-line portion where Britain is indifferent whether it trades or not.

Beyond the portion of the curve where it is indifferent to trade,

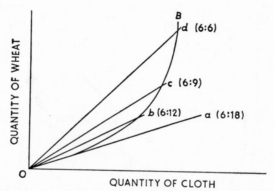

FIG. 3.2.   Britain's Offer Curve of Cloth (Demand for Wheat)

Britain is likely to offer less and less cloth for wheat as more and more wheat becomes available. In part, this will be because Britain wants wheat less; in part because cloth becomes more valuable as its supply is reduced through exports. At some point such as *d* Britain may be unwilling to give up any more cloth for additional wheat. At this point Britain's offer curve, interpreted as a demand for wheat against cloth, has unitary elasticity, in that it is prepared to offer only the same amount of cloth for larger amounts of wheat. As a supply of cloth offered for wheat, the offer curve has zero elasticity, since the supply of cloth is invariant to increasing amounts of wheat offered in exchange. The point to be noted is that the elasticity of the offer curve can be interpreted in various ways: as an import elasticity, reflecting the change in imports corresponding to a change in price; as an export elasticity, representing the change in exports associated with a change in price; or as a total elasticity, which is the percentage change in imports relative to the percentage change in exports at a point on the curve. The most usual concept of elasticity of the offer curve, used for example in Appendix D, is the import elasticity.

The offer curve is not an ordinary demand or supply curve, of course. As a demand curve, for example, it expresses the demand for one commodity (imports) in terms of the supply of another (exports), whereas the normal demand curve expresses the demand for a given commodity in terms of money. The money measure used, however, is price per unit, not total money spent. If the second commodity be regarded as money, which is possible, the offer curve would be a demand curve in terms of quantities of commodities against total amount of money. It would be a total revenue curve, as opposed to a demand curve, which compares quantity with average revenue per unit.

The British offer curve of cloth for wheat has been given in Figure 3.2. A similar curve for the United States is shown in Figure 3.3a,

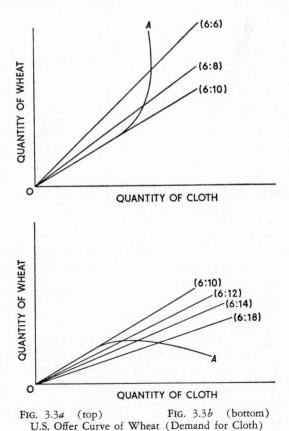

FIG. 3.3a (top)   FIG. 3.3b (bottom)
U.S. Offer Curve of Wheat (Demand for Cloth)

starting from the 6:10 domestic U.S. ratio, rather than the British ratio of 6:18. But there is no one to offer wheat for cloth at prices for cloth above 6:10. The real issue is what the United States will trade at lower prices for cloth, or higher prices for wheat. The offer curve must bend down, as in Figure 3.3*b*.

If the offer curves for the United States and Britain now be taken on the same basis, they will cross. This point (*P* in Figure 3.4) will

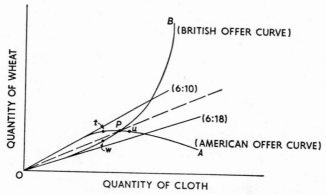

FIG. 3.4.   Law of Reciprocal Demand: Intersection of Two Offer Curves

show where our auctioneer would get the same price for wheat and cloth in both countries (*O–P*) and equal amounts of wheat and cloth exported and imported by the United States and Britain. At any other point than *P*—say, *t*—the United States would be willing to pay broadly as much wheat as at *P* for a good deal less cloth. But, for this amount of cloth, Britain is willing to accept a good deal less wheat, as indicated by the point *w*. Neither *t* nor *w* can serve as a point of equilibrium, because the terms of trade implied by the ray from the origin to each point do not suffice to clear the market. At the relatively high price for wheat in terms of cloth represented by *O–w*, for example, the British would offer only a small amount of cloth, and the United States would want considerably more (see point *u*).

Graham's Attack

A modern theorist, the late Professor Frank B. Graham, has attacked the law of reciprocal demand on the ground that it pays too little attention to supply. It pays, he suggests, none. It appears to make the theory of international trade the theory of trade with fixed quantities of production or initial trading endowments, such as trade in antiques or oil paintings by Renaissance masters, rather than a theory of trade in goods which are produced and reproducible.

Graham went further and stated that the existence of many countries and many commodities makes it likely that trade will take place at the ratio at which some country would interchange them without trade, rather than at some "limbo" ratio in between.

Graham was wrong on the subject of supply. While it is true that many of the classical economists used the law of reciprocal demand as if it took no account of supply, this need not be the case. In Appendix C we demonstrate geometrically, for those who care to learn, how supply enters into the offer curve along with demand.

Given his assumption of constant cost, Graham was right that the introduction of more countries (or more commodities) would leave the terms of trade less at the mercy of the vagaries of demand. With constant costs and two countries of more or less equal size, each specializes completely in one commodity and the terms of trade are indeterminate without demand. When more countries are involved, there is the strong possibility that some country will produce both the commodities after trade. Given constant costs, if one country produces both commodities, this determines the price ratio at which they all must trade.

If we abandon constant costs, however, and with it complete specialization, the fact that one or more countries produces two commodities after trade does not set the terms of trade. Every country may produce some of each commodity without this fact making the terms of trade determinate. With increasing opportunity costs, which is certainly the only realistic assumption, there is room for the law of reciprocal demand. What lies behind demand? Unfortunately the answer to this question requires us to master still another geometrical technique—the indifference curve.

Indifference Curves

The indifference curve may be compared with a contour line. A single curve represents a single level of satisfaction or utility, made up of varying combinations of two goods. Let us take our familiar (even tiresome?) products, wheat and cloth. The indifference curve $a–a$ in Figure 3.5a shows an example in which a consumer is indifferent whether he has 7 bushels of wheat and 4 yards of cloth (v) or 3 bushels of wheat and 8 yards of cloth (w), or any other combination which may be read off the same curve. It will be observed that the single indifference curve is convex to the origin and flattens out to become asymptotic to the axes at each end. After a certain point, as in offer curves, a consumer is unwilling to give up any more wheat simply to get more cloth, of which he already has plenty, or, at the other end, to lose more scarce valuable cloth for redundant wheat.

The single indifference curve represents the combination in which a consumer with a given utility level would purchase between two goods as the price between them is varied. The notion of price here takes us back to the example we used in the previous chapter, which is demonstrated again in Figure 3.1*a*. The indifference curve is made up of a series of points designating quantities of wheat and cloth, respectively, which would be bought with a given income at an infinite series of prices ranging between infinity and zero for wheat in terms of cloth. The same thing may be said in still another way. At a given price, the consumer with a level of real income indicated by a given indifference curve will consume the quantity of the two commodities indicated by point of tangency of the price line to the indifference curve.

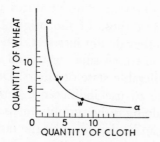

FIG. 3.5*a*.   Single Indifference Curve

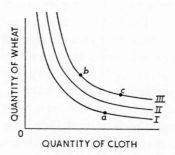

FIG. 3.5*b*.   Indifference Map

Like contour lines, indifference curves are arranged in maps in which the parallel lines indicate progress in the indicated direction from a lower degree of satisfaction (or altitude) to a higher. In Figure 3.5*b*, for example, point *b* on indifference curve *III* is taken to represent a higher level of satisfaction or welfare than point *a* on indifference curve *I*, even though it has more wheat and less cloth. The extra wheat is more than sufficient to compensate for the loss of cloth. Point *c*, where there is more of both, is clearly superior in satisfaction to point *a*, and the consumer is indifferent between *c* and *b*.

The higher branches of economic theory raise a difficult question about community indifference curves. It is agreed that the indifference map of an individual is conceptually satisfactory, and could be set down if any person could be found sufficiently confident of the logic and stability of his tastes to submit to questioning. If an individual believes that he is better off than he was before with 5 more bushels of wheat and 2 less yards of cloth—substantially better off—there is no one who can gainsay him. But there may be objection, it is suggested, to the notion that the *community* is better off with an average of 5 bushels more and 2 yards less. Some members of the community lose the cloth, while others gain the wheat. Who can say that the increase in satisfaction of the one is greater than the decrease in satisfaction of the other? Or if the changes are evenly distributed, there is still a problem if there are some who vastly prefer cloth over wheat and others with opposite tastes. In this case it is impossible to say that the gain of the wheat devotees outweighs the loss in satisfaction of the cloth addicts. Levels of satisfaction or welfare cannot be compared from one person to another.

These are real difficulties, as we shall see later in our discussion of commercial policy. If one group in the community is better off as a result of some action, but others worse, it is impossible to say how the welfare of the community as a whole has been affected. The change in income distribution where people have different tastes produces a new indifference map whose contours intersect those of the original. But indifference curves are only useful when they do not intersect. Intersecting curves imply that utility level *I* is sometimes superior to and sometimes inferior to utility level *II,* an intolerable state of affairs. Despite these difficulties, however, we continue to use indifference curves—although with caution. One basis for so doing is the simplifying assumptions that the tastes of the community can be described by the tastes of an individual, that these are consistent from one period to another, and that there is no change in income distribution. These assumptions are clearly contrary to realism. Another justification used by welfare economists has been the "compensation principle": If it is clear that the beneficiaries of a change in price have enough additional income to compensate (or bribe) the losers for their loss, and some left over, the new position represents an improvement. If the wheat addicts can afford to underwrite the losses of the cloth addicts, and the cloth addicts are not anxious to bribe the wheat addicts to abstain from trade, trade unambiguously makes possible an improvement in utility, whether in fact compensation takes place or not.

However unrealistic, the community indifference curve is schematically a neat device. In the first place, it provides us with the answer to the price at which wheat and cloth will be traded in the two communities with decreasing returns and in the absence of trade. The price which will prevail in a single market is that which is tangent both to the production possibilities curve (*AB*) and to the highest possible indifference curve (in this case curve *II*). Production and consumption will both take place, in the absence of trade, at this point of tangency. This is shown by point *Q* in Figure 3.6. At any point on a higher indifference curve—say, *t*—the quantities of wheat and cloth involved are beyond the capacity of the economy to produce. At any point on a lower indifference curve, satisfaction can be increased by shifting production toward wheat away from cloth, or vice versa. Point *r*, for example, represents the quantities of wheat and cloth which consumers would take at a price for wheat and cloth in terms of each other tangent to indifference curve *I* at *r*.

But, at this price, maximum production would require output at *v*. Let the student who has doubts refer back to Figure 2.4*b* and the

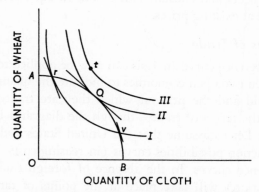

FIG. 3.6.   Indifference Curves, Production Possibilities Curve without Trade

discussion it brought on. The price of cloth is so high in terms of wheat that resources will be shifted from wheat to cloth. But this production cannot be sold at these prices. There is far too much cloth and far too little wheat to satisfy consumers, who at this price would consume more wheat and less cloth. In order to get rid of output, the price of wheat will have to be raised and that of cloth lowered. This means another shift of production from *v*. And so it would oscillate, first consumers and then producers dissatisfied with the combinations of wheat and cloth until a stable equilibrium is found at the point where the production possibilities curve is tangent to the highest possible indifference curve.

As long as decreasing returns exist, there will always be such a point. (And only one point.) While there is only one production possibilities curve, there are an infinite number of indifference curves which can be drawn representing infinitesimally small increases in real income. If these indifference curves do not intersect, as we assume they do not, any production possibilities curve must produce one point of tangency to a family of indifference curves.

The slope of this tangent is the price line. It is also the marginal rate of substitution in consumption, on the indifference curve, and the marginal rate of transformation on the production possibilities curve. When the price ratio equals the marginal rate of substitution in consumption, consumers are in equilibrium. When the price ratio equals the marginal rate of transformation in production, producers are in equilibrium. When the marginal rate of substitution in consumption equals the marginal rate of transformation in production, without external trade, producers and consumers are both in equilibrium, and markets are cleared at existing prices.

The Terms of Trade

The indifference curve analysis can now be applied to the problem of trade between two open economies to indicate the quantities of goods bought and sold and the price at which they are traded—frequently referred to as the terms of trade—though the diagrams become somewhat complex. Let us assume that the United States and Britain have different production possibilities curves (increasing costs) but the same set of indifference curves. In the absence of foreign trade, production (and consumption) will take place at the points of tangency to the production possibilities curves which are also tangent to the highest possible indifference curves. In Figure 3.7, these points are *c* in the United States and *d* in Britain. The tangents themselves, *C–C* and *D–D*, represent the prices at which wheat and cloth are traded in terms of each other in the United States and Britain before trade has been opened.

With the opening of trade, the amounts of wheat and cloth exported and imported in the two countries and the price at which they will be exchanged will be determined by parallel lines of equal length tangent to the respective production possibilities curves and tangent to a higher indifference curve. These lines, *r–t* in the United States and *k–m* in Britain, run in opposite directions from the production possibilities curves in order to reach higher indifference curves. The requirement that the lines must be parallel, or of the same slope, fulfills the condition that the prices in the two countries must be the same after trade is open, if transport costs be disregarded. The requirement that they be of equal length, as well as of the same slope, is in satisfaction of the necessary condition that exports of one country shall be equal to imports of the other. It should be observed that Britain's exports of cloth (*l–m*) are equal to the U.S. imports (*s–t*), while the U.S. exports of wheat (*r–s*) are equal to imports by Britain (*k–l*).

The effects of trade with different production possibilities curves and identical indifference curves are to make each country more specialized in production and less specialized in consumption. In both cases production slides farther along the production possibilities curve toward the output of the commodity for which the factors are most effective. Consumption, however, given the shape of the curves portrayed in Figure 3.7, tends to move in the other direction—more toward equality,

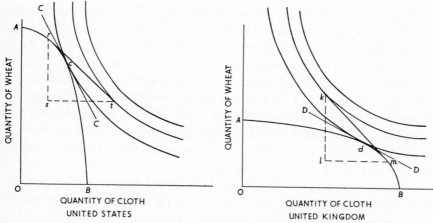

FIG. 3.7.   Trade with Identical Tastes, Different Factor Endowments

as the scarce commodity in each country becomes cheaper after importation.

While it is generally believed that countries are rather specialized in production and have broadly similar tastes in consumption, the shape of the indifference curves drawn in Figure 3.7 has no fundamental validity. Tastes (and hence indifference curves) may differ, as well as supply conditions. Indeed, as we shall see presently, trade is possible with identical supply conditions and different tastes. Whatever may be the indifference maps or supply conditions, however, trade is possible when the equilibrium prices in two countries without trade are different. Under these circumstances, there will be a new price at which it is possible for one or both to gain from exchange. In mathematical terms, trade is possible when the two countries find lines of equal length and slope which run from a tangency with the production possibilities curve of each country to a tangency with a higher indifference curve in one or both.

In general, the new indifference curve attained will be a higher one for both countries than that reached in the absence of trade. The student may, however, enjoy working out for himself a case in which a big country trading with a smaller one receives none of the gain from trade. The price in the larger country does not change, and without a price change no move to a higher indifference curve is possible. The country consumes what it consumed before but produces more of one product, now exported, and less of another (the new import). This means, of course, that the production possibilities curve must be a straight line over the relevant part of the curve with a slope equal to the international terms of trade. The more the post-trade price differs from the pre-trade price, for a given volume of trade, the higher the gains from trade for a given country. This is important to bear in mind in discussing the growth of trade of various countries, for example the widely mentioned fact that the trade of developed countries, grows faster than that of the less developed. If the difference between pre- and post-trade prices were to be narrow for developed and wide for the less developed countries, a smaller rate of increase in the latter may mean more substantial growth in gains from trade.

The student is reminded that there awaits him in Appendix C an exposition of a technique for putting offer curves, production possibilities curves and consumption indifference maps on the same diagram. The production possibilities curve and the consumption indifference map, in fact, are used to construct a trade indifference map from which the offer curve is derived. While the technique takes some time to master, for even the partially serious student it is worth it.

Different Tastes

The possibility of trade between countries with the same factor endowment and different tastes has already been mentioned. Two countries can produce wheat or rice equally well but, as consumers, rank them differently. Figure 3.8 illustrates this case. In the absence of trade, wheat is more expensive than rice in the country which prefers wheat to rice, and rice more expensive than wheat in the other. The opening of trade equalizes prices in the two countries and enables each country to move its consumption to a higher indifference curve by exchanging wheat for rice or the opposite. In this instance—the converse of the more usual case, in which tastes are more or less the same and factors differ—trade permits each country to specialize less in production and

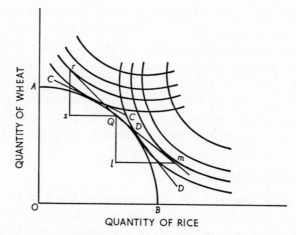

FIG. 3.8.   Trade with Identical Factor Endowments, Different Tastes

more in consumption. The explanation is that, prior to trade, each country had used for the favored commodity resources more suited to the product it did not prefer. In the bread-eating country, for example, land suited to rice production was used, in the absence of trade, to grow wheat. With trade possible, this land can yield a higher return in terms of satisfaction by growing rice, which is now exchanged for wheat.

Identical Factors—Identical Tastes

The basis for trade between countries with identical factors under increasing returns was set forth in the last chapter. Here it is necessary only to add the indifference curves which portray the demand side of the position. This is done in Figure 3.9. Identical tastes were implicitly

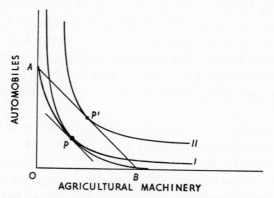

FIG. 3.9.   Trade with Identical Factor Endowments,
Identical Tastes, Increasing Returns

assumed in the discussion in Chapter 2, so that no further explanation is required. In the absence of trade, production is at point p in both countries. After trade begins and after producers in both countries have become aware of the possibility of economies of scale, production in one country will shift to the limit of the production possibilities curve, at either A or B, and the other country will be likely to shift to the other extreme. Under these circumstances, trade takes place to shift consumption in both countries to a higher indifference curve, i.e., to point p' on indifference curve *II*.

General Equilibrium

In its most general form, the answer to the first two questions raised by the classical economists reduces to the statement that what goods will be produced and the prices at which they will be traded will be determined by supply and demand and that the supply and demand for goods will both determine and be determined by the supply and demand for factors of production. The system of equilibrium is an interacting one.

The analysis of this chapter has been limited to two countries and to two goods. There are a number of economists who believe that the analysis is fundamentally altered if it is broadened to include more countries and more commodities. The majority, however, do not accept this view, believing that the two-country, two-commodity analysis is capable of extension, by means of a variety of techniques, to the more intricate and more realistic models.

Given, say, five commodities produced in each of two countries, these can be ranged in order of comparative advantage in each country. Initially one can say only that a country will export the commodity in which it has the largest advantage, and import the commodity in which its disadvantage is greatest. The question of whether it will export or import the three commodities between these limits will then depend upon the balance of trade. If the demand for imports of the commodity offering a large disadvantage is very great, it may have to export all four of the other commodities, given the nature of the foreign demand for them, to balance its accounts.

This concludes our presentation of the pure theory of international trade in its classical and neoclassical form. The next task is to make the picture more realistic, by relaxing some of the assumptions underlying it. In the next chapter we get away from the assumptions of fixed factor endowments on the one hand, and on the other, that of fixed production functions, a given technology, or what Professor Taussig used to call "a given state of the arts." In Chapter 5 we explore the case of the less developed countries that the classical theory of comparative advantage cannot apply to them because their situation departs from the classic assumptions in a variety of particulars, especially in their inability to shift smoothly and costlessly along the production possibilities curve, and their lack of perfect competition in goods and factor markets. Finally Chapter 6 lends verisimilitude to an otherwise unconvincing tale by introducing transport costs.

Summary

Ricardo answered the question of what commodities are exported and imported by stating that this will be determined by the law of comparative cost; Mill answered the question of what prices will rule in international trade by stating that this would be determined by the law of reciprocal demand. It was necessary to find a price which would exchange all the goods that one country had to sell for all that the other wanted to offer. Marshall and Edgeworth developed intersecting offer curves to show how this law operated.

But this analysis tended to submerge the effect of changes in supply. A diagrammatic analysis has been developed which combines production possibilities curves for supply with community indifference maps for demand. There are some difficulties posed by the community indifference maps, but they are used nonetheless. In the absence of trade, production and consumption will both take place at the tangent between the production possibilities curve and the highest indifference curve. With trade, it is possible to effect gains which carry each country beyond its production possibilities curve. Trade will take place at a price the same in each country, tangent to the production possibilities curve and a higher (for at least one country) indifference curve of the same length. This price line is then the hypotenuse of a right-angle triangle in which the other legs measure exports and imports.

The theory of trade is shown to belong to general equilibrium theoretical analysis in which goods are mobile but factors are not. One price reigns in one market—the terms of trade.

SUGGESTED READING

TEXTS

See Snider, chaps. iii and iv; Peter B. Kenen, *International Economics,* Foundations of Modern Economics Series (2nd ed.; Englewood Cliffs, N.J.: Prentice–Hall, Inc., 1967) (paperback) for less rigorous treatments, and Vanek, part iii and Kemp, part ii for more difficult. Excerpts from classical writers are represented in W. R. Allen, *International Trade Theory: Hume to Ohlin* (New York: Random House, Inc., 1965) (paperback).

TREATISES, ETC.

No brief paragraph can do justice to the bibliographical material on this subject. What follows, therefore, should be read in conjunction with the references to the literature in Appendices A and B. See Haberler, chaps. ix–xii; Viner, chaps. vii and ix; Stolper and Samuelson on the Edgeworth-Bowley box; articles by Leontief on the indifference curve, Samuelson on the gains from trade; Williams on increasing returns, in American Economic Association, *Readings in the Theory of International Trade*. Most of the articles on the pure theory in the American Economic Association, *Readings in International Economics* are cited in the bibliographies to Appendices A and B, but Haberler on "Some Problems in the Pure Theory" and Kenen on the effect of income redistribution on demand are worth noting. See also Kenen on "Nature, Capital and Trade," *JPE*, October, 1965.

Ohlin gives the best statement of the general equilibrium position in his chapters v–vii and xiii. This theory is presented mathematically by J. L. Mosak, *General Equilibrium Theory in International Trade* (Bloomington, Ind.: Principia Press, 1944). A linear programming solution to comparative advantage is given in R. Dorfman, P. A. Samuelson and R. M. Solow, *Linear Programming and Economic Analysis* (New York: McGraw-Hill Book Co., Inc., 1958), chap. v and especially pp. 117–21.

POINTS

J. B. Condliffe, *The Commerce of Nations* (New York: W. W. Norton & Co., Inc., 1950), gives an excellent account of the development of laissez-faire in the 19th century which makes useful supplementary reading. See especially chapters vi–viii and xiii.

The teacher who wants to illustrate the theory of comparative advantage in practice is referred to G. D. M. MacDougall's essay in American Economic Association, *Readings in International Economics;* B. Balassa, "An Empirical Demonstration of Classical Comparative Costs," *RE & S,* August, 1963; and R. M. Stern, "British and American Productivity and Comparative Costs in International Trade," *OEP,* October, 1962. An attempt to apply the theory to reality is set out in chaps. iii–v in C. P. Kindleberger, *Foreign Trade and the National Economy* (New Haven, Conn.: Yale University Press, 1962) (paperback).

| Chapter 4 | # THE COMPARATIVE STATICS OF TRADE: CHANGES IN TASTES, FACTOR ENDOWMENTS, TECHNOLOGY |

The Static Nature of Comparative Advantage

The basis for international trade discussed thus far rests essentially on static assumptions: with given tastes, given production functions, fixed factor endowments, and so on, a case for specialization and exchange can be made. We reserve for the next chapter a thorough statement of the objection to free trade raised by developing countries. This is largely built on dynamic arguments. But it is well at this stage to relax some of our static assumptions for the purpose of explaining part of existing trade, and indicating the nature of changes in the trade pattern even of fully developed countries. In particular we choose to depart from the initial assumptions of fixed tastes, fixed supplies of land, labor, and capital, and identical and unchanging production functions between trading countries.

Changes in Tastes

We need not spend much time with tastes. It is sufficient to point out that the analysis based on opening up trade between two countries which had never traded before predicates a gain from trade on the existence of fixed tastes unchanged by the fact of newly opened trade. This of course is highly unrealistic. Trade has many origins—the exchange of gifts between primitive tribes; the plundering of the Middle East by Europeans during the Crusades, or of Europe by Scandinavian pirates; the opening of the western hemisphere by Spanish, Portuguese, and English explorers. In most of these historical means by which trade began, the initial exchanges involved the creation of new wants, as well as their satisfaction. Tastes change with trade as well as trade satisfying existing wants more fully.

The point has significance beyond recalling the origin of cotton, muslin, sugar, and even tariffs, as Arabic words, or the introduction of tobacco, rum, and the potato from North America to Europe. Ragnar

55

Nurkse has pointed to the "demonstration effect" under which underdeveloped countries have learned about the existence of goods in developed nations which will lighten their burdens, satisfy their physical appetites, and titillate their innate sense of self-expression or exhibitionism. When modern methods of production are introduced into some particularly primitive societies, it is necessary to introduce modern methods of consumption. With the initiation of plantation cultivation of fruit, sugar, rubber, tea, and the like, there must come a change in the diet of native laborers and the replacement of the varied native subsistence fare by staple imported foodstuffs. With the alteration in the pattern of living, there may be a worsening in the nutritional level of the diet and dietary deficiencies.

When the price of exports rises with trade, or that of imports falls, with all tastes and means of production unchanged, trade may be said to result in an unambiguous gain for a country as a whole, leaving aside the distribution of the gain within the country, and the difficulties inherent in measuring the extent of the gain. But when the improvement in the terms of trade is accompanied by a shift in tastes in favor of imports, leading to an increase in demand for them, the case is not so clear. One can say that there is an improvement, as compared with the hypothetical case of increasing the demand for imports without satisfying it. A new want coming into existence along with trade to fill it, however, involves a departure from the classical assumptions and raises doubt as to the classical conclusion of gain. With the change in tastes there is a change in the consumption indifference map, as well as the trade indifference map, to use the jargon of Appendix C, and hence there is no basis for measuring gains or losses from trade.

There is some basis for thinking that the demonstration effect is stronger today than, say, before World War I. To take what may seem to be a trivial example, but one of some importance for international trade, international exchanges grew far in the 19th century without bringing about any substantial homogeneity of taste in dress, diet, consumers' goods, or cultural pursuit. Such is less and less true. Trade in Europe in the 19th century continued side by side with different styles of national diet and cooking: The British was distinct from the Continental breakfast, and on the Continent itself Italian, French, German, and Scandinavian cooking all differed. Today the Indo-Chinese complain that the native Asian breakfast is giving way to European eggs, bacon, and coffee; in Japan, rice is increasingly abandoned in favor of wheat; and Coca-Cola is a trademark known round the world. Demonstration effect is more significant for underdeveloped countries which frequently want to import—Swiss watches, British bicycles, and U.S. fountain pens at the most primitive level—before they have earned or arranged to borrow the necessary exchange. This possible source of disequilibrium will concern us in Part VI. But even between developed countries these changes in taste which come with the introduction of new goods are significant as the shift in American taste toward European products, including small cars, demonstrates. The former editor of the *Economist* has said that American high-speed printing machinery and construction equipment are so efficient that Europeans have to have them. In this case, the change in taste is responsive to a change in technology.

Changes in Factor Endowments

Tastes do not stand still, and neither do factor endowments. We can illustrate the impact of changes in factor endowments best, however, if we assume that tastes and technology are unaltered while factor endowments grow. Capital and population are the factors that grow. Land presumably does not, and may even shrink through depletion (although this, as are so many general statements, is subject to qualification: land can expand in an economic sense through changes in technology which may make old ore deposits useful, for example, and through capital investment, as in reforestation, and in new discovery, which seems to have run its course on this terrestrial globe, but may not have so far as the universe is concerned). Suppose we start with the simple case of a two-country, two-commodity, two-factor model, based on capital and labor, where capital and labor grow in the same proportion, with technology and tastes fixed.

It is intuitively evident, and can be demonstrated with the geometry of Appendix A, that with an equal expansion of the two factors, and no change in technology, the production possibilities curve will be expanded by pushing out evenly in all directions. In Figure 4.1, the production possibilities curve A–B will now become A'–B'. But what happens to trade, and to the terms of trade? The answer, as the answer to every question in economics at this level of generality, is "It depends." But this answer is not enough to satisfy the teacher, and the student must go on and explain what it depends on. It depends first on the position with respect to demand, and second on the shape of the other offer curve.

In Figure 4.1, let the triangle T–P–C represent trade before factor growth, with exports, T–P, being exchanged for imports, C–T, at the terms of trade, P–C. P is the production point and C the consumption. The operational trick is to find out what happens to production and consumption with growth at the same terms of trade as before. If it turns out that the country wants to trade more at the old terms of trade, it is likely that it is going to have to accept a lower price for its exports and pay more for its imports. If on the other hand, it wants to trade less, again at the original terms of trade, the outcome is likely to be the reverse: a higher price for exports and cheaper imports.

Since the growth of the production possibilities curve has been uniform, the production point P' on the new production possibilities curve $A'-B'$ will lie on a straight-line ray from the origin $O-P$, which intersects $A'-B'$ at P'. This is the result of the underlying linear homogeneous production functions, and unchanged terms of trade (as as-

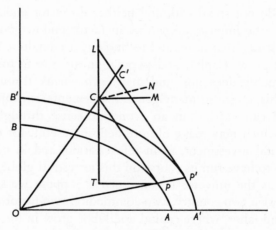

FIG. 4.1. Effect of Neutral Expansion of Production Possibilities Curve on Trade

sumed), $P'-C'$. The question is now what happens to demand. If a right angle such as $L-C-M$ is drawn with its origin at C, increased income from increased overall output will mean that the demand for both the A good and the B good expand, unless one of them is an inferior good. If we rule out inferior goods, the new consumption point has to lie within the triangle $L-C-M$. One possibility is that at the same price goods A and B will be consumed in exactly the same proportions with the enlarged income as with the smaller. This possibility would put the new consumption point on a straight-line ray from the origin through C. With this assumption it is now clear what will happen: line segment $P'-C'$ is parallel to and longer than $P-C$, which means that at the same terms of trade as before, the country would want to offer more of commodity A for more of commodity B. Its offer curve would have moved out to the right as in Figure 4.2. Unless the offer curve *A* faces is a straight line, such as *O–P* in Figure 4.2, the terms of trade will shift against the expanding country, as shown by the dotted line in the same illustration.

But there is no need for demand to be homothetic, as the condition of consumption in fixed proportions with expanding income and constant price is called. If the path of consumption with increasing income but constant prices, the so-called Engel's curve (of which there is one curve for every possible price), through *C* is steeper than *C–C′*, demand

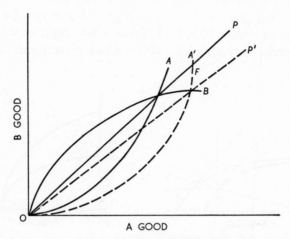

FIG. 4.2. Effect of Neutral Expansion of Production
and Homothetic Indifference Map on
Trade and Terms of Trade

favors the import good. Then *A* will want to trade even more than the amounts of exports and imports implicit in the length and slope of *P′–C′* and the market-clearing terms of trade, assuming *A* faces a *B* offer curve of less than infinite elasticity, will deteriorate still more. Indeed, the Engel's curve can favor the export good, for a bit, and *A* will still want to trade more of the *A* good for more of the *B* good, because its expansion of production possibilities for the *A* good exceeds its demand bias in favor of it. Draw a dotted line *C–N* exactly parallel to *P–P′* in Figure 4.1. If the Engel's curve follows this, *A* will want to trade the same amount before growth as after, and the terms of trade will remain unchanged. If the curve falls below it, demand favors the export good more than export production possibilities have grown, the offer curve in Figure 4.2 will shift to the left of the original, *O–A*, *A*'s trade will fall, and its terms of trade improve. But if the Engel's path cuts the $P'-L$ curve anywhere above $C-N$, the terms of trade will decline, provided that the foreign offer curve is not infinitely elastic, or a straight line.

But of course there is no need for the production possibilities curve to expand neutrally, with a symmetrical pushing out along its whole length. If the A good is capital intensive, and capital grows but not labor, the production possibilities curve will evidently grow in an export-biased fashion, as in Figure 4.3a. Or the factor which is intensively used in the import industry may be the one with the only or the greater expansion, as in Figure 4.3b. Note that growth can now be more than merely export or import biased. In Figure 4.3a a right angle set with its origin at P marks the boundaries within which growth can be defined to

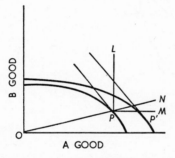

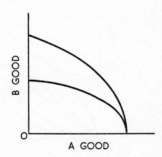

FIG. 4.3a.   Export-Biased Growth   FIG. 4.3b.   Import-Biased Growth

be import biased, neutral, or export biased. But on the production side, the tangency of the old price line to the new production possibilities curve can lie outside these limits, as at P' where growth is ultraexport biased. This occurs when with new production possibilities and the old trading price, the country will produce not only more of the export but positively less of the import good. Growth now necessarily worsens the terms of trade (allowing for less than infinitely elastic offer curve facing the country) so long as there are no inferior goods. And ultraimport-biased growth (not shown in Figure 4.3b) necessarily improves the terms of trade with the same qualifications.

Let us see if we can use this theoretical framework to say anything useful about the real world. First, we should note that in the next chapter, the less developed countries claim the terms of trade tend against them as they have ultrabiased export growth, with an import-biased demand. This means that after growth at the original terms of trade they would offer much more in the way of exports, and with higher incomes, want much more in the way of imports, the production of which declines under ultrabiased growth. This shifts out the offer curve and worsens the terms of trade. There is more to their story, but the analysis is suggestive.

Second, it is of some interest to show the position of the United States with regard to natural resource products. Land, as already indicated, is a complex factor of production. In a given state of the arts, land can be increased by discovery or reduced by depletion, or, simultaneously, both. But the factor resource, land, as indeed every factor, can only be defined in terms of a technological process. An innovation will expand or contract the amount of land viewed as an economic agent. Land bearing low-grade taconite ores became an economic resource only after the taconite-refining process was discovered.

It is hard to know whether, in the economic history of the United States since the Civil War, land has been an expanding, fixed, or a contracting factor. For some purposes, such as oil production, land was enormously abundant and is now relatively scarce. In other minerals, depletion has exhausted the richest deposits. But discoveries and improvements in technology continue. Drilling for oil takes place in the Continental shelf in the Gulf of Mexico; improvements in refinery techniques have just about reached the point where it will pay to extract oil from the abundant shales of the Rocky Mountain area. Land, the fixed factor, is seen to be subject to all sorts of changes.

If we assume land fixed, for purposes of illustration, and capital and labor growing together at a steady pace, the nature of comparative advantage may be seen to change. The United States used to be an exporter of a wide variety of metals and minerals. Now it is a net importer of all but two—coal and molybdenum. Copper, zinc, lead, iron, and especially oil which we used to export are now on a net import basis. Figure 4.4 shows a stereotyped representation of the nature of the change. The vertical axis measures land intensive goods; the horizontal axis, on the other hand, represents the goods embodying primarily labor and capital. The inner production possibilities curve, marked 1875, shows a strong specialization in land intensive production, which is in part exchanged for labor/capital intensive goods. With the passage of time, the shape of the production possibilities curve changes. Land is fixed, and capital and labor grow. Production possibilities in the land intensive product increase somewhat, as more capital and labor will

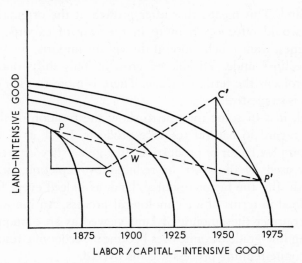

FIG. 4.4. A Schematic Representation of the Change in
U.S. Comparative Advantage in Land Intensive Commodities
to Comparative Disadvantage

produce more land intensive products even with land unchanged. But the production possibilities curve grows mainly to the right. By 1920, as the figure is drawn, the production possibilities curve is fairly balanced on the scales shown. By 1950, it is skewed in favor of labor/capital intensive products in place of its original skewness in the opposite direction.

The dotted line, P–P', represents the locus of points of tangency to the successive production possibilities curves, where production has taken place. C–C' signifies the path of consumption. To the left of the intersection, i.e., prior to about 1920 as shown on the figure, land intensive products were exported and labor/capital intensive products imported. After 1920, or thereabouts, when the curves intersect, the trade position was reversed. The United States exported labor/capital intensive products and imported the products of land.

This representation is of course purely schematic. It departs from reality in a hundred ways—two goods, constant technology, a fixed factor, incomplete specialization, and so forth. Problems of defining land intensive products make it impossible to pin down when the change from an export to an import basis occurred in minerals. It was probably more nearly after World War II than after World War I. Nonetheless, the demonstration has validity in a very broad sense and helps illustrate how comparative advantages change with factor growth.

Technological Change—Making Old Goods More Cheaply

The analysis of technological change in existing goods follows broadly the same analysis as changes in factor proportions, but with a vast number of complications which we will eschew. Production functions can change so that the same factor combinations can produce more goods than before; or the technological change can be biased in such a way as to save more of one factor than the other. Saving a factor is equivalent to increasing its quantity. It is intuitively obvious that an unbiased and equal technological change in both commodities is exactly the same as a proportionate increase in both factors. Unless demand is biased on an offsetting way, and unless the offer curve facing the country is infinitely elastic, the country will have to give up at least some of its potential gain from greater technological efficiency in reduced terms of trade. Similarly, unbiased technological change in one commodity will lead to export- or import-biased expansion of the production possibilities curve, as in growth of a single factor.

Biased technological growth is more complex. If there is biased growth in the export good which augments the abundant factor, this will lead to export-biased growth, in fact to ultraexport-biased growth since there are two tendencies working to expand exports. And biased technological growth in the import-competing good which augments the scarce factor will lead to ultraimport-biased growth. In between there are evidently a variety of intermediate cases, such as growth in the import sector which saves the abundant factor, or growth in the export sector which augments the scarce factor where one cannot say much without the specific data.

Factor Growth and Technological Change

While factor growth and technological change can be analytically distinguished, they may occur simultaneously or quasi-simultaneously in the real world to maintain a comparative advantage in a given commodity.

During the interwar period, for example, the United States was losing its comparative advantage in agriculture. Agricultural products which had represented 47 percent of U.S. exports in 1922–24 dwindled to 25 percent by 1937–39. Farm policies, including price supports, played a role in this deterioration, but one which we ignore. To a considerable extent the deterioration was the result of an increase in the price of labor which made a number of these commodities unable to compete in price on the world market.

Shortly before and during the course of World War II, however, a quasi-revolution occurred in U.S. agriculture. Machinery and fertilizer, plus new techniques of dry farming in wheat and irrigation in cotton, raised yields and especially labor productivity. A number of farm products which had been exported on the basis of land intensive comparative advantage could now be exported once more because they were capital intensive in a capital intensive country. Others, such as rice, linseed, soybeans, and Turkish tobacco which had been imported changed over to an export basis.

The position was possibly even more striking in coal. Successive changes in technology developed successively larger steam shovels for open-pit mining until the present 2,400-ton size capable of removing 80 tons of overburden in one bite. The cost of development of mechanized mines has gone up substantially compared to those with handloading facilities—from $2 per ton of output per year to $7 to $10—but the labor cost as a percentage of the price of coal has declined from 70 percent in the 1930's to 50 percent in the 1960's. The depletion of land has been more than offset by the improvement in technology with the result that coal has become an export product.

Changes in Technology—New Goods

Some years ago, Irving Kravis undertook an empirical investigation of the Heckscher-Ohlin theorem, looking especially to see if labor intensive exports were produced by especially low-wage labor, and found to his evident surprise that in virtually every country the exporting industries were those which paid the highest wage rates. What a country produced and exported, he decided, was what it had "available," i.e., the goods which its entrepreneurs and innovators developed. Availability meant an "elastic" supply. It did no good for a country to have the cheap labor to produce, say, transistors, if in fact it lacked inventors, or if the invention could be licensed, the innovators, entrepreneurs, skilled workmen, and so on, needed to produce them. This theory challenged the assumption of the classical doctrine that technology was the same all over the world.

A good deal of work has been done in pursuing this and other leads into the technological basis for trade in new goods. Linder, for example, suggests that it is not enough for a country to have entrepreneurs and innovators; it must have a broad local market. There must be, that is, a body of consumers in the home country interested in and able to buy a new product before manufacturers can develop the skills to make it cheaply and sell it abroad. This has been called the "spill-over" theory, in which exports grow out of domestic production. It applies only to manufactures, not to primary products. And it assumes, or asserts, that, few, if any products develop directly in world trade without having achieved importance in a domestic market. The student may interest himself in trying to think of counterexamples, such as Swiss watches, produced in volume during World War I by a small country on the border of two countries which needed timekeeping machinery but were too busy to develop it themselves; or Christmas tree ornaments exported by a non-Christian country such as Japan. But there is much in history to support the theory, and it can be dynamized to help explain how export products change as domestic income grows: another Scandinavian economist, Erik Hoffmeyer, observed the evolving character of U.S. trade in office machinery. At the earliest stage, U.S. innovators pioneered in typewriters, adding machines, and cash registers, and with their increasing use in the domestic market began to export them. With the passage of time, however, these relatively simple machines were widely produced abroad on the one hand, and replaced in the United States by more complex machinery. With time, therefore, the United States imported mechanical typewriters, adding machines, and so on, and exported electric typewriters and data processing machinery. In automobiles, higher U.S. income led consumers to want larger and more luxurious cars which priced themselves out of the export field. United States domination of the world automobile export market which characterized the 1920's gave way to a large import surplus, mainly in small cars which fitted foreign markets. Moreover two countries producing broadly the same type of goods will differentiate their output in an effort each to penetrate the market of the other, as when Fiats are sold in Germany and Volkswagens in Italy.

On this theory much trade in manufactures is based not on factor proportions but on a so-called technological gap. A thesis at M.I.T. on international trade in motion pictures observed that the United States pioneered in many film innovations, and that after each one—the feature-length picture, talkies, color, wide-screen, and so on—there was a surge of exports. After a lag, based on the need to see whether the innovation would succeed, and to imitate it, foreign producers followed suit. When the technology was widely known and adopted, the United States might or might not continue to export, or trade in differentiated products might move in both directions.

A similar study has been made for synthetic materials, identifying trade based on a technological gap, that due to economies of scale, and finally, resting on factor proportions, in the usual case, labor intensive goods based on low wages. The author notes that synthetic fabrics are not notably produced in the countries with cheap raw materials such as wood pulp (Sweden and Canada), or petroleum. In this field, trade starts with a technological breakthrough leading to a technological gap, is supported by scale economies, such as learning through production, which means that nothing succeeds like success, but may ultimately give way, when the technology has been widely disseminated and the limits of scale economies have been reached, to trade based on wage costs, or factor proportions.

This cycle in the life of a commodity has been generalized by Raymond Vernon who identifies stages of a product which is first

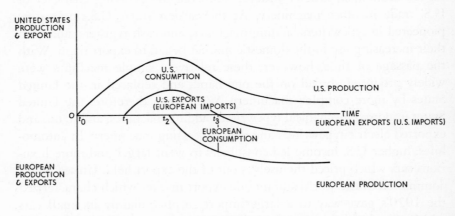

FIG. 4.5 Export Cycle of a Commodity in Which Innovation Leads to Exports and Imitation Abroad Ultimately to Imports

"new," then maturing (when it spreads to other industrialized countries than the originator), and finally standardized. Computers are at one end of the spectrum today, and textiles, leather goods, rubber products, and paper at the other. A British economist suggested many years ago that automobiles would turn out to be the textiles of tomorrow, and the recent entry of Japan into world trade in that product, after years of effort, suggests that this stage of standardization has just about been reached.

The cycle of a commodity can be illustrated with the stylized diagram in Figure 4.5. In the early stage of development, with time measured along the horizontal axis, the innovation and production begin in, say, the United States, at period t_0 (the invention may have occurred anywhere; what counts is the first commercial production). At t_1 begin exports from the United States, which are imports and consumption in Europe where quantities are measured negatively below the horizontal axis. At t_2 production begins in Europe. Vernon is interested in the question whether and when U.S. producers start facilities to produce abroad, but that subject will not engage us until Chapter 21. Whosever production it is, it substitutes for imports (exports of the United States) which decline, and may even turn into exports (U.S. imports at t_3 in Figure 4.5). This will occur if when the product has passed through the stage of "maturity" to "standardization," it turns out to have a high wage component that gives the comparative advantage, on a common technology, to Europe.

Much research is currently going forward on the connection between exports and high labor skills on the one hand, and exports and research and development on the other. The so-called technology gap between Europe and the United States in computers, electronics, nuclear energy, and space equipment is very much in the forefront of public discussion. If the 5 industries in the United States with the highest research effort, for example, are separated from 14 other major industries it is found that the former export four times as much per dollar of sales as the latter. Or the measures can be put in terms of scientists and engineers in research and development as a percentage of total employment. Whatever the measure, it is evident that U.S. exports, at least, have a high technological component and that many of these exports diminish or disappear when the technological lead of the United States narrows or is lost. Considerable debate currently swirls over the concept of a technological gap, which in many quarters is called a management advantage rather than a technological one. Indeed, in some industries, such as automobiles, technological change is largely confined to companies outside the United States. Whatever the outcome of this discussion, however, it lends realism to international trade to get away from the simple assumption of a given state of the arts, applied worldwide, and to recognize that innovation produces trade even though that trade may disappear or be reversed when the technology has spread.

Summary

The classical theory of comparative advantage gives an answer to the question of what products will be exported and imported, at what prices, and who will gain from trade, in a world of fixed tastes, fixed resources, and fixed technology. This static world no longer exists, however, if it ever did. Tastes change, particularly as the demonstration effect impresses one country with the articles of consumption or means of production developed in another.

The impact of changes in factor endowments on trade is tested by seeing how trade at the original terms of trade would be affected by the changes. Neutral growth, with the most neutral possible demand assumption (homothetic indifference curves), will lead to an expansion of the desire to trade at the old terms of trade. This will displace the offer curve in such a way as to expand trade and worsen the terms of trade, provided the foreign offer curve is not infinitely elastic. Changes in factor endowments may be biased in favor of exports or against them, and they may meet biased demand conditions which accentuate or offset (in whole or part) such production bias. Ultrabias in production, however, determines the outcome, provided there are no inferior goods.

Technological change can take place in cost reductions for old goods, or in the introduction of new. The former can be treated generally as if they were equivalent to changes in factor endowments. The introduction of new goods in one country ahead of others, however, gives rise to exports which are not related, in the short run at least, to factor endowments. The trade of the United States, for example, seems to be strongly influenced by the introduction of new products, although these are associated with a special factor, scientists and engineers engaged in research and development.

SUGGESTED READING

TEXTS

See Kemp, chap. vi; C. P. Kindleberger, *Foreign Trade and the National Economy* (New Haven, Conn.: Yale University Press, 1962) (paperback), chap. iv on "Technology."

TREATISES, ETC.

The most important article on factor growth and trade is "Economic Development and International Trade" in H. G. Johnson's *Money, Trade and Growth* (Cambridge, Mass.: Harvard University Press, 1962) reprinted in American Economic Association, *Readings in International Economics*. In this theoretical line, see also R. Findlay and H. Grubert, "Factor Intensities, Technological Progress and the Terms of Trade," *OEP*, February, 1959; and P. Bardhan, "International Differences in Production Functions, Trade and Factor Prices," *EJ*, March, 1965.

The literature on new goods referred to in the text is in order:

Irving B. Kravis, " 'Availability' and Other Influences on the Commodity Composition of Trade," *JPE*, April, 1956.

Staffan Burenstam Linder, *An Essay on Trade and Transformation* (New York: John Wiley & Sons, Inc., 1961), chap. iii.

Erik Hoffmeyer, *Dollar Shortage?* (Copenhagen: Ejner Munksgaards Forlag, 1958), appendix.

Gordon K. Douglass, "Product Variation and International Trade in Motion Pictures," M.I.T. thesis, 1963.

G. C. Hufbauer, *Synthetic Materials and the Theory of International Trade* (London: Gerald Duckworth & Co., Ltd., 1966).

Raymond Vernon, "International Investment and International Trade in the Product Cycle," *QJE,* May, 1966.

W. Gruber, D. Mehta, and R. Vernon, "The R and D Factor in International Trade and International Investment of United States Industries," *JPE,* February, 1967.

Donald B. Keesing, "Labor Skills and International Trade," *RE & S,* August, 1965; and "Labor Skills and Comparative Advantage," *AER,* May, 1966.

A relatively early paper in the discussion was M. Posner, "International Trade and Technical Change," *OEP,* October, 1961.

POINTS

On the possibility that automobiles will become a ubiquitous manufacture, see Sir Donald MacDougall, "A Lecture on the Dollar Problem," *Econ,* August, 1954, p. 196.

Figure 4.4 was developed by J. Vanek in *The Natural Resource Content of United States Foreign Trade, 1870–1955* (Cambridge, Mass.: The M.I.T. Press, 1963).

Chapter 5 | TRADE AND GROWTH IN DEVELOPING ECONOMIES

Trade and Growth in Developing Economies

The last chapter should have made clear the intimate connection between trade and growth, including growth based on factor accretion and that rooted in technological change. But the fairly optimistic conclusion that trade responds to and changes with growth, which it is hoped that chapter conveyed, is not universally shared. On the contrary, the less developed countries today are more or less united in believing that the path to growth does not lead through trade. Ragnar Nurkse made a distinction between growth in the 19th century which was on the whole led by exports, and that in the 20th, which, with the exception of the oil-producing and the developed countries, is not. Exports can be a leading sector in growth or a lagging. It is the view of the less developed countries, which dominate the United Nations Organization on Trade and Development (UNTAD) which met in Geneva in 1964 and New Delhi in 1968, that blame for the limited help the less developed countries get today from trade can be laid at the door of the developed countries. Before we address this issue, however, and the reply to it, it may be useful to look at the 19th-century experience more generally and that of the developed countries today, where trade abets growth rather than discourages it.

Export-Led Growth in 19th-Century Developing Economies

The developing countries of the 19th century were for the most part empty lands. As they filled up, they needed to acquire many products from abroad, which implied a need to export and borrow capital. The exports consisted for the most part in what the Canadian economic historian, Innis, has called "staples," and from which he developed a "staple theory" of trade and growth. Some products contributed much more to growth than others. Furs, for example, helped but little, since they required very high land/labor and land/capital ratios:

only a couple of Indians and a canoe per 100 square miles, perhaps; and they needed little transport to ship the beaver pelts to European markets for hat felt. Lumber and metals, on the other hand, led to farming to feed the labor force. The spread of wheat went hand in hand with the extension of railroads into the interior, and large-scale shipping to deliver the product to Europe, with room on the return voyage to bring settlers in bulk.

Douglass V. North has applied staple theory to the growth of the United States and suggested that the major forces for expansion in the early 19th century were associated with various products, some more than others, and wheat more than cotton.

The process by which one product stimulates, or does not stimulate, the production of others and thereby encourage growth, has been called "linkages" by Albert O. Hirschman. Forward linkages are found when new production makes a bulky material so cheap that industry is attracted to the area to take advantage of cheap inputs. Backward linkages occur when an industry needs inputs and creates such a strong demand for them that new industries spring into being to satisfy it. Staple theory went beyond forward and backward linkages to discuss the effect of a new industry on technological change—whether it stimulated and encouraged it or not—and on income distribution. In the Pacific Northwest, for example, the lumber industry with cheap stands of timber produced a local and remote market with high per capita incomes which attracted service and other industry to the location.

The linkages of staple industries had to meet a response. The guano industry of Peru in the 19th century needed labor, but since the local Indians would not serve, the exploiters of the deposits of natural fertilizer brought in Chinese coolies. Other factors had to be brought from abroad as well—capital, transport, and management. In some cases of economic growth today, as, for example, mining in Africa, the stimulus to the development of nearby farming was present, but since the African natives did not respond to it, the opportunity gave rise to immigration of European settlers to provide the needed food. The difference between the 19th- and the 20th-century experience in export-led growth in primary products may then be less the conditions of international markets than the capacity of the economies to respond to economic signals. Or the economy could respond but once. A classic article by Myint suggests that the plantation economies of the 19th century achieved a once-and-for-all improvement in technology which was not followed up by further technological change. Partly this was because the foreign planters made a great deal of money and saw no reason to alter the system, while native laborers lacked education and an opportunity to become entrepreneurs. Partly it was because of the nature of many plantation crops such as rubber, coffee, cocoa and coconuts, which took a long time to produce, so that agricultural experimentation by the individual planter was discouraged. Myint asserted that once-and-for-all technological change was followed by fossilization. It is of some interest to record that Belgian observers today complain that their foreign trade, relying on capital intensive products of slow technological progress such as semifinished iron and steel, glass, china, soda ash, and fertilizer, is fossilized.

Export-Led Growth in Industrial Leaders

The 19th century was distinguished by export-led growth not only in the "Regions of Recent Settlement,"—largely British dominions and the former colony represented by the United States. Then, as today, the industrial leader found markets abroad, both for old products, newly produced at lower costs, and for new products. In the first half of the 19th century, Britain, for example, developed export markets in cotton textiles, iron rails, locomotives, ships, and coal. Ultimately it failed to replace these items as they were imitated and produced abroad with new products, but turned instead to sell them more intensively in the colonies and dominions with colonial preference. But it was good while it lasted, and it bred resentment in the potential competitors. Alexander Hamilton in the United States and Friedrich List in Germany developed the infant industry argument for a tariff, based on increasing returns or decreasing costs. Tariffs, they held, were needed to prevent the headstart plus economies of scale leading to complete dominance by a foreign industrial leader. This argument is not entirely lost to sight in the less developed countries today.

Export-Led Growth in Developed Countries Today

Export-led growth today works perhaps through similar linkages, but the analysis emphasizes rather different factors. In postwar Europe and Japan, for example, the process started with technological change. This reduced export prices, and made it possible to sell more goods abroad in competition with other foreign producers. Most of these goods in which technological change took place were income elastic, i.e., demand for them grew rapidly as income increased (in contrast to the demand for the primary commodities produced in the developing countries, of which more below). But the process became a positive feedback one, so long as the developed countries had extra factors with which to

expand: an increase in productivity through new investment or technological change, or both, led to lower prices, more exports, which led to
more profits, more investment, lower prices, and more exports. The
process continued as resources, largely labor, were drawn from occupations of low productivity such as agriculture elsewhere in the economy,
or from abroad. Capital was formed from profits. Only when the economies ran out of labor in the first half of the 1960's did the positive
feedback process of export-led growth meet interruption.

Initial technological change was (much of it) imitation, and closing of the wide technological gap which existed between the United
States and other developed countries at the end of the war. Some of the
change led to import substitution, which when carried far enough leads
to exports, after the local producers take over first the entire market and
then sell abroad. But much of the change in Europe and Japan went
beyond imitation to innovation—*vide* Volkswagen and Sony. It was
helped by the European Common Market, and rapid growth in neigh-
boring countries. While plans for growth emphasized investment in
domestic industries and social capital, the lead in expansion was usually
taken by exports. The Italian case is particularly striking as moderniza-
tion in exports industries led export prices to fall in a world of creeping
inflation.

The Terms of Trade

The less developed countries today complain that they are unable
to follow the example of either the less developed countries of the
19th century or of the developed countries today. The reason, they assert,
is that the conditions they face are different. In particular, their spokesman, Raul Prebisch, insists, the terms of trade of less developed countries
are secularly declining.

Before we analyze the Prebisch contention about the terms of
trade, it is useful to say a few words about this concept, which is easily
misinterpreted. The terms of trade, as already made clear in Chapter 3,
is the relation between the prices of exports and the price of imports. In
barter trade, this is given either as $\dfrac{Px}{Pm}$, i.e., the price of exports divided
by the price of imports, or $\dfrac{Qm}{Qx}$, the quantity of imports divided by the
quantity of exports. Since the relative price of exports in such a diagram
as Figure 3.4 is the amount of imports one can get for one's exports,
these amount to the same thing when $PxQx = PmQm$, i.e., when the

value of exports is equal to the value of imports. (If the student divides $PxQx = PmQm$ by $PmQx$, he will find that $\dfrac{Px}{Pm} = \dfrac{Qm}{Qx}$). The $\dfrac{Px}{Pm}$ version is called the net barter terms of trade; the $\dfrac{Qm}{Qx}$ the gross barter terms of trade. It is not entirely clear how these uncommunicative terms crept into the jargon of economists, but they were adopted by Taussig and Viner and the rest of us are stuck with them.

A higher price for exports with the same price for imports, a lower price for imports with the same price of exports, or a larger volume of imports for the same volume of exports (with balanced trade) or a smaller volume of exports for the same volume of imports (again when $PxQx = PmQm$) is a favorable development in the terms of trade. The less developed countries claim, however, that the price of their exports is going down relative to the price of imports over time—an unfavorable change.

When trade is not balanced and $\dfrac{Px}{Pm} \gtrless \dfrac{Qm}{Qx}$, the net barter terms of trade differ from the gross barter. The latter become, on the whole, uninteresting since they may reflect less price movements than changes in the balance of payments, and even capital movements. Most reference, therefore, is to the net barter terms of trade, and when one reads "terms of trade" without qualification, one should think $\dfrac{Px}{Pm}$. This is a concept such as farm parity, which represents the relationship between the prices at which farmers sell and those at which they buy.

But like parity, the net barter terms of trade do not convey much meaning in their unqualified form. For one thing, prices can be held very high, but if sales volume falls off, raising the price of exports can overdo it. Opposite to the old joke "we lose a little on every sale, but, boy, do we have volume!" is the exact antithesis, "We make a big profit on every sale, but we don't sell much." Accordingly, the idea was developed of weighting the net barter terms of trade by the volume of exports. If export prices rise but volume falls off equally, this measure —called the "income terms of trade"—shows no change. The same concept is sometimes called the "capacity to import." It is obvious that if over the long run, $PxQx$ must equal $PmQm$, $\dfrac{PxQx}{Pm}$ determines Qm, or the volume of what the country can import. The less developed countries in fact say that they cannot change Px, or Pm or Qx so that their volume of imports, *Qm,* is determined for them. $\dfrac{PxQm}{Pm}$ is a superior

concept to $\dfrac{Px}{Pm}$ for the less developed countries' purposes. But the latter is the one usually employed.

When these concepts are applied to more than one commodity on a side, it should be obvious, we have to use index numbers. Instead of $\dfrac{Px}{Pm}$ for the net barter terms of trade, we use

$$\frac{Px_1}{Pm_1} \div \frac{Px_0}{Pm_0}$$

where 1 and 0 represent two periods in time. Here it is vitally important to make sure that the base year is a representative period. When the Agricultural Adjustment Act chose 1909–14 as the base on which to measure parity, it was because this was a particularly favorable period for farmers. Similarly, the British seem always to measure changes in their terms of trade from 1938 when they were the most favorable in the nearly 100 years between 1870 and the present. Conversely, the less developed countries today choose a base of 1950 when primary product prices soared sky-high under the influence of the outbreak of the war in Korea.

But the volume of exports and the choice of a base year are not all that's wrong with the net barter terms of trade as a measure of welfare. One must also take productivity into account. In the previous chapter it was noted that technological change of the most neutral sort worsens the terms of trade. But this does not mean that the country is worse off. It can be, as will be indicated later in this chapter. But typically what it means is that the country is sharing some of its improvement in productivity with its customers. With changing efficiency, the net barter terms of trade are distinctly misleading as a measure, as the farm population in the United States is unwilling to acknowledge in its insistence on parity. One ought to take into account the improvement in productivity as well.

Suppose export prices fall 10 percent relative to import prices, as measured from a suitable base year, but export costs have fallen 20 percent. The country is clearly better off. The concept used to express this is called the "single factoral terms of trade"—again a monstrous piece of jargon—which is given as $\dfrac{Px}{Pm} \cdot Zx$ where Zx stands for productivity in exports. (This expression should be adjusted, of course, for changes from a suitably chosen base period.) The "single" in this designation differentiates it from the "double factoral terms of trade" or $\dfrac{Px}{Pm} \cdot \dfrac{Zx}{Zm}$, which takes account not only of productivity in the country's exports, but also the productivity of foreign factors in the country's imports. The single factoral terms of trade is a much more relevant concept than the double factoral. We are interested in what our factors can earn in goods, not what our factor services can command in the services of foreign factors.

Related to productivity abroad, moreover, is a question of the quality of the goods imported. This is of some considerable relevance to the Prebisch claim, because coffee, copper, cotton, and so on, to stay alliterative, are roughly the same goods today that they were 50 years ago, whereas the price index of imports is not likely to have taken full account of the improvement in quality of automobiles, radios, petroleum-refining equipment, and trucks.

Further on the issue of whether the net barter terms of trade is the appropriate criterion for the distribution of the gains from trade between developing and developed countries, a distinction may be made between the terms of trade on merchandise alone, and those on goods and services in combination. Its importance is that some of the "price" in the export price level in the developing countries is attached to value added by foreign factors of production. If the price of exports rises, for example, and profits on foreign investment rise sufficiently to account for all of the increase in the price of exports, the local economy has not gained. Putting it this way is not likely to give much comfort to the less developed countries. But suppose the price of exports declines, and the return on investment declines as well. In this case the country is no worse off, when the net barter merchandise terms of trade would lead one to think it was. What is needed for deeper analysis then is the terms of trade on the current account of the balance of payments as a whole, not merely merchandise, or the terms of trade on domestic value added, sometimes called "returned value."

One further extension of this point pertains to transport costs, which will be discussed more fully in the next chapter. The merchandise terms of trade are generally given at border values, i.e., f.o.b. (free on board) for exports, and c.i.f. (cost, insurance, freight) for imports. If the country carries none of its own exports, and all of its imports, this is a good measure for merchandise and the transport account in the balance of payments. But this condition is unlikely to be fulfilled. And it is especially unlikely that the reciprocal of the merchandise terms of trade of a trading partner measured f.o.b. for exports and c.i.f. for imports will accurately reflect the terms of trade of a country. In his original work, Prebisch could find few terms of trade series for Latin America going back to 1870 and assumed that the Latin-American series would be the reciprocal of the British series. But this is not so. If transport costs decline relative to the costs of merchandise, as has been the case since 1870, the merchandise terms of trade of two trading partners can both simultaneously improve. Export prices in both cases are unchanged, for example, while import prices decline because of cheaper transport.

For all these theoretical and statistical reasons one cannot accept the Prebisch case that the terms of trade of the less developed countries have persistently moved against any particular group of less developed countries such as Latin America. But there is nonetheless something to the case.

Engel's Law, Biased Factor and Technological Change, and Monopoly

The case can be made that the changes in demand, factor growth and technology discussed in the previous chapter tend to operate, on balance, systematically against less developed and in favor of the more developed countries. Their effect is partly on the net barter terms of trade, and partly on the volume of trade, or the gross barter terms. But let us take the items one by one.

Engel's law states that as income grows, the demand for food grows less than proportionately. This is a law of pervasive importance in economic growth, with profound side effects in such questions, for example, as the necessity for the political importance of farmers to decline. To the extent that income elasticities determine the volume of exports, and to the extent that the less developed countries grow food-stuffs in a world of growing income per capita, the demand for their exports will grow more slowly than the demand for manufactured exports.

The last sentence is a highly qualified one, however. The less developed countries export coffee, tea, rice, tropical fruit, sugar, fats and oils, and other foodstuffs, but they also export products of high-income elasticity, not only oil, but also rubber, nonferrous metals, iron ore, diamonds, and so on. The volume of exports depends partly on income per capita, but also on population growth. And exports depend only partly on income elasticity abroad. To the extent that a developing country can produce them cheaply, and the potential importer abroad does not shut them off with protective policies, exports can grow through a competitive effect, as well as through income changes. Canada, Australia, the United States and Argentina took over the European market for grain in the 19th century from local farmers. And Japanese textiles grew not on the basis of income elasticities, but on cheapness.

As already mentioned in the previous chapter, factor growth and technological change in the developed countries seem biased in some considerable degree against the less developed countries. Not only is demand biased, through Engel's law, but capital grows faster than population (and land) and technology makes it possible to substitute capital for land and labor which the less developed countries have in relative abundance. Synthetics in rubber, silk, cotton, quinine, petroleum, fertilizer, and so on are part of this movement. More and more elaborate manufacture, so that a dollar's worth of raw material is worked up into higher and higher amounts of the finished product, is another. Thin coating in tin, and printed circuits which saved copper are only two examples which spring to mind. A smaller and smaller portion of final demand is therefore provided by the raw material producer.

Finally, the less developed countries assert that the terms of trade are governed in part by differences in the competitive situation as between the developed and the less developed countries. An increase in productivity in the developed world is likely to lead to no decline in price, as administered pricing diverts the increase in productivity first into higher profits and then into higher incomes for productive factors. In the less developed countries, on the other hand, a high degree of competitiveness among countries leads to lower prices, rather than higher factor incomes. The less developed countries give away more of their gains in productivity because of monopolistic competition abroad and more nearly perfect competition among them.

The Impact of Internal Conditions

The less developed countries tend to blame the environment in which they operate for the fact that they are unable, as they insist, to grow through trade as other countries have done. The terms of trade run against them, and the fault lies in conditions in the developed countries. Before this case can be accepted, however, it is necessary to explore whether there are circumstances within the less developed countries which contribute to the result. At least four possibilities have been explored in the literature: their inability to transform; their need for intermediate goods; disequilibrium in factor markets; and misallocation of resources through misguided protectionism.

The theory of comparative advantage assumes that a country can smoothly and costlessly adjust production along its production possibilities curve. It also implies that when a country invests additional resources in growth it does so in response to the price system. This implies that if the foreign offer curve is relatively inelastic it does not use its resources to expand export capacity but grows in import-biased fashion.

Figure 5.1 shows an offer curve, $O–T–A$ of a less developed country which is highly skewed in production. The offer curve is kinked because the country is fully specialized in the production of A-exportables and cannot expand its production at higher prices.[1] Intersecting B's offer curve at P, A gets substantial gains from trade but it has to be careful about growth. If its production possibilities grow only in

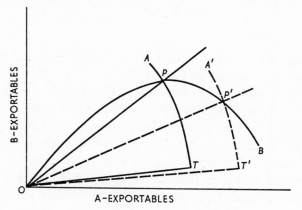

FIG. 5.1.   Adverse Terms of Trade through Growth

the A-good, it is ultrabiased and extends the offer curve down and to the right, as for example to $O–T'–A'$. This sharply worsens the terms of trade, from $O–P$ to $O–P'$. Under the conditions shown, where B's offer curve is inelastic, it is possible that growth in A leave it worse off than before, what Bhagwati has called "immiserizing growth" and Edgeworth called "damnifying." This means that the loss in the terms of trade has outweighed the increase in the production possibilities curve, which would normally have been expected to put a country on a higher consumption indifference curve; it ends up on a lower one, as in Figure

---

[1] The force of this statement cannot be seen by a student who has not worked through Appendix C which links the production possibilities curve to the offer curve. For those that have, the $O–T$ segment of the offer curve represents the constant cost portion of the production possibilities frontier. When the country is fully specialized and has no gains from trade, it will trade at T. At higher prices it cannot change output and it increases its consumption of the A-good only slowly.

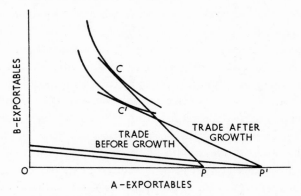

FIG. 5.2. "Immiserizing Growth": Ending Up on a Lower Consumption
Indifference Curve after Growth

5.2. The answer, of course, is not to foreswear growth, but not to grow
in a commodity facing inelastic demand.

The diagram shows one important point about the trade of the less
developed countries, however, which is often overlooked. A may not be
able to gain much from growth, but it obtains substantial gains from
trade at O–T–A in Figure 5.1. The contrast is with the position portrayed in Figure 5.3 where A and B with highly similar production
possibilities and tastes, as reflected in their offer curves, do not lose
much in terms of trade from growth, but have limited gains from trade

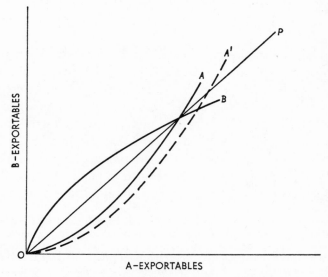

FIG. 5.3. Trade between Developed Countries with Limited Gains

to begin with. The less developed countries complaint that the growth of world trade has been largely among the developed countries over-looks the point that it is the gains from trade that count, not mere volume.

One reason A in Figure 5.1 may grow in the export-biased direction is because that is all it knows how to do. Resources may not be readily shiftable to the import-competing industry because of lack of complementary resources, or other friction. Another reason, cited by Linder, is that imports from B may kill off the import-competing industry, as British textile exports to India killed off the handicrafts, and free trade between Ireland and England after 1801 led Irish industry to collapse, and drove its population to seek work across the Irish Channel. When it is impossible to make a living in the import-competing industry, growth takes place in the export industry until it goes too far and loses the gains from trade which were originally substantial.

One alleged reason that the law of comparative advantage should not be applied to the less developed countries is that factor prices in these countries do not always reflect social marginal productivities. Suppose, for example, that there is disguised unemployment in agriculture, that is, labor employed which has a real marginal product below its money wage, and possibly as low as zero, while at the same time wages are high in manufacturing. Because wages are low in agriculture and high in manufacturing, it will appear that the country has a comparative advantage in agriculture and a disadvantage in industry. But if the social marginal product is still lower in agriculture than in industry, it will pay to shift workers from agriculture to industry, which may require interference in trade. The position may be illustrated in Figure 5.4 where the terms of trade cut the production possibilities curve at P, and trade lands consumption within the production possibilities curve at C, rather than on the curve itself at some point such as T (where the country might export either good, depending on demand conditions). Or the position can be summed up by stating that the case violates the condition of full trading equilibrium $P = DRT_P = FRT_T = DRS_C$ where P is price, DRT_P is the domestic rate of transformation in production, FRT_T is the foreign rate of transformation in trade, and DRS_C is the domestic rate of substitution in consumption. The case where factor prices do not reflect social marginal productivities, which has been put forward as an argument against trade, or for a tariff, by Manoilescu in the 1930's, and by Hagen more recently, rests on the fact that with noncompetitive factor markets, the market price of goods differs from DRT_P.

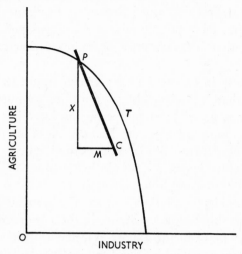

FIG. 5.4. Trade When Private Costs Do Not Reflect Social Costs

The third argument that the less developed countries should not follow the path of free trade, in addition to their inability to transform, and the failure of market prices to reflect social values, rests on the existence of intermediate goods, which are needed in relatively fixed proportions in many productive processes, and which the less developed countries cannot produce for themselves. If sufficient of these intermediate goods—fuel, iron and steel, cement, lumber, and so on,—are not imported, domestic resources cannot be fully utilized, since the possibilities of substituting domestic resources for imports are limited, and since they are needed together for production. Thus far, the trading problem of the less developed countries is no different from that of the developed, who equally depend on imported supplies of intermediate goods to keep their economies going, as they are forcibly reminded when some such event occurs as the closing of the Suez Canal to oil imports.

But Linder, who emphasizes the importance of intermediate goods, maintains that the less developed countries cannot solve their intermediate goods problem in the same way that the developed countries can. This is partly because their capacity to transform is more limited, so that their requirements are proportionately larger. This fact gives them an import minimum of capital equipment (for growth) and raw materials and fuel for maintaining existing capacity in operation. They may at the same time labor under the existence of an export maximum, based on the inelasticity of the foreign offer curve for primary products and their inability at an early stage of growth to produce and market finished manufactures. The problem arises where the import minimum exceeds the export maximum, leaving a foreign exchange gap. In this circumstance, the opponents of classical trade theory assert, it is necessary for the less developed countries systematically to cut down on imports of goods which they can make for themselves or do without (without affecting domestic factor use). This means in effect, import substitution for consumers goods.

Import Substitution

In the process of growth, domestic production replaces imports. This is a wholly normal process. Increased productivity in export industry leads to higher incomes which are spent on items first imported, but as the market grows, produced locally. As productivity in exports increases, the same output can be obtained for fewer resources; those freed may be attracted into import-competing enterprise through the price system. In Denmark, for example, exports of dairy products, bacon and eggs provided the income spillover for local industry to grow great under free trade and ultimately itself develop export markets in manufactures. Import substitution is therefore a natural concomitant of growth. But there is import substitution as a natural process and import substitution as a policy; they are not necessarily the same thing, nor do they necessarily lead to the same result.

In his classic pioneering study of growth, *The Conditions of Economic Progress,* Colin Clark observed that with growth, resources transferred from primary production (agriculture, fishing, forestry, and sometimes mining) to secondary production (manufacturing) and tertiary output (services). This is the result of Engel's law. But it is one thing to observe what happens in growth, and another to set out to grow by constructing a manufacturing sector. This is the fallacy of *post hoc ergo propter hoc* (after this, therefore because of this). The path to growth may lead through more efficient agriculture to a manufacturing sector which is built up as a spillover from the income increase generated by the primary sector. But to invest resources in a manufacturing sector as a planned policy may not lead to growth. By the same token, import substitution as observed historically is no warrant for applied policies of import substitution, which may end up producing the wrong thing at too high a cost.

Under the advice of Prebisch, Singer, Myrdal and others, however, most of the less developed countries have set about to meet their foreign exchange gap by import substitution in consumers goods. Where the country does face an offer curve of unit import elasticity or less, this is the economic course, since an enlarged volume of exports would lead to a lower return in value. But import substitution frequently takes off on its own, and reaches the point where the country in question spends more resources to acquire goods domestically than it would need to produce goods for export and transform them into the needed goods through trade. Where exchange rates are overvalued, domestic factor prices fail to reflect social marginal returns, and trade is restricted so that goods prices fail to reflect the foreign rate of transformation through trade. It is frequently impossible any more to know whether a country would do better to expand or cut down on trade, and in what goods.

A further discussion of these issues must wait until Chapter 10 when we discuss the commercial policy appropriate to the developing countries.

Summary

Trade was an engine of growth for the open lands of the 19th century and for the leader in the Industrial Revolution, Great Britain. Export-led growth is also a modern phenomenon in postwar Europe and Japan. In the 19th century, trade in some staples contributed more to growth than others, through linkages which stimulated other industry, or technological change. But linkages require a response, and when there was none locally, the stimulus turned abroad and led to enclaves cut off from the local economy.

Today's less developed countries, except for oil producers, expect little growth from trade. This is partly because of the world environment, in which the terms of trade are believed to turn systematically against the less developed countries; partly it is the result of conditions in the countries themselves. On the first score, the world environment, it is maintained that the developed countries grow with antitrade biased demand and antitrade biased factor growth and technological change. In addition, monopolistic competition among the developed countries and more competitive conditions of production in the less developed hurt the terms of trade of the latter. On the second score—conditions in the developing countries—their capacity to take advantage of the opportunities for growth presented by trade is restricted by inability to transform, i.e., to shift resources where they can earn the highest return; by the fact that factor and goods prices do not reflect social marginal productivities, and by a heavy dependence on imports of intermediate and capital goods for growth, and by full utilization of their resources at a time when an export maximum exists.

As a consequence of these circumstances in the world and within the developing countries many of the latter seek actively to substitute domestic production for imports. In so doing, they run grave risk of misallocating resources to wasteful uses.

In the course of developing the foregoing points, the chapter also expounded various concepts of the terms of trade, and distinguished between the volume of overall trade, and the volume of trade embodying substantial gains.

SUGGESTED READING

TEXTS

Gerald M. Meier, *International Trade and Economic Development* (New York: Harper & Row, Publishers, 1963; rev. and extended, 1967) has an excellent treatment and a large bibliography. On damnifying growth, see Kemp, chap. vi.

TREATISES

The views of Prebisch, spokesman for the less developed countries, are set forth in many publications, the latest available of which is United Nations Conference on Trade and Development, *Towards a New Trade Policy for Development,* A Report by the Secretary-General of the Conference (New York: United Nations, 1964). See S. B. Linder, *Trade and Trade Policy for Development* (New York: Frederick A. Praeger, Inc., 1967).

On the 19th century see Ragnar Nurkse, *Problems of Capital Formation and Patterns of Trade and Development* (London: Oxford University Press, 1967) (paperback). This is two small books published together, the latter of which, the Wicksell Lecture given in 1959, is the relevant one. See also Melville H. Watkins, "A Staple Theory of Economic Growth," *Canadian Journal of Economics and Political Science,* May, 1963; and H. Myint, "The Gains from International Trade and Backward Countries," *RES,* 1954–55. Bhagwati's essay on "Immiserizing Growth" is reprinted in American Economic Association, *Readings in International Economics.*

On the terms of trade, see Viner, p. 58 and C. P. Kindleberger's monograph, *The Terms of Trade* (New York: The Technology Press and John Wiley & Sons, Inc., 1956).

Hollis Chenery's "Patterns of Industrial Growth," *AER,* March, 1960, outlines how domestic production substitutes for imports over time.

POINTS

Douglass V. North's interpretation of early U.S. history in terms of export-led growth is to be found in *The Economic Growth of the United States, 1790–1860* (Englewood Cliffs, N.J.: Prentice-Hall, Inc., 1961). Hirschman's point about linkages is from *The Strategy of Economic Development* (New Haven, Conn.: Yale University Press, 1958). A study of modern export-led growth is Robert M. Stern's *Foreign Trade and Economic Growth in Italy* (New York: Frederick A. Praeger, Inc., 1967).

The reference to the Hagen article is "An Economic Justification of Protectionism," *QJE,* November, 1958.

Chapter 6 : TRANSPORT COSTS AND LOCATION THEORY

Transport Costs and Price Equality

The introduction of transport costs into the analysis of international trade disturbs the conclusion that international trade equalizes the prices of traded goods in the trading countries. If, in the absence of transport costs, our old friends, wheat and cloth, would have exchanged on a one-to-one basis, the necessity to overcome costs of

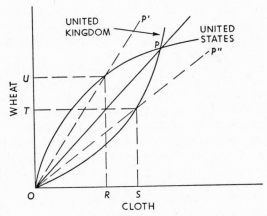

Fig. 6.1. General Equilibrium with Transport Costs

transport will make the import good more expensive in both countries and the export good less valuable. In the United States, for example, wheat might exchange for cloth at 8 bushels for 12 yards, while in Britain the ratio would be 8 yards for 12 bushels. The implications of this may be illustrated in diagrammatic form. In Figure 6.1, the British offer curve of cloth for wheat and the American offer curve of wheat against cloth cross at point P. But with transport costs, the price ratios in the two countries must differ, so that the line from O through P cannot be taken as the price in both countries. The effect of transport costs of both goods is represented by the angle formed by $O-P'$, the price in the United States, and $O-P''$, the price in Britain.

But these prices cannot solve the problem. At $O-P'$, the United States is willing to offer $O-U$ of wheat against $O-R$ of cloth. At P'', the United Kingdom is willing to offer $O-S$ of cloth for $O-T$ of wheat. Prices cannot differ and solve the equation of trade.

The difficulty, of course, lies in the fact that when transport costs are introduced, we really move to a three-commodity diagram, in which Britain offers cloth for wheat and transport and the United States offers wheat for cloth and transport. The difference between what the United States gets at the price $O-P'$ and what Britain is willing to offer in terms of cloth at the price prevailing in its country takes the form of transport. The offer curve analysis can be used to illustrate propositions involving transport costs only when these costs are expressed in terms of the traded goods themselves. Examples of this sort can be made up: Transport costs of oil and coal can be expressed in terms of the proportion of the delivered commodity used up in transit—immediately after World War II Silesian coal was sold by Poland in France even though the train journey and return required burning up one third of the original trainload of fuel. Or one can hypothesize commodities such as ice which arrive smaller than they start. In these cases, using the general equilibrium apparatus of offer curves or production possibilities and indifference curves, transport costs will require the price lines in the two countries to differ in slope by an amount representing transport costs in terms of the two commodities.

We can show the effects of transport costs somewhat more readily, however, if we fall back on partial equilibrium analysis. This shows the position before and after trade in one commodity only. The partial equilibrium analysis, though incomplete, is useful for a variety of purposes. In particular we shall find it invaluable in the analysis of tariffs, which appear in the next chapter, and of exchange adjustments, which we encounter in Chapter 15. The analysis is partial because it suggests the impact of trade on the demand and supply of a single commodity, priced in terms of money, without taking into account the repercussions on these demand and supply curves of changes in income, exchange rates, prices of other goods, or anything else, which may be affected. A demand curve can be drawn only with a knowledge of all other demand curves in the system, and it is valid only so long as all other demand curves in the system are presumed to be fixed. The Marshall-Edgeworth offer curve analysis, as well as production possibilities and indifference curves, all get away from considerations of money and income and represent a long-run equilibrium position. The partial equilibrium analysis, on the other hand, deals only with the immediate position after trade is begun and abstracts from secondary effects, repercussions, and adjustments.

Transport Costs in Partial Equilibrium

Figures 6.2*a* and 6.2*b* give the demand and supply of cloth in the United Kingdom and in the United States before trade. Both demand and supply represent quantities of cloth sought and available, respectively, against a given price per yard. The price in the United States has been converted by means of the existing exchange rate to the English

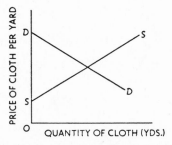

Fig. 6.2*a*. Demand and Supply for Cloth in the United Kingdom

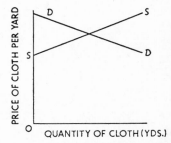

Fig. 6.2*b*. Demand and Supply for Cloth in the United States

unit of account, or perhaps it is the other way; it does not matter. The price of cloth in the United States is much higher, in the absence of trade, than the price in Britain.

To indicate what will happen after trade is opened, it is necessary to get both figures on the same diagram. This can be done in either of two ways. It would be possible to construct a new curve from the quantities demanded in the United States and United Kingdom at various prices by simply adding the two demands at each price and drawing a single new curve. The same could be done for supply. The intersection of the two new curves would be the new price, after trade is begun, in the absence of transport costs (and, to issue the warning for the last time, as an initial response). This is done in Figure 6.3.

The other method is portrayed in Figure 6.4. Here the four curves are put on the same diagram with the same vertical axis. The horizontal axis, however, runs in two directions from the origin. For the United States it runs in normal fashion from left to right, and for Britain it

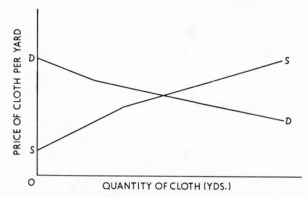

FIG. 6.3.   Demand and Supply for Cloth in the United Kingdom
and the United States

starts from the same point as for the United States but goes from right
to left. The U.S. demand and supply curves are exactly as in Figure 6.2*b*.
The British curves, however, are now inverted. The demand curve is
negatively sloped in proper manner, if one reads it from right to left. If
one is not careful, however, it appears to be positively sloped, like a

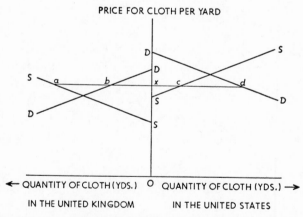

FIG. 6.4.   Partial Equilibrium Price for Cloth, No Transport Costs

supply curve. The supply curve, on the other hand, now looks something like a demand curve, though in the latter incarnation it would
have no vertical axis from which to start.

The new price after trade in the absence of transport costs is
calculated by the horizontal price line common to both curves which
will balance the excess of supply in the one country with the excess of

demand in the other. In Figure 6.4 the price line *a–d* settles at that level where *a–b*, the excess of supply in Britain, is equal to *c–d*, the excess of demand in the United States. Of course, *a–b* then represents exports and *c–d* imports. In Britain home production amounts to *a–x*, while home consumption is only *b–x*. In the United States, on the other hand, only those producers within the range *x–c* are efficient enough to compete with imports. The rest of consumption is satisfied by imports.

The partial equilibrium diagram is useful in showing how exports raise the price of a commodity above what would have been the case without trade and how imports lower the price. This is a truth worth emphasizing. When we put aside the fancy apparatus of production-possibilities and indifference curves, there is a tendency to remember merely that a good must be cheap before it can be exported from a country. This is true. But exports raise the price of the goods in which the country has a comparative advantage, as the partial equilibrium analysis shows. The U.S. exports wheat because it is cheap; wheat is less cheap in the United States than it would be without exports. The selection of the example of wheat underlines an important assumption which the student should note: that of decreasing returns. With increasing returns or decreasing costs, of course, exports cheapen commodities.

Thus far the partial-equilibrium analysis has been like that of general equilibrium—in the absence of transport costs. But transport costs can readily be included. Prices in the importing country will be higher than in the exporting country by a determinate amount: by the unit costs of transport. The solution is the same as that in Figure 6.4, except that the price line must now be broken at the vertical axis and continued at a higher level. The equilibrium price is that which equalizes exports and imports and is higher in the United States than in Britain by the costs of transport. This is shown in Figure 6.5, where *a–b* equals *c–d*, and *w–t* represents the costs of transport.

Costs of transport, the diagram shows, reduce trade below what it would otherwise be. No matter how frequently the theorist may abstract from them in his exercises, their existence means that prices in the exporting country are below what they would otherwise have been and that prices in the importing country are higher.

The notion of transport costs may be broadened to include all costs of transfer, mainly freight, but also insurance, handling, freight-forwarders' commissions, etc., and even tariffs. In the rest of the book we shall frequently mean transfer costs instead of transport costs, although transport is typically the most significant of these transfer costs and is always the inescapable one.

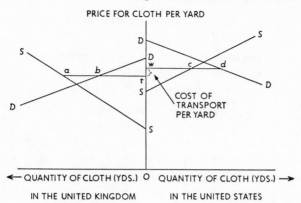

FIG. 6.5.   Partial Equilibrium Price for Cloth, Transport Costs

The Impact of Transport Costs

The existence of transport costs affects the theory of international trade in two ways. In the first place, it requires us to modify the answer given to the question of what goods are exported and imported. Price differences in two countries before trade must be wider than costs of transfer. In Figure 6.6, for example, transport costs, *w–t,* are wider than

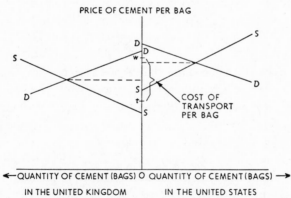

FIG. 6.6.   Transport Costs in Excess of Price Differences in Partial Equilibrium

the difference in price between the United States and Britain. The result is that international trade will not take place in this commodity, no matter what the factor endowments of the countries concerned or the factor requirements for its production. If transport costs did not exist, which means that all goods and services would be transportable in costless fashion, international trade would take place in every good and service. The existence of home goods has its origin in transport costs. Some goods, such as houses, for which transport costs approach infinity, can never take part in international trade.

A major cause of expanded world trade after World War II has been the progressive reduction of transport costs. This is partly owing to technological improvement which is discussed below. But a reduction of transport costs relative to production costs acts as a reduction in tariffs, expanding trade relative to output in already traded goods, and bringing goods into international commerce which had previously been home goods.

Some international trade is based primarily on transport costs and has little to do with a general theory of factor proportions. This is particularly true of local trade which takes place across a long international boundary. With the elimination of trade barriers as a result of the European Coal and Steel Community, Germany now exports steel to France in the north and imports steel from France in the south. This economizes transport. Or to take another example, Canada exports oil to the United States in the west and imports oil from Venezuela (by pipeline from Portland, Maine) in the east, so that its net comparative advantage is based on gross comparative advantage and disadvantage, which can exist simultaneously because of the importance of transfer costs. Or West Germany can export coal to the Netherlands down the Rhine while at the same time it imports coal into Hamburg from the United States.

But transport costs do more than serve as a cause of some trade and a barrier to other. With the fact that processing involves changes in weight and bulk, a knowledge of transport costs can be developed into a generalized theory of the location of industry, whether internationally or between regions, to form the link between industrial economics and industrial engineering. Location theory is a distinct and significant branch of economics. Classical trade theory tended to think of each region as a point, and all regions so close to one another that transfer could take place in costless fashion. To the location economist, distance is either a cost to be met or an input, practically equivalent to a factor of production, along with land, labor, and capital. In this latter connection, of course, the input is distance with a negative sign—or rather nearness. Nearness to the market, as productive land, makes it possible to produce a commodity for sale more cheaply. Without nearness or productive land, there is a cost to be overcome.

The theory of location of industry has validity even though the principles of location have not always been understood explicitly and followed by business entrepreneurs. Location analyses are now being made by industrial engineers in accordance with these principles. But industry follows locational principles in Darwinian or evolutionary fashion. Industry which has been well located has survived and flourished. Industry which has been badly located has tended to die through perennially low profits and business failure.

Not all evolutionary location is due to transport costs, of course. A good deal of industrial location is related to economics external to the firm—particularly in the form of a supply of trained labor—which have their origin in accidental or random occurrences and grow by agglomeration. Fichtel and Sachs, a bicycle firm, happened to locate their plant in Schweinfurt and to prosper. Various workmen split off and formed separate competing firms, staying close by in the hope of attracting other trained workers. The old firm and the new trained more workers. The result of several generations of this kind of growth was the development of one of the ballbearing capitals of the world. The location of the clock industry in Meriden, Waterbury, Derby, and Ansonia—a cluster of towns outside New Haven in Connecticut—was also due to accidental growth of this kind. With decreasing costs, an industry may evolve in a given location through an initial success, with the choice of location based on mere chance.

The Rationale of Transport Costs

It would be simple enough to take transport costs into account in the real world if they were proportional to weight and distance. But weight is by no means the only criterion relating to the goods shipped. Weight, bulk, and value are not all positively correlated. When a commodity is relatively valuable, it can bear a higher proportional charge to its weight than when it is relatively cheap. Orchids cost more to ship per pound than sand. This is a reflection of the fact that the market for transport services is not perfectly competitive as between different commodities. Transportation services have a large element of overhead cost in them which may be unequally assigned to different products carried. For cheap, bulky commodities, where transport costs are very large in relation to total value, on the other hand, the proportion of overhead charged must be kept low in order to make it possible to move the goods at all.

But there are many other aspects of transportation rates which indicate the imperfectly competitive nature of the market. Goods must move by fixed routes, and two different routes of different distance between the same points generally charge the same rate. So-called backhaul rates, or cheap rates given for cargoes on ships which would otherwise be returning in ballast to pick up a new cargo, are another indication of the same general phenomenon. The overhead costs are assigned mainly to the outward journey, and the backhaul rate can be kept cheaper because only direct costs must be met and any return in excess of these is clear profit. Examples of backhaul rates are to be found in the rate on coal from the lower lakes to Duluth, which is far cheaper per ton than the rate on iron ore from the head of the lakes to, say,

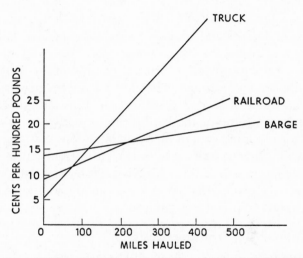

FIG. 6.7. Cost of Hauling 100 Pounds by Different Carriers for Different Distances (Adapted from E. M. Hoover, *The Location of Economic Activity* [New York: McGraw-Hill Book Co., Inc., 1948], p. 21.)

Cleveland. Conversely, in export trade, the rate on coal from Hampton Roads to Norway is $12 a ton, while the backhaul rate on iron ore from Narvik to Sparrow's Point in Baltimore is $4.50.

Not only do rates differ per commodity, depending upon its value or the direction of movement. The ratio of overhead to total costs will also vary, depending upon the form of transport. Once a commodity is loaded upon a barge, for example, it makes little difference whether it is hauled 10 or 500 miles. The overhead element is less significant in railroads, but still important. In trucking, it is of almost no importance, but direct operating costs are high. The result is that truck rates are cheap for short hauls but become increasingly expensive as the distance is increased. Figure 6.7 shows the cost per 100 pounds for carload lots of commodities by railroad, barge, and truck in 1939 and 1940, to illustrate the point.

Implicit in the data in Figure 6.7 is the high cost of handling, as contrasted with simple haulage. This is seen especially when the fixed path by which goods must move causes their transshipment from one type of transport to another. In a few cases, transport by two types of carriers is competitive with the use of a more expensive carrier for the entire journey. Part of the freight moving from Chicago to New York for export comes by rail the whole way, and part by barge to Buffalo and train (or by Erie Canal boat) thereafter. Frequently, however, transshipment from one means of transport to another involves such cost of handling that processing is undertaken at those places where transshipment is required.

Supply-Oriented Commodities

In terms of location theory, all commodities fall into one of three categories. They may be supply-oriented, market-oriented, or footloose.

Supply-oriented commodities are those in which the industrial processes tend to be located near the source of the major materials or fuel. These commodities are, for the most part, weight losing or weight saving in the course of processing or manufacture; or they may be products with heavy fuel consumption at a stage where the weight of the fuel (or its unique character) is important relative to the weight of the product; or they may be, particularly in agriculture, commodities which require preservation, grading, or standardization.

These industries or industrial processes will be located near the supply of the material or fuel in order to reduce procurement costs, which would otherwise include a large element for the transport of the materials. It is evidently sensible to concentrate ores near the mine, if the power or fuel can be found, in order to save on the bulk transport of waste material. It may, on the other hand, be necessary to move bauxite from Dutch Guiana to the Saguenay River in Canada, despite its bulk of unusable material, because the electric power necessary for the reduction of bauxite to alumina is unavailable in Dutch Guiana. (Atomic power may change this, and ultimately relocate all processes now strongly rooted to electric power.)

Cane crushing, the extraction of sugar from beets, the canning and freezing of vegetables and fish, and the grading of fruit are all supply-oriented industries. Frequently an industry will have a historic supply orientation which is no longer valid but will continue to remain where it is, more or less. Thus the textile industry in New England was originally attracted to waterpower sites on the Merrimac, Taunton, and Blackstone rivers; the paper mills on the Connecticut River were originally constructed near a supply of pulp, long since cut over.

The iron and steel industry abundantly illustrates the intricacies of supply and fuel orientation. When charcoal was used to produce cast iron, the industry was located at the iron mines—in the Catskills, Berkshires, Adirondacks—where wood for fuel was abundant. With conversion to coal, the industry became coal-oriented, particularly as 17 tons of coal were originally required for 1 ton of iron ore. Improvements in technology and the substitution of scrap for iron ore gradually reduced these proportions, but only after the industry in the United States had a historic orientation in the Pittsburgh, Cleveland, and Gary areas. With the prospect of higher prices for Mesabi iron ore in the middle of the 20th century, however, and imports of ore from Latin America, Africa, and Labrador, mills are moving toward the East Coast. In part, this is supply orientation toward iron ore and recovery scrap. To some extent, however, with new, huge, bulk carriers, the steel industry is overcoming transport costs. One of the remarkable phenomena of the postwar period has been the Japanese development of an exporting position in steel, using coal imported from the United States and iron ore brought from Australia. In part, it is market orientation, which was important for certain steel products such as shipplate, but which now becomes stronger throughout the industry. Changes in technology produce changes in location pulls in industry and in international trade.

The completion of the St. Lawrence Seaway halted part of this movement to the West Coast, especially for the steel industry of Cleveland using iron ore from Labrador. All great innovations in transport—new means of locomotion such as the steamship, railroad, pipeline, airplane, jet plane, and now the giant tankship and ore carrier, new techniques of handling cargo such as containers, or new routes made possible by the Suez and Panama canals have had wide repercussions on the character and size of international (and domestic) trade. Every reduction in transport costs thus brings about joint markets, opens new trade opportunities, and changes old ones. Isard has expressed the view that of all the innovations in economic life, those in transport have the most pervasive consequences in stimulating economic activity and altering its location.

Market Orientation

Some commodities such as bread have to be produced near the market because of their perishable nature (frozen bread, however, may eliminate the local bakery in the way that the automobile has led to the virtual demise of the corner grocery store). The product need not be perishable in physical terms. Other industries which are primarily service are pulled to the market where the service has to be rendered: gasoline stations, television repairs, plumbers, handymen. A major industry in international economics involves bringing the consumer to the site where the service can be consumed—the tourist industry. And this is one item in international commerce which has been strongly affected by innovation—in this instance the aircraft, first the transoceanic propeller plane, then the jet, and prospectively the supersonic transport.

Processes which add weight or bulk to the product are likely to be attracted to the market in order to minimize transport costs. Soft drink bottling is a good example. The extract may be manufactured in a single location, but the process of dilution and bottling adds so much weight and bulk that it must take place as close as possible to the point of consumption. The point may be made more generally in terms of assembled and packaged products. Assembly adds bulk. Automobile fenders, chassis, and frames pack more neatly in knocked-down form and ship more readily than the equivalent number of finished automobiles. Accordingly, there is a strong pull of the assembly plant to the market, though parts manufacture may remain concentrated. And the same principle applies in all assembly operations, whether of radios, electrical equipment, tire making, bookbinding, or wine bottling.

In some lines of activity where the buyer is concerned to compare values and service, the market area attracts the bulk of the suppliers. This has been called the "coalescence of market areas." It is represented in a city by the department store, theater, garment, financial, and similar districts. A new firm starting an insurance business will be unlikely to seek a new location in New York City but will rather try to find office space in the Williams Street–Maiden Lane area, where other insurance firms and the insurance brokers swarm. In international trade, the same effect is obtained by insurance centers such as New York, London, Munich (pre-World War II), and Zürich; style centers such as Paris, New York, and Rome; and the fur market of Leipzig. Coalescence of market areas is a phenomenon which occurs most frequently in service industries, where taste is likely to change.

In general, the early stages of production are likely to be supply-oriented and the later stages pulled to the market. To locate an industry at the early stages minimizes the costs of producing the article by keeping down the cost of transport of materials. At the same time, the establishment of an industry at the market will reduce costs of distribution of the product to the ultimate consumer. The transfer costs in procurement and distribution may be added, as in Figure 6.8, for different locations for an industry. The lowest point for the two types of costs will constitute the best location.

As the location of industry is moved from the source of material supply to the market, neither transfer costs of procurement nor those of distribution move in continuous fashion. Discontinuities occur for a variety of reasons but especially because of costs of handling due to the necessity for transshipment. Where transshipment is required both of materials on their way to processing and of finished products en route to

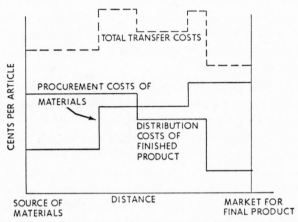

FIG. 6.8. Determining Minimum Level of Transfer Costs for Various Industrial Locations (Adapted from E. M. Hoover, *The Location of Economic Activity* [New York: McGraw-Hill Book Co., Inc., 1948], p. 31.)

market, there are likely to be sharp discontinuities in both curves, and a probable nodal point which will attract location. This is particularly true of ports, where a sea journey is transformed into a land journey. Ports as nodal points frequently attract supply-oriented industries dependent on imported materials and market-oriented industries which produce for export. Refining processes, whether of metals, oil, or sugar, are typically located at ports. Hamburg, Marseilles, and Southhampton all make soap and refine petroleum. The economics of pipeline transport is changing this currently, however, as it is more economical to transship crude oil by pipeline to the population center for refining than to carry the products there separately. And trans-Alpine pipelines save turnaround time on expensive tankers by shortening their voyages, at the same time that they deliver oil to consuming centers of Lyon or

Karlsruhe. But ports retain attraction for many industries such as automobile assembly plants, whether in the export trade, as the Ford plant at Manchester, England, or in imports, as the General Motors plant in Antwerp.

Where transport is performed on a single type of carrier, the economies of the long haul mean that processing is likely to be located at one end or the other, but not in between.

Footloose Industries

A number of industries have no strong locational pull either to supply or to market. The reason may be that costs of transfer are relatively unimportant; or the changes of weight and volume in the course of processing may be small. In these cases, following the proposition just enunciated, location is likely to be at either end of the transport chain, but not in between.

The textile industry has historically been loose-footed. Originally, cotton and woolen textiles had locational advantages on either side of the Pennines in northern Britain. Cotton manufacture was concentrated in Lancashire, and especially in the city of Manchester, because of the moisture on the western side of the mountains which prevented cotton thread from breaking. Another locational attraction was the port of Liverpool, at which cotton was unloaded from the United States. Woolens, on the other hand, were mildly attracted to the supply of wool east of the Pennines and the Yorkshire coal fields which furnished fuel. But none of these forces was strong. An industry in which cotton can be bought in Syria for manufacture in Japan and the cloth resold in the Middle East is evidently one in which transfer costs are unimportant. The same verdict applies to the woolen industry, where produce from Australia and New Zealand, manufactured in Leeds and Bradford, is reexported to the Antipodes.

The refining of crude petroleum into various fractions involves little change in volume or weight. Accordingly, the question of whether a refinery is installed at tidewater near the wells or at the market depends on other considerations. Historically, some oil refineries have been located in Texas and some at the market, as in Bayonne, New Jersey, or Marcus Hook on the Delaware River in Pennsylvania. Europe used to import refined products from the Gulf, the Caribbean, and the Middle East. Since World War II, however, refining operations have tended more and more to concentrate in Europe. In part this has been the result of commercial policy and a response to fears of expropriation. In part, however, it has followed from the fact that European consumption of petroleum products ceased to be concentrated strongly in the light fractions, especially gasoline. It made sense, in the interwar period, to refine Venezuelan crude oil in the West Indies and to export gasoline to Europe and residual fuel oil to the United States. Now that Europe consumes a more balanced set of products—tending in fact to need a higher proportion of fuel oil to gasoline now than the United States—it is wasteful of transport to separate the products at a great distance from the market.

Since transfer costs are relatively unimportant in footloose industries, processing costs count for more. It is in these industries—textiles, matches, oil refining, etc.—that the theory of comparative costs in its undiluted form operates to determine what a country exports and imports in the absence of direct intervention by the state in the form of tariff policy. By the same token, as we shall see, it is in these footloose industries that commercial policy can be most effective in distorting the operation of the law of comparative cost. Tariffs can readily be used to attract a market-oriented industry to a market, or a loose-footed industry; they can do little with supply-oriented industry.

Location Economics

This short chapter, intended to make some amends for the unreality of international trade discussion in abstracting from transport costs, should not be taken as a full-fledged introduction to location economics, to which it does much less than justice. This rapidly growing field requires detailed study of its own, and mastery of many more techniques than can be suggested in these pages.

Summary

The pure theory of trade has abstracted from a vital fact of life—the existence of transport costs. When this is reintroduced into the subject, it no longer follows that the price ratios between export and import goods are the same in the exporting and importing countries. Export goods must be lower in price to overcome transport costs; import goods higher. If transport costs are wider than price differentials in the absence of trade, trade cannot take place. This explains why many goods and services do not move in international trade.

The impact of transport costs can be illustrated with offer curves or in partial equilibrium.

Transport costs are not regular but vary according to the weight, bulk, value, perishability of the article, method of transport, and distance. Transport has to follow certain routes, and goods require handling in transport if the mode of travel changes. These characteristics make for complexity.

Three broad types of effects on the location of industry can be detected, emanating from transport costs. Supply-oriented industries are those in which weight and bulk of fuel or material are large in relation to value, and production involves weight-losing processes. These are generally the early stages of manufacture. The later stages of manufacture tend to be market-oriented, because assembly builds up bulk without adding weight. Goods which are valuable in relation to weight or in which weight and bulk do not change in process are likely to be loose-footed. Transport costs do less to determine their location than do the processing costs discussed in the theory of international trade.

SUGGESTED READING

TREATISES, ETC.

The classical work in international economics incorporating transport costs is Ohlin, especially Part III. From the side of location, reference may be made to a number of studies, and the literature discussed in them. August Lösch (translated by William Woglom with the assistance of Wolfgang Stolper), *The Economics of Location* (New Haven, Conn.: Yale University Press, 1954), is a pioneering attempt to produce a general equilibrium theory of economic location. It is uneven, brilliant in some passages and difficult in others. Walter Isard's *Location and Space-Economy* (New York: The Technology Press and John Wiley & Sons, Inc., 1956), is the most comprehensive statement of the subject. See also the subject of regional economics, on which John R. Meyer has written a survey article in "Regional Economics: A Survey," *AER*, March, 1963, with a comprehensive bibliography of 130 items. E. M. Hoover's *The Location of Economic Activity* (New York: McGraw-Hill Book Co., Inc., 1948) (paperback, 1967), from which several of the diagrams in this chapter were drawn, is a long-lived item as evidenced by its reprinting.

POINTS

The most careful study of transport costs within the United States is given in J. R. Meyer *et al., The Economics of Competition in the Transportation Industries* (Cambridge, Mass.: Harvard University Press, 1959). For a rather narrow discussion of the structure costs relative to value, see Carmella Moneta, "The Estimation of Transportation Costs in International Trade," *JPE*, February, 1959.

PART II

Commercial Policy

Chapter 7

COMMERCIAL POLICY—
TARIFFS

Eight Effects

Analysis of interferences with international trade—represented in this chapter by a tariff—can proceed through examination of various "effects" of its imposition. Our discussion is organized around eight such effects. They are:

1. The protective effect
2. The consumption effect
3. The revenue effect
4. The redistribution effect
5. The terms of trade effect
6. The competitive effect
7. The income effect
8. The balance-of-payments effect

Not all these aspects of the tariff refer to the same analytical viewpoint, and it is of the utmost importance to distinguish carefully at what level of interest the discussion runs. A tariff may be analyzed in terms of its impact on an industry, a region of a country, a factor of production, a country, or the world as a whole. An argument valid in terms of a given country will not be valid for the world, if the gain for the country is more than offset by losses of other countries, except under the particular circumstance that the international distribution of welfare can be improved by a redistribution of income in the indicated direction. A factor of production may gain from a tariff but only at the expense of other factors. Unless redistribution is required for welfare reasons (and is otherwise unobtainable), a tariff argument valid for a region is invalid for the country.

The Protective Effect

The protective effect can be illustrated in partial and general equilibrium, along with a number of other effects on the list. In Figure

7.1, Q–Q_3 represents imports at the price OP, prior to the imposition of a tariff. The tariff, P–P', is presumed to have no effect on the foreign offer price, because of the infinite elasticity of the supply of imports at the price OP. The protective effect is shown by the increase in domestic production Q–Q_1. The consumption effect is the reduction in total consumption, Q_2–Q_3. The revenue effect is the money amount received by the government on the new level of imports, the rectangle c, and is derived by multiplying new imports, Q_1–Q_2, by the tariff, P–P'. The redistribution effect is the quadrilateral a, which is the additional economic rent paid to the preexisting domestic producers, plus the rent paid to new producers above their supply price. In old-fashioned economic

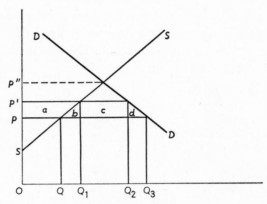

FIG. 7.1. Protective, Consumption, Revenue, and Redistribution Effects of a Tariff in Partial Equilibrium

terms it is an addition to producers' surplus derived by subtraction from consumers' surplus.

If it be assumed that the resources which are drawn into new production by the higher price were just on the margin of entry at the old price, and were earning a return equal to Q–$Q_1 \cdot O$–P in some other industry, the loss to the economy through the protection effect is limited to the area b. Similarly, if it be assumed that the expenditure diverted by the consumption effect to other products obtains a satisfaction equal to the marginal return under free trade, i.e., Q_2–$Q_3 \cdot O$–P, then the net loss in consumption is represented by d. These two areas, b and d, may be referred to as the deadweight loss of the tariff—all other losses in one direction being compensated for by a gain or change in another. They may also be called the cost of the tariff.

The size of the protective effect, relative to a given tariff, is evidently determined by the elasticity of the supply curve. If the supply curve is highly elastic, the protective effect will be large; if inelastic, small. A tariff is prohibitive when the protective effect is sufficient to expand domestic production to the point where it will satisfy domestic demand without imports. In Figure 7.1 the minimum tariff which will keep out all imports is $P–P''$.

The protective effect can also be shown in general equilibrium, but it poses some problems of exposition. In Figure 7.2, the tariff is represented by the difference between two slopes, that is, between the terms of trade $P'–C'$, and the parallel slopes tangent to the production possibilities curve and to the indifference curve. The tariff raises the internal price of the import good above its price in international trade (and lowers the internal price of the export good, which thus differs from the terms of trade). Internal equilibrium of producers and consumers requires that price be equal to the marginal cost of transformation between the two goods in production (the slope of the tangent at P') and the marginal rate of substitution in consumption (the slope of the tangent at C'). The tariff then is elusive to pin down, since it is the difference in slopes. In the illustration it is assumed, though this is not necessary, that the imposition of a tariff has left the terms of trade unchanged from the free-trade position, i.e., $P'–C'$ is parallel to $P–C$. The protective effect is the change in production, P to P', and the consumption effect is the change in consumption from C to C'. Note that if the terms of trade are unchanged, the country ends up on a lower consumption indifference curve as a result of imposing a tariff.

Note too, that we have refrained from saying, in Figure 7.2, which product is subject to a tariff. It could either be an import tariff on wheat or an export tariff on cloth, or some appropriate mixture of the two. In the case of an import tariff on wheat, the protective effect is increased production of the protected article. If the diagram represents an export tax on cloth, the "protective" effect is misnamed and should be regarded as a "destructive" effect, reducing the profitability of production of the export good. The Constitution of the United States prohibits export duties because the states in 1789 were unwilling to assign to the federal government this power to destroy export trades.

The protective effect of an import duty is almost always favorable for an industry or a region dominated by a single economic activity. The country as a whole may lose, but the particular industry which has its price raised is likely to benefit, at least in the short run. The resources engaged in an inefficient industry might do better in the long run to

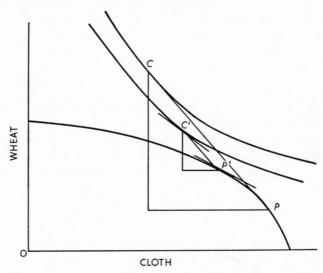

FIG. 7.2. The Protective and Consumption Effects of a Tariff in General Equilibrium

shift into occupations where they would be more productive. So long as they remain in the given industry, however, they gain from the tariff.

It follows that whenever a tariff is removed, an industry is hurt. This is by and large the case, and a number of attempts have been made to devise methods of offsetting the injury to an industry or the factory engaged in it from the removal of a tariff. But there will be times when an industry has gotten lazy and sluggish behind tariff protection, failing to take advantage of the opportunities for improving productivity by introducing new methods. In these cases, removal of the tariff may actually stimulate improvements in productivity through competition and help.

It further follows that a program of trade liberalization, such as the Reciprocal Trade Agreements Act in the United States, which promises to reduce tariffs without hurting anybody, is based on misrepresentation or stupidity. The Trade Expansion Act of 1962 finally recognized this and provided programs for alleviating injury—through extra unemployment benefits and retraining for labor, and special loans plus accelerated depreciation for industry—to meet, rather than evade, the necessity for reallocation into more efficient uses. But it has proved very difficult to administer these provisions of the act: import-competing industries tend on the whole to be inefficient, and it is very difficult to separate and cope with losses due to increased imports owing to tariff reduction as distinguished from losses due to inefficiency.

The Consumption Effect

The consumption effect is almost always adverse. When it is adverse, total consumption is reduced, by Q_2-Q_3 in Figure 7.1, or from C to C' in Figure 7.2; and the consumer pays more for each item he continues to purchase.

A region can be adversely affected by the consumption effect. Thus the South in the United States which sold its cotton on world markets was obliged by the northern tariffs on manufactures to buy its textiles and other manufactured products in a protected market at high prices.

The exception to the rule is the one argument for a tariff valid for the world as a whole: the infant industry argument. This argument is based on external economies or on imperfect competition, due, in turn, to imperfect knowledge or difficulties of entry. A demonstration was made in Chapter 2 that increasing returns or decreasing costs invalidated the law of comparative costs. If a tariff imposed on a good attracts into its production entrepreneurs previously unaware of the opportunities available or induces them to accumulate capital (or labor or land) in the amount required to achieve the economical scale of operations, the tariff may be said to be justified. There may be other and more desirable methods of calling attention to these opportunities—such as a subsidy. This lowers the price to the consumer rather than raises it, and in this way helps to broaden the domestic market. It has the disadvantage of requiring revenue rather than raising it. But it must be recognized that the infant industry argument, however much abused, is valid.

The infant industry justification for a tariff is frequently abused. The world is full of industries with tariff protection which never have achieved sufficient scale to be able to dispense with protection. The test, of course, is whether the industry ultimately is able to function without tariff protection after the economies of scale have been achieved and the infant has "grown up." But occasionally an industry will grow up without actually removing the tariff. The removal of the tariff is not the only test. The pharmaceutical industry in the United States, for example, operates behind a wall of protection which is evidently not needed in many lines, since the industry is on an export basis. The tariffs which aided the industry in getting started, or rather helped it to stay alive after World War I, are retained through inertia or as a defense against possible dumping (discussed in Chapter 9). If a protected industry develops to the point where it can compete in world markets, as many have, it has grown up.

Typically, the infant industry argument is used to justify the imposition of tariffs on an industry which had enjoyed the natural "protection" of trade disruption during war. This was the case of the famous "Corn Laws" imposed in Britain in 1819 to maintain the price of wheat at the levels reached during the Napoleonic Wars and so to prevent the collapse of grain production. The Corn Laws were not, in fact, removed until 1846, some 27 years later, nor was farming seriously disturbed until the 1880's. The Embargo of 1807 in the United States gave the textile industry a start which the Tariff Act of 1816 was passed to defend. The same argument was used to justify the protection of machinery and chemicals in Britain after World War I and of chemicals and pharmaceuticals at the same time in the United States. The object was not the procreation of infants but the prevention of infanticide in the cold, cruel world of competition. In these cases the costs of entry had already been met: the question was whether, with time, increased efficiency could make the industry normally profitable without protection or subsidy.

No other argument for tariff protection based on efficiency is valid for the world as a whole. With decreasing returns, specialization based on comparative costs ensures maximum output.

Tariff Factories and the Effective Rate of Protection

While the infant industry argument can be justified from a world point of view, great care must be taken, as pointed out, to apply it in individual cases. The theory of location may be helpful in this connection, as in the case of tariffs imposed on the finished product but not on parts or materials, to encourage foreign producers to establish tariff factories for final assembly or processing in the country in question. Pig iron and steel scrap may be duty free in Italy, for example, while semifinished and finished steel were subjected to high duties (before the European Coal and Steel Community). Equal encouragement can be given to factories working up raw materials for export by the imposition of export taxes on material such as jute, while the manufactured product, in this case burlap, is exported without impost.

Tariff factories pose certain problems for capital movements which are discussed in Part V, and especially Chapter 21. But a tariff on a final product when the raw material is free of duty raises an important question which has been much debated in the last few years under the designation of "the effective rate of protection."

Suppose the tariff on cotton textiles is 10 percent but that the value of cotton, which is imported free of duty, makes up 50 percent of the value of the final product. Since cotton is free of duty and can be imported by the textile manufacturers, the duty on cloth applies not to the entire price of cotton textiles, but merely to the value added by manufacture, i.e., half the total value. The nominal duty of 10 percent on the total value is really an effective duty of 20 percent on the value added.[1] For this reason schedules of nominal tariffs are said not to reflect adequately the real protective and consumption effects which are more accurately measured by the effective rate of the tariff. But the effective rate is not an unambiguous concept, resting as it does on the view that there is a fixed relationship between components and final product. Should input coefficients shift with price, as for example in iron and steel, where the inputs of iron, coal, and scrap steel alter with changes in their relative prices, the effective rate of the tariff cannot be readily computed. The effective rate of the tariff, therefore, is a partial equilibrium concept which assumes other things equal when in fact other things change. The formula for the effective rate is one equation with two unknowns, a system which is evidently underdetermined. One needs another equation to indicate how r in the footnote reacts to changes in t. But even though the effective rate may be less than a completely workable concept without some such simplifying assumption as fixed coefficients, it is highly useful in calling attention to the fact that things are not always (seldom?) what they seem.

A country which seeks to attract tariff factories will do well to bear in mind the location theory of the last chapter. Import tariffs have more pull on market-oriented and footloose industries than they do on supply-oriented, and export taxes are more effective on footloose and supply-oriented industries.

In the case of footloose industries, it makes little difference usually whether the process is located at the market or the source of supply, so long as it is not in between at a point which entails unnecessary handling. This leaves open the possibility that an importing country will tax gasoline and fuel oil, but not crude petroleum, in an effort to entice

---

[1] The formula for the effect rate of the tariff is $f = \dfrac{t - qr}{1 - r}$ where f is the effective rate of the tariff, t is the nominal rate, q is the rate of duty on components or intermediate goods, and r is the proportion of final product represented by imported or importable components. Where components are duty free, the formula reduces to $f = \dfrac{t}{1 - r}$. Where the same tariff obtains on finished goods as on components, i.e., $q = t$, then the effective rate is equal to the nominal rate, i.e., $f = t$.

the refining process to its shores—as France did for national defense purposes in the interwar period—while the crude petroleum-producing country will attempt to stimulate refining within its shores by an export tax on crude petroleum but not on refined products. The total effect would be a standoff, if the taxes were of equal magnitude, or a case of bilateral monopoly (a monopoly buyer facing a monopoly seller) in which the outcome is indeterminate. Only the consumer would lose.

These remarks are no warrant for taxing all exports of raw materials or imports of assembled products. Far from it. They should, however, convey the impression that this procedure makes more sense than putting export taxes on finished products and import taxes on raw materials and parts.

The Revenue Effect

Governments must raise revenue for a variety of public purposes, and from time immemorial foreign trade has been an object of taxation. In the United States 90–95 percent of all federal revenues came from the tariff in the 1850's. The less developed the country, the more likely it is that a substantial proportion of governmental revenues comes from tariff duties. This is less a matter of equity in taxation than of administrative convenience. Goods are easier to tax than the intellectual abstraction which is "income." And the flow of goods is constricted at ports of entry so that foreign is more readily taxed than domestic trade.

A tariff for revenue only is one where the protective and redistributive effects are missing. The consumption effect will be eliminated only under the limiting assumption that prices abroad fall by the full amount of the tariff, so that the tax is in effect borne by the foreign producer. A tariff for revenue only can be on goods which are not produced at home at all; or one where an equal tax is imposed on domestic production to eliminate the protective and the redistribution effects. Some economists have included in the tariff for revenue only a flat percentage tax on all imports. This is an error: the protective and redistributive effects are arbitrary and random, depending upon the amount of the domestic price increases and the elasticity of the domestic supply curves. But they exist.

In levying excise taxes to support tariffs, one should tax domestic production (including exports) or domestic consumption (including imports). If the tax is on production and all supply curves in a country are equally elastic, a flat rate of tax does not distort production. If supply curves differ, the welfare disturbance is minimized by taxing more heavily the less elastic supply curves, since this results in less distortion of production. By the same token, if taxes are levied on consumption, the distortionary effects of raising a given amount of revenue are reduced by taxing more heavily the less elastic demand curves since this minimizes the distortion of consumption.

The Redistribution Effect

The redistribution effect shown in Figure 7.1 represents a higher price, and higher profits, for existing producers. In the real world this may be much more important than the protective effect. The interests seeking tariff protection spend their time arguing the case of the marginal producer. The main drive for protection, however, is frequently the inframarginal supplier who will not be driven out of business by free trade but will make less profit.

The partial equilibrium diagram shows the redistribution effect as the transfer of consumers' surplus to producers in a single commodity. More fundamentally, tariffs will redistribute income among factors engaged in different proportions in producing different goods. Just as free trade raises the price of the abundant factor and lowers the price of the scarce, so a move away from free trade raises the price of the scarce factor and lowers the price of the abundant.[2]

In these terms, the tariff may represent an attempt by the scarce factor to reduce the trade which weakens its quasi-monopoly position. The drive to remove tariffs, on the contrary, can be equated with an attempt of the abundant factor to improve its position by widening its market. An increase in imports typically leads to an increase in exports, which raises export prices and the rate of return to the factor engaged intensively in export industry.

This analysis provides an insight into tariff history. The removal of the Corn Laws in 1846 is sometimes regarded as a response to the teaching of Adam Smith 70 years earlier. But the Corn Laws were imposed only after the Napoleonic Wars, already some 40 years after *The Wealth of Nations* had appeared in 1776. And the removal of the Corn Laws was engineered after the rising industrial and commercial classes (enterprise plus capital) became plentiful. These groups asserted their political ascendance with the Reform Bill of 1832. Having

---

[2] A geometric demonstration in general equilibrium can be provided by the box diagram set out in Figure B.1 in Appendix B. Here the tariff shifts production away from the factor-price-equalization points, R and U, and in the direction of the autarchic points, S and T. In so doing, it changes factor proportions and factor returns in both industries. This demonstration by Stolper-Samuelson reintroduced the Edgeworth-Bowley box diagram into international trade theory, as set forth in Appendix A.

achieved political power, they were able to increase their return, at the expense of the previously dominant agricultural classes who had engineered the tariff on wheat.

This same explanation in the United States setting ascribes the high tariff policies to capital in manufacturing attempting to maintain its scarcity value when land was plentiful and cotton and wheat would have benefited from free trade. This explanation does not fit 19th-century conditions well because of the greater importance of the infant industry argument. At the present time, however, it makes much more sense. Labor intensive types of manufacturing—shoes, textiles, pottery, hat bodies, and so on—are the strongest proponents of tariff protection. Large-scale manufacturing in mass production industries, on the other hand, employs a predominance of the abundant factor, capital, and is identified with exports. As capital became more plentiful than land and as the role of agricultural products in exports shrank, large-scale manufacturing industry swung from protectionism to export-mindedness, and agriculture from free trade to protection. This explains much of the reversal in U.S. trade policy.

The Republican party, long the stronghold of high tariffs, lost a great deal of its protectionist drive as states like Michigan contemplated their interest in automobile exports and organizations such as the Chamber of Commerce and National Foreign Trade Council responded to the foreign-trade views of farm machinery, business machinery, machine tools, and the oil industry. Some cultural lags remain: Southern states with a growing cotton textile industry clung for a long time to the free-trade position as if they still were predominantly exporting cotton. And Republicans from states such as Ohio attempted to emasculate the reciprocal trade agreements in reverent memory of McKinley. But the factor argument means that business, especially big business, has an interest in low tariffs, not high.

Here the monopoly and the free-trade argument come into some conflict in the United States. It used to be the argument of the liberal (in the laissez-faire rather than the left-wing sense) that free trade represented the general interest, while the tariff was the work of vested interests as big business. Today, the argument is found that since large companies with large volumes of capital are interested in freer trade—whether more exports which utilize capacity more fully and hold up prices, such as construction machinery, or more imports which lower costs, such as Middle East and Latin-American oil—free trade helps the monopolies while tariff protection favors the little fellow.

As regards big and little business, this may well be true. The economist must be neutral in this discussion, at least in his professional capacity, and simply point out what the relationships involved are in words as little loaded as possible. More specialization is more efficient, i.e., increases total product. More specialization, however, redistributes income in favor of capital and against labor. It accomplishes this by reducing the monopoly position of the scarce factor of production, which in this country is labor. Capital intensive industry may be big business, and labor intensive industry little. Nonetheless, higher tariffs increase the return to labor by reducing the supply of labor intensive goods, while freer trade increases the return to capital by increasing the demand for capital intensive goods. Some noncompeting groups of labor, as, for example, those which make up the bulk of the membership of the CIO, may regard their interest as associated with capital-intensive industry rather than labor intensive industry, and hence support freer trade. Conversely, small business is likely to side with labor intensive industry rather than capital intensive, even though it represents capital or entrepreneurship as a factor of production.

There is this much in the "cheap labor" arguments for tariffs, which, as normally put forward, is fallacious. If labor is the scarce factor, imports of labor intensive commodities, which are those in which the country has a comparative disadvantage, will reduce the return to labor. But this is not much. The cheap labor argument in its usual form is wrong, based on an erroneous labor theory of value and ignoring the obvious fact that countries with high wages are able nonetheless to export.

Government policy may deliberately strive to alter the distribution of income in the general interest. In Canada, it has been felt that a tariff on labor intensive products to stimulate the demand for and raise the price of labor is a necessity in order to encourage immigration, and to discourage emigration to the United States. This is important politically, of course, but helps to keep or move the population nearer some optimum level. Or a developing country could take the opposite tack and protect capital intensive products in the interest of stimulating profits and savings. This idea, which is reminiscent of the modern (Leibenstein-Galenson) arguments for investing in industries which will produce the greatest savings (rather than the greatest output per unit of input) was expressed as early as 1908 by Alvin S. Johnson. It requires, of course, positively sloped supply curves, that is, some low-cost producers whose profits can be built up by a substantial redistribution effect. If the supply schedule is relatively flat, and the tariff is just sufficient to expand domestic production (the protective effect) without large rents to the inframarginal units, a tariff cannot produce savings. But this sort of reasoning may be operative in Mexico where business profits are encouraged for their contribution to reinvestment and growth.

Noneconomic Arguments

When we leave the level of the industry and of the factor and move to national arguments for the tariff, we must recognize that there are some which are not economic and which are presumably excluded from the present discussion. In each case, the tariff involves a national loss which must be weighed against the gain in the other field.

Adam Smith admitted one such case, saying, "Defense is of much more importance than opulence." Clearly it is better for a country to continue as a going concern in the long run than to live at a higher standard in the short. But while the economist is prepared to admit the validity of this argument, he is forced by his common sense to suspect that many of the defense arguments put forward by special interests are rationalizations of positions which are really based on industrial interests. It is too much to say in this connection that "patriotism is the last refuge of a scoundrel," but it is easy for everyone concerned with the production of a given item to exaggerate its importance to the national interest, and easy for politicians who want to "do something" for a given area, to do so under the national defense label. In total war, everything is involved in defense. An inefficient watch firm, woolen manufacturers, the candle industry, and independent oil producers will all plead the need for tariffs in the national interest. The economist who has not thoroughly examined each case may nonetheless suspect special pleading.

One other noneconomic argument is concerned both with national defense and with sociology. German writers of the 19th century have argued for protection for agriculture to maintain the peasantry. In part this was to furnish a supply of soldiers for the army, since rural families were more reproductive than urban. In part, as recently in Britain, there has been a desire to maintain agriculture and the rural way of life—whether the life of the Junker baron or of the sturdy British yeoman. In France, protection against wheat imports provided in the 1880's and 1890's appears to have its origin in the urge to preserve the family and the family farm. The argument for maintaining the price of an import commodity in the face of a decline in price abroad—due to inelasticity of supply where factors cannot be shifted readily into other occupations—is both social and economic. We shall meet and discuss its counterpart in resources engaged in exporting which cannot be shifted into other occupations. This is the primary argument for intergovernmental commodity agreements in basic foodstuffs and raw materials, particularly minerals.

The Terms of Trade Effect

The static argument in favor of tariffs at the national level is that under the appropriate circumstances a tariff will enable the country to obtain its imports cheaper. In effect, the foreigner pays the duty, or some considerable part of it. This terms of trade argument in favor of a tariff may be demonstrated both with the partial equilibrium analysis and, more completely, with Marshallian offer curves.

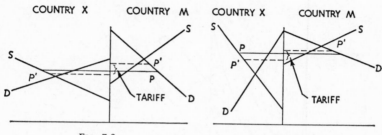

FIG. 7.3*a*.   FIG. 7.3*b*.
Tariffs to Improve the Terms of Trade—Partial Equilibrium

In the partial equilibrium case, Figure 7.3*a* shows the effect of a tariff in widening the spread between prices in the exporting and importing countries. *P* is the price with trade, before the imposition of a tariff, assuming no transport costs. *P'* is the price in each market after the imposition of a tariff. In this case, where the elasticities of demand and supply are roughly the same in both countries, the tariff will partly raise the price in the importing country and partly lower the price in the exporting country. If the price in the exporting country is lowered at all, however, the country gets the product cheaper.

It is true that the consumer in the importing country has to pay a higher price. But this is offset, so far as imports are concerned, by the revenue effect. If the redistribution effect can be ignored, the revenue effect, which is the tariff times imports after the imposition of the tax, is levied partly on producers in the exporting country. If the supply is very inelastic in the exporting country, as in Figure 7.3*b*, and the demand fairly elastic in the importing country, the imposition of a tariff will have only a small protective effect, i.e., imports will not be much changed, but they will be obtained much more cheaply.

The reader may be reminded that if the supply in the exporting country is very elastic, close to horizontal or constant costs, then the imposition of a tariff cannot improve the terms of trade at all. This is what the classical economists, for the most part, assumed.

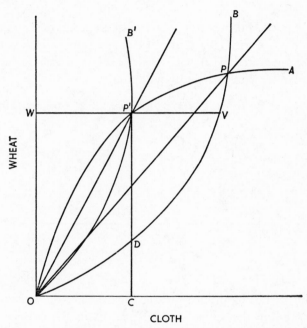

FIG. 7.4. Tariff to Improve the Terms of Trade—General Equilibrium

A similar demonstration may be made more completely with Marshallian offer curves. Figure 7.4 shows a pair of offer curves of Britain and the United States, *OB* and *OA,* respectively, which intersect at *P*. This gives a price *OP* between the two commodities, wheat and cloth. A tariff imposed by Britain on wheat from the United States may be represented by a new offer curve, *OB'*.

The tariff-distorted offer curve, *OB'*, may represent either an import tax on wheat or an export tax on cloth. As an export tax, Britain is now prepared to offer less cloth for a given amount of wheat, collecting the export tax in cloth. For *OW* of wheat, for example, it used to offer *WV* of cloth but now offers only *WP'*, collecting *P'V* in taxes. Or it used to be prepared to offer *OC* of cloth for *DC* of wheat, whereas now it requires *P'C* in wheat, collecting *P'D* as tariff.

The shift of the offer curve from *B* to *B'* changes the terms of trade from *OP* to *OP'*. This is an improvement for Britain.

The improvement in the terms of trade may or may not make the country as a whole better off. In retailing, profit per item can be very high, but if sales fall way off, total profit is less than if the rate of profit had been more modest. Analogously, there is an optimum tariff at which any further gain from the improvement in the terms of trade would be more than offset by the related decline in volume. This optimum represents that tariff which cuts the opposing offer curve at the point where it is tangent to the levying country's highest trade indifference curve. Beyond this optimum, improvements in the terms of trade are still possible, but they are accompanied by a decline in the volume of trade which more than offsets the gain. Short of it, there is room for improvements in the terms of trade not completely offset by the shrinkage in trade quantities. Appendix D presents a geometric derivation of the optimum tariff.

Note here, too, that the gain in terms of trade from imposing a tariff depends on the elasticity of the foreign offer curve. If the foreign offer curve were completely elastic, a straight line from the origin with the slope of *OP,* the imposition of a tariff cuts down trade but leaves the terms of trade unchanged.

But two can play at this game. If Britain can improve its terms of trade by imposing a tariff, so probably can the United States. The original British gain will accrue only in the absence of retaliation. But if both parties retaliate, both almost certainly lose. Figure 7.5 shows such a case in which tariffs imposed by Britain and the United States in retaliatory sequence *B, B', B''*, and *A, A', A''*, and so on, leave the terms of trade unchanged at the end but greatly reduce the volume of trade. Each country would have been willing to buy and sell much more at these terms of trade if the price relationship in domestic trade were the same. The successive increases in British tariff on food and the U.S. duty on clothing, however, have resulted in a high price of the imported commodity after payment of duty in each country and the necessity to curtail consumption at these prices. The imposition of tariffs to improve the terms of trade, followed by retaliation, ensures that both countries lose. The reciprocal removal of tariffs, on the other hand, will enable both countries to gain. This is an explanation, or a rationalization, of the reciprocal nature of the Trade Agreements Program in the United States and the General Agreement on Tariffs and Trade.

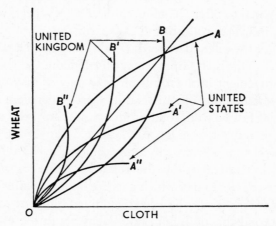

FIG. 7.5. Tariff to Improve the Terms of Trade—Retaliation

A subtle and difficult point may be worth making—although beginners would be well advised to skip the rest of this section down to "The Competitive Effect." A tariff may leave the price lower, rather than higher, than the free-trade position, and have negative rather than positive protection, redistribution effects, and a positive consumption effect. This can be illustrated in general equilibrium only after we indicate what the domestic price is in the tariff-imposing country. Look back at Figure 7.4. OP is the free-trade price; OP' the post-tariff terms of trade. But the domestic price in the tariff-imposing country, B, cannot be determined until it is stipulated how the tariff is collected. If the levy is an export tax on cloth levied entirely in cloth, the domestic price will be OPa_1 in Figure 7.6a. (OW of wheat exchanges for WV of cloth of which the B state gets $P'V$ and country A, WP'.) If the tax is collected in the import good, wheat, on the other hand, the price line will be OPa_2, since after the state subtracts $P'D$ of wheat, there will be only CD left for exchange against OC of cloth. If the state collects the tariff in some mixture of wheat and cloth, such as $P'M$ and MN respectively, this determines the local price OPa_3 which lies between the other extremes. But note that OPa_1, OPa_2 and OPa_3 all represent higher prices for wheat in terms of cloth than the free-trade price OP. The tariff raises the price of the import good in the tariff-levying country, even though the terms of trade improve for country B.

But as Metzler brilliantly pointed out, this need not happen. Take Figure 7.6b. Here the tariff is collected in terms of cloth (the export good) and the A offer curve is highly inelastic. It is now found that the internal price of wheat has fallen, OPa_1 requiring more cloth per unit of

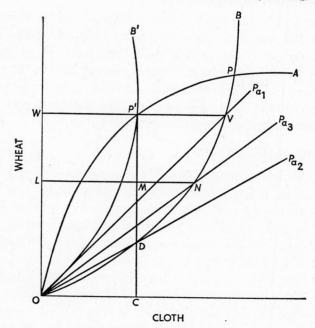

FIG. 7.6*a*.   The Domestic Price after a Tariff,
in General Equilibrium

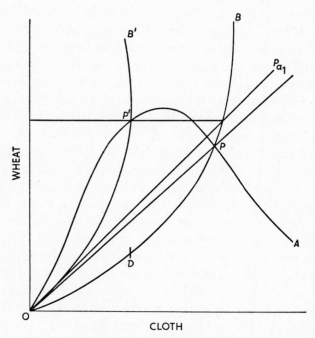

FIG. 7.6*b*.   The Domestic Price of the Imported Good
Lower after a Tariff, in General Equilibrium

wheat than *OP*. If the tariff had been collected in wheat, this would not have been the case, as inspection of point *D* indicates. But it is not a foregone conclusion that a tariff will raise the price of the import-competing good. The terms of trade effect may reverse the protection, consumption, and redistribution effects, and leave the import-competing industry and the scarce factor worse off, and the consumers better off. But this outcome must be regarded as unlikely.

The Competitive Effect

Autarky breeds monopoly. If foreign competition is kept out by tariffs, domestic industry tends to become sluggish, fat, and lazy. Or it may start that way, and resist the change which foreign innovation threatens for it by persuading government to impose tariffs. The competitive effect of a tariff is really an anticompetitive effect; competition is stimulated by tariff removal.

The competitive effect has been important both historically and currently. The Anglo-French commercial agreement of 1860, for example, is credited by some scholars with having pushed France into the Industrial Revolution, forcing its iron forges to convert from charcoal to coal, and its textile industries from hand-driven to power spindles and looms.

While many observers hold that the main impact of the European Common Market has been the achievement of larger markets and economies of scale, some of the most astute believe that its most significant result has been the breaking up of monopolies in such a country as France. Before the Common Market took effect, first in iron and steel, and coal, and then more widely, much of French industry could be described as made up of one or two large and relatively efficient companies which maintained a high, price umbrella over the heads of a number of small inefficient firms. This situation could exist because foreign competition was limited. Once the tariff walls came down, the smaller firms were forced to merge with or combine into larger, more efficient units or go bankrupt. It is true that the larger firms which survived competition with imports could always have lowered prices and forced the less efficient small ones to the wall. But among national firms, this sort of behavior was regarded as reprehensible. The same result could be achieved, with enlargement of volume and profit for the bigger firms which were efficient enough to export once tariff barriers abroad were lowered, by getting government to lower tariffs and have the foreign firm do in the local inefficient operators.

We come to economic integration in a later chapter, but it is evident that part of the interest of the British government in joining the Common Market is to stimulate sluggish firms in the country, and provide room for expansion of the lively ones. Not all British observers believe it will work. One poignant comment has been heard: "Not every kick in the pants galvanizes; some just hurt."

The Income Effect and the Balance-of-Payments Effect

The full explanation of the macroeconomic items on our list of effects must wait until the second half of the book. But enough can be said to indicate the nature of the problem. Tariffs cut spending abroad. The income not spent abroad will presumably not all be saved. Most will be spent at home. Under conditions of less than full employment, this will raise money and real incomes and employment. With full employment, however, it can only raise money income, through inflation, leaving real income worsened by the altered allocation of resources. With idle resources, it remains true, tariffs raise domestic spending and national income.

But this clearly is a beggar-thy-neighbor policy. The increase in spending in the tariff-levying country is at the expense of the previously exporting nation. Its income and employment are reduced. Thus while the income effects of a tariff are recognized, they do not come in for approval. But tariff reduction as an antiinflationary device does. This is a good means of cooling off an overheated economy, by mopping up the money supply with imported goods. It was used successfully by Germany in 1956. It should be used more widely, and doubtless would be, save for the unpopularity of unilateral tariff reductions with import-competing producers.

The balance-of-payments effect of a tariff is less certain than the money income effect. Like so much else in economics, whether a tariff will improve the balance-of-payments or not depends. What it depends on will be explored more thoroughly in Chapter 16. Here we content ourselves with saying that one must not regard the initial reduction in imports as the final balance-of-payments effect. That is merely the impact effect, which would remain unaltered only if the money not spent abroad were all saved in the tariff-levying country, and the loss of income in the affected exporter were all offset by macroeconomic action. If these conditions are not met, some, and possibly all, of the impact effect will be offset by repercussions through the system.

In today's tariff bargaining at the General Agreement on Tariffs and Trade (GATT), the world organization at Geneva which is the forum for tariff negotiations, it is agreed that balance-of-payments weakness is no basis for refusing to reduce tariffs. Reductions are reciprocal, so that the increase in imports from our reductions is likely to be offset by gains in exports from theirs. More than this, however; it is understood that while tariffs have side effects on the balance-of-payments, their main impact is on the efficient allocation of resources, and the efficient means of handling the balance of payments lie in broad macroeconomic policies rather than in diddling with rates of protection. One noted economist, J. Kenneth Galbraith, believes that tariffs are a useful instrument of balance-of-payments regulation, but he is exceptional in this, as in other respects. For the most part, economists regret the necessity to have to interfere with resource allocation for balance-of-payments reasons, and recommend that governments eschew it except as a last resort.

The Kennedy Round

In 1930 the Smoot-Hawley Tariff Act raised tariffs in the United States to their all-time height. Since then, and despite the depression, the direction has been down. The Reciprocal Trade Agreement Act, first passed in 1934 and regularly renewed, had two premises: first, that reductions should be mutual, and second, that reduction accorded to one country in an agreement, should be extended to other countries with which the United States exchanges most-favored-nation treatment. One exception to most-favored-nation treatment was recognized: agreement to enter into a customs union, which could take place slowly. Despite wide protest that it is illogical to permit 100 percent discrimination but not 99 percent, the customs union exception was regarded as a permanent giving up of tariff protection vis-à-vis a given country, as a marriage, whereas 99 percent reduction still retains the distinction between domestic and foreign firms.

After World War II, the Reciprocal Trade Agreements program was fundamentally altered by changing the bargaining from bilateral to multilateral, or rather to simultaneous bilateral bargaining, at which each "major supplier" bargaining with a partner, kept an eye cocked over his shoulder at what the generalization of his concessions would mean for other countries (minor suppliers) and what their concessions on other items would mean to him. These negotiations were carried out under rules laid down by the General Agreement on Tariffs and Trade, an executive intergovernmental agreement which did not require congressional approval.

Successive renewals of the Reciprocal Trade Agreement Act after the war, however, were increasingly burdened by congressional qualifications which narrowed the scope of bargaining. Negotiations had to be conducted product by product after hearings. An escape clause was called for to revoke concessions if a domestic industry was seriously injured by imports. Peril points were to be established by the Tariff Commission, setting limits below which tariffs could not be lowered by the Executive branch of the government except with full explanation. Each renewal limited the percentage points by which tariffs could be reduced. The no injury doctrine on which the program was originally based was hypocritical and increasingly strengthened the hand of the opposition. For these reasons, and because the formation of the Common Market in 1957 created a new situation, the Trade Expansion Act of 1962 set off in a new direction. The legislation provided for across-the-board reductions to 50 percent of the then existing tariffs, for tariff eliminations in cases of tropical products, or manufactures in which the European Economic Community and the United States together accounted for 80 percent of world trade in a commodity; and adjustment assistance for firms injured by imports, as already explained. GATT was given five years to complete its negotiations, and just got in under the wire before the U.S. government's powers to conduct negotiations lapsed at the end of June, 1967. The 100 percent authority of the U.S. Executive branch on items on which the United States and the Common Market were responsible for more than 80 percent of world trade proved to have no effect, because General de Gaulle in January, 1963, turned down Britain's first bid to join the Common Market. The 80 percent figure had been chosen so that it would embrace a wide volume of trade—but not items sold in important volume by the developing countries or Japan—provided that Britain joined the Common Market. When it did not join, the 100 percent authority proved to mean very little. As it turned out, the tariff reductions on items not withdrawn from negotiation by "exceptions"—a form of escape clause which negotiating nations could evoke, but which, if they did, reduced the enthusiasm for tariff reductions of trading partners—amounted to about 35 percent. This was regarded as a good, but not a scintillating result.

One interesting question was raised by the French during the negotiations, and slowed progress by more than a year. It was whether two countries with different tariff structures should lower their tariffs in the same proportion, or whether the country with a wider variance or disparity in its tariff structure should not reduce tariffs more than one with a more nearly uniform height. The question arose since the common tariff of the European Economic Community (EEC) was an average of the high rates of France, Italy, and Belgium and the low rates of the Netherlands and Germany, pulling most rates into a narrow range—about 12–15 percent—while the U.S. tariff had roughly the same average, with wider variance.

There is, of course, no final answer to this issue of disparities—or *écrêtements* in French. Take two tariff structures, as in Figure 7.7*a* and 7.7*b* in which various commodities are ranged along the horizontal axis and rates of tariff on the vertical. The French case amounted to asserting that even though the average tariffs were the same, an equal tariff bargain required the country with the wider disparity, as in Figure 7.7*b*, to reduce tariffs more than the country in Figure 7.7*a*.

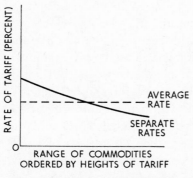

FIG. 7.7*a*. Range of Tariffs with
Narrow Disparity

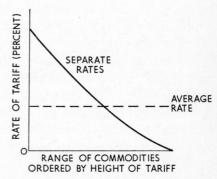

FIG. 7.7*b*. Range of Tariffs with
Wide Disparity

To be able to answer this question it is necessary to know the purpose of tariff reduction. If it is to expand the volume and value of trade, the French point is wrong. Equal percentage reductions in the two countries, on neutral assumptions as to elasticities, will, if anything, expand imports more in the case of the country with the wider disparity. A 50 percent reduction in the higher tariffs, for example, will reduce prices absolutely more and lead to a disproportionately higher increase in trade, after averaging, than in the country with the more uniform schedule. But if the purpose is to approach optimal resource allocation, the French case is a strong one. A uniform tariff across the board affords very little protection. Internally prices rise. As we shall have occasion to see more thoroughly, a 10 percent tariff on all imports is equivalent to a devaluation of the currency for imports by that amount, and after incomes and prices adjust to it, the protective effect is minimal. The disparate tariff has more important protective and consumption effects.

The Interaction of the Effects

The student must not get the impression that all eight effects of a tariff can operate with equal intensity at the same time. They are related to one another in many ways. The more the protective and consumption effects cut down imports, the less the revenue gained from a tariff. At the limit, of course, the tariff is prohibitive and yields no revenue. The more substantially the terms of trade change and lower prices abroad, rather than raise them at home, the less the protective and redistributive effects.

Some of the effects are complements, not substitutes. Thus the higher the protective and consumption effects, the larger the reduction in spending which stimulates domestic spending and income. And so it goes on. The student (and even the instructor) may gain insights into the variety of the possible results of a tariff by relating the various effects to one another. If the revenue effect is very large, what does this mean for the balance of payments? The answer, it happens, turns out to depend upon what happens to the terms of trade.

Alternatives to the Tariff

The presumptive case for free trade is hardly damaged by the demonstration in this chapter of the various effects which can be achieved by a tariff. This case, which we discuss again in Chapter 12, is essentially that free trade maximizes efficiency for any given distribution of income, allocating resources to their most efficient uses and distributing goods in such ways as to maximize consumer satisfaction. In addition, for any respect in which free trade falls short of the ideal, other and more efficient means than the tariff are on hand to correct the result.

Tariffs can, it is true, stimulate production, raise revenue, redistribute income within and between countries, expand employment, and alter the balance of payments. But other and more equitable devices available for these purposes do not have the undesirable effects of distorting the allocation of resources and limiting consumption.

The valid case for interfering with the price system where increasing returns go unexploited is better tackled through subsidies. These stimulate output without restricting consumption. Producers resist subsidies, however, and prefer tariffs. Somehow the latter are regarded as perfectly compatible with the ethic of private enterprise while the former are not.

Direct taxes and transfers are superior to tariffs for redistributing income within a country. They achieve the desired result with less distortion in production and consumption.

In transferring income between countries, international transfers are superior to tariffs to improve the terms of trade.

Finally, employment and balance-of-payments objectives should be approached with monetary and fiscal policies.

If anything that the tariff can do, something else can do better, how do we explain the enthusiasm with which countries all over the world impose tariffs and the painfully slow way in which they take them off?

The movement for tariffs is strong because producer interests in particular are more politically powerful than producer and consumer interests in general. In fact, the free-trade movement in Britain was, and that in the United States is, essentially a producer movement, representing those industries embodying advanced technologies, on the one hand, or abundant factors, on the other. A representative of the protectionist interests once complained with a fair show of reason that he thought it unfair that the protectionists were always charged with being selfish (and frequently vested) interests, while the free-trade movement posed as public-spirited and above material considerations.

Summary

The only valid argument for a tariff from the world point of view is the infant industry argument. For a nation, a variety of valid cases can be made: a tariff may be needed for defense or other noneconomic reasons; to raise revenue, improve the terms of trade, expand income, improve the balance of payments. The last three of these are beggar-thy-neighbor in that the gain for the country creates problems or losses for foreign countries. Their success assumes no retaliation.

Redistribution of income within a country can result from a tariff between producers and consumers of a given product, between producing and consuming regions, between the scarce and the abundant factor of production.

Anything that a tariff can do, some other weapon of economic policy can do better.

SUGGESTED READING

TEXTS

For an elementary but good treatment, see Leland B. Yeager and David G. Tuerck, *Trade Policy and the Price System* (Scranton, Pa.: International Textbook Co., 1966) (paperback). An advanced treatment is Vanek's chap. xvi.

TREATISES

The classical statement of the free-trade case was that by Haberler, chaps. xiv–xvii. Recently Meade's, *Trade and Welfare,* Part I, has advanced the argument a number of stages in subtlety. The revenue discussion in this chapter was based on one of his second-best arguments for tariffs, chapter xii.

The serious student should be aware of at least five major articles on tariffs, the Stolper-Samuelson article on income distribution, and the Scitovsky article on the terms of trade effect, in American Economic Association, *Readings in the Theory of International Trade;* and the Metzler, Lerner and Bhagwati and Ramaswami articles (on the Metzler effect, the symmetry of export and import taxes, and domestic distortions) in the American Economic Association, *Readings in International Economics.* Three other articles deal with important points treated in the text, though they are not so handily available: H. G. Johnson, "The Cost of Protection and the Scientific Tariff," *JPE,* August, 1960; R. N. Cooper, "Tariff Dispersion and Trade Negotiations," *JPE,* December, 1964, on disparities; and W. M. Corden, "The Structure of a Tariff System and the Effective Protective Rate," *JPE,* June, 1966.

A rather out-of-date history of the tariff in the United States (to about 1922) is by F. W. Taussig, *Tariff History of the United States* (New York: G. P. Putnam's Sons, 1923) (paperback). Modern accounts of GATT are contained in Gerard Curzon, *Multilateral Commercial Diplomacy* (London: Michael Joseph, Ltd., 1965), and Gardner Patterson, *Discrimination in International Trade, the Policy Issues 1954–65* (Princeton, N.J.: Princeton University Press, 1966).

POINTS

The point that tariffs may be used to speed the formation of capital by redistributing income in favor of savers was made by Alvin S. Johnson in "Protection and the Formation of Capital," *Political Science Quarterly,* 1908.

A convenient source of U.S. tariff schedules before and after the reductions under the Kennedy Round is the June 30, 1967, *New York Times,* although the print may be somewhat fine if it has to be read in microfilm.

Chapter 8

QUOTAS, EXCHANGE CONTROL, STATE TRADING, ECONOMIC WARFARE, EAST-WEST TRADE

This chapter deals with a host of problems of commercial policy generally, reserving until Chapter 10 the particular contentions of the less developed countries. The analysis broadly follows that laid down for tariffs with a variety of "effects" produced by interference with trade or its reduction. Space is lacking, and patience, to ring the changes on the eight effects of the previous chapter. The discussion will therefore be limited to significant differences from the tariff position.

Effects of Quotas

If a country has a fair idea of the shape of the demand and supply curves involved in a particular commodity, and if these are not particularly inelastic, there is little difference whether it imposes a tariff or a quota. If the quota is set at the volume of imports which would result from the imposition of a given tariff, the protective effect will be the same in either case, and so will the consumption and the redistribution effects. In the partial equilibrium diagram of Figure 8.1, for example, a tariff of 5 cents or a quota of 100,000 tons would each have the same effect in raising the internal price, reducing overall consumption, limiting imports, and encouraging domestic production.

There is, however, one considerable difference between a tariff and a quota, even where conditions underlying the market are known. This is in the revenue effect. Under a tariff, the area *abcd* in Figure 8.1 would be collected as governmental revenue in the importing country. If a quota of 100,000 tons is laid down, the price of imports is greater than before. Who will capture this increase cannot be determined in advance. If the importers have a monopoly of the trade and exporters are unorganized, the importers may succeed in obtaining it. If the exporters are effectively organized and the importers not, the terms of trade may swing against the country as the foreign exporters hold up the price. Or the government may issue import licenses to anyone it chooses; when

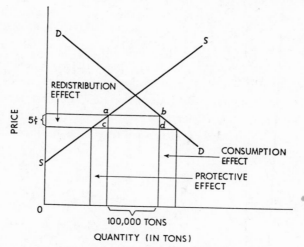

FIG. 8.1.   Tariffs versus Quotas in Partial Equilibrium

the U.S. system of issuing oil import licenses was shifted, under the Eisenhower administration, from previous importers to oil refineries, it made little difference for some companies which both imported and refined, but the difference for others could be reckoned in large amounts of money, approaching or surpassing a hundred million dollars a year. Inland refineries which had never used imported oil gained, and coastal refineries built to use imported crude lost, as the latter had to acquire the license to buy oil at the world price which was about a dollar a barrel below the domestic price. These licences turned out to be worth just about the difference between the world and the domestic prices.

Or the government of the importing country, by auctioning off import licenses, may succeed in obtaining for itself this increase in value due to scarcity, which economists sometimes call a "rent." This would make the quota the exact equivalent of the tariff, down to and including the revenue effect. The auction of import licenses is not used widely, however, so that the scarcity value inherent in the limited imports may accrue to either exporter or importer, depending upon the proximate conditions in the market. The greater likelihood is that importers will capture this rent. In any event, if the government does not auction off licenses to import, it must decide who imports on some basis: first come, first served (a rather messy system); traditional importers (which confers a monopoly on them unless room is left for new entrants); or some even more arbitrary system. The invisible hand of the competitive market must become visible.

In terms of offer curves, the situation can be set forth along the lines of Figure 8.2. If Britain, with the offer curve, *OB,* limits its imports of wheat to *OD,* the terms of trade between clothing and wheat may be *OP'* or *OP''* or any price between. Like the case of bilateral monopoly—with a monopoly buyer and a monopoly seller —the outcome is theoretically indeterminate. The new terms of trade, it will be observed, are either more or less favorable to the country imposing the quota. If the importers capture it, as has been suggested is

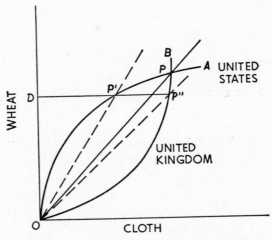

FIG. 8.2.   Effects of a Quota on the Terms of Trade

likely, the terms of trade are improved by a quota, to the extent that the foreign offer curve has an elasticity of less than infinity.

Origins of Quotas

If the protective and redistribution effects are the same under tariffs and quotas, provided that elasticities are not zero, why did quotas come to supplant tariffs so widely in the 1930's? The question is a fair one, and the answer consists of three parts. In some commodities in which quotas were first imposed, the supply position abroad was almost completely inelastic. Under these circumstances, a tariff could not increase the price in the importing country or reduce the volume of imports. The only effect of the tariff was to improve the terms of trade and to gain revenue for the government by taxing the foreigner.

But while under ordinary circumstances a country is pleased to have its terms of trade improved and governmental revenue enlarged, these were beside the point. The French, who first developed quotas, were concerned in 1930 neither to get wheat cheaper from abroad nor to balance the budget. They wanted higher wheat prices for French peasants. When the increase in the U.S. tariff diverted the bumper 1929–30 Australian wheat crop to Europe, no simple tariff could keep it out. With an inelastic supply of imports, it was possible to raise or maintain the internal price only by setting a lower and fixed figure on the volume of permitted imports. Figure 8.3 shows such a case. Country

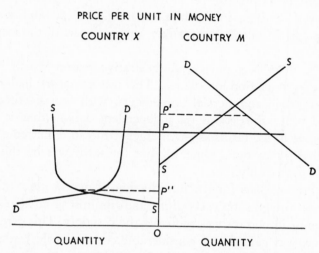

PRICE PER UNIT IN MONEY

COUNTRY X   COUNTRY M

QUANTITY   QUANTITY

FIG. 8.3.   The Imposition of Quotas in Partial Equilibrium
in the Face of Inelastic Supply

M wants to raise the price of the import good to achieve a redistribution of income to producers. Any reasonable tariff will fail to do this, since the terms of trade effect will be large, given the inelastic character of excess supply in country X. A quota which halved imports, on the other hand, would clearly raise prices from *OP* to *OP'*. Note that if this quota is imposed and country X does nothing about it, the export price in X will fall to something such as *OP''*. The imposition of a quota in M is therefore likely to be followed by some commodity stabilization effort in X.

Inelastic offer curves are met particularly in agriculture; and it is in this field, so often subject to domestic policies to guarantee farmers or peasants a "fair return," that quotas abound. Where price-raising efforts, required for domestic political reasons, would be defeated by imports, they are often supported by quotas which eliminate imports or restrict them to some tolerable amount.

The more general consideration which gives rise to the wide use of quotas for protection and redistribution of income is that the shape of the excess supply curve in exporting countries is unknown. How much of a tariff increase will prevent a price decline abroad from spreading to our country? It is difficult to answer this question if there is a single price abroad for domestic and export transactions. It may be impossible if foreign producers practice price discrimination and dump exports at prices lower than those in the home market. The possibility of such dumping, discussed in the next chapter, provides part of the inspiration for quotas.

Finally, there is a purely administrative reason which helps to explain the introduction of quotas. The use of tariffs had been so institutionalized in commercial agreements, with most-favored-nation clauses and other restrictions on independent action, that it was no longer possible to use tariffs as an emergency measure. Extreme circumstances called for extreme remedies, but the tariff was by this time a fair-weather device only.

The three reasons for the introduction of quotas, therefore, were inelasticity of foreign supply, certainty, and administrative flexibility. Of these, the most important was probably the certainty. This certainty, as we shall see, was gained at a considerable cost to world trade. Under some circumstances, however, a country will regard certainty as worth its share of this cost.

Quotas, Tariffs, and Monopoly

There is one further distinction between the effects of tariffs, on the one hand, and of QR's on the other. If there is a potential domestic monopoly protected by a tariff, it can charge only the international price plus the tariff. If it tries to raise prices above this level, it will lose sales to additional imports.

To change a tariff into a quota, even without reducing the existing volume of imports, may convert a potential domestic monopoly into an actual one. The domestic monopolist or combine can now raise its price secure from the potential competition of imports. This difference, which is set out diagrammatically in Appendix E, is of greater importance for manufacturing than for agriculture, and in such situations as that of Western Europe. Liberalization is a weapon against monopoly, even if the quota is replaced by an equivalent tariff.

The Balance of Payments

But the major reason for quotas in today's world is the balance of payments. This leads us to foreign exchange control, which is the subject of the next section. It makes no difference in Figure 8.1 whether the quota is 100,000 tons, or, at a world price of $3 a ton which is not altered by the imposition of the quota, or whether there is a foreign exchange allotment for the purchase of this commodity equal to $300,000. The administrative arrangements may differ; foreign exchange control is administered by a financial government agency and the quota typically by a commercial one. But the financial authorities must have the cooperation of the commercial administrators to ensure that the foreign exchange allotment does in fact result in the authorized imports, so that the trade aspect is inescapable.

Quotas on the whole range of imports, or foreign exchange control, are imposed because the country tends to import too much relative to its exports, and chooses to restore balance by selective controls on imports. It is usually assumed that administrative reduction of imports will do less harm than wider macroeconomic measures such as deflation or exchange depreciation. The price system, it is thought, would encourage the import of the wrong products, for example, luxuries for the rich instead of necessities for the poor. The purist would urge that if the import bill of goods under the price system violated the community's sense of social justice, the answer is to change the distribution of income through the tax system, rather than to allow an unjust system to continue, and to offset it in part by an inefficient system of importing. But the reply is that the societies that employ quotas or foreign exchange control typically are unable to muster up the political force to redistribute income. Foreign exchange control is a partial substitute.

Other Reasons for Foreign Exchange Control

The major purpose of foreign exchange control, with its central element of restricting imports (and collecting the full foreign exchange counterpart of exports) is the balance of payments. This is a topic we will reserve for later in the book. But there are other effects, similar to those of tariffs. An overvalued exchange rate, i.e., a rate which is kept above its natural level by controls, evidently improves the terms of trade. The restriction of imports may not get the country its imports any cheaper, because its purchases are likely to be too small to affect the prices at which it buys, but its high exchange rate for exports is a means of raising the price of those exports for which foreign demand is less than infinitely elastic. By raising the exchange rate, for example, Brazil, can raise the costs of all its highly competitive coffee growers, calculated in foreign exchange, and thereby hold up the foreign exchange price of coffee. The encouragement to imports of an overvalued rate means that import quotas must be established, usually favoring necessities and penalizing luxuries. To avoid the penalty to marginal exports, a multiple, foreign exchange rate system may be adopted, with low rates of exchange for marginal exports, and high ones for those which face an inelastic demand abroad. The multiple exchange rate system extended to imports gives an overvalued rate on necessities and a penalty rate (very low, as viewed from abroad, high in local currency per unit of foreign exchange) for luxuries. The administrative problem is formidable—usually impossible—to prevent undervaluation of export invoices (on which exporters have to turn in their foreign exchange) and overvaluation of import invoices (on which importers obtain foreign exchange from the financial authorities); and to make sure that traders sell and buy their exchange only at the appropriate prices. The rewards to deception are high and persistent. The system seldom works well for long.

A system of multiple foreign exchange rates can be equated to a system of tariffs and subsidies on imports and exports, with the same protective, consumption, redistribution, revenue, balance-of-payments, and so on, effects, whether positive or negative. If, for example, there are two rates of exchange, a high one for imports and a low one for exports, the government enjoys a considerable revenue from trade, buying exchange at low prices in terms of local currency and selling it for higher. There are also positive protection for imports and negative protection (i.e., a penalty) on exports. This is equivalent to a system of flat rate export taxes and import tariffs. Or the foreign exchange system could be a multiple rate one, which is equivalent to discriminatory taxation of exports, and varying rates of tariff on imports. The more complex the system, of course, the more expensive and inefficient it is to operate.

State Trading and Nontrading

In one sense state trading is an old-fashioned subject of international economics. Especially in central Europe, and especially before World War I, there used to be state monopolies of such commodities as tobacco and alcohol, and discussion of state trading to ensure that these large monopolies conducted their international business in such a way as to fit into the market pattern of private firms. In the charter for an International Trade Organization, drafted in 1948 but never ratified, the rule was adopted that state purchasing organizations should buy at the lowest price and sell at the dearest, as a private, profit-maximizing enterprise. In particular it should not give protection to domestic producers by paying more at home for a product than abroad, or discriminate as a monopsonist among foreign suppliers.

For a time after World War II, there was interest in so-called bulk-buying agreements among countries to replace the private international market with government purchases and sales. The thought was that with assured markets, the seller could concentrate on output and lower costs through economies of scale, sharing these economies with the purchaser in lower prices. In actuality, governments wrangled over prices which went up and down discontinuously as old contracts lapsed and new ones had to be rewritten, now in a seller's market, when the price went up, now in a buyer's when it dropped. Finally the scrapping of controls by the Conservative government in Britain in 1951 led to the abandonment of bulk buying by that country and many others.

There is one area, however, where states do as they like. This is in purchasing for their own use. Here there are no international rules nor any standard of conduct. All governments tend to buy at home. The tendency was accentuated during the depression, when "Buy British," "Buy French," and "Buy American" campaigns were urged on the public to expand employment. In the United States, the "Buy American" criterion for government purchases, which was laboriously reduced from 25 percent as a normal rate in the 1930's to 10 percent in the 1950's, was raised to 50 percent in the balance-of-payments weakness of the 1960's.

Governments pay no tariffs, so that perhaps some nominal preference for domestic supplies such as 10 percent is understandable. Buy local campaigns, like putting up a tariff during a depression, are clearly a beggar-thy-neighbor policy. And to jam up the rate to 50 percent, as the United States did in the early 1960's, is clearly to set up a double standard—no balance-of-payments tariffs or quotas for the private sector, because of international commitments, and near autarky for the government. For the United States to buy dairy products in Wisconsin for its troops in Germany, next door to Denmark, is evidently uneconomic—wasteful of real resources and causing the Department of Defense budget to run out faster than it otherwise would, thereby raising appropriations and the need for tax revenues.

Governments tend to buy at home under most normal circumstances. Larger governments are unwilling, for example, to buy arms from any country that is not a certain ally. And considerations of prestige require that the government officials ride in American limousines, rather than Daimler-Benz, and fly on American airlines. Many of these considerations are not even articulated. But the economic rule remains the presumptively correct one: one should buy in the cheapest market and sell in the dearest, whether household, firm, or government sector.

Trade among Socialist Countries

The same rule of buying in the cheapest market and selling in the dearest should apply to trade among Socialist countries, but it has proved very difficult to apply. After World War I, when the Soviet Union was the only Socialist country in the world, using the term in the Communist sense which excludes the Labor government and the Socialist parties of Europe, the Soviet Union used foreign trade as a device to achieve autarky. Sales of traditional exports—wheat, timber, furs, manganese, and so on,—were pushed to buy the machinery which would make the country independent of foreign supplies,—with great success except for a few commodities such as rubber and wool. But when the Eastern European countries and China arrived in the Socialist camp, it made no sense to pursue autarky. It was obviously necessary for Socialist countries to specialize and exchange among one another. The question was how to go about it.

Soviet planning with its emphasis on materials balances is regarded as biased against balanced foreign trade. Plan fulfillment as a prime target of administrative purpose means holding back on exports and speeding up imports to make good gaps in the plan. But foreign trade in independent plans in seven countries becomes even more difficult to regulate. The trade organization of the Soviet bloc, COMECON, has been searching for a fundamental way to organize the foreign trade of its members, without great success. Meanwhile, trade continues on an *ad hoc* basis, and even that gives rise to serious problems of deciding what countries export and import what commodities, at what price, and balancing the national value of exports against the value of imports on a multilateral basis.

Since the Soviet Union traded at world prices in the interwar period, one solution for the pricing problem in principle was to value trade among the bloc countries at world prices. This has proved difficult in practice. For bulky commodities, it is not clear what the world price of a commodity is in Eastern Europe, until a decision is made as to whether the Eastern bloc would export or import that commodity to the West. The price in North America or Western Europe is clearly inappropriate because of transport costs, but the question whether transport costs should be added or subtracted cannot be decided until it is clear which way the trade would go. For differentiated products, moreover, the question of quality can be decided only on an arbitrary basis: is the Moskvich more like the Renault, the Volkswagen or the Cortina? Studies of the prices actually used in Eastern trade suggest that the Eastern countries frequently trade with each other at higher prices than those at which they trade with the West. Various explanations have been used to account for this phenomenon, including trade discrimination, a "custom union effect" which has produced an island of higher bloc prices than those in the outside world, and rather arbitrary adjustment of prices after trade to help balance exports and imports.

But the more important problem is what goods to trade. Part of the difficulty lies in the lack of an efficient price system at home in each country. Real prices used in consumption and production differ widely because of heavy turnover taxes, which are added to imports and subtracted from exports to make it possible to trade abroad at all at arbitrary exchange rates. But even after prices are adjusted for taxation, they fail to reflect economic values. If capital is not regarded as a factor of production, capital intensive goods tend to be relatively cheap, overproduced, and exported, which is inefficient for the system as a whole. Planning techniques without prices, or with only implicit shadow prices, become too complex, even with computers, when seven systems have to be meshed, subject to the constraint that excess demand in one commodity in one country is matched by an excess supply in another, and that the value of all exports equals the value of all imports for each country, on a multilateral basis. These issues are solved in the West with prices and money. The Soviet bloc tries to operate without explicit prices reflecting scarcity values, and with a monetary system which is unsatisfactory so that its countries are unwilling to hold rouble balances. Thus far it is making slow work of it. COMECON has organized trade in ways variously described as "absolute advantage" or "empiricism," and resolved conflicts at the "highest political level," all the time seeking and failing to find an objective, scientific basis for international socialist specialization.

Economic Warfare

State interference in international trade may not necessarily be guided by the principles applicable to peaceful commerce under which a country is presumably interested in maximizing its economic well-being. A state, for example, may attempt to limit the output of another country, particularly of materials of war; or a state may attempt to depress markets in foreign countries for the sake of encouraging world revolution. Sometimes it is difficult to tell whether a country is selling abroad to depress world prices and thus make economic warfare against capitalist countries, or to pursue a comparative advantage, including, on occasion, getting rid of surplus production. Thus the Soviet Union has been accused of attempting to wreck the West by dumping wheat (in 1932) and since World War II on various occasions, tin, aluminum, and oil. While it is natural for Western competitors in these products to regard the Soviet sales as politically motivated, careful observers have in each case found an economic reason for selling which carried more conviction. Nonetheless, while improbable, the possibility exists that one country could use its powers of purchase and sale in international markets to achieve nonmilitary political designs on another.

Economic warfare is unhappily a much more usual phenomenon. Here the entire purpose of trade changes. In economic warfare conducted parallel with military operations, such as that waged by the Allies against Germany and Japan during World War II, the weapons included blockade, preclusive buying, agreements with neutrals to cut off trade beyond the range of blockade. Preclusive buying is perhaps the most interesting, since here the purpose of state trading is not to acquire what a country wants but to prevent the enemy from getting access to it. In frequent cases, as in the rival attempts to buy tungsten and tungsten ore (wolfram) in Spain and Portugal, or chrome in Turkey prior to Turkey's entry into World War II, the effect of the rival preclusive buying is to divide supplies much as before, to raise the price many times above its original relative value, and to expand output. In some cases, such as Swedish ball bearings, purchases were made to keep supplies away from the enemy; and the goods were mainly stored. Blockade-running British Mosquito aircraft could carry only a few tons of goods per trip in addition to their diplomatic traffic.

Short of "hot" economic warfare, there should perhaps be a stage of "cold" economic warfare. Here there is no military blockade imposed by force of arms, but one country will attempt to deny to its potential enemy those goods which are of extraordinary strategic interest to the latter's armament needs. The gain in slowing down the rate of armament of the potential enemy country, however, should be measured against its cost. Where no credit is extended, trade is a two-way balanced affair, and the restriction of exports involves a restriction of imports.

Success in the denial of exports should therefore be weighed against the impact of the loss in imported goods.

It is important to calculate in sober fashion the effectiveness of economic warfare on specific industries and specific programs. The impact of the economic blockade of Germany in World War I was exaggerated by the German General Staff to excuse its own short-comings. Even with aerial bombardment, the blockade of World War II had a supporting rather than a leading role in the defeat of the German armies. The difference between what a country needs to survive comfortably and what it can get along with at a minimum is substantial, as the oil sanctions of Rhodesia in 1967 and against Italy in 1935 amply demonstrate. There is first the task of making sure that sanctions are effective, and that small shippers in great number do not replace the large suppliers whose operations can be overseen. Next, even if total supplies are cut down, there is much fat to be cut through before one gets to muscle. For instance, much of the Rhodesian oil imports are normally used for nonessential purposes, which can be eliminated, without basic harm to the economy.

Moreover, a modern industrial nation is capable of shifting and adapting resources among industries, substituting one material for another with only a limited loss of efficiency. In consequence, except in the relatively short run, the denial to an enemy or potential enemy of materials for a particular industry results in diversion of other resources to this industry. If the country is industrialized on a fairly broad front and moderately adaptable, economic warfare will deprive it of resources in general rather than final weapons in particular. Viewed in this light, it is particularly important, in hot or cold war, to weigh the potential gain in minimizing the position of the other country against the cost to one's own.

Where the country is not highly industrialized, such as the Soviet Union or even more Red China, a further consideration enters. To deprive these countries of industrial products in the short run stimulates them to increase their industrial capacity in the long. Much depends upon the most probable time of trouble. To an economist, it might even make sense to sell war material to a potential enemy, if trouble were far away, to reduce his incentive to develop his own weapons and to lull him, if this were possible, into obsolescence.

East-West Trade

Trade between the private enterprise economies of the West and the state trading organizations of the Soviet bloc poses a variety of difficult institutional and organizational problems. But it has not been possible for the United States to tackle many of these because of its restrictions on trading with the East: an absolute prohibition on trading with Communist China and Cuba, and a restricted list of products which cannot be sold to the Soviet Union and the Eastern bloc. The position has eased somewhat since the passage of the rigid Battle Act of 1951 at the height of the Korean War, but President Johnson's efforts to relax congressional limitations on East–West trade to the end of detente in political relations with the Soviet Union meet strong emotional resistance and negative votes. Readiness of U.S. allies to trade and even to extend credits to the Soviet bloc makes maintenance of the contrary posture less and less effective.

Apart from the economic warfare aspect, which as the last section showed, may work contrary to the interest of a blockading nation if it lasts a long time, East–West trade raises questions of concern for political dependence, of one-sided economic advantages, of predatory dumping (to be discussed in Chapter 10), and of grave difficulties of settling the disputes which inevitably arise.

Fear of dependence on, say, Soviet trade on political grounds finds support in its sudden cutting off of purchases of Icelandic fish in 1948 and of sales of oil to Israel in 1956. But in its turn the United States abruptly reduced the Cuban sugar quota in 1960. There is risk of great dependence on any supplier or outlet, and Western governments may have to exert pressure, when they do, more overtly and publicly. The fact that Socialist trade organizations are governmental may enable them to squeeze a customer or a supplier more gradually. But the difference is probably small, since the trading organization in Eastern countries is different from the Politburo.

The one-sided economic advantage concerns Eastern bloc sales of primary products to Western developed countries, while purchasing products of high technological content. At the same time it seeks to buy primary products from the less developed countries and sell them arms, machinery, and machine tools. The West would like to buy output of the sophisticated Soviet space organization, particularly rocketry. This complaint rests on the contention that the Western price system does not in fact appropriately reflect relative scarcities as between primary and more advanced products. If we leave aside the military and space equipment which neither side sells to the other, it can happen that the economic prices at which various goods are traded in the West give large gains from trade to the East. This is the way competitive market economies work: sellers get the going price even though they would have been willing to accept less, and demanders pay the going price even though they gain a large consumers' surplus therefrom. The less developed countries get large gains from trade in this fashion as pointed out earlier. This does not bother us. We are interested only in maximizing our own income, and disregard, or react benignly to the gains of our trading partners. Such is the normal trading utility function. But it can happen that a country's utility function is more complex, and includes not only its own income, positively, but the gains of trade of its partner negatively. In this case, the West, for example, would be willing to trade with the East and enjoy gains from trade only if the gains of trade of the East were taken into account. There would be a trade-off between our gains and the East's gains. Such a utility function is clearly unChristian, to suffer from the good fortune and take pleasure in the losses of others. It equally violates the canons of laissez-faire economics. But there is no accounting for tastes, and economics takes tastes as given. If the West has such a utility function—as seems evident by its unwillingness to accord most-favored-nation tariff treatment to the East, though this involves some technical problems—it may be an argument for restricting trade on the ground that the East gains too large an advantage from it.

Predatory dumping will be explained later, but many western states are concerned that the Soviet Union will sell oil to Western Europe very cheaply, and then when it has turned away from other suppliers, jack up the price. It is possible. But the possibility requires an asymmetry in entry and exit, i.e., that at lower prices the oil companies outside the U.S.S.R. go out of business, and at higher prices, they fail to come back in. This seems unlikely, sufficiently so that the Soviet Union could hardly count on it. Much more likely is that Soviet oil production is excessive, and the pressure to market in Western Europe comes from distress selling, which comes from excessive investments in oil and gas because of planning error.

Even apart from these problems, however, the difficulties of expanding East-West trade very far are enormous, stemming from the wide differences in system, the difficulties in achieving mutual understanding, and especially the absence of surplus goods in the East available for sale. To a very considerable extent, East–West trade has been kept down by inadequate Eastern supplies, while the blame has been ascribed to Western policies. Eastern countries want to purchase on credit, and there are obvious limits on how far it is safe to go. If prices and foreign exchange are all in Western currencies, the technical burden on the financial side will be borne in the East (a naïve proposal of the Economic Commission for Europe some years ago to establish bilateral clearing between East and West predictably came to nothing). But there will still be difficulties of settling disputes. It will take many years to evolve an appropriate system for flourishing East–West trade. Meanwhile it is somewhat silly of the U.S. Congress to feel so passionately against it that it is willing to accept all the political blame for inhibiting it, at the expense of freedom for its exporters and importers and a great deal of political resentment in the rest of the West.

Summary

Quotas are like tariffs in their protective and redistributive effects. The revenue effect is lost, however, unless the state auctions off the licenses, and the terms of trade effect is undetermined. The quota must be administered, substituting the visible hand for the market place.

The advantage of a quota over a tariff is the certainty of its restriction of imports. This is important when price increases are sought, and to achieve balance-of-payments effects. Foreign exchange control, such as quotas, has impact on domestic prices, production, consumption, income distribution, terms of trade, employment, balance-of-payments, monopoly, and so on.

State trading used to be concerned with tobacco and alcohol monopolies. For a time, there was interest in bulk buying of primary products by state organizations. Today the state discriminates freely in its purchases and sales, especially as it is bound by no internationally agreed rules.

An important and difficult problem of state trading is the organization of specialization and exchange among Socialist nations.

Economic warfare is a particular form of interference by the state in trade with interesting analytical problems, but a limited record of accomplishments.

East–West trade presents a touchy political problem today in which institutional difficulties likely to inhibit a large-scale exchange of goods lie beneath an adamant refusal of the Congress to recognize changing conditions in the cold war.

SUGGESTED READING

TREATISES

The literature on quotas and foreign exchange control is all dated, as the problem has dwindled in importance since the immediate postwar and the interwar period, except for the less developed countries. See H. Heuser, *Control of International Trade* (London: George Routledge & Sons, Ltd., 1939); F. A. Haight, *French Import Quotas* (London: P. S. King and Staples, 1935); E. R. Schlesinger, *Multiple Exchange Rates and Economic Development* (Princeton, N.J.: Inc., Princeton University Press, 1952), emphasizes the revenue effect of exchange rates. For present systems of quotas an exchange control, see the annual volumes on restrictions published by the International Monetary Fund.

On state trading, the literature is again less than up-to-the-minute. See J. Viner, *Trade Relations between Free Market and Controlled Economies* (Geneva: League of Nations, 1943) and his article on the same subject in American Economic Association, *Readings in The Theory of International Trade.*

A good treatment of the Socialist trading system is F. L. Pryor, *The Communist Foreign Trade System* (Cambridge, Mass.: The M.I.T. Press, 1963). A strong viewpoint is taken in Robert Loring Allen, *Soviet Economic Warfare* (Washington, D.C.: Public Affairs Press, 1960).

On East–West trade see especially Committee on Foreign Relations, U.S. Senate, *A Background Study of East–West Trade* (Washington, D.C.: U.S. Government Printing Office, 1965); *East–West Trade,* Hearings before the Committee on Foreign Relations, U.S. Senate, 88th Cong., 2nd sess. (Washington, D.C.: U.S. Government Printing Office, 1964); and N. McKitterick, *East–West Trade: The Background of U.S. Policy* (New York: The Twentieth Century Fund, 1966) (pamphlet).

POINTS

The interesting implications of state nontrading are seldom discussed by economists. See however Michael S. Baram, "Buy American," *Boston College Industrial and Commercial Law Review,* Winter, 1966.

R. P. Manes, "Import Quotas, Prices and Profits in the Oil Industry," *Southern Economic Journal,* July, 1963, is useful in showing how the allocation of quotas redistributes profits.

Chapter 9

PRICE DISCRIMINATION
AND CARTELS

Kinds of Competition

The previous chapter was concerned with overall devices to modify or even to disregard the workings of the pattern of international prices on trade and the allocation of resources. Restriction of imports or exports can be calculated to give a monopoly or monopsony increased return, or, as in economic warfare, commodity agreements and much bilateral trading may spring from a feeling that the price system will produce an unsatisfactory answer and must be pushed aside in favor of quantitative controls and planning. The overall measures dealt with were those employed by governments.

Price discrimination, on the other hand, does not involve disregard of the price system. It is instead a manifestation of the workings of the price system under particular conditions of monopoly, monopsony, and separation of related markets. Instead of overall, we shall treat of differential techniques. For the most part we shall be dealing with the firm rather than with government.

The difficulty with the subject is that it uses everyday words which mean different things to different people. Competition, to an economist, means the process operating in an industry with a very large number of firms, where no producer and no purchaser can by his actions exert an influence over market price. Where the number of firms is smaller than this, so that an individual firm can control the price at which it sells or buys, competition is imperfect. Even in an industry which is imperfectly competitive, however, two types of price policy by the individual firm are possible. Assuming no cost differentials, the firm can sell to all buyers at the same net price; this approaches the competitive solution. Or the firm can sell at different prices to different buyers; this is price discrimination.

The businessman has a hard time seeing what the economist is talking about in all this; to the extent that he does understand, he dislikes what he hears and dissents vigorously. In the first place, he objects to the words used. He is not certain that he is favorably disposed toward "competition," since it calls to mind "cutthroat competition," which he knows he dislikes. The words "imperfect" or "monopolistic" competition are clearly invidious and disagreeable. So is "price discrimination," which calls to mind racial, religious, or national discrimination, which is disapproved conduct rather than "a discriminating taste," which is held in esteem.

Most of all, however, the businessman and the economist fail to talk the same language and to understand one another. To a businessman, it is competition when two firms sell in the same market at the same price. To the economist, this is competitive if no form of collusion exists and if it is the only market in which the firms sell. But if either or both firms sell in other markets at prices which yield them a different return than in the market in question, it is evidence of less than perfect competition. Where so much confusion and misunderstanding abound, it is necessary to proceed warily. In what follows we shall employ the reasoning and terminology of the economist and shall hope that the reader used to thinking in the terms of businessmen will withhold judgment until he understands what is intended.

Price Discrimination between Markets

In a single market, only one price prevails. This is true by definition—the law of one price, which says that only one price can obtain in one market. Where price discrimination is practiced, there must be more than one market which can be distinguished. This can occur in a fairly limited geographic area—see the different prices charged for first-run, second-run, and country movie houses; for professional services of doctors, lawyers, and others, depending on the patient's or client's income; and for the same article in the convenient corner store as opposed to the serve-yourself giant store at a shopping center some distance away from residential areas. In international trade, however, markets are already differentiated at a minimum by space, and may be further separated by differences of custom, habit, language, etc., even though other factors common in the domestic market—such as product advertising, snob appeal, or professional ethics—are absent.

If a seller has access to two separate markets and can exercise some control over price in one or both, it will pay him to sell at different prices if the elasticities of demand in the two markets differ. The general rule for the maximization of profit then holds: profit will be maximized where marginal revenue equals marginal cost. But the marginal cost of his output will be identical for sales in all markets, since we abstract from transfer costs. (The price we are discussing is the price f.o.b. the factory. Transfer costs are eliminated from calculations of price, revenue, and cost.) The crux of the matter then becomes the difference in marginal revenue in the two markets.

The seller may ignore the difference between the markets. In this case he will add average revenue curves and marginal revenue curves. Where the marginal cost curve intersects the combined marginal revenue curve will give the production point of maximum profit. In Figure 9.1, with average and marginal revenue curves added for markets A and

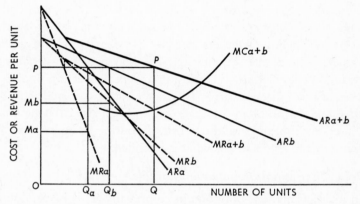

FIG. 9.1. Aggregated Demand Curves—No Price Discrimination and Inequality of Marginal Revenue

B, the quantity OQ will be produced and sold in the two markets, at the same price, OP. The quantity OQ will be made up of OQa sold in market A and OQb sold in market B. But observe that the sale of OQa units in market A produces a marginal revenue of OMa, while OQb sold in market B gives a higher return, OMb. A policy of identical or flat pricing in two markets with different elasticities means that a higher marginal return is earned per unit sold in one market than in the other. The profit of the seller could be increased by shifting sales from the less elastic to the more elastic market.

Price Discrimination

This can be made clear by putting the two sets of revenue curves on different sides of the vertical axis, as is done in Figure 9.2. This diagram, which omits the marginal cost curve, shows the same marginal and average revenue curves in markets A and B, but no totals. The A

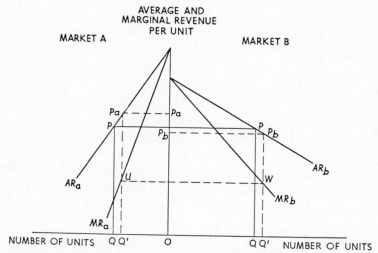

FIG. 9.2   Discriminatory Pricing by a Seller—Equating Marginal Revenue
in Two Markets

curves are to the left of the vertical axis and run from right to left. The
B curves perform in the usual manner. The quantity QQ is the same as
OQ in Figure 9.1 and is also the same amount as $Q'Q'$. In this diagram,
however, we can see that a shift of QQ' from market A to market B will
equate marginal revenues ($Q'U=Q'W$). This will result in price
discrimination, a higher price (OP_a) in A, the market with the less
elastic demand, and a lower price (OP_b) in B, with the more elastic
demand.

The fact that price discrimination can take place at all is due to the
quasi-monopoly position of the seller and the fact that he can, whether
because of monopoly, because the other few competitors in the business
will follow his leadership, or because of a cartel agreement, fix his price.

It will be noticed that the higher price is charged by the discriminating seller in the market with the less elastic demand curve, and the
lower where demand is more elastic. This underscores the monopolistic
nature of discriminatory pricing. A maximum return is reached when
the seller exploits to the full through price discrimination the inelasticity existing in each separate market. The limiting case is reached where
the seller singles out in a separate market each potential buyer and
charges him what he is willing to pay as a maximum for each unit. In
these circumstances, the seller captures for himself the whole area under
the demand curve. Under perfect competition the average revenue curve
is completely elastic, or horizontal, and marginal revenue equals aver-

age revenue. If one market is highly competitive, the discriminatory price solution comes to simply selling at a monopoly price in one market. In the other the discriminating seller has no power over price and has to sell at the market. Here average and marginal revenue are identical, and marginal cost equals price, which is the competitive solution. Marginal revenue in the other market is the same as in this market, but the monopoly price charged is higher.

Notice that the difference in delivered prices between two markets cannot exceed the costs of transport between them. If the difference were wider than this amount, it would pay others to undertake arbitrage, buying in the cheaper market and selling in the dearer. On this account, price discrimination is much more prevalent in heavy products than in light.

Discriminating Monopsony

Less frequent in international trade is the discriminating buyer, or monopsonist, who is sufficiently big to take account of the effect of his

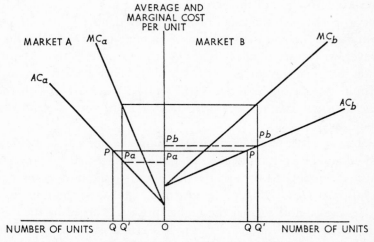

FIG. 9.3. Discriminatory Pricing by a Buyer—Equating Marginal Cost in Two Markets

purchase on price (see Figure 9.3). The monopsonist may be a big company, such as the De Beers syndicate which dominates the market for uncut diamonds, or a state trading organization, which goes in for bulk buying. It is an organization big enough to take account of the effect of its purchases in raising the prices it pays for goods. Accordingly, it will shift purchases from the less elastic source of supply to the more elastic and pay a lower price in the former than the latter, in order to reduce its overall cost. It will equate the marginal cost of supplies in the two markets.

Note that the competitive buyer equalizes the delivered cost of his purchases, not the cost f.o.b. from different destinations, while the discriminating monopsonist equalizes marginal cost on a delivered basis. The return to the seller excludes the cost of transport, but the cost to the buyer most definitely includes it.

Overhead Costs

It may be helpful to think of price discrimination in terms of overhead costs. After a company covers its overhead costs in one market, it is in a position to sell in another market at whatever that market will bring above variable costs. This is implied when it is stated that marginal cost is the same in the two markets, but focusing attention on overhead costs helps to prevent exclusive attention on different elasticities of demand.

Opponents of price discrimination want overhead costs assigned to different markets in proportion to the units sold in each. This means that average costs, rather than marginal costs, should be the same in two markets. The difficulty of this position is underscored in questions of joint supply, where it is impossible to assign overhead costs to one item or another and price is determined by demand and marginal cost, with overhead costs covered where they can be. One of the best examples of this in international trade is petroleum products.

What is the average cost of crude oil, gasoline, aviation gasoline, diesel fuel, lubricants, fuel oil, and residual? Marginal costs can perhaps be computed, but how should overhead costs be allocated? The sellers, as all sellers do, allocate overhead costs to those products which can cover them in the market. Residual fuel oil has in the past sold for less than the value of its crude oil content, in order to be sold at all in competition with coal. As the price of coal has risen, however, it has been possible to shift some part of the overhead costs of the production and refining of oil to the residual product. The day may not be far distant when the by-product which bore no share of overhead costs becomes a principal product which carries some or all of it. Examples of this shift are found in coking coal in the Ruhr. Prior to about 1929, coke for steel was the main product and coal-tar derivatives the by-product. The development of the German chemical and explosives industries in the interwar period, however, made coke the by-product and resulted in its sale as common fuel even to farmers. Overhead costs, which had been assigned mainly to coke, then became shifted to the coal-tar chemical products.

What effect does the existence of overhead costs have on the theory of comparative costs? There is a temptation to say that it modifies it greatly. A country which would have no comparative advantage in a product may be able to export if overhead costs are assigned to the domestic market, or to other joint products. How can costs be compared internationally if one country calculates on the basis of average total costs, and the other on the basis of average variable costs?

There can be no doubt that the existence of overhead costs and the possibility of assigning them in various ways does raise questions for the theory of comparative costs, in the short run. It in fact turns it into a theory of comparative demand. It is demand which determines where overhead costs can and cannot be assigned. If residual fuel oil bears a small part of overhead in the U.S. petroleum industry, and gasoline is similarly placed in Europe, which enables these products to be exported, this is because of demand conditions.[1] But in the long run, of course, all costs are variable when full capacity is reached, and the expansion or addition of plant is necessary.

Price Discrimination and Policy

The fact of market control over price by buyers and sellers gives rise to certain dilemmas of public policy. It also poses troublesome issues for business enterprise. Under perfect competition, abstracting from transfer costs, the same price should be charged to every buyer. Under perfect competition, moreover, each firm is encouraged to maximize its profits. Public policy in free enterprise societies embraces both objectives of policy: profit maximization and nondiscriminatory (flat) pricing. But when a firm is large enough to affect its prices, the two objectives are incompatible.

If profit maximization and flat pricing cannot be reconciled under imperfect competition, which should be favored? If the same price is charged net to all customers, the company foregoes some additional income. If different prices are charged to different customers, the latter complain of unequal access to materials, or competitors complain of

---

[1] The student must not make the mistake of thinking that the theory of comparative advantage is destroyed by making it possible for two countries to charge overhead costs to home sales and dump abroad the same product, so as to sell this product to each other. This is impossible because of the law of one price which requires the imported product to be sold at the same price as the domestic. The dumping in one good can only go in one direction, and simultaneous dumping in different directions must take place in different products.

unfair competition. If the same price is charged to all customers, the seller has to ration his sales in the more profitable market.

It is difficult, as a rule, to obtain data on private behavior in this area. Firms are naturally secretive about their pricing practices. A somewhat garbled story in the *Journal of Commerce* reported a survey of 138 manufacturing companies in the United States undertaken by the Export Managers Club of New York in 1953, which showed that:

> 70 of the group, or 50 per cent, maintained the same prices for both markets;
>
> 10 per cent quoted lower prices on foreign than on domestic sales;
>
> a slightly higher proportion (than 10 per cent) charged higher prices on foreign sales;
>
> a fairly large number (the remaining 30 per cent?) used a flexible pricing system, varying their prices according to the competitive situation abroad.

There is no way of telling how representative this sample is of exports of finished manufactures or of total exports, or whether those companies charging higher or lower prices did so persistently or merely found themselves in that position at the time of the survey and could be said typically to use a "flexible pricing system." But however accurate a reflection of the position as a whole, the survey suggests policy differences among the 138 private firms.

More research is needed in this area, but it is at least clear that there is frequently an arbitrary character to business policies with respect to foreign pricing. A company which operates largely in the domestic market and only occasionally sells abroad is likely to use a more "flexible" price policy on foreign sales. Thus the famous increase in the price of steel by the United States Steel Company of May, 1962, which was rescinded after President Kennedy's outburst against it, was to apply to domestic sales only and not to foreign. Automobile prices in Europe are typically altered separately as between the home and foreign markets, and an increase in Volkswagen prices for home purchase in 1964 when foreign prices were left unchanged produced a similar reaction of Prime Minister Ludwig Erhard at that time. As the proportions of foreign and domestic business approach equality, there is a tendency to shift to flat pricing. If, however, the export market is very large in relation to the domestic, prices in the two markets may again be set independently. Further differences will turn on the absolute size of foreign sales, and on the practice of the industry, governmental policies, and so on. It was observed in the British devaluation of 1949, for example, that some British companies thought of the prices of their products as determined in sterling and initially marked down dollar prices by the full amount of the devaluation. This was true of many manufactured products—lawn mowers, automobiles, bicycles. As costs rose, the sterling prices picked up and dollar prices started back toward their original level. In other instances, however, such as Scotch whiskey, it was recognized that the price was set in the foreign market, and the domestic price was raised, or not, depending upon whether flat or independent pricing existed.

The fact of equal prices in separate markets, whether for sales netted back or of purchases including transport, does not eliminate discrimination, though it makes it a mild sort which approaches the competitive solution. The competitive solution is identical prices *and* equality of marginal revenue and marginal costs. When costs in the two markets differ or demand curves have different slopes, equality of marginal revenue in the two markets (to limit our discussion to sales) will produce different prices, and equality of price will produce differential returns. Some discrimination is inevitable. The rationing of markets with flat pricing is generally the milder form of discrimination.

The objection to price discrimination is the objection to monopoly. The buyers in the country with the less elastic demand suffer. The Economic Cooperation Administration attacked the (European) practice of charging higher prices for steel in the export trade than those charged at home. The reasons for the practice were (1) the economic one of maximizing profit; (2) to hold down the level of home prices; and (3) to improve the competitive position of the steel-consuming industries at home. The effects of this pricing, however, were uneconomic utilization of resources in the selling country, which produced too little steel—the objection to all monopoly; the "unfair" imposition of higher costs on the foreign steel-consuming industries; and the incentive to develop new steel capacity in the importing countries, which was not economically justified.

While the U.S. government objected to dual pricing, through the Economic Cooperation Administration, no stand on the matter was taken by any country in the General Agreement on Tariffs and Trade. Governments were urged to act in a competitive fashion, but no such requirement was imposed on private enterprise. It could not be, because it is far from clear whether the firm should prefer, of the two-horns of the dilemma, flat pricing or profit maximization.

Some large firms act to maximize not short-run but long-run profit. This may favor flat pricing over price discrimination. Flat pricing offers no basis for retaliation or adverse action by foreign governments. It has a ring of fairness about it. Purchasers cannot complain of unequal treatment. Competitors are unable to argue unfairness. Even taxing authorities are confronted with an unambiguous position. This last point was raised by the action of the Saudi Arabian government which objected to the discounts given by the Arabian-American Oil Company on oil sales to its owning companies on the ground that the company's profits, on which the government levied an income tax, were in reality being transferred abroad. Charging the same prices to all customers, all the time, may maximize long-run profits by earning goodwill even when short-run profits are less than their possible peak.

Dumping and Reverse Dumping

Charging different prices in different markets is called, in international trade, "dumping." The word is unfortunate. Its origin goes back to the case of the manufacturer with an unsold supply who "dumps" the excess abroad in a market in which he does not normally sell, in order not to break the price in his own market. By default, more than anything else, the practice of sale at different prices in two markets has become "dumping." The height of absurdity in nomenclature is reached when the manufacturer sells abroad at a higher price than at home. This is called "reverse dumping"—the notion existing that he is then dumping in the domestic market.

Dumping is simply price discrimination. It takes place when the demand abroad is more elastic than the demand at home. It arises only because of the monopolistic element in the home market. In reverse dumping, the demand abroad is less elastic than the home demand, whether because competition abroad is less keen than at home or for any other reason. In this case it is possible to exploit the inelasticity of demand of the foreign market by higher prices abroad than at home, balancing marginal revenue in the two markets.

In some cases, such as the steel industry, foreign and domestic prices will go separate ways, and the U.S. industry dumps or reverse dumps as the occasion calls for. Prices outside the United States expressed in dollars tend to fluctuate in a wider range than prices in the United States. At times they are above those in the United States, and reverse dumping takes place; at times below, and market positions are maintained only by dumping.

Various kinds of dumping have been distinguished, including mainly sporadic, predatory, and persistent. Sporadic dumping is the sort which occurs when a company finds itself with distress goods on its hands which it wants to dispose of without harming its normal markets. It is engaged in by companies which typically stay clear of foreign markets and only occasionally find themselves with more inventory than they can hope to dispose of in orderly fashion through their normal outlets. For this company, the demand abroad is more elastic than the demand at home, where it wants to preserve its quasi-monopolistic position. Or it may regard the cost of the goods as already sunk (i.e., marginal costs ex transport costs as zero), and cut its losses abroad by selling the goods for anything that can be realized.

Predatory dumping is selling at a loss (as measured by average costs but not by marginal) in order to gain access to a market, to drive out competition, or for any other short-run cause. Predatory dumping is followed by an increase in prices after the market has been established or the competition overcome. Foreigners are frequently accused of this sort of price conduct by U.S. producers. It is difficult to establish cases. American textile producers after the removal of the embargo in 1814 charged that British exporters were dumping in the American market to drive them out of business. However valid, the argument was a powerful factor in the passage of the Tariff Act of 1816.

The reduction of sales price is only one way to get a product established in a foreign market. Another is to engage in extra costs, to advertise, to establish a distribution system, and to obtain an acceptance of the product in the new market. Increased selling costs—indulged in briefly—are almost exactly the same as predatory dumping, except that the harsh condemnation implicit in the adjective in public understanding does not apply.

Persistent dumping occurs when a producer consistently sells at a lower price in one market than in another. As a rule, this occurs when the firm regards two markets differently from the point of view of overhead costs. Suppose, for example, that average variable costs are low relative to average total costs, and that average fixed costs can be covered in the domestic market. Additional sales at any price above marginal costs in the foreign market will increase the profits of the firm. It may then pay a firm to dump persistently. An example of this is the motion-picture industry, in which, prior to 1948, the cost of many motion-pictures used to be covered in exhibition rentals in the United States, where marginal costs were low, especially if no new sound track was required, and where foreign sales at almost any price would increase profits. Overhead costs are not prorated between markets on the basis of quantity sold, and persistent dumping may be profitable to the firm. Most economists regard persistent dumping as beneficial to the importing country and harmful to the exporting country, in which consumers are charged a monopoly price. The analogy in domestic trade with which some students will be familiar is the well-known Filene's basement in Boston where the department store puts on sale at rock-bottom prices distressed goods bought up all over the country which other merchandisers are anxious to prevent from being sold to reduce local prices in their areas.

In the usual case, dumping and reverse dumping are thought of in relation to the foreign market as a whole, contrasted with the home market. Price discrimination operates on the side of exports much like the tariff with a most-favored-nation clause as regards imports. A tariff (or import subsidy) changes the relative price of imports at home as compared with those abroad. Price discrimination, which regards all foreign markets as one, brings about changes in relative prices at home and abroad.

Price discrimination, which takes advantage of different demand elasticities in different export markets, might be called differential dumping; it is more nearly akin to tariff discrimination, applying different rates of tariff to imports from different countries. To achieve equilibrium of the firm, marginal revenue should be equalized in each separate market, which means a variety of different prices. From the point of view of the markets, however, dumping, which makes a distinction only between the domestic and the foreign market, is less discriminatory than that which separates the various segments of the export market.

Most economists regard dumping as a vicious policy, much more to be condemned than tariffs. Unconsciously, these writers hold that while it is legitimate for a government to make distinctions between its citizens and foreigners (so long as it does not make invidious distinctions among foreigners), it is inadmissible for a firm to do so. The intervention of the government is charged with the general good—even though it may be used to advance a private interest. The producer in a position to discriminate, on the other hand, is a monopolist, in whole or in part, working for his own interest.

Trade Restrictions against Dumping

A wide number of countries impose penalty tariffs or quotas against goods which they believe are being dumped within their borders from abroad. For this purpose dumping is usually defined not in terms of f.o.b. price discrimination but as sale below average costs of production. The facts are always difficult to establish, but in addition, the theory is questionable. The economist's defense of persistent dumping has just been made. Sporadic dumping which pushed distress goods into a foreign market can evidently be upsetting to businessmen in the same way that any competition is, but it too evidently benefits the consumer. Most feared presumably is predatory dumping, with the argument being that the foreign seller drives out the local competitor and then raises prices higher than ever before and mulcts the consumer.

The question arises, however, why, when the price is raised again, does the former local competitor who has been driven out, not effect a reentry into the now profitable business? If he can, the possibility of pillage is eliminated. If he cannot, why not? It may be that the predatory dumper achieves economies of scale, and can keep the price permanently lower. This shifts the argument back to persistent dumping, and is presumably a gain. It is conceivable that there is an irreversibility in the system, so that producers driven out cannot effect a reentry when the price is subsequently raised, but it is not self-evident.

The subconscious producers' bias which most of us have, and which makes us mercantilists in instinct, operates here to make us typically applaud antidumping measures. Thus a measure of poetic justice appears in the European Economic Community retaliating against the U.S. escape clause withdrawal of tariff concessions on Wilton carpets and flat glass by imposing tariffs on polyethelyene (plastic) which the American chemical industry had been accused of dumping in Europe.

But the international trade theorist must beware of succumbing too quickly to instinct. Countervailing measures against alleged dumping are obnoxious because they reduce the flexibility and elasticity of international markets and reduce the potential gain from trade. From 1846 to 1913 when Britain followed a free trade policy, distress goods in any part of the world could be rid of in London which was the Filene's basement of the world, to the benefit of the British consumer and of the overseas producer. With antidumping tariffs everywhere, adjustment after miscalculations which result in overproduction is much less readily effected.

The Basing Point System

A special form of price discrimination which gives rise to much misunderstanding is that involved in the basing point system and its variants. The economist, it will be remembered, is concerned with identical prices for different consumers at the point of production. The basing point system, on the other hand, has been devised to ensure that prices paid by purchasers are identical on products delivered from separate points of production. To the economist, the "competitive" price is measured by identity of prices to different customers at each mill. To the businessman using the basing point system in one of its forms, the essence of competition is the identity of price from different mills to each customer.

In a basing point system, prices in a given market are calculated by taking the price at a given benchmark or "basing point" and adding freight from that point to ultimate destination, no matter where the goods are produced. If, in fact, the goods are delivered from farther away than the basing point, the company making the sale "absorbs freight," i.e., pays that part of the freight cost in excess of the cost from the basing point itself. If the goods are produced at a place nearer the consumer than the basing point, the customer is charged "phantom freight," i.e., freight costs which are not incurred. Most businessmen are

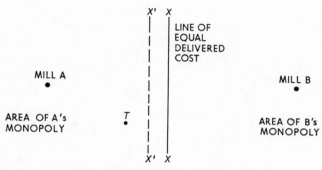

FIG. 9.4. Spatial Competition

prepared to recognize that charging phantom freight is somewhat less justifiable a practice than absorbing freight.

Frequently there will be no formal basing point system but merely two or more points of production engaged in marketing a product in which freight costs are a significant portion of delivered cost. Here each producer will enjoy a monopoly position with respect to nearby customers and those who are located in the direction away from the other mill. Costs of the delivered product will be higher as customers are located farther away from each mill until one crosses over the watershed line dividing the two markets. The position is indicated in Figure 9.4, starting with prices at mill A and mill B, which may be assumed to be identical.

In this position, competition may take two forms. Mill B may sell to customers on A's side of the line *X–X,* say at point *T,* at the prices charged by A. Or B may lower prices to all its customers at once, which would move the line to the left, as indicated by $X'-X'$, and undersell A in the intervening territory.

To the businessman, the first method is competitive because identical prices are being charged to the customer, whatever the origin of the goods. To the economist, the first method is discriminatory because it gives the customer at T a discount over the rest of B's customers, when prices are netted back to f.o.b. mill. The economist regards this pricing method as a prime example of the uneconomic character of price discrimination. It saves transport to serve point T from A. When goods move from B to T, there is crosshauling, which is prima facie evidence of waste. Goods moving from east to west to T pass goods going from west to east to other customers of A located to the left of $X-X$.

The system of flat f.o.b. pricing, on the other hand, appears to the businessman as noncompetitive. Each mill has its own customers, to the west and east of the line $X-X$, and any extra production on the part of A or B cannot be sold, at competitive prices, in the territory of the other mill. The economist suggests, in reply, that the whole range of the watershed line $X-X$ is an area of competition. If B has extra production or lowers his costs, the general good calls for this to be recognized in lowering the price at the mill, B. This will share the gain with all of B's existing customers and will shift from A to B some customers who now lie within the market sphere of B on an f.o.b. mill system. Carried to an extreme, where each customer becomes a separate base on which to fix prices, it would be possible for A to charge the same delivered price to all its customers, in disregard of real economies of transport, which should attract consuming industries to locations near the mill.

In international trade these basing point or other spatial monopoly competition examples have been found in oil, cement, steel, coal, and similar standardized bulky products. In oil, for example, the world price system used to be based on the Gulf of Mexico with delivered prices everywhere in the world calculated "Gulf plus" which meant the Gulf price plus freight. Where a fundamental change occurs in supply or demand conditions, the shift to a new basis may call for some transitional freight absorption before the new pattern of trade emerges and becomes stabilized.

Take crude oil. Initially, when the Persian Gulf was able to supply only a limited market, the price there was Gulf of Mexico plus freight as on the solid line in Figure 9.5. (It is assumed in this diagram, contrary to fact, [a] that the various producing and consuming points are arranged in a line geographically, [b] that freight is proportional to distance, and [c] that freight rates are constant through time. The first

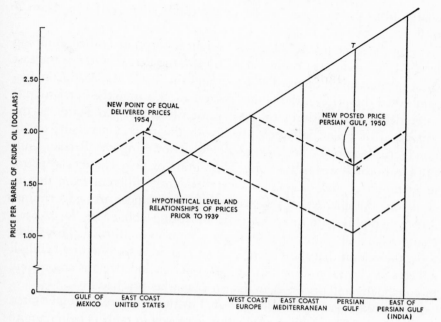

FIG. 9.5.   The Geographical Pattern of Crude Oil Prices (Stylized)

two assumptions provide a good enough approximation to reality for analytical purposes; but the problem raised by the structure of freight prices, and their variability, will be dealt with presently.) So long as the Persian Gulf could serve only India, in part or in whole, there was no need to change the price system from Gulf of Mexico plus. As Persian Gulf production grew, however, high profits were made on this price basis. Production grew and to expand sales, special discounts were given, first to the U.S. Navy, then to other customers. After the Persian Gulf area had taken over the entire market on the far side of the Gulf of Mexico, it began selling on the near side, which involved freight absorption, or Gulf of Mexico plus freight to the Persian Gulf, less freight to say the east coast of the Mediterranean. After a time, and in historical fact with the pressure of the Economic Cooperation Administration, a separate posted price was established for the Persian Gulf on an independent basis, as in the top dashed line in Figure 9.5. The local discounts and freight absorption then constitute transitional steps to an overall price change which would otherwise involve a convulsive change, if the Persian Gulf meets western hemisphere competition on the west coast of Europe, e.g., in the British market, of twice the freight charge from the west coast of Europe to the Persian Gulf (i.e., from T to W).

By the same token, there was freight absorption (called dumping by the U.S. producers) on initial sales from the Persian Gulf to the east coast of the United States. Depletion and the Texas Railroad Commission raised the price in the United States. After a time the Persian Gulf succeeded in establishing the east coast of the United States as the watershed of equal delivered price, with the further necessity, on an nondiscriminatory f.o.b. pricing system, of lowering the Persian Gulf price as in the lower dashed line. The timing of price changes in petroleum products, and the pattern, were evidently different from that in crude oil. But changes in the structure of trade under a nondiscriminatory geographic pattern of prices would bring about very large price changes if no discounts or freight absorption were allowed. This seems to be the reason that the European Coal and Steel Community, while it adheres in general to f.o.b. pricing, does not exclude freight absorption, or equal delivered prices, as an industrial market practice.

A word about the problem created by the structure of freight rates. In oil, about 50 percent of production is moved in tankers belonging to the large oil companies; another 30 to 40 percent is obtained on long-term charters from shipping company owners (largely Norwegians and Greeks), and only a small proportion is handled in spot voyage charters for which the rates are fixed for each voyage. Since only a small portion of supply has to submit to marginal changes in the whole demand, spot tanker rates tend to move in highly volatile fashion, moving as widely as United States Maritime Commission (USMC) standard (a hypothetical base which fixes the relationship among various standard voyage runs) plus 200 percent, when the market is strong, to USMC minus 40 or 50 percent when tonnage is redundant. (The market cannot go below USMC minus 50 percent or so because at lower rates owners cannot cover variable costs and prefer to keep their boats tied up.)

The question is what should customers be charged for freight. In a competitive market, price should equal marginal cost, and the marginal cost of transport on a single voyage is clearly set by the spot rate. But this would involve moving up and down the whole structure of oil prices in Europe and the United States and possibly adjusting the trade pattern, every time there was a change in the thin and unrepresentative spot tanker market. The industry, producers and customers alike, disliked this solution. The alternative was to find a representative rate, hypothetically one which new oil companies entering the trade for the first time could charge on a continuing basis. The first approximation of such a rate, the London Brokers Tankers Award (LBTA), was the average quotations by five London brokers on a hypothetical two-year time charter. This was changed every six months, and delivered oil prices adjusted. LBTA was found unsatisfactory for a number of reasons, and a shift was made to the quarterly Average Freight Rate Assessment (AFRA), which consisted in an average of rates on an existing mix of spot and time charters, in current service. This average, instead of marginal conception failed quite to meet the theoretical need since it indicates rates at which past charters have been fixed, rather than the rate which a new entrant planning to enter the business and remain in it for a time should charge. A subsequent change was made to Intrascale, the details of which are not known to the writer.

The volatility of spot rates, however, creates a need for an objective standard by which a company can charge for transport rendered by its subsidiaries.

A similar problem existed in coal, where the marginal cost of coal in Europe was set by the cost of shipments from the United States. This cost included the price of coal from West Virginia or Ohio delivered to Hampton Roads, Virginia, plus a sizable amount, usually more than the f.o.b. price of coal, of tramp ship freight to Europe. To have allowed the price of all European coal amounting to 250 million tons as an order of magnitude, to change with the movement in price of the marginal supply of roughly 30 million tons, was held to be unthinkable, especially as the price fluctuations in the tramp ship market had no relation to demand and supply in coal. The European Coal and Steel Community and the various national coal authorities within it and outside in Europe, established or permitted administered pricing policies which ignored the changes in the delivered cost of the marginal supply from the United States.

Cartels

A cartel is a business agreement to restrict competition in matters of markets, price, terms of sale, conditions, and so forth. Whether this agreement is explicit and contractual or implicit and habitual is a matter of some semantic dispute but of little real economic interest. If businessmen understand one another's reactions to the same phenomena so well that they can act in the knowledge of the reactions of the others, there is no need for formal agreement. Legally, there may be no cartel; so far as the economics of the matter are concerned, the business agreement exists.

The content of cartel agreements, whether implicit or set out in formally negotiated documents, may differ. Some, such as the electric light cartel, may be concerned with fixing prices; some, like the "as-is" agreement of 1928 in the petroleum industry with marketing arrangements (no company was to produce or market in any country in which it was not already established, i.e., everything stayed "as is"); some with patents, such as the arrangements between I. G. Farben in Germany and Du Pont and Standard Oil of New Jersey in the United States; some with conditions of sale, and so on. But the essence of them all is that competition is limited by international business agreement.

A host of new problems concerning international business agreements has arisen in connection with direct investment, discussed in Chapter 21, and with the international licensing of patents and technological secrets. If a company in the United States owns a subsidiary in Canada it is likely to determine which of them sells to a third, say the Australian, market. This seems normal: a company with two plants in the same country decides which one should fill a certain order, and if it is trying to make money, it is likely to fill it with the plant in the better (i.e., cheaper) position to do so. But the Canadian government may believe that the opportunities for companies within its borders are restricted by such an understanding or an agreement. Patent rights are typically awarded country by country, so that market differentiation is condoned or even authorized by the patent procedure. But some firms are reluctant to license technology at all, and some reluctant to license without an understanding as to what markets the licensee shall serve. And this comes close to restraint of trade.

Business agreements occur in standardized products costly to transport, such as those mentioned in the discussion of the basing point system; in raw materials and some primary products subject to inelastic demand and inelastic supply, such as those which form the subject of intergovernmental commodity agreements treated in a subsequent chapter; and in some highly differentiated goods, such as pharmaceuticals, and complex chemicals, such as rayon, nylon, synthetic rubber, and dyes which operate within the sphere of patent control. In addition, shipping services themselves are likely to have their rates regulated by so-called shipping conferences.

In most of the products covered by these areas, entry of new competitors is limited, and exit is unlikely. Entry may be limited because of a natural monopoly, as in mercury, nickel, sulphur, potash, and so forth; because of the large amounts of capital needed to get started from scratch, as in oil, or aluminum; by government regulation, as in pepper, quinine, rubber, coffee; or by patent control, as in dyes, photographic supplies, optical instruments, electronic equipment. Exit is limited by the fact that large amounts of capital or the governments in question cannot afford to withdraw quietly from the business in case of losses. The result is that when price competition does occur, it is likely to be cutthroat in character and self-defeating.

Cutthroat competition is a phenomenon of oligopoly or a limited number of sellers. A price war may spread widely, in gasoline markets, by means of linkages between local markets. But essentially the problem arises because of competition among a limited number of competitors struggling for one another's business. The price is reduced below average cost, below marginal cost, and in some cases, such as in the famous railroad wars or a 1946 freight rate war on the east coast of India, below zero. Ten rupees, for example, may be given to the customer for each ton of cargo shipped between Madras and Calcutta. At this juncture the freight lines can profitably ship cargo of great weight and little value over their competitor's facilities. The self-defeating nature of this competition is evident. A predatory price cutter can sometimes force other concerns out of business if the firm's resources are much greater than those of its competitors. In this case, too, price competition is self-defeating. In the oligopolistic case, price cutting generally comes to a halt through agreement to maintain prices well before any firm has come to the end of its resources.

While the economist objects to cartels and to the elimination of price competition, he increasingly recognizes that perfect competition cannot exist in an oligopolistic industry. He is therefore prepared to settle for something such as "workable" competition. By workable competition is meant, of course, that in which price cannot get too high because new entrants will be encouraged to come into the industry and may do so unhindered by capital costs, patent restrictions, lack of access to raw materials, or other barriers; and that in which price cannot get too low because existing firms will be encouraged to quit and to shift their efforts into other more profitable lines.

Cartel Policy

A number of interesting questions respecting cartels present themselves in international trade. It is argued by some that cartels cannot endure without government support; the case of the British governmental tariff action in behalf of the Iron and Steel Federation in its dispute with the European iron and steel cartel in the 1930's is cited. Some think that private cartels are superior to intergovernmental agreements or bulk buying contracts because private cartels dissolve under the impact of diverse interests of individual producers. There is a body of American opinion which holds that international cartels are subversive of the national interest in self-preservation and that the member of a cartel somehow loses his patriotism—but this is difficult, if not impossible, to sustain.

What interests us primarily is the question of public policy toward international (and, if you like, national) cartels. Three possible lines of action present themselves: One may ignore them, attempt to break them up, or work out a way of living with them in which their worst features are softened or eliminated.

The policy of ignoring cartels attracts a wide body of conservative opinion. Laissez-faire, a rule derived from competitive conditions with freedom of entry and exit, becomes perpetuated into a rule with validity after the underlying conditions which justified it have changed. There are those who are unable to make intermediate distinctions between monopoly and perfect competition. But the tenor of this chapter may have persuaded the reader that there are many shadings. If regulation is appropriate to monopolies such as public utilities, then the principle of laissez-faire—hands off business under any and all circumstances—has been breached.

The notion that it is possible to restore perfect competition by breaking up cartels, insisting upon the disintegration of combines and trusts, and enforcing arm's-length bargaining between separate stages of production in vertically integrated industries is perhaps more idealistic as a policy, but at the same time more naïve. Economies of large-scale production, especially in highly capitalized industries, may be in some part irreversible.

The third alternative has the drawback of being much less clearcut than the other two. In part, it requires publicity for written agreements among firms and certain limitations on the content of such agreements, such as forbidding the division of markets and restriction on entry. In addition, it requires the instilling of restraint in pricing and of approximating, to the maximum degree consonant with the long-run interests of the owners of the business, the behavior of the trade under competition, including flat pricing. This involves restraint in the exercise of monopoly and oligopoly power. It is this third alternative which the European Economic Community is trying to develop. Prohibitions against cartels are combined with provision for the registration of industrial agreements for clearance, in much the same way as the British special courts on restrictive business practices distinguish between good and bad business agreements, and approve of the former.

The difficulty with the pursuit of this third line, however, is the absence of objective criteria. How high should profits be in oligopolistic industry? What is a fair price, a fair share, a fair profit? In part, the basic difficulty occurs in the period of transition. Under perfect competition, with freedom of entry and exit, maximization of the short-run interest, i.e., of short-run profit, is a satisfactory rule and accords with the national interest. With its use, resources will be properly allocated among industries. Under imperfect competition, where a company is attentive to its long-run interest and long-run profit and is prepared to ignore short-run opportunities to increase profits, there may also be a satisfactory outcome. Companies will then abjure exploitation of monopoly positions because of fear of reprisal; will limit short-run profit maximization in favor of more security. The intermediate period is where the troubles press. Here companies have power but continue to exercise it in accordance with the rules applicable to the day of impotence of the private firm.

Summary

Perfect competition means that no individual buyer or seller has control over price, i.e., that the demand and supply curves facing the individual firm or consumer are infinitely elastic. In the real world of international trade, however, firms in many industries are of such a size that they can affect price.

When demand curves in different markets have different elasticities, a profit maximum is reached by charging discriminatory prices. The higher price is charged in the market with less elasticity. Or, looked at in different terms, a disproportionately high share of overhead costs may be allocated to the market with the less elastic demand curve.

Dumping is merely price discrimination. Sporadic, predatory, and persistent dumping have been distinguished in theory. While governmental action to prevent predatory dumping may be justified, when its existence is clearly established (a difficult matter), sporadic dumping performs a highly useful service for the seller, and persistent dumping is a benefit to the buyer.

Spatial price discrimination in international trade raises the question of basing points or stipulated places used for calculating price regardless of the place of production. The economist generally regards the basing point system as less competitive than the system of identical prices for all buyers at the point of production, plus actual transport. The basing point system requires freight absorption or phantom freight when production takes place elsewhere than at the basing point. This involves price discrimination, but may be a necessary transitional step to new price patterns.

Cartels are international business agreements to regulate price, division of markets, or other aspects of competition. They occur in industries with less than perfect competition. If the cartel is eliminated by some action, imperfect competition will still exist. This fact argues against the policies of either ignoring cartels or eliminating them by fiat, and in favor of a policy of regulation and publicity. In the present state of economic theory, however, no consensus exists as to how cartels should be regulated.

SUGGESTED READING

TEXTS

Snider, chap. xiii.

TREATISES

See Haberler, chap. xviii. E. S. Mason, *Controlling World Trade* (New York: McGraw-Hill Book Co., Inc., 1946) and J. Viner, *Dumping* (Chicago: The University of Chicago Press, 1923; reprinted by Augustus M. Kelley, Publishers, 1967) are out of date in terms of examples and later theory, but still useful.

See C. Edwards, *Control of Cartels and Monopolies: An International Comparison* (Dobbs Ferry, N.Y.: Oceana Publications, Inc., 1966).

POINTS

A useful discussion of European Common Market cartel policy is in Jesse Markham, "Competition in the European Common Market," Joint Economic Committee, *Factors Affecting the United States Balance of Payments* (Washington, D.C.: U.S. Government Printing Office, 1962).

The international oil industry has recently become the object of a great deal of study. Among the latest and best books are H. J. Frank, *Crude Oil Prices in the Middle East* (New York: Frederick A. Praeger, Inc., 1966); and J. E. Hartshorn, *Oil Companies and Governments* (London: Faber and Faber, Ltd., 1967).

Chapter 10

COMMERCIAL POLICY FOR THE DEVELOPING COUNTRIES

As Chapter 5 indicated, the 75 or so developing countries of the world—apart from the Soviet bloc and the developed West (Western Europe, North America, the British Dominions and, on an honorary basis, Japan)—are unhappy about the conditions of world trade within which they pursue economic development, and seek actively to change them. In particular, they believe that the development of world trade is unfavorable to their growth; that the markets in which they sell primary products are unstable, with adverse repercussions on sustained development efforts; that the terms of trade are evolving systematically against them; and that they are discriminated against in trade in manufactures. For the most part they blame the fact that trade is not a positive factor in assisting growth on the world trade environment and the policies of the developed countries. The developed countries, on the other hand, while sympathetic with the ambitions of the less developed countries, assert that the difficulty lies in the inability of these countries to take advantage of the opportunities available to them. The crux, they believe, is not weakness of world demand but rigidity of less developed country supply. There is this much agreement that the less developed countries are caught in a dilemma. To achieve greater stability of primary product prices and an improving trend, they need economic development and the capacity to reallocate resources into other activities; to pursue programs of economic development, which cost foreign exchange, they need stability and a better trend of prices.

This chapter is divided into the commodity problems on the one hand, and the less developed country demand for import preferences for manufactured exports in the developed countries on the other. The potentiality of regional tariff preference in economic development will be reserved for the next chapter.

169

Commodity Price Stabilization

The less developed country case about commodity prices, as just noted, has two main aspects. One concern is with short-run instability, the other with trend. The basic case about instability was made as long ago as 1952 in a United Nations study which pointed out that from 1900 to 1952 primary product prices rose or fell on the average of 14 percent a year. Price changes do not necessarily imply changes in export proceeds, of course, since the volume of exports can change in the opposite direction, but the data showed that the volume of exports tended to move less than price, and often in the same direction, to compound the instability.

It has been widely agreed, without much evidence until the studies of Coppock and MacBean, that instability of export proceeds complicates the problem of economic development by interrupting the flow of imports, and hence of domestic investment. Case studies by MacBean, however, cast doubt on this conclusion. Investment in the less developed countries seems to have been well insulated from instability in export prices by a number of factors: offsetting volume changes, expenditure for imports out of foreign exchange reserves, and restrictions on imports of consumers' goods. But instability, or at least excessive instability, is clearly undesirable. Some movement of price around the long-run equilibrium trend is useful to pay speculators to hold the crop, in the case of agricultural commodities, which are harvested in a few months and consumed over the year. But there is generally more, and almost certainly too much.

The causes of instability in primary products can be summarized as changes in demand or supply reacting against inelastic supply or demand curves. In the case of agricultural crops, supply moves in response to weather. Moreover, planting can take place in response to one set of price signals, and the harvest occur under different circumstances. With products of long gestation, such as tree crops, and including especially coffee, cocoa, rubber, there are strong cobweb or lagged responses. When the price rises today, planting cannot affect supply for five years or more. This may mean five years of high prices and high planting before a large volume of supplies presses on the market and drives prices down.

In minerals, the instability tends to arise from variation in demand which is subject to cyclical swings and from speculation, both of which run demand up and down against a relative inelastic supply.

In some commodities, particularly sugar, much of world output is traded under preferential arrangements outside the world market, so that the spillover of changes in national demands and supplies impinges on a relatively small world market, which exaggerates price fluctuations.

A wide variety of remedies for price instability has been offered. There are schemes for fixing maximum and minimum prices, as in the International Wheat Agreement; buffer stock plans, as in tin; export quotas, as in coffee; and various financial measures, ranging from International Monetary Fund assistance to countries experiencing export price declines to varied export taxation.

The International Wheat Agreement fixes maximum prices at which the exporting countries guarantee to make stipulated amounts of wheat available to the importing countries, and minimum prices at which the importing countries agree to purchase fixed amounts of wheat from the exporters. The range between is left for the price system to operate in, to encourage output when crops are short, and to discourage them in periods of glut. The system can work only if governments intervene when a limit is reached, to make available exports at the maximum price or to purchase imports at the minimum. In fact, prices under the Wheat Agreement have been almost continuously at the maximum, so that the U.S. and Canadian governments have been obliged to make wheat available for export below domestic prices in the United States. The narrower the range between maximum and minimum prices, of course, the more nearly the system approaches a system of export and import quotas; on the other hand, the wider the range, the more nearly the scheme resembles the free market. The object of the exercise is to forecast and agree on a range within which price will fluctuate most of the time, with the limits coming into operation occasionally to moderate extreme swings. This objective, however, has not been achieved.

Buffer stock arrangements call for an international authority to set a range of prices, and to buy the commodity at the minimum and sell at the maximum. If its funds are too small, and the price rests long at the minimum, it will, of course, be unable to hold the price up. If its stocks of the commodity are limited, and the price stays long at the ceiling, it will be unable to hold the price down after it runs out of supplies. The larger its resources, the more effectively it can carry out its task. The tin scheme ceased to stabilize when it ran out of tin and was obliged to let the price go up.

Export quotas are perhaps more a device for holding up the trend of prices than for stabilizing variation around an equilibrium level. In coffee, agreement among major producers of Latin America and Africa limits the amount that can be exported, although if the price were to move up, the enlargement of quotas would be quickly accomplished in view of the heavy burden of accumulated stocks. The need for an international agreement arose because export restriction by the major supplier, Brazil, encouraged expansion of output and even new entry on the part of other Latin-American countries, but largely East African producers. The central feature of the agreement is that quotas are policed by the importing countries, most significantly the United States, since the smaller exporting countries tended to exceed quotas and inch into the Brazilian export position. The West African Cocoa Marketing Board which marketed the cocoa of Ghana and Nigeria when they were colonies of Britain acted largely as an export quota scheme, feeding supplies to the market in an effort to stabilize the price. The attempt to replace the marketing board with a commodity agreement in cocoa proved very difficult since the cocoa-growing countries were for many months unable to agree on relative quotas, and the consumer countries, mainly the United States, objected to the minimum price as too high.

Maximum-minimum price schemes, buffer stock and export quota agreements together pose the critical questions for a stabilizing commodity plan: How much room is left for the price mechanism to guide the market itself; How far should the scheme be automatic or discretionary; should there be consumer representation; Who finances the holding of stocks; Is there room left for new entry; Is there a mechanism for restricting output as well as exports in export quota plans, so as to prevent the buildup of unsold supplies; Should programs be permanent or only to overcome a particular imbalance; Should the plan deal with one commodity at a time, or a wide range? The implications of many of these questions are obvious, and need no gloss. But a few points may be less than self-evident.

Who holds or finances stocks has a substantial impact on balances of payments. If buffer stocks are held in the importing countries, for example, exports are stabilized during, say, a business cycle, whereas if the stocks are held by the exporting countries, price may be stabilized, but exports are not.

Export quotas are designed to hold up price. But does the benefit accrue to the grower or to the country? If the grower gets a high price, he has an incentive to go on producing at a high level. Production quotas may be introduced, but are not always effective, as illustrated by U.S. acreage restrictions which led to closer planting and heavier applications of fertilizer. The ideal scheme economically is to have a high price for export, but a low price to the grower to hold down production. This gives a substantial revenue to the government. If the scheme is one for stabilization, rather than merely to raise prices, the funds should be kept intact for a period of low prices when growers may be given a higher domestic price than the export price. But the economically desirable solution is not always politically or administratively feasible. Producers of export crops are often important politically and are unwilling to submit to what is in effect heavy export taxation; even if they do so, governments in prosperity seldom have the restraint to set aside foreign exchange reserves from large export taxes. The West African Cocoa Marketing Board piled up a large surplus in sterling but then yielded to pressures from the growers to raise prices and dissipate the reserve.

Automaticity, it was felt, would have helped with the last problem. Bauer and Paish recommended that the West African Cocoa Marketing Board pay the farmers in effect a moving average price, paying, for example, one half of the current price plus one third of the retained proceeds of the previous three years. Managers of a buffer stock scheme may be given set limits at which to buy and sell, or they may be allowed discretion to respond to market forces.

The question of whether commodity plans should be temporary or permanent cuts across whether they are wanted to change the long-run price or merely to stabilize around it. The U.S. government was initially entirely opposed to commodity agreements. In the 1948 Havana conference which produced the draft charter of the International Trade Organization, the position was loosened to provide for temporary agreements, limited to five years with a possible renewal for another five years, to meet a situation of particular imbalance such as a burdensome surplus in a commodity, after which it was expected to be left on its own. By the time of the so-called Haberler report of 1958 under the auspices of the General Agreement on Tariffs and Trade, permanent agreements were respectable. (The difficulty was that they were still not workable.)

Finally, the question continuously brought up by the less developed countries was: Why was it necessary to deal with commodity agreements one at a time, whereas there were apparently economies of scale and room for bargaining, in dealing with more than one, and even with all major commodities in international trade? The Food and Agricultural Organization staff and the former French Minister of Agriculture, M. Pisani, have talked of "planning" the flow of primary products in international trade. Most of this discussion is vague and amorphous, without a specific plan. One concrete but unacceptable version of it is to establish commodity backing for international money, either for its own sake, or as part of monetary reform.

It is difficult to the point of impossibility to make commodity agreements function effectively in a single commodity. As Professor Johnson says, the whole trick is to estimate the long-run equilibrium price. A United Nations group of commodity experts pronounced that the adequate, fair and equitable price sought by the less developed countries was in fact the long-run equilibrium price (although the representatives of the less developed countries seemed uneasy about the admission). The theoretical conclusion is one thing; to estimate the equilibrium price and to plot its future course, is something else again. But the difficulties extend beyond the technical. Producer pressures have been universally more effective in pushing for a high price than consumer or governmental representatives in holding price to the equilibrium level. The result is that there are strong incentives to expand, to violate the restrictions, or to undertake new production in new areas outside the agreement. The result in the long run is overproduction and breakdown.

The rationale of dealing with many prices at once is that each country will be willing to agree in price supports for the other fellow if he is getting his share. Presumably it is easier to negotiate the whole network of primary product prices than to take them on one at a time. This is a most dubious proposition.

In some formulations, the "planning" of commodity prices reduces itself to providing commodity markets, producers, and buyers with better information on the present and future state of production and consumption. This is always desirable. So-called study groups under the authority of the commodity wing of the United Nations, however, seem invariably to lead to attempts to raise prices, and not merely to provide market information.

Financial Devices

Rather than operate directly on commodity prices, one line of attack is to work with the financial consequences of price instability. One of the successful fruits of UNCTAD at Geneva in 1964 was the agreement of the International Monetary Fund (IMF), to make credits available more automatically to countries which suffer a fall in export proceeds because of the decline in export prices. One fifth of a country's IMF quota was the so-called commodity *tranche* (a French word for "slice" which has wide usage in international finance) to which different rules and more automatic access applied than to the so-called credit tranches.

If a country had tremendous discipline, it could stabilize its economy itself over cyclical rises and falls of prices. Start first with the rising portion of the cycle to get off on the right foot. Export taxes skim off rising prices from producers' incomes, and these permit the authorities to accumulate foreign exchange which they "sterilize," i.e., hold idle and prevent from enlarging the domestic money base. When prices turn, export taxes are removed, the foreign exchange is sold to permit imports to continue and the local currency is used to pay exporters more than their prices at existing exchange rates in international markets.

The late Ragnar Nurkse thought it undesirable to use export taxation for this purpose, as it distorted relative prices between export, import-competing, and domestic lines of output. He wanted to use general taxation to run a domestic and foreign exchange surplus in the boom to be disbursed in balance-of-payments and budget deficits in depression. This would minimize the distortion of relative prices.

But this calls for a standard of fiscal management which is beyond the powers of the developed, much less the less developed countries. As the West African Cocoa Marketing Board's experience demonstrates, large sums of foreign exchange held for the uncertain future are scarcely proof against the political urge to spend. The advantages of the IMF commodity tranche are that one can start from a fall in prices, rather than have to wait for an initial rise, and the repayment is a requirement. Many of us force ourselves to save in contractual ways— through insurance, pension plans, and even Christmas clubs, because it is so hard to summon up the self-discipline to pay ourselves back when we borrow from our savings.

Another device which has not been accepted is to make financial assistance, or perhaps insurance based on premiums paid by all trading countries, available to countries which suffer adverse shifts in their terms of trade of a certain magnitude. Under one scheme, a country with a 10 percent gain in its terms of trade over the base year, would have to pay part of its gains over to a pool which would be distributed to countries suffering losses of 10 percent or more. Under the insurance plan, all countries pay a small proportion of exports as a premium and countries which suffer poor price experience are accorded the proceeds. Since the developed countries are expected to have relatively stable prices, this amounts to more aid from them than insurance for them. But the technical details of these international schemes proved impossible to overcome: Are the net barter terms of trade really a valid measure of the gains from trade? (Chapter 5 argues that they are not.) How is it possible to match contributions into the pool with the demands on it, under various postulated conditions? Pencil and paper work had a difficult if not impossible time in finding past periods when these schemes would not break down unless the initial period were chosen with great skill or luck.

"Commodity" dollar proposals which go back to Benjamin Graham some years ago, have been supported by Frank D. Graham, and by J. Goudriaan of the United Nations commodity experts. A variant of the idea embodying international monetary reform was proposed to the Geneva 1964 conference of UNCTAD by three distinguished economists, Nicholas Kaldor, Albert Hart, and Jan Tinbergen. In essence the schemes provide that national or, in the latter instance, world monetary authorities attempt to stabilize a (world) price index of primary commodities, by buying a fixed bundle of commodities when the price index fell below the agreed range, and selling it when it rose above. There would be no attempt to fix the price of any single commodity. The whole bundle would be bought and sold whenever commodities were traded. Provision would have to be made, on infrequent occasions, to change the proportions of a bundle when some commodity or other became too scarce or too abundant. But the effort would be to stabilize the index, not particular commodities, by issuing new money when the index fell, and redeeming it when prices rose substantially.

The monetary features of the plan take us a little ahead of our plotted course, though we shall have to deal with them briefly. But first note some interesting features: (1) many commodities which are not readily stored—petroleum products, meat, eggs, coal, many fats and oils, fruit, and fish have to be left out of the scheme altogether, and the cost of storing and turning over stocks of others is a substantial expense; (2) the incidence of the system is highly arbitrary and if it were extended to primary commodities generally would benefit the developed more than the developing countries. Consider wheat, cotton, wool, corn, bacon, butter, and so on. It would perhaps be possible to order the list so as to eliminate the major commodities produced by the temperate zones. But commodities do not regulate themselves between the developed and the developing countries without overlapping, and it would be difficult to exclude the former while covering the main less developed countries; (3) the occasions for changing the commodity bundle to accommodate underlying changes in the demand and supply situation, which went beyond the power of the price system to settle within the stable average, would pose tough bargaining sessions at best.

The main issue, however, is the monetary one, and the question is whether one stabilizes the terms of trade of primary products by fixing their average in money terms. The answer is almost certainly no. If the long-run position of primary commodities deteriorates as a result of adverse relative shifts in demand or supply, with demand growing more slowly and supply, or ease of entry, more rapidly, the terms of trade are going to turn against the less developed countries. This is a real phenomenon. If an index of money prices of these commodities is stabilized, this means inflation of the prices of manufactured goods. More and more primary products will be offered to the monetary authorities; increasing supplies of new money will be created, and they will be spent in greater relative amounts for manufactures, to drive their prices up. Like so many ideas in the monetary field, what appears to be an ingenious device to stabilize turns out on second thought to be an engine of inflation.

Commodity Cartels

A number of commodities produced by the developed countries—nickel, diamonds, aluminum, timber, iron and steel in the United States, and so on—fail to show declining terms of trade. In some of these there is real scarcity—for example, timber. In others the organization of the industry in the hands of a few companies keeps production restrained and prices up. Where entry is limited, as in nickel and aluminum, which require rare ore deposits or huge amounts of capital to develop, prices can stay high for a long time. Where entry cannot be controlled, however, short-run high prices tend to erode. Chiselers, as they are regarded by the established producers in the trade, make price concessions in order to expand their share of the market. Large discounts are available below quoted prices.

What is of particular interest in the world oil trade is the attempt by an organization of producing countries, the Organization of Petroleum Exporting Countries (OPEC), to hold the price up itself after the companies had proved unable to do so. OPEC makes no bones about its policy: to hold prices up, and if possible, to restore prices to their level before the reduction of August, 1960. The method is of some interest: taxation of the oil companies' income calculated at posted prices rather than the discounted prices at which it is necessary to sell in order to hold a company's share of the business. This is equivalent to an export tax, which lowers production and, with some inelasticity to the foreign demand curve, raises prices abroad. But little can be done to curb new entry. Exploration and development continue outside the original members of OPEC, in Lybia, Egypt, Algeria, and Nigeria, and new producers do not join unless they are entitled to bring a substantial market share into the arrangement. As Malaya found out in rubber in 1928, and Brazil in coffee, Cuba in sugar, and so forth, holding the price up in the short run encourages new entry in the long run and brings the price ultimately down.

Preferences for Manufactures

One of the demands of the less developed countries at UNCTAD in Geneva in 1964 was for preferences in the developed countries in manufactured goods. It was thought too much to ask for free trade in such products; the developed countries were presumably entitled to discriminate in favor of domestic producers against foreigners. But within the totality of foreigners, the less developed countries wanted to be given a preference over other developed countries.

This demand was rejected by the United States. Other developed countries were not so adamant, although it is not clear that they would have been willing to go along if the United States had not taken on the onus of rejection. Professor Harry G. Johnson adduces a great many of the objections to preferences for the less developed countries—that they would generate friction, involve government surveillance and control, build new vested interests, and open Pandora's box for other discrimination by countries and of wrangles as the countries of the world sought to discriminate in a "fair" way. Nonetheless he believes that the idea deserves serious consideration for political reasons. The less developed countries believe they have a grievance: that GATT cannot or will not help them; that the developed countries discriminate among themselves and against the less developed countries, and it is time they stopped.

There is no doubt that the less developed countries have a strong case against present discrimination against them. The 80 percent clause of Trade Expansion Act of 1962 discussed in Chapter 7—that tariffs be eliminated on products on which the United States and the Common Market account for more than 80 percent of world trade—was deliberately and explicitly designed to lower tariffs more on the items which the less developed countries had little or no share of the market. It failed to work, because of Britain not joining the Common Market, but the intent was clear. Then there is the Textile Agreement under which the exporting countries agree to limit exports of textiles to the developed countries, especially the United States, not because they want to limit exports, but because they are told that if they don't, they will be limited for them by quotas in the developed countries. The United

States was a bit slow, but much faster than Europe, in removing quota restrictions on Japanese trade. The fact is that the low-wage manufactures that the less developed countries are able to produce impinge on the sensitive, vote-conscious, labor-intensive, import-competing sectors of the developed countries, where it is politically very difficult to welcome the competition of imports. Reduced barriers and free trade are welcomed in commodities produced by other developed countries— products made by the rich for the rich, the less developed countries would say—but a poor man who wants to break into the game is fenced off with quotas, or even made to impose them himself, to save the reputation for no quantitative restrictions which the developed countries cherish. The claim of the developed countries that their tariffs on manufactures are low is unacceptable, according to Johnson, because of the theory of the effective rate of protection. Textiles, in particular have high proportions of low-duty imported fiber so that effective rates are much higher than nominal rates.

The developed countries will maintain that things are not as bad as the less developed countries paint them. Tariffs in the developed countries are low. The Textile Agreement provides for a 5 percent expansion in quotas each year, which over time will permit a very considerable expansion of imports from the less developed countries. And the less developed countries were given a handsome present at the Kennedy Round of GATT in having the mutual concessions of the developed countries extended to them under the most-favored-nation clause, without being asked for reciprocal concessions. But these professions of goodwill can be refuted. If one moves from nominal to effective rates of tariff, the duties of the developed countries do not seem low: Balassa, for example, suggests that the nominal rates of the United States and the Common Market on textile fabrics, at 24 and 21 percent are in reality effective rates of protection of 51 and 52 percent, respectively. The 5 percent expansion in the Textile Agreement is more than used up by new quotas which are imposed as soon as new supplies come to the United States from countries previously uncovered. And the benefit of uncompensated reductions in tariffs under the Kennedy Round is of scant value to the less developed countries since the bulk of the manufactured products which concern them are covered by quotas or were held out of the developed country bargaining by the exceptions procedure.

There can be no doubt but that the less developed countries have a strong case of discrimination against them. But the answer is to remove the discrimination, not to swing to positive discrimination in their favor.

Australia made a political gesture of solidarity with the less developed countries by providing them with preferences in some manufactured goods lines. But these are circumscribed with quotas, which limit imports to a small fraction of domestic production. The path through discrimination leads back to the quotas, quota-bargaining, and governmental control of trade which throttled trade in the 1930's and early postwar period and which it took so much time to dismantle. The effort should be applied to lower duties in general, i.e., to a chance to compete with local producers on more even terms, not merely to have an advantage against other potential exporters.

And the long-run prospects look favorable. Countries grow in part through merely adding capital and labor; fast growth, however, typically involves reallocating labor from less to more productive activities. The import-competing lines of labor intensive goods are on the whole low-wage and low-profit activities in the developed countries. The resources engaged in them should be transferred out into more productive lines. During a depression these jobs are better than no jobs at all, and the depression mentality makes it difficult to reduce tariffs in labor intensive lines. But when full employment is consistently maintained, as has been the case in the United States in recent years, and widely in Europe, it pays a country to reallocate labor from import-competing activities to domestic or exporting. The balance-of-payments considerations cannot be ignored; we treat them in Parts IV and VI. But the instincts appropriate to a depression economy are a treacherous guide in a full-employment one.

This much can be said for action like that of the United States in the Textile Agreement, or of Europe in preserving employment in coal. Liquidation of an industry with unproductive employment should not be precipitous. It takes time to transfer workers to other locations, where plant and housing must be constructed, or to attract new industry to the work site. Tariffs and quotas to slow down the rate of change make sense. But they should be disappearing tariffs or quotas, which decline by, say, 20 percent of the original amount each year for five years.

Reciprocity versus Nondiscrimination

The long period of difficult negotiation over the Kennedy Round and the complaints of the developing countries in UNCTAD led some observers to suggest that the time had come to effect a new approach to trade matters. Johnson put it that if a choice had to be made between reciprocity and nondiscrimination, it might be time to choose reciprocity and to let nondiscrimination go. He argues that reciprocity is based on mercantilism, that there is much to be said for nondiscrimination, and that the choice between the two principles is false. Despite this, he is concerned that the less developed countries can make little headway in the world if they are committed under GATT to both reciprocity and nondiscrimination. They would perhaps prefer to get rid of both principles. A group of developing countries has submitted to the Special Committee on Preferences of UNCTAD a scheme for general preferences of the developing countries in the developed countries which would be given without reciprocal concession. But if it were necessary to make a choice between the two principles, Johnson predicts that reciprocity will be retained and nondiscrimination will be lost.

The politics of this position are readily understood, but the economics leave much to be desired. Apart from the balance-of-payments argument, and the terms of trade, which is irrelevant in the particular context, there is no valid argument for reciprocity in a full-employment world. It is possible with optimal discrimination to improve world welfare over the nondiscriminatory basis, but assurance that discrimination would be optimal would be hard to obtain or believe. The developing countries are right in wanting infant industry protection for getting industries started, and market outlets abroad for those that prove successful. The first implies nonreciprocity. The second might benefit from preferences. It will do better in the long run with low or zero tariffs. If the less developed countries have to conserve their ammunition, they had better address lower tariffs than preferences which imply continuing tariffs and retention of labor intensive industries in developed countries.

SUGGESTED READING

Treatises, Etc.

The most thorough treatment of the subject is found in the eight volumes prepared for the UNCTAD conference at Geneva in 1964, including one on commodity problems and another on trade in manufactures (New York: United Nations, 1964). Volume III contains the Kaldor-Hart-Tinbergen proposal referred to in the text. A thorough concise treatment, though the text takes exception to parts of it, is Harry G. Johnson, *Economic Policies toward Less Developed Countries* (Washington, D.C.: The Brookings Institution, 1967) (paperback, Frederick A. Praeger, Inc.). On commodity agreements, see J. W. F. Rowe, *Primary Commodities in International Trade* (Cambridge: Cambridge University Press, 1965) (paperback). See also A. I. MacBean, *Export Instability and Economic Development* (London: George Allen & Unwin, Ltd., 1966) and Joseph D. Coppock, *International Economic Instability* (New York:

McGraw-Hill Book Co., Inc., 1962). On trade preferences see Sidney Wein-traub, *Trade Preferences for Less-Developed Countries* (New York: Frederick A. Praeger, Inc., 1967), and a short popular plea K. S. Sundara Rajan, "Tariff Preferences and Developing Countries," in *Finance and Development,* December, 1966.

Studies of the foreign trade of particular developing countries are worth-while, see for example, William O. Freithaler, *Mexico's Foreign Trade and Economic Development* (New York: Frederick A. Praeger, Inc., 1967).

POINTS

The estimate of the average nominal and effective rates on textile fabrics in the United States is from Bela Balassa, *Trade Liberalization among Industrial Countries* (New York: McGraw-Hill Book Co., Inc., 1967), Appendix, Table 3.1, p. 180.

The experience of the West African Cocoa Marketing Board is discussed in P. T. Bauer and F. W. Paish, "The Reduction of Fluctuations in the Incomes of Primary Producers," *EJ,* December, 1952.

A popular study by the Committee on Economic Development on "Trade Policy toward Low-Income Countries" (New York, 1967) recommends preferential tariff reductions extended by the developed to the developing countries without counterpart. This discards the principles of both nondiscrimination and reciprocity.

Chapter 11

ECONOMIC INTEGRATION

The Theory of Customs Union

Integration is one of the polysyllabic words such as co-operation, coordination, and organization which does not mean anything until it is given content. We will define it later. But the discussion of integration after World War II started with Viner's book *The Customs Union Issue* and especially with the concepts of trade creation and trade diversion. These concepts again need content. The idea of trade diversion underlined a paradox which has come to take a large place in the theory of economic policy. Not every step to reduce tariffs results in more and more gainful trade. Eliminating trade barriers between two trading partners may not improve world efficiency, if the trade diversion effect outweighs the trade creation effect. Ultimately this developed into the "theory of the second best," which holds that if one cannot achieve the best—perhaps free trade—it may be wrong to take off some tariffs, and better to put others on. But we get ahead of our story.

The theory of trade creation and trade diversion can be illustrated in both partial and in general equilibrium. The position in partial equilibrium is shown for a single commodity in Figure 11.1 Assume, in Figure 11.1, that $D-D$ and $S-S$ are the demand and supply curves of a "home" country which imports $M-M$ of a product with a tariff WH. The world price OW is assumed to represent an infinitely elastic supply schedule, which eliminates adverse terms of trade effects on the rest of the world after the formation of the customs union. In short, the world price is fixed no matter what happens. The partner's supply is also assumed to be infinitely elastic at the price OP. Before customs union the prospective "partner," facing the same tariff as the rest of the "world," is out of the market, since its pretariff price is higher than that in the outside world. After the union with no tariffs against partner, and the tariff WH still applying to imports from the rest of the world, all imports come from partner and none from the rest of the world.

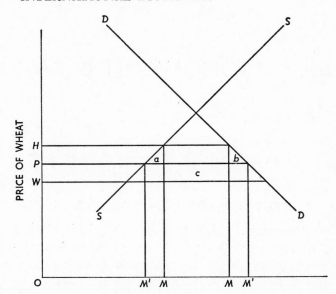

FIG. 11.1.   Trade Creation and Trade Diversion in Partial Equilibrium

Customs union between "home" and partner then results in a net trade creation gain equal to the triangles *a* and *b* (trade expands from MM to $M'M'$ but $M'M \cdot OP$ represents merely the employment of partner's resources instead of domestic resources, and $MM' \cdot OP$ is the corresponding shift of consumption expenditure from domestic to partner's markets. The trade diversion deadweight loss is measured by *c*, representing a shift in imports from cheap world sources to the higher cost partner. In addition to these net deadweight gains and losses, there is a variety of gross shifts which the student may profit from thinking about. For example the total value of imports is diverted from the world to the partner. Why is this not all loss? Or what happens to the tariff revenue which the home state used to receive? (Part of it goes to reduce prices to domestic consumers; the rest to pay producers in the partner country. The domestic country is worse off than before by this latter amount, which is *c*, since the loss of revenue is not entirely made up by gains to consumers.)

In this one commodity, the gains from customs union are evidently greater, because of more trade creation, the greater the elasticities of demand and supply in the home country (or the flatter the demand and supply curves in the figure), the wider the cost differences between home country and partner, and the smaller these differences between partner and the world. On the other hand, the trade diversion loss is greater, the less elastic the demand and supply curves in the home country, and the smaller the cost differences between home and partner, and the wider they are between partner and the world.

Viner thought of the gain from trade creation as coming from cheaper production in the partner than in the home country, and trade diversion as the shift from cheaper world output to the more expensive output of partner. He did not deal with the consumption gain. This was because he lacked the modern analysis of the demand side with indifference curves, and for convenience assumed that the country always consumed goods in fixed proportions, regardless of price. Thus in Figure 11.2*a*, consumption is divided between the two goods X and Y in

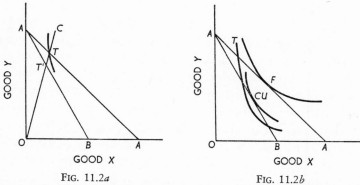

FIG. 11.2*a*   FIG. 11.2*b*

Customs Union with Fixed Production; The Consumption Effect in General Equilibrium

proportions indicated by the straight-line ray from the origin, *O–C*. The country concerned produces the Y good at the upper point *A* before and after customs union. The world terms of trade are *A–A*, and the country consumes at *T*. The consumption indifference curve is not tangent to the world traded price line at that point, because the domestic price has been distorted by the tariff. After customs union, the terms of trade of the country worsen and consumption retreats along the consumption path from *T* to *T'*. By assumption there is no change in the proportions in which the goods are consumed. But this is hardly realistic, as the Figure 11.2*b* shows. The free-trade position would be *F*. With a nondiscriminatory tariff the country trades at world terms of trade, but consumption is distorted from *F* to *T*, landing the country on a lower indifference curve. With customs union, it is claimed, the position will shift to a consumption point like *CU* which may or may not be on a higher consumption indifference curve than *T*. As drawn in Figure

11.2*b*, it is on a higher curve; the price of the imported good has declined, and this makes consumers better off. (But depending on the shape of the indifference curves, it might be lower.) Thus even with production fixed, customs union may (but need not) improve the position through providing cheaper consumption.

This analysis does not go undisputed. It is claimed that it makes some curious assumptions. To handle the issue as a case of general equilibrium, the government of the country imposing the tariff is assumed to give back the revenue it collects to consumers who spend it in accordance with their collective indifference map. But if production cannot change, if the government does not need revenue, and if trade continues at world terms of trade, the tariff is a curious one. Its purpose is merely to change the price at which consumers buy. Where a tariff has been imposed for the sole purpose of distorting and limiting consumption in the imported good, it seems evident that a reduction in the tariff is likely to produce an increase in welfare. With more normal assumptions, the question is whether the change in consumption from a customs union leaves the country better off or not, after the tariff has been replaced by taxes needed to maintain the government's revenue.

Customs union can also be shown in general equilibrium, using offer curves, which allows us to show three countries *A*, *B*, and *ROW*, the rest of the world, and two commodities *X* and *Y*. The exposition is difficult, because there are a lot of possibilities. *A* and *B* may trade mostly with each other, and only an excess with *ROW*, or they can both have a comparative advantage in the same product and import the other from *ROW*. In Figures 11.3*a* and 11.3*b*, *O–A* and *O–B* represent free-trade offer curves which indicate these separate conditions. The problem is to arrive at a combined offer curve for the union. In Figure 11.3*a*, the combined offer curve is derived by drawing a series of price rays from the origin (not shown) and marking off the distance between the *O–A* and *O–B* curves. Two curves of the locus of these differences can be drawn, one at lower prices for *X* (higher for *Y*), going to the right—an excess demand for *X* and supply of *Y*—and the other at higher prices to the left. At the price at which the free-trade *O–A* and *O–B* curves intersect, there is evidently no excess demand or supply for either commodity, as the market is cleared. In Figure 11.3*b*, on the other hand, the two curves are added to form the *A + B* curve, which is done by summing the distances along price rays from the origin.

The same procedures can be used to net or sum tariff-distorted offer curves. This is done in Figures 11.3*c* and 11.3*d*. The tariff-distorted offer curves, it will be recalled from Chapter 7, are displaced in

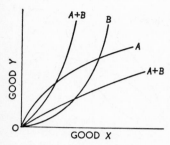

FIG. 11.3*a*. Summing Free-Trade Offer Curves to Arrive at Net-Offer Curve

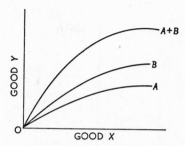

FIG. 11.3*b*. Summing Free-Trade Offer Curves to Arrive at Gross Offer Curve

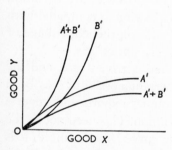

FIG. 11.3*c*. Summing Tariff-Distorted Offer Curves Net

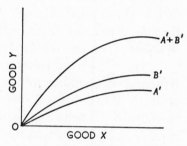

FIG. 11.3*d*. Summing Tariff-Distorted Offer Curves Gross

uniform percentages toward the axis of the demanded good. The simple addition of the *A* and *B* and *A'* and *B'* offer curves (the primes standing for tariff-distorted curves) in Figures 11.3*b* and 11.3*d* gives no difficulty. The summed *O–A'* and *O–B'* making up the *O–A'* + *B'* curve is exactly the same as if the *O–A* + *B* curve had been displaced by a tariff. But the shape of the excess tariff-distorted curves in Figure 11.3*c* has changed: both *O–A'* + *B'* curves more quickly approach the *O–A'* and *O–B'* (simple tariff-distorted offer curves) because mutual trade has been cut down.

Now we are ready to see what happens with customs union, and the difficulty is that there is no unique answer. In Figure 11.3*f* nothing happens. *A* and *B* exchange good *Y* for good *X* before with separate tariffs; they continue to trade *Y* for *X* with a joint tariff. The tariff-distorted summed offer curve (*A* + *B*)' is the same as the sum of the separate tariff-distorted offer curves, *A'* + *B'*. In the other case, where the two countries were trading with each other before customs union, the tariff-distorted offer curve *O–(A + B)'* differs from the relevant

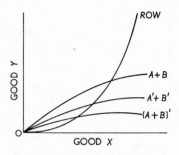

FIG. 11.3e. Trade Diversion in
General Equilibrium

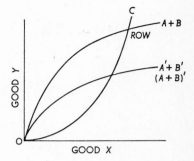

FIG. 11.3f. Customs Union with
No Effect

$O–A' + B'$ curve. As drawn, the former cuts the $O–C$ offer curve at a
point to the right of the latter, and shows trade diversion. But this is not
a necessary or even a typical result. The offer curve of the customs union
may be the same, trade expanding or trade narrowing as compared with
the case with separate tariffs. Everything depends on the exact shape of
the offer curves and their elasticities over the relevant ranges.

The right-hand column of diagrams offers a trivial case, and the
left-hand set is indeterminate. But one important possibility has been
omitted. In every case covered so far, each country exports and imports
the same goods before and after the customs union. This need not be the
case. If A and B have roughly similar offer curves, for example, it is
possible for B to switch sides when the change from universal tariffs to
customs union takes place. It would be tedious to draw a new set of
curves, but contemplate Figure 11.4 which shows B with two offer

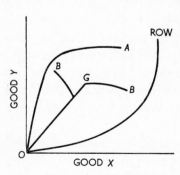

FIG. 11.4. Trade Diversion when
Country B Switches Traded
Commodities

curves, one at higher prices for Y than
OG, at which it would trade Y for X, and
the other at higher prices for X, at which
it would switch sides. With nondiscriminatory tariffs, assume that A and B trade
Y for X. With a customs union, B
switches to X, and the tariff-distorted
offer curve of the union is sharply contracted. This is trade diversion with a
vengeance.

In his original book, Professor Viner
stated that trade creation was more likely
to occur when the two countries forming
the customs union were competitive, and
trade diversion if they were complementary. This fails to put the issue
in its full complexity, and our diagrams help but little. Moving from

the tariff-distorted offer curves $O–A'$ and $O–B'$ in Figure 11.3c to the free-trade curves in Figure 11.3a is trade creating within the union. What it does to trade with C is indeterminate. Trade creation within the union can be said to arise because some protected industries were put out of business by imports, i.e., the economies turned out to be competitive. But in Figure 11.4, A and B may be said to be competitive in one sense, that is, they both are better at the production of Y as compared to ROW. But if customs union means that A and B trade with each other and only a small excess with ROW, they are complementary after the fact of trade diversion. The point is perhaps better put that trade creation involves suppression of tariff-protected activities in the customs union, whereas trade diversion involves expansion of tariff-protected activities in the union.

Trade creation and trade diversion are not purely hypothetical concepts. In U.S. history the foremost example is the customs union between the plantation agriculture of the South and the nascent manufacturing of the North. These were not separate countries, but they were different regions in terms of factor proportions, factor prices, and comparative advantage. Before World War I, in fact, trade between the North and the South was conducted much like international trade and unlike internal trade. Little capital moved south or labor north. With factor immobility, factor prices failed to equalize, and it paid to employ different factor proportions. The South had a labor and land intensive agriculture; the North a capital intensive manufacturing industry.

The inclusion of the agricultural South in the customs area of the North, which is what a common customs meant, required the South to buy in a protected market while it was selling in a free market. Like country A in Figure 11.4, it was required to buy its X from the high-cost producer B, instead of on the cheap world market represented by ROW. The price of its imports increased, and its terms of trade were reduced. This economic exploitation of the South by the North is generally regarded as a factor contributing to the War between the States.

A further example can be given from the history of Germany, in which Zollverein, or customs union, actually preceded political union by many years. The Zollverein was formed in 1834; Bismarck united Germany under the leadership of Prussia in 1870. In 1879 the first of the increases took place in the tariff on grain. This was combined with a tariff on steel; but Germany was in the business of exporting steel, so that the tariff was useful only in widening its scope for dumping. The tariff on rye, on the other hand, raised the cost of living of the worker in western Germany well above what it would have been, had Germany bought its grain on the world market. Customs union thus involved the exploitation of the working classes by the Prussian Junkers, who were both soldiers and managers of estates which grew rye. After World War II unsophisticated observers thought that West Germany would be harmed by being cut off from its traditional source of food in the east. As it turned out, however, West Germany gained by being able to obtain its food abroad at low world prices, rather than from protected high-cost farms in the east.

The net impact of trade creation and trade diversion effects of the European Common Market is difficult to weigh. Within the union, the gains from trade creation in industrial products are substantial. This is because of high elasticities in these competitive production lines. Trade diversion in manufactured goods is probably relatively unimportant for the world, if not for the individual countries left out, because of the limited differences in cost for most goods between the countries in the union and the outside world. But trade diversion is likely to be substantial in agricultural products, where Germany, and Britain if it succeeds in getting entry, are called upon to shift purchases of temperate commodities from the Commonwealth and the United States to the relatively high-cost production of France, and of tropical products from Latin America and the independent African states generally to former French colonies in Africa, the so-called French Community.

The trade diversion effect may not be serious for the world because of the narrowness of the difference in cost between the excluded outside seller and the favored inside one. It will still be painful to the outside seller. This is why the British, Danes, and Norwegians were so anxious to join, and the neutrals (Austria, Sweden, and Switzerland) and the underdeveloped countries (Greece and Turkey) so concerned to find a basis of association. Trade diversion also adversely affected the United States, which, however, was able to mitigate the economic hurt of discrimination in industrial products by establishing facilities to manufacture inside the Common Market boundaries. The United States was in any event prepared to pay the economic price of European integration to obtain the political benefits in the form of strengthening the Free World. But the other outsiders—Japan (where cost differences in manufactures were substantial), the Commonwealth, and the producers of tropical products which were discriminated against by the preferential position in the Common Market given to former colonies—all these were adversely affected. The U.S. Trade Expansion Act of 1962 attempted to reduce this hurt by providing for mutual lowering of tariffs. If the tariff, WH in Figure 11.1, is reduced below WP, the home country will buy nothing in the partner which, in its turn, will buy for the first time in the world market. The more countries join the customs union, and the lower the common external tariff, the less will be the extent of trade diversion and the more nearly will the customs union approach the free-trade ideal.

The Dynamic Effects of Customs Union

Trade creation and trade diversion are static effects of customs union or trade integration. There is some doubt as to their importance. A number of scholars have sought to measure the effects of tariff reductions, both total and partial, and the impact on national income usually turns out to be exiguous, to use a fancy word, or very small. Imports, say, are 20 percent of national income. Elimination of a 10 percent tariff may expand trade to 22 or 24 percent of income. But the change is not a clear gain for national income, as partial equilibrium diagrams such as Figure 11.1 remind us. The protective effect and the consumption effect are represented, not by the total change in trade, which includes resources, but by the increment in trade times the change in price made possible by the new arrangements, in the case of trade creation, the higher price for exports and the lower price for imports. Even if this is substantial, we end up with a small measure of the static gain.

Not all the gains are static, however. Dynamic gains include economies of scale, the stimulus of competition, and the stimulus to investment. Economies of scale were touched upon in Chapter 2. As specialization takes place, costs may fall for a number of reasons: because of specialization and learning to make the product more effectively through repetition; through developing a higher skilled pool of available labor; through spreading a number of capital items of a lumpy character more thinly per unit of output; and so on. These matters are discussed more thoroughly in courses in intermediate theory. Economies of scale are the great hope of customs unions among less developed countries; they may occur in customs union among manufacturing countries through product specialization which enables manufacturers in two countries to concentrate on particular sizes or models of a product, rather than to make a full line (this is even sometimes the result of a business agreement); and they are much debated. Many Europeans assert that the advantage of the United States is that it has a large internal market which enables its manufacturers to achieve economies of scale. The opponents point to the efficiency of many small companies, and the sluggishness of some large, and note that countries like Sweden and Switzerland have efficient manufacturing where the market extends beyond the national boundaries. The importance of economies of scale cannot be demonstrated. This gives us students of international economics much to argue about.

The competitive effect has been touched on earlier in Chapter 7. Professor Scitovsky believes that this was the most important impact of the European Economic Community (EEC) or Common Market. As suggested in the earlier discussion, high tariffs foster monopoly in which one or two large companies preside over a larger aggregation of small, inefficient producers. The big companies like the quiet life and prefer high prices to substantial volume, which they could achieve to drive out the little firms, if they chose. With lower tariffs, the big companies are forced to compete, and the little to merge, combine, become efficient, or go under. This effect has been particularly observed in France. It may be a function of lower tariffs within the EEC, or of their anticipation.

Finally among the dynamic effects, the change in relative prices and the prod to competition stimulate investment. This may be domestic investment, to take advantage of new trading opportunities or under the spur of competition attacking from abroad. One important aspect of the change in domestic investment is the pull of market-oriented industry to the frontier nearer markets in the trading partner. This is hard on such regions as southern Italy, southwest France or southeast Germany which lie far from the markets in the union partners. New investment to take advantage of opportunities is accompanied by disinvestment in industries adversely affected by trade creation, i.e., the import-competing industries which are no longer able to make a go of it. The investment stimulus of new industries is likely to be greater than the disinvestment discouragement in old industries, unless there is substantial excess capacity available. On this score, customs union may be said to be inflationary.

The possibility that investment will decline in the remote and backward portions of a newly integrated area has led to special measures to assist them. Thus the EEC established a European Investment Bank to undertake new ventures in the adversely affected portions of the Six. This constitutes explicit acknowledgement that in the absence of policy certain parts of the integrated area will suffer.

In addition to the dynamic stimulus to domestic investment, however, there is the possibility of inducing investment from abroad. This is of two kinds. There may be rearrangement of existing foreign capacity in the community to take advantage of the new conditions. This effect is identical to the pull to the border in the market-oriented industries, with this difference, that domestic firms are not likely to cross the border, and foreign firms, without roots in the particular country, may be drawn across. Or the trade-diverting effect of the customs union may induce foreigners who have served the various national markets by exports and now are discriminated against, to substitute tariff factories for trade. American firms undertook massive investment in Europe after about 1955 for a variety of reasons (or excuses), and the EEC may have been one or the other. To a considerable extent in the judgment of more than one writer, the effect of the EEC was not so much that it provided the marginal conditions under which a close calculation revealed that it was better now to invest in Europe than to provide that market from the United States. Rather it called attention of manufacturers who had neglected to notice investment opportunities in Europe, that here was a growing, vigorous market from which outsiders might be expelled and which it was useful to join.

Economic Integration

In some definitions, economic integration is nothing more or less than free trade. This, for example, is the definition of the Dutch economist, Jan Tinbergen in his *International Economic Integration*. Most economists go further. One touchstone is whether or not one can get rid of the customs officers on the frontier. Even when they are not required to collect duties, there are still sanitary regulations and other invisible trade barriers, and much more far reaching, in the usual case, the question of excise taxes. Tobacco, alcohol, perfume, and so on are usually taxed internally. If the taxes differ in two countries, it is necessary to post collectors to prevent the smokers and drinkers from running supplies into the state with the higher taxes from the state with the lower—a problem not unknown in the United States, despite a uniform federal excise tax system—because of differences in state excises. Or if one state's system of general excise taxation differs from that of another, there is a problem. The answer, before the officers can be removed, is "harmonization" of taxation of all goods. We will return to this question in Chapter 13.

Are customs union plus harmonization of goods taxation enough to constitute economic integration? It evidently depends on the definition. Balassa's definition is the absence of government discrimination. In goods, this means customs union plus harmonization. For factors it may mean much more: freedom of migration (see Chapter 14, and parallel or identical policies in the fields of money, foreign exchange, regulation of capital markets, et cetera. The "et cetera" includes the special goods field of agriculture. But assume that two countries agreed on a customs union and tax harmonization, and then one froze wages while the other let them rise. Or the divergent policy could be foreign exchange depreciation. The policy outside the tariff field would evidently expand exports and hurt imports, thereby changing the balance of payments and altering the basis on which the customs union had been agreed. It has been suggested that customs union is a halfway house on the way to a wider economic integration, a halfway house in which it is not possible to stay forever. The members must move on toward economic integration more broadly, however specifically defined, or in time the customs union will break down.

The absence of government discrimination is perhaps not the ultimate definition of economic integration. Suppose Iceland and New Zealand were to adopt regulations granting each other's nationals not most-favored-nation treatment, but national treatment, i.e., treatment identical with each country's own nationals over a wide area. There might be customs union, harmonization of tax policy, and even parallel policies in other fields. Would this result in economic integration? Evidently not.

The reason an Iceland-New Zealand customs union of this sort would not result in economic integration is that whether or not governments discriminate between the two countries, Nature does. By putting them in separate hemispheres, both East–West, and North–South, Nature has reduced the economic contacts between Iceland and New Zealand to what one may presume, without being burdened by the facts, is virtually zero. So it is not government discrimination alone that counts.

This brings us to a definition of economic integration which makes it a standard of measurement, but one which, like absolute zero in low-temperature physics, is never reached. Economic integration is factor-price equalization. This can be produced by trade, without factor movements, by factor movement without trade, or by some combination of the two. But any interference with trade, whether by tariffs or transport costs, prevents goods prices being equalized, and therefore factor prices. And discrimination can be carried on by governments or by the public.

Take first transport costs. The reason that an Iceland–New Zealand customs union would fail to produce economic integration is that distance would prevent an equalization of goods prices. In addition to distance, moreover, two such widely different countries are almost certain to be completely specialized, thus eliminating another of the significant assumptions of the factor-price-equalization theorem. Both points make clear why the EEC was a much more serious step in the direction of integration than the free-trade area among Britain, the three Scandinavian countries, Austria, Switzerland, and Portugal. France, Belgium, the Netherlands, Germany, and Italy share common frontiers, across which transfer costs, after the removal of tariffs, are zero. The countries of the European Free Trade Association (EFTA) are spread out in an enormous circle around the EEC, with long distances between many of them, whether physical as between Portugal and Sweden, or economic between Austria and Switzerland where the economically important areas are divided by mile after mile of Alps. The issue is of prime importance also in the Latin-American Free Trade Area (LAFTA) where countries which are contiguous are not necessarily close economically. Argentina and Chile with a long common border find it cheaper to ship steel around by sea than to lug it up over the passes of the Andes. In economic terms, therefore, Buenos Aires is not much nearer Valparaiso than the Sparrows Point plant of the Bethlehem Steel Company in Baltimore.

Next is the possibility of private discrimination, even when governmental discrimination has been eliminated. When Benelux (the economic union among Belgium, the Netherlands, and Luxemburg, which preceded the EEC and was absorbed into it) finally lifted the barriers to the movement of capital and labor between the two countries, nothing happened. The Dutch preferred to keep their capital in Holland, and the Belgian workers preferred to live and work in Belgium, both despite the possibility of higher monetary rewards from the newly permitted migration. Thus private discrimination prevents economic integration.

Under the factor-price-equalization definition, economic integration is likely never to be fully achieved. The definition is useful, however, as a standard. The content of integration then becomes one price, as in the law of one price. In one market there is one price, and if there are transactions and one price, there is, in effect, one market. It permits us to say that the labor market in the United States is not integrated, since wages are not the same everywhere, and that the market for Negroes and whites is still not integrated, despite governmental prohibition of discrimination, because Negroes earn less than whites even when they have entry to the same jobs. The test of whether customs union works toward integration is whether it narrows factor-price differences.

Some Lesser Problems of Customs Unions and Free-Trade Areas

The difference between a customs union and a free-trade area has been implied, but not explicitly stated. In the former, there is a single schedule of customs duties, adopted by all countries. In the latter, countries retain their old tariff levels, and merely waive the collection of duties on commerce with members. Both systems have their problems.

In a customs union, the development of a single tariff schedule is a difficult task. First, there is the problem of arriving at a common tariff nomenclature. There is no unique way to classify goods. Most countries have their own system, and when two or more systems are joined, the task is to develop a new one which is agreeable to all. Like all classification systems in a world of change, moreover, there are different rewards and penalties for retaining an old system and for altering it frequently in the light of new conditions. The one gives comparability in time; the other best suits current problems. The experts of the EEC spent several years working out a common tariff nomenclature, even before it was time to set the rates.

Then come rates. GATT rules, which authorize customs unions, state that the common tariff must be no higher than the average tariffs of the countries which go to make it up. There are problems both in measuring the height of a tariff, and in choosing a suitable average of more than one. The simplest system of measuring the height of a tariff is to average separate *ad valorem* tariff rates. This is misleading, as there should be a weighted average. What weights? To weight by actual trade is likely to give a biased result, since the higher the tariff, the more it keeps out trade and the lower its impact. A prohibitive tariff would get no weight, which is absurd. The correct system of weighting is the values which would be achieved under free trade. There is no way of knowing this without an enormous amount of information on elasticities. A proxy for free-trade weights is domestic consumption; here goods which enjoy a prohibitive tariff (a strong protective effect) enter the index.

We noted earlier under the discussion of disparities in the Kennedy Round (page 126), that the Belgian, French, and Italian tariffs were reduced in the EEC averaging and the Dutch and German tariffs raised. Observe that this means more trade creation for the first group, and more trade diversion for the second. The discussion of trade creation and trade diversion earlier in this chapter assumed a constant and uniform rate of tariff. But if any country raises its tariff, trade diversion is evidently accentuated, and for those that lower, the reverse occurs.

Once given the common tariff, what happens to the financial proceeds? They evidently must be divided among the members. How? A simple system is to have each country keep the proceeds it collects; this is more practical than equitable. Should the Netherlands keep the duties on goods for Germany which enter at Rotterdam on their way up the Rhine, or Italy for goods transshipped across the Alps from the Mediterranean? But to trace goods to the country of consumption and assign it the duties is to require more organization than is desirable. The Rome Treaty of 1957 turned this question over to be resolved by the commission which was asked to submit a proposal to the council made up of the foreign ministers.

In a free-trade area, there is no problem about dividing customs receipts: to each his own. But differences among tariff schedules give rise to a problem because of the possibility of arbitrage, that is, entering the goods into the free-trade area in the country with the lowest duty and then reshipping them to another country with a higher. This problem may not be serious when the countries are far apart, as Portugal and Norway, or Switzerland and the United Kingdom in EFTA: the saving in tariffs is likely to be less than the added transport costs. But the problem is sufficiently significant to require control. This is provided by certificates of origin. Goods going from one member of a free-trade area to another are accompanied by a certificate of origin, issued to attest that the goods originated in the member country and not in a third country. The process of issuing such certificates, and verifying the facts, is tiresome, but inescapable.

EEC's Special Regime for Agriculture

The Rome Treaty of 1957 which created the EEC, after the partial "functional integration" in iron and steel and coal of the European Coal and Steel Community, proposed a special regime for agriculture. This sector is a problem in virtually every country and was supported by subsidies and restrictions on trade in particular ways in each member country. No country except the Netherlands was willing to let its farmers compete in world markets. But most countries were unwilling to apply simple tariffs for the reasons suggested in Chapter 8 under "Origin of Quotas."

The negotiations on agriculture proved to be difficult politically. There was initially the question of the system, and then that of details under the system. The system adopted was one of a sliding tariff of the sort that Britain used at one time under the Corn Laws. First a domestic support price for separate commodities in the Common Market is determined. The sliding tariff is the difference between this support price and the world price. If domestic supplies are short, and the price tends to rise above the support price, the world price plus tariff (equal to the support price) will bring it down. If on the other hand, the crop is heavy, the domestic price will sag, and the tariff will become a prohibitive one. The student should have no trouble figuring out the partial equilibrium diagrams. The tariffs on agriculture, incidentally are paid into a special fund designed to modernize EEC agriculture.

The system was one thing. To agree on support prices proved much more difficult. Germany, where the Christian Democrat party depended on farmer support, wanted a high price for wheat. France, where agricultural efficiency was rising rapidly, was afraid that a high price would keep too many men on the land, and produce a larger surplus than Germany could absorb. These negotiations were complicated by U.S. insistence in the Kennedy Round negotiations that provision be made for quota minimums representing amounts of wheat, cotton, soya beans, and so on, that the Common Market would continue to import despite the sliding tariff.

The British application to join the Common Market was made the first time and again the second, on political grounds. But their very different agricultural system poses serious problems. The British start with world prices of foodstuffs, and add subsidies for farmers. To move to the EEC system will require, or would require, a large increase in the price of foodstuffs, and the difference between the world price and the new high prices would be paid to modernize French, German, and Italian farms, since the British are already efficient.

Regional Integration among Developing Countries

The most successful case of economic integration thus far is the European Economic Community. Regional integration is a device often recommended for the developed countries, however. Some have come to fruition, such as the Central American Common Market (CACM), or are struggling to make the grade (as LAFTA). Others have broken up already, such as the West Indian Federation or the arrangements on the East coast of Africa among Kenya, Uganda, and Tanganyika. Some have been for years in the talking stage—the Arab League. Others are now being talked about for the first time, among the Maghreb countries of Tunisia, Algeria, and Morocco, and the Asian countries of the Philippines, Malaya, and Thailand.

The purpose in all cases is to industrialize. National markets are thought to be too narrow. A regional market may be able to support modern industry. There is much less interest in trade creation through destroying inefficient producing units existing in the member countries, than in trade diversion—shifting purchases from the rest of the world to member countries, and more constructively, the achievement of economies of scale. If the countries are going to industrialize anyway, it is best to do it with minimum inefficiency.

But the difficulties are great. On the economic side, the lagging country becomes frightened that by giving its partners free access to its market, it will never be able to start any industry. Thus Bolivia refuses to join LAFTA on the ground that it would impede its development, rather than assist it. It regards LAFTA as a device to speed up the development of Mexico, Argentina, and Brazil—now leading in industry in the area—at the expense of the slower countries.

Various devices are being developed to meet this objection. The lagging country may be given special treatment. This may consist of investment assistance, as in Europe. Or the obligations of the less developed countries to the others may be reduced. In the EEC, the association agreement covering Greece and Turkey provides that Greece and Turkey get access to the markets of the Six, but that the reciprocal reduction of their duties is delayed for five years. (Immediately after the agreement was signed, however, worry was expressed in Athens about what will happen in 1970.) Similar asymmetric treatment of the laggards is promised in LAFTA. In CACM, made up of five very small countries, industries are assigned to countries, with each country being assured of a share in the industrialization process. Special transitional steps may be taken in advance of total integration by countries on roughly the same level of development. In LAFTA, a so-called Bogota group consisting of Colombia, Chile, Ecuador, Peru, and Venezuela has agreed to a joint development commission and other integration measures. But the political difficulty remains. Regional integration provides the hope of industrial gains and the reality of losses to a competitor. If the latter pile up too high, the country is likely to withdraw.

The fact is that despite their geographic proximity, the less developed countries are not economically unified. They are typically more competitive than complementary, and their competitive interests make it hard for them to form a community. Forming a single land mass with good communication as they do, the EEC members for the most part have an economic advantage over the outside world in the markets of the community. In the developing countries, many of them with only exterior lines of communication as noted for Argentina and Chile, there is no natural unity, and the artificial unity of political resolve is difficult to sustain. The fact that benefits for one member are costs for the others is divisive.

If the political difficulties can be overcome, however, there can be little doubt that industrialization in large units is better than industrialization at the same levels of protection in five times that number. The question may be raised, however, whether economic integration into the world market may not be more efficient because trade creating than regional integration of a trade-diverting sort.

SUGGESTED READING

TEXTS

See Snider, chap. xi; Vanek, chap. xviii; Clement, Pfister and Rothwell, chap. iv; and B. Balassa (ed.), *Changing Patterns of Foreign Trade and Payments* (New York: W. W. Norton & Co., Inc., 1964) (paperback), part ii.

TREATISES

On a theoretical level, see Bela Balassa, *The Theory of Economic Integration* (Homewood, Ill.: Richard D. Irwin, Inc., 1961); R. G. Lipsey, "The Theory of Customs Unions: A General Survey," in American Economic Association, *Readings in International Economics* and a vast literature, among which the outstanding theoretical items are:

Jacob Viner, *The Customs Union Issue* (New York: Carnegie Endowment for International Peace, 1953).

Tibor Scitovsky, *Economic Theory and Western European Integration* (London: Unwin University Books; reprinted with a new introduction, 1962) (paperback).

James E. Meade, *Problems of Economic Union* (London: Oxford University Press, 1953).

On Europe, see, *inter alia:*

Lawrence B. Krause (ed.), *The Common Market: Progress and Controversy* (Englewood Cliffs, N.J.: Prentice-Hall, Inc., 1964) (paperback).

F. B. Jensen and I. Walter, *The Common Market: Economic Integration in Europe* (Philadelphia: J. B. Lippincott Co., 1956) (paperback).

Miriam Camps, *Britain and the European Community, 1955–1963* (Princeton, N.J.: Princeton University Press, 1963).

On Latin America:

Victor L. Urquidi, *Free Trade and Economic Integration in Latin America* (Berkeley, Calif.: University of California Press, 1962) (paperback).

Miguel S. Wionszek (ed.), *Latin American Economic Integration: Experiences and Prospects* (New York: Frederick A. Praeger, Inc., 1966).

Sidney Dell, *A Latin American Common Market?* (New York: Oxford University Press, Inc., 1967).

POINTS

Tinbergen's definition of integration is given in *International Economic Integration* (Amsterdam: Elsevier Publishing Co., 1965).

A useful source on the Central American Common Market is Ingo Walter and Hans C. Vitzhum, "The Central American Common Market: A Case Study on Economic Integration in Developing Regions," in New York University, Institute of Finance *The Bulletin,* No. 44, May, 1967.

For theoretical argument in favor of economic integration among developing countries, see C. A. Cooper and B. F. Massell, "Toward a General Theory of Customs Union for Developing Countries," *JPE,* October, 1965.

Chapter 12

THE CASE FOR FREE
MULTILATERAL TRADE

The last few chapters have suggested that there are many cases where tariffs or subsidies are justified, and many circumstances in the real world when countries in fact interfere with foreign trade. Modern theorists, moreover, make a very weak case for free trade, arguing only that free trade is better than no trade, and even some trade better than no trade, but being unwilling to say anything as strong as that free trade is better than restricted trade. How then can economists, with a weak basic case, and recognizing so many exceptions, go on uniformly recommending free trade as the best commercial policy? We have saved the case for free multilateral trade for this last chapter in Part II on commercial policy to see how much of the classic doctrine of free trade is left or can be salvaged after modern economics theory has chipped or hacked away at it with qualifications. We proceed by discussing efficiency conditions with two and then more countries, and then the distribution of welfare between countries. Thereafter we recur to the theory of the second best, which suggests that even if free trade is best not every step toward free trade should be taken. Finally, in the light of all the possible violations of efficiency conditions, the possible desirability of altering the distribution of welfare, and the dangers of moving toward free trade piecemeal, we get back into line with most economists in arguing for free multilateral trade as a general presumption.

Merits of the Price System

Leaving aside for the time being the question of equity or welfare distribution, the case for free trade rests at basis on efficiency. Provided certain conditions are met, the invisible hand operating under free trade will produce a maximum of world output for a given distribution of income or welfare. Resources will be allocated among various activities and goods will be distributed among consumers, so as to produce the greatest possible volume of satisfaction for the distribution of welfare. It will be impossible to make any one person or group better off without making some other person or group worse off. This is called (after the great Italian economist) Pareto optimality.

We come to the conditions and assumptions shortly. Assuming these conditions, however, and within the limitations of the assumptions, free trade works to equate goods prices everywhere (abstracting from transport costs), which will eliminate any further gain from trading; to equate the prices of goods to their marginal costs, which assures optimum production; and to provide that factors earn the same in every industry, apart from differences in productive capacity, which assures optimum allocation of resources. If social and private marginal value are everywhere equal to social and private marginal cost, society has reached an optimum of efficiency in the allocation of resources, the production of goods, and the distribution of goods. This may not be an optimum welfare position, because of the distribution of income which may leave differences in the significance of income for different income recipients. But for the moment we are discussing efficiency rather than equity.

The case for free trade rests on the view that it is the most direct approach to Pareto optimality, and that the distributional arguments can be taken care of in ways which do not distort efficient allocation of resources. But the conditions are far-reaching. There must be no marked divergence between social values and market prices, either for goods or factors. Such divergences, as the last chapters have shown, do in fact occur. Market prices may differ from social values—apart from governmental interference for redistributional purposes—because of scale economies and diseconomies, of monopoly and monopsony, and because of nonoptimal taxation. Divergences at the factor level may be the result of rigidities and other distortions of factor prices from social marginal products. Rigid factor prices may result in unemployment. While we have discussed most of these at some stage during the last few chapters, it is well to recapitulate.

Demerits of the Price System

When external economies or diseconomies exist, social marginal value diverges from the private marginal value given by the market. Private costs may overstate long-run social costs, as in the infant industry case: a tariff on imports, or better a subsidy on domestic production, is needed to develop for producers the new cost conditions which enable them to reduce price.

Internal economies of scale, which may persist due to lack of competition arising from ignorance or lack of access to complementary factors such as land or capital, similarly produce a divergence between social and private value and reduce economic efficiency below the optimum.

External diseconomies receive less attention. These may exist where depletion enables private value to be higher than social value. Private costs which fail to take account of depletion of natural resources or pollution of air or water understate social costs, and production is excessive. Here the remedy is to require replaceable resources to be replaced (in farming or lumber), or steps to eliminate pollution. Where the resources are irreplaceable, as in mining, there is much to be said for taxation—not on imports but on domestic production, where the country is on an import basis, or on exports if the country sells abroad. The heavy taxes on oil profits in countries such as Venezuela and Iraq have as their justification the replacement of wasting natural resources by man-made capital assets to maintain the productivity of the economy. (Note that as land is depleted and capital built up, the transformation schedule must change and with it comparative advantage.) The external economies or diseconomies may be dynamic, as well as static. It is, for example, sometimes argued that primary product exports may yield a higher return than import-competing manufactures, but that manufacturing has training effects, through a learning process, which lead to increased productivity over time, while the gains from specialization in export products are once-and-for-all.

Where competition is imperfect, the results achieved by free trade again fall short of the efficiency optimum. Monopoly unduly restricts production and raises private above social value. Monopsony unduly restricts consumption and holds private below social value. In goods markets, these results flow from the existence of market power, along with the existence of overhead costs. They can also stem from ignorance, habit, and tradition. Consumers purchase in the expensive rather than in the cheaper market for any of these reasons or because they lack the capital to act in economical fashion. Producers may fail to foresee how permanent a shift in demand is against their product.

It is not only firms which have overhead costs and which act with imperfect foresight. The same is true of factors. Factors may be badly allocated, with crowding of factors in some lines and scarcity in others, through lack of awareness of opportunities, inability to forecast their duration, or costs of moving. Labor has difficulty in transferring between occupations, except insofar as the alternative employments exist side by side in the same locality. There are costs of changing jobs—of selling one house and buying another in a different locality or of merely moving and starting a new home. Labor is mobile over a generation; young people hesitate to enter a shrinking industry unless family and local traditions are very strong; and the overhead costs of moving for young people fresh from schools and colleges are low or nonexistent. But the fact of depressed areas of highly specialized resources—the coal miners of Appalachia, the Negro farmers of the South, and the shoe and textile workers of New England—attest to the immobility of labor.

Real, as opposed to financial, capital, of course, is even more immobile, although less so than land. Capital is completely mobile only over the long run as it wears out in one location and is replaced in another through the investment of depreciation allowances. This takes time, which may run as long as 20 years. In the short run, an individual may be able to move his capital, if he can sell his textile mill in New Hampshire, let us say. But this is not mobility of economic capital, since the buyer puts in what the seller takes out. In economic terms, the equipment may have some mobility, if it can be transported or sold as secondhand machinery or as salvage or scrap steel. The building, however, is unlikely to be movable, and the capital it represents can be shifted only in the long run.

If firms and factors are frequently unresponsive to price signals in the market, and so fail to bring about equality of social and private value, they sometimes actively produce divergence by responding excessively to price change. The cobweb theorem mentioned in Chapter 10 is illustrative of this phenomenon. A higher price for potatoes this year produces too many next year, which leads to a low price then and a shortage the year after. Each rise in price elicits too large an increase in output to bring about equilibrium; each decline too large a decrease.

How far the price system can serve as a guide to investment in new capacity remains a debated point. There are economists who attach great significance to the time lag which supervenes between the recognition of the need for new capacity—during which the supply of consumers' goods is inelastic with response to price increases—and the time when the new capacity is completed and goes into production. If this period is long, as it will be in capital intensive processes, there is danger that the persistence of scarcity and high prices during the period of capital formation will lead to the establishment of what ultimately proves to be excess capacity. The inability of the price system adequately to guide investment decisions in this regard is charged with much of the responsibility for the business cycle.

Alternatives to the Price System

This book is concerned with international trade and not with comparative economic systems. It may nonetheless be worth mentioning that the possible weaknesses of the price system to which reference has been made do not imply that any alternative system—whether cartel or government planning or state ownership—is superior or, for that matter, worse. What appears to be important is the size of the decision-making unit and the scale on which decisions are taken. Monopoly industry, governmental planning, and competitive industry, in which all entrepreneurs are culturally identical and respond in the same way to the same stimuli, are likely to react in the same direction to a change in demand or supply. There may be differences in the speed with which they recognize errors of judgment—this is an advantage claimed for private enterprise. But both will differ from a situation in which tradition decrees what is produced and how, or in which production is carried on by a number of small firms whose views are arrived at independently.

It is probable that the price system works with more effective response, and with less chance of excessive or erroneous response, when the economic society is composed of many firms, each actively trying to maximize its income but each with independent views on the course of events. The exact form of the alternative does not make much difference if it means either that the society ceases trying to maximize or that an industry responds as a unit.

This situation leads to the conclusion that the price system works with greater efficiency as one approaches the classical assumptions of perfect competition and constant costs, i.e., infinitely elastic demand and supply curves, with less efficiency as one departs from them. Viewed in this light, the change in the theory of international trade since its classical development has been a change in analysis only in limited degree. For the most part it has consisted in a revision of the underlying assumptions.

Efficiency and Welfare

The optimum in terms of efficiency would also be the optimum welfare position under either of two circumstances: first, that it made no difference what the distribution of income was, because a dollar of income produced the same amount of welfare no matter who received it; or, second, that the distribution of welfare did not change as one moved toward the efficiency optimum. Unfortunately neither of these assumptions is tenable. Accordingly, even if the price system worked well enough to produce an efficiency optimum, it is by no means certain that this would maximize world welfare.

The classical economists of course recognized that the marginal utility of income was different for rich and poor, so that it was inappropriate to assume that a dollar of income was a dollar of welfare for every income recipient; they also understood that a change toward freer trade redistributed income so that one cannot claim that free trade produces more welfare than protection even if free trade produces more goods at less cost than protection. They nonetheless held that free trade, like honesty, was the best policy.

Modern welfare economists have two hypotheses by which they attempt to say something about free trade and welfare. One device is to assign weights. If country A's income is worth one for every $1 of income, and country B's, one half, then it would be possible to calculate whether free trade produced more welfare than a given position of protection by deriving a weighted result. If free trade turned the terms of trade in B's favor, and lost A 10 but gained 18 for B, this would reduce welfare on the weights indicated: A's weighted loss of 10 is greater than B's weighted gain of 9. But, on the basis of equal weights, free trade would produce gain for the world of A and B. If equal weights are assigned to income recipients in all countries, free trade produces an optimum of welfare. If A's weight is one and B's zero, on the other hand (a highly nationalist point of view), the welfare optimum is the optimum tariff which will improve A's terms of trade to the maximum possible without a counterbalancing decrease in quantity.

The system of weights, which is one form of international social welfare function, should be extended to income recipients within each country. Free trade will distribute income in A against the scarce factor and in favor of the abundant one. If the abundant factor is rich, and the scarce poor, free trade may be a worse position in terms of welfare than the protected position. But of course it would be possible to adopt free trade and redistribute income through fiscal policy.

The other hypothesis is the so-called compensation principle. Situation one is better in terms of welfare than situation two if the gainers in welfare in moving from two to one gain enough to be in position to compensate the losers, and still have something over. This reduces welfare comparisons to those in efficiency: any time there is an increase in the value of total output, it follows that the gross gainers would be in position to compensate the gross losers. But of course such compensation rarely occurs. The progressive income tax, and transfer payments to the needy who may become unemployed, go a short part of the way to provide compensation. But for the rest, the compensation principle remains a pure hypothesis.

Provided that the price system works efficiently to produce a material optimum, there is no doubt that free trade produces a welfare optimum, either with equal weights for countries and income recipients within countries or with the compensation principle, also between and within countries. But this is a trivial truth. Every country has rich and poor, and some countries are richer than others. From the free-trade position, then, it would be possible to impose tariff barriers and other interferences with trade which would improve welfare within and between countries. This is far different, however, from saying that any interference with free trade improves welfare. Some trade barriers transfer income from the poor in the protecting countries to the rich within their borders, and internationally from impoverished countries to wealthy. Unless one knows the distribution of income, there is just as much reason to believe that a movement away from free trade will worsen the welfare position as that it will improve it. Nay, there is more; and for two reasons.

First, the free-trade position tends to produce overall more income. For any given distribution, more is better than less; for any random distribution, moreover, more is better than less. Since there is no presumption that free trade worsens the distribution, there is a presumption that the total welfare position is superior when efficiency is higher than when it is lower. Second, the rich are more likely to have political power and to exercise it than the poor. In consequence, tariffs are likely to favor the rich, and the removal of tariffs, the poor. If the internal welfare function calls for shifts of income from rich to poor, there is a second presumption in favor of freeing trade. The sum total of these two presumptions, however, is not sufficiently high to make an overwhelming case.

Part of the difficulty is that the price system both allocates resources and distributes income. It used to be thought that within an economy the price system and the tax system specialized and divided functions: the price system was used to create an efficiency optimum; the tax system to redistribute income and welfare. This is no longer true even within a closed economy; the existence of cartels, monopolies, price parity formulas, cost-of-living clauses in wage contracts, and so on, demonstrates the extent to which the price system has been used to affect the distribution of welfare. Perhaps the division of function never really existed except in the minds of economists. Internationally, however, no such division of function was possible, because the countries of the world were not bound together in a common budget and so were not linked through taxes. The price system is responsible both for efficiency in the allocation of resources and for the distribution of income and welfare internationally. The price system then tends to produce a maximum of efficiency, to the extent that it operates effectively, and achieves a distribution of income and welfare between countries. This welfare distribution is not necessarily the optimum. For the same distribution of welfare, however, free multilateral trade produces more welfare all round than autarchy.

One important feature of the price system when it operated with a considerable degree of competition was that its decisions were accepted as the impersonal judgments of a sort of fate. The market in a competitive society represents a collective judgment, different from the arbitrary or quixotic decisions of government, monopoly, or a foreign country. An adverse decision administered by the market gives less ground for retaliation through market forces or through extra-market action. Adam Smith regarded the market's actions as those of an "invisible hand." One of the strongest arguments for free multilateral trade with any considerable degree of competition is that it gives an objective basis for the allocation of resources and the distribution of income both nationally and internationally.

One possible qualification must be admitted. Free trade is both the optimum material position for all countries for a given distribution of welfare and the possible optimum for the abundant factor in the economically more advanced country. If all countries are of equal size and power, and income is distributed relatively evenly among them, the first consideration is relevant. If one country is more advanced technologically than the others and of greater economic (and political) power, then free trade may represent an optimum position for the existing distribution of income, but welfare may be capable of increase through a redistribution of income brought about by trade barriers.

If tariffs are justified by the international redistribution of income from a rich country to a poor, the Free Trader has still one more string to his bow. His alternative: adopt free trade and international income transfers. Or to put it another way, if it agrees that welfare should be transferred to the tariff-imposing country, let the country which has a tariff applied against its products adopt an offsetting subsidy. The price distortion produced by the tariff will be corrected by the subsidy. One

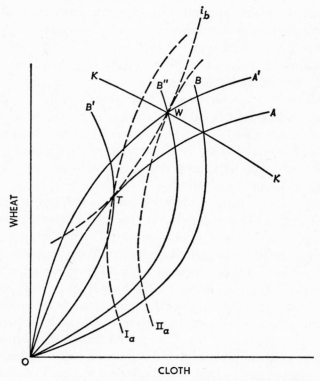

FIG. 12.1. Replacing the Optimum Tariff by an International
Transfer

country taxing imports and the other country subsidizing them is equivalent to a subsidy from the second to the first country, or an international transfer.[1]

This seems a fairly unrealistic suggestion for dealing with international trade, but there is one relevant case: at the United Nations
Conference on Trade and Development in 1964 the developing countries suggested that the European nations which maintain high taxes on

[1] For the student who has studied the appendices and especially C and D, it should
be observed that it is not enough for A to counter B's optimum tariff with an optimum
subsidy. What is required is a reduction in B's tariff plus A's subsidy, which will in
combination keep B on the same indifference curve attainable by the optimum tariff but
make A much better off. In Figure 12.1, B's original optimum tariff displaced the B
offer curve to B', which enabled B to reach the trade indifference curve i_b. A subsidy on
exports by A, displacing its offer curve from A to A', combined with a reduction in B's
tariff so that the offer curve is displaced from B' to B'', keeps B on indifference curve i
(moving from T to W) but enabled A to advance from indifference curve I (at T) to
indifference curve II at W. This exercise underlines the truth that the contract curve, K—K,
is an optimum locus where one country cannot benefit without another country losing.

coffee, tea, and cocoa should eliminate those taxes. It was originally thought that this would expand consumption and developing country exports. But the idea occurred to a number of people that if these import, tariff for revenue only (since there is no local European production) taxes were removed in Europe, the developing countries could replace them with export taxes. Europe would lose revenue, and the developing countries would gain revenue. Production and consumption would still be inefficient, but the shift of tax revenues from the importers to the exporters would be equivalent to foreign aid (and require the same budgetary steps). In short, intergovernmental economic assistance is superior to the optimum tariff, as it accomplishes the sought-after transfer of welfare without distorting production and consumption. The Free Trader repeats: there is nothing a tariff can do that something else cannot do better.

The German School has consistently regarded free trade as the ideological weapon of the dominant country. A number of economists have considered the attempts of the United States to achieve a multilateral convertible world of lower tariffs in the same category. There can be no doubt that the distribution of income internationally will be different with trade barriers than with free trade, and the total material level lower. If the social welfare function or set of value judgments called for a shift of income from export interests to import-competing industry in the United States or if the terms of trade could be turned against the United States by tariffs abroad and the international social welfare function required a shift of income from the United States to other countries, the free-trade optimum position in material terms would not represent the desirable position in terms of welfare.

Free trade is necessarily nondiscriminatory trade. And the case against discrimination is a solid one, despite the demand of the less developed countries for preferences in manufactures. If the less developed countries require help to get a start to achieve economies of scale, subsidies are better than tariffs that are relaxed in a discriminatory fashion. Perhaps even better than export or manufacturing subsidies by the developing countries would be import subsidies by the developed countries, having the international distribution of welfare in mind. This is perhaps perfectionism. But nondiscriminatory trade in which imports are bought in the cheapest market and sold in the dearest to the extent needed to equalize prices (adjusted for transport costs) is the efficient ideal. If the price system is allowed to produce efficiency and transfers are undertaken to achieve international equity, the slogan of "trade not aid"—which would distort trade in order to redistribute welfare better—does not stand up.

The Case for Multilateral Trade

In a world of more than two countries the case for free trade becomes a case for multilateral trade and convertible currencies. If free trade takes place only between pairs of countries and, because of inconvertibility, each segment of paired trade must be in balance, the overall criterion for a free-trade maximum of efficiency is breached. Goods will be bought in markets other than the cheapest and will be sold for less than the dearest price. This follows because of the necessity to balance. If a single pair of countries shows an export surplus for A and an import surplus for B, with all buyers and sellers maximizing their gain, balance will require the redirection of A purchases from a cheaper source to B, or a shift of A sales to a less profitable market than B.

Multilateralism requires convertibility. The export surplus earned by A in B's currency must be convertible into C's exchange to requite the gross deficit incurred by A in trade with C. The difficulty in a world of interconnected trade balances is that the maintenance of convertibility of a country's currency is not solely within its capacity. The currency of the countries with which it has export surpluses must be convertible if it is going to meet its gross deficits. In a system of interlocked export and import gross balances, convertibility requires that each country maintained overall balance simultaneously or that any country with a net deficit have reserves which it is prepared to spend, in a medium of exchange acceptable to the country or countries with which it has gross deficits.

The Conditions Needed for Free Trade

The presumption in favor of free trade comes down partly to the argument that interference in trade has a comparative disadvantage in meeting the economic or social condition which is said to call for tariffs. Thus if the problem is that wages in manufacturing are too high in a less developed country the remedy is not to put a tax on the good, but to subsidize manufacturing employment. This hits at the source of distortion, rather than producing an offsetting one, which incidentally results in misallocations elsewhere in the system. Similarly the alternative to a tariff in the case of external economies is a subsidy, this time not on the employment of the factor, but on the output of the good.

Where monopoly prevents the realization of Pareto optimality, it must be remembered that freeing up trade helps to destroy monopoly and to assist competition. The general argument against free trade because its conditions are not met backfires, and free trade helps.

The argument to achieve a socially desirable distribution of income through transfer of aid rather than interference in trade is more difficult. Aid has not developed very far, nor the sort of tax cum subsidy that, as we have just seen, can substitute for aid. In the long run, the international community needs to build the common objects of expenditure, such as budgets for the United Nations and its specialized agencies, to permit international transfers as a regular matter by unequal incidence of costs and benefits. A market is different from a budget. Markets are used for efficient allocation; budgets for income redistribution. Until international budgets are substantial in relation to national money incomes, the scope for automatic income redistribution through international spending and taxation will be limited. Redistribution of income through national budgets helps make the income distribution decreed by the national market more tolerable although such groups as farmers refuse to accept it even then and insist on efficiency-distorting price supports. In the long run, readiness to submit to the dictates of the market is assisted by the existence of devices for sharing income which exist alongside the market and mitigate its most severe consequences on income distribution.

The Theory of the Second Best

If it be granted that complete free trade will result in an optimum position in which social (and private) marginal value equals social (and private) cost, it does not follow that any movement toward free trade improves an existing protected situation. If social value diverges from social cost throughout an economy, any tariff removal will improve the position if it, on balance, reduces the total divergence. This it may do. But it may not. The reduction of the tariff in one commodity may narrow the divergence in this commodity but give rise to an increase in trade in another commodity in which the divergence was larger. To determine whether a partial freeing of tariffs is good or bad, Professor Meade has devised a theoretical system of adding, algebraically, the weighted divergences of social marginal value from social marginal cost. A net reduction in divergences is an improvement; an increase is a setback.

Suppose Britain reduces the tariff on wine from France. This narrows the divergence between the social marginal value of wine and the social cost in Britain and increases its consumption. This much is a gain in welfare. But many additional effects may occur. The increase in wine consumption in Britain may lead to increased consumption of a complementary product with a large divergence, or decreased production of a competitive product with a small or no divergence. Similar distortion may take place in the country expanding exports. If the tariff reduction is discriminatory, it is necessary to take into account the effect on, say Germany, which may or may not be able to sell its wine elsewhere, or ceases its production. Until one has a view of the total effects on consumption and production in all the affected countries, weighted in each case by the divergence between social value and social cost, one cannot really judge whether a given tariff reduction improves or worsens the welfare position. In some cases where free trade as a best solution is impossible, a second-best measure may be to impose a tariff on a single commodity. And, similarly, a partial step toward tariff reduction may not be a second-best solution.

This sounds somewhat overintellectualized, but it is easy to provide a simple demonstration. Suppose a country had a tariff of 10 percent on all imports. To lower the tariff on raw materials without changing it on finished goods results in an increase in protection, as we saw in the discussion of the effective rate of the tariff, not in an approach to freer trade. The reduction in the divergence between social marginal value and social cost in raw materials is more than offset by the increase in output of the protected manufactures where a large divergence exists. As Professor Meade puts it, not every step upward necessarily helps to climb the highest hill. If one is on a foothill, it may be necessary to go down for a bit and to cross over to the main slope.

We encountered the theory of the second best briefly in the previous chapter in connection with customs unions. Here a tariff reduction which stops short of overall free trade (the first best) may be trade creating and second best, or trade diverting and third, fourth, tenth or nth best as compared to nondiscriminatory tariffs.

The Burden of Proof

There is something of a temptation at this stage to say that no holds are barred and anything goes. The efficiency conditions for a Pareto optimum are not usually met; the international and domestic distribution of income are rarely satisfactory; and from a condition of divergences between social and private marginal values, any particular reduction in trade barriers may lead toward or away from an optimum of efficiency and welfare. But one can say more.

In the first place, there are some strong presumptions. Since tariffs improve the terms of trade, the richer countries should take off tariffs first.

In taking off tariffs, a country should take off tariffs on substantial amounts of trade, so that the reduction of the discrepancy between private cost and social value will be as wide as possible.

A country should reduce tariffs more on goods with a high divergence between private and social marginal value, than on goods with a low. Where the divergence is the result of the tariff, it should reduce high tariffs before low tariffs.

In multilateral trade, a country should equalize the severity of import restrictions by lowering restrictions on goods of high divergence and raising them on goods of low divergence, if necessary to maintain balance of payments equilibrium, both on all goods from any one country and as between countries.

The fact is that while specific interference with trade to correct a specific departure from the assumptions for Pareto optimality, or to achieve a particular redistribution of income may be justified on second-best grounds—because the first-best method of dealing with the difficulty was ruled out for some reason—this is a far different thing than arguing that since economists as a rule don't know whether tariffs help or hurt, you might just as well put them on as take them off. The presumption lies in favor of freer trade, even though not all steps toward freer trade are desirable. Professor Haberler suggests that tariffs and quotas are like poison, helpful in small doses for particular ills, but poison nonetheless, to be kept on an upper shelf of the bathroom closet and used with great discretion. Or perhaps free trade should be likened to honesty, which is the best policy, as is well known, particularly because it is not then necessary to remember what you said, but must be held in check on limited occasions. Or as Mr. Churchill said about democracy, a very poor system of government, but better than any alternative. The difficulty with removing the strong presumption against interference with trade is that tariffs and quantitative restrictions are unlikely to be used correctly to meet ills which are correctly diagnosed. If we may recur to democracy, it is well known that benevolent despotism is the optimum form of government, just as optimum trade interventions are the best way to handle trade. The task with despotism is to keep it benevolent, and with interventions to keep them optimal. In the long run it is better to try to improve the workings of democracy and to correct the ignorance, monopoly, rigidity, and other divergences which would justify exceptions in the case for free trade.

Social versus Economic Goals

Professor Haberler's summary of international trade policy says that it calls for not only keen analysis but also historical, political, and social judgment, and that economic history may have more to offer than economic theory. The point is apt. When social goals and efficiency fall out, the tradeoff between them is not immediately obvious. To the economist, it was evident when the price of wheat fell in the 19th century because of the expansion of settlement onto the rich lands of North America, Argentina, and Australia, that the European farmer was doomed. Social policy, however, insisted that it was impossible economically to wipe out such a large class of the community, particularly one which embodied national virtues (France) or which provided footsoldiers (Germany). Karl Polanyi stood aghast that in Britain it was possible for a tradition of laissez-faire to permit a social class to be destroyed in the interest of efficiency.

But French experience in high protection for an agriculture which felt no pressure to modernize until the 1950's was not a happy one. Some tradeoff between social protection and economic efficiency is required which will slow down the rate of social change to a tolerable pace but ensure that it is accomplished. Today's equivalent are the miners everywhere in Europe who must be reallocated to higher earning occupations as quickly as can socially be done to allow the Continent to depend primarily on oil for its fuel (with stored supplies if need be for protection against the danger of Arab blockade) and U.S. coal for those uses in steel where it serves as a chemical rather than as a fuel. How long is long for coal miners? For wheat farmers, it seems likely that 15 years was too short in Britain, and 80 years too long in France.

By the same token, however, the comparative advantage of a year or two should not be allowed to decide the issue for all time. In the famous chicken war of the late 1950's, the Common Market sought to limit imports of chicken from the United States to give Dutch, Belgian, and German farmers a chance to catch up with the head start of a few years which the broiler houses of Maine and Delmarva (*Del*aware, *Mary*land, and *Virginia*) had staked out. (France bought no American chicken on a sanitary pretext, alleging that its treatment with hormones somehow corrupted it). American farmers, the U.S. Department of Agriculture, and the U.S. Department of State resisted any attempt to restrain imports on the high moral ground of laissez-faire, and the small head start. But here was a footloose industry, using farms literally as factories, with no real comparative advantage in the United States. A couple of years of protection would suffice to overcome the industry's teething troubles. It is hard not to feel great sympathy with this case for restricting trade.

It is thus reasonable to believe in the doctrine of free trade but unreasonable to be doctrinaire about it. Perhaps we may give the last word to the economic historian, as Haberler suggests, and quote from William Woodruff's *Impact of Western Man:*

> Especially important in England was the ideal of "Free Trade." "Free Trade" was identified with civilization; out of greater international coordination would come the economic cosmos of the world; "Free Trade" was peace and progress; "Free Trade" would provide a natural harmony and order in human affairs. . . . Britain in its trade policy was by no means altruistic; it was not regard for great economic truths or high moral purpose that led Britain to abandon the protection of its agriculture, industry and shipping; it was the hope of economic gain. Yet some of the noblest and ablest minds in Britain believed in the dream of "Free Trade" . . . and not for pecuniary reasons alone.
>
> "Free Trade" proved to be an illusion. Its fault was the overwhelming importance it gave to economics; especially in its attempt to apply to the world something that was built up on premises specifically English. But it was never a mean illusion, and it helped to strengthen the commercial ties binding nation and nation. . . .

Summary

The case for free trade depends on the fulfillment of certain conditions for efficiency—no monopoly, external economies, distortions of market price from social values, and so on,—and an acceptance of the income distribution it provides. But free trade plus other action to correct the distortion is better as a rule than trade intervention. Where the international distribution of income should be altered, trade and aid may be better than "trade not aid" which distorts efficient resource allocation.

The theory of the second best states that when the conditions for free trade cannot be achieved, not every move toward free trade takes an economy to a more efficient or more equitable solution.

While particular measures to interfere with trade may advance national and international welfare, the presumption lies in favor of freer trade and against intervention. Intervention must be used with restraint. Whenever social and economic objectives seem to clash in the short run, the efficient solution is likely to be the socially desirable one in the long run.

SUGGESTED READING

TREATISES

Meade, *Trade and Welfare*, part iv; Caves, chap. vii; and the reviews of the theory of trade, cited in the "Bibliographical Note" following Chapter 1. See also the papers by Baldwin, Haberler, Bhagwati and Ramaswami, and Fleming in Part 3 of American Economic Association, *Readings in International Economics.*

POINTS

Polanyi's attack on laissez-faire on social grounds is in *The Great Transformation* (New York: Farrar and Rinehart, Inc., 1944); the reaction of European governments and farmers to cheap overseas wheat in the 19th century is discussed in C. P. Kindleberger, "Group Behavior and International Trade," *JPE,* February, 1951. The citation for Woodruff's book is *Impact of Western Man* (New York: St. Martin's Press, Inc., 1966), and the quotation is from p. 12.

PART III

International Resource Allocation:

Taxation and Migration

INTERNATIONAL TAXATION

Elements of Public Finance

From at least the time of Adam Smith, the recognized task of public finance has been to raise the revenue necessary to pay for government expenditures with a minimum of distortion of resource allocation and in ways which conform to the community's standards of equity. These revenue, allocation, and equity considerations, which are not always readily harmonized, correspond to five of the eight effects we have treated under tariffs, exchange control, and exchange depreciation. The revenue effect is identical. The impact on resource allocation is the protective effect on production and consumption. Equity is represented by the redistribution effect within a country and the terms of trade changes between countries. Much more recently, since Keynes, economists have occupied themselves further with the impact of taxation and government expenditure on total output and income. This corresponds to the income or employment effect of tariffs. The effects of taxation on competition are highly complex and lie outside the scope of this chapter which refers only to the other seven effects. The one aspect of tariffs left over to which there is no correspondent in domestic taxation is evidently the balance-of-payments effect.

The student who has progressed thus far should not be surprised, therefore, if we invite his attention to the impact on trade, international investment, and international migration (to be discussed in the next chapter) of the existence of differing systems of taxation. The subject is under vigorous discussion internationally in connection both with efforts at economic integration and the operations of the international corporation. While we do not deal with the international corporation at length until Chapter 21, it is convenient to touch upon the tax aspects here. There is basis for the belief that much of this discussion exaggerates the importance of differences in systems of taxation, which have existed among states in federal systems without producing problems of overwhelming significance and has been one-sided in dealing with taxation but ignoring national differences in benefits. It may nonetheless be useful to provide an analytical basis for handling it.

Our interest is international economics rather than government finance. Accordingly we work through a number of problems using very simple assumptions, having in mind that alternative assumptions would modify many of our results. We assume, for example, that the corporate income tax falls on the corporate stockholder, though it is recognized that whether this tax can be passed forward to consumers or back to the factors of production is not a settled question. Similarly the incidence of excise and turnover taxes is assumed to fall forward on the consumer, while that of the employment tax including social security taxes rests on labor. This assumption runs contrary to a recent view expressed by international oil companies that excise taxes levied on fuel oil in Europe in an effort to raise its price to protect coal have fallen on the companies themselves. They argue that the present state of competition in the oil industry results in a highly elastic demand for the products of the individual company and prevents the tax from being passed on.

Government Activity and Comparative Advantage

The mere existence of government distorts comparative advantage. Assume country A without government of any kind, and country B with. Both government expenditure and taxation in B are virtually certain to alter the basis for comparative advantage which would have existed without them. On the expenditure side, it might be assumed that government takes factors off the market in exactly existing proportions, so that the Heckscher-Ohlin basis for trade is unaltered; and that expenditure affects no demand or supply schedules through complementarities or substitution effects. These are hard assumptions to swallow. But on the tax side there is virtually certain to be distortion. Excise taxes clearly distort, except under the most extreme assumptions; and even progressive income taxes which leave price proportional to marginal social cost distort the input of effort by making leisure more attractive relative to work. Public finance experts have devised the theoretical device of a lump-sum progressive income tax which leaves marginal rates of return unchanged and thus is not distortionary in terms of effort. Unfortunately, this tax is universally recognized as impossible to apply, and remains an intellectual curiosity.

We thus start from the proposition that governmental activity distorts comparative advantage, and this would be true if all the countries of the world had the same philosophies of government expenditure and taxation. But where there are differences in governmental systems of taxation—to limit ourselves to one side of the coin—the effects on international economic behavior can be far-reaching.

The Impact of Differences in Tax Systems, I: Trade, National Firms, No Factor Movements

Domestic excise taxes are like tariffs in their effect on consumption, revenue, the terms of trade, internal income distribution, the balance of payments, and national income. Since they apply at home as well as to imports, however, they do not have protective effects. The six effects they have are not without importance, at home and abroad, which is why the coffee- and oil-producing countries want the members of the European Common Market to lower their excise taxes on coffee and gasoline.

Our concern is less with the impact of domestic excise rates than with differences in their rates between countries. There will be instances, where the consumer can escape the payment of any excise tax at all: he has left one tax sovereignty, and, in transit by ship or airplane, or pausing in the customs free portion of an international airport, he has not yet entered another. When he does, he will typically have a tourist's exemption from customs duty which enables him to escape taxes in both countries. But this loophole is not likely to be very large. Where the tourist exemption is large, the quantities of articles subject to excise tax—liquor, tobacco, and so on—which may be imported by tourists are typically limited. We refer rather to the distortion induced by differences in excise rates between countries, much like the comparable distortion along state lines in the United States with different taxes on gasoline, cigarettes, and alcoholic beverages.

Where rates are low and the excise tax is levied at the retail level, the distortions in trade introduced by differences in rates are relatively unimportant. They are limited to the border, and to what the individual consumer finds it worthwhile to transport. Where the tax applies at a higher stage of production or distribution, however, say on the gasoline refiner or the coffee roaster, it is necessary to apply excise duties along with tariffs at the border. Thus far no problem. But, as noted in Chapter 11, when two countries form a customs union, the fact of differences in excise taxes above the retail level does pose a choice: either submit to the tax-induced and distorted trade, with consumers individually buying in the low-tax country, or maintain customs inspectors at the border for the sole purpose of collecting domestic excise taxes. To escape the dilemma there has arisen strong pressure to harmonize excise taxes.

Such harmonization generally takes the form of equalization and evidently has revenue, equity and allocational effects in those countries where rates are changed.

If one looks just at the tax side, there is an important gain from harmonization in simplicity. But it is by no means clear that this gain is a net one. To do the job completely it may be necessary to harmonize benefits as well. Assume two countries with two different tax systems: one has public schools financed by a tax on alcoholic beverages and cigarettes; the other private schools without the taxes. To harmonize the tax systems without doing something about the benefits will evidently be awkward, giving rise to budget and allocation problems in one country or both.

The difficulties posed by differences in rates become still more complex with different systems of applying taxes to foreign trade. In the European Common Market these have been particularly acute for turnover taxes on the one hand, and social security taxes on the other. The French value-added tax is theoretically a great improvement over the turnover tax levied on the entire value of output at each stage of production because the turnover tax favors vertical integration to escape the impact of the tax.[1] In contrast, the value-added tax, called, in France, T.V.A., or *taxe sur la valeur ajoutée,* would result in the same level of taxation on a product whether produced in a series of stages by separate firms or by a single integrated company. In practice, its collection is complex, the whole tax being levied at each stage, with credits given for taxes paid at earlier stages of production. The French tax authorities favored the "destination" principle under which they would remit the tax on exports and levy a turnover tax on the whole value of imports. West German experts, by contrast, argued in favor of the "origin" principle under which they would allow imports free of turnover tax, but require the tax to stand on exports.

Note that the budget effect is unimportant in each country. Assume for the sake of argument that exports and imports are equal in each country, and will be unaltered by the tax. It evidently makes little difference to the budget whether the French or Germans tax exports or imports at a given rate. But the other effects may be highly significant. If France follows the destination principle, and Germany the origin, German sales to France get taxed twice, once by Germany and once by

---

[1] Note that the standard view in public finance, in contrast to that used for convenience in the text, is that the value-added tax differs more fundamentally from the turnover tax in that it is passed backward as an income tax, while the turnover tax is passed forward.

France, whereas French exports to Germany escape tax in both jurisdictions. This will distort production in favor of France and against Germany, improve the French balance of payments (making the appropriate assumptions about the elasticities), worsen French terms of trade, and so on.

This problem first presented itself in the European Coal and Steel Community and was thought to be serious. A distinguished committee of economists was appointed under the chairmanship of Professor Jan Tinbergen of the Netherlands to examine it and make recommendations. The French, in particular, thought that the Germans should adopt their system as a matter of harmonization. But the economists observed that so long as the bilateral balance of payments between the two countries was appropriately balanced in the long run, it made no difference. Any tax distortion in favor of France and against Germany was balanced out by a somewhat higher exchange rate. The balance-of-payments, terms of trade, production, consumption, and so on effects of the taxes could be offset by equal and opposite influences on the side of the exchange rate. Like other distortions between social and private marginal values, the tax system had already been absorbed into the general equilibrium system. The experts recommended that the problem be ignored.

This recommendation is no longer universally supported by economists, on the ground that exchange rate changes are much more general than even the very general turnover tax. Depreciation which will correct the distortion in the current account between these two countries will produce new distortions in capital items between them, and in all payments and receipts with third countries. Exchange rate changes are a meat-ax when a surgeon's scalpel is needed. The Common Market countries chose not to settle the problem by ignoring the tax difference and adjusting the exchange rate.

Instead, on mutual trade they initially adopted the French system of taxing the user rather than the producer. This meant remitting taxes on exports and applying them to imports, retaining the customs inspectors. Since the rate of French T.V.A. tax was higher than the German *Umsatzsteuer* (turnover tax) applied on final output, it further meant that while French and German steel sold in competition was taxed at the same rates in each country, German steel in France was taxed at higher rates than French steel in Germany. The German steel manufacturers objected to this system which they regard as discriminatory, and blamed it for the fact that Volkswagens were made in Germany to a considerable extent out of French sheet steel. There thus arose pressure for harmonization, to remove both the customs inspectors and the basis for allegations of discriminatory treatment. The outcome was that Germans adopted the T.V.A. on the destination principle, applying the tax to imports and subtracting it from exports, which amounted to a modest devaluation.

Harmonization of excise taxes without harmonization of the total fiscal system (including benefits) produces new distortions. To take just revenue, it reduces the revenue of the government whose tax system had relied most on excise taxes, and increases the revenue of that which had used such taxes least. Pressure to harmonize any one aspect of the economy seems to lead to new pressures to harmonize further. The end is the merging of fiscal sovereignties, which in the European Economic Community still lies some distance ahead.

French pressure to harmonize social security taxes seems to have less a broad integrative purpose at its basis than the wish to impose on the other members of the Common Market the same disabilities under which France labors. It is paralleled by French insistence on equal pay for men and women in the rest of the Common Market as well as in France. This legislation distorts resource allocation and trade in France. If applied through the Common Market it would eliminate relative distortion among the Common Market countries at the expense of increasing it between such countries and the outside world. The question of social security arises in particularly significant form for Britain joining the Common Market. British social security is paid for to a considerable extent by general taxation on incomes at progressive rates, rather than entirely by employer and employee taxes on employment. For Britain to adopt the French or Continental system would alter the distribution of income in Britain against the worker and in favor of the well-to-do who are most affected by general taxation. If on the other hand, each country retains its own internal system, the differences in social security financing by themselves would make labor costs higher in France relative to Britain, and distort comparative advantage.

2: Trade, International Firms, No Factor Movements

Differences in excise taxes between countries which affect resource allocation, revenue, equity, and the balance of payments have been discussed in the previous section. But it is self-evident that with international firms similar effects will flow from differences in income-tax systems, even if factor movements do not occur. Domestic firms produce and pay income taxes at home. International firms have a choice as to where they produce and pay income taxes. This choice is evidently affected by differences in definitions of income and differences in income tax rates, as firms maximize not profits in general but profits after tax.

Domestic firms maximize after-tax profits, of course, but firms in the same business in the same country pay the same rates of tax, apart from monopolized clever legal stratagems. Where a single firm operates in the same business in two countries, it is evident that other things equal it will tend to produce a given good in the country with the lower rate of corporate income tax, with all the effects on allocation, revenue, international and domestic income distribution, employment, and balance of payments that that implies.

Some business spokesmen argue that a case can be made for taxing business only where production takes place. The case runs that a company which has to pay income tax in its home country is handicapped vis-à-vis its local competitors who pay only one tax, or foreign investors from other countries who, in accordance with their national laws, may pay taxes only in the country where production takes place. The counterargument is that the foreign firm brings certain advantages to its foreign investment as well as certain disadvantages: its cheap capital, special technology, or superior management on the one hand, as well as the cost of conducting business at a great distance from its home office on the other. It is illogical to insist that it should be relieved of all possible disadvantages while being permitted to keep all its advantages.

That the company should pay local taxation accords of course with the benefit theory, under which taxation is a payment for services provided, such as police and fire protection, rather than this and something more, such as a contribution to a community budget. One U.S. government official tried to justify U.S. taxation of income from foreign operations, regardless of taxes paid at the other end, largely on the ground of the protection accorded by the U.S. government to the property of its citizens abroad. It is true that governments have an obligation, which they are not always able to discharge, to protect the property of citizens abroad, but the immediate protection of the property is under the charge of the local government. And both jurisdictions cannot tax. Most countries negotiate treaties with other friendly powers to eliminate double taxation which would limit or even eliminate economic intercourse between them. Whether double taxation is better or worse than the activity which eludes both jurisdictions is a philosophical question which each student must answer for himself. But taxation at either end is better than taxation at both or none, in terms of resource allocation, and equity, if not perhaps in the one case, revenue.

In the next section it will be shown that taxation limited to the country of production leads to factor movements where national differences in rates exist. Even apart from this stimulus, however, it can be demonstrated that this basis of taxation raises questions of equity. The equitable principle holds that people with the same incomes should pay the same tax. Income produced might be a satisfactory basis for taxation in terms of allocation, but incomes received or earned constitutes a more equitable basis. The United States attempts to take equity into consideration by taxing income received from subsidiaries abroad at the U.S. rate (48 percent above $25,000 a year, 52 percent prior to the tax reduction of 1964), at the same time allowing a credit against the tax due of corporate income taxes paid abroad. If the tax abroad is 48 percent or higher, the amount due in the United States is nothing. If it is below 48 percent, the tax is the difference between the amount paid and 48 percent.

The credit for income taxes paid abroad exerts some pressure for harmonization of rates. When the Arabian-American Oil Company (Aramco) began to remit substantial dividends to the United States, the Saudi Arabian government put into effect a corporate income tax with rates at 52 percent. This tax did not affect Aramco, which had to pay 52 percent of its profits to some country, but there were changes in the national tax receipts of the United States and Saudi Arabia, in national balances of payments, and in the international distribution of welfare. In effect, the Arabian government taxed the U.S. government through the intermediary of the oil company.

The deferral of the U.S. tax until income was received in that country further constituted a stimulus to international investment. An opponent of this basis of taxation can point to the equitable argument that domestic taxpayers are obliged to pay corporate taxes on the basis of earnings, rather than dividends. He can regard the deferral basis as an interest-free governmental loan so long as the earnings are not remitted. The suggestion has even been made that the deferred basis of taxation be retained, but that taxpayers be charged interest on earnings not remitted of which they have the use. The defenders of the deferred basis, on the other hand, point to the impossibility of remitting earnings from some countries with exchange control, and to the importance for world welfare of increases in U.S. foreign investment. The Treasury officials supporting a change in the law from the dividend to the earnings basis, argued the weak position of the U.S. balance of payments as justification of the measure which would speed up the remittance of earnings and slow down U.S. foreign investment. In the end, the Congress decided against the Treasury position and in favor of that of industry with overseas interests. The action made no difference in most countries where foreign tax levels were at or above those in the United States, so that no tax was due. Elsewhere, however, tax was to be paid in the United States on dividends received, not funds earned overseas.

Where it faces different systems of taxes in two countries, a company with subsidiaries in both will naturally and inevitably try to maximize its profit in the country with the lower rates of tax. This will not maximize social output in one of the countries and may not do so on a world basis. In addition it creates a problem for the taxing authorities. What is the income which can be said to be earned in a given country?

At the limit, where these are joint costs, the problem is insoluable. Suppose that the Trans-Arabian Pipeline Company crosses Arabia, Jordan, Syria, and Lebanon and earns a profit from transporting oil through its pipe. How much of the profit was earned in each country? Saudi Arabia with the longest mileage of pipe argues for distance as a basis for allocating profit. Lebanon with the terminal insists that the biggest geographical contribution is made by the two countries where oil is put in and taken out of the line. Jordan and Syria are left to maintain that what is significant is that the national borders have been violated, and that the profit should be divided equally among the four countries. But the problem is economically insolvable and must be resolved in quasi-political terms. One response to this "jointness of profit" was the proposal of the Saudi Arabian government to tax income on oil produced in its territory at every stage of production from the oil well to the consumer's gas tank, i.e., on transport by pipeline and tanker, refining, storage, and distribution. This obviously raises a question of overlapping jurisdictions, and whether the writ of the Saudi Arabian government can be made to run abroad. But most probably the attempt was made to justify a tax raise to force a price rise, as indicated in Chapter 10.

Where there is one country and one company with subsidiaries or a mother corporation abroad, the approach may be to "construct a profit," as the Internal Revenue Service does in the United States from time to time when it does not concur in the statement of profits recorded in intercompany dealings. A tax commission in country A which does not approve of the profits reported by the subsidiary within its boundaries of a corporation located in B, may determine what it thinks the profits of the subsidiary should be and charge a tax on the basis of that determination. The criterion in economics may differ from that which is laid down in law, but can be stated briefly: what would be the profit made by a reasonably efficient competitive entrant into the business? If the tax authorities felt, for example, that the taxpaying subsidiary was paying too large royalties to the parent company for the use of patents, or was entitled to discounts on purchases from the parent which it was not receiving, the standard would be whether a separate efficient competitor would have been able to obtain lesser royalties or discounts from posted prices. But it is easier to state the principle than to apply it.

The company may find itself in the worst of all possible worlds, with its production in one country, for example, taxed on the basis of the posted price, and its subsidiary in the consuming country taxed on the basis of estimated discounts. This would mean that taxes are levied in both countries on more profits than the combined company produced. The more that governmental tax authorities move to "construct profits," the closer the likelihood of this happening. But it is probably not very widespread, or there would be evidence of a movement to spin off subsidiaries into independent companies.

More realistically, a company may find itself between two countries, one of which is trying to assist it but is frustrated by the other. The corporation income tax of Israel, for example, is divided into two parts, one amounting to 28 percent, and another constituting 25 percent of the remaining 72 percent, or 18 percent of the original net income. The two steps together make an income tax of 46 percent. In order to stimulate foreign investment, Israel has granted a concession of a free period of 5 years within the first 10 years of a corporation's existence, the 5-year period beginning with the first annual net profit, during which the second step of the income tax, i.e., the 18 percent, is remitted. But this does not stimulate investment by U.S. investors. While Israel remits its tax, the United States does not remit its. An American corporation which was excused from this 18 percent would be obliged to pay it, with the 2 percent ordinarily due (48 percent less 46 percent) to the United States. Israel has concluded a so-called tax-sparing agreement with the United States, providing that any tax concession granted by one country to the nationals of another would be spared of additional tax by the other. The Treasury Department has not, however, pressed the Senate for ratification. Israel has succeeded in concluding tax-sparing agreements with Sweden, Italy, West Germany, and a number of other countries. The bulk of foreign investment in Israel, however, is owned by U.S. nationals.

The U.S. Revenue Act of 1962 was aimed particularly at one form of tax evasion or tax avoidance felt to be inequitable. This is the establishment of a nonproducing corporation for the sake of taking advantage of differences in tax rates, widely called a "tax haven." One example might be the establishment of a sales corporation in a Swiss canton which offers low income tax rates to nonproducing corporations (for which it has to provide few benefits). Sales from the United States are routed through this corporation, which employs a considerable number of clerks for copying invoices at higher prices than those used for exporting. "Profits" accrue to the Swiss corporation which are available for reinvestment abroad so long as income tax in the United States is on a dividend basis—and no dividend is paid to the U.S. parent company. Whether this is tax evasion, which is illegal, or tax avoidance which is taking every advantage available under the law, will depend upon the exact circumstances.

A third country may be involved. France has a tax treaty with Switzerland under which the 24 percent withholding tax on royalties which applies to every other country is not collected. An American firm with a subsidiary in France charges it patent royalties which it orders paid to a Swiss tax haven. With taxation on the basis of dividends, and the funds used abroad rather than returned to the United States, no tax is collected beyond the nominal few percent due the Swiss canton.

3: Tax Differences and Factor Movements

In his *Trade and Welfare,* Professor Meade contrasts two countries using different bases of taxation. The one, interested in minimizing distortions in efficiency, taxes output; the other, emphasizing the principle of equity, taxes income. In these circumstances, it is evident that factors of production are under a strong compulsion to commute—like citizens of New Jersey and Connecticut who work in New York City and used to escape state income tax. A man works in the country taxing income received, and lives in the country taxing income produced, thereby achieving the best of all possible worlds. Other things equal, different tax systems produce distortions in resource allocation, including an undue use of resources in transport, not to mention effects on equity, revenue, employment, and the balance of payments. The country that taxed production would receive inward transfers in the form of emigrant's remittances, but experience the capital outflow of new saving.

But even where both countries adopt the same system, there may be significant effects from differences in rates. Capital and labor will move to the area of lower taxation, to work, if the tax is on production, to reside, if it is levied on income received. Only the double-barreled form of taxation employed in the United States, taxing income earned in the country and income earned abroad (to the extent not already taxed abroad up to the U.S. level) avoids distorting factor movements.

Even here U.S. laws on personal income tax stimulate some movement. Citizens of the United States who reside 18 months abroad are exempt from U.S. income tax on income earned abroad. Where matched by a parallel exemption abroad, this exemption is a stimulus to foreign residence, with effects on U.S. trade, investment, and since World War II, foreign technical assistance of various kinds. The Revenue Act of 1962 set limits on the amount of incomes which were exempted in this fashion. This was to cut off the inequitable use of the provision by a few people, mostly movie stars, of very large incomes. Never staying long enough abroad in any one place to be subject to foreign taxation, they could escape U.S. income tax by remaining away for 18 months. Here the distortion was neither efficient nor equitable.

The United States is not above resort to tax competition to stimulate factor movements. "Operation Bootstrap" in Puerto Rico involves remission of corporate income tax for a period of 10 years after the establishment of an enterprise in the territory. It is possible, however, that the tax concessions served less to subsidize companies which moved to the island than to call to their attention the opportunity available there, and in particular the availability of inexpensive trained labor.

The competition need not only take the form of kinds or levels of taxes. The definition of income is also clearly a variable which affects the statement of income. Higher depreciation allowances in Germany and France in the 1950's exerted strong attraction for U.S. investors. By reducing the level of taxable income in the short run, the higher depreciation rates serve, like the deferral of U.S. income tax until dividends are remitted, to make available interest-free funds to the investing concern. Some people stress that these loans never have to be paid back so long as the company does not shrink in size. By the time that taxable profits on this year's investment have risen, because the asset is 100 percent depreciated on the books even though its serviceable life is not yet finished, accelerated depreciation on a new investment keeps profits understated and the interest-free loan need not be repaid. The 7 percent investment credit in the U.S. Revenue Act of 1964 was intended as a direct stimulus to investment in this country; it reduced the margin favoring U.S. investment in France and Germany, however, and served to that extent to harmonize tax laws as called for by the integration process discussed in Chapter 11.

Summary

The traditional three goals of taxation—allocative efficiency, revenue, and equity—are matched in international economics by the five of the eight effects discussed for a tariff: production and consumption, revenue, and redistribution within and between countries. Income stabilization, which the public finance experts added later, is matched by the employment effect. The only additional impacts in the international sphere are the balance-of-payments and competition effect.

Differences between national tax systems may produce distortions in these various aspects of the economies, which may be partly offset by comparable distortions in benefits, or by exchange rate adjustments. Reduction in the costs of transport and the lowering of tariffs have increased the residual distorting effects of excise taxes, and exerted pressure for their harmonization.

With international firms, the distortions are extended to the location of production and investment. Firms maximize income after tax, and take differences in taxes into account. The geographical location of income, important to determine which government can tax it, and affecting the international distribution of welfare (like the terms of trade effect) and the balance of payments, poses difficult problems. While a firm can minimize taxation by its operation, it may work out that a firm is overtaxed by two governments each "constructing a profit" for tax purposes on a different basis. The chapter discusses tax sparing by one government of concessions made by another, and tax havens or methods of evading taxes by the establishment of corporations for no purpose other than taking advantage of low tax rates.

Differences in tax systems and differences in rates under the same system also exert pressure for factor movements of labor and capital. One important difference in the tax systems is how income is defined, and especially how much depreciation is allowed as a deduction from income.

SUGGESTED READING

TEXTS

On the problem of the integration of fiscal systems, see Balassa, *The Theory of Economic Integration,* chap. xi.

TREATISES

See Meade, *Trade and Welfare,* chap. xxv; L. B. Krause and K. W. Dam, *Federal Tax Treatment of Foreign Income* (Washington, D.C.: The Brookings Institution, 1964); and Carl S. Shoup (ed.), *Fiscal Harmonization in Common Markets* (New York: Columbia University Press, 1967), 2 vols.

Students who have occasion to look up actual tax systems should be aware of the "World Tax Series" on national systems, published by the Harvard Law

School International Program on Taxation. Up to the middle of 1967, volumes had appeared on Australia, Brazil, Colombia, France, Germany (F.R.), India, Israel, Italy, Mexico, Sweden, the United Kingdom, and the United States.

POINTS

The work of the Tinbergen Committee is entitled: High Authority of the European Coal and Steel Community, "Report on the Problems Raised by the Different Turnover Tax Systems Applied within the Common Market" (Luxemburg, 1953). A subsequent study recommending fiscal harmonization was produced under a committee presided over by Professor Fritz Neumark of the University of Frankfurt, and entitled *The EEC Reports on Tax Harmonization,* an unofficial translation of the *Report of the Fiscal and Financial Committee* of the EEC and the reports of subcommittee A, B, and C (Amsterdam: International Bureau of Fiscal Documentation, 1963).

The negative response of the business community to the Kennedy administration proposals for changing the tax on foreign income from a dividend to an earnings basis, is set forth in many hearings before congressional committees and in business publications. For the view that business should be taxed only where production is carried on, see the testimony of E. G. Collado, Vice-President of the Standard Oil Company of New Jersey, in *Hearings* before the House Ways and Means Committee on the President's 1961 Tax Recommendations, Vol. IV June 5, 1961) at p. 2674.

Chapter	THE INTERNATIONAL
14	MOVEMENT OF LABOR

Most textbooks on international economics, and most courses, steer clear of the question of migration. This is probably only partly due to the pious classical assumption of factor immobility between countries. This assumption applies as well to capital, but capital movements, as Part V will reveal, have been accommodated into the corpus of the subject. In part, it may be thought to have been overwhelmed in importance by trade; the fact that Europe exported 60 million people overseas between 1851 and 1960 and that today, approximately 4 million migrants in Europe are working outside their native country, however, suggests that migration is not small. President Roosevelt once addressed the Daughters of the American Revolution, it will be remembered, as "Fellow Immigrants." The more likely reason is that the subject is thought to belong rather to sociology or demography than to economics. More recently, however, with the reduction in transport costs, there has been a renewed interest in the economics of international migration and national migration policy. The latter may lie largely in the social field, but the economic questions are neither uninteresting nor unimportant.

The International Labor Market

There has always been a limited international market for labor. Workers commute to jobs across frontiers in Europe, between Windsor, Canada, and Detroit, Michigan; and Brownsville, Texas, and Montamoros, Mexico. Casual workers journey from country to country in search of work, moving particularly northward with the harvest or in the construction season, whether they are Mexicans in North America, or Italians, Greeks, and Spaniards in Europe. Government administrators in colonies, businessmen managing foreign subsidiaries, planters, Peace Corps recruits, and increasingly professional and technical consultants spend varying amounts of time in economic roles outside the country of their permanent residence. And long-term or permanent migration is a familiar phenomenon, as masses of people have been driven abroad by one or another kind of trouble or attracted abroad by economic opportunity.

An international market for labor may be said then to exist. But classical economists were right to the extent that it is a most imperfect one. The return to common labor is not equalized around the world. And even within specialized noncompeting groups the equalization is far from complete. Indeed, equalization of wages does not take place within a country, except in broad terms and for some professional and technical classes; some labor economists make a lot (too much) of the fact that there is variability in wages for equal skills in the same town. Between continents, the returns to labor differ persistently, despite the fact that labor can move to a limited extent in overseas migration, and despite the tendency for international trade to bring about some equalization of factor prices as discussed in Chapter 2.

In Europe, since about 1955, however, the international labor market has become more efficient. There is increased movement across borders between developed countries, but the major change has been a northward movement, especially to Switzerland, Belgium, France, and Germany, first by Italians and then by Greeks, Spaniards, Portugese, and Turks. Foreign workers comprised as much as 30 percent of the Swiss labor force before restrictions were imposed in 1964, much higher than Belgium, 10 percent; France, 9 percent; and Germany, 4½ percent. But their importance is greater than these numbers, as the student of marginal analysis knows. Since the foreign worker is without strong ties to any one location away from his native heath, his mobility makes a vital contribution to the improvement of the European labor market at the margin. European wage rates have converged sensibly in the period since 1955, with emigration raising wages along the Mediterranean and immigration holding them down relatively in the north. Factor-price equalization, however, has not been achieved either for worldwide professional and technical labor, or for common labor in Europe, much less for common labor between continents.

There is doubt that the factor-price equalization model is relevant for intercontinental migration. This migration, as we shall see also in the case of capital follows well-worn grooves rather than spreads evenly over the world in response to economic signals. The design of many flows is political and related to noneconomic or quasi-economic considerations. Thus as subjects of the Queen, West Indians had the right to migrate to Britain, until that right was modified; and Algerians and members of the French *Communauté* had strong cultural ties to France. The British emigrate largely to the English-speaking dominions or the United States. Even when cultural and political considerations are not initially present, moreover, migration is a positive feedback process which follows a learning pattern. The movement is initially small and slow, as the early migrants overcome inertia. Once the channel is opened up, however, institutions are built which make it possible to move large numbers.

The Patterns of Labor Movement

Of particular interest among the world patterns of labor movement to our country are the waves of immigration to the United States in the period up to 1914, bringing in large numbers of English, German, Scandinavian, Irish, Italian, and eastern European immigrants. Each wave had a pattern of cumulative growth. Small numbers of pioneer emigrants made a successful start, sent for their relatives and friends, and the movement snowballed until the wave died down for one reason or another. Economic historians have debated whether the pull of opportunity was greater than the push of economic difficulty. In any case, however, it seems clear that these forces acted only against the background of a long-run migration cycle, which may or may not have had its origin in economic circumstances. In the burst of emigration from Ireland in the 1840's, the potato famine provided the push. Conversely, given the large-scale movement from Italy and eastern Europe with its beginnings in the collapse of the European wheat price in the early 1880's, the size of the annual flow was affected by conditions in the United States, slowing down as a consequence of the panic of 1907 and picking up with the subsequent revival.

Professor Brinley Thomas has detected a broad pattern in the Atlantic community, in which long cycles, connected with construction, were counterposed in Europe and North America, and produced rhythmical movements in migration. Large numbers of people were left stranded in rural occupations in Europe by the improvement in agricultural productivity in the first half of the 19th century and in the second half by the technological advance in transport, which made possible grain imports from the rich plains of North and South America, Australia, and the Ukraine. The Industrial Revolution created opportunities for work in European cities. In the upswing of the long construction cycle, the rural exodus was directed internally to the industrial cities. In depression, however, when it was necessary to pause and consolidate the domestic economic position, the rural reserve went abroad. One regulator of the movement, directing the Scandinavian, German, and British peasant now to the city and now to North America and (for the British) the Antipodes, was the terms of trade. When they favored Europe, economic opportunity at home was high in textiles, coal, and steel, and ultimately engineering trades and the chemical industry. In the slump, the terms of trade turned against Europe, and capital and labor went abroad.

This pattern is sketched in broad strokes, of course, and does not fit parts of the picture. In southern Italy, Hungary, Poland, and Russia, there was little industry to attract the rural surplus. For a long time it stayed put. When it moved, it headed almost entirely abroad. It has been said that the southern Italian was regarded as an object of derision in the industrial cities of Milan or Turin, and was more at home in New York or San Francisco—once, that is, the movement had gotten under way. It is interesting, too, to note that the migrants upon their arrival in the United States found their way into limited occupations and limited places of residence. Much of this was largely accidental. It is claimed that the Irish settled in Boston in greater numbers than in New York because the transatlantic fare to the former port was five shillings cheaper. German communities in Milwaukee and St. Louis, Swedish groups in Minnesota, Norwegian in the Dakotas, Polish in Baltimore and Buffalo, and Polish and Russian Jews in New York emphasize that the migrants were seeking their own kind, in the beginning, to provide a transition to life in the new world. Construction attracted Irish and Italian labor; Germans and Scandinavians went in for mixed and grain farming; northern Italians for truck gardening; Polish, German, and Russian Jews into the garment industry.

The imposition of immigration quotas by the United States in 1921 and 1924 is explained largely on social grounds. The cumulative flow of migrants from southern and eastern Europe, cut off by the war, showed signs of sharp revival. The check to cumulative emigration provided in Britain, Germany, and Scandinavia in the 19th century by industrial development and rising real incomes had never taken hold elsewhere, and the natural rate of increase had shown no signs of diminishing. Potential immigration was accordingly large. Its restriction posed grave social and economic problems for the affected areas, but its continuance would have done so for the United States and other receiving areas as they filled up.

The growing consciousness of international differences in levels of living has led to significant streams of immigrants to Britain from the poorer portions of the Commonwealth, especially Malta, the Indian subcontinent, and the West Indies. This influx created economic and social problems which led in 1962 to a change from completely free immigration, by people in search of work, to immigration limited to workers already in possession of jobs.

War and its aftermath bring large-scale movements of population, again largely for social reasons. The Turkish expulsion of Greeks, Armenians, Jews in 1921, the eastern European expulsion of German colonists and residents from east of the Oder-Neisse line in 1945, and the displacement of Arabs from the territory made into Israel in 1948 or occupied in 1967, provide examples of strict war origin. The vast movements of Hindus and Moslems between India and Pakistan after independence and partition in 1947, and the westward infiltration from behind the Iron Curtain, culminating in the escape of hundreds of thousands of refugees from Hungary in 1956, reflect social, political, and religious differences. The problem of economic and social settlement of these masses of people is a serious one. East Germans were absorbed into Western Germany with some difficulty but later became a basis of West German prosperity. Jewish refugees from all over the world, including eastern Europe and Arab countries, are welcomed in Israel. The Arabs who fled to Jordan in 1948 and the new influx of 1967 consisted of people of limited education and skill who did not want to migrate but wanted only to return to their homes under Arab sovereignty. Few large groups of refugees have a ready reception. Countries seeking immigrants tend to specify requirements which demand youth, skills, capital, and frequently specialized occupations, including farming. When they do not insist on unmarried men younger than 30, they prefer families of western European emigrants, and typically the Dutch farmer now in surplus because of the loss of his emigration outlet to the former Netherlands East Indies. The result is an indigestible refugee problem which private, national, and international action, through the United Nations Works and Relief Agency, finds a heavy burden to support, and which the International Refugee Organization has been able to do little to reduce.

Many cases of political refugees can be cited without direct reference to wars, but simply to oppressive regimes. Until August, 1961, a large segment of the East German skilled labor force escaped to the more prosperous conditions of West Germany through Berlin. As Castro's government in Cuba swung further left in the early 1960's, more and more Cubans flocked to Florida. Hong Kong has been a focal point of refugees from Red China who are particularly numerous in times of famine on the mainland. Often, religion and politics are mixed: the Puritans and other early American colonists got away from the Anglican Church, Jews fled pogroms in Czarist Russia, other Jews escaped Nazi persecution of the 1930's, and even the individualistic Dukhobers left Russia at the invitation of the Canadian government only to continue their stubborn noncooperation with any civil authorities.

The European Labor Market

Not every country in Europe welcomes foreign labor. In some, such as Britain, trade union opposition keeps down readiness to import workers. In Scandinavia, there is a Common Market for Labor limited to Scandinavians, with the largest movement having been from Finland to Sweden, but all the countries are reluctant to admit workers from the Mediterranean area, and justify this reluctance by saying that the southern labor would find the northern climate dark and cold. As a member of the European Economic Community, the Netherlands has subscribed to the Rome Treaty providing for freedom of movement of labor within the Community; it is not, however, aggressive in recruiting labor in Italy. The other northern members of the EEC not only have welcomed the movement of labor within the Community to the point of sending recruiting agencies abroad, but have extended the same generous provisions for national treatment (not most-favored nation) to Spain, Portugal, Greece, and Turkey. Until their labor shortages became so acute in the first half of the 1960's that foreigners with their limited skills could not meet them, these countries depended on foreign labor for a significant contribution to growth, a contribution which is measured not by the proportion they constituted of total labor, but by their contribution to holding wages down and thereby profits up, at the margin.

Once inflation hit, costs rose, profits were squeezed, and the long upswing from the early 1950's to the mid-1960's in Europe was over. The pressure to hire more foreign workers was relieved, and the regular turnover of workers who had filled their contracts and were returning home with their accumulated "target" savings, reduced the numbers of foreign workers in northern Europe. But the position was very different from the 1930's when the French forced the Poles and Italians in their country to return home, by canceling their police permits, rounding them up and shipping them out.

The returning foreign worker runs the risk of being disenchanted with life at home. Australia, which used to recruit, in Britain, the white immigrants it insisted on, now extends its search and finds that Mediterranean workers, who have been to northern Europe and returned south, make excellent prospects. The experience of higher standards of living and better working conditions abroad makes them intolerant of life at home. But then Australians assert that the immigrant from Britain does not become a real Australian until he has taken his first trip "home" to Britain.

One complex pattern of migration is found in Canada, where immigrants come from the United Kingdom and emigrants leave for the United States. Among the latter are young people who go to the United States for an education and decide to stay on, as many students from other countries would do if the student visa did not require them to leave the country for at least two years. Recently education has been equated with investment in human capital, which has led to attempts to estimate whether Canada gains or loses on balance on capital account, i.e., in terms of the education which it contributes to emigrants and gains from immigrants. Only about 10 percent of the immigrants entering Canada represent a net gain in numbers. But it was found the gain in education is much higher than this, since trained Britons immigrate, and relatively young and less educated Canadians emigrate.

Does Emigration Benefit the Sending Country?

If we leave out convulsive population movements mentioned in the second previous section, an interesting question which has received some discussion from economists is whether emigration is a good thing. It has been argued against it that sending grown people abroad permanently is a form of capital export: the country of emigration raises them from birth, feeds, clothes, and educates them through an unproductive period; and then loses them as they begin to reach a productive stage. This loss of a productive worker is comparable to the export of productive capital, except that not in all cases does the exporting country get a return on the net marginal productivity of the labor, over and above the maintenance and replacement costs (subsistence).

If the workers were slaves, sent abroad to produce a higher return than at home, and if their net product above subsistence were returned to the capital-exporting country, the capital-exporting analogy would be appropriate, provided that the slaves were raised for the purpose of earning a return. As a rule, however, population growth is independent of the opportunities for emigration, at least in the short run; the choice is not between investing resources in productive workers for migration abroad or investing these resources in more productive domestic lines. It is rather whether labor stays home in unemployment or underemployment, or seeks a job abroad. The resources invested in raising the labor to working age can be regarded as sunk. It is then a question whether a positive return on these resources is possible or, to put it otherwise, whether it is possible to relieve the pressure of the unemployed on the domestic labor market through emigration.

If, in fact, emigration means escape from the long-run check to population growth, it may be wasteful in terms of real income per head. The ideal policy would be not to allow emigration until the Malthusian barrier has been broken and family limitation is used to maintain the per capita income.

Even with population growth at a rapid rate, large-scale emigration may produce real income for the remaining population if the rate of remittance to the home country is high. For temporary workers with a savings target, this provides a country not only with foreign exchange but with savings, although these are not always invested in the most productive possible way. For permanent workers, including those who are temporary *ex ante* but become permanent *ex post,* the rate is a function of the ties in the society, partly cultural in character and partly a reflection of the time period that the migrants have been away. In the early stages of migration, when men precede their families, income is remitted home to dependents and relatives, including sums saved to enable these to join the breadwinner. Later, as whole families are united abroad, remittances will decline to the level needed to assist relatives beyond the immediate family. Finally, as a generation passes, remittances dwindle to a trickle. Cultural change has altered the pattern as well as the time profile. In the 30 years before World War I, immigrants into the United States lived in ethnocentric groups in this country and moved only slowly to acquire the standard of living of the second- and third-generation families in the country as a whole. Today, the cultural hold of the immigrant group is virtually nonexistent, since numbers are so small, and the pressure is strong on the occasional immigrant, such as the Hungarian refugees, to adjust quickly to the American standard. Even if it were easy and convenient to remit to relatives abroad behind the Iron Curtain—which it is not—social pressures to be assimilated to the new level of consumption reduce the capacity.

But there are more elements in the calculation. An emigrant will earn more abroad than at home, and may consume less (if his family remains home), so that savings are increased on two scores, and improve the capital/labor ratio. But the capital belongs to him, not to the country, and he presumably consumes (or saves) the income from it.

The external effects which go wider are the tax on this income, and the change in factor prices and combinations throughout the economy.

If there were no external effects of any kind, it could be argued that what a man did was entirely his business. If he earned more in one country or another, he consumed or saved more, and in either case the savings accrued to him. If all factors were paid their marginal product, changes in factor endowments brought about by migration have these impacts on taxes and other factor prices, but that's all. The concern that many people feel about the "brain drain" of talented professional youth leaving the less developed countries is overdone, according to this calculation. The main effects cancel out. If a scientist leaves Britain, he takes his production with him, but he also takes his income representing a claim on goods equal to his marginal product. Much of the analysis of migration, according to this way of looking at it, stresses the loss in output, but not the equal claim on the output of others.

The external effects cannot be overlooked, however. Abundant and therefore cheap scientists and engineers, doctors, or even economists, are an external benefit for other factors in the nation, and a scarcity of technical and professional personnel is a diseconomy. Above a certain minimum these effects are relatively unimportant. Thus the Netherlands and the Scandinavian countries, for example, export professional personnel because they cannot employ all their educated nationals at socially acceptable levels of remuneration. But larger countries can benefit from large numbers of scientists, to limit ourselves to one category, and small and poor countries may be dangerously close to the minimum needed as a fixed input critical to other activities. Emigration which pulls the numbers below these minimum levels is harmful to output in general.

These external effects are, for the most part, incalculable. This is especially true of the highest quality of scientist—the Fermis, Von Neumanns, Von Brauns,—who change the course of scientific and technological history.

By no means all emigration is deleterious. A case can be made that when there is open or disguised unemployment, a distortion of factor prices in the language of Chapters 10 and 12, emigration helps to get rid of it. The point is limited to unskilled labor. If disguised unemployment means that the marginal product is zero or close to zero, this inhibits investment. Why install machinery when there is in effect free labor, or rather family labor which must be paid anyhow? When enough labor is drawn off so that marginal product rises to the wage, it pays to calculate the returns on investment. Emigration thus stimulates investment, technological advance, and growth. In these cases, as the experience of the Mediterranean countries in the 1950's and 1960's shows, high emigration rates were accompanied by high rates of growth.

But it must not go too far. Below some optimum population, the economy has trouble supporting the variety of activities it needs, as Goldsmith's *Deserted Village* and the ghost towns of the West remind us.

Does Immigration Benefit the Receiving Country?

Whether immigration will benefit or hurt a country depends upon the country's resources of capital and land, relative to population, and the dynamic effects of the movements in question. Australia, Canada, Brazil, and similar large, underpopulated countries are interested in immigration of selected types of workers—young, farmers, skilled factory workers, and so on—because their resources are large relative to labor supply, and because the social overhead capital in countries of vast expanse typically produces increasing returns. Broadly the same investment in interurban roads, railroads, and harbors, for example, is required for a large population as for a small one, and a given population may be well below the optimum.

There is nonetheless likely to be capital expenditure needed as a consequence of immigration. Housing is a particular requirement, where the indivisibilities inherent in a transport network do not exist, and along with housing comes the provision of local overhead capital—schools, intra-urban transport, including streets, hospitals, and so forth. A considerable volume of investment in Australia today is linked to immigration requirements.

In Israel and Western Germany, the large-scale inward movement cannot be said to have hurt these countries, in the long run, despite the fact that they were well above the optimum population at the beginning of the movement in terms of social overhead capital. The reasons lie in the dynamic aspects of the movement. Israel's readiness to receive all Jewish refugees who were able to leave the countries where they constituted minorities contributed substantially to the spirit of dedication which evoked long hours of work and acceptance of low levels of consumption. These were extra market phenomena which the economist has difficulty in explaining in terms of marginal productivity. In Germany, the dynamism lay partly, but only partly, in the evocation of a national effort. In large measure it operated through short-run pressure on wages, which held profits high, out of which a compulsive and even neurotic drive to work and invest by entrepreneurs rebuilt German capital at a rapid rate.

But immigration does not always bring one's co-religionists or co-nationalists, and even when it does, as in the case of the Palestinian Arab refugees in the Sinai peninsula and Jordan, there is no necessary dynamic result. (In these cases, the receiving countries discouraged efforts of the refugees to improve their economic conditions since this might have implied an acceptance of the view that they were not entitled to return to their land in Israel.) The return of the European settlers from Algiers to France after the settlement of 1962 has an effect halfway between the stimulation of the East German refugees for West Germany and the deadening impact of the Jordanian Arabs.

Apart from external economies in social overhead capital and dynamic forces, immigration has effects on total output and on income distribution. It has been suggested by Lerner that where diminishing returns exist, and where on that account marginal product is below average product, it might be possible for the receiving country to alter the market distribution of income after immigration in order to bribe existing workers to accept an inflow of labor. Immigration lowers the marginal product of labor and hence wage rates; and raises the rent of unchanged factors such as land and capital. Government, however, could pay new workers their marginal product, but old workers their old wages, using part of the increase in rent in the system to make up the difference between the new and old marginal product. Since the marginal product in the new country is higher than in the old, everyone benefits from this operation.

To a certain extent this happens automatically, at least in the short run. Immigrants form a noncompeting group which takes on the dirty jobs that no one in the rest of the economy wants—the Italians who move into farm, hotel, and other service jobs, plus some in heavy industry, and free the Swiss to transfer to skilled work and offices. The immigrants may be sought because native labor is not available for particular tasks which would be remunerative with cheaper labor available from abroad: the slaves needed to make cotton planting pay in the 1830's and 1840's kept down wage rates in cotton-farming areas. Similarly, the importation of Mexican wetbacks and Puerto Rican truck farm hands lowers wage rates at the margin. The pressure to halt immigration was primarily social but partly economic, the latter stemming from the newly powerful trade unions which emerged from the war.

Or the immigration may be needed to keep down wages in general, as in Germany. In part this may be the net effect of separate plants looking for workers, which ends up in the government establishing recruiting agencies overseas. Or it may be conscious. An authoritative writer on Latin America asserts that support for immigration into these countries comes from employer groups who are anxious to hold down wage rates and maintain rates of profit. As we have had occasion to observe in discussing tariff policy, one policy may recommend itself from an overall point of view, but another be adopted for distributional reasons where the factor or group which benefits wields political power. In this instance, however, it seems likely, as in the support given for free trade by Manchester liberals in the 1840's and Detroit manufacturers in the 1950's, the distributional argument and the total efficiency argument overlap. While population is growing rapidly in many of these countries, such as Brazil and Venezuela, they are currently underpopulated relative to resources and already possess an efficient network of social capital.

Apart from its economic merits, however, the proposal is highly academic for social reasons. In the long run, the immigrants will want to be assimilated in the receiving country and to end discrimination against them in wages. Social and cultural conditions, including the color of their skins, will affect how rapidly this comes about. But the pressure will be ineluctable.

Cosmopolitan Migration Policy

From a strictly economic point of view, which we are not warranted in taking in this discussion, the optimum policy for the world with respect to migration would be freedom of movement to equalize wages among those countries where the rate of population growth had shown some check. If there were no social and political inhibitions to movement, countries of immigration among them would experience a decline in wages, while wages would rise in countries of emigration. If the overpopulated country has not experienced the Malthusian revolution, however, unlimited migration can only equalize wages by reducing them abroad, as the reduction in the surplus population through emigration is replaced by natural increase.

This position is not fundamentally altered by the demographic counterrevolution in North America and in some countries of western Europe under which the large family is sought, despite its effect on the level of material income per capita, because large families are regarded as good in themselves. The enlarged family should be counted as part of real income. Income increases at a fixed income of $6,000 per family as family numbers rise from four to six, despite the decrease in income per capita from $1,500 to $1,000.

A special problem is posed by migration from a country where family limitation prevails to one where it is not needed, with the consequence of a return to much larger families. Ireland in the last half of the 19th century limited the rate of population increase by late marriages. Emigrants from Ireland to the United States were able to obtain incomes and marry at a much earlier age, with the result that the birthrate of the immigrants from Ireland was very much higher than that of the society they left. This case should probably be counted as one in which the Malthusian revolution had not been accomplished.

Technical Assistance

Current interest in economic development of underdeveloped areas, with its emphasis on technical assistance, suggests that the international transmission of technology through personal visits is a new phenomenon. It is not so. Flemish weavers taught their secrets to the British woolen industry in the 13th and 14th centuries. Somewhat later Lombardy merchants and bankers led the commercial revolution in London. After the Industrial Revolution, British engineers built the railroads of the Continent, and British textile and steel workers communicated their skills to French, German, and Italian factories and mills. Up to about 1830 it was illegal in Great Britain to export machinery, for fear of competition; but master workers coming to the United States smuggled it out or reproduced it upon arrival from drawings.

There are, to be sure, differences in the extent and character of international diffusion of technical capacity now as compared, say, to the 19th century. International organizations, national governments, and international corporations provide new institutions for this transmission which are evidently more efficient than the single worker or engineer, or the limited colony of workers. The result is that international travel and foreign residence of skilled personnel, professional and manual, have reached new heights each year since World War II. Crews of Texas oil drillers can be encountered anywhere; teams from Morrison-Knudson, Krupp, and similar construction enterprises are found from Afghanistan to Zanzibar; economists from Scandinavia and the British dominions —which produce impressive surpluses for export—are found advising central banks, planning boards and treasuries in Asia, Latin America, and Africa. A special kind of technical assistance, not always of a very high technical caliber, but certain to spread an awareness of modern economic life and of the capacity of man to improve it, is the Peace Corps of the United States and its smaller European and British equivalents.

Freedom of Movement and Social Integration

Reduction in transport costs relative to income means that the populations of the world can mix with one another on an increasing scale. They become more aware of each other in other ways than travel,—through motion pictures, magazines, radio and television, including live television by Telstar. But there is a significant difference between the interest of the outsider and the familiarity of the habitué, who feels at home in what was once a strange environment. The social barriers against outsiders begin to be overcome when there have been so many trips that the traveler stops counting them. In some occupations persons have now stopped counting trips to Europe and Asia, as they once stopped counting trips between the East and West Coasts, and before that trips from Washington to New York or Los Angeles to San Francisco.

Much of the world is still far from mobile. Some of it is in the stage of first trips. But increasingly people are beginning to feel at home over wider areas. The Harvard Business School graduate of the 1930's probably had strong preferences for work in a region of the United States—East, South, Middle West, Far West; the graduate of the 1950's was usually content to work anywhere in the United States. Today's graduate is willing to be hired for work (for an American company and at an American salary) anywhere in the world. The parenthesis in the last sentence indicates the room left to go. By the end of the century it seems inevitable that factor price equalization will have taken care of the salary part, and social integration of the need to work with his fellow countrymen.

The trend is clearly in this direction, to extend freedom of movement, on a scale which leads to social integration, to more and more groups and classes in societies in more and more countries. The mobility poses problems for countries with few facilities which are or feel threatened by the loss of particularly intelligent, well-trained and energetic individuals. Love of country (and difficulties in learning foreign languages) will retain some. Interest in the different and narrower differential returns will attract similar people from abroad. That the movement of peoples will become an increasingly important aspect of international economics, however, there can be no doubt.

Summary

Labor moves across international boundaries in limited amounts, and generally in structured paths. Some movement is daily, seasonal, institutionalized through companies and governmental bodies, and some permanent. The pattern of migration in the 19th century tended to be synchronized with alternating long cycles in Europe and abroad. Waves of emigration from Britain, Ireland, Germany, and Scandinavia initially built up in cumulative fashion, and then came to a halt, as the difference in wage rates narrowed between Europe and the areas of settlement. From Italy and eastern Europe, however, the migration built up cumulatively until cut off by war and immigration quotas. Birthrates remained high, and there was no substantial domestic industry to assist in absorbing the rural surplus.

Large-scale European movements, largely from the Mediterranean countries to Switzerland, Belgium, France, and Germany have helped to create a European labor market. The Common Market for Scandinavia, and Britain and the Netherlands stand largely aloof from this movement.

Emigration benefits the sending country through remittances, improvement in the terms of trade as a result of expanding production abroad, and relief for structural unemployment. In one sense, however, the raising and education of able-bodied workers constitutes a capital investment when it is not clear that overpopulated countries should export capital. Emigration may also attract the most vigorous elements in a society. Immigration is desirable for a country, provided the process of social assimilation is not serious, if its population is below optimal. In addition, immigration may be undertaken for structural and distributional reasons. Immigration, however, may have dynamic effects in other circumstances which outweigh adverse economic considerations.

Technical assistance is provided partly by the written word, but most effectively through the international movement of people. Increased mobility is leading to wider intermingling on social and economic bases.

SUGGESTED READING

TEXTS

S. Enke and V. Salera, *International Economics* (3rd ed.; Englewood Cliffs, N.J.: Prentice-Hall, Inc., 1957), chap. xvi; Kemp, chap. ix.

TREATISES, ETC.

Brinley Thomas, *Migration and Economic Growth* (Cambridge: Cambridge University Press, 1954), studies the experience of the Atlantic migration and contains a detailed bibliography. On migration in Europe and the creation of an international labor market, see C. P. Kindleberger, *Europe's Postwar Growth: The Role of Labor Supply* (Cambridge, Mass.: Harvard University Press, 1967), especially chaps. ix, x.

H. Jerome, *Migration and Business Cycles* (New York: National Bureau of Economic Research, 1926), examines whether the push of depression is more significant than the pull of prosperity abroad. Meade, *Trade and Welfare,* chap. xxvii, studies the effects of factor movements.

POINTS

H. Grubel and A. Scott have produced a series of interesting papers on the "brain drain." See *AER,* May, 1966; *JPE,* August, 1966; and *AER,* March, 1967.

Bruce Wilkinson has a chapter on "Human Capital Values of Canadian Immigration and Emigration," in his *Studies in the Economics of Education* (Ottawa: Department of Labor, Dominion of Canada, July, 1965).

PART IV

The Adjustment Process

Chapter 15

THE PRICE MECHANISM OF ADJUSTMENT

We now move from the world of microeconomics and the discussion of what products are exported and imported at what terms of trade, to that of macroeconomics, and in particular the world of balance-of-payments adjustment. The transition is not an abrupt one, as the title of this chapter indicates: the word "price" might suggest we are still in a microuniverse. But the price we are interested in applies to the whole economy. It is either the price of the country's money, i.e., the rate of foreign exchange; or, at a fixed rate of exchange, the price level. But it is not both. If one doubles all prices and halves the rate of exchange, nothing has happened. For the most part we shall assume that prices are constant and that the rate of exchange is altered. This implies the flexible exchange rate system. But it could be the other way, with a fixed exchange rate and changing price levels, which is what is supposed to happen under the gold standard and the fixed exchange standard. Discussion of actual international monetary arrangements is postponed until virtually the end of the book. Our interest here is in the mechanics and the intellectual tools.

We start, as implied in the preceding paragraph, along partial equilibrium lines. In this chapter we discuss the price mechanism as if income were constant; in the next chapter income as if price were constant. In Chapter 17, we set forth what little can be said with income and price both free to move. And in the final chapter of Part IV, we illustrate the adjustment process with a particular form of disturbance, the transfer of capital from one country to another, where the task is to show how the monetary transfer gives way to a real transfer in goods and services, changing the balance of payments (exports minus imports) to produce an export surplus for the lending country and an import surplus for the borrowing.

The Fluctuating Exchange Rate

When demand exceeds supply at a given price, the position can be restored to equilibrium by changing demand, changing supply, a little of both, or by changing price. In international trade, when the demand for a currency differs from the supply for it at the rate of exchange, one way of clearing the market is to change the exchange rate. At the new rate, demand is equal to supply, in the short run.

But the change in the exchange rate has more important effects. It changes the relationship between the prices of internationally traded goods—goods exported and imported, and goods produced domestically which are close competitors of imports—and the prices of domestic goods which do not enter into international trade. An increase in the prices of internationally traded goods will expand the production of exports and of import-competing goods which are now more profitable, and will curtail expenditure on imports. A decrease in the prices of internationally traded goods, relative to domestic goods, on the other hand, would increase imports and lead to a contraction of exports.

Depreciation of a currency will increase the domestic price of internationally traded goods if we assume that world prices are unchanged. Suppose that the world prices of cotton textiles and wheat are represented by their New York prices and stand at 30 cents a yard and $2 a bushel, respectively. Leaving out of consideration costs of transportation, with sterling at $4 per pound, the London prices of these commodities will be 1s. 6d. per yard for cotton textiles and 10s. per bushel for wheat. If the value of the pound sterling is changed by the foreign exchange market, still assuming world prices unchanged, the sterling prices of these commodities will be affected. A depreciation of the pound to $2.40 will raise the price of cotton textiles to 2s. 6d. per yard and that of wheat to 16s. 8d. per bushel. Cotton textile manufacturers will be disposed to expand their production and sales abroad, which increases exports; domestic producers will raise more wheat at the higher price, which will enable millers to limit imports.

An appreciation of the pound from $4 to $5, however, would lower the prices of textiles and wheat to 1s. 2d. and 8s., respectively, which would discourage exports and encourage imports.

Even if we abandon the assumption that the world price remains unchanged, the first effects of depreciation will be to encourage exports and discourage imports, while the converse will be true of appreciation. Suppose that sterling depreciates from $4 to $2.40 but that instead of the sterling prices of cotton textiles and wheat rising to 2*s*. 6*d*. and 16*s*. 8*d*., respectively, the world prices fall in New York to 18 cents and $1.20. In London, the price of cotton textiles is still 1*s*. 6*d*. and of wheat 10*s*. There may be no incentive to alter foreign trade in Britain, with prices unchanged; but there will be in the rest of the world. It is less profitable to produce wheat for export to Britain at the lower price, so that British imports will decline; and since the goods bought from England are cheaper than before, it pays to buy more. British exports will increase.

A change in the exchange rate alters the relationship between prices of internationally traded goods in two countries. At one limit and the other, the price change will occur all in one country, while the price in the other remains unaffected. In the normal case with only two countries, prices will change somewhat in both and will alter the relationship of internationally traded to domestic goods in both countries.

There will be secondary effects operating through income, if only those which are brought about by the initial repercussions on foreign trade. These will work in the opposite direction from the foreign exchange rate change. A depreciation of the exchange rate, for example, will expand exports and reduce imports. But both the expansion of exports and the reduction of imports will increase national income, and this will tend to decrease exports and expand imports. These secondary effects may be offset through action of the monetary or fiscal system; or they may be exaggerated through policy decisions or mistaken action. Price is then not the whole story in adjustments brought about through exchange rates. But it bears the initial impact.

The complications of the income movements set off by exchange rate changes are left for Chapter 17. At this stage the task is to go into how much exports and imports are affected by changes in exchange rates. This involves a discussion of elasticities of demand and supply in foreign trade.

Excess Demand and Supply Curves

The elasticity of demand for imports is higher than the elasticity of demand for the product as a whole if there is any elasticity to the domestic supply schedule. Similarly, the elasticity of the supply of exports is higher than the elasticity of the supply curve as a whole if there is any domestic consumption of the export product and the domestic demand curve has elasticity greater than zero. These propositions may best be illustrated by the process of consolidating domestic demand

and supply curves into a single curve representing excess demand or excess supply. It is this last excess demand or excess supply curve which is the operational schedule in international trade.

Figure 15.1a shows an ordinary set of curves representing the domestic demand and supply of a given commodity, say wheat, expressed in terms of money prices. Without international trade, the market would be in equilibrium at the price P. At a higher price, supply would exceed demand; at a lower price, demand would exceed supply. These amounts of excess supply and excess demand, derived by subtract-

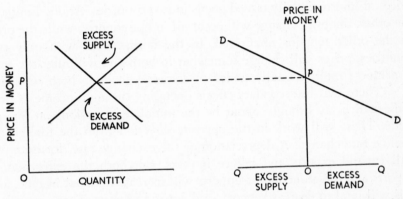

FIG. 15.1a. Domestic Demand and Supply in the Importing Country

FIG. 15.1b. Excess Demand for the Import Good

ing the demand curve from the supply curve at prices above OP, and the supply curve from the demand curve at prices below it, can be transferred in a single curve to another diagram, such as Figure 15.1b. This is a curve representing excess demand. Above the price OP, the excess demand is negative (or excess supply). Note that the excess demand curve has greater elasticity than the domestic demand curve. If domestic production were nonexistent or had zero elasticity, i.e., were a fixed amount, the slopes of the two curves would be identical. If domestic production were infinitely elastic, the excess demand curve would be infinitely elastic at the same price.

The position in the exporting country is shown in Figure 15.1c, and the excess supply, available to the importing country, derived in Figure 15.1d. Notice that this is calculated in the currency of the importing country. This means that the two curves can be put together on the same diagram and used to indicate the equilibrium of the interna-

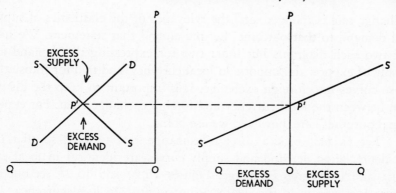

FIG. 15.1*c*.   Domestic Demand and Supply in the Exporting Country

FIG. 15.1*d*.   Excess Supply of the Export Good

tional market in the single commodity, expressed in the currency of the importing country. This is done in Figure 15.1*e*. We can use this simple variation on the usual demand and supply, partial equilibrium diagram to study exchange depreciation.

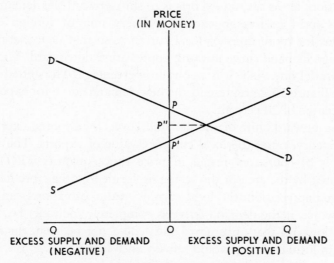

FIG. 15.1*e*.   Partial Equilibrium Representation of Trade in One Good with Excess Demand and Excess Supply Curves

Exchange Depreciation

Take two of these diagrams showing excess demand in one country and excess supply in another to indicate what happens when a foreign exchange rate is changed, and the relevance of the elasticities of supply and demand to that outcome. Let me amend that statement. We need not two such diagrams but four: two for expressing the demand and supply of exports and imports in local currency, and two for translating these curves into foreign exchange. It is important to keep the distinction between the local currency and foreign exchange clear. For expositional purposes here, however, we use both.

Let us first pick a foreign exchange rate of one, so that our pre-depreciation demand and supply curves are identical in local currency and in foreign exchange. Figures 15.2*a* and 15.2*b* set out the curves for exports in the depreciating country, in local currency, and foreign exchange, respectively. If we assume only one export commodity, the horizontal axis measures the volume of that good; or it can measure exports as a whole with units of the individual goods chosen to represent the same amount of money (10 oranges, ½ bushel of wheat, 1/2,000 of a Rambler) at existing relative prices.

What is the effect of a change in the exchange rate? Let us concentrate only on the local currency diagrams. The impact of a depreciation, let us say, on exports is to shift upward the demand curve, which is fixed in foreign exchange. Every unit of foreign currency exchanges for more units of local currency, so that depreciation shifts the foreign demand curve upward, appreciation downward. The shift is not a parallel one, since it is a constant percentage. The dotted demand curve in Figure 15.2*a* represents the new demand curve for exports after a depreciation of 20 percent.

The upward shift of the demand curve for exports, expressed in local currency, raises the local currency value of exports. The value of exports is of course expressed in price times quantity (PQ) and is represented by the area of the rectangle formed by their product. With exchange depreciation, the local currency value of exports cannot fall. At the worst, if the demand curve is completely inelastic, i.e., straight up and down so that an upward shift could not be seen, the value of exports in local currency would remain unchanged.

Depreciation may, however, expand, reduce, or leave unchanged the local currency value of imports. Depreciation involves an upward shift in the supply curve, which is fixed in foreign exchange as shown in Figure 15.2*c*. Whether the value of imports will rise, fall, or remain unchanged depends upon the elasticity of demand for imports. If this elasticity is unity, the value of imports will remain unchanged. If it is less than one, it will increase. If it is greater than one, it will fall.

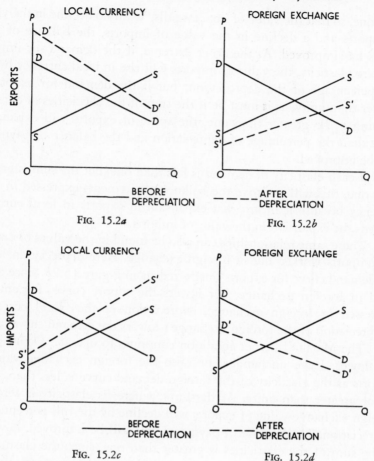

FIG. 15.2*a*

FIG. 15.2*b*

FIG. 15.2*c*

FIG. 15.2*d*

Excess Demand and Excess Supply of Exports and Imports, in Local Currency and in Foreign Exchange, before and after Foreign Exchange Depreciation

The Marshall-Lerner Condition

These relationships have led to the development of the Marshall-Lerner condition which states, in effect, that depreciation will improve the balance of payments of a country and appreciation worsen it, if the sum of the elasticities of demand for a country's exports and of its demand for imports is greater than one. Take first the case where the elasticity of demand for exports is zero. Exports in local currency are now no smaller than before. If the sum of the elasticities is greater than one, this must mean that the elasticity of demand for imports is greater than one, so that the value of imports falls. With no decline in the value of exports and a decline in the value of imports, the balance of payments has improved. At the other extreme, if the demand for imports has zero elasticity, the value of imports will rise in local currency by the full percentage of the depreciation; but if the demand for exports is greater than unity, as it must be if the sum of the elasticities of demand is going to be greater than one, the value of exports will expand by more than the percentage of depreciation and the balance of payments will be improved.

If each elasticity of demand is less than one, but the sum is greater than one, this will improve the balance of payments expressed in local currency because it means that expansion in exports in local currency exceeds the expansion in the value of imports.

These same relationships can also be found in the values of exports and imports worked out in foreign exchange. Here depreciation leaves the demand curve for exports unaffected, as in Figure 15.2*b,* since this is fixed in foreign exchange, but lowers the supply curve. For imports expressed in foreign exchange, depreciation of the "local currency" (appreciation of the foreign exchange) lowers the demand curve.

The Marshall-Lerner condition continues to operate. Depreciation can lower, leave unchanged, or raise the foreign exchange value of exports as the elasticity of the foreign demand curve is less than, equal to, or greater than unity. At the limit, where its elasticity is zero, the foreign exchange value of exports will decline by the full percentage of depreciation. The balance of payments will still be improved, however, if the sum of the elasticities is greater than one, since the elasticity of demand for imports must now be greater than one. This means that the value of imports will be reduced by more than the percentage of depreciation. Depreciation can leave imports unchanged in foreign exchange or reduce them; it cannot serve to increase them. With zero elasticity of demand for imports, the foreign exchange value of imports will be unchanged; but if the demand for exports has an elasticity greater than one, the foreign exchange value of exports will rise and the balance of payments will be improved.

The Marshall-Lerner condition, which is derived algebraically in Appendix F, is broadly correct if supply elasticities are relatively large and if the balance of payments is in equilibrium to begin with. But the supply elasticities may be relatively low, as was the case, for example, with Scotch whiskey in Britain at the time of the 1949 devaluation, or as is likely to be true under conditions of full employment. In this circumstance, the Marshall-Lerner condition is sufficient for balance-of-payments improvement but not necessary. With low supply elasticity, the price of exports will not fall so low in foreign exchange, and foreign exchange earnings will not decline to the same extent with a low elasticity of demand, as would have been true with infinite supply elasticity. Compare, in Figure 15.3, points *a* and *b*. Since the slope of the demand curve between *a* and *b* has an elasticity of less than one, the higher price at *b* more than makes up for the decline in volume.

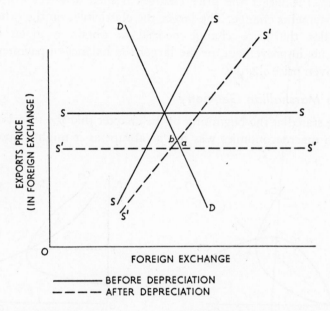

FIG. 15.3. The Market for Exports in Foreign Exchange before and after Devaluation, with Infinite and Low Supply Elasticities

Accordingly the sum of demand elasticities can be less than one (but not much less) and still improve balance of payments when supply elasticities are low.

The condition that the imbalance of trade must not be large to begin with is grounded in the characteristics of percentages. If the sum of the elasticities is greater than one, the percentage increase in exports will always be greater than the percentage increase in imports, or the percentage decrease in foreign exchange will be smaller. But if imports are very large, relative to exports, the absolute increase in imports may be larger in local currency, or the absolute decrease in imports smaller in foreign exchange. This worsening of the arithmetic $(P_xQ_x - P_mQ_m)$ balance of payments is accompanied by an improvement in the geometric balance $\left(\dfrac{P_xQ_x}{P_mQ_m}\right)$.

The Marshall-Lerner condition emphasizes the critical nature of unity for the sum of the elasticities. But for substantial improvement in the balance of payments from exchange depreciation, the sum should clearly be much higher, nearer four, or five, or six. The smaller the elasticities, the larger the price changes needed to effect a given balance-of-payments change. The larger the elasticities, on the other hand, the smaller the price change needed to obtain a given balance-of-payments improvement, or the larger the balance-of-payments effect from a given price change.

The Marshallian Geometry

We stated at the beginning of the chapter that the transition from micro- to macroeconomics was not as abrupt as it might appear. This

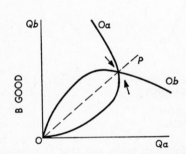
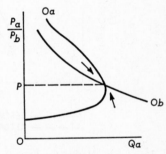

FIG. 15.4*a*. Stable Equilibrium with Offer Curves

FIG. 15.4*b* Stable Equilibrium with Marshallian Offer Curves

can be shown for the exchange market, with the geometry Marshall used for offer curves, by diddling with the prices of goods and of units of exchange. The exercise shows that the stability conditions in international trade are the same as the Marshall-Lerner conditions for the foreign exchange market. But while it appears that the device shows the market in general equilibrium, it really does not. To make the demonstration work incomes must remain fixed and also goods prices in domestic currency.

Offer curves, as shown in, say, Figure 15.4*a,* represent quantities of one good supplied or offered against quantities of another good demanded. Both curves are expressed the same way. But it is possible to convert them to more nearly ordinary demand and supply curves. The price of the *A* good in terms of the *B* good goes on the vertical axis, and quantities of the *A* good on the horizontal axis as in Figure 15.4*b*. The *A* offer curve is readily transferred from quantity–quantity to price–quantity space as a supply curve. At low prices for the *A* good, *A* will offer no *A* for *B;* hence the positive intercept on the vertical axis. After a certain price has been reached, moreover, *A* is unwilling to supply more *A* at higher prices, since the income effect from the higher price outweighs the substitution effect and it consumes the *A* good itself. Accordingly the supply curve will bend backwards.

The *B* offer curve in Figure 15.4*a* can be expressed as a demand curve, showing how much of the *A* good *B* demands at various prices. Provided this good is not subject to Giffen's paradox, which will make consumers want less of it at lower prices and more at higher, the curve falls negatively from left to right, or at least has an elasticity not less than zero—or straight up and down. As Figures 15.4*a* and 15.4*b* are drawn, the market is stable. There is one price which clears the market, *O–P*. And this price, as the arrows show, is a stable equilibrium. At higher prices, supply exceeds demand, so that there is downward pressure on price which restores equilibrium. At lower prices, demand exceeds supply, which drives price back to the equilibrium level.

Both diagrams can be converted into representations of the exchange market. In Figure 15.4*a*, fix the domestic price of the *B* good at one unit of *B*'s currency, no matter what happens to the terms of trade, and the same for the *A* good in *A*'s currency. The terms of trade are now the same as the exchange rate. They show how much one unit of the *A* good exchanges for a unit of the *B* good and how much one unit of the *A* currency exchanges for a unit of the *B* currency. Likewise for Figure 15.4*b*. This looks like a general equilibrium representation of the exchange market, since these are offer curves rather than the obviously partial equilibrium diagrams shown earlier. But the other things that must be equal include national income and the domestic prices of the separate goods.

The stability condition with usual offer curves is that they intersect each other from the inside. This is the same as the Marshall–Lerner condition, that the sum of the import elasticities of demand is greater than one. The student (and his instructor) are left to work out the proof with the help of Appendix D which shows how to calculate the import elasticity of an offer curve, though they may need help from Meade's *Geometry*. We will provide a counterexample shortly. But in the right-hand drawing, the equivalent equilibrium condition is that the net of the elasticity of demand (which is negative) minus the elasticity of supply must be less than zero, or that the supply curve must cut the demand curve from below and from the left. The two conditions are the same. Converting a demand curve to a supply curve, as is done for A in the Marshallian demonstration, reduces its elasticity by one (a unit elastic demand curve when converted becomes a zero elastic supply curve). There is the complication that the Marshall-Lerner condition is generally given in absolute terms, without regard to signs, which have to be watched in the Marshallian version. But stability means that offer curves intersect from the inside, or that the sum of the import elasticities is greater than one; in the Marshallian offer curves it means that the supply curve cuts from below and left, or that the elasticity of demand (negative) minus the elasticity of the supply curve (positive or negative) is less than zero. (If the demand elasticity is zero, for example, the supply elasticity must be positive).

Unstable Equilibrium

But offer curves are not required by Nature or man to be stable, nor are exchange markets. Consider Figure 15.5*a*. At the price $O–P$, Oa

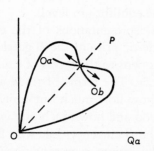

FIG. 15.5*a*. Unstable Equilibrium with Offer Curves

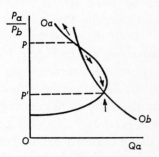

FIG. 15.5*b*. Unstable Equilibrium with Marshallian Offer Curves

cuts Ob from the outside, not the inside. At higher prices for A, B wants more of the A good and A offers less. The price will go still higher. $O–P$ may clear the market, but any departure will be cumulative. Or contemplate Figure 15.5*b*. A higher price for the A good than $O–P$ produces an excess of demand over supply, driving the price up, and a lower price an excess supply, driving the price down. $O–P$ is an unstable price here, too, whether this is a goods market, or an exchange market. In the latter case each good is fixed in local currency price, the vertical axis represents the exchange rate, the horizontal axis quantities of foreign exchange.

The possibility that the sum of the elasticities will be less than one (in the Marshall-Lerner formulation) will be discussed presently. Notice now that Figure 15.5*b* has a stable equilibrium at *O–P'*. At lower prices the demand for *A* exchange exceeds supply; at higher, supply exceeds demand. And there must be another stable equilibrium above *O–P*. At some very high price of the *A* good, country *A* will increase its offer, and at some high price, *B* will want none. Accordingly the curves must intersect again higher up with a stable intersection. Every unstable equilibrium is bounded by two stable ones, barring freak cases of free goods. In Figure 15.5*a*, the offer curves have not been extended for very high prices of *A* and *B*, but will intersect twice again, and with stable equilibria.

The fact that unstable equilibria are bounded by two stable intersections does not dispose of the problem of an unstable exchange market. One country may prefer one stable point, while another country may prefer the other. In Figure 15.5*b*, *B* obviously prefers the lower stable intersection with high prices for its product, while *A* prefers the undrawn one high off the diagram. Moreover the unstable area gives trouble. If there is a deficit and the sum of the elasticities is less than one (with large supply elasticities, as in a depression), the balance of trade cannot be improved by depreciation, but appreciation will improve it. Because of the inelasticity of the demand abroad for the country's exports, increased exports would reduce foreign exchange earnings, but a higher exchange rate and smaller exports will raise them. By the same token, cheaper imports will expand quantity less than the decline in price and reduce the value of imports. Some economists have used the unwillingness of countries to try appreciation as a remedy for a balance-of-payments deficit as a *reductio ad absurdum* of the position that elasticities are low in the real world. But where elasticities are high in the long run, even though low in the short, appreciation is a dangerous device to use to remedy a deficit. The short-run advantage from the monopoly position in exports and the monopsony in imports quickly melts away.

Elasticity Optimism and Pessimism

During the depression of the 1930's, there was considerable doubt whether depreciation would improve the balance of payments, and a whole school of thought grew up which became known as elasticity pessimism. In the postwar period, on the other hand, apart from the developing countries where pessimism still prevails, most economists have turned into elasticity optimists. The change is often thought of as due to improvements in reasoning and measurement. Much of it, however, seems better explained as the result of changed conditions.

Elasticities vary with many circumstances: with the number of sellers and the size of a particular seller in relation to the size of the market, the amount of domestic production or consumption, the size of price changes, expectations, the time allowed for reaction, and especially market conditions, and alternative outlets or sources. A few words on each point may be useful.

It is well known that the demand for the product is less elastic than the demand for the output of an individual seller. At the extreme, the demand for wheat is price-inelastic; the individual farmer can sell all he can produce at a constant price. On a moderated scale, the same is true in international economics. A country small in relation to the market will have higher elasticities than a country which is large. The very large country may have only the same elasticity as the elasticity of the product. It is a price maker, rather than a price taker, to use the phrase of Metzler. Brazil in coffee, Ghana in cocoa, Malaya in rubber and tin face inelastic demand curves and cannot expand the value of exports through price reduction, or, the same thing with unchanged domestic prices, exchange depreciation.

Earlier in this chapter, a demonstration was offered that excess-demand and supply curves of a country have higher elasticities than national product demand and supply curves. The excess demand curve includes the product demand curve plus the elasticity of domestic supply; the excess-supply curve includes the product supply curve plus the elasticity of domestic demand. These effects are larger for manufactured products than for some primary products, particularly that class known as "colonial" products. If consumption of coffee, cocoa, or bananas in a producing country is of low elasticity, adding the demand elasticity to the product supply elasticity does not change it much. Since there is also no production of these commodities in the developed world, the product demand elasticity and the import elasticity abroad are identical.

Size, expectations, and time can all be dealt with together. The outcome depends on consumer reactions in demand elasticity and on producer reactions in supply. For price changes which are small, not expected to last, and which do not last, it is not worthwhile to make adjustments in production and consumption. When the price change is large, is expected to continue, and has lasted for a time, however, it pays to adapt.

But the major question is what the alternatives are, and particularly whether the world is depressed or prosperous. In depression, demand and supply elasticities are low for price decreases, and depreciation fails to work well. Appreciation, however, is likely to be effective in producing an adverse balance of trade, since there is extra capacity to produce supply, and marginal demanders drop off when the price is raised. Conversely in periods of prosperity, demand and supply elasticities are high for price decreases: in a seller's market, people turn avidly to the country which cuts prices, and adjustment is easy in declining lines because of alternative opportunities. (Conversely for price increases.) Accordingly it is not surprising that the econometricians for all their inability to agree exactly how to go about measuring elasticities in international trade, find higher elasticities now than in the 1930's, with a rise in the optimism felt about the effectiveness of exchange depreciation.

Terms of Trade and Depreciation

What will happen to the terms of trade with depreciation? We avoid the temptation to say that they decline because the price of exports falls in foreign exchange and the price of imports rises in local currency. It is now evident that the comparison must be made in the same *numéraire*. Having avoided one temptation, we succumb to another. The answer, like our answer to most questions in economics, is "It depends." And when the matter is advanced one stage, the usual reply is again called for: "It depends on the elasticities."

Three main positions have been staked out. To the ultraclassicists such as Graham and his students, the terms of trade are likely to be unchanged because a country typically deals at world prices, on which it has no effect. Depreciation raises domestic prices of both exports and imports by the full percentage of depreciation, since the ordinary country faces an infinite demand elasticity for its exports, and an infinite supply elasticity for its imports. The foreign offer curve is a straight line. The terms of trade are given.

The classic, as opposed to the ultraclassic, position is that depreciation worsens the terms of trade and appreciation improves them because a country specializes in exports but not in imports. It has an effect on the price of its exports, that is, but none on imports. The classic assumption has been tested and found to be correct as a general rule. It is particularly true of the larger developing countries.

But the classic assumptions do not hold in all cases. A country can specialize in imports and generalize in exports, i.e., have a larger monopsonist position in imports than its monopoly position, if any, in exports. The outstanding example here is Britain, whose terms of trade improved with depreciation in 1931. Partly this was the result of dynamic effects, but largely it was because the world depended on the British import market to sell its foodstuffs and materials, so that world prices of British imports fell more than world prices of British exports.

Partial versus Complete Elasticities

As stated with tiresome but useful repetition, the elasticity approach is based on partial equilibrium analysis. Exchange depreciation produces changes in exports and imports which can be calculated from elasticities because we assume other things equal. But while it is satisfactory to regard other things as equal for all intents and purposes in microeconomic analysis of the demand and supply for one commodity, the exchange rate is something different. A change in this price produces changes which reverberate throughout the economy, altering incomes and goods prices over a wide range, so that other things cannot be taken as equal. At the very least, if exports rise and imports fall, there will be an increase in domestic spending which changes domestic money income. We need then not partial elasticities, which assume other things equal, but total elasticities which take all effects into account. The elasticity optimists are not disposed to regard the difference between partial and complete elasticities as a serious problem. The elasticity pessimists fear that total elasticities are lower than partial elasticities, or even that the repercussions of exchange devaluation within the economy may produce a rise in nontraded goods prices and all incomes, which would mean that nothing happened. If the exchange rate falls, and all prices and incomes rise by a like amount, the system is homogeneous, and the only change that has occurred is in the unit of account.

Changing Prices and Fixed Exchange Rates

This analysis can be applied to the situation when the exchange rate is fixed, but the price level moves. Domestic inflation, as appreciation, worsens the balance of payments through price effects. The inflated country is a better place in which to sell at the old exchange rate, and a poorer place from which to buy. Deflation of prices, if it could be produced, would improve the balance of payments. This is the mechanism by which the gold standard was supposed to have worked, the so-called price-specie-flow mechanism, which more logically would have been called, the specie-flow-price mechanism. If a country gained gold (specie), this added to the money supply, its prices rose, and the balance of payments turned adverse. If it lost gold, it was assumed to deflate its money supply, reduce prices, and improve the balance.

Note one important assumption in this reasoning. There is assumed to be continuous full employment, and no relation between money income and imports or exports, apart from the changes produced by the price elasticities. But if real income does change, or if changes in money income, apart from changes in real income, do have an effect on spending on imports for any reason, the changes will be in the same direction. Inflation raises prices, increases money income, and may lead to some increase in real income. All three work in the direction of more imports.

Finally note that inflation which worsens the balance of payments, followed by an equivalent depreciation which improves it, will restore the original position of prices, money income, and trade, apart from a dimensional change. This is a widespread pattern among developing countries. The question of particular interest is whether the sequence works the other way, and has causal significance; i.e., that depreciation leads to inflation which offsets its impact on the balance of payments. But first we need to discuss the impact of income changes on the balance of payments, assuming prices constant.

Summary

How effectively the price mechanism will work in international trade depends upon the elasticities of demand and supply. If these elasticities are high, as they would be if the classical assumptions of perfect competition, factor mobility, and constant factor proportions were realized, small price changes would produce large changes in exports and imports. This means that a deficit in the balance of payments could be corrected by a small price change or that the terms of trade would not have to move much.

Elasticities of demand and supply, however, are difficult to deal with in the real world. The elasticity for a given good will change through time and with different degrees of price change. In addition, methods of measurement leave much to be desired. Despite these handicaps to conclusive statements, it is probably true that elasticities in international trade are less now than they were 50 years ago.

The Marshall-Lerner condition requires that the sum of the elasticities of demand—the demand at home for a country's imports and the demand abroad for its exports—be greater than one if depreciation is to improve its balance of payments. This is true whether one deals in the foreign currency or the domestic currency balance. The condition assumes that supply elasticities are high and that the deficit in the balance of payments is not large. If the sum of the elasticities is less than one, currency appreciation will improve the balance.

Price changes cannot be isolated from income changes.

SUGGESTED READING

TEXTS

Yeager, chaps. vi and viii.

TREATISES

See Meade, *The Balance of Payments*, Part IV; and essays by Robinson and Machlup in American Economic Association, *Readings in the Theory of International Trade*, Nos. 4 and 5. See also Egon Sohmen, *Flexible Exchange Rates: Theory and Controversy* (Chicago: The University of Chicago Press, 1961), and on a mathematical level, G. Stuvel, *The Exchange Stability Problem* (Leiden: Stenfert Kruese, 1950).

A. Marshall, *Money, Credit, and Commerce* (New York: Macmillan Co., 1924), Appendix J; and A. P. Lerner, *The Economics of Control* (New York: Macmillan Co., 1944), are the original references for the Marshall-Lerner condition. Modern citation may be made of L. A. Metzler, "The Theory of International Trade," in American Economic Association, *A Survey of Contemporary Economics* (Philadelphia: The Blakiston Co., 1948); and A. O. Hirschman, "Devaluation and the Trade Balance," *RE & S*, February, 1949.

POINTS

The long econometric discussion after the war on the size of the elasticities in international trade is summarized by A. C. Harberger in "Some Evidence on the International Price Mechanism," *JPE*, December, 1957. Harberger is an elasticity optimist.

M. Michaely presents evidence in support of the classical presumption that depreciation will worsen the terms of trade because a demand for a country's exports is less elastic than its demand for imports (i.e., it specializes in production and generalizes in consumption) in *Concentration in International Trade* (Amsterdam: North-Holland Publishing Co., 1962). For a discussion of one-commodity exporting countries, 1913 and 1953, see P. L. Yates, *Forty Years of Foreign Trade* (London: George Allen & Unwin, Ltd., 1959) Table 121 and Appendix Tables 37–45 which present shares of different commodity export markets.

Chapter 16 · INCOME CHANGES AND INTERNATIONAL TRADE

The Assumptions

We now turn from the world in which prices changed and incomes were fixed to a world of constant prices and changing income. This is an analytically interesting world, but it may be no more realistic than the one we have left. And it behooves us, before we enter, to have clearly in mind the various assumptions under which it operates. A few of the major ones are set out here by way of introduction. Others, among them some no less important, will be encountered as we go along.

In the first place, if prices are constant, any change in money income is a change in real income and output. In the next chapter when income and prices both change, we shall have to worry whether imports should be related to real or to money income. The requirement that prices are constant implies that there are unused resources ready to be taken up into production with an increase in spending, or factors ready to withdraw from current employment if spending falls. Full employment is excluded by assumption.

The identity of net national product and national income with constant prices is worth noting. In a closed economy, product and income are identical. But in an open economy they can diverge if the terms of trade change. Suppose output is unchanged from period one to period two but the terms of trade fall owing to a rise in import prices. Net national product is unchanged, but real income must fall. With constant prices, however, this distinction need not worry us. The terms of trade cannot change; and output and income are identical.

Second, we assume away time by using a simultaneous multiplier. Changes in income take time, and it is possible to divide time into spending periods and trace through who pays what to whom at each stage of the process. But the simultaneous multiplier shows the end

271

result of a smoothly operating period analysis. It is neat in exposition. We use it.

Third, all balance-of-payments deficits and surpluses are assumed to be financed in some fashion or other by gold movements, short-term capital, or other means. At this stage the means do not interest us.

As we proceed, other important assumptions will be introduced and explained. A few may be listed here for convenience: functions are linear and constant; imports are for consumption or investment but not for reexport; exports are sold exclusively out of current production. There is no government expenditure nor any taxes.

The Import Function

The relationship between imports and national income is expressed in a variety of ways. One of these is the average propensity to import. This relation is simply the dollar value of imports as a percentage of total national income (M/Y) or the proportion of national income spent on imports. The average propensity to import may vary from low values of 2 or 3 percent, as in the Soviet Union, to 20 to 40 percent in small, highly specialized countries, such as Norway, Belgium, or New Zealand. Too much significance should not be attached to differences in average propensities to import; much will depend upon the size of a country as well as the degree of specialization. Each community in the United States may be as specialized as each community in, say, Britain; but if the United States includes within its borders areas as economically diverse as Maine, Texas, Florida, and Wyoming, the sum total of its communities will find it less necessary to import than those of Britain. Divide a country in two without disturbing trade patterns, for example, and you very much increase the average propensity of each part to import.

More important than the average propensity for many purposes is the marginal propensity to import. This is the *change* in imports associated with a given change in income. In algebraic terms it is dM/dY, where d stands for "the change in." If imports rise by $100 million, when income increases by $1 billion, then the marginal propensity to import will be 0.10.

The marginal propensity to import is likely to differ from the average propensity to import. Two typical cases may be cited. Brazil, for example, supplies most of its basic needs but has a standard of living close to the subsistence level. Improvement in the standard of living leads to the import of new types of goods not available at home. In this case the average propensity to import is low, but the marginal propensity may be high. Contrast with this the case of a country like Britain, which imports a number of necessities such as wheat and tobacco (and movies?) and produces luxury products at home. In this case the average propensity to import is high, but the marginal propensity low.

The relation between the average propensity to import and the marginal propensity is expressed by the ratio called "income elasticity." This is more usually thought of as the percentage change in imports associated with a given percentage change in national income. If a 5 percent increase in national income produces a 10 percent increase in the value of imports, then the income elasticity of imports is relatively high—to be exact, 2. If, on the other hand, a 5 percent increase in national income produces a change in imports of only 2½ percent, then imports are income inelastic, or 0.5. When a given percentage change in income leads to an equal percentage change in imports, the income elasticity of demand for imports is unity, or 1.

Expressed in algebraic terms, income elasticity is measured by $(dM/M)/(dY/Y)$, which is the percentage change in imports associated with a given percentage change in national income. Since

$$\frac{dM/M}{dY/Y} = \frac{dM/dY}{M/Y},$$

income elasticity can be computed by dividing the marginal propensity to import by the average propensity. If these are the same value, the income elasticity of imports is unitary, or, in other words, a given percentage change in national income will produce a change of equal percentage in imports.

The average propensity to import at various levels of national income is the import schedule or propensity to import. This is shown in Figure 16.1, where $M(Y)$—in mathematical language, imports as a function of national income—is the propensity to import of the econ-

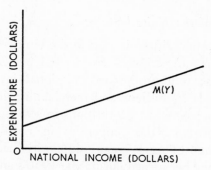

FIG. 16.1. The Propensity to Import

omy. It does not pass through the origin at 0, because at zero national income some imports may still be bought from abroad out of reserves. The marginal propensity to import is the slope of $M(Y)$. The assumption that $M(Y)$ is a straight line is, of course, an unreal simplifying aid to analysis.

The use of mathematic symbols to represent the various propensities and elasticities must not beguile the reader into thinking that the numerical values of these concepts for a country are constant under all conditions and circumstances. We shall assume that they are, but this is only for simplicity. In the real world, for example, the marginal propensity of a country to import may in actuality differ sharply between one given year during which the increase of national income occurs in the manufacturing sector of the economy, and another, when it occurs in the agricultural. Or the marginal propensity to import may differ for a country in depression and prosperity or in mild prosperity, with excess capacity available in domestic industry, as compared with an inflationary boom of full capacity, when additional purchases in the short run can only be made abroad.

Still once more, the marginal propensity to import will differ between one period of prosperity in which the upswing in national income is generated by long-term investment in, say, housing, which in the United States uses little imported material, and another boom in which short-term investment in inventories is large, or one in which the autonomous change occurs in expenditure for durable consumers' goods. The marginal propensity to import has proved high in business cycles in which inventory investment was prominent, as in 1936–37 and 1949–50. It tends to rise as full employment capacity is reached. It is convenient for theoretical analysis to think of the marginal propensities as fixed and eternal. It is dangerous to get so used to this teaching device that we drift into thinking of them as unchanging in the real world.

Propensities of the United States

The average propensity to import in the United States is now just over 4 percent. This means that 4 percent (4.1 percent to be exact) of national income is spent on imports. National income in 1966 in current prices was $610 billions and merchandise imports $25.2 billions. (In 1966, income was $526 billions in 1958 prices and imports $24.2 billions, to make the propensity in real terms—on 1958 prices—4.6 percent.) This average propensity had been declining slowly over the years, but turned during the 1950's and 1960's. Early in the 19th century it stood at 10 percent. After World War I, it fell to 7 percent, and after World War II to 3 percent. Since full European recovery, however, the trend has turned, and imports have risen relatively to national income. Such a reversal had been anticipated because of depletion of raw materials, which was expected to lead to more complete reliance on imports. In actuality, the substantial increases in imports in the period after World War II occurred in manufactures as the American consumer became more conscious of the variety of products available throughout the world.

The marginal propensity to import in the United States has been close to 7 percent (6.8 percent in 1965 and 7.4 percent in 1966). This means that 7 cents out of every additional dollar of income is spent on imports. But this marginal propensity to import can change, as pointed out, depending upon the circumstances of the period. In the 1950's it tended to be 4 percent or identical with the average propensity of about 4 percent. In the middle of the 1960's, with the U.S. economy reaching full employment, more of national income spilled over into imports than was true when unemployment was substantial.

With the average propensity to import at 4.1 percent in current dollars and the marginal propensity to import at 7.4 percent, the income of elasticity of demand for imports amounts to 1.8.

In what follows we assume that imports are entirely for consumption rather than investment or to hold as capital assets. This is an unreal but useful assumption and implies that imports are an alternative to domestic spending and extinguish income. The implications of relaxing this assumption will be explored subsequently.

Exports and National Income

As already noted, we assume that exports take place out of current production rather than from past production, such as disinvestment of inventories, or transfers of existing assets, such as antiques and rare paintings. This means that exports increase income.

Exports, moreover, are assumed to be a constant at every level of national income rather than a positive or negative function of income. Figure 16.2 shows this relationship. Implicit in it is the assumption that the country exports commodities which it either does not consume at all or for which its demand is income inelastic. This assumption is appropriate for a primary producing country—Dutch Guiana exporting bauxite but consuming none of it, or Australia exporting wheat and wool. But it is unrealistic for those countries which export manufactured products, particularly consumers' goods. In Britain, exports and consumption, and exports and investment are both competitive rather than

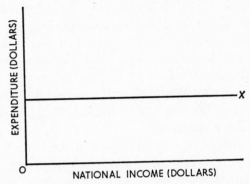

FIG. 16.2. Exports Constant at Every Level of National Income

independent as we show them. An increase in income under this circumstance will lower exports, and exports may be taken as a falling function of income. In what follows, this complication is ignored.

The Multiplier in a Closed Economy

We propose to construct the foreign-trade multiplier by analogy with the domestic. This means representing the simplest kind of system in which there are savings and investment schedules (but no government expenditure, taxes, transfers, or similar complications). Savings are a rising function of national income with a negative vertical intercept (i.e., dissaving occurs at zero national income), as in Figure 16.3*a*. Investment is a constant at every level of national income, as in Figure 16.3*b*. Superimposing the investment on the savings schedule in Figure 16.3*c* gives us the equilibrium level of national income, Y, where

Income produced = Income received = Income spent

Income produced is the sum of consumption goods and services and investment goods $(C + I)$; income received equals consumption

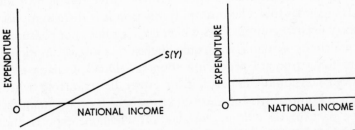

FIG. 16.3*a*. The Savings Schedule   FIG. 16.3*b*. The Investment Schedule

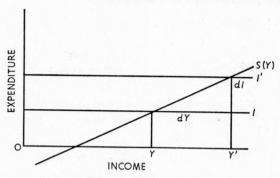

FIG. 16.3c.   The Multiplier in a Closed Economy

plus savings $(C + S)$. We define investment goods to include any goods originally intended for consumption and not sold. On this definition the value of consumption goods produced equals the value of consumption goods consumed. From this,

$$C + I = C + S$$
$$C = C$$

Therefore

$$I = S .$$

The equilibrium level of national income, therefore, is that level where the investment and the savings schedules intersect.

If now there is an autonomous change in the investment schedule, from I to I' in Figure 16.3c, national income is increased. The amount of the increase is determined by the increase in investment and the domestic multiplier. Using the symbol d for the change in, we want to find dY from dI. This is done either geometrically from the characteristics of the triangle combining them in Figure 16.3c, or by simple algebra. In Figure 16.3c, dY is dI times the reciprocal of the slope of $S(Y)$. The slope of $S(Y)$ is $\dfrac{dS}{dY}$, so that the multiplier, by which we have to multiply dI to get dY, is $\dfrac{1}{\dfrac{dS}{dY}}$ or $\dfrac{1}{MPS}$, where MPS is the marginal propensity to save.

Algebraically, $I = S$ at equilibrium levels of national income. Therefore in equilibrium

$$dI = dS .$$

Dividing both sides into dY, we get

$$\frac{dY}{dI} = \frac{dY}{dS} \quad \text{or} \quad \frac{1}{\frac{dS}{dY}} \quad \text{or} \quad \frac{1}{MPS}.$$

This is the domestic multiplier in a closed economy. The change in income equals the change in investment times the multiplier,

$$dY = \frac{dI}{MPS}.$$

The question now presents itself, what is the foreign-trade multiplier? Assume a change in exports, dX, what is dY? Or $\frac{dY}{dX}$, the foreign-trade multiplier, equals what?

The Foreign-Trade Multiplier—No Savings, No Investment

In an open economy with foreign trade, goods produced (Y) plus imports (M) are equal to goods bought ($C + I$) plus goods exported (X). It is assumed, still, that there is no government. If there are no savings and no investment, all income is spent on consumption and Y must equal C.

Since

$$Y + M = C + I + X$$

and

$$I = 0, Y = C$$

∴

$$X = M$$

and exports are equal to imports at equilibrium levels of income. Given the schedules of exports and imports, as in Figures 16.1 and 16.2, one can determine the level of national income. This is done in Figure 16.4,

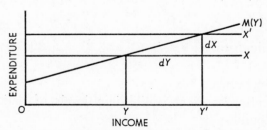

FIG. 16.4. The Foreign-Trade Multiplier, No Savings

which combines the two early schedules exactly as Figure 16.3*c* combined 16.3*a* and 16.3*b*.

By comparable steps, we can derive the foreign-trade multiplier for this simple economy. If exports shift from X to X', the change in income, from Y to Y', is the change in exports multiplied by the reciprocal of the slope of the import schedule, or the reciprocal of the marginal propensity to import. In algebra

$$X = M$$

at equilibrium levels of national income.

Therefore in equilibrium

$$dX = dM .$$

Dividing both sides into dY we get

$$\frac{dY}{dX} = \frac{dY}{dM} \quad \text{or} \quad \frac{1}{\dfrac{dM}{dY}} \quad \text{or} \quad \frac{1}{MPM} .$$

Any continuing increase in exports in an open economy without domestic savings or investment will raise the equilibrium level of national income to the point where the increment of new exports is matched by an equal increase in imports. With no savings, the increased spending injected into the system by the increased exports can be spent on consumption (which increases income) or spent on imports. In a period multiplier, at each round of spending current income is divided between consumption and imports, and every increase in income is also divided between them (though perhaps on a different basis if the marginal propensity differs from the average). Income will continue to grow because of increases in consumption until the cumulative increase in imports offsets the autonomous injection of new spending from exports.

A shift in the import schedule will also affect national income, as Figure 16.5 illustrates. Here exports remain unchanged, but imports are assumed to be reduced at each level of income from what they would have been. Such a shift in the import function may occur because of a change in tastes, or an internal shift in the distribution of income, or any one of a number of possible causes. It might have been caused by a rise in prices brought about by foreign inflation or by a tariff, except that we have excluded price changes from our analysis by assumption. It should be noted that the actual level of imports does not change. Under the conditions assumed, the reduction in the readiness to import at the old

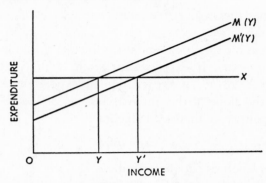

FIG. 16.5. The Foreign-Trade Multiplier, Shift in the Propensity to Import

national income leads to such an increase in income that imports are built up again to their original level. The shift *of* the schedule, that is, is matched by a movement *along* the schedule. If the propensity to import were changed by an increase in tariffs, for example, the defenders of the tariff might argue that the tariff had no effect because the level of imports was unchanged. This would not be true. There would be no balance-of-payments effect because the shift *of* the import schedule would give rise to a change in income sufficient to produce an equivalent shift *along* the import schedule in the new position. The income effect, that is, would wipe out any balance-of-payments effect. (This is the discussion of the income effect, and the first installment of that on the balance-of-payments effect of a tariff, which we have owed the reader since Chapter 7).

Note that with no savings or investment, exports always equal imports. This is the world of David Hume, in which it made no sense to try to increase exports, since all increases in exports would be offset by increases in imports. Hume used the specie-flow analysis, relying on price rather than income. But it works more effectively through income, provided that there are no savings. Hume's law that exports equal imports is the foreign-trade equivalent of Say's law of markets that demand equals supply. And it is equally invalidated by the introduction of savings.

The Foreign-Trade Multiplier—Savings

With savings and investment present, the equilibrium condition of national income is still

$$I = S,$$

but investment (I) breaks down into two parts, domestic (I_d) and foreign (I_f).

$$I_d + I_f = S .$$

Foreign investment is the difference between exports of goods and services and imports of goods and services.

$$I_f = X - M .$$

Substituting this in the previous equation we get

$$I_d + X - M = S$$

or

$$I_d + X = S + M ,$$

which is the basic equilibrium condition of national income in an open economy.

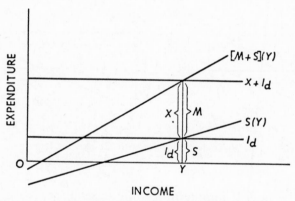

FIG. 16.6.   The Foreign-Trade Multiplier with Savings and Domestic Investment

This is readily diagrammed by adding the domestic investment schedule in Figure 16.3*b* and the export schedule in Figure 16.2, on the one hand, and the import and savings functions in Figure 16.1 and 16.3*a*, respectively, on the other. This is done in Figure 16.6.

The multiplier is now the reciprocal of the slope of the sum of the two functions $M(Y)$ and $S(Y)$, and will be the same for an increase in exports or an increase in investment. To take the former only, in algebraic terms, with domestic investment constant at all levels of national income and

$$X + I_d = S + M ,$$

the change in exports must be equal to the change in savings plus the change in imports. Expressing this as

$$dX = dS + dM ,$$

we can divide both sides of the equation into dY and derive

$$\frac{dY}{dX} = \frac{dY}{dS + dM} ,$$

$\frac{dY}{dX}$ is k (the multiplier) ,

$$k = \frac{dY}{dS + dM} \quad \text{or} \quad \frac{1}{(dS/dY) + (dM/dY)} \quad \text{or} \quad \frac{1}{MPS + MPM} .$$

The diagram has been drawn in Figure 16.6 so that $I_d = S$ and $X = M$, at the equilibrium level of national income Y. This is not

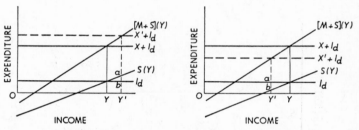

FIG. 16.7a. Increase in Exports   FIG. 16.7b. Decrease in Exports

The Foreign-Trade Multiplier with Changes in Exports

necessarily the case. If long-term lending takes place, X can exceed M, provided that S exceeds I_d by an equal amount sufficient to maintain the equation $I_d + X = S + M$. With a higher level of exports than X, say X' in Figure 16.7a, exports will exceed imports by the amount ab, the amount by which savings will exceed domestic investment. If exports were to fall to X' in Figure 16.7b, however, imports would exceed exports, and domestic investment would exceed savings. The export surplus in the first case can be regarded as a deduction from savings; generally, however, it is thought of as positive foreign investment. In the second case the import surplus may be regarded either as a supplement to savings or as negative investment to be subtracted from I_d.

The new equilibrium of national income where savings differ from domestic investment by the amount by which exports differ from imports, care being taken to get the signs right, emphasizes that we have been talking about national income equilibrium, not balance-of-payments equilibrium. Any leakage, whether into imports or savings, is good enough to offset the factors tending to raise income. And the student will recall that we abstracted from balance-of-payments difficulties, at an early stage in this chapter, by assuming that any foreign-trade balance could be financed.

It will be appreciated that the leverage working to change national income at each stage is the change in consumption based on the increase in income in the previous period. On this basis, the analysis can be broadened to include other leakages, such as taxes and corporation profits.

Income Changes and the Balance of Payments

Figures 16.7*a* and 16.7*b* are appropriate enough for illustrating the equilibrium condition for national income. They fail, however, to show very clearly the effect on the balance of payments. For this purpose it is useful to express the equilibrium condition of national income in another way. Instead of

$$X + I_d = S + M,$$

we can transpose I_d and M, and get

$$X - M = S - I_d,$$

which is to say that the balance of payments on current account equals the difference between savings and domestic investment. This can equally be diagrammed. It requires only that we subtract the import from the export schedule, on the one hand (Figure 16.1 from Figure 16.2), and the domestic investment from the saving schedule, on the other (Figure 16.3*b* from Figure 16.3*a*). This is done in Figure 16.8. The combined $X–M$ schedule is downward sloping because the upward-sloping import schedule is subtracted from a constant level of exports. This indicates that the balance of payments is positive at low levels of national income and declines as income rises. The $S–I_d$ schedule is upward sloping because savings increase with increasing income and have a positive sign, while investment is constant. The intersection of the two schedules gives the equilibrium level of national income and the balance-of-payments position. In Figure 16.8 as drawn, the two schedules intersect with zero balance of payments. But as already indicated at some length, this is not necessary.

This diagram is not well suited for showing the multiplier, but it can indicate what happens to the balance of payments, as well as to the national income, as a result of a change in any of the four schedules. An increase in domestic investment will displace the $S-I_d$ schedule downward to $S-I'_d$ because the negative term is increased. This will raise national income from Y to Y' and open up a balance-of-payments deficit. The deficit $(X-M)$ is less than the amount of the increase in investment (dI_d) because the movement along the schedule, represented by increased savings, partly offsets the shift of the schedule, represented by additional investment.

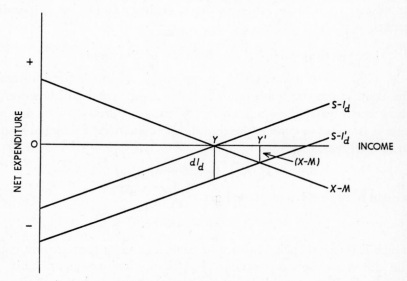

FIG. 16.8.   The Balance-of-Payments Effect of a Change in Investment

One can as readily explore the impact of changes in the other schedules—an increase or decrease in exports, which would move the $X-M$ schedule up or down, respectively; a change in the import schedule down or up, which would have the same effects on the $X-M$ as a whole; or a change in the propensity to save. Increases in exports, decreases in imports, decreases in investment, and increases in savings all help the balance of payments. And movements in the opposite direction hurt it.

We can see from this diagram what it would mean if exports declined with increased income because of the competition between exports and consumption or investment such as occurs in a number of countries selling manufactures, like Britain. The negative slope of the $X-M$ curve would be steeper; the balance-of-payments effect of a given shift in any of the schedules would be greater; and the income effect would be reduced.

Foreign Repercussion

An important extension of this analysis may be introduced by the foreign repercussion, which is the effect of the change in exports and/or imports on national income abroad, and the backwash effect which this has on foreign trade and national income at home. If the country we are considering is small in relation to the outside world, the foreign repercussion can be neglected. An increase in such a country's imports will not stimulate income abroad by significant amounts. And even if there were a noticeable effect on income abroad, the repercussion may still be small if the marginal propensity of the countries affected to import from the original country is small. An increase in income in New Zealand may be sufficient to raise income in Britain (through the resultant increase in British exports to New Zealand and the multiplier), but it is unlikely to have any further repercussion in New Zealand because the British marginal propensity to import from New Zealand, let us say by way of illustration, is so small.

With large countries, however, the foreign repercussion is likely to be significant. The United States accounts for virtually 40 percent of world money income. An expansion in U.S. income increases its imports from the world, the world's money income, and in turn the world's imports from the United States. This feedback raises U.S. income still further. Where the system will come to rest depends upon the marginal propensities to save and import in the United States, and those in the rest of the world as well.

The interaction can be set out in a series of stages, as in Figure 16.9. At stage 1, the United States increases its domestic investment (to Id'), which spills over into imports from the rest of the world, i.e., the movement along the import schedule from the position at Y to that at Y'. To the rest of the world this appears at stage 2 as a shift of its export schedule. Exports rise, and with them by means of the multiplier, income, and in turn imports. This last shift feeds back to the United States as an increase in exports, which helps to dampen the original import surplus, but raises income still further, inducing still another increase in imports. Back to the rest of the world: exports rise, income, and imports ditto. And so on. Successive stages of smaller and smaller changes could be diagrammed until the system came to rest.

A simultaneous geometric representation of the foreign repercus-

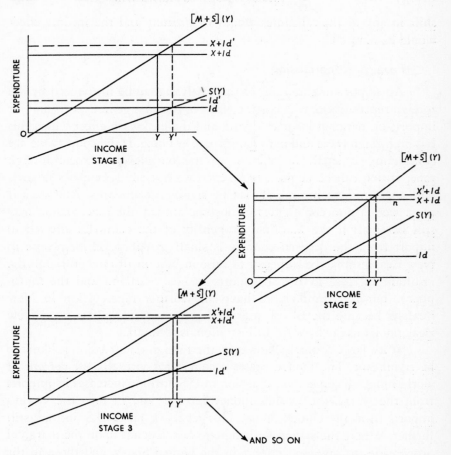

FIG. 16.9. The National Income Multiplier, with Foreign Repercussion, by Stages

sion has been worked out in which national income in each of two countries is expressed as a function of national income in the other. In Figure 16.10, for example, national income in A is expressed as a function of national income in B. Even if B's income is zero, A's income will be what it is from consumption, investment expenditure, and government expenditure in A, which are entirely independent of what is taking place in B. This independence is shown by the fact that the sum $Ca + Ida + Ga$ is a horizontal line, which means that it is constant at all levels of B's income.

Exports in A create income, however, whose size is not independent of the level of income in B. In Figure 16.10, B is assumed to import from A even at no income. This creates some income directly

(*Xa* at the vertical axis) and, through the foreign-trade multiplier in A, induces some further increases in consumption (*dCa*). As B's income increases, A's exports increase and, with them, the induced increase in spending dependent on exports.

The total of the three lines indicates the level of income in A at various levels of national income in B.

A similar representation of income in B as a function of income in A can be drawn on the same diagram. This is done in Figure 16.11,

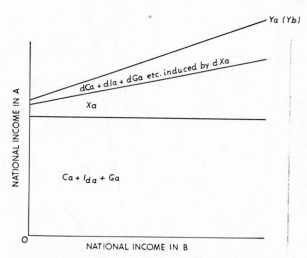

FIG. 16.10. Income in A as a Function of Income in B

where line *A* reflects income in A as a function of income in B, and line *B,* income in B as a function of A. If these two lines intersect in a stable system, the interaction between the national incomes of the two countries is indicated. Now, if national income in B rises because of a change of any sort—let us say, in this case, because of an increase in investment in B—the line representing B's income as a function of income of A will be displaced to the right, since B's national income will be higher even if national income in A is zero. In Figure 16.11, line *B* is displaced to *B'*. This will raise national income in A from *Y* to *Y'*. Notice that national income in B has increased by more than the displacement of income, i.e., that the distance between *Y* and *Y'* along the *B* axis is greater than the amount by which the *B* function was displaced. This is because the increase in investment in B raised national income in B, imports from A, and hence national income in A, imports from B (or B's exports), and national income in B again.

This analysis can be used to demonstrate the interaction of national incomes in two countries (or in one country and the rest of the world taken as a whole) under a variety of circumstances. A change in the marginal propensities in B, whether to save, to import, to tax, or any other, will alter the slope of the curve of B's income as a function of income in A. This will produce a change in national income in both countries. A change in tastes in B which decreases domestic consump-

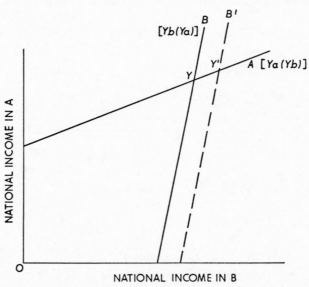

FIG. 16.11. Simultaneous Representation of the Foreign Repercussion

tion in B and increases imports from A will displace both curves simultaneously but will lead to a unique new equilibrium, so long as the two curves continue to intersect. This diagrammatic analysis, which is needed where the foreign repercussion is important, is capable of handling all the various foreign-trade multipliers.

The derivation of these multipliers is given in an appendix to this chapter. Here it is sufficient to give a pair of formulas, one for a change in foreign trade and one for a change in domestic investment. The foreign-trade multipliers depend, of course, on the marginal propensities to save and import at home, which determine how much of the original increase in exports will be spent on consumption at home, in the first instance, and on the marginal propensities to save and spend abroad, which determine, first, how much of a change in income abroad is brought about by the original decrease in consumption and, second, how much of this is communicated through imports back again to A. The formula for the multiplier for an autonomous change in exports is

$$k = \frac{1}{MPSa + MPMa + MPMb(MPSa/MPSb)} \,.$$

This multiplier in A will be larger as

> the marginal propensity to import in A is smaller,
> the marginal propensity to save in A is smaller,
> the marginal propensity to import in B is smaller,

and

> the marginal propensity to save in B is larger.

The first two propensities cut down the leakage of income in A and ensure that the first and successive doses of expenditure arising from the increase in exports will be larger than otherwise. The effect of a small marginal propensity to import in B is to increase the multiplier in A, since it limits the induced decline in A's exports resulting from any decline in income in B. Finally, the larger the marginal propensity to save in B, the smaller will be the decline in income and the smaller, in turn, the induced decline in A's exports.

All these relationships can be expressed inversely, of course, but we may limit ourselves to one. If the propensity to import abroad is large, the multiplier in A will be small because the decrease in income abroad will be quickly translated into decreased imports as an offset to the original increase in A's exports.

The multiplier for an autonomous change in home investment is

$$k = \frac{1 + (MPMb/MPSb)}{MPSa + MPMa + MPMb(MPSa/MPSb)} \,.$$

This value is larger than the multiplier for an autonomous change in exports, because the foreign repercussion is working in the same direction as the increase in domestic investment, rather than against it, as in the case of the change in exports.

One reminder may be useful before we leave the foreign-trade multiplier and the foreign repercussion. If the rest of the world (country B in our illustration) is large relative to country A and consists of many countries, the foreign repercussion can be neglected. Each country may have a large propensity to import overall, but its marginal propensity to import from country A is likely to be small. The foreign repercussion is a negligible element, that is, in the foreign-trade multiplier for Guatemala and New Zealand and Egypt. It can, however, be neglected only with great peril in a discussion of the foreign trade of the United States or of western Europe.

The student must once again be warned that the discussion in this chapter, though complicated, has relied upon a wide range of simplifying assumptions which serve to clarify the exposition of basic principles. In light of present (and still unsettled) discussion on income determination, it is worth pausing to pay tribute to some of the important qualifications to the basic model.

Mainly through empirical studies in the postwar period, it has been realized that the multiplier relationship described here, though valid as a tendency, is far from an adequate description of reality. The consumption (or savings) function may not be a straight line, for, as incomes increase, the marginal propensity to save may increase. Indeed, as with the permanent income hypothesis, increments in income that are considered windfalls may be entirely saved. Variables other than current income show significant effects upon consumption and savings behavior, including past income and consumption levels and past savings now embodied in wealth held as real property, stocks, bonds and savings deposits. And, of course, price changes occur over time.

With the admission of time into the system, we run into the problem of lags and the possibility of accelerators, which operate in a dynamic world lying beyond the static model outlined above. The investment functions employed have been linear and horizontal, unchanging with respect to income changes. But changes in income, say through increased consumption, may induce changes in the level of investment. As production of consumption goods increases to meet higher final demand, especially as full capacity of the system is approached, investment is increased to provide new machinery and equipment for further expansion of output. As long as the rate of increase of consumer demand is itself increasing, there will be a growing demand for investment goods. Once the rate of increase falls off, investment demand will fall absolutely. With less investment, the multiplier will work to decrease income, hence also to decrease consumption. With this line of causality in mind, accelerator-multiplier models have been developed to describe business cycles and fluctuations around a long-term growth trend.

In foreign trade there may on occasion be an effect comparable to the domestic accelerator. We may call it the "foreign-trade accelerator." An increase in exports leads through increases in investment to an import surplus. The increase in investment may take place in the export industries themselves: an increase in American tourist expenditure in London may lead to the construction of more hotels. Or the general prosperity created by expanded exports may lead to new investment in industries producing for home consumption.

This accelerator effect may be also demonstrated in successive steps. In the first period there will be an increase in exports. This will raise national income and consumption in the second. The increase in exports and induced consumption requires an enlargement in capacity, so that the third period produces an increase in investment, which in turn stimulates income and consumption. And so on.

The simple accelerator itself has fallen into disrepute in theoretical and empirical literature due to its restrictive assumptions. And since most national income theorists work with closed economies, the trade economist must wait while the complex arguments over closed systems are settled before applying the results to a many country world. But just as accelerators exist in domestic economies and produce the business cycle, so may they, from time to time, and under particular circumstances, be found in international economics. And when they are, an increase in exports, starting from a balanced position, will produce an import surplus, or a decline in exports, an export surplus.

The Sum of the Marginal Propensities to Import

In a two-country world, it makes a considerable difference for many problems whether the sum of the marginal propensities to import is greater than, equal to, or smaller than one. Start from an increase in spending in A, matched by an equal decrease in B. Provided that the marginal propensities to save in the two countries are equal, if the sum of the marginal propensities to import is exactly one, national incomes will be unchanged in the two countries taken together and the balance of payments will turn against A and in favor of B by an amount equal to the change in spending. If the change in spending is 100, and the marginal propensities in each case are 0.5, the demonstration is easy. A's increase in spending is half on domestic goods and half on imports. Imports rise by 50. Similarly B's decrease in spending is half on domestic goods and half on imports. Its imports fall by 50. The decline of 50 in exports and increase of 50 in imports in A turns the balance of trade against it by 100, and this disinvestment offsets the original increase in expenditure to maintain national income. The converse holds in B.

If the values in A and B are somewhat altered but the sum of the marginal propensities to import still amounts to one, the same results hold. If the marginal propensities to import are 0.4 in A and 0.6 in B,

A's exports fall by 60, while imports rise by 40 to produce the identical outcome.

If the sum of the marginal propensities to import exceeds one, the balance-of-payments change is greater than the original change in spending. Take *MPM*'s of 0.5 in A and 0.6 in B. The initial impact will be an increase in 50 of imports in A and a decline of 60 in exports. The disinvestment represented by the initial balance-of-payments deficit of 110 exceeds the original increase in spending in A, and A's income declines. Conversely, B's income will increase because the export surplus exceeds the decline in expenditure.

If the sum of the marginal propensities to import is less than one, on the other hand, an increase in expenditure in A and a decrease in B will result in an increase in income in A, a decrease in income in B, and a balance-of-payments change which is less than the original changes in spending. This is generally regarded as the normal case. It is believed that countries spend more on home goods than on imports because of transport costs, which make it impossible for many heavy and perishable goods to move in trade at all. If A's *MPM* is 0.3 and B's is 0.2, an increase in spending of 100 in A matched by an equal decrease in B will produce an initial balance-of-payments deficit for A (surplus for B) of 50, and leave an extra 50 of domestic spending in A, and the contrary in B, to produce changes in national income in the directions indicated. What the final changes in the balance of payments and national income will be, however, cannot be told without knowledge of the *MPS*'s and the multipliers.

The Money Supply

The bright student who has gone beyond Keynes in macroeconomics to the rediscovery of money will observe that this chapter and Chapter 15 paid virtually no attention to the money supply. Money was mentioned in connection with the price-specie-flow mechanism and the price level in Chapter 15. It has not been referred to in this, despite the development of the Hicks and Patinkin systems which incorporate the money supply into spending. Let this student be patient as well as bright. We save the impact of the interest rate until much later, Chapter 26, in fact, when we can bring short-term capital movements into the adjustment process. Some economists believe that the money supply has a fairly direct impact on imports, through switches between savings and imports, i.e., that the interest rate is one of the prices which should be taken into account in the previous chapter. Others think that spending is a function of the money supply, rather than of income. In this day and age when capital is free to move, however, both these connections seem less important than the role of the money supply on short-term capital movements. We wait.

Summary

While Hume was concerned with price effects and our interest is in income, Hume's law that exports equal imports is valid only under conditions of no savings. In the absence of savings, an increase in exports will increase income to the point where sufficient additional imports are created to offset exports. The amount by which national income will increase is the increase in exports times a multiplier equal to $1/MPM$. But if savings take place, the increase in exports will be balanced by increases in imports and in savings, provided that investment is unchanged. In this case the multiplier is $1/(MPM + MPS)$.

The foreign-trade multiplier expresses the change in income caused by a change in exports or in investment in an open economy in which income spills over into imports.

If the effect of the change in imports on income abroad is significant and if the effect of income changes abroad on a country's exports is again appreciable, there is a foreign repercussion. More complex formulas are now necessary to express the relationships among savings and import propensities in the countries involved.

If an accelerator is at work so that an increase in income due to a rise in exports leads to an increase in investment, the increase in exports may produce a larger increase in imports and turn the balance of trade unfavorably.

SUGGESTED READING

TEXTS

See Yeager, chap. v. An old, but complete treatment is given by D. B. Marsh in *World Trade and Investment* (New York: Harcourt, Brace & Co., Inc., 1951).

TREATISES

Meade, *The Balance of Payments,* Parts II and III, gives a simultaneous analysis based on a generalized technique for solving problems. F. Machlup, *International Trade and the National Income Multiplier* (Philadelphia: The Blakiston Co., 1943) (reprinted by Augustus M. Kelley, Publishers, 1965), is an early work but uses a period analysis. Some teachers swear by Lloyd A. Metzler, "Underemployment Equilibrium in International Trade," *Econometrica,* 1942. Among the pioneer writing, see J. M. Keynes, *The General Theory of Employ-*

ment, Interest, and Money (New York: Harcourt, Brace & Co., Inc., 1936), chap. xxi.

The refined treatment of the foreign repercussion used in the chapter is taken from R. Robinson's interesting "A Graphical Analysis of the Foreign Trade Multiplier," *EJ,* September, 1952.

Another graphical analysis which the student may enjoy is J. Black, "A Geometrical Analysis of the Foreign-Trade Multiplier," *EJ,* June, 1957.

POINTS

Modern econometric model-building relying on this sort of income analysis is found in chapters in L. Klein and A. Goldberger, *An Econometric Model of the United States, 1929–1952* (Amsterdam: North-Holland Publishing Co. 1955); and by R. Rhomberg and L. Boissonneault, in J. Duesenberry, G Fromm, L. Klein and E. Kuh (eds.), *Brookings Quarterly Econometric Model of the United States* (Chicago: Rand McNally & Co., 1965). The latter includes price, has exports dependent on world income, and disaggregates imports.

Chapter 17

INTERACTIONS OF INCOME AND PRICE

The Assumptions

We move now from the worlds of price changes with income constant and income changes with prices constant to a more realistic world in which income and price are both free to move. The difficulty with this world is that it is, so to speak, underdetermined. Anything can happen: there are too many unknowns and not enough equations. It is impossible to discuss international adjustment with this many degrees of freedom. We are obliged, therefore, to pose certain problems, and to see how the mechanism works under more narrowly specified conditions.

The mathematical language of that paragraph—"underdetermined," "number of unknowns and equations," etc.—should not distress the student lacking competence and/or confidence in mathematics above the high school level. This is the sort of subject which lends itself to mathematical treatment, perhaps, but we shall remain in the highly simplified world of prose. The reasons lie not only in the possible fears of the reader but also in the competence of the writer.

Out of a wide variety of possible cases, we will discuss six types. They are:

1. The balance-of-payments and income effects of devaluation
2. Depreciation under full employment
3. Structural inflation and income redistribution
4. Flexible exchange rates with balanced trade
5. Changed productivity
6. Changes in income and price abroad

The Balance-of-Payments and Income Effects of Devaluation

We may start out by reviewing the simple fact that the balance-of-payments effect of devaluation and the income effect are closely linked. In Figure 17.1, let us assume that depreciation shifts the $X–M$ schedule upward,[1] because the sum of the elasticities is greater than one. The net improvement in the balance of payments will be less than the amount by which the schedule is displaced, because the initial balance-of-payments effect produces an income effect, that is the shift from Y to Y' consequent upon the shift of the $X–M$ schedule to $X'–M'$.

What determines how much the initial impact of depreciation will be cut down? The answer is obvious: it is the slope of the $S–Id$ schedule. If this is very steep, so that the multiplier is very small, the final balance-of-payments effect will be very much like the initial impact. But if the $S–Id$ schedule is relatively flat, the income effect will greatly modify the balance-of-payments effect in the long run.

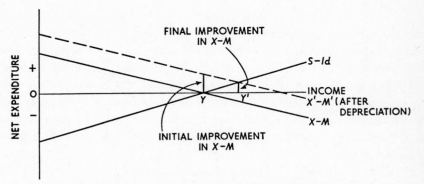

FIG. 17.1. The Balance-of-Payments Effect of Depreciation

This emphasis on the income effect of exchange depreciation leads us to make the further point that some exchange rate changes are undertaken not for their influence on the balance of payments, but to promote income expansion or to hold it down. This was the point of the Canadian effort in 1961 to get the Canadian dollar down from $1.05 in terms of U.S. dollars. Or upward revaluation of the exchange can be adopted as a counterinflationary move: witness the New Zealand revaluation of 1948. Similarly in 1961, the German mark was revalued upward by 5 percent largely to dampen down the overheating of the economy. Whether the income or the balance-of-payments effect will be

[1] Observe that we have to be careful in using the income diagram for cases where prices change. In this diagram, money and real income are identical, and since prices are constant under all circumstances, a change in the $X–M$ schedule can be independent of changes in $S–I_d$. Not so when prices change. Strictly speaking we should stay away from the income diagram; but we propose to use it circumspectly.

the more pronounced depends, of course, on the slope of the *S–Id* schedule. When this schedule is flat, depreciation produces pure inflation, as in Figure 17.2 and the balance-of-payments effect is nil. When it is steeply sloped upward, the balance-of-payments effect will be large and the income effect small. Without knowing what is going to happen to savings, the monetary authorities can get fooled, adopting exchange rate change for balance-of-payments reasons and getting an income effect (if the marginal propensity to save is much lower—and the

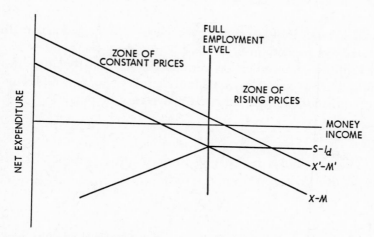

FIG. 17.2.   Failure of Depreciation to Improve the Balance of Payments
in Absence of "Money Illusion," Etc.

multiplier much higher—than estimated), or seeking an income effect and achieving a change is the balance of payments.

Depreciation under Full Employment

So much follows on the Keynesian analysis, which requires that the supplies of other factors be elastic, i.e., that land, labor, and capital are available in abundance at constant prices, and that changes in money income are equivalent to changes in real income. The literature which produced the Marshall-Lerner condition was for the most part fashioned during the great depression of the 1930's, when this was broadly true. But does it apply under conditions of full employment?

Note that the final improvement in the balance of payments in Figure 17.1 can be regarded either as the initial improvement in the balance of payments, less the increase in real income times the marginal propensity to import; or as the marginal propensity to save times the increase in real income. The net improvement in the balance of payments is matched by an increase in savings.

The point may be put algebraically. The equilibrium condition of national income is

$$Y = C + Id + G + X - M.$$

If we transpose a bit and change signs, we get

$$X - M = Y - (C + Id + G).$$

The balance of payments on current account is equal to Income produced less Expenditure.

Professor Alexander has introduced into the literature the term "Absorption" to cover the expenditure terms $C + Id + G$. Using A for absorption and B for the balance of payments, he puts it

$$B = Y - A.$$

This also holds for changes from a given position. Using small letters to designate changes in variables,

$$b = y - a.$$

The change in the balance of payments equals the change in output less the change in expenditure.

With less than full employment, the balance of payments can be improved by increasing output more than absorption, or by sliding along an $S–Id$ schedule which is positively sloped. But under conditions of full employment, such as obtain in underdeveloped countries and have applied in developed countries for most of the period since World War II, it is by no means clear that Y can be increased. In these circumstances, the possibilities of improving the balance of payments by depreciation, Alexander insists, turn on whether absorption can be reduced. What is the mechanism by which exchange depreciation can increase savings or decrease absorption?

One possibility is "money illusion." Suppose savings are a positively rising function of money income rather than of real income. This implies "money illusion," i.e., that spending habits respond to money incomes without reference to the level of prices. Under exchange depreciation, people would reduce the proportion of income spent if money incomes rose, despite the fact that prices were rising along with them and real incomes were constant. It would in fact leave us in the position indicated by Figure 17.1, provided the horizontal axis represented "money income" and not "real income" as well. An upward shift in the $X–M$ schedule would intercept the $S–I_d$ schedule at a higher money income and identical national output, but real savings would increase and the balance of payments would improve.

Another possibility is found in the so-called Pigou-effect, named after the famous Cambridge economist. With a constant money supply, an increase in prices and money income may produce an increase in savings, Pigou thought, as consumers try to build back the real value of their cash balances which have depreciated because of the rise in prices. The standard question is put in terms of what would happen if all prices and incomes were doubled but money remained the same. There would clearly be an incentive to restore the old relationship of liquid and fixed money assets to real income, and the savings schedule would shift upward in relation to real income. This then is another possible avenue by which depreciation could lead to a decline in absorption and an improvement in the balance of payments. But it is unlikely to be a major force to be counted upon.

Or the money supply can have an impact in another way. The rise in prices and income against a constant money supply may raise interest rates, which produces more savings along savings schedules which respond to the interest rate. This would be true in a very classical and non-Keynesian world.

The main hope for improvement in the balance of payments with full employment probably lies in its effects on the distribution of income, which may affect absorption. If imports bulk large in ordinary consumption, depreciation raises the cost of living and reduces the real incomes of workers, civil servants, teachers, pensioners, and so on, who have fairly fixed incomes. They will save less. But the rise in prices in the foreign-trade sector—exports and import-competing industry—will increase profits here, and this will, in the first instance at least, lead to new savings. Whether absorption will on balance decrease over the longer run depends in part on whether new investment is undertaken in the foreign-trade sector in response to the higher rate of profit, which would increase absorption again, or whether—a different response—the society is prepared to accept the major changes in income distribution without resisting them.

Much depends here on institutional forces: the political strength of labor, the readiness of various income groups to use every weapon at their command to resist any decrease in their share of the total income. Where wage rates are tied to the cost of living, as in the Scandinavian countries, there is almost no prospect of effecting substantial income redistribution, and increased savings, through depreciation. Or where, as in France, the separate income groups—peasants, workers, civil servants, veterans, industrialists,—use every means, including strikes and violence, to prevent any reduction in the real income of the group, depreciation is unlikely to work in this way. It was only with the advent of strong government under de Gaulle in 1958 that French devaluation was successful—a devaluation which reduced the real income of labor and agriculture in favor of the business sector. In the long run, it may be noted, economic growth offsets the losses of these sectors, but in the short run there can be no doubt that the balance of payments was improved at their expense.

Unless one can count on income redistribution, money illusion, the Pigou effect, or some other means of increasing savings as a function of a given real income, according to Alexander's view, exchange depreciation is unlikely by itself, with full employment, to improve the balance of payments. If real output cannot be expanded, there must be a decrease in absorption: a decline in consumption, or a decline in investment. If depreciation does not decrease absorption, prices will rise internally with depreciation, and the change in the exchange rate works like a change in dimensions from yards to feet, which alters the length of nothing.

But economists now agree that Alexander leaves out one important step: the possibility of expanding real income by means of depreciation through resource reallocation. Assume a balance-of-payments deficit with full employment. The exchange rate is overvalued. This means that resources have been drawn out of exports and import-competing goods into domestic lines. Correcting the exchange rate leads to resource reallocation which improves real income. The extent of the improvement is ambiguous, quite apart from any particular case, because the change in prices gives rise to an index number problem. Measured in terms of before devaluation prices (the Laspeyres index), the income change will read differently from the measurement in terms of postdevaluation (Paasche index) prices. But despite the measurement difficulty, the improvement exists. And if absorption can be held down while income expands, there will be room for improvement in the balance of payments even without a cut in absorption. Various writers attach greater and less importance to this effect, with Professors Machlup and Sohmen regarding it as central. Whatever the relative weights attaching to absorption and reallocation under full employment, it remains true that neither can be neglected.

Exchange Devaluation, Structural Inflation, and Income Redistribution

In Alexander's analysis, equal (and limited) importance is attached to money illusion, the Pigou effect, and income redistribution. But there can be little doubt that the redistribution effect is at the core of the explanation of much Latin-American devaluation, along with what is called in that area "structural inflation." Take Argentina, or Brazil, or Chile. The pattern runs something like this. Rising labor costs and a fixed exchange rate result in a cost and profits squeeze for exporters, and, together with freedom of city workers to import, a balance-of-payments deficit. The fixed exchange rate with full employment redistributes real income in favor of the urban workers. The real income of this group is improved still more by the increase in imports, at the expense of the national reserves.

When it becomes necessary to halt the deficit, devaluation effects a shift of real income from urban workers to rural export interests, as the cost of living rises along with export prices. Profits which go into savings rise at the expense of real wages, which depresses total consumption and cuts back absorption. In some extreme forms, this Latin American thesis about devaluation holds that the income redistribution effect of depreciation is more important than any balance-of-payments effect, and in fact that devaluation is sought by exporters as a measure of income redistribution to offset the wage rises of the laboring classes. In this analysis, both groups save little and consume a lot, so that there is not much improvement in the balance of payments from devaluation. Or the point can be made differently. It is the failure to achieve an effective redistribution of income in favor of saving classes, including the government which taxes profits, that prevents depreciation from improving the balance of payments. Each group which feels its real income being cut raises prices, withholds product, or goes on strike until its money income rises to offset the increased cost of living owing to the higher prices of imports. The end result is that domestic prices and money incomes rise by the full percentage of depreciation and the system is homogeneous. Structural inflationists claim, with what reason it is hard to judge, that exchange depreciation cannot help the balance of payments.

Flexible Exchange Rates with Balanced Trade

The interaction between the price and income effects of exchange rate changes can be seen in a different perspective. Suppose a country adopts a flexible exchange rate system so that the balance of payments is always in balance. Will this enable the economy to maintain an independent monetary and fiscal policy so as to stabilize domestic money income without repercussions from foreign influences? Many economists have thought so. In a pathbreaking article, Laursen and Metzler have concluded that it will not.

Let us set the stage by noting the balance-of-payments behavior of the economy. When changes in the demand for exports or supply of imports occur, the economy adjusts to them readily and smoothly by means of changes in the exchange rate and costless and speedy reallocations of domestic resources. If, for example, the demand for exports falls off, the exchange rate will depreciate to the point where newly induced exports, or reduced imports, automatically offset the original change. If the demand for exports increases, exchange appreciation leads to displacement of incremental exports, or the stimulation of incremental imports, to match the initial change. The balance of payments is always in balance. The amount of spending on domestic resources is constant, as a first approximation, because the change in foreign spending on exports is matched either by other changes in spending on exports, as a result of depreciation, or by other changes in spending on the domestic output of import substitutes, as imports change. If exports fall, for example, and imports fall to match, the decline in foreign spending for exports is counterbalanced by an increase in domestic spending on import substitutes. This calls for a smooth and frictionless transfer of domestic resources from the export sector to the import-competing sector. Assuming that this can be achieved, will not domestic income be stabilized?

Laursen and Metzler put the issue as one of the impact of changes in the terms of trade on domestic total expenditure. The balance of payments may be left unaffected by the change in foreign demand or supply, but the terms of trade will be affected. How will changes in the terms of trade affect national income and expenditure?

In the two-country, two-commodity model, there can be no employment effects because this barter model implicitly uses Say's law. All income is spent. Changes in real income cannot affect savings, because the model has no room for savings. But if savings are allowed, there is a question, and there may be a problem.

In order to answer this question, we need to provide further assumptions about the economy. We need to know, in particular, how the rate of saving is related to changes in the terms of trade. A variety of such assumptions has been provided by a variety of economists.

Laursen and Metzler took as their assumption that savings are a function of real income, and that an improvement in real income from an improvement in the terms of trade will increase savings, a reduction reduce them. This led them to conclude that a favorable shift in the terms of trade will reduce national income by raising real income and increasing savings. An improvement in the terms of trade, they concluded, is deflationary. Conversely, a worsening of the terms of trade through depreciation was regarded as inflationary through its effect in increasing expenditure (reducing savings) because of a reduction in real income.

Stolper worked from import prices (rather than the terms of trade) directly to savings, using the assumption that savings and imports were competitors for the consumers' dollar. In this circumstance, an increase in import prices (worsening of the terms of trade) led to a reduction in spending on imports (elasticity greater than one) and an increase in savings. Total spending declined, and income fell. When imports were cheaper, on the other hand, savings were drawn down to buy more goods from abroad, which led to an expansion of spending.

According to Laursen and Metzler then, an improvement in the terms of trade was deflationary; according to Stolper, inflationary; and vice versa for a worsening of the terms of trade.

The Laursen-Metzler assumptions can be criticized as highly limiting. A large change in the terms of trade—say 10 percent—will produce a much smaller change in real income. If the average propensity to import is 20 percent, this change in the terms of trade will affect real income by 2 percent. Under no circumstance can a 2 percent change in real income produce a very large shift in savings or expenditure.

More fundamental, an increase in real income arising from lower import prices cannot be very deflationary, since any considerable deflation would reduce real income and restore the level of real expenditure to its level before import prices fell. It seems likely, rather, on the Laursen-Metzler assumptions, that the country will end up with some small decline in money income but a small increase in real income and real expenditure.

The Stolper assumption, in its turn, has been criticized as unrealistic. There is less justification for assuming that imports and savings are alternatives than the opposite, i.e., assuming that cheaper imports mean more saving.

What will happen to imports, savings, and domestic expenditure as a result of changes in the price of imports depends on the structure of a country's trade. If price elasticity is high, the substitution effect will be substantial but the income effect will be small. There will be a substantial increase in imports; a necessity to shift the resources released from the import-competing sector into exports to balance trade; but very little change in overall spending or saving. No substantial change in income arises from the model as it exists. Dynamic changes can occur, however, because of failure of adjustment to be that smooth. Thus, for example, the expansion in exports may require more investment in export industry than is provided by the savings released from the import-competing sector.

If the price elasticity of demand for imports is low, the substitution effect will be small but the income effect will be large. Some part of the increase in income will be saved, and money income may fall to some extent. But much will be spent. At higher real income, more is consumed as well as more saved. Resources will be released from the export sector and transferred to domestic occupations.

The classic example offered by the real world is that of Britain in the early 1930's, when a rise in the terms of trade increased real income substantially, because of the inelastic nature of the demand for foodstuffs and raw materials, and provided real income which spilled into domestic housebuilding (investment rather than consumption).

It is, in short, difficult to generalize about the interactions between the terms of trade and domestic spending. The nature of the income effect and the substitutability between imports and domestic goods will differ from country to country and circumstance to circumstance.

Productivity Change

Assume two countries, A and B, each producing one good and consuming two, i.e., each completely specialized in production but generalized in consumption. Now introduce a change in productivity in A. Whether this improves or worsens the balance of payments of A will depend upon the elasticities and the marginal propensities, and on whether the increased real output of A is reflected in higher money incomes, lower prices, or both.

To the extent that the increase in productivity takes the form of higher money incomes, the increase in output may worsen the balance of payments, assuming that imports are not an inferior good. More income means more spending on imports. Country B, with unchanged income and facing an unchanged price for its imports, experiences no initial reaction. The consequence of an increase in its exports is likely to include a rise in prices, an increase in imports through the multiplier, and a worsening of exports because of increased prices; but the net effect will be favorable in the absence of any perverse dynamic changes such as accelerators, since it starts with an increase in exports. And if B's balance of payments improves, A's worsens.

If the increase in productivity took place in the form of unchanged money income but lower export prices, the balance-of-payments effect will depend, in the first instance, on the sum of the price elasticities of demand. If these are greater than one, the balance-of-payments effect is favorable to A; if less than one, unfavorable. An income effect follows the balance-of-payments effect and offsets it in part, but only in part, assuming the sum of the marginal propensities to import less than one.

If the productivity change leads to a partial rise in money income and a partial decline in price, the income and the price effects will move in opposite directions or together depending upon the relative size of the two movements and whether the sum of the price elasticities of demand for imports is greater or less than one.

This is a highly simplified model. All productivity changes are export biased if production is limited to one commodity; and competitive effects in third countries producing the same good are neglected. But the model is interesting in showing, from still another angle, how income and price changes may be related.

Changes in Income and Price Abroad

Our final case poses the question whether a country's balance of payments is affected more by income or by price changes when incomes and prices abroad change in the same direction. Incomes and prices at home are neglected. The income change abroad is important for our exports, through the foreign income elasticity of demand which is assumed to be high. The price change abroad is supposed to be important for our imports, on the assumption of low domestic price elasticity.

It can be seen that these assumptions, like the others of this chapter, are rather particular. But it can happen that income elasticity abroad can be significant for exports, if our exports are manufactured goods; and imports price inelastic, if imports are necessities such as food-stuffs and raw materials. The problem is posed largely for Britain and Europe.

The income and price effects may be opposed in this way for Europe particularly in the business cycle. In world depression incomes fall abroad and so do prices. British exports fall and so do imports. Which effect is the stronger? In world boom, the opposite occurs: world incomes rise and with them exports, but world prices rise, which makes imports cost more. Which is the more significant in determining the cyclical behavior of the balance of payments, the income effect or the price effect?

The answer to this question, as to all those above, is that it depends on the circumstances. How price elastic is the domestic demand for imports; how income elastic is the demand abroad for your exports (their imports); how wide are the swings of income; how elastic is the supply of goods abroad which determine the amplitude of price fluctuation? So much is obvious.

What is not permitted, however, is for a country to complain of its lot in the world by pointing to one effect now and a different effect later. A European writer has suggested that industrial countries of western Europe suffer from the income effect in world depression and from the terms of trade effect in periods of boom. No reference is made to the income effect in boom, or to the terms of trade effect in depression.

Or a spokesman for underdeveloped countries bewailed the "fact" that these countries suffer from the terms of trade in depression, and tend to let inflation get out of hand in boom, so that their balance of payments is always in deficit.

If we look squarely at both the income and price effect when they thus operate in different directions because of price inelasticity, we can suggest that there may be different stages of boom and depression, with different income and price impacts. Take a country with substantial world trade as Britain which used to export income inelastic and import price inelastic products. Starting from some normal level, such a country benefits from world depression and is hurt by world prosperity. In depression, prices of imports fall while demand for exports is sustained; in prosperity, the terms of trade become adverse, without any substantial expansion in export volume. The price effect outweighs the income effect.

If, on the other hand, the demand for imports is only slightly price inelastic and the foreign demand for imports highly income-elastic, the country benefits from booms and is hurt by depression. The income effect outweighs the price effect.

It could happen that a country's demand for imports was price inelastic, and the demand for its exports rather income elastic, under conditions where prices rose only slightly during the early part of the boom and much more during the late stages after full employment was reached or closely approached. In these circumstances, the country might gain from world prosperity before full employment and price inflation, when the income effect prevailed over the price effect, but lose in the peak stages of the boom, when the positions were reversed.

The answer here then is that almost anything can happen, and that whether the income effect is more significant than the price effect when they work in opposite directions on a country's balance of payments depends upon the kind of country one is dealing with and the nature of the conditions which produce the price and income changes. In industrial countries which export income elastic products and import price inelastic, the income effect is likely to be more significant than price, except perhaps at the peaks of booms. But for some industrial countries whose exports are income-inelastic, such as textiles, this may not hold, and so on.

Elasticities versus Absorption

The quarrel between the elasticity optimists, on the one hand, and the absorption school, on the other, is one which is rooted in the academic development of economics. In price analysis, we use partial equilibrium elasticities, assuming other things, including income, equal. Similarly, in income analysis, we tend to use models which usually require an assumption of unchanged prices. When incomes and prices both change, we could use either general equilibrium price elasticities—of the *mutatis mutandis* (changing those things which ought to be changed) type rather than *ceteris paribus* (other things equal)—and changing, among these other things, income; or we can use an absorption approach, in which the propensities to spend reflect not only consumers' response to changes in real income, with prices fixed, but also changes in relative prices. The elasticity approach is inadequate if it is partial. Ditto for the income approach. When the elasticities approach is generalized to include changes in spending, or the income approach to include changes in prices, they merge into one another.

It is wrong, as we have suggested, to regard the elasticities approach as appropriate for the impact of devaluation on the balance of payments, and the income approach as suitable to the analysis of changes in internal monetary and fiscal policy. As the song puts it, you can't have one without the other. The impact of devaluation on the balance of payments is indeterminate until one states what happens to income; ditto income changes . . . prices.

The change in the balance of trade and the change in saving are equal by definition. The equation

$$X - M = S - I_d$$

is an identity rather than a behavioral or policy equation. But the student of macroeconomics will recall that while $S = I$ in the Keynesian closed system *ex post*, it does not always equal it *ex ante*. If one could guarantee *ex ante* equivalence between the change in the balance of payments and the change in saving net of domestic investment, it would make no difference in projecting balance-of-payments estimates whether one used the elasticities or the absorption approach. The elasticities approach to the balance of payments, lying through trade, calls for estimates of exports and imports separately and assumes that income and spending will accommodate themselves to the trade. The absorption approach, on the other hand, operates by looking at savings and domestic investment, and assumes that the trade will fit. But if the identity only holds *ex post,* it becomes necessary to choose between the two approaches. International economics has not reached agreement as to which is the more useful.

The *Brookings Report* on the balance of payments of the United States for 1968 (written in 1963, and hence a forecast) worked with the trade figures. It assumed that prices would rise more in Europe than in the United States, and that the balance of payments would improve in consequence, as a result of favorable elasticities. In his review of the Brookings study, Professor Johnson attacked it with vigor for failing to justify its forecast in terms of absorption. Similar differences can be found in estimates of the balance-of-payments position of the less developed countries, with one group looking at trade prospects, the other at marginal propensities to save and coming out with very different results.

For short-run balance-of-payments changes, the elasticities approach seems superior to the absorption approach. Savings equals investment *ex post,* but not *ex ante,* as high profits result in say unintended savings which have as their counterpart the balance-of-payments surplus; or unintended investment—in inventories because of inability to sell the goods abroad—results in an excess of investment over domestic savings which matches the trade deficit. The parallel with domestic income determination is exact. The *ex ante* schedules for savings and investment have long-run validity, but the operation of the elasticities can produce unintended positive or negative savings or investment which make the *ex post* identity work out.

It can work the other way: an unintended decline in investment as in Germany in 1967 can lead to a large surplus in the balance-of-payments, as imports decline along the propensity to import schedule, and goods which cannot be sold to domestic consumers and investors are exported. Here the elasticities are passive.

What is worth remembering, however, is that in equilibrium an export surplus must be offset by some net savings, an import surplus by net investment (net investment less domestic savings). It is often useful to try to identify who in the system is doing the domestic investing and saving, and to try to judge whether this is an intended or transitional position they find themselves in.

SUGGESTED READING

TEXTS

See Clement, Pfister and Rothwell, chap. 7.

TREATISES, ETC.

The absorption approach was introduced by S. S. Alexander in "Effect of a Devaluation on a Trade Balance," American Economics Association, *Readings in International Economics*, and has been attacked by F. Machlup in "Relative Prices and Aggregate Spending in the Analysis of Devaluation," *AER*, June, 1955, and "The Terms-of-Trade Effects of Devaluation upon Real Income and the Balance of Trade," *Kyklos*, No. 4 (Bern), 1956. Alexander revised his first view in "Effects of a Devaluation: A Simplified Synthesis of Elasticities and Absorption Approaches," *AER*, March, 1959.

One of the earliest attempts to incorporate income and price analysis into the same framework was A. C. Harberger's "Currency Depreciation, Income and the Balance of Trade," *JPE*, February, 1950. Only a few months behind were the papers by S. Laursen and L. A. Metzler, "Flexible Exchange Rates and the Theory of Employment," *RE & S*, November, 1950; and W. F. Stolper, "The Multiplier, Flexible Exchange Rates and International Equilibrium," *QJE*, November, 1950. The productivity case is discussed by H. G. Johnson, in "Increasing Productivity, Income-Price Trends and the Trade Balance," *EJ*, September, 1954.

POINTS

For a case study of the redistribution effect, see Carlos F. Dias-Alejandro, *Exchange-Rate Devaluation in a Semi-Industrial Country: The Experience of Argentina 1955–1961* (Cambridge, Mass.: The M.I.T. Press, 1966).

The references in the text on elasticities versus absorption are to W. S. Salant *et al.*, *The United States Balance of Payments in 1968* (Washington, D.C.: The Brookings Institution, 1963) (paperback), which is given a sharp review in H. G. Johnson, "The International Competitive Position of the United States and the Balance of Payments for 1968: A Review Article," *RE & S*, February, 1964. See also Bela Balassa's comparison between Rosenstein-Rodan's estimate of the developing countries need for foreign assistance through projection of domestic investment and saving, and GATT's estimates through foreign-trade forecasts, in "The Capital Needs of the Developing Countries," *Kyklos*, No. 2, 1964.

Chapter 18 | THE TRANSFER PROCESS

We can wind up the preliminary discussion of the adjustment process, and introduce Part V on capital movements by discussing how capital is transferred from one country to another. Lenders in one country save in local currency; borrowers in the other country as a rule want largely their own, a different local currency. How the money is transferred through the foreign exchange market and how the real capital is transferred between the countries in the form of an export surplus on the part of the lender, and an import surplus for the borrower, is a standard adjustment problem. It is one that Professor Taussig of Harvard and his students worked on in connection with the experience of Britain, Canada, Argentina, France, Australia and other countries, in an attempt to verify the classical theory of trade adjustment represented by the price-specie-flow mechanism. In debating the feasibility of German reparations payments after World War I, Keynes and Ohlin, along with most other prominent economists of Europe and the United States who joined in the controversy, assisted in developing the theory of international trade in important respects.

As an exercise in adjustment, the transfer discussion was not concerned with what happened after capital had been put in place, or who owned it and received the income from its marginal product. It was interested almost entirely in the manner in which physical capital was transferred between countries as a result of borrowing, or how payments which did not necessarily result in capital formation, such as reparations, produced a physical transfer of goods and services from one country to another. Reparations or tributes would not be regarded as capital movements today but as transfers of income. It is still appropriate for us, however, given our interest in the adjustment process, to treat reparations and voluntary international transfer payments, such as Lend-Lease, Marshall Plan, and AID assistance, as capital movements.

310

The Transfer Process

Borrowers of long-term capital desire command in the short run over purchasing power. By and large, however, they desire goods. To get capital without saving, which is to invest or consume without producing, it is necessary to borrow or to liquidate accumulated assets. A country gets capital from abroad in a real sense only when it gets goods or services, over and above the value of the goods it exports. A country lends abroad when it produces more than it consumes and invests at home, the difference representing the excess of exports over imports.

The goods and services borrowed or loaned need not be capital goods. The illustration most frequently used to drive this point home is that of a loan between two islands in, let us say, the South Pacific, each occupied by a tribe of natives. One island and tribe may be designated as A, the other as B. If B borrows from A to build a new hut for the B chief, the real movement of capital may take one of several forms: (1) net imports of building materials, together with assorted craftsmen to assemble them; (2) services of native field workers from A who tend the coconuts in B while the B natives build the hut from indigenous materials; or (3) consumption goods—yams, coconuts, and other food—to enable B's population to work on the hut without the necessity of worrying about their subsistence.

When industry or government in one country borrows in another, it frequently is interested not in foreign but in domestic purchasing power. How the borrower gets purchasing power in his own country relates to the money transfer. But how this money transfer, in turn, leads to an import surplus, which is the only real way that capital can be loaned between countries, is called the "real transfer." The money and real transfers are interrelated, as we shall see. When one or the other or both offer difficulties, we may have a transfer problem.

The Classical Mechanism

Classical economic theory had one answer for the transfer problem under the gold standard and another under fluctuating exchange rates. In the former, the money borrowed in London, for example, was sold for dollars. This depressed the pound sterling to the gold export point and led to a gold inflow to the borrower, which we shall call the United States. Prices declined in England as a result of the contraction of money resulting from the gold outflow. Conversely, prices rose in the United States because of the increase in means of payment. If bank rates were raised in England to halt the gold outflow by attracting short-term capital, the contractive process would still take place, though probably on a reduced scale. This is a topic for later consideration, one we come to in the next chapter. But the loss of gold or the inflow of short-term capital in the lending country, plus the increase in interest rates, would be contractive and depress prices. In the United States, the gain of gold or of short-term claims on London, the expansion of the money supply, and lower interest rates, all work to raise prices.

The lower prices in England and higher prices in the United States would produce an export surplus in the former, import surplus in the latter. This involves the assumption that the sum of the price elasticities of demand is greater than one. The resultant export surplus of Britain and import surplus of the United States is the real transfer.

The real transfer in goods reverses the original gold movement or subsequent short-term capital movement. As British exports exceed imports, gold returns to the Bank of England, or the London money market is enabled to repay the short-term capital borrowings from New York. When the entire capital movement has been transferred in goods, the gold or short-term capital movement has been reversed completely, and everything remains in balance if we ignore the effects of the interest payment and of the productivity of capital. The decline in export prices in Britain and the rise in prices in the United States will change the terms of trade in favor of the borrower and against the lending country during the process of transfer; but when real transfer has been completed, the terms of trade will revert to their original status.

The classical view of the transfer mechanism under the paper standard follows along familiar lines. The attempt by the borrower to sell pounds for dollars leads to a depreciation of the pound, in the absence of stabilizing short-term capital movements. The depreciation of sterling and the consequent appreciation of the dollar encourage the lender's exports and the borrower's imports and discourage the borrower's exports and the lender's imports. As Britain develops an export surplus, the original borrower buys the dollars he needs for expenditure in the United States. Money transfer and real transfer take place simultaneously. When all the funds (and capital) have been transferred from London to New York, the export surplus of Britain vanishes and the depreciation of sterling is corrected, as the demand for dollars is reduced and the export surplus of Britain creates a demand for sterling which can be satisfied only at a higher rate.

The addition of stabilizing short-term capital movements to the picture makes it more closely resemble the gold standard mechanism. If in the beginning, as sterling begins to depreciate, speculators who believe it will remain at par over the long run buy it at a small discount, their offerings of dollars enable the original borrower to achieve the transfer of purchasing power. The expansive effect of the short-term capital outflow from the United States and the contractive effect of the short-term capital inflow into Britain—still to be explained—will act like the gold movement, though with less certainty and force, to raise prices in the United States and to lower them in Britain. Whether short-term capital movements take place or not, the terms of trade normally turn against the lending country as a result of transfer.

Flaws in the Classical View

Objections to the foregoing analysis were directed mainly to the process under the gold standard. Three points were made: first, that some of the proceeds of the loan might be spent in Britain in the first place. This was readily conceded. There is no need for the marginal propensity of the borrowers to spend borrowed funds abroad to be the same as the country's marginal propensity to import. To the extent the proceeds are spent immediately, transfer takes place automatically in real terms with no money transfer effected or required.

Second, it was argued that prices could not be raised in the United States and reduced in Britain, since a number of goods were traded in both, and the law of one price required that they be quoted at the same price in a single market. If wheat was $2 in Chicago and 16s. in Liverpool, it was impossible for the price to rise in one and decline in the other, since they were tied together. This objection, however, was in error. Wheat which was exported from the United States to Britain could be expected to rise in price in both markets; woolens which were exported from England to the United States, to fall in both. What the classical economists were talking about were sectional price levels. To look at the matter from the standpoint of the United States, export prices were expected to rise along with domestic prices. But import prices, determined in Britain, would fall. And the reverse would be true in England. After a purely formal correction for the law of one price, the classical mechanism was unaffected by this criticism.

The third and most fundamental objection in theory was to the reliance on the quantity theory of money. This explanation might have had operational validity in the 17th and 18th centuries, when the economy was more or less in continuous full employment. It might still serve as a reliable guide for prediction in periods of inflation, such as war. But in the short run the quantity of money was little indication of the level of prices. To put the matter succinctly in modern terms,

changes in money can occur without bringing about changes in spending, and changes in spending sometimes affect employment without
producing changes in price.

But these theoretical objections were less significant than the facts.
What distressed Professor Taussig about the classical theory, which he
had helped to perfect and which his students had sought to verify, was
that the transfer process in the real world worked far more smoothly
than one could have imagined from the classical explanation. Time was
presumably required for changes in money supply and prices and then
in exports and imports. In actuality, the balance of payments adjusted
itself to changes in borrowing (or vice versa?) with remarkable speed
and precision and without marked pressures leading to gold flows or
exchange rate changes.

Modern Theory

What the classical theory had neglected were changes in spending
and income and their effects on the balance of payments through the
marginal propensity to import. More was involved than the fact that
borrowers sometimes spent part of loans directly in the lending country.
On this portion of the loan, the marginal propensity to import (on the
change in spending power) may be said to be one. And, to this extent,
transfer takes place automatically. But on the portion of the loan spent
at home the increase in domestic expenditure raises income which spills
over into imports, and this transfers part of the loan. How much of the
loan will be transferred in this fashion depends upon a number of
factors. These include the marginal propensities to import and save in
the borrowing country, the course of money income in the two countries, and the response, if any, of domestic investment.

It has been enunciated as a theorem that if the marginal propensity
to save in the borrowing country is positive and if domestic investment
in the borrowing country is changed by no more than the amount of the
loan, with no induced changes in investment in either country, changes
in income in the two countries will not be sufficient to transfer the
whole loan through induced changes in imports. This theorem may be
illustrated, in a general way, with the multiplier diagram as in Figure
18.1*a*, using one country only, a continuous borrowing and investment
rather than a single nonrecurring transfer, and eliminating all effect of
the foreign repercussion.

Given a marginal propensity to save of 0.1 and to import of 0.3, in
the borrowing country, the sum of *MPM* + *MPS*, which is the reciprocal of the multiplier, will be 0.4, and the multiplier will be $2\frac{1}{2}$. If $10

million of new borrowings from abroad are spent within the borrowing country as additional investment, the increase in income which results is $25 million, the increase in savings $2.5 million, and the increase in imports $7.5 million. The downward displacement of the $S–I_d$ schedule by the $10 million increase in I_d transfers only three fourths of the loan. The remaining $2.5 million, offset by new savings in the borrowing country, will press on the foreign exchange market, tending to increase the supply of the exchange of the lending country and the demand for that of the borrower. Real transfer of this portion of the loan will

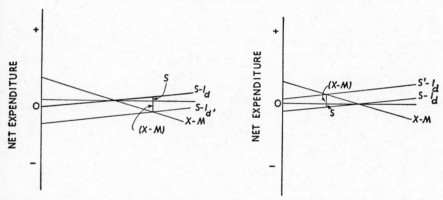

FIG. 18.1*a*. Incomplete Inward Transfer with Increased Investment   FIG. 18.1*b*. Incomplete Outward Transfer with Increased Savings

require something akin to the price-specie-flow mechanism on the fixed exchange standard or depreciation of the lender's currency under the paper standard.

The same is true if outward transfer is attempted by an increase in savings in the lending country, as shown in Figure 18.1*b*

Observe, in the first of these simple examples, without foreign repercussion, that if the *MPS* had been 0 (and the multiplier 3.3), the full amount of the loan could have been transferred through income changes. Or with the *MPS* unchanged at 0.1. if there had been a positive slope to the investment schedule of 0.1 or higher, the full amount of the loan, or more, could have been transferred. To summarize, the theorem states that if the marginal propensity to save is positive and if there is no accelerator or other positive slope to the investment schedule, less than the full amount of the loan will be transferred by income changes.

Adding the foreign repercussion does not change matters greatly if that country undertakes to save the monies to be transferred and is also "stable in isolation," i.e., if that country also has a marginal propensity to spend on consumption and investment which is less than one, or if its $S-I_d$ curve is positively sloped. This has been shown in a period analysis in Lloyd Metzler's classic article, reprinted in the 1949 American Economic Association, *Readings*. It can readily be demonstrated in other ways.[1] The essence of the argument is that the help which comes to A's import surplus from B's direct decline in income and imports is greatly offset by the stimulus to B's exports and income from A's increased imports.

This, however, is a much oversimplified model. A variety of its

---

[1] It may interest a few readers to compare results with and without the foreign repercussion, using Meade's simultaneous technique, referred to earlier (page 293).

Without foreign repercussion, and with an MPM_a of 0.3, an MPS_a of 0.1 and an MPC_a of 0.6, a loan of $10 million spent in A increases A's income by $25 million and its imports by 0.3 times that amount, or $7.5 million.

If the same values for the propensities exist in lender B, the change in income can be computed from a matrix in which A and B are listed as spenders vertically in columns, and as recipients of spending horizontally in rows. A's marginal propensity to spend at home (MPC_a) is in the upper left-hand box; its marginal propensity to import (i.e., spend in B), immediately below it. B's propensity to spend at home is in the lower right-hand corner, and its propensity to import above it:

Receivers	Spenders	
	A	B
A	MPC_a	MPM_b
B	MPM_a	MPC_b

The equilibrium condition for national income in each country is that total spending equals total income. If there is an autonomous increase in spending of $10 million in A, and a similar decrease in B, one can derive two equations:

$$10 + MPC_a \times dY_a + MPM_b \times dY_b = dY_a$$

and

$$MPM_a \times dY_a - 10 + MPC_b \times dY_b = dY_b ,$$

where dY_a and dY_b (or more simply a and b) are the changes in income A and B. Filling in the marginal propensities, we have two equations and two unknowns:

$$10 + 0.6a + 0.3b = a$$
$$0.3a - 10 + 0.6b = b$$

If we succeed (after several tries) in solving, we find a and b each equal to a little less than 14.3 million, an increase in A, and a decrease in B. B's export surplus is now based on an increase of approximately 4.3 million in exports and a decrease of 4.3 million in imports, for a total improvement of 8.6 million, as compared with the previous 7.5 million. So long as both countries are stable in isolation, then, it adds something, but not very much, to have spending change in both rather than in simply one without repercussion.

If the lending country does not cut its spending by 10, however, the rise in spending in the borrower, plus foreign repercussion will succeed in transferring $4.3 of the $7.5 millions, as income rises in B almost as much as in A ($42.9 as against $57.1 million) and increases rather than reduces B's imports.

assumptions must be altered in discussion of the real world. These assumptions relate to:

1. The course of spending and income in the lending country
2. The course of spending and income in the borrowing country
3. The marginal propensity of the borrower to import out of borrowings
4. The responses of the banking systems, etc.

The variability which may be experienced within these assumptions is so wide that it is impossible to make any general statement about the extent to which income changes can transfer theoretical international capital movements. It may be fair, however, to conclude from the capital transfers which surprised Professor Taussig that income changes are likely to transfer normal capital movements smoothly, and, from the German reparations experience, that some capital transfers will be very difficult to effect.

The course of spending and income in the lending country will be affected by a variety of factors. These include the way in which the capital to be transferred is raised and the rapidity with which exports increase because of increased spending by the borrower. On the first of these, let us suppose, on the one hand, that the funds are raised through an increase in saving or a decline in investment or an increase in taxes required to collect a reparation payment to be paid abroad. Under any of these circumstances, spending and income will fall in the lending country, and this will help transfer the capital abroad by reducing imports and freeing goods for export. On the other hand, however, the capital may be raised by credit creation or other inflationary means. In this case the process of real transfer will be rendered more difficult, since the increase in exports generated by foreign spending will raise income in the lending country and tend to work against the transfer by increasing imports and limiting exports.

While spending may fall or rise in the lending country, its course is predictable with somewhat more certainty in the borrowing country. Most borrowing is undertaken for capital formation purposes, and this generally means an increase in spending and in money incomes. But a country receiving reparations from abroad may not respond by lowering taxes or undertaking governmental investment. It may use the receipts merely to pay off the government debt. If this fails to lower interest rates and, by this means, to increase other investment, spending and national money income in the receiving country may not be affected. A considerable part of the reparation payment can still be transferred through a reduction in spending in the paying country, but the task of transfer is rendered somewhat easier if both countries alter their spending schedules.

If the banking system in either country permits a multiple expansion or contraction of credit based on the initial changes in savings or investment or upon the movement of short-term credit needed to finance the loan pending real transfer, the normal expectations derivable from the foregoing must be amended still further. This reaction could be subsumed in the remarks about the course of income in the two countries, but it is well to make explicit mention of it.

Most of this wide range of variability can be put into a complex mathematical formula. Rather than do so, however, we may summarize by saying that international capital transfers in money may be transferred in goods through income changes, in part, *in toto,* or in excessive degree (i.e., a larger real transfer than the original money payment), and that real transfer will be fully or excessively effected, the greater the extent to which, other things being equal,

1. Spending and income fall initially in the lending country in the process of raising the money capital
2. The loan is spent by the borrowers in the lending country
3. Money income rises in the borrowing country, due to
    a) A low marginal propensity to save
    b) A positive marginal propensity to invest
    c) In the case of reparations, a readiness to reduce taxation or increase government investment, or of domestic investment or consumption to respond upward to a reduction in government debt
4. The foreign repercussion of both countries is low
5. The banking systems of both countries respond to the movements of short-term capital and gold

Conversely, the less that the above conditions are realized, the greater is the likelihood that the capital will not be fully transferred through income changes arising out of the capital transfer itself. Under these circumstances, gold flows will be needed on the gold standard, which may induce income changes of a banking origin; or an exchange rate adjustment will be needed to accomplish the remaining transfer through price changes.

Borrowing Money for Increased Liquidity

In the last few years, the possibility has been suggested that some small portion of international borrowing may be for the purpose of acquiring money as such. The classic assumption that foreign money was borrowed only for obtaining capital assets has been modified in the light of recent monetary theory which points out that asset holders balance portfolios at various levels of wealth. If real assets are added to a portfolio, it is likely that liquid assets will be increased too. Borrowers in A selling securities in B are likely to spend the proceeds mostly perhaps to acquire real assets, but partly to expand their holdings of A money. Moreover, the multiplier increase in A's income from the spending will require an increase in the A money to finance a higher volume of transactions. The increase in the A money supply called for by the changes in assets and income may well limit the completeness of the transfer mechanism, whether through income or price. This idea certainly disturbs the neat classical conclusion that the completion of the transfer would restore gold, short-term capital, money supplies, and so on, to the *status quo ante*.

The possibility that countries borrow to some extent for the sake of adding to the money supply was developed by an economic historian exploring the transfer mechanism as it operated in the United States in the 19th century. We may then postpone its further discussion until we assemble a series of case histories of transfer in the real world.

The Terms of Trade and Transfer

A favorite question asked by the classicists was: What happens to the terms of trade under transfer? If the price mechanism takes the lead in transferring the capital, the terms of trade will evidently turn against the lender and in favor of the borrower. In order to sell more goods abroad to achieve the export surplus, the lending country has to reduce prices either through deflation or through depreciation. To become a more profitable market in which to sell, the borrowing country must raise the prices of its goods either through inflation or through appreciation.

The possibility of transfer through changes in the marginal propensity to import or through income changes, however, alters this. Assume that the investors have a marginal propensity to import out of borrowed funds equal to one and spend the whole loan in the lending country. If they buy the goods that the new savers have foregone, no price will change anywhere in the system, and the terms of trade will remain unaltered. If they buy export goods and the savers economize on import goods, the terms of trade may turn against the borrower. And if the money capital in the lending country is created by bank credit rather than through new saving, there will be an increase in net spending in the lending country, prices are likely to be bid up, and the terms of trade will also turn against the borrowing country and in favor of the lending.

Terms of Trade and Income Changes

When income changes bear the brunt of the transfer, the change in the terms of trade, if any, will depend upon the extent of the income changes in opposite directions in the two countries, the relative propensities to spend on home goods and imports, and the elasticities of supply. The difficulty with these cases, however, is that they need two different types of analysis which can be combined only with difficulty. The use of income changes and multipliers assumes linear propensities to save and import, which, in turn, depend upon constant prices based on idle resources. Terms of trade analysis, on the other hand, assumes full employment and general equilibrium. If the terms of trade change, this alters the propensity to import and possibly that to save, which affects the multiplier analysis. While the analysis cannot be made accurate within the scope of this chapter, we may be able to say something of a rough nature about it.

Turn back to Figure 18.1a. In this we assumed no foreign repercussion and ignored the lending country. Let us now assume that the money loan was raised by credit creation rather than new saving, so that total spending in the lending country was initially unchanged. Total expenditure on the products of the borrowing country increased by $25 million, representing $10 million of the original loan and $15 million of induced consumption. The increase in expenditure in the lending country consisted only of the $7.5 millions of increased exports. If the elasticities of supply in the two countries are anything comparable and not infinite, the terms of trade will turn in favor of the borrowing country.

If income changes occur in both countries, the same general principle holds good and can be put to use. What happens to total spending for the lender's goods as contrasted with the borrower's? If the net change in money income in the two countries is zero, the increase in income in the borrowing country being offset by the decline in the lending, and there are no savings, the criterion is whether the sum of the marginal propensities to import is greater, equal to, or less than one. This can be illustrated with matrices used in the footnote on page 316.

Suppose the two MPC's and the two MPM's are both alike, and equal, respectively, to 0.6 and 0.4 as indicated in the accompanying matrix. The sum of the MPM's will be less than one; the increase in spending on A's goods by A will exceed the decrease in spending on A's goods in B; the increase in spending on B's goods by A will be less than the decrease in spending on B's goods by B. Net spending on A's goods will increase; net spending on B's goods will decrease. The terms of trade will clearly turn against B and in favor of A:

Receivers \ Spenders	A	B
A	MPC_a +0.6	MPM_b −0.4
B	MPM_a +0.4	MPC_b −0.6

If, on the other hand, MPC_a and MPC_b are each 0.4 and the two MPM's 0.6, it is evident, or should be after reflection, that the decline in B's spending on A's goods is greater than the increase in A's spending on A's goods; while the increase in A's spending on B's goods exceeds the decrease in B's spending on B's goods. Net spending increases on B's goods, decreases on A's, and the terms of trade favor the lender.

Where the sum of the marginal propensities to import is equal to one, and there are no savings, net spending in each commodity is unchanged, and the terms of trade cannot change. It makes no difference to the terms of trade whether the marginal propensities to import are smaller or larger than 0.5, as the following matrices may be used to illustrate:

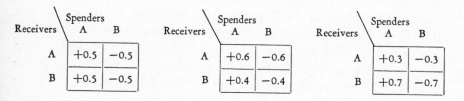

Receivers \ Spenders	A	B
A	+0.5	−0.5
B	+0.5	−0.5

Receivers \ Spenders	A	B
A	+0.6	−0.6
B	+0.4	−0.4

Receivers \ Spenders	A	B
A	+0.3	−0.3
B	+0.7	−0.7

The assumption of MPS's equal to zero is exactly equivalent to a general equilibrium geometric model with two commodities, two countries, and the transfer effected in kind. Making the transfer in kind takes care of the spending changes. The terms of trade will favor the borrower if the sum of the marginal propensities to import are less than one; or, what amounts to the same thing (again on reflection), if MPC_a is greater than MPM_b, or if MPM_a is less than MPC_b.

If there are savings, if the amount of spending change is different in the two countries, or if the supply elasticities are unequal, the simple criterion of the sum of the marginal propensities to import no longer holds. It is easy to cope with savings. Given equal changes in spending, the terms of trade will favor the borrower if the marginal propensity to consume in the borrower exceeds the marginal propensity to import in the lender *and* if the marginal propensity to consume in the lender exceeds the marginal propensity to import in the borrower. The sum of the marginal propensities to import is no longer a valid criterion, as the following matrix suggests. There the sum of the marginal propensities to import is less than one; but it is clear that there will be a net decrease in spending on A's products, and a net increase on B's, producing a change in the terms of trade in favor of lender B.

Receivers	Spenders A	B
A	+0.3	−0.6
B	+0.3	−0.2
Saving	+0.4	−0.2

In the usual case, where spending in the two countries is not identical and of opposite direction, it will be necessary to know the changes in income and the propensities to spend on home goods and imports in the two countries to forecast their terms of trade, given equal supply elasticities. The essential question is how much more (or less) is spent for the goods of the lender and the borrower. To the extent that the rise in income is likely to be greater in the borrower than in the lender and that the propensity to spend on home goods is higher than the propensity to import, the terms of trade will tend to favor the borrower. If the typical case of capital transfer, however, involves a rise in income in the borrower in excess of that in the lender, but a marginal propensity to import in excess of that to spend on home goods and the reverse in the lender, there is no normal outcome. It will be necessary to ascertain the exact amounts of spending on the goods of the two countries.

Terms of Trade and Supply Elasticities

In the real world the assumption of equal supply elasticities is almost certainly invalid. Assume that there are equal increases in spending for the goods of both borrowing and lending countries. Which country is favored by the terms of trade will depend upon the elasticities of supply. If the borrower is a raw material country and the lender a manufacturing one, the terms of trade of the borrower are likely to improve, since the increase in spending drives up prices, at least in the short run, without expanding output by a great deal. This is in contrast with the position of the lender, assuming the existence of some excess capacity, where the increase in spending tends to expand output but to bring little increase in prices.

Summary on the Terms of Trade

Most readers will mop their brows at this point and conclude that one cannot say much about the terms of trade under capital transfer. Sad but true. The terms of trade depend upon the extent of the income changes, on balance; the relative propensities to import and to spend for home-produced goods, again on balance; and the relative supply elasticities. More accurately, this is the extent to which income changes will affect the terms of trade. If income changes fail to transfer all the capital, additional capital is left to be transferred through price changes. The income impact on the terms of trade may be outweighed by the direct price changes.

But the position is by no means hopeless. We shall attempt below to make a distinction between normal and abnormal long-term capital movements, which may help us. We may anticipate its conclusion enough to suggest that, under normal capital movements, income changes in the borrowing country are more likely than parallel changes in the opposite direction in the lender and that income changes are likely to be sufficiently wide to transfer all the capital—and sometimes even more. This suggests that the net change in spending is likely to be an increase. The terms of trade will now favor the country in which the greater part of the increase is spent or the country with the lower elasticity of supply for the sought after goods, or both, or the net of the two effects if they move in opposite directions.

It is hard to predict which country, in the typical case, will receive the bulk of the spending. The borrowing country will need imported goods if it is underdeveloped, because it probably lacks a capital-goods industry. At the same time, much capital formation consists of construction which must be done in place. Probably, on balance, the borrowing country will spend more for its own output than for the output of the lending country; but the case is not open and shut.

When it comes to supply elasticities, however, there would seem to be a stronger presumption that the supply elasticity of the borrowing country will be less than that of the lending. Lending countries are typically more developed and have greater capacity to expand output in the desired lines. Even if the majority of the net increase in spending is directed to the goods of the lending country, if this majority is not large, it may well be that prices rise further in the borrower than in the lender.

On this showing, which is not conclusive, there is something of a presumption that the terms of trade will favor the borrowing country and be adverse to the lender under "normal" conditions. Borrowing countries typically undertake a considerable amount of capital formation from local resources, and typically have little impact on the prices of exports in the lending countries, because of their high supply elasticities. It seems probable that the literature overemphasizes the importance of the terms of trade effect for normal international lending, and the presumption that the terms of trade favor the borrower is positive, but small.

This presumption does not, however (repeat *not*), extend to a tribute, reparations payment, or other unilateral transfer in which it is impossible to generalize about the likely income changes, propensities, and supply elasticities. The movement of the terms of trade will be dictated by these considerations, and no strong presumption exists in any direction.

Chicken or Egg

Another classical question for debate was whether real transfer typically followed, led, or occurred simultaneously with the money transfer. Under paper standard conditions without short-term capital movement, the real and money transfers must take place simultaneously, since the borrowers can sell the borrowed foreign exchange for their own currency, if they do not spend it directly, only when an excess supply of the domestic currency is created through an import surplus. But under the gold standard, or under a flexible exchange rate with stabilizing short-term capital movements which afford an approximation of the gold standard, the question remains open. And the answer—characteristically in economics—is any one or all.

Professor Taussig and his students thought of the capital movement as the autonomous factor and of the import surplus of the borrower as induced. This pattern has certainly occurred many times. But it is not a necessary order of things. A country can embark on a program of investment financed locally through credit expansion. The resultant inflation will lead to an import surplus. Foreign borrowing, late in the process, can fill the gap. One reason to borrow abroad may be that the rate of interest locally may have been increased by the central bank as part of its measures to protect the currency in response to the adverse balance.

At the other extreme is the case in which no new expenditure takes place in the borrowing country until the money has been borrowed abroad, or, as in the case of reparations payments, the capital movement is clearly autonomous and the balance-of-payments adjustment, if it takes place at all, is induced.

But there need be no necessary causal leadership in either direction. The money transfer and the balance-of-payments adjustment may both respond equally and simultaneously to deep-seated factors. Such causal factors may be the long-run relationship between the propensity to save and domestic investment opportunities. An excess of investment outlets within a country, relative to the supply of new savings, will tend both to produce inflation and an import surplus, on the one hand, and to induce investors to seek funds abroad, on the other. A clear and intimate connection between the capital movement and the current account imbalance may, but need not, reflect mutual dependence rather than causality.

Transfer in the Real World

This chapter may conclude with some brief examples of long-term capital transfer, successful and otherwise, to illustrate these principles. There is no reason to depart from the familiar examples with which the literature deals. We shall therefore present the Canadian experience of 1900–13 and touch on the American borrowing of the 19th century. We contrast the Franco-Prussian indemnity with German reparations after World War I. The stabilizing capital movements in central and eastern Europe after World War I will then be compared with the destabilizing movements which succeeded them. Finally, we shall treat the normal capital outflow from the United States in the 1920's and the abnormal inflow in the subsequent decade.

Canadian Borrowing, 1900–13. The classic verification of the theory of international adjustment is Viner's *Canada's Balance of International Indebtedness, 1900–1913.* Professor Viner calculated the amounts of Canadian borrowing both directly from issues on the London market and indirectly by estimating other items in the balance of payments. He worked out the monetary mechanism by means of which Canadian banks maintained their first line of reserves in dollar balances in New York, rather than gold held in Canada. And finally, he "proved" the classic price-specie-flow mechanism, and the role in it of the terms of trade, by showing that domestic prices in Canada rose most, export prices less, and import prices least, and the Canadian borrowing was transferred inward in an import surplus which just about matched the borrowing.

At the time of his study, the Dominion Bureau Statistician R. H.

Coats had quite a different picture of the sequence of events. In his view the capital inflow did not give rise to the boom; rather the reverse: the boom which had started in 1896 finally produced the capital inflow. Interest rates and prices had been rising before the capital flow started. And exports had been rising, not falling, as investment in railroads extended the land accessible to grow grain for European consumption.

A number of scholars recently have reviewed Viner's findings in the light of the income theory, and even of growth theory which accounts for the expansion of exports, and find that these explanations, which accord with that of Coats, fit the facts more closely than the classic price-specie-flow mechanism. But Viner's study remains a landmark in the progress of international economic analysis, as it posed the issues against the background of data, and gave rise to successive attempts to make the theory conform to the data.

American Experience in the 19th Century. In studying long cycles in the balance of payments of the United States in the 19th century, J. G. Williamson observed that gold movements failed altogether to conform to the pattern prescribed by the price-specie-flow mechanism. Instead of gold inflows occurring at the beginning of a capital inflow and being reversed by real transfer, they occurred all during the inflow, and were reversed only when the cyclical inflow had ended. The capital inflows were the result of long (Kuznets) cycles in U.S. investment, often construction. These required an increase in the money supply. Borrowing abroad was needed partly to transfer to the United States real goods and services, but partly also to shore up the strained banking system with gold specie. Instead of two markets which had to be cleared as in the classic mechanism—in securities and goods—there were three markets, in goods, money, and securities. In the periods of intense activity in the United States, excess demands for goods *and money* were cleared by an excess supply of securities—i.e., selling bonds in London. Only after the boom had subsided and the money supply was shrinking, was gold shipped back abroad.

This interesting insight into the transfer mechanism will be of use to us subsequently when we discuss the balance-of-payments disequilibrium of the United States in the 1960's. For the moment, however, it remains an important qualification to the classic explanation of the role of money in effecting transfer.

The Franco-Prussian Indemnity. The Franco-Prussian indemnity of 1871 led economics into a great deal of trouble because it created a precedent for German reparations after World War I when the conditions basic to the payment were altogether different. Germany won the brief war of 1870. In addition to the cession of Alsace and Lorraine, it levied an indemnity of 5 billion francs. Interest brought the sum to 5,301 million francs. The transfer of the French title to the Alsace-Lorraine railroad, worth 325 million francs, reduced it to less than 5 billions. Almost 750 millions was transferred in gold, silver, and German bank notes. This left $4\frac{1}{4}$ billions to be transferred through the foreign exchange market in a few installments.

France raised the French franc value of the indemnity by two large loans amounting to $4\frac{1}{2}$ billion francs paid in 1871 and 1872. A considerable part of the subscription to these loans came from abroad, both from foreigners who found the investment attractive and from patriotic Frenchmen who sold foreign investments. Both forms of subscriptions created the foreign exchange which the French government could purchase with the proceeds of the loan. Together they amounted to more than 4 billion francs. The rest of the loans were subscribed out of new savings, partly encouraged by higher rates of interest, partly stimulated by the appeal to patriotic Frenchmen to save and help pay the indemnity to wipe out the blot on French national honor.

Paying 750 millions in bullion and bank notes, and $4\frac{1}{4}$ billions mainly in exchange produced by the liquidation of French holdings of foreign securities and by foreign subscriptions to French issues, would seem to have disposed of the transfer issue. Not at all. It merely set the stage for transfer. The real capital outflow took place as France reconstituted a portion of its portfolio of foreign securities and paid off foreign subscriptions to French *rentes* (bonds) over the next half decade. Exports rose from a level of 2.9 billion francs in 1870 and 1871 by 1 billion in 1872 and remained at 3.9 billion francs through 1875. Imports rose, however, only from 2.9 to 3.6 billion, which produced an export surplus of 300 million, on the average, for the four years from 1872 to 1875. This was the amount of real transfer of the indemnity. More capital outflow, and real transfer, took place in the rest of the decade.

The real transfer was aided by the relative deflation in France, which increased taxes to pay interest on the loans and raised interest rates to help sell them. It was also materially promoted by the German inflation up to 1873. This German inflation was partly the result of the acquisition of gold in part payment of the indemnity. More significantly, perhaps, it occurred simultaneously with the shift of the German monetary standard from bimetallism, in which both gold and silver were included in the German reserves, to gold alone.

The German inflation partly assisted in the transfer by increasing direct imports of goods from France. In part, the process was more roundabout. French sales to Britain increased; German sales decreased. Britain consumed the same goods as before but merely shifted its source of supply. The same result could be achieved through British exports. German imports from Britain increased; French imports (relatively) decreased. Britain could sell the same volume of goods as before but helped transfer the capital by shifting exports from France to Germany.

The difficulty for economics posed by the Franco-Prussian indemnity was that it made reparations payments appear transferable between countries, provided that the mechanism were handled properly. In retrospect, however, it appears that this unilateral payment could be effected only because the French were desperately anxious to do so and because Germany acquiesced in permitting an increase in spending. The contrast of the failure to transfer German reparations after World War I made clear that the 1871 episode had been a special, not a general, case.

German Reparations, 1919–31. That France would require reparations from a defeated Germany in 1919 followed automatically from the facts of 1871. But for payment to be effected required a duplication of the position of 1871, or another set of equivalent circumstances. Neither condition was met.

The facts of the 1919 schedule—the breakdown under inflation and the new basis in the Dawes Plan of 1924; the collapse after 1928, producing the ill-fated Young Plan of 1930, closely followed by the Hoover moratorium of June, 1931—none of these will be set out here. For our purposes it is sufficient to observe that Germany did not deflate, nor did the reparations recipients expand expenditure, to produce the required export surplus and import surpluses, respectively. The German government tried to raise the reparations payments in marks through taxation, and this taxation was deflationary. But the increase in the rate of interest and the enthusiasm of the newly established international investment bankers in New York defeated this. Governmental deflation at the national level was offset by provincial and local inflation, as industry and local governments borrowed abroad for spending, on balance.

Nor did Britain and France adjust their spending to fit projected reparations receipts. They regarded reparations receipts not as a new source of income which must be spent to raise national income by a multiple, but as a means of debt reduction. Reparations failed to contract expenditure in the paying country, on balance, or to enlarge expenditure in the recipients. Transfer proved impossible except on the basis of borrowed funds.

The payment produced an important economic controversy. Like so many such debates, no clear winner or loser emerged. In debate with Ohlin, Keynes reached the conclusion that reparations could not be paid (correct, though for the wrong reason). He believed that price elasticities were too low and that Germany could not expand export receipts by lowering export prices. This might have been true, but it was never tested because Germany did not reduce export prices. Ohlin, on the other hand, discounted Keynes's worries about price elasticities of demand as he focused attention for the first time on the possibility that transfer would be effected not through price shifts but through changes in income. He failed, however, to perceive that none of the countries involved were pursuing the internal policies which transfer called for.

With the halt in U.S. long-term lending to Germany in 1928, this means of paying reparations and enjoying the net import of commodities was no longer available. In 1929 the gap was filled by short-term borrowing, and Germany still experienced a small import surplus on trade account. Beginning in 1930, however, the position changed drastically. Deflation in Germany reduced imports from $3.25 billion in 1929 to $2.53 billion in 1930 and $1.66 billion in 1931. Exports were sustained fairly well, and the balanced trade condition in 1929 was converted to an export surplus of $230 million in 1930 and $715 million in 1931. Real transfer was effected through deflation.

This episode is regarded rather differently by different observers. To some it suggests how effective income changes can be in adjusting the balance of payments. To others it is a reminder that adjustment of the balance of payments at any cost is likely to result in $5\frac{1}{2}$ million unemployed, or 30 percent of registered workers—hence Hitler and a world war.

Hyperinflation and Capital Movements. The period after World War I in eastern and central Europe illustrates the effects of different kinds of capital movements—long- and short-term—under conditions of freely fluctuating exchanges, and also provides an insight into capital transfer. In most of these countries inflation was inevitable after the war, as households, firms, and governments all simultaneously tried to spend more than their income. Gold and foreign exchange reserves were quickly dissipated, and foreign exchange rates were allowed to depreciate.

The currencies of these countries could be said to be valued in two markets: internally in terms of prices; externally in foreign exchange. In the early stages of depreciation, stabilizing speculation took place in both markets. Internally, observing that prices were rising, consumers postponed expenditures in the expectation that they would come down again. At the new level of income and higher prices, consumer saving balanced government deficits and business investment. Externally, foreign speculators, surprised at the low prices for the zloty, mark, shilling and other currencies, bought them in the expectation of their return to initial or prewar pars.

The foreign stabilizing capital inflow supported the foreign exchange at a rate higher than would otherwise have been the case. In the exchange market the value of speculative purchases plus exports equaled imports, so that the capital inflow was transferred in goods. This import surplus had a braking effect on internal inflation, too, and, together with the consumers' savings, kept the external value of the currency above the internal value. In this phase the currency was overvalued in the foreign market relative to the domestic market.

But expectations of lower commodity prices and higher exchange rates were doomed to disappointment. After a time, the speculators became thoroughly disillusioned and reversed their positions. Consumers spent their income as fast as it was received and, to the extent made possible by past savings and bank credit, faster. The effect on the level of internal prices was explosive. In the external market foreign speculators reversed the field and took their losses, selling the currencies they had bought for the rise. And capital flight began, as domestic holders of currency sold it for foreign exchange.

No net capital movement out of these countries could take place, however, unless exports exceeded imports. With a freely fluctuating exchange and no gold support, depreciation had to proceed far enough to make, say, Poland a cheap place in which to buy before anyone with Polish marks (later the zloty) to sell for pounds could make the exchange. A domestic holder of capital could get pounds if he found a person willing to give up pounds for Polish marks. This would be the case only if the holder of pounds took a speculative view in favor of the Polish mark. After a time this was practically excluded. Or he could buy sterling if the depreciation in the exchange market proceeded faster than the internal depreciation, so that the exchange was undervalued and goods were cheap in Poland despite the rapidly rising price level. In this way an export surplus developed to transfer capital abroad. Some short-circuiting of the process took place after a time. Instead of attempting to buy foreign exchange at ruinous prices, a holder of the hyperinflated currency would buy goods which he would ship abroad for sale in foreign exchange. This method of capital export created its own export surplus and added to the internal inflation. But the explosive character of inflation under destabilizing speculation in both internal and external markets was so marked that it quickly brought about the collapse of currencies and the necessity for their stabilization or replacement by Draconian measures.

After World War II, with the memory of the postwar hyperinflations of 25 years previous fresh in their minds, those countries which failed to maintain adequate controls or to institute monetary reforms reached the stage of explosive hyperinflation much faster. There was no stage of stabilizing speculation internally or externally, since no one believed in a return to normality. All who could took flight into foreign currencies or goods. After World War I the final breakdown of the mark took place in December, 1924, and the depreciation of the zloty was checked in the same year. This was six years after the Armistice. But in 1945–46 the Hungarian pengo lasted only nine months after V-E Day before its value fell to one octillionth.

Normal Capital Movements. Some economists make a distinction between normal and abnormal capital movements. In one sense, all international capital movements are abnormal, if we adopt the classical assumption that factors of production do not move internationally. But if we grant that capital does move, though insufficiently to equate interest rates among countries, a distinction between normal and abnormal movements may be appropriate.

During the 19th century, private capital moved from countries where it was plentiful and cheap to those where it was scarce and expensive. London, Paris, and Amsterdam lent. The rest of the world borrowed. Capital flowed from the low-interest rate countries to the high-interest rate countries.

It is clear enough that the London capital market will fix a rate of interest on Union Pacific Railroad bonds which will equate the return on capital, after allowance for risk, to the other rates in the London market. We are not talking in terms of this subjective discount, which operates internationally in the same way that it does within a country: a single rate of interest will prevail in a capital market in an abstract sense, even though the market yields on governments and grade B bonds will differ. The theoretical rate of interest is net of subjective risk. The market rate is not.

For present purposes, however, a normal capital movement is one from a country with a lower rate of interest to one with a higher, dealing not in subjective or theoretical rates but in market terms. An abnormal movement is one which runs from a high-interest rate country to a low.

Some capital movements, abnormal in this restricted sense, are entirely normal insofar as business practice is concerned. Thus, for example, amortization payments or periodic repayments of principal are abnormal to the extent that the original loan was normal, in that the debtor high-interest rate country is making payment to the low-interest rate lender. Similarly, investments by a trust anxious to diversify its portfolio may run uphill in "abnormal" fashion, though they may constitute sound disposition of funds. But capital flight from an under-developed country is abnormal in an important respect in the balance of payments, whereas capital movements to such a country are typical and easily handled through the payments mechanism.

Normal Transfer. A normal capital movement is virtually certain to be spent in the borrowing country and to increase national income and imports. Exceptions occur. We have just discussed the German case, in which the bulk of the inflation caused by foreign borrowing—but not all—was offset by governmental deflation to pay reparations. But, as a general rule, borrowing by high-interest rate countries is borrowing to spend. Deflation may not occur in the lending country. This is relatively unimportant, if income expansion in the borrower is assured.

The 19th century lending was of this normal variety. So was the lending, with the partial exception noted, of the United States in the 1920's. Net long-term lending averaged close to $800 million a year from 1924 to 1928, inclusive, and no difficulty was experienced in its transfer. Gold movements were relatively small, on balance and gross, and can be explained largely in terms of short-term capital movements.

Abnormal Transfer. The capital inflow to the United States in the 1930's, however, was of an entirely different order. Fleeing for safety from taxation, devaluation, and outright confiscation, it failed either to decrease expenditure in the "lending" country or to expand it in the "borrowing." It has been said that the United States did not need foreign capital in the 1930's. This is true; but it fails to make clear why it did not use it. Foreign purchases of American securities raised their prices, relative to what they would otherwise have been; but United States firms did not respond by issuing more securities. Foreign purchases of bonds lowered interest rates, but no significant number of new borrowers chose to borrow. The demand for capital in the United States was inelastic with respect to the price of securities and the rate of interest at this time.

It does not inevitably follow that a normal or downhill movement of capital from a low-interest rate country to a high will be spent by the borrower or that an uphill movement in the other direction will not be.

But the presumption runs in this direction. On this account, transfer takes place fairly readily from the capital rich to the capital poor country. It is more difficult to effect from the poor to the rich.

The balance-of-payments behavior of the United States after World War II presented a very different picture in which the transfer process became complicated by a subtle switch in the character of government donations, along with an increase in capital outflow through new issues, direct investment, and American purchases of existing foreign securities. Part of the story must be left for later discussion of the equilibrating process. Here it is important only to indicate that the U.S. balance changed from insufficient capital movements to meet the current account surplus in the interwar period, to insufficient current account surplus to meet the capital outflow plus donations, especially after 1958.

The early postwar period of reconstruction saw the United States as the one major source of output in a world of grave material shortages. Other countries were anxious to borrow, receive aid, and spend reserves to obtain import surpluses of goods and services. United States assistance under the postwar schemes and the Marshall plan could be said to have been induced by the current account surplus. After the outbreak of the Korean war, with its necessity to rearm in Europe and the Far East, and after the decision to undertake assistance to programs of economic development abroad, the position changed. The current account surplus declined substantially. When the capital outflow picked up after the restoration of convertibility in 1958, complete transfer was not effected, despite a rapid rise in the current account surplus from 1958–1964.

There was no problem in transferring capital inward to the developing countries. In part, however, these countries borrowed from the United States but had import surpluses with Europe. There was also a capital outflow from the United States to Europe which was not transferred fully in goods and services. Long-term capital flowed from the United States to Europe; dollars piled up in European hands to fund the movement.

Whether this movement should or should not have been transferred remains an open question. Some observers, such as Professor Machlup, think yes. Another point of view is that this movement is a response not to deep-seated differences in savings and domestic investment in Europe and the United States, but to monetary phenomena, of the sort that complicated the transfer process in the United States in the 19th century. The issue must remain unresolved until Part VI.

Summary

The transfer process is the means of effecting a real capital movement from one country to another. In the case of autonomous unilateral payments, there is a money or purchasing power transfer and ultimately a real transfer in goods. Classical economic thought believed that transfer was brought about by the price-specie-flow mechanism. Modern economists, beginning with Ohlin, have looked to income changes.

There is no need, however, for the purchasing power movement to precede the real movement.

What happens to the terms of trade during transfer will depend upon the net movement in income in the two countries, upon the net marginal propensities to spend on domestic and imported goods, and upon the supply elasticities.

The theory of transfer was built on Canadian experience in borrowing before World War I and on unilateral payments such as the Franco-Prussian indemnity and German reparations after World War I. It has been applied, in a case of fluctuating exchanges, to the currency disorders after World War I. Monetary phenomena connected with borrowing disturbed the classic conclusions in the U.S. borrowing of the 19th century, and may do so currently.

It is much easier to transfer capital from capital rich countries to capital poor, than in the opposite direction. After World War II, however, and after a long period of failing to fund in lending its real capital transfers, the United States failed to transfer *in toto* its capital movements and governmental grants for economic development.

SUGGESTED READING

Treatises, Etc.

See Haberler, chaps. vii and viii, and Viner, *Studies in the Theory of International Trade,* chaps. vi and vii. J. W. Angell's *The Theory of International Prices* (Cambridge, Mass.: Harvard University Press, 1926), summarizes the theory to a relatively early point. Carl Iversen's *Aspects of the Theory of International Capital Movements* (Copenhagen: Ejnar Munksgaards Forlag, 1935) carried the story forward a decade. Bloomfield's monograph, noted below, brings it to 1950.

The major studies in the verification of the classical views on transfer are:

J. H. Williams, *Argentine International Trade under Inconvertible Paper Money, 1880–1900* (Cambridge, Mass.: Harvard University Press, 1920).

J. Viner, *Canada's Balance of International Indebtedness, 1900–1913* (Cambridge, Mass.: Harvard University Press, 1924).

R. Wilson, *Capital Imports and the Terms of Trade* (Melbourne, Australia: University of Australia Press, 1931).

H. D. White, *The French International Accounts, 1880–1913* (Cambridge, Mass.: Harvard University Press, 1933).

Other monographic literature on the subject consists of:

A. I. Bloomfield, *Capital Imports and the American Balance of Payments* (Chicago: The University of Chicago Press, 1950).

M. Fanno, *Normal and Abnormal International Capital Transfers* (Minneapolis, Minn.: University of Minnesota Press, 1939).

E. E. Fleetwood, *Sweden's Capital Imports and Exports* (Stockholm: Natur och Kultur, 1947).

R. Nurkse, *Internationale Kapitalbewegungen* (Vienna: Verlag Julius Springer, 1935).

J. G. Williamson, *American Growth and the Balance of Payments, 1820–1913, A Study of the Long Swing* (Chapel Hill, N.C.: University of North Carolina Press, 1963).

Viner's monograph has been rewritten in the light of more recent theory in two articles: G. M. Meier's "Economic Development and the Transfer Mechanism, 1895–1913," *Canadian Journal of Economics and Political Science,* February, 1953, which emphasizes the income mechanism; and J. C. Ingram's "Growth and Canada's Balance of Payments," *AER,* March, 1957, which focuses on the effects of growth. A book, John A. Stovel, *Canada in the World Economy* (Cambridge, Mass.: Harvard University Press, 1959), reworks the material entirely.

An excellent treatment of capital movements in the period following World War I is in R. Nurkse's, *The Course and Control of Inflation after World War I* (Princeton, N.J.: League of Nations, 1946).

The journal literature on transfer is rich and varied. A good start on it is to be found in the American Economic Association's collections. See especially Metzler on transfer through income changes and the Keynes and Ohlin articles in American Economic Association, *Readings in the Theory of International Trade,* and Samuelson and Johnson in Part II of the American Economic Association, *Readings in International Economics.*

For a useful independent view of the case histories see chap. xv entitled "The Transfer Problem: Theme and Four Variations," in Fritz Machlup's *International Money, Debts and Gold* (New York: Charles Scribner's Sons, 1964).

POINTS

The matrix technique on which the chapter leaned is set out by Meade in *The Balance of Payments,* pp. 36, 88–93, and 125–48.

PART V

Capital Movements

Chapter 19

SHORT-TERM CAPITAL MOVEMENTS

Types of Capital Movements

A number of attempts have been made to categorize capital movements. They have been divided into "induced and autonomous," "stabilizing and destabilizing," "real and equalizing," "equilibrating, speculative, income and autonomous." The most usual division, however, is into short-term and long-term. Here there is an objective criterion on which to base the classification. A capital movement is short term if it is embodied in a credit instrument of less than a year's maturity. If the instrument has a duration of more than a year or consists of a title to ownership, such as a share of stock or a deed to property, the capital movement is long term.

While the distinction between short- and long-term capital movements is clear cut, it does not necessarily reveal what brought the movement about or what its effects in the balance of payments are likely to be. For these purposes we need to divide capital movements by motivation and by role in the balance of payments. In terms of motivation, we will want to know whether a capital movement is equilibrating, speculative, undertaken in search of income, or autonomous. In the balance of payments, it may be induced or autonomous, stabilizing or destabilizing. Since the causes and effects of short- and long-term capital movements differ, however, we must uncover these aspects of the subject as we go along.

Classification according to instrument, moreover, does not really indicate whether a capital movement is temporary or quasi-permanent. Many changes in foreign deposits take place slowly over long periods of time: for example, an Arab sheikh with deposits hidden in a numbered account in Zürich is holding instruments payable on demand; in a more fundamental sense he has made a long-term capital movement from the standpoint of his country and of Switzerland. European speculation in the New York stock market in the 1920's and 1930's used the instruments of long-term investment—equity shares in companies—but demonstrated a high rate of turnover and only a brief loss of liquidity. A European central bank which buys U.S. government bonds rather than short-term bills is still holding monetary reserves and not making a real long-term investment.

But no basis of classification is good for all purposes. As a point of departure we divide short-term capital movements by instrument and by holder.

Short-Term Credit Instruments and Holders

Short-term capital movements of, say, the United States can take place through changes in claims of U.S. residents on foreign residents or in liabilities of U.S. residents owned to foreign residents. The U.S. residents involved may include the government, the Federal Reserve System, commercial banks, other money market institutions (including other types of banks, financial intermediaries, security brokers, dealers, private speculators, and so on) and industrial and commercial firms. The short-term instruments are typically central bank deposits, commercial bank deposits, bills, acceptances, overdrafts, open-book credit, and even bank notes. A list of the most important instruments associated with each major category of resident would look as follows:

Holder	Claims	Liabilities
U.S. Treasury	Deposits in foreign central banks Debts to U.S. government coming due in a year	Foreign holdings of U.S. government debt, including long-term debt held by foreign monetary authorities
Federal Reserve System	Deposits in foreign central bank	Foreign central bank deposits with Federal Reserve Banks Federal Reserve notes held abroad
Commercial banks	Deposits in foreign banks Bills held abroad Overdrafts for foreign account	Deposits due to foreigners Overdrafts abroad
Money market institutions	Deposits in foreign banks Bills held abroad	Deposits due to foreigners Overdrafts abroad

Commercial and indus- trial firms	Due from foreign firms (including subsidi- aries) Deposits in foreign banks Bills held abroad	Due to foreign firms Acceptances due to for- eign holders Loans from foreign banks

The list makes no attempt to break down the assets and liabilities by currency, i.e., into those denominated in dollars and those in other currencies. It further omits forward exchange contracts, which are neither an asset nor a liability, but a contract to acquire an asset in the future in exchange for another. It includes the long-term government bonds held by foreign monetary authorities, since these highly liquid assets, readily salable in an active market, are virtually indistinguishable from the maturities of less than one year. No such list can claim to be complete in all respects. But the present one suffices to show the range of possible variation. It is important to observe that while the list gives bank deposits and bills of exchange as the major instruments of short-term capital at various levels, bills of exchange were more important in the 19th century and deposits more so in the 20th.

Short-Term Movements and Gold

On the gold standard, short-term capital movements, like gold, had two functions, one in the balance of payments and the other in the banking system.

In the balance of payments, short-term capital movements occasionally gave rise to movements of gold, but generally substituted for them. The short-term movement giving rise to a gold movement may occur, for example, when the current account is balanced. Exports of goods and services equal imports of goods and services, and there is no need for international payments on that score. In these circumstances, however, an outward short-term capital movement takes place: it may be an autonomous movement of capital in fear of taxation; a speculative movement which foresees an appreciation of a foreign currency; an income movement responding to an increase in the discount rate abroad or a reduction in the rate at home. If the current account is sluggish in reacting to the capital outflow, a gold outflow will occur. Or a central bank may merely convert into gold its foreign exchange holdings on a center which maintains convertibility. In all these cases, a short-term capital movement gives rise to a movement of gold.

In the more normal relationship, however, the short-term capital movement substitutes for gold in the balance of payments. A country has an export surplus. Instead of acquiring gold abroad, it adds to its foreign exchange reserves. Thus the gold exchange standard grew out of the gold standard; the members of the sterling bloc use sterling rather than gold as their primary international reserves. National monetary authorities outside the United States and the Eastern bloc built up their dollars more than their gold from 1938 to 1964, and their gold more than their dollars thereafter to 1967. In 1938, gold and dollars were $11.4 billions and $474 millions; at the end of 1964, they were $25.4 billions and $15.8 billions; at the end of June, 1967, $27.1 billions and $14.1 billions, everywhere respectively.

Gold and the Money Supply

Before setting out the impact of short-term capital movements on the money supply, it may be helpful briefly to review how gold movements produce monetary changes. Much depends upon the nature of the banking system and its ratios of central bank reserves to central bank liabilities, and member bank reserves (deposit liabilities of the central bank) to member bank deposits. Under the gold standard, an outflow of gold typically leads to a multiple contraction of money. The credit base is reduced, and member banks, because of traditional or legal requirements to maintain certain reserve ratios, are obliged to call loans and sell investments. If the central bank also operates on a reserve basis which is effective, there may be considerable leverage. The credit pyramid in the United States, operating at its maximum and neglecting any effect on note liabilities of the Federal Reserve Banks, used to call for a contraction of $3 in Federal Reserve credit for every $1 loss in gold. This total shrinkage of $4 in member bank reserves would produce, in turn, a decrease of $20 in member bank deposits or money, assuming an overall reserve ratio of 20 percent. This internal reserve requirement is no longer taken seriously in the United States, however; the provision for gold backing for Federal Reserve deposit liabilities has been eliminated by the Congress, and the President has asked Congress to relieve the Federal Reserve System of the need to maintain a reserve ratio against its liabilities in the form of Federal Reserve notes.

The British system, prior to the suspension of gold in 1931, operated somewhat differently. Here the liabilities of the central bank were not geared to gold in a simple multiple ratio, but above a certain minimum, called the "fiduciary issue," all liabilities of the Bank of England were matched one for one by gold. Incrementally, a change in gold holdings by the Bank of England produced a change of only the same amount in central bank liabilities. Since the joint-stock banks maintained lower reserves with the Bank of England, however, at about 11 percent, an outflow of a pound sterling in gold would lead to a shrinkage in the money in circulation of roughly £9.

On this showing, an outflow of gold under the gold standard leads to a multiple contraction of money in use. Conversely, an inflow of gold may result in multiple expansion.

Short-Term Movements and Money

An outflow of short-term capital may operate as an inflow of gold, leading to multiple expansion in the money supply. Conversely, an inflow of capital may lead to multiple contraction.

These relationships are most readily demonstrated by reference to the gold exchange standard, starting with an initial export surplus to be financed. Under the gold exchange standard, an outflow of capital to offset the export surplus typically took the form of an increase in the foreign exchange holdings of the central bank on a gold standard country. This exchange, taken to be as good as gold, forms the basis for a possible expansion in central bank credit. Even without this expansion, however, it provides the basis for an increase in member-bank reserves of the same amount, and hence for a multiple expansion in money. In response to a gain of 100 local currency units' worth of foreign exchange, the balance sheet of the central bank would show the following changes:

CENTRAL BANK

Assets	*Liabilities*
Foreign exchange.............+100	Member bank reserves........+100

The balance sheets of member banks, in turn, would be changed as follows:

ALL MEMBER BANKS

Assets	*Liabilities*
Reserves with central bank....+100	Exporters' deposits...........+100

The exporter who acquired the exchange which is sold to the central bank might just as well have acquired gold. The short-term capital outflow substitutes for a gold inflow, not only in the balance of payments but also in providing the basis for an expansion in the money supply.

Another form which the capital outflow may take is a reduction in liabilities to foreign banks. Suppose the export surplus which gives rise to the capital outflow is paid for through a reduction in foreign central bank deposits with the central bank of the reporting country. The balance sheets will then read as follows:

CENTRAL BANK

Assets	*Liabilities*
No change	Member bank deposits........+100
	Foreign central bank deposits..−100

ALL MEMBER BANKS

Assets	*Liabilities*
Reserves with central bank....+100	Exporters' deposits...........+100

The short-term outflow in this form has the same effect on the level of member bank reserves as a gold inflow or an increase in central bank reserves of foreign exchange. The effect at the central bank may be different, however. If the central bank regards its liabilities as all of equal importance insofar as they require it to maintain liquid assets, there is no effect on the credit policy of the central bank. If, however, the central bank typically worries about accumulations of liabilities to foreigners, because it regards them as subject to sudden withdrawal, but is not similarly concerned about liabilities to member banks, even this change on the asset side may produce a relaxation of credit policy. The reduction in quick liabilities to foreigners may induce the central bank to expand the credit base, just as an increase in foreign assets, whether gold or foreign exchange, would have done under our earlier examples. This form of short-term capital outflow may thus substitute fully for gold inflow. But this effect on the central bank is less certain than the effect in increasing member bank reserve balances and leading thereby to multiple expansion.

This asymmetry between the expansionary effect of an increase in foreign exchange assets and the contractive effect of an increase in liabilities to foreigners has led many experts to conclude that the gold exchange standard is on balance inflationary, and others to think that it automatically destroys itself by piling up its liabilities too high. Gold is money. Short-term capital is money when it represents an asset of a central bank, but not necessarily a subtraction from the money supply when it stands for a liability of a central bank. It may be irrational for a central bank to base its policy on changes in gross assets (i.e., gold and foreign exchange assets) and not on net assets (gold and foreign exchange less liabilities to foreigners), as the United States did from

1950 to about 1957. Thereafter, however, it became conscious of the need to worry about changes in net gold and foreign exchange.

Here is an important reason for making a distinction between short-term and long-term movements of capital. The former may have a monetary function; the latter as a rule do not. In fact when we think of short-term capital we tend to think of capital in its financial manifestation: of credit, banks, deposits, and the like. When the question concerns long-term capital, it is frequently desirable to think of capital as physical assets rather than in financial terms. We must occasionally contemplate the physical aspects of short-term capital movements, to be sure, or the financial character of long. The bright economist is the one who knows when the general rule does not apply. For the most part, however, short-term capital approaches money; long-term capital does not.

The accumulation of foreign dollar claims on the United States, which *in toto* have risen from $4.8 billion at the end of 1947 to $29.6 billions at the end of June, 1967, has worried some observers. This worry is usually expressed in the use of a ratio of foreign dollar claims to the U.S. gold reserves. Since the claims are now greater than the gold reserves ($13.1 billion in June, 1967), and, with the considerable likelihood of a further "worsening" of the ratio as U.S. payments deficits continue, such calculations are the source of handwringing both in and out of the government. The fear is, in effect, that if all dollar liabilities were cashed in at once, we would no longer possess sufficient gold reserves to meet our obligations. Others answer with a banking analogy, insisting that there is no need to deduct foreign claims from the gold reserves, since foreigners are most unlikely to withdraw the whole amount in gold. No bank is sufficiently liquid to meet all its deposits if they are suddenly and simultaneously withdrawn. The sterling area, for example, operates more or less effectively with liquid reserves of the British authorities amounting to less than one third of short-term liabilities to foreigners. It is necessary to have regard not only to the amount, but also to the character of the deposits.

But the ratio of reserves to foreign short-term liabilities suffers another important weakness. These liabilities are not the only possible claimants on the reserves. A foreign run on the dollar or sterling, or any other currency, can under conditions of currency convertibility be followed by a domestic run. No amount of reserves would be proof against this. Foreigners may be expected, perhaps, to turn against a gradually weakening currency before domestic holders, which makes the reserves to foreign short-term liabilities ratio of some significance. But it is clearly wrong to think of the last foreigner getting clear before the first domestic holder leaves. Hence equality of reserves and liabilities to foreigners has no special significance.

Primary and Secondary Changes in Money

The extent to which short-term capital movements substitute for gold in the money supply will depend upon where in the banking system the assets are held and where the liabilities are recorded. Much depends upon what we regard as money. Here it is defined to include all domestic demand deposits, but not the deposits of foreigners. This is somewhat arbitrary, and one could take the view that foreigners earn money (through their exports) and spend it (on their imports) so that their deposits should not be regarded as different from those of domestic residents. Nonetheless, the velocity of circulation of foreign deposits is probably different from that of resident demand deposits, and money is generally defined to exclude them.

The changes in money supply brought about by short-term capital movements can be broken down into the primary, secondary, and tertiary. Note well that our concern is with changes in money, not income. We are dealing with multiple expansion and contraction of means of payments, not multiplier effects on income. The primary expansion or contraction in the money supply is that which results directly from the balance-of-payments surplus or deficit on current account. Exports exceed imports. This means that there is a net expansion of money in the hands of exporters. Or imports exceed exports. This means that import transactions extinguish money over and above that amount of money created by export transactions. These are regarded as the primary expansion and contraction.

The change in the money supply from the current account of the balance of payments must be combined with domestic credit creation or extinction to give the total change in domestic money. This is a tautology. As such, it is not very interesting. Some economists have tried to ring the changes on simple equations relating to credit creation and the balance of payments surplus or deficit to the change in money supply, and to study statistical data on these series. But it is impossible to "specify" the model, that is, to know whether credit creation produces deficits because the money supply is held constant, or deficits lead to the necessity for credit creation, or any one of a variety of other possible relationships. In developed countries, at least, this research has hit a dead end, because there is no unique causality.

Credit creation and contraction may not be independent of the balance of payments, as implied in the last paragraph. Secondary changes in money may occur as a result of short-term capital movements which affect member bank reserves. Suppose exports exceed imports, and these are paid for by a reduction of foreign monetary authorities' deposits with the central bank. Member bank deposits increase; the offsetting increase in exporters' deposits is the primary expansion in money. But on the basis of the excess reserves thus created, it is possible to undertake new lending leading to a secondary expansion.

Conversely, an import surplus which resulted in a reduction in member bank deposits and an increase in foreign central bank deposits with the central bank would lead to secondary contraction through the loss of reserves. Secondary expansion and contraction assume, of course, that there are no excess reserves.

If the central bank operates on a reserve basis, and is prepared to expand its discounts or open-market investment purchases when it gains reserves or reduces its foreign liabilities, or contract when it loses reserves or when its foreign liabilities increase, the resultant monetary change can be called the tertiary effect. But for most purposes the tertiary effect can be ignored. The secondary change in the money supply then includes any and all changes in money resulting from the change in net claims on, or liabilities to, foreigners.

If the secondary change in money supply leads to a change in national income, through changes in liquidity, interest rates, and consequent changes in domestic investment, these must be distinguished from those which take place through the multiplier. The creation of income through net exports, or its extinction through net imports, is the multiplier change in income. If the primary and secondary changes in money accompanying the changes in income produce a further change in domestic spending and income, this may be regarded as the banking income change. And this banking income change is still different from any income change induced by a current account surplus or deficit through the international accelerator. It is not necessary to give this change a designation, since we mention the accelerator so seldom that we can be explicit on each occasion.

Note this. A foreign central bank intent on its own interests may find itself conducting open-market operations in the United States. If it buys deposits at the Federal Reserve Bank with gold it expands our reserves. If it buys gold with deposits it contracts. But even when its dollar reserves are unchanged, it can affect the New York money market. To switch Federal Reserve deposits to a commercial bank or to use them to buy acceptances or government paper expands the money base; to build up deposits at the Federal Reserve through selling short-

term paper or transferring deposits from commercial banks is contractive. A world banking center must learn to offset the meaningless
changes in reserves arising from international transactions in the same
way that it responds to seasonal and similar changes in the note circulation.

The Role of the Commercial Banks

But to return to short-term capital movements and the money
supply. In the examples we have worked through, the change in assets
or liabilities has taken place at the central bank. There is nothing which
requires this. Suppose the short-term capital outflow took the form of an
increase in commercial bank holdings of foreign exchange, much as the
Australian banks used to hold sterling directly as reserves, in addition to
their deposits with the Commonwealth Bank. The primary expansion in
money now takes place as the banks increase their holdings of foreign
exchange and their liabilities to exporters. Whether secondary expansion will occur or not, however, is dependent upon whether the commercial banks are permitted to count foreign exchange as part of their
reserves or, with reserves in excess of the legal limit, whether they feel
safer with these added assets and therefore more in a mood to expand
loans and investments. Some secondary expansion may therefore occur,
though it is not so likely as in the case where the change in assets was
located at the central bank.

The short-term capital outflow can take the form of a decrease in
foreign deposits at the commercial banks. There will be no secondary
expansion unless the banks have been worried about the size of their
liabilities to foreigners and, relieved at the reduction of this potential
drain, feel inclined to expand loans and investments. The banks must be
in a position legally to do so through the existence of excess reserves.
These may be held because of lack of investment opportunities in a
depression; they may reflect simply fear that foreign deposits are less
"permanent" than domestic, so that more caution than that required by
law is desirable.

The Money Market

As a third alternative, the short-term capital movement may be
financed in the market rather than by the commercial or the central
banks. In this case the secondary expansion of money is unlikely to take
place, and even the primary expansion may be excluded. Suppose that
the export surplus is financed by a speculative short-term capital out-

flow. The seasonal surplus in the balance of payments of the United States was financed each autumn, prior to World War I, by speculators who bought sterling when it was cheap and planned to sell it later in the spring when it was dear (and the balance seasonally weak). Deposits of exporters would have increased, but those of speculators would have been drawn down. On balance, there has been no change in the money supply. But there is still a way to finance the increase in income. The expansion in balances in the hands of exporters is an expansion in what monetary economists call the "transactions circulation," i.e., those deposits which are used in the purchase of goods and services. The speculators, however, have paid them money, not from the transactions circulation, except in the unlikely event that the funds were newly saved, but from accumulated working funds pending investment. These belong to what is sometimes called the "financial circulation." In consequence, while the total supply of money is unchanged, the transactions circulation increases at the expense of the financial circulation, and the increase in national income due to the export surplus can be financed.

Finally, if the exporters financed the short-term capital outflow themselves, there would be no money change. Net exports take place. Assume that the exporters allow the foreign importers six months to pay. The export surplus is financed by an outflow of capital provided by the exporters. If the exporting house discounts bills or gets additional credit from its bank, then money is increased, whether the short-term capital is extended directly by the bank or indirectly through a bank loan to the export firm. If the exporter needs no additional financing, his deposits are drawn down, those of his suppliers of goods and services are built up, and the amount of money in circulation is unchanged. But the exporter cannot finance the shipment unless he had idle funds previously—in which case these may be regarded as having belonged to the financial circulation—or unless he is going out of business. In the latter circumstances a planned shift of funds from the transactions to the financial circulation does not take place, because the funds are moved abroad.

Varied Possibilities

This by no means exhausts the possibilities. Dealing with a capital outflow, we have not treated a reduction in liabilities to foreigners on the part of importing houses as a means of financing the export surplus, and what this may mean for the money supply. The indefatigable student, and the enthusiastic one, may work through these examples, as well as all the variations on the same theme associating a capital inflow with a contraction of the money supply. The essential points to retain, however, are these:

1. How does one define money for the purpose of this exercise? Are foreign deposits money? Is the financial circulation money? On the narrowest definition, an export surplus financed by short-term capital movements leads to a primary expansion of money, and an import surplus so financed to primary contraction. On a wider definition, the amount of money may remain unchanged, although significant changes take place within the overall total.

2. The general rule governing the secondary change in the money supply resulting from short-term capital movements is that its certainty will vary with the distance of the movers of the funds from the central bank. If the short-term capital is moved on the books of the central bank itself, whether through assets or through liabilities, the secondary expansion can and will take place, unless excess reserves prevent. If the funds are moved by commercial banks, there is still some chance, but less. If the nonbanking market finances the movement, the secondary expansion is impossible.

Let us return to the short-term capital movement which gives rise to a gold movement, rather than one which substitutes for it. A short-term capital outflow takes place when the current account is balanced. The consequence is a loss of gold. The loss of gold leads to a primary and secondary contraction of the money supply. But the short-term capital outflow may lead to offsetting primary and secondary expansions. The result would be a standoff. The primary and secondary changes induced by the short-term capital outflow may be less certain than those resulting from the gold exports. In this case the net result might be a contraction of money, even though there was no decline in national income to be brought about because of an import surplus. We shall recur to this shortly in discussing the role of stabilization funds in ensuring that unwanted monetary changes do not result from the movement of hot money.

Short-Term Capital, Speculation, and the Rate of Interest

Under the 19th-century gold standard, the rate of interest moved short-term capital and played a considerable part in bringing about adjustment in the balance of payments. It is important to observe that this requires that the various sections of the money market—dealers, banks, central banks—be willing to speculate, i.e., to take an exchange position, or to maintain an imbalance between its short-term claims and liabilities denominated in foreign currencies. If no one were willing to take a speculative position in sterling, the only effect of increasing the discount rate in London would be to increase the forward discount on the currency (or reduce the premium). Any capital inflow in response to the change in the rate of interest would be hedged in the forward market, in order to avoid the exchange risk. Unless the increased sales of forward exchange, offsetting spot purchases, lead to speculative forward purchases, which, by assumption, they do not, the attempt to sell forward will fail to find buyers, and the rate will fall. When the forward discount is equal to the interest rate differential, there is no advantage in moving hedged funds to the high-interest rate money market.

The use of the discount rate as a means of inducing short-term capital movements thus requires speculative capital movements in which the exchange risk is not covered. This condition prevailed in the 19th century. A foreign trader was, on the whole, indifferent as between assets in sterling or in his own currency and cared very little about which currencies his liabilities were denominated in. With the exception of the period from 1797 to 1816 during the Napoleonic Wars, the pound sterling had been immovable in terms of gold since 1717, while the value of the dollar, apart from a slight adjustment in 1834 and the suspension of specie payments from 1861 to 1879 because of the Civil War, had also been fixed in relation to gold since 1792. Expectations concerning exchange rates were inelastic, and speculation was stabilizing. Under these conditions, interest rate changes induced movements of short-term capital.

The classical view of the role of the discount rate on the gold standard was that it operated through credit to alter prices, and thereby to affect exports and imports. In its most elaborate treatment by Hawtrey, the theory suggested that wholesalers operated in the London market on borrowed funds. A rise in the rediscount rate, by increasing the cost of carrying goods, would tend to make them sell. This would lower prices, encourage exports, discourage imports. A reduction in the discount rate, on the other hand, however, would induce them to expand their inventories. The impact of their buying on the market would drive prices up, discourage exports, encourage imports. In this way, the bank rate was believed to influence the balance of payments on the gold standard. An increase or decrease in the discount rate would attract or repel gold by encouraging and depressing exports and imports.

Subsequent investigation has suggested that short-term capital movements in a world of stable expectations short-circuited this round-about process. An increase in the discount rate led to an inflow of gold into the London market through its effect in encouraging lending to London and discouraging borrowing from it. At a higher discount rate, borrowers would tend to pay off bills coming due in London, rather than renew them; and foreign banks would think twice before discounting bills drawn in sterling, preferring to hold them for their own account and earn the higher return. In either case, a capital flow toward London would be set in motion and lead to a gold inflow. Conversely, a decline in the rate of interest would lead to a capital outflow, which would have to be matched by a gold outflow, as more bills would be drawn on London and more bills would be discounted there.

So powerful was this short-circuit device that a gold flow resulting from the balance of payments on current account could be halted and reversed through opposing short-term capital movements. Through years of experience, the Bank of England learned that the remedy for a crisis, whether in domestic or in foreign payments, was to raise bank rate rapidly and to lend freely at the high rate. Liquidity was available to the market as a whole, but only upon payment of a penalty discount rate.

Note that this sort of speculation that existed in the 19th century and is developing today, after the establishment of convertibility in 1958 and the alignment of the guilder and the Deutschemark in 1961, differs markedly from that which took place in the 1920's and 1930's. In that interim, people took speculative positions because they expected an exchange rate to change. In the 19th century, and increasingly today, people are willing to hold a variety of foreign currencies because they expect exchange rates to be unchanged. This is especially true of the relations of the Common Market, the Swiss franc, and Scandinavian currencies to the dollar—both the New York dollar and dollar assets and liabilities of European financial institutions. It is not true for sterling, in which foreign exchange positions are carefully watched. But the casual ignoring of exchange risks among other major world currencies has the interesting feature that while it makes short-term capital highly responsive to interest rate changes, it makes interest rate changes less and less available for domestic monetary purposes. The attempt to raise or lower interest rates for domestic as opposed to balance-of-payments reasons will be swamped by short-term capital flows.

Destabilizing Movements

Under circumstances of flexible exchange rates, or fixed rates which are subject to frequent changes, exchange risks will be avoided or taken with deliberation. If exchange risks are avoided, short-term capital movements cannot take place (apart from prospective changes in the current account, a tricky point, best ignored by all but the *aficionado*). When short-term movements do occur because exchange risks are consciously undertaken, they may be stabilizing or destabilizing. In a world of monetary mess and frequent rate changes, such as that between 1919 and 1958, short-term capital, when it was not controlled, tended to operate with elastic expectations in a destabilizing way. In these circumstances, an increase in a discount rate would often lead to a capital outflow, rather than an inflow. It would be taken not as a sign of strength indicating the readiness of the authorities to protect the balance of payments but as a sign of weakness, and as a preliminary to eventual currency depreciation.

A similar destabilizing movement took place from New York and especially London to Frankfurt and Amsterdam in the spring of 1961 after the 5 percent upward revaluation of the Deutschemark and the Dutch guilder. The international money market regarded this shift in the rates not as a final change, but as the first bite of the cherry. Instead of foreign funds in Germany and the Netherlands moving home with their profit, new funds moved in.

Under destabilizing speculation, an import surplus leads to capital outflow and increased loss of reserves rather than to the inflow which would finance the balance of payments on current account and render the reserve movement unnecessary. Conversely, an export surplus leads through a rising exchange rate and reduced rate of interest not to the offsetting capital outflow, which stabilizing speculation would produce, but to a capital inflow which brings about an embarrassing addition to gold and exchange reserves, excess banking reserves and monetary superabundance. Short-term capital movements came to be regarded in the interwar period as a menace to international stability rather than as an instrument in its achievement. An early step in the defense of a currency with a persistent disequilibrium was the forbidding of movements of capital.

If the current account is in rough balance, a destabilizing capital outflow will produce a gold outflow, and an inflow of capital a gold inflow. It may happen that the monetary effect of the capital movement offsets that of the gold movement. Such was the case, for example, when foreign central banks acquired dollars during the "gold scare" of 1937, in the expectation that the U.S. dollar was going to be appreciated through a reduction in the Treasury gold-buying price. Gold was exchanged for dollars. The Federal Reserve System acquired a new asset in the form of gold and a new liability, a deposit of a foreign central bank. So long as the increase in the gold ratio of the Federal Reserve System led to no change in reserve bank credit outstanding, the expansionary effect of the gold was offset in full by the contractive effect of the short-term capital inflow. But, as we have already suggested, this need not be the case. If the foreign balances are held in accounts not with the Federal Reserve Bank of New York but with a commercial bank, a net increase in member-bank reserves will have taken place, and a net secondary expansion of credit is possible.

There may be occasions when it is desirable to permit this net effect of the gold movement which overwhelms the opposite tendencies of the outflow of short-term funds. But, as a rule, countries prefer to have their monetary policy unaffected by destabilizing capital movements. The devices worked out to offset the net monetary impact of "hot money movements" were the exchange stabilization fund and gold sterilization.

Stabilization Funds

The first stabilization fund was the British Exchange Equalization Account, established in 1932 to moderate movements of the exchange rate after the abandonment of the gold standard by the British in September, 1931. Like so many other economic institutions, the uses of the Exchange Equalization Account (EEA), were originally only dimly perceived. The primary focus of the authorities when it was established was upon variations in the exchange rate. In its actual operation, it did little stabilizing of exchange rates because it was unwilling to take exchange risks, converting rather the foreign exchange it bought each day into gold which it brought back to British shores.

Ultimately the Exchange Equalization Account came to be used less to affect the exchange rate than to protect the London money market from the excessive changes in liquidity which the movements of hot money would otherwise produce.

The Account was originally equipped with sterling bills. It was in a position to buy foreign exchange (and convert it into gold) to meet a capital inflow, but it would have been helpless before an outflow since it owned no gold or foreign exchange to supply to foreigners in exchange for sterling. But the EEA's bills—actually short-term government obligations—could be issued (or sold) in any amount. When a foreigner bought sterling, the EEA would sell sterling bills for the same amount and buy foreign exchange (ultimately gold). The foreigner was supplied with a sterling asset, and the sterling authorities acquired gold which they held outside the banking system. No secondary expansion of the money supply could occur as a result of a capital inflow.

Whether any primary expansion took place depended upon how one defined money and upon how the foreigner chose to hold sterling. If the foreigner held a deposit with a joint-stock bank, money had increased if foreign deposits are included in the definition of money, but otherwise not. In the latter case the joint-stock bank was likely to buy the bills sold by the Exchange Equalization Account:

BALANCE SHEET OF EEA

Assets	*Liabilities*
Gold......................+£100	Bills........................+£100

BALANCE SHEET OF JOINT-STOCK BANKS

Bills......................+£100	Due to foreigners...........+£100

If, on the other hand, the foreigner chose to hold bills directly himself, then there was no increase in money under any definition. The foreigner gave up foreign exchange convertible into gold for sterling bills, and the Exchange Equalization Account gave up bills for gold. The British government had to pay interest on these bills, which the foreigners earned. This was the price paid for permitting the capital movement, which it would have been costly to prevent without producing untoward effects.

The bright student may have observed that if the foreigner holds deposits and the joint-stock bank bills, the effect will be contractive in money terms. The liabilities of the banks have increased, but not their primary reserves. If their primary reserve ratio was just being met before the capital inflow, they now have a deficiency. The Bank of England frequently undertook open-market operations to rebuild the deposits with the Bank of the joint-stock banks and to prevent deflationary consequences from short-term capital inflows and expansive repercussions of outflows.

These so-called trimming operations called for small Bank of England purchases of bills in the face of a large capital inflow and large EEA sales of bills, to keep the monetary system on an even keel.

Later when foreigners withdrew funds placed in the London market, the entire process would be reversed. The Exchange Equalization Account would sell gold for foreign exchange, and in turn, sell the foreign exchange for sterling. The sterling would be used to retire Treasury bills in the London market. Foreigners, on the other hand, would sell British Treasury bills for sterling (or sell sterling which would lead the joint-stock banks to sell Treasury bills) and buy foreign exchange which would lead their central banks to buy gold. The earlier transaction would have been reversed without an impact on the London money market, after a small trimming operation of the Bank of England. The Bank, in this connection, would sell bills to mop up primary reserves no longer needed by the joint-stock banks after their foreign deposits had contracted.

These stabilization-fund operations were successful, as already noted, because the Exchange Equalization Account was equipped with sterling and because the forces it was called upon to neutralize produced a capital inflow. If it had held gold or foreign exchange, it would not have been well placed to meet an inflow but could have coped with an outward movement. To meet an outflow, a stabilization fund needs gold; an inflow, domestic money or near money.

United States Stabilization Fund

The United States Stabilization Fund was originally established with part of the gold "profit" which came from the revaluation of the gold stock of the United States from $20.67 an ounce to $35 in 1934. With $2 billion of gold at the new value, the Fund was in an admirable position to finance a capital outflow. Confronted with a capital inflow, however, it was helpless. In order to provide dollars to foreigners, it had to obtain dollars. This it could do only by selling gold to the Federal Reserve Bank of New York. The first result of this transaction is as follows:

FEDERAL RESERVE BANK OF NEW YORK

Assets	Liabilities
Gold.......................+$100	Stabilization Fund deposit....+$100

When the Stabilization Fund now spends its dollars to buy foreign exchange offered to it by foreigners who seek refuge for their funds, the reduction in Stabilization Fund deposits results in an increase in deposits of member banks. This, of course, provides a basis for multiple expansion of money which the Fund was established to assist in preventing.

Gold Sterilization

Open-market operations are the means of preventing a capital inflow from affecting the credit base when the Stabilization Fund lacks power to borrow dollars. As gold increases in the balance sheet of the central bank, discounts and securities should be reduced, to leave the total volume of member bank reserves unchanged. Assuming that the foreigners hold their funds in the form of deposits with the commercial banks, this policy requires no stabilization fund and is called simply "gold sterilization." The sterilization of a capital outflow which leads to a loss of gold calls for open-market purchases of securities by the central bank.

In 1936–37, the U.S. Treasury pursued a policy of gold sterilization without calling upon the Federal Reserve System to assist with open-market operations. Normally, when gold was sold to the Treasury by gold arbitrageurs, it would replenish its balances at the Federal Reserve Bank. In order to sterilize the imported gold, however, it chose to pay for gold with its balance, which it brought back to normal not from the deposit of gold certificates but from borrowing in the money market. The new borrowing needed to buy the gold acted as an offset to the increase in member bank reserves in the same way as would a sale of government securities by the Federal Reserve System.

If the gold inflow takes place as a consequence of an export surplus on current account rather than a capital inflow, a policy of sterilization cannot prevent a shift of money from the investment circulation to the transactions circulation. This finances the multiplier expansion of income: money in the hands of exporters and their suppliers increases; money in the investment circulation declines as the Treasury or the Federal Reserve System sells government securities to the money market. Complete sterilization, which would smother the income as well as the monetary effects, would call for buying the gold with money raised through an increase in taxes. The government surplus (new savings) would then offset the export surplus (foreign investment). The increase in net taxation would take money out of the transactions circulation as fast as the export surplus put it in.

The Basel Agreement

It may not be enough for a country which experienced a destabilizing short-term inflow to take offsetting steps in its money market, nor for a country losing capital to offset the contraction in monetary reserves. There will possibly be need to support the balance of payments of the country losing gold. Central bankers have become increasingly aware of the need for joint action by monetary authorities on both sides of the fence. In the spring of 1961, when the heavy movement of capital took place, largely from London to Frankfurt and Amsterdam, the Continental central banks bought and held sterling under arrangements worked out in Basel at the Bank for International Settlements.

Private holders of sterling dumped it on the foreign exchange market. Official sources bought it. This eliminated the net capital movement. Monetary effects might be felt, as liabilities to foreigners were shifted from the commercial (joint-stock) banks and the money market to the Bank of England. These would call for off-setting open-market operations. Similarly in Germany and the Netherlands, it was necessary to mop up the excess liquidity of the money markets after the capital inflow.

The success of this *ad hoc* informal arrangement growing out of monthly meetings and close cooperation among central bankers raises a question which we reserve for Part VI. Is it good enough to rely on informal and flexible arrangements, or are new institutions (or alteration of old) required to spell out the rights and obligations of the various parties? There is much to be said on both sides: until one can foresee all the various ways in which problems can present themselves, it is of course better to keep flexible, like the Basel Agreement. On the other hand, the French and especially the Netherlands central banks tried to help out the Bank of England in 1931, and got stuck with a lot of depreciated sterling. Can national institutions take on international risks without explicit political authorization such as enabling legislation would provide?

Central Bank Dealings in Forward Exchange

There is one more means of meeting speculative attacks on a currency besides the use of reserves and support from abroad. This is intervention in the forward market. When the market is selling dollars for foreign currencies, the Reserve Bank authorities may support the dollar not in the spot market with gold, but by feeding forward sterling, marks, Swiss francs, and so on, to the market, i.e., buying forward dollars. Some of the individuals seeking to acquire foreign currencies may be content in this circumstance to keep on holding spot dollars, and to satisfy their urge to acquire foreign exchange by buying it forward. If, however, they should insist on holding spot foreign currencies, the reduction in the rate on forward foreign exchange induced by the Federal Reserve's sales will encourage interest arbitrageurs to enter the market. These arbitrageurs will buy spot dollars and sell them forward, i.e., sell foreign currencies spot and buy them forward. Their spot operations will provide the counterpart to the spot foreign exchange outflow. Their forward operations will match the sales of the authorities. The result would be that foreign holders of dollars would be able to exchange them for foreign exchange without causing a reduction in U.S. gold reserves.

This operating device, recommended by Keynes in the 1920's, has been used only sporadically in the interwar and immediate postwar period. It is not suited to cope with a serious disequilibrium in the balance of payments, since the monetary authorities must ultimately deliver the foreign currencies they have sold forward—despite the fact that for a time they can keep swapping their contracts forward as they mature. The forward contracts in fact serve as a kind of mortgage or encumbrance on the national exchange reserves.

But forward operations of central banks are useful to meet short sharp speculative attacks on one or another currency which can be expected to reverse themselves over time. They have been described by the Treasury as the outer perimeter of the defenses of the dollar, a short-run device which by preventing sudden losses of reserves maintains confidence and reduces the nervousness of the foreign exchange market.

Forward operations can also serve domestic monetary purposes. A central bank which has experienced a large capital inflow may choose to offset it domestically not by selling off its portfolio of government securities but by forcing the commercial banks to hold foreign exchange rather than additional reserves. The technique is to undertake swaps, the sale of spot foreign exchange and the purchase of similar amounts forward. The commercial banks are forced to buy only by the fact that more interest can be earned in this fashion, at the rates set by the central bank, than on domestic liquid investments. The Bank of France undertook such swaps in sterling in 1927, and the Bank of Italy in dollars in 1965. Convenient as these central bank dealings in forward exchange may be for domestic monetary policy, they may mislead foreign authorities, who take a different view of official and private banking balances owned abroad in their market. Thus the dollars held by Italian commercial banks seem to be those of private institutions, when they are in reality merely held temporarily and the ultimate ownership is in official hands.

Exchange Control

In the 1930's it was thought that the only effective means of coping with destabilizing short-term capital movements was exchange control. Easy money policies directed to fight unemployment had led to vast pools of liquid funds. In a world of aggression, foreign threats, taxes regarded as confiscatory, and civil war, capital outflow could take place—so long as it was deemed necessary to maintain money markets liquid—without warning, and on a scale with which governments had difficulty in dealing. (If governments had been willing to let interest rates rise, asset holders could not have converted their domestic asset into currency to present for foreign exchange, since they would have been "locked in," i.e., able to achieve liquidity only at a price at which some other asset holder was willing to part with his liquidity.)

The Articles of Agreement of the International Monetary Fund produced at Bretton Woods in 1944 embodied this conclusion in favor of control of short-term capital movements into international prescription. But whatever the merits of the argument in favor of control over capital movements, the difficulty in the real world is to enforce it. The proceeds of exports must be collected; underinvoicing must be prevented. Foreign securities must be prevented from going abroad; nationals must be forestalled from taking the national currency (a noninterest bearing form of debt) abroad and all foreigners and nationals from bringing it in. The credit terms of foreign transactions must be regulated to prevent imports from moving to a cash or even prepayment basis and exports to longer and longer credit terms, thus moving capital abroad by means of the "leads and lags." Professor Mikesell has stated that if there is anything we have learned about international economics in the postwar period is that it is impossible to control capital movements without controlling the balance of payments as a whole.

Capital Movements under the Paper Standard

Under the freely fluctuating paper standard, stabilizing capital movements may take place on short-term account and limit the extent of exchange rate adjustment, or destabilizing movements may occur and widen it. History abounds with examples of both kinds. There is considerable difficulty, however, in forecasting which kind of speculation will take place.

Keynes once proposed that the distance between the gold points on the gold standard be enlarged—presumably by widening the gap between buying and selling prices of the central bank. The purpose of this proposal was to encourage short-term capital movements of the stabilizing variety by giving speculators more profit from foreign exchange bought just short of the gold import point and sold close to the gold export point. The proposal for permitting the foreign exchange rate to fluctuate without official intervention had provision for forward rates which it was hoped would bring out stabilizing speculation. As we observe in Appendix H, however, the establishment of a forward market is no guarantee that speculation will be of the stabilizing variety. If it is, the foreign exchange rate will move within a narrow range around the long-run equilibrium rate, much as an automatic pilot anticipates deviations from the course of the ship or airplane and makes adjustments in advance. If not, however, destabilizing speculation will exaggerate the deviations, like a servomechanism "hunting" in unstable oscillations, far each side of the norm.

Note the interesting position of speculation in the Canadian dollar during the period of flexible exchange rates from 1950 to 1961. Here short-term funds responded to changes in the exchange rate in a stabilizing way: Rhomberg found that a one-cent change in the exchange rate induced a $45 million movement of short-term capital, appreciation leading to outflows, depreciation to inflows. This market was relatively unconcerned by interest rates. In the long-term capital market, on the other hand, differences in interest rates produced substantial movements in capital flows whereas investors ignored the exchange rate.[1] This led to the curious reestablishment of the dominance of interest rate policy by the back door: changes in long-term interest rates led to movements of long-term capital, which produced changes in the exchange rate. These in their turn led to short-term capital flows. Thus the change in the long-term capital market was communicated to the short, rather than vice versa, and the exchange rate became a dependent rather than an independent variable. Note also that the increase in interest rates led to deflation by the curious route of attracting foreign capital which produced currency appreciation.

If the foreign exchange rate is not left to adjust to market conditions by itself, without assistance, but the authorities intervene to iron out daily, seasonal, or cyclical fluctuations, the authorities themselves will undertake short-term capital movements of a stabilizing variety. When the balance of payments is temporarily adverse, the authorities will supply the market with foreign exchange. This short-term capital inflow (reduction of foreign assets) may lead to primary and secondary contraction of the money supply in exactly the same way as if the currency had been on the gold standard. If there is a temporary surplus, on the other hand, the authorities will be called upon to absorb the

---

[1] This is probably because it was thought that over the long run the Canadian dollar would be worth just about a U.S. dollar, with cumulative departures from parity unimportant between the issuance of a bond and its retirement over its 20-year or so life. The investment was largely undertaken by American insurance companies in Canadian provincial and municipal bonds, and both parties could afford to take a long view.

redundant foreign exchange rather than to permit an increase in the rate; and the capital outflow may act as an expansive force. To the extent that official short-term capital movements operate to steady the foreign exchange rate, the country might just as well be on the gold standard, especially since the stabilizing capital movements are carried out by the central bank or other official body likely to be operating with central bank funds or credit.

Statistical Explanations

Modern econometric investigation has not ignored short-term capital, but progress is slow. One investigator finds that short-term capital movements are not interest sensitive; another that they are. In some work, the largest influence on short-term flows from the United States turns out to be the changes in foreign trade, which short-term flows finance. There is disagreement as to what would be the best proxy for speculative activity, or whether a stock adjustment model (in which portfolios of assets are rearranged when the interest rate changes) is superior or inferior to one based on flows. Should one regress capital against differences in interest rates or changes in these differences? Successive writers criticize the econometric models of the earlier economists in the field as yielding biased estimators, but successive attempts to penetrate the mysteries continue to yield low correlation coefficients.

This is the path of progress in science. The disagreements are so deep that the subject must be left for the nonce to econometrics, rather than transferred into international economics. In the long run, however,—and not too very long—the inductive work must be married to the deductive at the textbook level.

Summary

Short-term capital movements are those embodied in instruments of less than a year's maturity. They can substitute for gold or give rise to a gold movement. When they substitute for gold, they have the same primary effects on the money supply and may, but are unlikely to, have the same secondary effects. They give rise to gold movements when the short-term capital movement is destabilizing.

A number of devices have been used or proposed to deal with short-term capital movements. In a period of stabilizing speculation, their course has been effectively controlled by changes in short-term interest rates. Stabilization funds and gold sterilization have been evolved to permit destabilizing movements, without experiencing their monetary and banking effect. Central bank dealing in forward exchange, long since proposed, has begun to evolve into a more effective instrument. Exchange control, once thought useful to suppress them, has proved in practice difficult to administer.

Thus far the econometric tests of the theory of short-term capital movements have proved inconclusive.

SUGGESTED READING

TREATISES, ETC.

See C. Iversen, *Aspects of the Theory of International Capital Movements* (Copenhagen: Ejnar Munksgaards Forlag, 1935), especially chaps. ii, iii, and xiii; Bloomfield, *Capital Imports and the American Balance of Payments, 1934–39* (Chicago: The University of Chicago Press, 1950) especially chaps. ii, v, and viii; and C. P. Kindleberger, *International Short-Term Capital Movements* (New York: Columbia University Press, 1937; reprinted Augustus M. Kelley, Publishers, 1966).

For detailed accounts of the working of the Exchange Equalization Account, see N. F. Hall, *The Exchange Equalization Account* (London: Macmillan & Co., Ltd., 1935).

For a discussion of speculation and forward exchange, which goes beyond the confines of this chapter and into the world of Chapter 23 and Appendix H, see H. Grubel, *Forward Exchange, Speculation and the International Flow of Capital* (Stanford, Calif.: Stanford University Press, 1966), and William H. Branson, "The Capital Account in the United States Balance of Payments," an M.I.T. thesis of 1967.

POINTS

R. G. Hawtrey, *Currency and Credit* (London: Longmans, Green & Co., 1919), contains the exposition of the effect of short-term interest rates on the price level and the balance of trade. The evidence that the system did not work this way is furnished in W. E. Beach, *British International Gold Movements and Banking Policy, 1881–1913* (Cambridge, Mass.: Harvard University Press, 1935).

For a comparison of changes in money supply and the balance of payments, see Robert Triffin, *The World Money Maze* (New Haven, Conn.: Yale University Press, 1966), appendix.

Accounts of official United States operations in the forward exchange markets are contained in various issues of the New York Federal Reserve Bank *Monthly Bulletin.*

The reference to Rhomberg's findings about the movement of short-term capital in response to changes in the Canadian exchange rate is to R. R. Rhomberg, "Canada's Foreign Exchange Market," *SP*, April, 1960.

For a discussion of the econometric work on short-term capital movements, see J. L. Stein "International Short-Term Capital Movements," *AER*, March, 1965, the work of Bell and Kenen, cited by him, and criticism of Stein and his reply in *AER*, June, 1967.

Chapter	LONG-TERM PORTFOLIO
20	CAPITAL

Long-Term Debt

This and the following chapter discuss a few of the various forms of long-term capital moving between national economies. This deals mainly with debt; the next with equity or ownership capital accompanied by control. Between them is an important vehicle for capital movements which we neglect, capital movements through existing equity securities unaccompanied by control. In the interwar period there was an important movement of European capital into the New York Stock Market, which did not subside after 1929 or even after the post-World War II European recovery. The latter development, moreover, set in motion a reverse flow of U.S. private investment into European (and Japanese) equities, both through private dealings and through mutual investment funds. We neglect this traffic in shares. Much of what we have to say about debt in this chapter and direct investment in the next will apply to it.

The traditional form of long-term lending is the bond. For 100 years, up to 1914, the sterling bond dominated world financial markets. For a period from 1919 to 1930, the New York bond market assumed the role previously played by London. But this interlude was brief. Excessive lending, international disequilibrium, depression, the collapse of export markets, the notoriety given to certain questionable practices by bond promoters, all combined to turn the investor away from foreign bonds, except for those of Canada, which have never really been regarded as foreign. With few but perhaps gradually increasing exceptions, moreover, borrowers no longer liked fixed obligations in an uncertain world. The foreign bond fell on evil days.

Late after World War II with the reestablishment of convertibility of European currencies the New York bond market experienced a revival. European capital markets were compartmentalized. Those like

364

the Swiss and Dutch which had low rates of interest limited issues to relatively small amounts. Other, which could handle larger sums, had high rates. The New York long-term market gradually overcame its antipathy to foreign issues and gradually undertook new issues of bonds not only for Canada and Israel, the latter with a large element of charity about them, but also for European, Dominion, and Japanese borrowers. The net was smaller than the gross, since European investors, impressed with the breadth and liquidity of the New York market, bought dollar bonds issued by European borrowers, even though the rate of interest on New York issues was below that obtainable in Europe. So substantial was the expansion of the market that, given the weakness of the U.S. balance of payments, the Treasury authorities in July, 1963, imposed a prohibitive tariff on new securities, the Interest Equalization Tax, or IET. The market then moved to Europe, where so-called dollar bonds, i.e., bonds denominated in dollars, were issued and bought, by borrowers and lenders, outside the United States. Although such a market was smaller than the dollar bond market when it was located in New York with the strength of U.S. investors behind it, it remained, at close to $1 billion of new issues a year. An amount well in excess of the foreign bond markets—both national and international—available in Europe.

If the foreign bond is no longer dominant in international lending it is nonetheless worth study. Its behavior differs from that of other forms of long-term debt, such as term bank loans and government lending, because foreign bonds are sold to private investors. The borrower may be governmental, but the lender is not. Investment banks underwrite the sale of bonds which are distributed through the capital market to private institutions and individual investors, whose concern lies with safety of principal and flow of income. The private character of the lenders gives bonds a distinct pattern of behavior affecting both the level of income in the borrowing and lending countries and the balance of payments.

The eclipse of the bond after 1928 or 1929 led to new forms of foreign lending. Some was private banking, some government lending at long term, some government banking. From 1930 to the 1950's private long-term lending by banks had been limited to advances against gilt-edged security, such as gold, or to loans made with governmental guarantees. In the 1950's, there was renewed banking interest in medium-term financing of international trade in part under the provisions of the little used Edge Act of 1919, and in part with the help of an Export-Import Bank program of credits and guarantees. After the IET

European borrowers switched to long-term bank loans from the United States until the Gore amendment to the IET made the tax apply also to bank loans of more than one year. Governmental lending has been carried on partly through banking institutions such as the Export-Import Bank in the United States and, since 1946, partly through international agencies such as the International Bank for Reconstruction and Development (IBRD), the Inter-American Development Bank, the European Investment Bank, and the Asian Development Bank. Other governmental lending has taken place through specially created institutions such as the Lend-Lease Administration, the Economic Cooperation Administration, the Mutual Security Agency, the International Cooperation Agency, and the Agency for International Development, or has been arranged for particular purposes such as ship disposal or disposal of surplus commodities.

We may restrict ourselves, therefore, to private lending through the bond market, and government lending in its many long-term forms. The flow of capital through bank loans can be neglected on the grounds that it conforms largely to the principles of one or the other.

Foreign and Domestic Investment

Foreign investment is similar to domestic investment in that it increases income and employment in the process of capital formation and ultimately enlarges capacity for higher income after the capital has been formed. On the first score the real transfer of capital abroad through an export surplus gives rise to a multiplier increase in domestic incomes, leading to expanded domestic employment. On the second score the increased income made possible by foreign investment differs somewhat from that through domestic capital formation. It is national income which is increased, not geographic product since the nationally owned capital is located abroad. Conversely, when a country borrows from abroad, its geographic product is increased through the addition of new capacity, but national income grows by less than geographic product because some part of the increase in output accrues to foreign-owned factors as foreign income.

There is, of course, a decided difference in effect on factor proportions. Foreign investment leaves domestic factor proportions unchanged, and forestalls an increase in the capital/labor ratio, which would have raised the marginal product of labor and lowered that of capital, had the capital been invested domestically. One should accordingly expect labor to oppose foreign lending, in the same fashion that it has in the past approved of tariffs on labor-intensive imports. In recent years such concern has begun to be expressed by labor, but primarily in the direct investment field, where the connection between the foreign investment and local jobs can be clearly seen.

One old distinction made by Keynes turned on the location of the physical assets. The private investor runs risks whether he invests at home or abroad. If he makes a mistake in judgment and his investment proves worthless in case of domestic investment, the physical assets at least are within the national boundaries but accrue to foreigners if it be foreign. This distinction is an appropriate one if the risk he incorrectly judges is that of confiscation by government authority without adequate compensation. But it cannot be made for economic risks. A worthless factory or railroad is worthless whether at home or abroad; and an asset with some salvage value can be sold for that value, again whether at home or abroad.

With perfect international capital markets, there would be one interest rate all over the world. But of course such perfect capital markets are far from achieved. There are risks of default and confiscation, which require a subjective risk premium, different for each country, before capital will flow from a safe home market to countries abroad. Moreover, most investors and borrowers are myopic in that their horizons are restricted to the home territory, both for investments and for loans. (This is not necessarily irrational, as there is a cost to obtaining information on investments and opportunities for loans abroad.)

Economists like to play with the idea that it would pay a country to limit the movement of capital abroad, if the unrestricted movement of capital lowered the interest rate abroad. The domestic price of capital under optimum lending should be equal to the marginal rate of return on foreign capital, not the average rate, if the two differed, as would be the case if the lending country were a pricemaker in the world capital market. The analogy with the optimum tariff is exact. Under an optimum tariff strategy it pays to limit exports and/or imports, if the nation's trade has an impact on world prices, to equate relative prices at home to marginal rates of transformation abroad, not average rates. So with lending. There is even a small literature which combines the optimum tariff with the optimum level of foreign lending. This literature contributes to theoretical elegance more than to practical relevance. Not only do countries hesitate to undertake beggar-thy-neighbor intervention in world markets in the capital field, but the institution of the long-term contract, with no possibility of continuous recontracting, makes the impact of today's prices on the return on outstanding issues of limited significance.

Institutional Pattern of Lending

The imperfection of the international capital market may have been diminishing prior to the IET, as a consequence of better communication and transport in the modern age, but it is still marked. Well-established attitudes of investors, practices of investment banking houses, governmental intervention, and controls have all contributed to confining capital movements to well-worn paths. To use a hydrological analogy, capital flows not as broad rivers which equalize levels over a vast area, but as water in irrigation canals and ditches which bring moisture to some areas and not to others, even though they be on a lower level and may need it more. In these circumstances, the understanding of capital movements calls more for the techniques of the historian who can explain where the channels of capital flow were dug, than the analysis of the economist who merely describes the supply and demand for capital in separate markets without indicating how, and to what extent, they are connected.

From about 1825 to 1850, British foreign lending was largely to Continental borrowers, with the largest amounts sought for railroads and the associated supplying industries. With the revolutions of 1848, however, British investors turned away from European loans to lending to the Empire, the United States and gradually to the Middle East and Latin America. The emphasis continued on railroads, although the fact that colonial issues qualified as trustee investments, i.e., as approved for investors requiring very safe securities, helped sell the bonds of colonial governments at rates approaching British government yields. The movement of capital to specific countries would follow a learning process growth pattern: loans to Argentina, for example, started slowly in the 1880's and spurted from 1885 until the crash of Baring Brothers in 1890.

After getting its railroads started with British help, France turned to lending elsewhere on the Continent, largely for railroads and industrial banks rather than developing capital issues for other French industries. French financiers and engineers contributed importantly to the development of Germany, Italy, Spain, and Austria. The high commissions received by French banking houses, and the corruption of the press by foreign borrowers, led to the flotation of numerous dubious issues.

The Czarist government for example managed to issue in Paris loans which it could not sell or refund in London or Berlin.

It is a still open question whether British and French foreign lending diverted abroad capital which could have been profitably employed at home. The City of London and the Paris bourse were widely accused at home of having slowed down the growth of Britain and France prior to World War I by lending abroad for purposes of lower economic utility than loans refused at home.

In the interwar period, the demands of capital for reconstruction took London and Paris out of international lending, except for a continued flow of British loans to the Empire, then in process of becoming the Commonwealth. New York took over as the world's financial center and went in for an orgy of foreign bond issues, particularly for Germany and Latin America. Big underwriting commissions led to abuses, including the high-pressure selling of bonds by investment banking subsidiaries of New York banks at times when they had private knowledge of the borrower's default. New York also took the place of London as the provider of investment capital to Canada, with U.S. insurance companies which deny that they buy foreign bonds, ready to admit in the next breath that of course they buy Canadian.

The revival of the New York bond market in the late 1950's until it was hit over the head with the IET was largely for European borrowers, the Dominions, and Japan (apart from the IBRD, and Israel). Most of the developing countries needed still to establish their credit worthiness. Mexico was one that did. The IET did not apply to Canada, to the less developed countries, or to Japan up to a limit of $100 millions a year. Despite its exemption, however, Mexico chose to borrow in the Euro-dollar bond market in 1967, at higher interest rates, in an effort to maintain its good credit standing in the New York market.

Government Control

The effect of qualifying colonial issues for trustee investment in Britain has been mentioned. In France, in the 19th century, the Foreign Office attempted to foster loans for its allies, and restrain them for others. In the United States in the 1920's, the State Department asked the financial community to advise it of contemplated loans, so that it might enter an objection to a loan whose purposes were contrary to U.S. foreign policy. The basis for possible objection was purely political and had nothing to do with the soundness of the loan in question. Later, when the Securities and Exchange Commission was established, foreign borrowers, including foreign governments, were required by law to file a registration statement with the commission, prior to the issuance of new obligations, setting forth a host of financial data by which the soundness of the loan might be judged. These data included balance-of-payments statements, as well as material on the national income, government expenditure and receipts, and so forth. The SEC passed no judgment on the merits of a particular loan but was concerned solely to ensure that the borrower made full disclosure of information which would enable a purchaser of the bonds to judge these merits for himself.

Diplomatic representations are also made by governments in connection with default on obligations to their nationals by foreign governments. In another day, not long ago, U.S. Marines were used to protect U.S. property abroad and to assist foreign countries in the recognition of obligations to American investors. Today, questions of default are regarded as primarily the concern of private groups, such as the Council of Foreign Bondholders in the United States. These groups are entitled to and receive the support of their governments in presenting their cases, to such an extent in Britain that the United Kingdom council is regarded as a quasi-official body. This concern and assistance of government, however, are far from "control."

Government has been associated with international lending in other ways. The Johnson Act of 1934, for example, prohibited borrowing from the public by foreign governments which were in default on obligations to the U.S. government. This act, passed at the peak of isolationist sentiment in the United States, did not have to be repealed to enable the United States to lend to Britain in the early stages of World War II. It did not apply to the government itself or to its subsidiaries as the Reconstruction Finance Corporation. Even if it had, there might still have been room for the United States to lease or give equipment to other nations, under some such authority as that of the Lend-Lease Act of 1941, so long as it did not lend money.

Governmental controls have, then, been used to interfere in the private process of foreign borrowing and lending for the political reasons or for the protection of domestic investors. Increasingly, however, the major purpose of controls on capital movements has been the protection of the balance of payments. This was the aim of the IET. Most countries use not a tax but rather direct controls. The Capital Issues Committee in London, established in 1931, gives or refuses permission to foreign borrowers to sell their bonds in London, and when permission is given, may require the borrower to take his place in the queue, i.e., to wait in line to sell his bonds so that the market will not be choked with too many issues at once. Little by little Britain has felt obliged to cut down on lending until in the spring of 1966 it said it could no longer provide loans for the Dominions, and especially for those countries such as Australia and New Zealand which had continuously borrowed in London. We have touched in Chapter 18 on why and when transfer of capital fails to take place. We return to this issue under the discussion of balance-of-payments equilibrium in Chapters 24 and 25. At this stage of the discussion, however, the student should bear in mind that capital flows are occasionally (perhaps frequently) judged to be excessive in balance-of-payments terms, and give rise to efforts to curb them directly or with taxation.

Stabilization Loans

Two general types of governmental (and banking) loans may be distinguished: the stabilization loan and that for financing particular exports of the lender or imports of the borrower. Like others, this distinction cannot be rigidly maintained. The British Loan of $3\frac{3}{4}$ billion of 1946, for example, was intended primarily as a stabilization loan, to enable the British government to maintain convertibility of sterling into dollars; but it was recognized that a year would have to go by before it would be possible to achieve convertibility and that during this time some of the loan, at least, would have to go to pay for imports needed for British reconstruction.

Purely stabilization loans were made to replenish foreign exchange reserves, especially during the 1920's. Many of these were made by governments, but in some cases, particularly the Dawes and Young loans, the American tranche was subscribed by private banks or by the public. In World War I the British government asked J. P. Morgan and Company to act as its agent in stabilizing the pound sterling in the New York market, buying pounds with dollars whenever the rate fell below the rate stipulated by the British authorities. Later, the same banking house loaned the British government funds for this purpose.

Closely resembling stabilization loans are colonial loans contracted in Britain, where the proceeds are held in deposit in London as backing for the currency in the colony (rather former colony, since all are now independent). The sterling area system gave rise to a controversy in the early 1950's, based on the contention that rich Britain was exploiting the colonies by making them lend to it. Many of these colonies had monetary systems in which the local money was backed to the extent of 100 percent by foreign exchange, which was sterling held in London. A certain amount of outrage was felt that these countries had to produce an export surplus and lend it to the United Kingdom, in order to be able to expand their money supply.

A full discussion of the colonial monetary system would lead us far afield.[1] But the point should be made that the system does not require that the money supply must be earned. It can be borrowed. Colonial or independent governments linked to the sterling system can borrow at long term, hold the funds on deposit, and issue domestic money against the sterling deposits. The cost is only the difference between the long- and the short-term rate, rather than a real cost in resources less the earnings on the exchange reserves. And against this cost there is the benefit that if holders of the local money choose to convert it to imports—an outcome which is contrary to expectations, but has a positive statistical probability—there is foreign exchange available to meet the drain. The colonial monetary system involves the colonies lending short, but borrowing long, and London lending long and borrowing short. London performs the banking function for the outlying country. This is not exploitation.

Stabilization loans and those to finance imports differ from those for purchasing power in general, in that they are sought in order to get command over foreign purchasing power and present no transfer problem. The fully successful stabilization loan may never be used. Its existence convinces speculators of the strength of the currency, so that speculation becomes stabilizing. In these circumstances the long-term stabilization loan is balanced by short-term borrowing as the funds are held unused on deposit in the lending country. No money changes hands, and no real transfer takes place.

Occcasionally, for psychological effect, a stabilization loan is made in gold. It was a frequent suggestion after World War II that $1 billion or some such sum in gold be loaned to the Bank of France and paraded through every town and village in a showcase, to persuade the peasantry of the strength of the currency and induce it to dishoard its louis d'or, napoleons, and eagles (all gold coins). The suggestion was, of course, partly or largely ironical, but it indicates that stabilization loans need not be used.

---

[1] In those far-off fields we would make the point that the 100 percent reserve system is a good one for an open economy, with variable exports, so long as the 100 percent rule applies at the margin, but not on the average. In other words, it is efficient in a wide open economy, to have a loss of reserves pull down the money supply by an equal amount, but there is no need to back the bottom dollars—perhaps half of the total or 60 percent—with foreign exchange.

Borrowing to Finance Imports

Prior to 1913, and to a lesser degree up to 1929, foreign borrowing had as its purposes to get resources in general cheaply. Interest rates were lower abroad than at home. A country in need of purchasing power to undertake investment or even to make up a budget deficit borrowed abroad when the risk premium demanded by foreign investors were less than the difference in the rates of interest at home and abroad.

During the depression, risk premiums rose, and domestic interest rates in the money markets of the developing countries tended to decline under cheap money policies. Purchasing power in general could be obtained at home. Foreign loans were sought to meet deficits in the balance of payments.

In today's world of development, another element has been added to the analysis. When a country can reallocate resources and faces a sufficiently elastic demand for exports so that it can readily convert domestic resources into imports via exports, its only need for foreign loans for growth is to add to total resources for investment, i.e., to make up for any deficiency in savings. But not all countries are capable of such transformation. Imports may be a bottleneck to growth because of fixed ratios of foreign equipment in investment, and of intermediate goods needed to utilize existing capacity. The stock of automobiles and trucks may need imported petroleum products to operate, or steel may need imported coal or iron ore. If domestic resources cannot be readily transformed into imports, either because of difficulties of reallocating resources internally at the existing level of output, or because of inelasticity of the demand for exports, foreign loans may be needed for imports.

McKinnon has suggested that in a simple growth model, in which growth depends on capital, the capital may be divided into foreign and domestic elements, each with different capital/output ratio, or a different relationship between the rate of growth and capital. It could happen that with abundant capacity to transform domestic resources and relatively elastic demand for exports, the bottleneck to growth which foreign loans are needed to break is merely domestic savings. Or foreign loans may be needed to buy bottleneck imports until capacity to produce exports or import substitutes is sufficiently enlarged. Or one bottleneck may bind for a while, and later the other. In Figure 20.1a, the relationship between the domestic savings and the foreign exchange constraint on growth is drawn so that it is the former which binds. In this case foreign loans are needed for general purchasing power, not to purchase

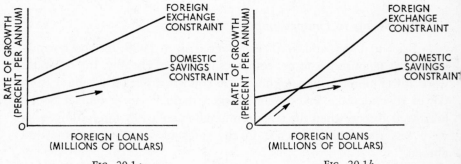

FIG. 20.1*a*   FIG. 20.1*b*

The Contribution of Foreign Loans to Domestic Growth under Differing Assumptions about the Capacity to Transform Resources into Imports

specific imports. But in Figure 20.1*b,* the foreign exchange constraint is the binding one for a certain distance, until productive capacity has been sufficiently expanded. After that the limit is total savings. Attempts have been made to apply this analysis in more elaborate form to particular developing countries in connection with programming international aid.

Tied Loans

The incapacity of the borrowing country to transform gives rise to the necessity to borrow specifically for purchasing imports. The difficulties of the lender in effecting transfer have led to the device of tying loans to the purchase of specific exports.

During the depression, loans were frequently made for the purpose of stimulating exports. The Export-Import Bank in the United States, for example, the Export Credit Guarantee Department in Britain, and similar organizations in other countries selling capital equipment found it necessary to provide governmental credit to continue to export machinery during the depression when the private international long-term market for capital collapsed. Here the purpose of the loan was to sell the exports. In some countries, such as Germany, moreover, there was never any thought of separating the finance from the sale of goods. But the problem posed by tied loans today is otherwise. Foreign loans or other forms of assistance are sought by the developing country. In order to prevent these loans from weakening the balance of payments of the United States, as the most notorious example, the loans are tied to expenditure in the United States.

Such tying of course violates the principle of Pareto optimality in which one should always purchase in the cheapest market. It would only happen by the rarest coincidence—at least in peacetime—that the cheapest market for the capital was also the cheapest market for the various imports to be bought with the proceeds of the loan. To the extent that tying is effective, it raises the cost of goods, or reduces the value of the loan. The International Bank for Reconstruction and Development has estimated that the price level on which tied loans are spent is some 30 percent higher than the cheapest sources.

But tying is not always effective. Money is fungible, and accountants over time achieve a certain low cunning. In partial equilibrium, with other things equal, a new loan which is tied will achieve its purpose. But other things have a habit of refusing to stay equal. Contemplate tied aid, for example. If military aid is available but economic aid is not, a country can switch its own resources from military to economic expenditure, and in effect maintain the old level of military effort and expand the economic. Or vice versa. It can shift a development project it was planning to undertake with the proceeds of exports to the lending country to a loan basis, and use the free exchange from exports for other purposes. Especially if it can transform its resources, a country can minimize the cost of tied loans (or tied aid) by using the loans (or aid) for inframarginal purposes, freeing up untied exchange for use at the margin.

In many countries, however, such capacity to transform is limited. Suppose such a country is interested in a domestic investment. In this circumstance, tying loans to the foreign exchange content of an investment can present a considerable obstacle.

Let us assume that a country wants to undertake the construction of a railroad as part of a program of economic development. The total cost of the project amounts to $100 million. Of this total, $50 million, we may say, represent the foreign exchange value of materials and equipment which must be bought from abroad; the remaining $50 million constitute costs to be incurred in local currency.

Under a system of tied loans, only $50 million could be borrowed in the United States, since the borrower must specify what U.S. goods are to be purchased with the loan. The United States may or may not be the cheapest place to buy the goods, but the loan is tied to U.S. goods. The remaining $50 million expended locally are likely to give rise to a foreign exchange requirement. Whether they will or not will depend upon how the local funds are obtained. If they are acquired through new savings or through taxation which reduces consumption, then the expenditure is not inflationary, i.e., does not increase national money income or imports. If, on the other hand, as is frequently the case, some part or all of the local expenditure is financed through credit creation or deficit spending, the domestic expenditure will spill over into new imports. How large an increase in imports will occur depends, of course, on the marginal propensities to import and save, leaving aside the foreign repercussion. But there is no foreign exchange from the loan available to finance the incremental imports. The transfer process works only for the first round of spending. Any increase from subsequent rounds of spending will have to be paid for out of reserves or, if these are inadequate, will lead to depreciation or foreign exchange control.

The Project Basis for Loans

The International Bank for Reconstruction and Development started out to make what were essentially tied loans, although the officials of the bank deny that they can properly be called such. Loans were made on a project basis, i.e., a borrowing country had to indicate the purpose for which the loan was sought, and this could not be so vague as "to fill the deficit in the budget." Moreover, the borrower originally was required to specify what new imports were needed for the project, and where these would be bought. If it approved the project and regarded the imports as reasonable, the bank was then prepared to lend the moneys needed to finance the imports.

This procedure, which the bank has now altered, was objectionable on two scores. It was "discriminatory," and it was likely to increase rather than mitigate the foreign exchange difficulties of the borrowing country. The discriminatory feature is found in the fact that the bank loaned currency which the country expected to spend, rather than loaning purchasing power in general. In a completely nondiscriminatory system, loans would be provided from the cheapest source—that is, the money market with the lowest interest rates—and the proceeds of these loans would be spent where the goods sought were cheapest. Dollars might be borrowed and spent in Britain, or, as during the 19th century, pounds might be borrowed and spent on the Continent. To lend only the currencies to be spent is to require the borrower either to borrow in the dearer market for loans or to buy in the dearer market for goods, unless the cheapest markets for goods and loans are the same. This objection was not perhaps important in practice up to 1950, because goods as well as loans were cheaper in the United States. But the principle of tying the currency of the loan to the currency of the projected import is discriminatory.

In the second place, a loan limited to the cost of imports needed for a project is insufficient to balance the international accounts except in the limiting case where all the local expenditure is raised in a deflationary fashion. Any inflationary financing of local expenditures of the project will raise income and imports and unbalance the international accounts. Purchasing power in general is neglected in favor of a limited amount of foreign purchasing power in particular. These loans and projects worsened rather than improved the country's balance of payments.

Capacity to Absorb Capital

The International Bank, which we will discuss at greater length below, has argued that the problem it faces is not lack of funds but lack of projects. The capacity to absorb foreign loans, it holds, is limited. What determines the capacity to absorb loans?

The earlier analysis in terms of alternative bottlenecks—foreign exchange or total savings—is relevant here. If there is no bottleneck, the capacity to absorb capital is a function of the cutoff point at which projects of diminishing productivity cease to be interesting. The payoff which indicates the limit may be a rate of productivity of 20 percent a year, or 10 percent or 5 or zero. But the view that the capacity to absorb capital is limited, or kinked, supposes there are more bottlenecks such as administrative capacity, skilled labor needed in fixed proportions, or the engineering talent to prepare project proposals for submission to the IBRD. Many of these bottlenecks could be broken by more foreign loans used to hire specific talent from abroad, although the concept may implicitly assume that the country uses its own administrative or engineering talent. When it is recognized that the notion of a limited capacity to absorb capital rests on the existence of bottlenecks, it would seem sensible not to accept the limit, but to break the bottleneck.

Countercyclical Lending

It is sometimes argued that long-term lending should be used as a countercyclical device—expanded in depression, contracted in prosperity. This, it is thought, would have two effects: first, to assist in stabilizing business conditions in the lending country; and second, to stabilize balances of payments.

This works out satisfactorily in an economic model. Let us imagine that country A has business cycles due to fluctuations in domestic investment, but that the rest of the world, called B, maintains stability of national income and of interest rates. In depression, the long-term rate of interest is likely to decline in A, making it a more attractive place for B to borrow. In prosperity, on the other hand, the rate of interest increases, making it a less desirable source of investment funds, so that foreign lending declines. Foreign lending expands in depression, contracts in prosperity, and serves as a balancing device to offset all or part of the changes in domestic spending in A.

More is called for than simply the funding of the export surplus which results from the decline in income and the consequent fall in imports relative to exports. This is a task for short-term capital movements, needed to sustain the level of exports. Countercyclical foreign lending, however, would produce a positive expansion in exports. In Figure 20.2 national income has decreased from Y to Y' as a result of a

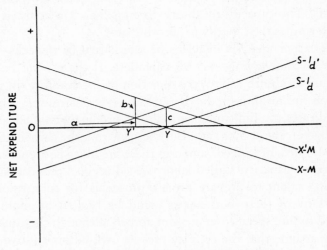

FIG. 20.2   Countercyclical Foreign Lending

decline in investment which shifted the $S-I_d$ schedule upward to $S-I_d'$; the movement along the $X-M$ schedule produces the export surplus, a. But countercyclical lending calls for an upward shift in the $X-M$ schedule, say to $X'-M$, in which the upward shift by b produces an export surplus of c ($=b$) at the original level of income Y. The derived export surplus, a, is wiped out by the reinduced imports.

The Cyclical Pattern of Lending

There is nothing really wrong with this model except that it is not particularly relevant to today's world.

Prior to 1914, international long-term lending, particularly by Britain, tended to be countercyclical except at the turning points. The position was as if there were a given fund of investible resources: when home investment boomed, foreign borrowers went without, but when recession set in at home, loanable funds sought new opportunities for investment abroad. On occasion, home and foreign investment moved together at the turning points, recovering together in the early stages, and declining together in the period of early recession. Cairncross has elaborated this model to suggest the role of the terms of trade as an allocator of these capital resources: when the terms of trade went against Britain in depression, capital moved abroad; in the succeeding boom when prices overseas fell, the terms of trade favored Britain and home investment.

But this pattern, which represented a broad tendency rather than a detailed description, changed after World War I. Private long-term lending tended to be correlated positively with domestic investment, again with the exception of the turning points. The reason is to be found in the familiar acceleration principle.

The decline in domestic investment which leads to a fall in income and imports also affects the prospects for investment abroad. Exports of the foreign country have fallen. In consequence, its national income declines. The country therefore becomes a less attractive place to which to make loans. This is the simple acceleration principle: increases in investment abroad will follow increases in sales, not decreases. In addition, however, the decline in exports in the potential borrower dims the outlook for transfer of interest and amortization on new loans through the foreign exchanges. The higher the level of exports, the more credit a country appears to foreigners to deserve; the lower, the less creditworthy it seems to be. The acceleration principle makes foreign loans fluctuate positively in the business cycle through variations in the profitability of the export sector in the borrowing country and in its balance of payments.

It is true that the recession phase of the cycle is an excellent time in which to make profitable loans, provided that one can be assured that recovery will ultimately follow. This argument for countercyclical private lending applies as well to domestic loans or purchases of securities. The reason why business is depressed, however, it that not enough people are convinced of the inevitability of recovery.

The positive correlation between domestic and foreign investment is not perfect, however, and may become particularly involved at the turning points. This is due to the behavior of the rate of interest. In late 1928 and early 1929, for example, when the expansion phase of the business cycle in the United States brought about a sharp rise in stock-market speculation and in the rate of interest, foreign lending slumped badly as the call money market bid for funds for use in brokers' loans. Immediately after the crash, moreover, interest rates declined and led to a short-lived revival in foreign lending. The interest rate pattern peculiar to a given cycle may cause foreign long-term lending to deviate in some degree from the fluctuations in domestic investment. By and large, however, private lending will be high in prosperity and low in depression, as the overall force of the accelerator swamps any balancing effects which may be produced through changes in relative interest rates.

The cyclical movement of long-term capital thus accentuates the cyclical problems of countries engaged in the production of primary products. In depression their supply of foreign exchange is reduced on two scores: exports are cut and, with them, foreign borrowing. From the point of view of the lending country, there is a double source of instability—domestic investment, which builds cumulatively up or runs cumulatively down, to produce changes in national income, and foreign investment, which acts in the same way.

A shift from private to government long-term lending does not change this position as much as one would be inclined to think at first blush. In the first place there are the lags of recognition and execution which may delay help to the next phase of the cycle when it is not needed. The idea of countercyclical spending on domestic public works runs afoul of the fact that much government spending—on roads, schools, post offices, hospitals, and so on—either is not capable of being postponed through a long period of prosperity or is positively geared with the cycle. In prosperity, for example, the expansion of private housing must be accompanied by roads, schools, and so forth, furnished by public funds. In the same fashion, many of the purposes for which foreign governments are anxious to borrow, and other governments or international institutions are willing to lend, either will be related to the expansion phase of a business cycle on exports or will not be postponable so that they may be accumulated for depression.

The International Bank for Reconstruction and Development was required by its articles of agreement to do what it could to smooth out business cycle fluctuations: "The purposes of the bank are: . . . (v) To conduct its operations with due regard to the effect of international investment on business conditions in the territories of its members."

In the event, however, it has stated that its primary task must be economic development, and any major attention to anticyclical timing would come into conflict with this concern.

One can, and below we do, argue that foreign investment is a second-best alternative to domestic investment undertaken simultaneously in a number of countries, or in the case posed in Figure 20.2, investment at home by itself. The international economic position is always most effectively assisted by undertaking home remedies for home difficulties. But even if it were highly desirable to offset home depression by foreign lending in the present pattern of international capital movements, it does not seem very practicable.

Cumulative Lending

If foreign investment is broadly similar to domestic investment (and equally difficult to manipulate anticyclically), it follows that a country with a deficiency of investment opportunities at home relative

TABLE 20.1

ANNUAL AMOUNT OF 20-YEAR LOANS REQUIRED, AT VARIOUS INTEREST RATES, TO MAINTAIN AN ANNUAL EXPORT SURPLUS OF $1,000,000,000*

(Billions of Dollars)

Year	Percent				
	2	3	4	5	6
5th...............	1.35	1.38	1.43	1.47	1.52
10th...............	1.81	1.92	2.03	2.16	2.31
15th...............	2.44	2.65	2.90	3.18	3.50
20th...............	3.28	3.67	4.14	4.68	5.32
25th...............	4.41	5.08	5.90	6.88	8.09

* It is assumed that the sum of interest plus amortization on each loan is paid in equal installments.

to savings should lend abroad, and a country with a deficiency of savings at home relative to investment opportunities should borrow abroad. But there are those who worry about the necessity to keep on lending or borrowing. It is objected, for example, that foreign loans cannot long offset a deficiency of domestic investment opportunities because of interest and possible amortization. Suppose, it is argued, a country wants to maintain an export surplus on current account of $1 billion annually. The first year it can lend $1 billion abroad. The subsequent year, however, it will have to lend $1 billion more, plus enough to enable the foreign borrowers to pay interest on the first year's loan and amortization, if the loan contract calls for regular repayments. The higher the rates of interest and amortization, the more rapidly will the rate of lending increase to sustain the stipulated export surplus. Table 20.1, taken from an article by Hinshaw, shows the effect of interest at various rates with amortization. In another table which we do not reproduce, the compound interest arithmetic is carried still further; $46.90 billion would have to be invested as a perpetual loan without amortization if one assumes 8 percent interest and calculates the requirement for the 50th year.

This analysis is applicable to amortization, which is an abnormal capital movement involving difficulties of transfer unless offset by new capital lending. The Export-Import Bank, and increasingly the International Bank for Reconstruction and Development, must undertake each year a substantial amount of new loans if they are to avoid the contractual repayments on old loans producing an inward movement of capital to the dollar area from weaker currencies. To help equalize marginal efficiencies of capital, movement of capital from capital rich to capital poor countries should involve perpetual loans, such as fixed assets which are kept intact, or British consols. In fact, however, the loans are made for short periods and involve periodic repayments of principal.

The requirement of amortization is a further illustration of the fallacy of composition: useful in the case of an individual loan, it complicates foreign lending as a whole by constituting an uphill movement of capital unless offset by new loans.

Leaving aside amortization, the charging of interest on old loans seems to raise a problem. If lending stops, the payment of contractual interest turns the balance of trade against the lending country. The rate of increase in foreign loans outstanding must equal the rate of interest received on foreign loans to prevent such a shift. If the productivity and income of a country grow at the same rate as the level of the rate of interest at which it lends abroad, and it, on this account, lends abroad at the same rate, the balance of trade, other things equal, will remain constant.

But this analysis is uninteresting. It is partial equilibrium in character when it should not be, holding other things equal when in the nature of events they must alter. It makes no sense to cling to the objective of maintaining a constant export surplus as the only way of offsetting an existing excess of savings over investment opportunities, if in fact the receipt of income from abroad raises spending for consumption and gives employment to the resources involved. Nor is the borrowing country condemned to borrow in order to pay interest, if in fact the original loan is invested productively and yields an income out of which interest can be paid. The problem of a geometric growth of lending to stay in the same place would be a real one only if all income from loans were saved, on the one hand, and all loans were consumed rather than invested in capital formation, on the other.

Take first the lending country. It lends and receives an income in the first year. This income has a multiplier effect just like, or almost just like, an increase in exports. The moneys from abroad will be partly spent on domestic goods, partly spent on imports, and partly saved. The amount saved in the first round of income creation reduces the multiplier below that for normal exports, so that the foreign interest multiplier may be somewhat smaller than the foreign-trade multiplier. It is analogous to the balanced budget theorem known to students with a knowledge of the finer points of income analysis. That portion spent at home in the first and respent in subsequent rounds of spending, however, will employ part of the resources previously engaged in foreign investment. Progressively the need to maintain an export surplus will diminish.

The Need to Borrow Interest

In the borrowing country, the notion that a country must borrow to pay interest on old loans is unacceptable. Latin-American observers are continuously comparing debt service on old loans with new loans, often making statements such as "The United States is taking more out of Latin America in profits and interest than it is putting back in new investments." Domar in an article worked out that the balance of payments of a borrowing country would turn adverse unless the rate of growth of total lending was equal to the rate of interest on outstanding loans. Put into a formula

$$R = \frac{a + i}{a + r}$$

where R is the borrowing country's balance of payments (the ratio of debits to credits), a is the rate of amortization, i the rate of interest on outstanding loans and r the rate of growth of new loans. So long as i is less than r, R is less than 1 and the balance of payments remains favorable.

But this analysis is far from complete. It is appropriate, perhaps, to lending for consumption to people at the subsistence level. As loan sharks know, if a poor man falls behind and has to borrow, his borrowing has to increase geometrically. But when loans are contracted for productive purposes, each loan should pay its own way, producing new exports, or saving on old exports, sufficient to pay its debt service.

Under the Domar–Latin-American analysis, it would be impossible to borrow for a single project without going increasingly into debt, which is absurd. What should be compared is not new lending with old interest, but new lending with new imports for capital investment, and old interest with the increase in exports and decrease in imports arising from the producvitity of old investment. If subscripts 0, 1, 2, and so on, indicate time, L stands for loans, X and M for exports and imports, and i for interest, the balance of payments at the several stages (amortization being left out) should look like this:

$$\text{(Stage I)}$$

$$\frac{M_0 + dM_{cap_0}}{X_0 + L_0},$$

where $L_0 = dM_{cap_0}$ is the transfer process;

$$\text{(Stage II)}$$

$$\frac{M_0 + \left(iL_0 - dM_{L_0}\right) + \left(dM_{cap_1}\right)}{X_0 + \left(dX_{L_0}\right) + \left(L_1\right)}, \text{ etc.}$$

Thus iL_0 (the interest on the original loan) should not be matched against L_1 (the borrowing of the next period) but with $+ dX_{L_0}$ and $- dM_{L_0}$ (the increase in exports and decrease in imports made possible by the productivity of L_0. This is done in the line encircling them. And new loans, if any, should be used for transfers of new goods ($L_1 = dM_{cap_1}$), not to pay interest on old debt.

The reasoning must be qualified in some cases: where a project has a long period of gestation, its productivity does not produce exports or import substitutes immediately. Here it is necessary to borrow the interest until production gets under way. But this merely says that the real amount of capital borrowed is more than the face amount by the accumulated interest to the period of production. The High Dam at Aswan, for example, which took 10 years to get production under way, cost $1 billion or so in face amount of capital plus 10 years' interest. Or the borrowing is for domestic projects and the country is facing an exchange bottleneck as in Figure 20.1*b*, or is unable to transform resources. In this case, it must be expected that the country will ultimately be able to achieve increased productivity which it can direct into export-increasing or import-reducing activities, or the case is similar to a consumption loan. And consumption should be financed by aid, rather than lending.

If the borrowing country does not need to borrow the interest, neither does the lending country have to lend it. Britain at the end of the 19th century did lend roughly each year about as much as it received as interest on its outstanding debt, but there is no analytical connection between the two items in the balance of payments. Individual recipients of income from overseas investment mingled that income with income from domestic sources, and then divided disposable income between consumption and savings, and the latter into savings invested at home and savings invested abroad. Some corporations directly reinvested foreign earnings abroad (as well as remitted dividends to Britain). But there was and is no necessary connection between overseas earnings and overseas investment.

Debt Service Ratio

The increase in postwar borrowing by developing countries has recently excited interest that some countries may have borrowed too much and be on the verge of default. The shorthand measure for the extent of a country's involvement is the ratio of its debt service—interest and amortization—to the current value of exports. This ratio on the average was under 5 percent on public debt for the developing countries after World War II until about 1955. Thereafter it rose to more than 10 percent in 1965. A number of countries have defaulted in this period—Argentina, Brazil, Chile, Turkey, and so on. Others have been rescued by international consortia. Still others, such as Indonesia and Ghana, which contracted debt for military operations and spectacular but impractical development projects, face very high debt service ratios and a strong possibility of the need to readjust external commitments.

The debt service ratio is hardly the neatest possible concept. As the ratios on the previous page indicate, interest should be related to the increase in exports and the decrease in imports. Equally or more important in the background are the capacity to transform resources from one sector to another, the productivity of new investment, and the marginal propensity to save out of increased income. Where a country maintains an overvalued exchange rate, with domestic inflation in excess of external depreciation, the outlook for its ability to maintain service on its debt is dim. The tendency to single out a particular ratio as critical in analysis is understandable, but the message of this chapter is that the economist must have his eye on a wide variety of aspects of international borrowing. Particularly critical are that loans should be invested productively; that some considerable portion of the productivity should be skimmed off, part to pay debt service, and part to save for new projects; that the economy must be able to reallocate resources from domestic to export and import-competing activities, to transfer the productivity subtracted for debt service abroad; and that the economy must not be otherwise mismanaged. These are perhaps rigorous conditions in today's world, but their fulfillment would make it possible to abandon a whole series of illogical views and expedients in the field of foreign lending from tied loans to insistance on the lending of the interest on past loans.

Summary

There are many forms of foreign capital movement but the traditional one, which had virtually died out but is now coming back, is the foreign bond. Foreign investment is like domestic, insofar as multiplier and growth effects on national income are concerned. There are differences in effects on factor proportions.

Capital flows internationally in deep channels dictated by institutional considerations as well as by differences in the marginal productivity of capital. Government control has been an important influence. Government also developed as an important international lender, making stabilization loans and loans to finance particular projects, or particular exports or imports.

There is general objection to tied loans, on the ground that they depart from the welfare maximizing principle which calls for borrowing in the cheapest market for capital and buying in the cheapest market for goods. The project basis for loans is analytically unacceptable because of its tied feature, and in addition because borrowing countries typically need help in financing their general balance-of-payments deficits created by investment projects, not merely the projects' foreign-exchange content.

Countercyclical international lending is no more feasible than domestic countercyclical spending. It is a fallacy to think that foreign lending (and borrowing) must continue cumulatively, if once undertaken, as the lender must relend the interest on old loans, along with the new loans needed to maintain an export surplus, in perpetuity and at a geometrically progressing rate.

The debt service ratio which relates interest and amortization on outstanding foreign debt to the value of exports is a crude measure of a country's capacity to borrow abroad, invest productively at home, and service its debt.

SUGGESTED READING

TEXTS

Kemp, chaps. xiii, xiv. For a good account of 19th-century lending, with tables and references to the literature, see William Woodruff, *Impact of Western Man,* chap. iv, including notes to tables and bibliography. See also R. F. Mikesell, *Public International Lending for Development* (New York: Random House, Inc., 1966) (paperback).

TREATISES, ETC.

For institutional treatments, see the Royal Institute of International Affairs, *The Problem of International Investment* (London: Oxford University Press, 1937); C. Lewis, *America's Stake in International Investments* (Washington, D.C.: The Brookings Institution, 1938); *The United States and Foreign Investment Problems* (Washington, D.C.: The Brookings Institution, 1948) and R. F. Mikesell (ed.), *U.S. Private and Government Investment Abroad* (Eugene, Ore.: University of Oregon Books, 1962).

For accounts of 19th-century lending by Britain, see L. H. Jenks, *The Migration of British Capital to 1875* (New York: Alfred A. Knopf, Inc., 1927); H. Feis, *Europe: The World's Banker, 1870–1913* (New Haven, Conn.: Yale University Press, 1931) (paperback, W. W. Norton & Co., Inc., 1966); C. K. Hobson, *The Export of Capital* (London: Constable & Co., Ltd., 1914); A. K. Cairncross, *Home and Foreign Investment, 1870–1913* (Cambridge: Cambridge University Press, 1953); and R. E. Cameron, *France and the Economic Development of Europe, 1800–1913* (Princeton, N.J.: Princeton University Press, 1960).

On the pure theory, see R. A. Mundell, "International Trade and Factor Mobility," in American Economic Association, *Readings in International Economics;* R. W. Jones, "International Capital Movements and The Theory of Tariffs and Trade," *QJE,* February, 1967; and M. C. Kemp, "Foreign Investment and the National Advantage," in *Economic Record,* March, 1962.

POINTS

The distinction between the foreign exchange and the savings bottleneck to growth is made in R. McKinnon, "Foreign Exchange Constraints in Economic Development and Efficient Aid Allocation," *EJ,* June, 1964. This approach to the foreign capital needs of a country is applied by Adelman and Chenery to Greece in the *RE & S* for February, 1966, and by Chenery and Strout to Israel in *AER,* September, 1966. An ambitious exercise in its application to Colombia is J. Vanek, *Estimating Foreign Resource Needs for Economic Development* (New York: McGraw-Hill Book Co., Inc., 1967).

On the capacity to absorb capital, see John H. Adler, *Absorptive Capacity* (Washington, D.C.: The Brookings Institution, 1965).

The compound interest problem is discussed in R. Hinshaw, "Foreign Investment and American Employment," *AER,* May, 1946; W. S. Salant, "The Domestic Effects of Capital Export under the Point Four Program," *AER,* May,

1950; and E. D. Domar, "Foreign Investment and the Balance of Payments" *AER,* December, 1950.

The debt service ratio is analyzed in a series of books by Dragoslav Avramovic and others of the Economics Division of the IBRD, the latest of which is D. Avramovic *et al., Economic Growth and External Debt* (Baltimore, Md.: The Johns Hopkins Press, 1964).

An excellent institutional discussion of the requirements of an integrated capital market is given in European Economic Community, *The Development of a European Capital Market* (Brussels, 1967).

Chapter 21   DIRECT INVESTMENT

Perhaps the most sensitive area in international economics today is direct investment. The United States tries to restrain direct investment abroad by its companies, to limit damage to its balance of payments. Less developed countries fear exploitation. European states and the Dominions worry lest their control over domestic resources be diluted by foreign ownership. Prohibitions or restrictions are issued against investment in certain lines of activity which are regarded as peculiarly vulnerable or wasteful—natural resources, banking, retail trade, defense industries, newspapers, soft drinks. Conditions are laid down that there must be local participation, foreign exchange brought from abroad, training, local component manufacture, domestic research, exports, and so on. And still the scope of international corporate operations mount. We explore first the theory of direct investment; then the impact on the balance of payments in both investing and host country, and finally a series of charges made against foreign corporations: that they are expensive, exploitive, monopolistic, competitive, and so on. The chapter ends on a projection of the future of the international corporation and the pressures it puts on the international community to harmonize policies over a wide range of functions.

The Theory of Direct Investment

It used to be thought that the major difference between portfolio and direct investment was that direct investment involved control, whereas portfolio investment did not. Control was a legal concept and rested on 100, 98, 51, or 48 percent ownership of the equity of a foreign corporation. Or control was thought of in decision theory terms, and meant that the head office made decisions respecting foreign operations, within a clearly laid-out scheme, on such questions as choice of top personnel, new products, capital budgeting, research and development, and dividend policy. But direct investment was a capital movement combined with control and perhaps other elements much as technology.

It was observed, however, that direct investment often did not involve a capital movement. A firm would undertake investment abroad with funds borrowed in the local country. It might provide the equity in foreign exchange, but if it were going into a joint venture, this equity investment might take the form of patents, machinery, technology, or other real considerations. Once the investment became profitable, moreover, it grew from local borrowing and reinvested profits. Direct investment represented not so much an international capital movement, as capital formation undertaken abroad.

Other theories were not lacking. In one view direct investment was akin to gambling. A firm undertook a small investment abroad and tried to pyramid it into a large stake, much as a gambler leaves his winnings on the table. It was noticed that 50 percent of profits on direct investment was reinvested on balance, so the rule of thumb developed that direct investment withdrew half its earnings and pyramided the other half. Or direct investment was the last stage in a technological cycle, along lines touched on in Chapter 4. First comes domestic production, then exports, and when imitation abroad is about to take over, the company undertakes production abroad. This is akin to the "defensive investment" concept of Alexander Lamfalussy. Some investment, he asserted with reference to domestic capital formation, is motivated not by the desire to make profits but in order to avoid losses. The marginal rate of return on this investment is equal to any other, measuring from the expected loss to the low profit. But the average is low. It is better to enter a market with a low expected profit, than to get pushed out of it altogether. This theory is related to a business view: direct investment is undertaken where there are large and growing markets. It is markets, not profits, which guide it. Where markets exist, profits will be found in the long run.

Monopolistic Competition

While each of these explanations has a piece of the truth, none has the power and the generality of that of Stephen Hymer, in his M.I.T. thesis on "The International Operations of National Firms." In this view, direct investment belongs to the theory of monopolistic competition rather than that of international capital movements. A local company has an advantage over a foreign company, other things being equal. It is expensive to operate at a distance, expensive in travel, communication, and especially in misunderstanding. To overcome the inherent native advantage of being on the ground, the firm entering from abroad must have some other advantage not shared with its local competitor. The advantage typically lies in technology or patents. It may inhere in special access to very large amounts of capital, amounts far larger than the ordinary national firm can command. Or the company, as in petroleum refining or metal processing, may coordinate operations and invested capital requirements at various stages in a vertical production process, and because of its knowledge of requirements at each stage, and the heavy cost of inventories, be able to economize through synchronizing operations. It may merely have differentiated products built on advertising. Or it may have truly superior management. But some special advantage is necessary if the firm is going to be able to overcome the disadvantage of operating at a distance.

The firm must be able not only to make higher profits abroad than it could at home, but it must also be able to earn higher profits abroad than local firms can earn in their own markets. For all its imperfections, the international capital market would be expected to be able to transfer mere capital from one country to another better than a firm whose major preoccupations lie in production and marketing.

The implications of this theory of direct investment are many. For one, direct investment will not occur in industries with pure competition. Few farmers operate overseas, nor do retail distributors other than Sears Roebuck, or many representatives of the textile, clothing, leather and so forth, industries. Second, a company is not interested in acquiring local partners in a joint venture, seeking to keep the good thing for itself;[1] at the same time, the local investors naturally resist the suggestion that they should buy the shares of the parent company: the return on the overall stock is diluted as compared with the profitability of the local situation which they observe. Third, direct investment takes place in two directions in the same industry, which would not be the case if the movement were based on general levels of profit. In part this is because of differing advantages resulting from differentiation and specialization. But in part it is a peculiar phenomenon of oligopolistic

---

[1] There is something of an irrationality about this attitude, of course, if the minority shareholding is sold for a favorable enough price. But there is another compelling reason against joint ventures: that the interests of the majority and minority shareholders are almost certain to diverge: the one wants growth, the other wants dividends; or the one wants to maximize the earnings of the subsidiary, whereas the other is interested in the earnings of the entire company and will slight the interest of a particular subsidiary on occasion in the broader company interest.

competition: each firm must do as the others to prevent another from getting an unanticipated advantage. Thus Lever Brothers operates in the United States in soap, and Procter and Gamble in Britain; Shell in the United States in oil and Esso in its various markets, and similarly for Knorr and Heinz in soup, Agfa and Kodak in photographic supplies, and so on. When one automobile company builds a small and inefficient plant in Brazil, 15 more follow. Like the leader in a sailboat race, one must not let the second boat split tacks, but cover it to protect one's lead.

The oligopolistic character of direct investment is easily misunderstood. To the local inefficient competitor, the difficulty is that the foreign invader competes too vigorously. As in the case of the chain stores in the 1920's and 1930's, the local monopolist decries the large firm from outside the district because it competes, although he accuses it of monopoly. And firms such as R.C.A. which teamed up with Siemens of Germany in the computer field, or General Electric with Machines Bull of France, did so not to extend a monopoly but to gather strength to challenge the industry lead of International Business Machines. This increases international competition. The contrary example is furnished by the 1967 purchase from the Norwegian government by Alcan Aluminium Ltd. of Canada of a 50 percent interest in the Aardal Og Sunndal Verk, an aluminum smelter that had been "a source of price competition that had vexed the entire industry." Buying up a competitor tends to restrain trade. But one cannot judge whether any particular takeover or investment increases or reduces competition without examination of the particular facts.

Firms maximize profits within an horizon which extends in time and space. Horizons change. Prior to about 1950, the Campbell Soup Company had few if any foreign branches outside Canada, whereas the Heinz company had almost 57. The former was preoccupied with its domestic operations; the latter, finding domestic competition stiff, had expanded especially abroad. After 1950, however, the Campbell Company put on a drive to expand overseas. In the same way the chemical industry in the United States, and the pharmaceutical, had been so busy, prior to World War II, fending off foreign competition that they had not contemplated foreign operations. In the depression of 1954 after fulfilling the bulk of their planned postwar domestic investments, they lifted their eyes to the world horizon and started to invest abroad. As already indicated in Chapter 11 the Rome Treaty of 1957 perhaps stimulated U.S. foreign investment more through calling attention to existing profit opportunities than it did by creating new ones. Up to the beginnings of the Common Market, rapid and substained European growth had passed unnoticed over the horizon of many large firms which would have been capable of investing there. With the formation of the EEC, the horizon suddenly was enlarged to encompass Europe, and investment in Europe as a whole soared.

This theory of direct investment can be summarized with reference to a simple formula used in elementary economics for capitalizing a perpetual flow of income

$$C = \frac{I}{i}$$

where C is the value of an asset or obligation, I is the stream of income it produces and i is the market rate of interest or profit. Thus, the student will remember, a perpetual bond with a face value of $1,000 bearing a 4 percent coupon (an income of $40 per year, or I) will sell for $1,333 ($C$) when the market rate of interest (i) stands at 3 percent. Hymer's theory of direct investment states that foreigners can pay more for an earning asset, such as a business, in country A, than residents of country A, not because they are content with a lower i, but because they can earn a higher I. It will happen, to be sure, that international capital markets are less than perfect, and that differences in i contribute to the flow of capital. But the behavior of direct investment,—the readiness of investors to borrow in the host country at the same i as residents face, its concentration in oligopolistic industries, its movement in two directions, and the insistence on complete ownership—indicate that it is capital I not small i which dominates.

The Balance of Payments of the Investing Country

There is controversy over the impact of direct investment on the balance of payments in both the investing and the host country. We deal with these successively. The United States imposed a Voluntary Credit Restraint Program (VCRP) in February, 1965, in an effort to slow down the outflow to Europe on direct investment, and to stimulate the remittance of dividends, asking originally 400 corporations, later extended to 700 and then 900, to undertake each to alter the company's impact on the balance of payments so as to produce a 5 percent improvement. Attention was focused not on restraining investment, but on limiting its impact on the balance of payments. Expanded exports, reduced imports, increasing the remittance of dividends, shifting financing from the United States to foreign sources of loans, all counted equally with a reduction of overseas investment. There is evidence, however, that direct investment of U.S. firms had been unduly large in 1964 as many companies anticipated some form of restraint, following upon the Interest Equalization Tax on portfolio investments in 1963, and increased their foreign holdings beyond normal requirements.

There is no dispute as to the character of various impacts of direct investment on the balance of payments of the investing country, and little on the relative size of the effects. Controversy centers on the choice of the model. It is agreed, for example, that direct investment stimulates direct exports of equipment, components, and inventories, indirect exports of other products in a company's line, newly sold by reason of the company's presence abroad; other positive help to the balance of payments comes from rents and royalties on patents and technology and most important of all from the flow of interest and dividends, though not all profits are remitted home. On the negative side are the displacement of exports by new production abroad; some imports of foreign output for the domestic market, but most of all the initial investment. There is little or no discussion in macroeconomic terms of the way the transfer mechanism works. All the items under discussion stem directly from the foreign investment process.

In his early formulation of the problem, Bell used only a few variables, broken down as follows:

Balance-of-Payments Improving	*Balance-of-Payments Worsening*
Export stimulus and fees.........19	Capital........................100
Remitted earnings.............. 6	
Total (annual)...........25	100

The earnings took place year after year, beginning with the second period. The question turned, however, on what was the appropriate assumption to make about the capital outflow. On the basis of a single investment, the balance of payments turned adverse in the first year by $100, but improved each year thereafter, with the cumulative total 0 by the end of the 5th year, and everything thereafter gravy. But Bell considered this model to be naïve. If one shifted the foreign investment schedule up by $100, and had $100 newly invested each year, the cumulative deficit would grow to $250 at the end of the 4th year, would decline annually thereafter, but would not reach zero until the 9th year. Even this may not be the most realistic model. Between 1957 and 1961, U.S. direct investment grew at 25 percent a year. Extrapolating this percentage, each $100 of direct investment pays for itself in 5 years but the cumulative adverse effect of the total on the balance of payments rises forever.

The business community argued hotly against the schedule shift and the constant rate of increase models, in favor of the single injection. Of course. But there really is no ideal answer as to which is the appropriate model. It depends on the question asked. The geometric progression model is silly, to be sure, for anything but a relatively short period of time. Trees never reach the sky, and babies who double their birthweight in five months and triple it in a year, end up weighing positive and not infinite numbers of pounds, stone, or kilograms. But as between the single injection, schedule shift, or spurts of geometric growth, there can be no scientific answer as to the best model.

One business group, the National Industrial Conference Board (NICB), sought to make a distinction between the "incremental" and the "organic" approaches to direct investment. The former singles out one investment at the margin and tries to work out its implications. The NICB understands the logic of this approach, but rejects it as unrealistic. In its view, foreign investment is all of a piece. To maintain the profitability of old investments, it is necessary to undertake new. To halt the outflow is not only to cut off future returns, but to undermine the continuation of the present stream of dividends. A firm operating abroad must move with the market as the latter grows; to stand still is to lose market position, which is to begin to die. It is hard to judge the merits of the biological argument, which has overtones of mysticism about it. If the foreign investment is profitable, it is possible to reinvest profits; if it is not, there may be doubt whether expansion is warranted. The economist tends to be skeptical in the face of such argument, but it is easy to understand how businessmen feel this way.

If progress on the proper choice of a model is difficult, it has been possible to refine the variables. A Brookings study divides the effects into:

Balance-of-Payments Improving		*Balance-of-Payments Worsening*	
Export stimulus	10.6	Capital	100
Remitted dividends	8.1	Import stimulus	6.5
Royalties and fees	2.3	Loss of exports	(none)

With these numbers one injection pays off in the 6th year, a steady flow in the 11th year, and a flow growing at the rate of 22 percent a year never pays off. The annual investment under the last approach reaches numbers such as $53 billions in the 20th year, with the export stimulus $37 billions and so forth.

One observer raises a still further question: suppose a new investment of $100 is undertaken with no money transfer, the equity consisting of goods and other valuable considerations transferred in kind, and the remaining capital raised through local borrowing or through reinvestment of profits on existing investment. In this case the positive effects of investment start immediately and grow. The model which starts out with a negative impact of $100 is by no means the only possible one. The reply to this, however, is that the coefficients used in the various models were derived from balance-of-payments statistics. If one poses a different problem, one needs to work out a different set of coefficients. If you eliminate the $100 initial investment, you must change the other positive and negative numbers.

In summary, one can conclude that direct investment worsens the balance of payments in any one year when it is large, but that over time it helps. There may be something to the view that one must keep on investing year after year to continue to reap the dividends of the past, but probably not much. As in so much else in the world, today's crisis is the enemy of long-run health. And to justify taking action which is helpful in the short run, harmful in the long, it is important to be sure that today's "crisis" is indeed critical.

The Impact on the Balance of Payments of the Host Country

The impact of direct investment can be regarded as negative for the balance of payments of both the investing and the host country if the one concentrates on the short run and the other on the long. And so they do. The host country regards direct investment as "expensive." A small investment with little balance-of-payments impact in its early years will develop through reinvestment into a company with a sizable remittance of dividends abroad. In not infrequent cases, a comparison is made of the initial investment and the annual flow of dividends years later. In an early and notorious case, the Australian public became agitated in the early 1950's when it learned that one year's profits of General Motors–Holden Proprietary, Ltd., ran 14 percent of sales, 24 percent of funds employed, 39 percent of shareholders' equity, and 560 percent of General Motors original investment. Dividends paid from these profits amounted to 11 percent of funds employed, 18 percent of shareholders' equity, 260 percent of the original investment and 8 percent of the Australian dollar export receipts for the year. All this occurred despite the fact that the company had priced the Holden car—occasionally held to be the forerunner of the Corvair—at a level which failed to clear the market. There was a six-months' waiting list.

The General Motors–Holden case has been explained by one scholar as an example of the gambling money thesis: direct investments grow at rapid rates because the companies plow back profits on the basis of some rule of thumb. The consequence is that the original investment pyramids rapidly, and ultimately returns a stream of income which is large in relation to the original investment. Possibly. But this will only work if the product makes money, if, that is, the direct investor produces and sells a product which the public wants. Not all direct investment can make profits to reinvest, and no direct investor will plow back profits unless the prospect for further profit is bright. Instead of being expensive, the direct investment may be regarded as efficient, in that it provided at limited cost an automobile which the Australian public wanted very much.

On this score it is not legitimate to compare the subsequent rates of profits or dividend with the original investment. They are appropriately compared to total funds employed and with the foreign equity. Reinvestment each year must count as a separate and additional investment, so long as the investor had the option of taking his profits out. Reinvestment and pyramiding are not inevitable. In the last chapter we saw that investors don't have to lend the interest on past debts, nor do borrowers have to borrow it. Similarly, an initial direct investment does not always grow exponentially; such reinvestment as does take place is entitled to a return of its own.

One small point may be made about how Holden sales were financed. The introduction of a new product may produce a shift in demand to it. If total demand is unchanged, an increase in purchases of the Holden will involve decreases in purchases of other goods, which will cut back imports directly in part, and for the rest release resources which can be transferred into export-increasing or import-decreasing occupations. If, however, purchases of the Holden are all financed on credit—say installment loans—there will be an increase in total spending and an increased strain on total resources, leading to an import surplus. But the strain on the balance of payments should be blamed not on the direct investment so much as on the credit expansion.

A third point of considerable importance is that General Motors–Holden made its large profits behind substantial tariff protection. In July of 1966 when the Japanese Toyota automobile managed to take over $7\frac{1}{2}$ percent of the total market with imports into Australia, the Tariff Board raised the tariff from 35 to 45 percent *ad valorem* to ensure that the market was supplied by domestic manufactures instead of imports. The higher the tariff needed to maintain the marginal inefficient producer, the larger the profits of the inframarginal efficient producer. It is impossible to know what the General Motors–Holden profits were in the 1960's because so great was the outcry in the 1950's that General Motors bought up the minority stockholdings and transformed itself into a private company, with a single owner, which is under no obligation to publish its accounts. But to the extent that the Australian Tariff Board maintains high tariffs on imports, the General Motors–Holden profits (the redistribution effect in Figure 7.1) is the result of Australian, not foreign company action.

More fundamentally, when direct investment makes large profits, it is a sign that supply is very small in relation to demand, and that new entry is called for to expand supply to the point where only normal profits are made. It would be desirable from the national point of view for a domestic producer to take advantage of the opportunity. But the high profits are there for the foreign investor because domestic enterprise is incapable of filling the vacuum. In the General Motors–Holden case, the high profits performed the function that they are supposed to do under the capitalist system; the success of General Motors–Holden was followed by the establishment of Australian subsidiaries of other world automobile companies such as Ford and Daimler–Benz which would have restored profits to normal levels had it not been for the tariff. The high profits were needed as a signal of where output should be expanded. The monopoly power of the direct investor may preclude new entry. But where it is based on efficiency and skill, as in the General Motors case, imitation, not suppression is called for.

It is of some considerable interest that the rate of profits on U.S. direct investment in Australia went down sharply after 1960 when import controls were relaxed. Of all the points made about the expensive character of direct investment, and its impact on the balance of payments then, it appears that the protection afforded to the foreigner through trade controls may be the most important. Monopolies and oligopolies make higher than normal profits. Tariffs and quotas protect monopoly positions. Governments which raise tariffs to give more monopoly protection have the capacity to reduce rates of profits on direct investment.

The Exploitation of Less Developed Countries

Particular attention has been paid to the role of direct investment in less developed countries.

In discussing the performance of the Iraq Petroleum Company in Iraq, Edith Penrose held that the company had "exploited" the country because it had earned a return higher than the minimum it would have been willing to enter the industry for. But the use of so pejorative a word runs the risk of confusing the analysis. The Iraq Petroleum Company, like any direct investor, has an advantage to exploit—whether technology, outlets for oil, or access to large amounts of capital. Initially Iraq's advantages are limited—merely sovereignty over oil-bearing sands. But this is a bilateral monopoly situation—the confrontation of a monopolist with a monopsonist, for which there is no determinant solution. Moreover, there is so much room between the maximum that each party to the contract might hope for, and the minimum that it would be willing to take, that any solution can be called exploitive of one party or the other or both, if exploitation is defined as receiving a higher price than the minimum acceptable.

Bargaining between the company and the country in this situation calls for the analysis of nonzero sum game theory, akin to love and war, where the range of possible solutions runs from both happy (peace), one happy the other unhappy (victory), to both unhappy (devastating war). A more fruitful mode of analysis is to observe how the relative bargaining strength of some hypothetical country and company change through time, and as a consequence of policies. Initially, the advantage lies entirely on the side of the company. The underdeveloped country lacks markets, technology, capital, management skills, which the company brings to the bargain. All the country has is the natural resource. Unless it can induce a great many companies to bid against one another for the concession, unrestricted by divisions of territory such as the Red-Line agreement which assigned concessions in the Middle East north of a red line on the map to the British and those south to the United States, it has to take what is offered. If there is a gunboat in the harbor during the negotiations, its room for negotiation is still further restricted.

With the passage of time, however, the balance of bargaining strength shifts. The company is committed for a large investment. It may no longer have all the skills on its side, because native personnel has been technologically trained by the company, at the country's insistence, and government personnel has acquired economic sophistication about the industry. With proven reserves, the risks for new entrants are much reduced, which increases the readiness of competitors to enter. As the old agreement comes to an end, or if it can be abrogated, the new terms much more favorable to the country replace the original arrangement. The companies make an attempt to "hold the line," as for a while was done in the petroleum industry with the 50–50 agreements under which the company and the local tax authorities divided equally profits plus royalties. But the bargaining position fails to come to rest. The country tends to enact new conditions: an overvalued exchange rate at which the company must buy its local currency, for example, or a requirement that taxes be paid on the posted price rather than the sales price which includes discount. New concessions provide for a 40–60 division, or a 25–75, and the old concessions have gradually to be brought into line. The original bilateral bargain approaches the competitive solution. In the end the country may "exploit" the company by forcing it to accept less-than-normal profits, maintained just high enough to prevent it from withdrawing. And in many cases, of course, the countries go farther, and the companies do withdraw.

Seen in this light, the appropriate policy for underdeveloped countries is not to keep out direct investment but to embrace it and gradually to invade its monopoly—learn its technology, and management skills, build capital through taxation and government surpluses, to eliminate reliance on foreign capital, and develop direct marketing.

The International Corporation

It is an interesting question of economics whether markets or corporations are better devices for allocating resources among competing uses. The imperfections of markets have been discussed in Chapter 12. The possibility that international corporations may not maximize the efficient use of given resources has been touched upon in this chapter. But a case can be made that the development of the large international corporation in the 20th century will prove in the long run to be a more effective device for equalizing wages, rents, and interest rates throughout the world than trade conducted in competitive markets by small merchants. The analogy is with the national corporation which in the United States after about 1890 helped to equalize wages, interest rates, and rents within the country's borders, by borrowing in the cheapest market (New York) and investing where it was most productive in terms of costs and markets. The resultant movement of capital and shift in demand for labor was probably more effective in, say, raising wages in the South and lowering interest rates there than either trade by local companies or the limited direct movement of factors.

Today more and more companies are lifting their horizons from the national to the international scene, contemplating a wider and wider geographical range of alternatives on where to borrow, build, sell, undertake research, buy. The giant oil, chemical, automobile, tire, food-processing, and similar firms cover the world. Companies with subsidiaries in 40 or 50 countries are no longer rare and those with 5 to 10 are common. To the extent that these companies coordinate the operations of firms in different markets with a view to achieving monopoly profits, and succeed in preventing new entry through imitation, it is not clear that they maximize welfare. To the extent that these companies buy in the cheapest market and sell in the dearest—with reference both to factors and goods—they provide an institutional network which may go farther than trade flows to equalize factor returns and improve welfare throughout the world.

It is not clear that international corporations do act in a nondiscriminatory way. Brash observes that General Motors–Holden started out in Australia with a rule which said that purchases would be made in the United States unless the products concerned could be obtained 10 percent cheaper in Australia, and shifted over time to a criterion which said that products would be bought in Australia unless they were 10 percent cheaper elsewhere. Neither rule is justified. There is something to be said, to be sure, for rules of thumb which minimize the cost of decision making and do not require a purchasing agent to get quotations from all over the world before he buys tacks. Costs of information are high, and some implicit rule for small amounts and differences as small as 10 percent may be justified on this account. If the General Motors regulations meant no more than this, they are understandable. If the discrimination is deliberate, however, and runs contrary to the rule of profit maximization when the facts are known, it suggests that corporations feel the need to have a citizenship, and that discrimination in favor of the country of citizenship can be the enemy of efficiency.

The international corporation is not truly international in another respect, despite the accusations of the Marxists. Each one has a home office, and a home unit of account in which it keeps its liquid assets as well as calculates its maximization of profits. The truly cosmopolitan corporation which is prepared to move head office and liquid assets out of any country whose currency is weak is yet to arrive. Few have even reached the position of national corporations in the United States which frequently such as General Motors, have two head offices in Detroit and New York, for production and finance respectively. But the Arabian American Oil Company (Aramco) with production in Saudi Arabia, top management in New York, and accounting in The Hague may be a portent of the future. It is a sign of the times, however, that the Saudi Arabian government wants the head office moved from New York to Dahran.

That the large international corporation has not yet developed to its ultimate extent can be seen by looking at the balance sheet of any large American corporation which separates out earnings and assets and possibly sales in the United States and abroad. It will be seen that

402 · *INTERNATIONAL ECONOMICS*

earnings are higher on foreign investment, and on foreign sales, than in the United States, whether for General Motors, Du Pont, Gillette, Corn Products Refining, Standard Oil Company of New Jersey, or whatever. This is partly a consequence of risks. But even if we had data on earnings per share and per dollar of sales in countries where the risks are little if any higher than in the United States, say for Canada, Australia, or the United Kingdom, the returns are still going to be higher abroad for the U.S. corporation (and higher in the United States for the foreign corporation with investments here) because the companies feel that they belong somewhere in particular and go afield only for a higher than ordinary return. When it earns an equal return (after risk) on every dollar and dollar equivalent invested everywhere in the world, the large corporation can be said to be truly international.

Efficiency and Citizenship

Writing on *Canadian-United States Economic Relations* for the Royal Commission on Canada's Economic Prospects, Brecher and Reisman set up the proposition that foreign ownership of Canadian industry was of little consequence because a Canadian and a foreign company in Canada, both trying to maximize profits, would operate in the same way. Things equal to the same thing are equal to each other. The analysis of this chapter, however, suggests that there may be a difference in behavior owing to differences in horizon. The international company faces a wider range of alternatives on many fronts—investments, taxes, purchasing, recruitment, and so on. Often its choice will be governed by efficiency; sometimes it will respond to its ownership-country citizenship and against the dictates of efficiency. In either case, its interests may differ from those of the host country. Or it may seek to be a good citizen in the host country, which in some cases may involve departure from the efficiency standard, and from the short-run interests of the owner-country.

A sharp conflict arises over differing interpretations of jurisdiction. The U.S. government takes the view that the foreign operations of U.S. companies are a matter of U.S. government concern. In questions affecting the U.S. balance of payments, antitrust policy, foreign policy, and so on, our government considers itself authorized to issue orders to U.S. corporations. They should export more from the United States to their foreign subsidiaries, and import less, to improve the balance of payments; cease exporting to Communist China from foreign subsidiaries, to carry out U.S. foreign policy; withhold from the French government high-efficiency computers which are sought to expand the French nuclear capability and hence run counter to U.S. views on proliferation; and so on.

Foreign governments regard these instructions as an attempt to assert sovereignty over what happens under their jurisdiction. A corporation organized under the laws of Canada, for example, must respond to Canadian instructions on balance-of-payments policy, not to the United States. International law lies outside our jurisdiction. But we may observe the difficulty that an international corporation faces when two governments tell it to behave in different ways. On political questions, the economist has nothing to say. In the realm of economics, he can suggest that one objective criterion is what contributes most to efficiency.

On occasion, the international corporation itself will depart from the standard of efficiency. Such is the case, for example, when it suppresses competition, charges arbitrary internal (transfer) prices to itself for the sake of minimizing overall taxation, discriminates in favor of one or another or source of supply in the interest of citizenship, and so on.

But on occasion, governments will lay down regulations for national purposes which depart from the efficiency criterion and run counter to the normal operations of an international corporation which happens to be efficient. Most studies of direct investment raise a question whether the parent company prevents the subsidiary from contributing to exports. The question is seldom asked whether comparative advantage favors exports, or why the international corporation would not want to fill orders from the low-cost source of supply. Where direct investment has been attracted by a tariff to an import-competing activity to ask whether the firm exports is to pose a nonsense question. Or at the behest of one group or another government may prevent foreign investment in a monopolized industry—banking or retail trade or mining. The socialist or antibig business economist (not identical) suspects that government is right and big business wrong when they disagree; the laissez-faire school thinks business right and government wrong. The eclectic position taken here is that both business and government may adopt policies which are inimical to the cosmopolitan standard of international efficiency. Some of these may be second-best policies— prohibition of foreign investment in soft drinks, when the first-best policy would be consumer sovereignty and equitable income distribution but the country lacks the political capacity to achieve them. Some may be self-seeking at the expense of others—monopoly on the part of business or—the same thing—optimum tariff policies by governments. But while the true believer of Eric Hoffer may uphold one side or the other, the analytically more respectable position is that to make a judgment one needs the facts.

It will frequently be the case that the international corporation is more efficient than the local protected one. It is mobile. Its horizon is wide. It is capable of adjusting to changes in tariffs, and in fact prefers free trade. Its interests are cosmopolitan, not national.

This gives rise to the paradox that in the European Economic Community the most European corporations are in fact those owned in the United States. French companies are located in France, and would not shift locations to Belgium, Germany, Italy, or the Netherlands if there were a change in the efficiency conditions. An American-owned corporation would. As Mediterranean labor, which is mobile between the northern countries because it has roots in none, the U.S. or Anglo-Dutch corporation which operates in many countries is more truly European than the company confined by its national tradition and citizenship to one.

Governments put other things above efficiency, and countries may have economic independence in their social welfare function along with efficiency. The trade offs are hard to evaluate. Similarly, corporations have more than profits in their objective functions, including the quiet life for corporate executives. There is a temptation for the international corporation to simulate a series of national corporations, each a good citizen of the country in which it operates, and ready to turn away from opportunities for profit which may raise questions of national policy. But that is not the corporation's role. The institution is economic, not political. Its purpose is to make profits, not to maximize its longevity. Corporations are required to obey laws, and this is as it should be. It is not that it is too high a standard to ask them to interpret the national will and to carry it out; it is the wrong standard.

Harmonization of National Policies

Operating in a variety of national jurisdictions the international corporation has a chance of maximizing profits by moving operations to the most beneficial jurisdiction, or getting the worst of all possible worlds by being penalized everywhere. It may, as we have seen above, evade or avoid some or all of corporation taxation, be taxed reasonably on its operations by only one jurisdiction, or suffer from double taxation. And the same applies in antitrust, balance of payments, research and development, and other areas.

To limit departures from efficiency, customs unions find themselves obliged to harmonize excise taxes. As the corporation acquires international mobility at lower costs, harmonization will be required in other fields, and not only in customs unions but throughout the world. It is necessary to sort out which country has jurisdiction in balance-of-payments questions, and whether it is not possible to exclude from the armory of balance-of-payments weapons, policies which distort efficient international business allocation. This would be a rebuff for the United States. On the other hand, the world could do worse than to accept the U.S. position that all trading nations have an interest in a reduction of competition in an industry through merger between two companies with significant positions in the world market for a product, no matter where such merger occurs.

One way to harmonize policies is to adopt laissez-faire. This is not possible in taxation, nor wise in such fields as the maintenance of competition. Bit by bit in the international monetary field, a meeting of minds has developed, and the adoption of common points of view. If the international corporation is not going to get a long start on national governments, a similar effort is required in the regulation of international corporate behavior.

Summary

The foreign operations of domestic corporations, or direct investment, belong to the theory of monopolistic competition rather than to that of international capital movements. This theory explains better than any other the industries in which direct investment takes place, the cross currents, and the borrowing abroad.

The impact of direct investment on the balance of payments of the investing country is adverse in the short run, helpful in the long. The question as to what is the appropriate model for a balanced judgment remains open. Conversely the balance of payments of the host country is helped in the short run and may be hurt in the long. This is especially the case if profits on direct investment are helped by loose credit policies and by high tariffs.

Direct investment by developed countries in less developed is not properly regarded as exploitation without defining the terms. Typically the advantage in a bilateral monopoly situation starts out all on the side of the investing company and gradually shifts to the host country.

The international corporation is likely in future to become an important vehicle for equalizing the returns to factors of production and spreading technology internationally, as the national corporation has done domestically. Where the international corporation is faced by national jurisdictions with conflicting interests, it may slide between them, or it may be penalized by double penalties or conflicting commands. Harmonization of tax, antitrust, balance-of-payments, and so on, policies will help, especially if such policies put efficiency above citizenship as criteria for corporate behavior.

SUGGESTED READING

TEXTS

Roy Blough, *International Business: Environment and Adaptation* (New York: McGraw-Hill Book Company, Inc., 1966).

TREATISES, ETC.

There is little in the way of synthetic treatises in the field. See J. N. Behrman, "Promoting Free World Economic Development through Direct Investment," in R. F. Mikesell (ed.), *U.S. Private and Government Investment Abroad* (Eugene, Ore.: University of Oregon Books, 1962) and, more heavily relied upon by this chapter, Stephen H. Hymer, "The International Operations of National Firms: A Study of Direct Investment" (doctoral dissertation, M.I.T., 1960).

The monographic literature is booming. Among the outstanding items, see:

Donald T. Brash, *United States Investment in Australian Manufacturing Industry* (Cambridge, Mass.: Harvard University Press, 1966).

John H. Dunning, *American Investment in British Manufacturing Industry* (London: George Allen & Unwin, Ltd., 1958).

Allan W. Johnstone, *United States Direct Investment in France* (Cambridge, Mass.: The M.I.T. Press, 1965). (The student who reads French should take a look at the literature in that language, such as Gilles-Y. Bertin, *L'Investissement des Firmes Etrangères en France* (Paris: Presses universitaires de France, 1963).

Michael Kidron, *Foreign Investment in India* (London: Oxford University Press, 1965).

A. E. Safarian, *Foreign Ownership of Canadian Industry* (Toronto: McGraw-Hill Book Company of Canada, 1966).

Arthur Stonehill, *Foreign Ownership in Norwegian Enterprises* (Oslo: Central Bureau of Statistics, 1965).

A large-scale research project on the foreign business operations at the Harvard Business School under the direction of Raymond Vernon will shortly begin producing more material.

Among the periodical literature, see H. W. Singer, "The Distribution of Gains between Investing and Borrowing Countries," in American Economic Association, *Readings in International Economics;* and Edith T. Penrose, "Foreign Investment and the Growth of the Firm," *EJ,* June, 1956, and "Profit Sharing between Producing Countries and Oil Companies in the Middle East," *EJ,* June, 1959.

POINTS

The reference for the discussion of the impact of direct investment on the U.S. balance of payments are P. W. Bell, "Private Capital Movements and the U.S. Balance-of-Payments Position," in *Factors Affecting the United States Balance of Payments* prepared for the Subcommittee on International Exchange and Payments, Joint Economic Committee, 87th Cong., 2nd sess. (Washington, D.C.: U.S. Government Printing Office, 1962); and J. W. Polk, I. W. Meister, and L. A. Veit, *U.S. Production Abroad and the Balance of Payments: A Survey of Corporate Investment Experience* (New York: National Industrial Conference Board, 1966). (To call production by foreign subsidiaries of U.S. corporations "U.S. Production Abroad" seems peculiarly ethnocentric.)

An especially interesting study of attitudes toward the facts of U.S. investment in Europe is Christopher Layton, *Trans-Atlantic Investments* (Boulogne-sur-Seine: The Atlantic Institute, 1966).

The concept of defensive investment mentioned in this chapter is from A. Lamfalussy, *Investment and Growth in Mature Economies* (Oxford: Basil Blackwell & Mott, Ltd., 1961).

The view that national firms and international firms behave identically is set out in I. Brecher and S. S. Reisman, *Canadian-American Economic Relations* (Ottawa: The Government Printer, 1957), chap. viii.

Chapter	INTERGOVERNMENTAL
22	ECONOMIC ASSISTANCE

Prior to the middle of the 20th century, the government's role in international financial transactions was largely limited to occasional foreign borrowing, and to the control of private flows. There were exceptions. The Louisiana purchase from France and the Alaska purchase from Russia were significant capital transactions of the United States. The British government granted subsidies to colonies (which might be regarded, however, as internal transactions) and occasional military assistance like that of £10 million annually to support the Arab Legion in Jordan.

In war, the record was different. Allies typically shared treasure as well as blood. President Coolidge's view of the Allied war debts of World War I as a commercial obligation ("They hired the money, didn't they?") sounded strange to many ears even in the 1920's. The British had provided subventions to their continental allies against Napoleon, without the need to justify it.

Disaster also evoked intergovernmental assistance. The International Red Cross is only semigovernmental, but the United States took official action in transferring its share of the Boxer indemnity to Chinese relief, and governmental assistance was invoked in the Tokyo earthquake and fire. The largest role internationally in disaster was left to private charities, but government was not wholly passive.

In retrospect it seems inevitable that the role of government should expand in international economics, as it has done domestically. The origins of the domestic expansion have been war and depression: in 1929 the governmental budget accounted for less than 5 percent of national income, as compared with 20 percent today, and 50 percent at the peak of the war effort in 1944. Most of the increase in the role of government domestically is due to war—past, current, and prospective. But some substantial amount of today's 20 percent is attributable to domestic transfers (apart from interest on debt contracted in wartime) such as social security, aid to education, housing, and roads. In exact parallel, most of the international governmental transactions in the 1960's are caused by defense expenditure, but some have their origin in a new principle of international transfers or sharing between countries.

Table 22.1 sets out the record of international economic assistance

TABLE 22.1

SUMMARY OF U.S. FOREIGN GRANTS AND CREDITS BY PROGRAMS, JULY 1, 1940 TO
DECEMBER 31, 1965
(Millions of Dollars)

	War Period (*July 1, 1940– June 30, 1945*)	Postwar Period (*July 1, 1945– December 31, 1965*)
Total grants....................................	48,128	84,371
Military aid..................................	380	36,165
Economic and technical assistance................		29,900
Farm products disposal.........................		5,768
Civilian supplies..............................	813	6,002
Lend-lease...................................	46,728	
Other (includes UNRRA, post-UNRRA, and special country programs)............................	207	6,536
Less: Reverse grants, returns, and prior grants converted into credits.....................................	−7,882	−4,894
Net grants...................................	40,246	79,477
Total credits.................................	1,095	30,169
	329	9,540
Export-Import Bank............................	329	9,540
Agricultural trade development and assistance......		3,907
Lend-lease and surplus property..................	349	1,562
Country program loans.........................		7,410
Prior grants converted into credits...............		2,747
Other.......................................	417	5,003
Less: Principal collections........................	−380	−11,780
Net credits...................................	715	18,389
Other assistance		
Net accumulation of foreign currency claims.......		3,334
Net foreign aid................................	40,961	101,200

SOURCE: U.S. Department of Commerce, Office of Business Economics, quarterly report, *Foreign Grants and Credits by the United States Government* (Washington, D.C.: U.S. Government Printing Office, various issues).

of the U.S. government from the beginning of Lend-Lease in March, 1941, to the end of the war and from July 1, 1945 to December 31, 1965. The amounts are impressive. Their evolving distribution by areas (and very broadly by character) is set forth in Table 22.2. An account of this development of U.S. assistance is set forth below. But it is important to remember that the United States is by no means the only country in the world supplying aid. Official flows, which include some capital lending and guarantees on practically commercial terms, amounted in 1965 to 1.08 percent of national income in France, 0.90 percent in Belgium, 0.75 percent in Portugal, 0.67 percent in the United States, and 0.64 percent in Australia. Comparable figures are not available for the Soviet Union which entered into competition with the Western powers in military and civilian assistance as early as 1954.

TABLE 22.2

OUTLINE OF AID AND PREDECESSOR NET COMMITMENTS BY FISCAL YEARS, 1949–66, THROUGH DECEMBER, 1966
(Millions of Dollars)

Category and Region	Marshall Plan Period 1949–52 (4 Years)	Mutual Security Act Period 1953–57 (5 Years)	Mutual Security Act Period 1958–61 (4 Years)	Foreign Assistance Act Period 1962 through Dec. 1966 (5½ Years)	Total 1949– Dec. 1966
Grand total	14,505	9,142	7,416	12,040	43,103
Development loans	...	...	1,987	5,871	7,859
Technical cooperation/development grants	86	574	702	1,596	2,958
Defense support/supporting assistance	14,089	7,837	3,624	2,506	28,056
Other, including international organizations	331	731	1,103	2,066	4,231
East Asia	706	3,068	1,808	1,170	6,753
Vietnam	...	784	681	1,380	2,845
Near East and South Asia	1,088	2,024	2,556	4,079	9,748
Africa	4	120	666	1,093	1,883
Latin America	19	246	570	2,846	3,681
Europe	12,469	2,296	453	10	15,229
Nonregional	218	604	681	1,461	2,965

SOURCE: Agency for International Development, *Operations Report* (Fiscal Year, 1967).
NOTE: Figures do not in all cases add exactly because of rounding.

Defining Economic Aid

When the United States was the only country making assistance available directly, there was little difficulty in defining it. This country could determine its own definition, and that was that. In a world of more than one aid provider, however, comparisons are called for, and these call for some definition of what economic aid is. Unfortunately, there is little agreement on what should be included under the heading. Grants would seem clearly to belong, provided one can distinguish a grant from a purchase. A grant from A to B presumably lets B do something it wants to do. Suppose it persuades B to do something A wants it to do. Is this a grant or a purchase? Or suppose they both want it but it is not worth doing on some impartial outside judgment? Or suppose there is no cost to A? French subventions to former French colonies to keep them in the French camp in international affairs, or U.S. surplus disposal abroad (before the surplus stockpiles dwindled) are capable of raising philosophical questions.

But most countries, and the Development Assistance Committee of the Organization for Economic Cooperation and Development (OECD), count not only all grants, no matter how closely they resemble purchases, and all surplus disposal. They also include government and even private loans on commercial terms. This cannot be justified in economic terms. To an economist the amount of the assistance must be regarded as the difference in present value of the loan on the one hand, and the obligation to repay on the other. This difference for hard loans is zero, and they are not assistance. For loans at rates of interest below the market rates which are used to convert the flow of interest and amortization into present value, the proportion of assistance is measured by the proportion of the difference from market rates. For soft loans, repayable in foreign currencies, one has to perform the difficult exercise of calculating the mean of the probability distribution that the interest and capital repayment will be useful to the lender without an implicit foreign exchange discount. To take a simple case, assume that the chance of being able to convert the debt service into foreign exchange, or to spend it for useful goods and services without an implicit discount was exactly half. The soft loan may at market rates of interest then be regarded as half aid, half business.

As already suggested, these subtle calculations are altogether ignored, and aid is aid, no matter how closely the terms approach the market. Germany whose aid consists to a great extent of short (but longer than a year) export credits, or on the official flow, export credit guarantees, insists that these are as much foreign aid as a 40-year, 3 percent loan repayable in foreign currency. The world is storing up problems on these counts, especially when it comes to settle debt repayment schedules by countries which default on outstanding obligations and are obliged to reschedule and write down their foreign obligations.

While we deal for the most part with U.S. aid, we touch at various places in the chapter on multilateral assistance, and on developed country aid more generally, particularly as manifest in the problem of burden sharing which is under continuous review in the Development Assistance Committee (D.A.C.) of the OECD.

Lend-Lease, Mutual Aid, and Military Relief

The principles of Lend-Lease are generally familiar. Goods (not money) were provided to U.S. allies without payment, on a basis to be settled after the war. A number of these countries in turn provided mutual aid to U.S. Armed Forces in their countries. Lend-Lease aid consisted in military equipment and military and civilian supplies. Mutual aid was made up of services rendered to the American forces, including civilian labor, rents, supplies of domestically available produce, and moneys distributed as troop pay to American forces for local expenditure. This mutual aid amounted to $7,882 million, or 16 percent of Lend-Lease in the opposite direction. In the case of Belgium, the value of mutual aid exceeded that of the Lend-Lease, and ultimate settlement involved a net payment by the United States to Belgium.

Precipitously at the end of hostilities, President Truman and Secretary of State Byrnes halted Lend-Lease, in line with their commitments to the Congress. Goods in transit were delivered, and specialized goods ordered were allowed to be finished and shipped. Lend-Lease procurement facilities were used for prime civilian items such as wheat and gasoline, but only against full cash payment. For past items, settlements were negotiated. A few items in short supply were asked to be returned. Some goods of prime civilian use not yet consumed but in storage or transit were regarded as transferred at full cost on long-term loans. The majority of military equipment and supplies which had been consumed were written off against the contribution of other countries to the war. At the same time, a considerable amount of U.S. equipment abroad, capable of civilian use, including trucks, tires, tents, military clothing, as well as food, was declared surplus and made available to allied countries under surplus property loans for 28-year terms at low rates of interest.

Lend-Lease was available to active allies. Liberated countries which did not enter Lend-Lease agreements were recipients of military supplies for civilian use—to maintain order in the zone of military operations—under the so-called Plan A. Bills were later submitted by the Army for these supplies, and these were consolidated into surplus property settlements. Austria and Italy, which had a status between liberated and defeated countries, received military aid from the United States and Britain before they were transferred to international support from the United Nations Relief and Rehabilitation Agency (UNRRA). United States support for the civilian populations of Germany and Japan was provided under a military budget item entitled Government and Relief in Occupied Areas (GARIOA).

UNRRA and Post-UNRRA Assistance

It was recognized during the course of the war that there would be serious problems afterwards. To this end were organized UNRRA to provide relief and rehabilitation as its name indicated; the International Bank for Reconstruction and Development, which was to complete the reconstruction and make the transition to the peacetime problem of development; and the International Monetary Fund to organize payments in the reconstructed financial world. Much as economists (and perhaps a few other classes of people) would like intergovernmental assistance to operate on the basis of objective economic principles from which political considerations are absent, it seems a counsel of perfection, impossible of achievement.

UNRRA was constituted partly with money and procurement machinery, largely in the United States, and partly with surplus U.S. Army stocks, which enabled it to begin operations rapidly. Its major contributors initially were the United States (72 percent), the United Kingdom (18 percent), and Canada (6 percent). The remaining contributions, including that of the Soviet Union, were small. The first tranche, or share, amounting to $1.3 billion, was allocated mainly to countries behind the Iron Curtain, since the countries of Western Europe either were contributors, had foreign exchange reserves, or were occupied. When it came time to vote a second tranche, the British wanted to transfer Austria and Italy from military relief, where their share of the cost was greater, to UNRRA. Canada decided to channel its aid direct to Britain. And the Soviet Union, as a price of agreeing to these changes, insisted that the "separate countries" of Byelo-Russia and the Ukraine be entitled to receive rehabilitation supplies. The United States with only 1 vote in 17 on the council, despite the fact that it contributed 78 percent of the second tranche (its original share plus the Canadian), resolved to avoid the necessity to bargain about its aid in future. With the allocation of the second tranche, UNRRA was wound up. A post-UNRRA relief program was provided by the United States largely for Austria and Italy, as deteriorating relations with Yugoslavia, Poland, and Hungary colored the U.S. view of their relief requirements.

Export-Import Bank and the Anglo-American Financial Agreement

It was recognized, in the summer of 1945, that the International Bank and Fund would take time to begin operations, and that something was needed to tide over until they did. To this end the capital of the Export-Import Bank was raised by $3 billion. Loans were made for reconstruction purposes to liberated countries like France, and to Latin-American allies. For a time $1 billion was earmarked for a loan to the Soviet Union. When it failed to apply, or did not receive an application—but in any event after the worsening of political relations—the money was made available to other borrowers.

Shortly after the Export-Import Bank capital expansion, it became clear that neither it nor the International Bank would be sufficient to cope with the financial problem facing the United Kingdom. This was especially the case after the abrupt termination of Lend-Lease. In the fall of 1945, a British delegation under Lord Keynes came to Washington to negotiate a very large amount of assistance to put Britain back on its feet and enable it to play a role in the postwar reconstruction of other countries. Aid to Britain was justified under the so-called key-currency principle which Professor John H. Williams had enunciated in opposing the Bretton Woods Bank and Fund. He had held that it was a mistake to try to get all countries back on their feet simultaneously but rather that one currency at a time should be restored to strength and relied upon as a pillar of support for others. Lord Keynes had envisaged a substantial loan of $5 billion or more on an interest-free basis; or possibly as a grant. The United States was willing to provide only $3,750 million, however, and on the basis of interest and repayment of principal. It insisted that the British resume currency convertibility within 12 months of the receipt of the loan. When these 12 months were up, in July, 1947, Britain had succeeded in negotiating no agreements for scaling down or blocking the substantial sterling accumulations of its colonies and allies, had permitted substantial export of capital to South Africa and Australia, and had been unable to prevent withdrawals for Belgium and Argentina. Convertibility brought with it a run on sterling which in six weeks had exhausted the bulk of the loan. Foreign exchange restrictions were then restored.

The Truman Doctrine and the Marshall Plan

By the spring of 1947 it became clear that UNRRA, the International Bank, and the Fund were going to be insufficient to meet the postwar reconstruction needs of Europe, even with the Export-Import Bank capital enlargement and the Anglo-American Financial Agreement. A severe winter and spring had set back agricultural and industrial production, but even before that the reconstruction and restocking of the economy of Western Europe were far from complete. Countries such as France and the Netherlands were running short of exchange reserves, even after Export-Import Bank, Fund, and Bank loans, and were not in a position to pay their way.

In December, 1946, the British government decided that it was unable to continue providing support for the civilian population of its zone of occupation in Germany, and the United States took that over. In February, 1947, Britain felt obliged to discontinue financial support of Greece. President Truman responded by announcing a program of military and economic assistance for Greece and for Turkey, which was similarly threatened by aggression.

In June, 1947, Secretary of State George C. Marshall made an address in which he suggested that if Europe were to devise an overall plan of recovery to replace the piecemeal, patchwork approach followed thus far the United States would view it favorably. A Committee for European Economic Cooperation drew up such a program. While it was being discussed, an Interim Aid program was put into effect to tide over especially France and the Netherlands. On April 3, 1948, the Marshall Plan went into effect, contemplating an expenditure of some $16 billion over four years. The Soviet Union did not participate, nor did it permit the participation of its satellites. Western Germany, which had carried through a monetary reform in June, 1948, was shifted from GARIOA to Marshall-Plan assistance. The level of aid for 17 countries from Iceland to Turkey was scheduled at $5.2 billion a year and was expected to decline to zero after June 30, 1952.

It is difficult to evaluate the Marshall Plan in detail because the outbreak of fighting in Korea two years later, in June, 1950, substantially changed the character of the problem. Economic assistance to Western Europe declined on, or ahead of, schedule. But military assistance rose substantially. Nonetheless there is general agreement that the aid was effectively used and made a substantial contribution to the European economic recovery from which the subsequent brilliant spurt of growth took off.

Military Assistance and Defense Support

The Korean hostilities underlined the weakness of the defensive position in Europe and the necessity to take new military measures. The North Atlantic Treaty Organization, covering a somewhat smaller number of countries than the 17 members of the Organization for European Economic Cooperation, undertook a program of defense expenditure with a number of international aspects. One was the provision of military equipment by the United States to its allies. Another involved the purchase of equipment by the United States from factories in Europe, for ultimate use either by United States or by other European forces. A third was the provision of certain overhead defense installations: airfields, pipelines, storage depots, and so on, called by the French the "infrastructure" (in English, not underfoot, but overhead).

In an important sense, buying military assistance in the cheapest market cannot be called military assistance. We are not used today to hiring mercenaries, as George III did Hessians, and there is even something of a loss of prestige involved in using foreign equipment and relying on foreign defense contributions. But if each country ceased to rely on the patriotism of its armed forces, defense might well be an item of international commerce. One could buy defense, as one now buys bananas, coffee, tin, and rubber. To some considerable extent, then, military assistance is not so much assistance to others as a purchase for domestic consumption.

Supporting assistance involves the provision of civilian assistance to enable a foreign country to devote more of its own resources to defense needs. In the United States, military assistance has been operated by the Department of Defense, and supporting assistance by the Agency for International Development, as successor to the International Cooperation Administration (ICA), and the Economic Cooperation Administration (ECA). On March 31, 1967, two thirds of the $336 millions fiscal 1967 commitment of supporting assistance had been allocated to Vietnam. Laos received $34 millions, Jordan $25 millions, Korea $12½ millions and the Dominican Republic $10 millions.

Technical Cooperation and Development Assistance

Point Four of President Truman's Inaugural Speech in 1949 called for a bold new program of assistance to underdeveloped countries. The content of this program turned out to be mainly technical assistance, largely in the fields of agriculture, public health, and education. This has been carried out partly through the United Nations machinery, which in turn is divided between the specialized agencies such as the World Health Organization (WHO), the Food and Agriculture Organization (FAO), the International Labor Organization (ILO), etc., and partly through experts hired directly by the United Nations. In addition, there has been a large bilateral U.S. undertaking, governmental and private, and among the latter through foundations, religious bodies, and various sorts of private arrangements. In due time, Soviet technicians went abroad under various assistance projects. The United States initiated the Peace Corps, a body of persons, largely young, and to some extent inexpert, with a strong zeal for participating in the task of training the broad masses of the underdeveloped countries.

At a very early stage after the enunciation of the Point IV program, it became clear that technical assistance was not sufficient by itself to bring about self-sustaining growth in underdeveloped countries, and that there was need for capital assistance beyond that available through private investors and the international agencies. The United States year by year made increasing amounts of such assistance available, partly again through the United Nations, but largely directly for a host of purposes. Initially the emphasis was defense, and the assistance was administered by the Mutual Security Agency, which was the successor organization to the Economic Cooperation Administration which had operated the U.S. end of the European Recovery Program. As the work expanded, the MSA was succeeded by the International Cooperation Administration, and later by the Agency for International Development, with the appropriate initials, AID. The Development Loan Fund was created within ICA in 1958 to administer loans to underdeveloped countries. Public Law (P.L.) 480 was passed in 1954 to make food surpluses available to underdeveloped countries outside commercial channels against payment in local currency. In 1961, the Inter-American Development Bank, long sought by the Organization of American States, was established primarily with U.S. dollars to make loans for social as well as economic purposes, going beyond the scope of the work of the International Bank for Reconstruction and Development, the Export-Import Bank, and the Development Loan Fund. In the same year the United States signed at Punta del Este the Alliance for Progress under which it undertook to assist an expanded program of economic development in Latin America which would be supported, in those countries, by measures of tax and land reform. A similar Asian Development Bank was organized in 1966 and opened its doors in 1967.

In 1967, AID provided purely economic aid in two main forms: project aid consisting of particular capital, technical, and supporting assistance projects; and program aid of Development Loan Fund and Alliance for Progress loans, and also supporting assistance. As already noted in Chapter 20, economists prefer program to project loans, thinking the latter partakes of the fallacy of misplaced concreteness. The agency wants to shift to more programs; but Congress likes projects. Congress is also responsible for a trend to loans from grants, with the latter being reserved for technical and supporting assistance. Important congressional voices want to reduce foreign aid sharply, and others want to concentrate assistance on a limited number of countries. One important feature of AID operations is a program of guarantees of private investments against particular hazards, and specifically against the risks of war, expropriation, and inconvertibility of the exchange for remittance of earnings and capital.

Intergovernmental Assistance Problems

The foregoing pages do little more than identify the various forms of intergovernmental economic assistance in which the United States has participated in the last 20 years. In the space that remains in this chapter, not much more can be attempted that to indicate some of the problems and dilemmas to which such assistance gives rise. The astute reader will recognize that some of these dilemmas have had their domestic analogues which time has managed to solve without undue difficulty. It used to be thought, for example, that unemployment insurance ran grave risks of undermining the incentive to work. It may be that time will also be found to settle decisively, in one way or another, certain issues which now appear more delicately balanced. The problems concern the nature of the need for assistance, the principles on which aid should be granted, conditions, and so forth.

Aid for Limited Purposes versus Provision of Resources in General

During the provision of Lend-Lease to Britain a serious problem related to the size of U.S. assistance was the extent to which Britain was to continue normal exports. These exports used up resources which would otherwise have been devoted to the war and would therefore have reduced the need for assistance. Whether Britain should be left further in debt to its peacetime trading partners, and with a minimum of normal export trade at the end of the war, is unimportant for the present discussion. The essential point is that any assistance program must consider not only the particular use of the resources made available but the totality of the resources under the jurisdiction of the receiving country.

This principle is not always observed. The project basis for the loans of the International Bank for Reconstruction and Development has been noted. Similarly, the Economic Cooperation Administration was concerned to trace through the use of the steel made available to, say, France under the Marshall Plan, whereas it should have been concerned with the efficient use of all steel, or in fact all resources which might have been used to manufacture steel. It is a clear-cut and relatively easy to ensure that appropriate use is made of particular economic assistance. But only total resources are relevant.

This principle raises an important point concerning military assistance and defense support. It has been proposed that both these categories of aid be separated from the question of assistance for economic development and handled through the budget of the Defense Department in the United States. But the distinction between aid for defense and aid for development is a difficult one to keep sharp. Given a fixed military program in a recipient nation, foreign aid for that program releases resources for economic development; and, conversely, given a fixed development program, economic development assistance contributes to military capacity, or consumption, or any other expansible item. The separation between economic and development assistance is only valid if each is determined separately, assuming every other expenditure fixed. If both remain to be determined, they are inseparable.

The same can be said about the project approach to development initiated by the International Bank and followed by the Agency for International Development. To allocate assistance for capital projects ensures that it is not wasted only on the untenable assumption that everything else is unchanged. More frequently the project would have been undertaken anyhow; to assist it is to assist consumption, or capital exports, or some other diverse purpose. Economic assistance in particular turns out in the usual case to be economic assistance in general. And it is justified or wasted, depending upon how effectively the country uses its own general resources. What is relevant is not the single project, but the total program, which is why AID economists prefer the program approach. The position is exactly the converse to the principle of economic warfare enunciated in Chapter 8. Bombardment (or blockade, and so on) deprive the enemy of resources in particular, rather than resources in general, only when he has no capacity, or is not allowed time, to transfer resources from one occupation to another.

The Appropriate Amount of Aid

In wartime the determination of the appropriate amount of aid is relatively easy. The United States should help Britain rather than use its resources on its own military effort, so long as a dollar of resources in Britain buys more firepower delivered against the enemy than a dollar of resources in the United States. This principle may have to be modified to take account of national pride, the indivisibility of military effort, and similar considerations. But at basis, the calculation is straightforward.

In peacetime, on the contrary, there is no single criterion. It might be argued that aid should be continued until income per capita is equal in the two countries, but this requires a world rather than a national point of view, and few are prepared to urge it.

Under the Marshall Plan, country programs were adopted, and aid was sought to make up the balance-of-payments deficits resulting from these programs. But this was fallacious. As Machlup pointed out, the programs depended upon how much finance could be found for the resulting balance-of-payments deficits, not the deficits on unalterable programs. And when the first approximation of investment programs of the Committee on European Economic Cooperation produced a four-year deficit of $30 billion, the Committee was able to amend the program when Messrs. Clayton and Douglas informed them that this was more than the United States was likely to support.

Not only does the program determine the deficit, rather than the other way about, but to calculate aid on the basis of deficits is to distort incentives and to put a premium on inefficiency. A country which contributes its own resources to capital formation through a rigorous program of austerity will have a smaller deficit than the country which is unable to marshal savings for productive use, and deserves more rather than less aid, according to the principle that the Lord helps those who help themselves. Subsidies, like taxes, can be distortionary in terms of effort. To minimize this distortion, there is something to be said for having the amount of assistance fixed, so that the benefits of its additional efforts accrue to the assisted rather than to the assisting country. Theorists have devised the ingenious (but impractical) scheme of lump-sum progressive taxes, levied on expected earning power. The fixed amount of the tax makes the marginal return from additional effort equal for people of different incomes and minimizes distortion of effort. Similarly, lump-sum subsidies, not necessarily on a progressive basis, would minimize the perverse effects of a subsidy to inefficiency involved in basing economic assistance on the amount of a country's deficit.

Perverse incentives abound in economic aid, in the small as in the large. To provide food to India to aid in preventing famine, lowers grain prices and takes the edge off the peasants' urge to grow grain.

The national goal must take into account the available resources, but is likely also to rely on some combination of the historical, the desirable, and the feasible, the last in terms of domestic as well as foreign availabilities. Thus, under the Marshall Plan the goal of Britain involved a standard of living higher than that in Italy, but the projected

Italian standard was higher in relation to prewar than the British because of the poverty of prewar Italy.

Some years ago, Millikan and Rostow proposed that each country's capacity to absorb capital could be uniquely defined, and that those countries below a certain level of income per capita should be accorded all the assistance they could absorb, in a program of developed country aid to economic growth. The contrast with the vagueness of the appropriate amount of aid under the Marshall Plan is sharp. The concept to absorb capital has been discussed two chapters back. But the Millikan-Rostow proposal is especially interesting as an example of the view that aid should be determined solely by economic goals. The reasoning may be questioned on two scores. In the first place, it is hard for the donor to ignore opposition in foreign policy, riots in the street before the embassy, burning of the United States Information Agency library, and the like. Foreign aid is a tool of foreign policy, and the self-denying ordinance which says it will not be used is hard to adhere to. Second, as already pointed out, it is impossible for the donor to ensure that the aid will be used for the purpose for which it is given. Economic aid to India and Pakistan can be used against each other rather than for economic development. Jacob J. Kaplan, a professional economist and a foreign-aid hand of 20 years' experience, characterizes aid exclusively for economic development as a gimmick, along with other gimmicks, which the Washington authorities have resorted to because of unwillingness to face the reality that foreign aid is a tool of foreign policy.

A final dilemma is encountered in connection with competitive assistance from the Soviet Union. Should aid from the Soviet Union entitle a country to more, the same, or less aid from the United States? More is the competitive answer, which the underdeveloped countries would like. On the other hand, if the country can only absorb a limited amount of capital, its requirements are reduced by the availability of other aid. But in any practical situation the response of the United States to Soviet aid to an underdeveloped country could be neither substantially to increase its aid nor to cut it by the amount of Soviet aid, but something in between.

Indirect Assistance

There is no need for assistance to a country to be direct. In some cases, indeed, it is not clear which country is being helped. Under the Hyde Park Agreement of 1941, the United States made available goods on Lend-Lease to Britain which were shipped to Canada and used there in connection with the Canadian war effort on British behalf. This can properly be regarded as aid to Britain if Canada would have been unable to assist Britain in its absence. But if the Canadian assistance would have been forthcoming in any event, and to this extent, the Lend-Lease amounts recorded for Britain in fact aided Canada.

This form of indirect assistance has developed on a much larger scale in the postwar period. The Anglo-American Financial Agreement was recognized as an attempt, through assistance to Britain, to help other countries of the world, including the Dominions and Latin America. By means of this loan, the British were able to buy, and the Dominions and Latin America able to sell, goods which might not otherwise have moved in trade. Later in the European Recovery Program, offshore procurement by the United States in Canada and Latin America financed with convertible currencies the sales of these countries to Europe.

During this stage of the recovery in Europe, there was widespread trade discrimination against so-called luxury goods in Europe in the hope of acquiring dollar surpluses for use in buying necessities from North America. Aid to Europe could thus be given by U.S. purchases of lemons from Italy for delivery to Germany. Italy was helped to sell products for which it could not otherwise hope to receive dollars; Germany received lemons it would not otherwise have been able to enjoy. This system, however, was admittedly stopgap, and required the financing of particular transactions.

The awkwardness of administering offshore purchases led to the development of conditional aid. Suppose France and Britain each have a deficit of $100 with the United States but that France in addition has $50 in deficit with Britain, which is a British surplus. The United States can now finance the total balance-of-payments deficits of the two countries ($150 for France and $50 for Britain) or their separate deficits with the United States ($100 each). The total of U.S. aid is the same in either event. In the former case, $50 of the $150 made available to France must be conditional on France's buying its normal imports from Britain and paying $50 in convertible exchange; or if $100 is given to each country, $50 of the amount given to Britain can be made conditional on its financing (by gift or loan) its balance-of-payments surplus with France. It is evident which of the two systems France and Britain will each prefer. And either system will introduce distortion into normal trade patterns. For France, $150 will tend to make it indifferent whether it buys the British goods; and $100 to Britain will make it indifferent whether it supplies the French requirements. Accordingly, the system of conditional aid, which functioned through the Intra-European Payments Scheme, was abandoned in 1950 in favor of the European Payments Union (EPU).

Under EPU, United States contributed $500 million plus to the OEEC to be used to finance multilateral settlements among the countries of Europe. All intra-European trade was multilateralized, i.e., bilateral balances in intra-European trade were converted into balances due from or owed to EPU. Every country had a quota which was divided into five shares or tranches. Debtors paid dollars (or gold) and received credit, in varying proportions for each tranche, and creditors in turn received dollars and made credit available, according to the following schedule:

Tranche of Quota	Debtors		Creditors	
	Dollars Paid	Credit Received	Dollars Received	Credit Given
	(In Percent)		(In Percent)	
1...................	10	90	0	100
2...................	30	70	50	50
3...................	40	60	50	50
4...................	50	50	50	50
5...................	70	30	50	50
Average............	40	60	40	60

On the average, debtors on clearing account would pay in enough dollars to requite creditors; but the fund was obliged to have assets to take care of the occasions when more credit was being extended to debtors than was being provided by creditors. Such would be the case, for example, if most debtors were operating at the first or second tranche receiving 90 percent or 70 percent in credit, while a few persistent creditors were making available only 50 percent in credit. This was the purpose of the U.S. provision of capital which was maintained and not used up.

The European Payments Union was wound up in 1960, replaced, after convertibility had been achieved for most of the members, by the looser European Monetary Agreement of little operational importance. Outstanding credit and debit balances were funded into long-term debts; the capital was set aside to make loans for special needs of the underdeveloped members (Spain, Portugal, Greece, Turkey) of the Organization for Economic Cooperation and Development, which succeeded the Organization for European Economic Cooperation, including Canada and the United States as members, and was concerned with the

Atlantic Community's economic responsibilities in the world, rather than merely European recovery.

The European Payments Union was an enormous success. A great deal of the credit belongs to the ingenuity of its creators, and the goodwill of the participating countries. Some, however, is ascribable to the fact that its early persistent debtors, Austria, Greece, and Turkey, had their deficits made up by the United States, and did not therefore soak up the assets of the Union. It had an important theoretical weakness—that to require all countries to balance their payments within the system assumes that all can also balance them without, and that no country happens to balance its total trade with a gross surplus inside used to pay a gross deficit outside. But this theoretical lack failed to be significant, partly because the major external deficit—in dollars—was being funded otherwise—and partly because the other major currency in which a deficit was possible was sterling, with the whole sterling area included in the payments union.

But the mechanism which worked so brilliantly in Europe has not been tried outside of it, despite the urgings of Latin-American and Asian advocates. These areas would find the theoretical weakness hurtful, and they lack the positive assets which made the EPU work—a large volume of intra-European trade plus impressive political cohesion. In Asia and in Latin America, each member of such a payments union would hope to use it to earn currencies to spend outside. This is manifestly impossible. In consequence, the calls for similar payments arrangements elsewhere in the world have faded.

Conditions of Aid

There is almost general agreement among political scientists, if not among politicians, that the major condition of economic assistance should be that the particular country is doing its best to improve its position. This poses the dilemma of incentives discussed above. But it also raises a host of other questions, ranging from the purely political to economic conditions of aid which can be construed as undue interference.

The purely political questions lie outside the scope of an economics text but are nonetheless (or all the more?) real. Does Pakistan get more aid than India, on some comparable basis, because Pakistan has joined the Southeast Asia Treaty Organization, while India is a strict neutralist? Is aid for Yugoslavia a good thing when Tito remains Communist? Is help to Polish reconstruction indirect assistance to the Soviet Union by relieving it of a burden, or does it more significantly increase the independence of Poland from the Soviet Union? The U.S. Executive Branch of the government has decided that aid to these members of the Communist bloc, but not food for starving Communist China, is politically useful. The legislative branch tends to vote against this aid in an election year, however.

Apart from such larger political questions, however, there is a variety of lesser dilemmas of a quasi-political or political character which involve economic issues. Do the benefits of aid go largely to one class inside a country; and does action by this class block economic development, or recovery, in a significant measure? Does the country oppose private enterprise and drive away foreign capital which could lessen its requirement for foreign assistance? Does foreign aid enable the internal political forces to escape the necessity to face hard decisions, such as how the burdens of recovery or economic development shall be shared, and thus to postpone effective domestic action? Or can the conditions of aid be used by the constructive forces within the aided country to persuade other domestic interests to follow the policies which will most speed development. A discouraging test of this proposition has been under way in the Alliance for Progress in Latin America. Aid was offered mainly on the basis of progress in reforms—the imposition of taxes to balance the budget and check inflation, and agricultural reform in the interest of democracy and agricultural productivity. Aid officials wanted reform first, as a condition of aid; Latin-American government officials, worried lest they be voted out of office, wanted aid as a condition of reform. On the whole, the latter carried the day. Currently, a new condition of aid is being laid down: progress in integration of the Latin-American market as decided, once again, at Punta del Este, Uruguay, in April, 1967. It remains to be seen how effectively the Latin American governments will cope with the political obstacles in the road to this objective.

One method devised in the European Recovery Program, and extended in some of the development assistance programs such as those involving surplus agricultural products, has been to require U.S. agreement to the disposition of the local currency counterpart of U.S. aid. Commodities representing U.S. aid are not given to consumers and firms but sold for local currency. The use of these "counterpart funds" has important consequences. If they are saved, i.e., used to retire public debt, and particularly central bank loans to the national treasury, the deflationary impact of the assistance is evident. They may, however, be used for capital formation or even for regular expenses, which would maintain or increase the level of national income and give rise to increased imports.

The requirement that the United States approve the disposition of these funds involves this country's representatives in a discussion of the financial aspects of the recovery or the development program. The significance of this involvement may vary widely. At one limit, as in Britain in the European Recovery Program, the deflationary impact of the piling up of counterpart funds can be fully offset by other Treasury and central bank operations. The British went for several years without making any proposals regarding the use of counterpart funds, leaving it obvious that they resented the necessity to obtain U.S. permission. At the other extreme, however, a country such as Turkey built much of its financial policy around the use of counterpart funds and sought U.S. advice on this policy in its total aspects. When inflation in a country has deep political roots, to withhold counterpart funds sought to pay normal governmental expenses may overthrow the government in a financial crisis. The limits of the technique are thus evident. But in other cases, the requirement that the United States approve the disposition of counterpart funds gave useful leverage to a finance minister or central banker fighting a political battle against internal forces of inflation by enabling him to appeal to necessity from without.

There are some who believe that aid should be given without strings of any kind. This may be appropriate in a few cases, such as between Britain and the Dominions, where the aiding country and the aided operate at the same level of political and economic sophistication and understand one another fairly completely. But it is otherwise naïve. At the minimum, the aiding country should know how the country being assisted proposes to use the help and have some idea of whether it is capable of carrying out its intentions. And if it approves of the goals, all other conditions should be directed to their efficient achievement. On the political side, this suggests that short-run objectives should be minimized as irrelevant or even capable of interfering with the long-run political goal of political and economic independence. In economic terms, it means merely that the country use its resources as efficiently as it can.

One condition which the United States attached to most of its assistance programs—Lend-Lease, the postwar settlements, the Anglo-American Financial Agreement, and the Marshall Plan—was that the recipients dedicate themselves with the United States to the construction of a world trade and payments system of a multilateral, nondiscriminatory character. It was relatively easy for the recipients to provide an affirmation of faith which lacked operational significance (except for the disastrous requirement of convertibility in the British loan). They were doubtless, too, sincere in this affirmation at the time it was given. Some observers object to the requirement of subscribing to long-run principles. Not every country can afford to ignore its short-run for its longer-run interests, and there is a danger, when repeated professions of faith are sought, that they may come to mean little more than the hymns intoned by those about to be fed by the Salvation Army.

Loans versus Grants

The religious objection to interest on loans, in pre-Reformation Europe and in much of the Muslim world today, was based on the ethical injunction not to take advantage of the distress of others. In economic conditions where the harvest was variable, borrowing took place in times of distress, and for consumption. To charge interest was to exploit a brother's bad luck.

When lending became predominantly for capital formation rather than for consumption, the Christian Church modified its opposition to interest. Since the borrower was going to benefit from the loan, he could afford to pay for the use of the capital which the lender was temporarily giving up.

Similar ethical considerations seem to dominate the question of whether international economic assistance should take the form of loans or grants. Military assistance and defense support take the form of grants because the *quid pro quo* is the contribution of the recipient to the joint military effort. For the rest, disaster rehabilitation and reconstruction assistance are largely on a grant basis, while economic development or reconstruction assistance which enlarges capacity is regarded as suitable for loans. The failure to recognize the ethical aspect of reconstruction assistance was responsible for evoking the moral outcry against the collection of the war loans after World War I and against the precipitous halting of Lend-Lease after World War II.

Note that these distinctions, which are applied only loosely, turn on the nature of the demand. From the point of view of the suppliers, it might be noted that international economic assistance involves giving up of real resources, that this is painful, and that it therefore ought to be on an interest-bearing loan basis. The fact is that the supply side is considered only in a few cases, such as aid in the form of surplus commodities. These were given away or loaned on a soft basis calling for repayment in local currencies (which were then allocated for economic development) because the cost of the loans could be regarded as sunk. The Commodity Credit Corporation has already acquired the commodities. To lend them abroad involves no pain of parting with scarce resources but rather relief from the embarrassment of redundancy. Now that the surplus stocks are gone, there is still little cost to P.L. 480 aid; basically it is aid to U.S. farmers, not aid to foreign consumers. The evidence is that wheat acreages were cut, not raised, despite widening famine in 1967, because American wheat prices had been soft and needed stiffening before the 1968 elections.

Some observers try to make a distinction between assistance for social overhead capital—roads, ports, schools, hospitals, and so on—which it is felt should be given on a grant basis, and that for industrial capital, which is appropriate for loans. Others believe that assistance which increases the capacity of a country to export or to replace existing imports can be appropriately charged on a loan basis, whereas assistance to a mainly internal project which does not directly help the balance-of-payments position should be granted. Still a third point of view in favor of grants rather than loans would select those projects with a long delay between the start of the investment and the payoff in increased productivity as deserving grants.

None of these points of view has much validity. If social overhead capital is productive, that productivity shows up somewhere in the economy and a portion of it can be captured by the government and used for repayment if the governmental fiscal machinery is adequate. If it is not adequate, or if great uncertainty attaches to the question whether the investment will be productive, then a case for grants rather than loans exists. The fallacy of insisting that each project provide for its own repayment has been dealt with earlier. What is needed is capacity to subtract the necessary part of the increase in productivity from consumption, and to reallocate a sufficient amount of the economy's resources, at the margin, into export- or import-competing lines. If resources cannot be reallocated, then again there is a case for a grant (but not much prospect for growth). Finally, the existence of a long delay between the start of a project and the payoff means only that the capital cost of the project is larger than the aggregated annual costs by the interest on the amounts expended in the earlier years prior to completion. If the productivity of the project is justified after the capital has been calculated at a higher amount in this fashion, then the larger loan which would be needed to pay interest in the interval to completion is also justified.

The social ethic need not limit grants to cases of distress, or for maintaining consumption, while loans are exacted for increased productivity capacity or increased consumption. An international social welfare function could call for grants to countries with per capita incomes less than a given level, whether they used the assistance for consumption or capital formation, and loans to countries above that level. It makes a curious kind of logic to give billions to the United Kingdom to maintain its consumption above $750 per capita (say) while insisting on lending capital to India to get its income per capita up from $60.

The point to be emphasized is that the issue of loans or grants is not an economic one but moral, ethical, and social. One shares within the circle of family and friends, and deals on a business basis outside it. And some relationships change between friendship and business in complex and unpredictable ways.

Bilateral versus Regional versus International Administration

An additional political issue to which we give only slight attention is the question of administering aid programs. The difficulty faced by the United States in UNRRA has been mentioned earlier. With 78 percent of the cost and only 1 vote in 17 on the disposition of the funds, the United States might have been able to continue with UNRRA if there had been an objectively determined set of principles on which aid was to be divided. But when the division of aid is settled politically, it behooves the provider to safeguard his interests.

The division of aid is a political matter. Within the European Recovery Program, the United States asked for a recommendation by the 17 countries as to how aid should be divided, while it retained the right, through bilateral agreements, to approve the level of aid to any individual country. The multilateral recommendation was important in deflecting dissatisfaction about the level of the assistance for any country from the United States to the Organization for European Economic Cooperation. The retention of the right to veto aid for any one country was important to ensure that the objectives would be met in every case.

The task of arriving at a multilateral recommendation to the United States was a difficult one, and required an underlying basis of political cohesion. It is not clear whether this basis is present in other areas of the world; whether, that is, the Arab countries could agree on a basis of sharing a given amount of assistance made available to them as a group, or the Far Eastern countries, a given amount for them. In the Colombo Plan, as the Marshall Plan, all aid is bilateral, as all development plans are unilateral rather than coordinated. The Colombo Plan has in fact no permanent secretariat, as did the OEEC, but one which meets only a few weeks each year to draft a report.

The Alliance for Progress had a procedure for relieving the donor countries (mainly the United States) of the political "heat" of with-holding aid from those countries which are not making progress toward self-sustaining growth, or in cutting down aid below what a country thinks it is entitled to. Nine so-called wise men from the member countries, chosen for their economic competence and judgment, but not without a sense of political balance, were called upon to make the final decision as to the distribution of aid. Ultimately the wise men resigned in a body because their judgments were not accepted by the Alliance—another classic instance of the short-term clash between economic the-ory and political fact.

Voting power in the International Bank for Reconstruction and Development and in the International Monetary Fund and United Nations Special Fund recognizes these dilemmas by which the providers of assistance must have the right to refuse it, unless there is an agreed and unambiguous set of principles for its use. Lacking this right, assist-ance develops into taxation. When one pools sovereignty with other countries, one agrees in advance to abide by the outcome of the total decision, made according to agreed procedures. Taxation is appropriate in this circumstance. But when sovereignty is retained, intergovern-mental assistance means that the ultimate decision to give or withhold aid must rest with the donor. It is nonetheless desirable to widen the basis for agreement as far as possible and achieve international and regional recommendations for the character, scope, and division of aid.

Distributing the Burden of Aid

The recovery of Western Europe and the balance-of-payments difficulties of the United States raised the question at the end of the 1950's whether the burden of aid was equitably distributed. To analyze this issue one must raise still further questions. The first of these is whether the balance of payments is related to a country's share of an international obligation.

Economists are virtually fully agreed that, in principle, the basis of distributing a burden should be income (or possibly wealth) but not the balance of payments. The balance of payments should adjust to the burden of aid, rather than the share of aid adjust to the balance of payments. A poor man should not give more to charity than a rich just because he has managed to save in one year at a time when the rich man has been forced, at his standard of living, to borrow. At the same time that this is said, however, the improvement in the Western European balance of payments has served to attract attention to the fact that many of these countries had been gaining rapidly in income and wealth without taking on major responsibilities in intergovernmental economic assistance.

The problems of computing an appropriate basis for sharing aid to underdeveloped countries in terms of income are formidable. First is the question of determining what comprises aid, as discussed at the outset in this chapter. This has two parts: the categories of aid to be counted, and the valuations used for different types of aid. Where surplus commodities are included in aid, for example, should they be counted at their full market value, the market value less government subsidy, or should some credit be subtracted for the benefit to the donor government from disposing of a burdensome surplus? Professor Rosenstein-Rodan arbitrarily counts P.L. 480 contributions of the U.S. government as aid at two thirds of the market value, and defense support at 20 percent of cost. Or take technical assistance. If the United States sends one high-priced, high-expense account technician to a country, should that count as a multiple of or equal to a lower salaried, more modest level-of-living technician in the same field from Japan, Israel, or Western Europe. This problem is particularly acute in evaluating defense contributions to NATO, where the Turkish government properly resents the low value assigned to its contribution of low-pay infantry, as compared with the high-priced American soldier, making the valid point that their fighting values are not related in the same multiple as their monthly salaries.

But assume that aid can be consistently defined and valued. We then need to relate it to each country's real income per capita. Money income, compared in a common unit such as dollars is not adequate, since national income definitions differ and since foreign exchange rates overstate the value of the moneys of developed countries and understate that of the less developed. But correct for this, too. We now have to decide whether the contribution to aid should be proportional, progressive, or regressive, and whether there should be a cut-off point, as $600 on the U.S. personal income tax, below which no contribution is called for.

Unhappily, the Development Assistance Committee does none of these things. The 1 percent rule is proportional, and applies to aid defined to include commercial transactions, without correction for overvaluations or surplus disposal. The world is still a long way from burden sharing of the sort that is undertaken by "communities." But the direction seems inescapable.

Summary

With the rise of government transactions in general, there has been an increase in the volume of international governmental business

432 · *INTERNATIONAL ECONOMICS*

and nonbusiness transactions. These were large during the war, and continued at an impressive scale through relief, rehabilitation, reconstruction, and, more recently, in technical and capital assistance for economic development. The resurgence of interest in national and international defense arrangements has led to an increase of intergovernmental business and assistance in this area.

It is difficult to distinguish aid for particular purposes from aid in general unless the particular purposes are served in partial equilibrium with everything else equal. There are problems and dilemmas to be faced in determining the appropriate amount of aid in a given case: financing deficits is clearly wrong; capacity to absorb capital is ambiguous; there is no objective basis for determining whether a given goal aims too high or too low. There are also interesting issues concerning which countries receive aid; and some means are available for using the same funds to assist two or more countries in different ways. The European Payments Union is an example of a particular form of indirect assistance which is not extendable to other areas. Intergovernmental economic assistance involves an almost inevitable watering down of the lines of division of national sovereignty, and interference by one nation in the affairs of others. Counterpart funds are one means for doing so, with widely varying degrees of effectiveness. The decision whether aid should be on the basis of loans or grants cannot be made on economic grounds but involves ethical and moral considerations. Similarly, the decision whether to administer aid on international or bilateral grounds is a political one. There are reasons for encouraging international bodies to propose, while national donors dispose.

Still in process of evolution are international principles and machinery for distributing the burden of intergovernmental assistance appropriately.

SUGGESTED READING

Texts

See J. N. Behrman and W. E. Schmidt, *International Economics* (New York: Rinehart & Co., Inc., 1957), chaps. xvii, xix, xx; T. C. Schelling, *International Economics* (Boston; Allyn and Bacon, Inc., 1958) chaps. xxvi, xxvii, and xxviii. See also Peter B. Kenen, *Giant among Nations* (New York: Harcourt Brace & Co., Inc., 1960), chaps. viii and ix.

Treatises

Robert E. Asher, *Grants, Loans and Local Currencies* (Washington, D.C.: The Brookings Institution, 1961) (paperback).

I. M. D. Little and J. M. Clifford, *International Aid* (London: George Allen & Unwin, Ltd., 1965) (paperback).

Harry G. Johnson, *Economic Policies toward Less Developed Countries* (Washington, D.C.: The Brookings Institution, 1966).

John A. Pincus, *Economic Aid and International Cost Sharing* (Baltimore, Md.: The Johns Hopkins Press, 1965).

John A. Pincus, *Trade, Aid and Development: The Rich and Poor Nations* (New York: McGraw-Hill Book Co., Inc., 1967).

Outstanding in the periodical literature are P. N. Rosenstein-Rodan, "International Aid for Underdeveloped Countries," *RE & S*, May, 1961, which is a large-scale exercise in calculating the needs of world aid, and their appropriate burden sharing; J. A. Pincus, "The Cost of Foreign Aid," *RE & S*, November, 1963; and W. E. Schmidt, "The Economics of Charity: Loans vs. Grants," *JPE*, August, 1964.

Soviet aid to underdeveloped countries, barely referred to in the crowded chapter above, is reviewed in Marshall I. Goldman, *Soviet Foreign Aid* (New York: Frederick A. Praeger, Inc., 1967).

POINTS

The Millikan-Rostow book referred to in the text is M. F. Millikan and W. W. Rostow, *A Proposal: Key to an Effective Foreign Policy* (New York: Harper Bros., 1957).

The OECD Development Aid Committee (DAC) publishes an annual review of the policies of the developed countries. The 1966 volume is by Willard L. Thorp, Chairman of DAC and entitled *Development Assistance Efforts and Policies* (Paris: OECD, September, 1966).

A highly useful series of case studies is available in W. G. Friedmann, G. Kalmanoff, R. F. Meagher, *International Financial Aid* (New York: Columbia University Press, 1966).

J. J. Kaplan, *The Challenge of Foreign Aid: Policies, Problems, Possibilities* (New York: Frederick A. Praeger, Inc., 1967), is a popular book, highly critical of congressional antipathy to aid.

PART VI

*Balance-of-Payments Equilibrium and
International Monetary Arrangements*

| Chapter | THE FOREIGN EXCHANGE |
| 23 | MARKET |

A foreign exchange transaction is a purchase or sale of one national money against another. Prior to 1913, the instruments traded in the foreign exchange market were bills of exchange, largely bankers' acceptances, drawn by exporters on importers and accepted by the importers' banks. These were near money, rather than money. Today, transactions are almost entirely in demand deposits, which are money. There is thus no need to quibble about the word "money" in the foregoing definition.

More significance should be attached to the word "national." There is a temptation to say that a foreign exchange transaction involves the purchase or sale of a domestic money for a foreign money. This temptation must be resisted. "Domestic" implies residence, which is a proper concept for the balance of payments in the next chapter, but misleading for the foreign exchange market. Economic literature is full of references to the New York foreign exchange market, or the London, Paris, or Frankfurt markets. In economic terms, these are imprecise. We should instead refer to the foreign exchange market for the dollar, pound, French franc or Deutschemark, wherever they may be traded.

The point may be illustrated by postulating a movement of funds from New York to the Euro-dollar market in London. There is a movement from domestic to foreign money, but not a foreign exchange transaction. To regard the Euro-dollar as foreign money may seem curious, but it is not domestic money, and it is surely money (or, if a time deposit, "near" money).

Perhaps a better illustration of the importance of the nationality of money and the unimportance of residence is to point out that the demand and supply of foreign exchange need not clear the market in New York. If there is an excess supply of pounds, it can be sold for dollars in London, or if there is an excess demand for pounds, it can be satisfied by selling dollars for pounds in London. The foreign exchange market is the market for a national currency anywhere in the world, as the financial centers of the world are united in a single market. This unity has not been a permanent feature, however, since there have been periods of political and economic upheaval, as in the 1930's and 1940's, when exchange controls and other devices effectively segregated national exchange markets. In any event, national markets among the major currencies have been closely united since the late 1950's.

Functions of the Foreign Exchange Market

The three functions of the foreign exchange market are to effect transfers of purchasing power, to provide credit for foreign trade, and to furnish facilities for hedging foreign exchange risks. Of these by far the most important is the transfer of purchasing power—from one country to another and from one currency to another. The means of effecting these transfers is identical in broad outline with that used in domestic trade, through the clearing of payments in opposite directions.

International Clearing

The foreign exchange market effects transfers of purchasing power through a clearing process which is the international analogue of the domestic clearing that takes place informally between banks of the same community, in city clearinghouses, within a Federal Reserve district, and in the Interdistrict Settlement Fund. Exporters in one country have claims abroad, and importers have payments to make abroad. Goods move between countries, but payments take place within countries, by means of the clearing mechanism, except for the settlement of net balances.

In what follows we leave aside the possibility that international trade will take place in a Euro-currency, for example, that European firms are willing to hold dollars in the Euro-dollar market and buy and sell goods to each other and with U.S. traders against dollars. Such a system seems to be in process of evolution. But assume that national and domestic money are identical. A country pays for its imports with its exports. Exporters in a given country receive payment in domestic currency from the country's importers, who thereby pay domestic currency for their purchases from abroad. Goods and credit instruments move across the border, but payments in domestic currency takes place within the country as part of the clearing process. Figure 23.1 provides a stylized illustration of this basic proposition. The exporter in the United States ships goods to the importer in Britain; and the importer in the

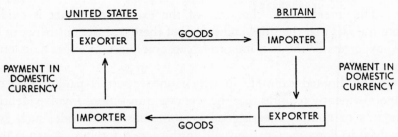

FIG. 23.1.   International Clearing through the Foreign Exchange Market

United States acquires goods from the exporter in Britain. The U.S. exporter is presumably paid by the British importer, and the British exporter by the U.S. importer. But in an ultimate sense the U.S. importer pays the U.S. exporter and the British importer the British exporter. The detailed way in which this is done will depend upon the way in which the transactions are organized.

Suppose the British importer buys dollars to pay his obligation to the U.S. exporter. How are dollars produced in the London market? Evidently by British exports to the United States for dollars. Dollars paid by the U.S. importer to the British exporter are bought by the British importer and paid to the U.S. exporter.

Or the transaction can proceed in sterling through the medium of the New York exchange market. The U.S. exporter draws a sterling bill on his British customer and discounts it with his bank. The bank then sends it to London for rediscount, selling the resulting sterling to the U.S. importer who needs it to discharge his debts for goods bought in Britain.

If we omit the case where the British importer starts off with a supply of Euro-dollars, and the U.S. exporter accepts payment in them, the variety of possible combinations which will clear the market can be summarized as follows:

Foreign Exchange Transaction	*Payment by British Importer to U.S. Exporter*	*Payment by U.S. Importer to British Exporter*
U.S. exporter sells £ in New York to U.S. importer.......	Payment in £	Payment in £
British exporter sells $ in London to British importer..	Payment in $	Payment in $
U.S. exporter sells £ to (buys $ from) British exporter.....	Payment in £	Payment in $
U.S. importer buys £ from (sells $ to) British importer..	Payment in $	Payment in £

The international character of the exchange market is evident from the fact that the third and fourth of these transactions between the two exporters or the two importers can take place in either London or New York.

This limited example in which one export is paid for by one import evidently requires that the separate transactions involve identical amounts of money. Clearing on a more substantial scale, such as is involved in domestic clearings and in the actual foreign exchange market, occurs for instruments ranging over an almost infinite variety of amounts, with large sums on each side canceling out and leaving only small net balances to be settled. But the essence remains simple. Like any other clearing arrangement, the foreign exchange market carries out payments, in this case internationally, by simultaneously clearing debts owed in both directions.

The clearing need not be bilateral. In fact, trade thrives best when the clearing takes place on a multilateral basis. Malaya earns dollars from its sales to the United States, which it pays to Britain for chemicals, enabling Britain to pay dollars for its purchases of machinery in the United States. Or Canada, by means of the exchange market and multilateral clearing, exchanges wheat and bacon sold to Britain for automobiles and coal bought from the United States. The clearing function of the foreign exchange market applied multilaterally enables countries to effect exchanges of goods far too intricate to negotiate without the use of the international means of payment provided by foreign exchange. These multilateral payments are usually effected in a major world currency, sometimes called a "vehicle currency" to illustrate its pivotal role. The pound sterling was such a currency up to 1913, and to lesser degree to 1931. The dollar has filled the role in the postwar period after 1945. Thus a German importer may buy dollars with which to buy francs to pay for French goods. The dollar market against both DM and French francs is so much broader than the direct DM-French franc market, that the transaction may be cheaper in the roundabout way. In this manner, the dollar becomes a part of many transactions in which U.S. residents are not direct participants.

The Eastern trading bloc organized by COMECON suffers from the fact that the ruble is not sufficiently hard for the trading countries to be willing to hold it. In consequence, clearing is inefficient because it is bilateral, rather than multilateral.

When a country's claims arising from foreign transactions differ from its payments, there is a balance which must be handled—an excess demand or supply of foreign exchange (supply or demand for the national currency). This may be taken off the market by speculators, short-term capital movements, the monetary authorities, or gold movements, or the price must change. The possibility of imbalance at the margin complicates the foreign exchange market, and opens up a variety of possible outcomes. But the basic function of the market is discharged in dealing with the inframarginal transactions, that is, in clearing payments against receipts in transactions with foreign countries.

Credit Function

In addition to its primary function of clearing payments, the foreign exchange market is also called upon to provide credit. We do not propose to discuss this matter in great detail. This is more properly a subject belonging in books on the techniques of foreign trade, and involves detailed discussion of the credit instruments used in the foreign exchange market. Here we propose merely to make clear that the credit function falls into two parts: the national and the international.

That international trade requires credit follows from the fact that all trade does. It takes time to move goods from seller to purchaser. Someone must finance the transaction for this period, and possibly for longer. In the normal case, credit will be needed as well by the exporting firm during the period required to manufacture the goods and by the importer for the time between his payment for the goods and his receipt of payment after selling them in their original or processed form. But if the exporter can finance manufacture and the importer can finance marketing, credit is necessary for the transit of the goods. If the importer pays cash, he may be said to finance the transaction. If the exporter holds the accepted bill of exchange for his own account or finances the export through an open-book credit to the importing house, the exporter undertakes the financing. In general, however, when the special credit facilities of the foreign exchange market are used, the foreign department of a bank or the bill market of one country or the other will be called upon to extend the credit.

In the 19th century the world financed its trade in sterling. Exporters to London drew bills of exchange on London. The London discount rate was below that in other centers. Foreign banks therefore discounted their sterling bills and repatriated the proceeds to their own money markets. A New York bank, for example, which could earn 8 percent on its money at home and only 4 percent in London would be foolish to hold sterling bills. In discounting for its local exporter it had used the New York rate, but it rediscounted in London at the lower rate. This meant that a three-month bill for which it has paid 98 (8 percent a year is 2 percent for three months) could be rediscounted for 99. With the London rate typically lower than rates abroad, there was a strong incentive to draw bills in sterling and to discount them in London. In this way London financed its import trade.

London, however, also financed its export trade. London banks would have earned a higher return by encouraging their exporting customers to draw bills in foreign currencies which the banks would hold to maturity. But this would have involved taking an exchange risk which these banks were unwilling to undertake. During the period the bills ran, the foreign currencies might change in value. Accordingly, the London banks were resigned to earning the lower rate of interest available in their own market. British exporters drew their bills in sterling, and these were discounted and held to maturity in London. This involved an exchange risk for the foreign importers, who received goods for which they had to pay in foreign currency in three months. But since sterling provided the world's standard of value, exchange risks in sterling were taken unhesitatingly. In this manner, London financed its imports and exports, representing a substantial part of the rest of the world's exports and imports, respectively. In addition, London financed a considerable amount of trade which did not touch British shores, by discounting sterling bills drawn by exporters in second countries on importers in a third.

The Euro-Dollar Market

The credit function of the foreign exchange market has changed drastically since the decline of the sterling bill of exchange. United States export and import trade was increasingly financed in dollars, which also were used to provide trade credits to the rest of the world, producing a high correlation between short-term capital movements from the United States and changes in merchandise trade. (Dollar credits were not widely used for financing trade between second and third countries, however, as New York bankers instinctively tied their credit to U.S. trade.) After 1958, and the restoration of currency, convertibility in Europe however, there grew up, partly accidentally, a complex institution called the Euro-dollar market by means of which the United States and many other countries provided credit.

A major factor which gave rise to the Euro-dollar market was Regulation Q of the Federal Reserve System which fixed the rates of interest paid on time deposits but did not apply to time deposits owned by foreign accounts. Competition of New York banks led returns on such deposits in 1958 and 1959 to rise $\frac{1}{4}$ of one percent above the

Regulation Q ceilings. This in turn induced banks in London to bid for dollar deposits which they in turn re-lent to New York. Moreover, some depositors, such as the official agencies of the Soviet Union, found it convenient to hold their dollar accounts in Europe, largely London, out of the jurisdiction of American authorities. European lenders and borrowers in dollars also found it convenient to trade in dollars in London, rather than New York, because of the identity of the time zones, without the need to limit trading to the few hours a day when European and U.S. banks were open simultaneously.

Through the 1960's, the Euro-dollar market grew rapidly. Other currencies than dollars were traded outside their domestic markets. By 1967, bank liabilities in Euro-currencies of eight European countries were $14.7 billions in dollars and $3.6 millions equivalent in other Euro-currencies. (Additional "Euro-currencies" are held in Canada and Japan.) The major location of the market is London. Depositors consisted of European central banks, firms and individuals, and banks, firms and individuals in the United States and in third countries outside Europe. Borrowers at the end of 1966 consisted especially of U.S. banks which had borrowed $2.5 billions the previous summer during a credit squeeze, British municipalities, and a variety of European firms, some perhaps subsidiaries of U.S. corporations, seeking cheaper credit than that available to them locally.

Many transactions in Euro-dollars involve no foreign exchange component. Where U.S. depositors hold dollars in London and U.S. banks or firms borrow dollars in London to be used in the United States, the Euro-dollar market is a simple extension of New York. The balance of payments of the United States is affected, the way the figures are compiled, but there is no foreign exchange transaction. Where, however, the deposits are owned by a European account, there usually has been a past foreign exchange transaction by which the dollars were acquired; and where the funds are borrowed for use in Europe, it is usually necessary to convert them to local currencies before they can be used. The depositor has a long speculative position in foreign exchange (dollars), and the borrower a short position.

The Euro-currency market is still in process of development as an institution, so that it is impossible to discuss it definitively. This much can be said, however, that it has surprised financial and economic observers by its flexibility, and especially by its capacity to furnish large amounts of short-term credit to countries in need of assistance. In 1963 and 1964, the Italian money market borrowed close to $1.5 billions from the Euro-dollar market without undue strain; and in July, and

August, 1966, U.S. banks borrowed about $2.5 billions. At the end of 1966, a number of central banks including the Swiss National Bank and the Federal Reserve Bank of New York, fearing a year-end credit squeeze in the Euro-dollar market, undertook to deposit more dollars in it for a brief period to prevent a sharp run-up of rates. To many observers this was the beginning of international open-market operations in an international credit market. The interesting contrast is between the Euro-dollar, or Euro-currency, market which has evolved in a pragmatic, step-by-step way, and the plans for monetary reform which we will discuss in Chapter 27.

Hedging Function

The third function of the foreign exchange market, in addition to clearing and credit, is to provide hedging facilities. An importer with foreign currency to pay abroad in the future, runs the risk that the price of the currency will rise between the time the obligation arises and the time it must be discharged. To cover himself against this risk the importer can deposit funds abroad now equal to the prospective debt, or he can buy forward foreign exchange. By the same token, an exporter with funds coming due in foreign exchange runs the risk that the rate of exchange will fall between the time he enters his contract and the payment date. For cover, he can borrow abroad, sell the foreign exchange for domestic currency, and use the proceeds of his exports when received to pay off the debt, or he can sell his expected foreign exchange forward. Covering an exchange risk is called hedging. Hedging can be done through the spot market, if the trader has cash or credit facilities, including credit facilities abroad. A forward contract is simpler.

A forward contract is a contract to buy or sell foreign exchange against another currency at some fixed date in the future at a price agreed upon now. No money passes at the time of the contract. But the contract makes it possible to ignore what happens to the exchange rate, or almost to ignore it. There is no way the trader can protect himself against what the changes in the exchange rate will do to or for his competition. An importer establishes the rate at which he buys foreign exchange and the foreign prices of the goods. But if the foreign exchange depreciates (and the prices of goods do not change *pari passu*), his competitor will get a bargain which will affect the importer's transaction.

The existence of a forward market makes it possible to hedge an exchange position. It also makes it possible to speculate without possessing domestic funds or having a credit standing abroad, provided that one has a sufficient credit standing to be regarded by one's bank as a suitable customer for forward exchange. What constitutes an exchange position, which should be hedged by one who is unwilling to hold a speculative position, is a complex question. Contracts to buy and sell goods at fixed prices should be hedged. The average commercial trader has enough to worry about in his own product line without concerning himself additionally to forecast the course of the foreign exchange market. But the possession of cotton in London is not equivalent to a position in sterling: if sterling changes price, the cotton also changes in price and in the opposite direction, since its price is determined in dollars. On this account, the cotton does not involve an exchange risk, and it should not be hedged. On the other hand, if a trader possesses goods in Britain which are specially produced for the British market or costly to transport, so that they have to be sold against sterling, this is equivalent to an open position in sterling.

Financial assets pose even more complex questions. Demand and time deposits in a foreign currency imply a foreign exchange risk, and should be hedged through a forward sale unless one deliberately welcomes the exchange risk (assuming, of course, that there is no future liability against which the deposit is held). Equities, such as land, or shares, should not be covered, since they may be expected to change in price oppositely to the exchange rate. The most interesting question relates to long-term, fixed-money claims, such as bonds. Here is clearly an exchange risk, but nearly all forward markets are very thin for contracts beyond 6 months or a year, and it makes little sense to try to cover a 10-year asset in dollars with a 3-months' forward sale. In the world of risk averters, the international long-term capital market is likely to dry up when exchange rates change frequently. On the other hand, the movement of long-term capital between the United States and Canada did not cease when the exchange rate was flexible, largely, this writer thinks, because the market took the view that the Canadian dollar would be somewhere near the U.S. dollar in the long run, near enough, in any event, to compensate for the wide difference in interest rates.

An important question is whether the existence of a forward market fundamentally changes the character of the exchange market. The short answer is no. A longer response is given in Appendix H. The short answer can be expanded here beyond the single word already given. At the opening of this section, it was indicated that hedging can take place through the spot market—holding funds abroad against future requirements, or borrowing funds abroad and transferring them through the spot market. Assuming adequate facilities, the cost will be the same whether one goes through the spot or the forward market. Take the case of an exporter who either borrows abroad and sells the proceeds through the spot market (ultimately paying off the debt through the payment for exports), or sells his exchange forward. In the first instance, he pays interest on the foreign loan, but earns interest on the proceeds of the spot sale deposited in his bank at home. If the interest rate abroad is 6 percent and that at home 4 percent, he pays a net of 2 percent interest per annum for the benefit of having his exchange risk covered. If he operates through the forward market, it will also cost him 2 percent per annum. With interest rates at 6 percent abroad and at 4 percent at home, forward foreign exchange will sell at a discount of 2 percent per annum. If it were higher than this, it would pay financial houses to put funds abroad at 6 percent and sell them forward at less than the 2 percent per annum discount. By this means they would earn more than the 4 percent interest rate available at home. Or if the discount on foreign exchange (premium on our exchange) were greater than 2 percent, it would pay foreigners to put their funds here, earning 4 percent, plus the premium of more than 2 percent, which would be a return greater than the 6 percent available on domestic loans. In the real world, the forward exchange rate, calculated in terms of percent per annum, discount or premium, departs from the difference between the two interest rates, or "interest differential," up to $\frac{1}{2}$ percent either side under normal conditions. Interest arbitrage, the process of moving spot funds and covering them forward, is unwilling to operate for a return less than $\frac{1}{2}$ percent per annum above the return available at home. Over the years, however, the number of people satisfied with smaller margins, down to $\frac{1}{8}$ of a percent, has increased.

In time of stress, interest arbitrage considerations may be overwhelmed by speculators using the forward market to take exchange positions, rather than to avoid them. When this occurs, and the amount of arbitrage funds is overwhelmed by the volume of speculation, or even reduced by official restrictions, the forward market may not clear itself through offsetting interest arbitrage funds. On such occasions the forward rate can diverge widely from the interest parity and the forward market can become an expensive facility for hedging.

Arbitrage

To discuss interest arbitrage before arbitrage in general is to get ahead of our story. In interest arbitrage, a position in the spot is cancelled against a position in the forward market. In ordinary arbitrage, a foreign exchange trader will move in and out of a single currency at the same time. It is arbitrage which keeps the market for a given currency unified all over the world.

Suppose a change in demand for pounds occurs in New York. The increase in the dollar rate on pounds will be practically instantaneously communicated from New York to London by arbitrage. The rate for the pound cannot exist at $2.4010 in New York with the rate for the dollar at $2.40 in London, because it would be profitable for arbitragers to buy pounds at $2.40 in London and sell them at $2.4010 in New York. This would increase the demand for sterling in London and the supply in New York and would continue until the prices became the same or differed by no more than the cost of telegrams and interest. Arbitragers are not speculators. Except for a matter of moments, they have no open position in foreign currency. They make their profit from buying *and* selling foreign currencies, in the course of which they end in the same currency in which they started.

Two-point arbitrage is that in which the arbitrager finds a spread in the price of his own currency in two markets, generally his own and one abroad. Three-point arbitrage would involve the purchase of francs in New York, their sale in Paris against pounds, and the sale of pounds for dollars in either London or New York. In this case it is assumed that the rates are identical for the franc in Paris and New York, and for the pound in London and New York, but not for the pound and franc in London and Paris. A three-point deal by an arbitrager in New York would then accomplish simply what two-point arbitrage in francs and pounds would do from either London or Paris. Three-point arbitrage occurs only when exchange dealers in the local market are unaware of the opportunities or forbidden to take advantage of them. It is rare.

Arbitrage is the mechanism which makes two markets, physically separate, a single market in an economic sense. A single market is defined as the place where buyers and sellers of an article trade it at an identical price. In the same market only one price exists. Where the same price exists continuously for the same commodity, there is one market. Where there are two markets and the costs of buying in one and selling in the other are small, arbitrage will produce essentially one price and one market. Where arbitrage cannot take place for one reason or another—for lack of knowledge of the facts of the other prices, because of inadequate communication, or because of prohibitions— prices between markets will differ. In the last case, when arbitrage is prohibited, large price differences will encourage covert trading because the rewards for operating contrary to the law are great.

In the absence of exchange controls the foreign exchange market for a currency, including all countries where it is traded and with which arbitrage takes place, is among the most nearly perfect markets of the world. This is because money is the most homogeneous of articles and because it can be transferred instantaneously. The wheat markets in Chicago and Liverpool were closely linked in normal times, but not so closely as foreign exchange markets. The international gold market on the gold standard represented a series of markets separated within certain limits by the costs of transferring gold from one country to another. But, for foreign exchange, the cost of the telegrams and the loss of interest on the money for the period of time it is tied up in arbitrage are very small in relation to the amounts of money which may be transferred. The time element is practically eliminated. Accordingly, the price of sterling in New York cannot differ by much or for long from the reciprocal of the price of the dollar in London. Arbitrage is the force which prevents the single market from separating into two markets.

The Foreign Exchange Rate

The supply and demand for foreign exchange determine the foreign exchange rate within certain constraints imposed by the nature of the foreign exchange system under which the country operates. Assuming no foreign exchange controls, traders, banks, and speculators will trade in the market under any system. Under the gold standard there will also be gold arbitragers. Under the fixed-exchange standard short of gold, there will also be the monetary authorities. And these monetary authorities may also operate under the flexible exchange rate standard or the gold standard.

The simplest system, though not necessarily the best, is the flexible exchange standard without intervention by the authorities. The price of foreign exchange is determined by the demand and supply for foreign exchange, which are in turn determined by domestic and foreign prices of goods and services, domestic and foreign awareness of trading opportunities, international capital movements, the anticipations of speculators as to the future course of exchange rates, and so forth. The market clears itself through the price mechanism. Some academic authorities insist that such a market will be stable, with speculation acting to hold the market down in the short run when demand exceeds the supply at the old price, or to hold it up under the opposite circumstances. We will postpone discussion on the flexible exchange standard until Chapter 27.

Under other arrangements, however, the movement of the exchange rate is bounded. Under the gold standard, the limits are set by the costs of moving gold from one market to another, the costs including not only transport, insurance, and handling charges, but also interest during the time gold arbitragers have their funds tied up. The mint parity in Figure 23.2 has no effect except to set the limits of the gold export and gold import points. It is calculated by dividing the price of a given amount of gold in one currency by the price of the same amount in another. If an ounce of gold costs $35 in the United States, and 292s.

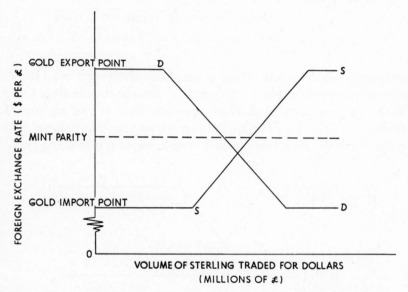

FIG. 23.2.   Establishing an Exchange Rate between the Gold Points under the Gold Standard

in London, the mint parity is $2.40 ($35 ÷ 292s. = $2.40 ÷ 20s.). Gold arbitragers then see to it that the two currencies do not depart from the mint parity by more than the cost of moving gold. In Figure 23.3*a*, demand and supply were equated within the gold points (but with no pull to the mint parity), with the demand and supply curves equal to *D–D* and *S–S*, respectively. A change in demand to *D′–D′* leads to gold exports. In Figure 2.3*b*, a shift in supply from *S–S* to *S′–S′* leads to gold imports.

The role taken by gold in these illustrations can be assumed by speculators, if they believe that the exchange will stay within the gold points in the long run and that it pays to buy foreign exchange when the

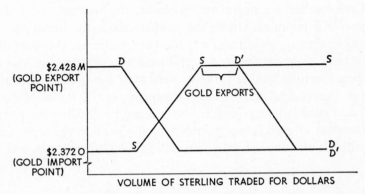

FIG. 23.3*a*.   Demand for Foreign Exchange Partially Satisfied by Gold Exports

rate approaches the gold export point. Here short-term capital move-ments substitute for gold movements, as already discussed in Chapter 19. Or the monetary authorities can intervene in the market. The British authorities, for example, support sterling or hold it down, within a range narrower than that dictated by the cost of transporting gold.[1]

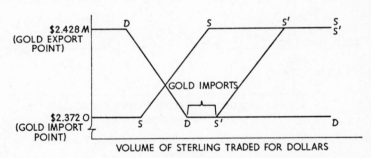

FIG. 23.3*b*.   Supply of Foreign Exchange (Demand for Local Currency) Partially Satisfied by Gold Imports

Types of Intervention

The defense of the foreign exchange rate may be undertaken for monetary authorities by speculators who intervene before the gold

[1] The operations of the Bank of England and the Exchange Equalization Account in sterling are more complex than suggested by these paragraphs because there is no fixed gold price, but the London price of gold can change. The British authorities can therefore affect the pound sterling by operating either in the foreign exchange rate for the pound, or in the London gold market. Selling gold for sterling in London supports the pound by lowering the London gold price and encouraging gold arbitragers to buy sterling with foreign currencies and gold with sterling. In recent years, however, the Bank of England's management of the London gold pool has been passive, rather than active, supplying gold to the market when demand is brisk, and mopping it up when it is abundant.

points are reached, by gold arbitragers, or, as just indicated, by the monetary authorities themselves. When the monetary authorities intervene, there are the questions of, first, which set of authorities does so, and second, how. On the first score, for example, assume that there is an excess supply of A's currency, or an excess demand for B's. To keep the A–B exchange rate from changing, the monetary authorities in B may intervene to buy up the A currency, supplying B currency to the market, or the A authorities may be required to sell off gold or B currency, or to obtain B currency by one or another of various devices, such as swaps, loans, and selling B currency forward. Where B buys up the excess supply of A's currency automatically, the total reserve bank credit in the system is expanded. Where A draws on existing balances of B's currency, total monetary reserves of the system are reduced (A's reserves are reduced, and B's are not increased). Where A pays gold to B, total reserves in the system are unchanged.

Some of the implications of these forms of monetary authority intervention in the foreign exchange market have been discussed— notably central bank dealings in forward exchange in Chapter 19; and others such as the role of the International Monetary Fund remain to be explored below. Here it is useful to explicate swaps and so-called Roosa bonds, two of the so-called "perimeter defenses" of the dollar developed since 1960.

Swaps are a means whereby two sets of monetary authorities can acquire claims on each other. Assume that the Bank of England seeks a short-term credit in dollars to meet pressures in the sterling market. Under its agreement with the Federal Reserve System it would credit the Federal Reserve with say £100 million and would itself receive $240 million credited to its account with the Federal Reserve Bank of New York. There is no net short-term capital movement, but the Bank of England is better placed to meet an excess demand for dollars. (Likewise the Federal Reserve could be the one seeking credit; the initial phase of the swap is the same.) Such swaps could be irreversible, i.e., final transactions. In actuality, they have been almost entirely temporary transactions which are reversed after a fixed period of time under the terms of the original contract. Indeed, the term "swap" in the foreign exchange market means that a forward contract is involved. Thus the central bank swaps include a spot exchange of currencies with a contract to reverse the exchange at a specified future date.

Market swaps are also common, either by individual traders or by central banks. The Italian authorities, as noted earlier, use swaps with Italian commercial banks as a means of domestic monetary control, or to limit the volume of dollars held overtly in official reserves. The Italian authorities will sell dollars to banks under repurchase agreements (i.e., forward contract to buy dollars back at a fixed lira price). The spot and future rates are set so as to make the investment attractive to the Italian banks, with a forward rate on the dollar better than that generally available in the market. Since banks pay in spot lira under the swaps, local bank reserves are drawn down and lira credit is tightened. At the same time, the published foreign exchange reserves of Italy are reduced, as spot exchange is transferred to private holders against forward purchases.

The Federal Reserve System has constructed a network of swap or mutual credit agreements with foreign central banks which amounted to $5,030 million by 1967. Any credits drawn under the agreements were limited in time, so that they were less useful to defend the foreign exchange rate than would have been foreign exchange or gold owned outright. For temporary pressure against the currency, however, like the forward contracts discussed in Chapter 19 with which they have many similarities, they serve well. It is because they are useful in the short run while more basic adjustment measures are getting under way, that they are called perimeter rather than main defenses.

"Roosa" bonds are less a device to meet current pressure than one to relieve potential future strain. Where the excess supply of A's currency is met by B purchasing it, B has a demand claim on A. Such a claim, which may be used to purchase gold, may be funded into a long-term claim, denominated in A's currency. But, it may be given additional attractiveness to B by a funding which causes a guarantee of its value in B's currency, against the possibility of a devaluation in A's money. This device, named after the then Undersecretary of the Treasury, Robert V. Roosa, has been used extensively with foreign currency bonds issued to the authorities in Austria, Belgium, Germany, Italy, and Switzerland. In effect, they substituted future liabilities against current ones, much like the swaps or forward contracts.

The Foreign Exchange Market and the Balance of Payments

As an introduction to the discussion of the balance of payments in the next chapter, it is useful to ask how a record of foreign exchange transactions differs from the balance of payments. These differences will occur in valuation, timing, and coverage.

The differences in valuation between a record of foreign exchange transactions and the balance of payments is that the former mirrors what happens in the world, while the latter records transactions on a consistent basis, perhaps f.o.b. (free on board) or f.a.s. (free alongside ship) for exports and imports, or f.o.b. or f.a.s. for exports and c.i.f. (cost, insurance, freight) for imports. The importer may take delivery from the exporter at the factory, at the dock, at the customhouse in the importing country, or at the warehouse in the importing country, and pay for such freight and insurance as may be involved. The balance of payments, on the other hand, must treat the merchandise trade consistently, and put in the necessary offsetting items for freight and insurance to accord with what has actually transpired.

Timing is concerned with when transactions are recorded, and the choice of time is among orders, deliveries, receipts, or payments. The foreign exchange record evidently deals with payments: the balance of payments with shipments for exports and receipts for imports (these may differ by a few days which means that this month's or year's exports from X may be recorded as next month's or next year's imports in M). But the relationship of payments to deliveries (to take only one) is by no means uniform. If all goods are consistently sold on three-months' credit, there would be the problem of having a portion of this year's exports for balance-of-payments purposes count in next year's record of foreign exchange transactions. But the relationship varies. Some goods normally are prepaid, some paid at the time of shipment, and some paid with a lag. Bent Hansen recorded the surprising fact that, at a given point in time, close to 10 percent of Swedish exports were prepaid. And the relationship can change as expectations about a national currency change. When there is a likelihood that a given currency will be devalued, foreign importers slow down payments, and foreign exporters speed up collections, to give rise to a "leads and lags" problem. Normally the question is of little or no importance: payments lag or lead deliveries by a small and constant margin. But if, in any one year, as a result of a change in the speculators' view of a currency, the imports of a country which had been sold on 3-months' credit shifted to a cash basis, and its exports moved from a 3-months' basis to 6-months' credit, the balance of payments (exports and imports) may remain unchanged, but the country receives 9 months' payments for exports in its foreign exchange transactions, and is required to pay for 15 months of imports.

The most interesting aspect of the question today is coverage. The balance of payments covers transactions between residents of a country and foreign residents. The summary of foreign exchange transactions is limited to exchanges of the national for a foreign currency. The balance of payments includes, and the record of foreign exchange transactions excludes the following: barter; private compensation (where credits and debits in a single currency are cleared within an international firm, or between firms which clear outside the foreign exchange market); transactions in Euro-dollars where the dollars come back to the United States and are held here. On the other hand, a foreign exchange record includes, and the balance of payments excludes (since it deals only in net capital movements) gross capital transactions in foreign exchange. But this question is less interesting for a discussion of the foreign exchange market than it is for the balance of payments, to which we now turn.

Summary

A foreign exchange transaction is a purchase or sale of one national money against another. The functions of the foreign exchange market are three: to clear payments between countries; to provide credit for the foreign-trade sector, both within and between countries; and to provide hedging against exchange risks. The credit function of the foreign exchange market has been developed in recent times in new ways by the Euro-dollar market. The forward market used for hedging does not fundamentally alter the behavior of the foreign exchange market.

Arbitrage is the practice of buying and selling a currency simultaneously to take advantage of spreads in the price for it in separate locations, or as between the spot and forward market, for different time periods. The arbitrager takes no exchange risk. Arbitrage makes one market of two, whether it be the market for sterling in New York or for the dollar in London, or the market for spot and forward sterling against dollars. With freely available and plentiful arbitrage funds, the forward rate will tend to the interest differential.

The foreign exchange rate is determined by the foreign exchange market in ways which are affected by different monetary institutions. Under the freely flexible exchange rate without government intervention, changes in price clear the market. Under the gold standard, gold arbitrage at the gold points, offset an excess demand or excess supply for foreign exchange. Speculation near the limits of exchange rate fluctuations may clear the market. Or the authorities may buy up the excess supply or satisfy the excess demand, with the aid of various devices to acquire foreign exchange.

A record of foreign exchange transactions differs from a balance of payments in valuation, timing, and coverage.

SUGGESTED READING

TEXTS

See Yeager, chap. ii. For advanced treatments, see Vanek, chap. v, and Kemp, chaps. xvii, xviii.

TREATISES, ETC.

See Alan Holmes and F. H. Schott, *The New York Foreign Exchange Market* (2d. ed.; New York: Federal Reserve Bank of New York, 1965); M. N. Trued, *United States Official Operations in the Foreign Exchange and Gold Markets* (Washington, D.C.: U.S. Treasury Department, 1965). The Euro-dollar market is discussed in articles by O. L. Altman in *SP* for March, 1961, March, 1963, and March, 1965, and in the *Annual Reports* of the Bank for International Settlements since 1964. An elementary account entitled "The Decade of the Euro-Dollar" is provided in *The Economist* for July 8, 1967.

POINTS

The difference between the balance of payments and a record of foreign exchange transactions is set out in the International Monetary Fund's first *Balance of Payments Yearbook* for 1938, 1946, and 1947.

The best discussion of leads and lags, but an advanced one, is Bent Hansen's *Foreign Trade Credits and Exchange Reserves* (Amsterdam: North-Holland Publishing Co., 1961.)

The definitive work on the gold standard is W. A. Brown, Jr., *The Gold Standard Re-Interpreted, 1914–34* (New York: National Bureau of Economic Research, 1934), 2 vols.

Chapter 24

THE BALANCE OF
PAYMENTS

Purposes

The balance of payments of a country is a systematic record of all economic transactions between the residents of the reporting country and residents of foreign countries during a given period of time. Such a record may be useful for a variety of reasons, large and small. The major purpose of keeping these records is to inform governmental authorities of the international position of the country, to aid them in reaching decisions on monetary and fiscal policy, on the one hand, and trade and payments questions, on the other.

The distinction between monetary and fiscal policy, on the one hand, and trade and payments on the other, emphasizes the manyfold nature of the balance of payments. First came the statistics for trade, which were kept primarily to measure the resource flows between one country and another. To these records of goods and ultimately services, there was added information on other payments and receipts in foreign exchange, as monetary authorities wanted to be assured that the country could go on buying foreign goods and meeting payments in foreign currency when they became due. More recently, with the development of national income accounting and the depression of the 1930's, the balance of payments has been used to measure the influence of foreign transactions on national income.

Each of these three approaches to the balance of payments can be thought of as linked to a separate system of domestic accounts: the resource approach to the input-output table; the foreign exchange budget approach to the sources and uses of funds statements of the economy; and the national income approach of course to the national income accounts. As all three domestic sets of accounts are interrelated, the differences among the separate approaches do not lead to very wide differences in balance-of-payments accounting, as explained below.

Balance-of-payments statistics are being increasingly refined to serve these broad purposes, with quarterly, regional, and detailed break-downs, and to throw light on particular problems of international commerce as well.

Definition

The balance of payments of a country is "a systematic record of all economic transactions between the residents of the reporting country and residents of foreign countries." This seems straightforward enough. But it also raises questions. For example, who is a resident? What is an economic transaction?

Tourists, diplomats, military personnel, temporary migratory workers, and branches of domestic companies are regarded as residents of the countries from which they come, rather than the country where they are. These decisions are arbitrary, but since the rest of the ac-counting is adjusted to them, that fact makes little difference. Some of these decisions which make sense from one way of looking at the balance of payments make little from another. Thus the Italian balance of payments, adjusted to fit national income categories, treats permanent and temporary migrants entirely differently, although there is very little difference between them (i.e., some temporary workers are in fact permanent, and vice versa). The earnings of permanent workers are part of national income abroad, and all that enters into the balance of payments is their remittances to Italy as a "transfer." The earnings of temporary workers abroad, however, are sales of services which form part of Italian national income and go into the foreign accounts as ex-ports; their local expenditures for room, board, and so on, are imports, and *their* remittances are an internal Italian transaction which are ex-cluded from the balance of payments. Whichever way it is done makes no difference for the total balance; but the national income approach in this case is the enemy of the foreign exchange budget approach, which would be interested in knowing directly how much is remitted from abroad by emigrants.

Economic Transactions

An economic transaction is an exchange of value, typically an act in which there is transfer of title to an economic good, the rendering of an economic service, or the transfer of title to assets from one party to another. An international economic transaction evidently involves such transfer of title or rendering of service from residents of one country to residents of another.

Normally an economic transaction will involve a payment and a receipt of money in exchange for the economic good, the service, or the asset. But it need not. In barter, goods are exchanged for goods, and in private compensation, assets against assets. Moreover, some goods are transferred to other ownership as a gift, without expectation of payment. In each case, there is an international economic transaction, and the necessity to make an entry in the balance of payments. But some entries are made where there is no international "transaction" in the sense of an international payment: the foreign subsidiary of an American corporation earns a profit in its foreign operations and reinvests it in the country where it operates, without paying a dividend to the parent company. There are those who insist that this should go into the balance of payments as a credit on current account, receipt of profits, and debit on capital account, new investment, even though no international payment takes place. Or a *contra* item may be required to offset some overstatement elsewhere in the balance of payments, as we shall see below in the treatment of the transport accounts. Here is the necessity for an entry even though the transaction may be purely domestic.

Balance-of-Payments Accounting

In theory, the balance of payments is kept in standard double entry bookkeeping under which each international transaction undertaken by residents of a country results in a debit and a credit of equal size. An export is a credit for the movement of goods; the means of payment for that export would show up as a debit—the new claim on a foreign company, or bank, the purchase of a foreign security (capital outflow), the acquisition of gold, and so on. Conversely, imports (a debit) might be paid for out of an increase in liabilities to foreigners, or by reduced claims on foreigners (both recorded as credits). In actuality, the Department of Commerce measures only one side of physical transactions, and the net of the changes in assets and liabilities. Where one side of the transaction is caught by the accountants, say a CARE package sent abroad which results in an export but no balancing claim on foreigners, it is necessary to put in a contra item, in this case "donations" (a debit). It is not always possible to have sufficient knowledge of transactions to effect a complete record of international transactions. Some items can only be estimated. Others are carried out by individuals who, unlike bankers, brokers, security dealers, and large corporations, do not report regularly on their foreign operations. The result is that it is necessary, after summing total credits and total debits, to put in an item for "Errors and Omissions" to strike a balance between the two sides of the accounts. Where nonrecorded transactions are large and tend to all be in one direction, the residual "Errors and Omissions" item may be sizable in comparison with other items in the accounts.

Balances within the Total

While total credits equal total debits, by definition, policy questions often call for an analysis of various groups of items within the total. At least five separate types of balance have been distinguished—the merchandise balance, current account balance, basic balance, the balance on regular transactions, and the balance settled by official transactions. Each one matches up selected credits with selected debits, and asserts that the net of these is significant, presumably in sign and amount. A surplus occurs when credits exceed debits; a deficit, when debits are greater than credits. Since total credits and debits are equal by definition, or would be in a perfect recording system where errors and omissions were zero, as we shall assume, the balance of some items of the balance of payments implies a corresponding balance (with reverse sign) of all other items as well. The student is warned that some tabulations are made on the "reverse sign" basis and that a surplus can show up with a minus sign.

The Merchandise-Trade Balance

The most usual, and the least interesting, balance is the merchandise balance

$$X_{\text{merch}} + M_{\text{merch}} = 0 \tag{1}$$

where X_{merch} is exports of merchandise (a credit, or plus) and M_{merch} is imports of merchandise (a debit, or minus). This balance has some resources significance, but services belong in the input-output table along with goods. It made more sense in the days of the mercantilists when services played only a minor part in balances of payments. It has less point today. A large merchandise import surplus may be balanced by shipping, interest and dividends, tourist and other service income, quite apart from the capital account. It is useless from the foreign exchange budget and the national income approaches. There is a temptation to excoriate the attention given to the merchandise balance as evidence of the fallacy of misplaced concreteness—thinking a concept to have analytical significance because it refers to objects with bulk and solidity. One aspect of the merchandise balance, however, can justify the attention it gets in the press. The data are among the earliest received on the balance of payments for a recent period. As such,

X_{merch} and M_{merch} serve as proxies for exports and imports of total goods and services, X and M, respectively. But it is correct that the merchandise balance receives too much attention.

The Current Account Balance

The current account balance, including services with goods, allows us to set out the other principal items in the balance of payments along with exports and imports of goods and services:

$$X + M = 0 = LTC + STC + G \qquad (2)$$

where LTC is a long-term capital ($+$ or credit for inflow, $-$ or debit for outflows), STC is a short-term capital (with the same signs) and G is gold ($+$ or credit for exports, $-$ or debit for imports). Errors and omissions, transfers and similar complications are omitted.

When exports consist of newly produced goods, and imports go into final use, the current account balance has interest for national income accounting. As noted in Chapter 16, $X - M^1$ is a foreign investment, positive or negative:

$$X + M = Y - (C + I_d + G). \qquad (3)$$

When $X + M$ is positive, the country is gaining net claims on the rest of the world, and foreign transactions are a stimulus to national income. It is solvent, even if it is borrowing funds from the rest of the world to buy long-term securities, so long as $X + M > 0$, and the assets it acquires are worth what has been paid for them. With net domestic investment also positive, the net worth of the country is increased. This current account balance is thus like the break-even or zero-profit position in a profit and loss statement. Obviously, this analogy should not be carried too far. An economist who asks firms to maximize their profits would be calling for a strict mercantilist policy if he asked nations to do the same, that is, to maximize their current account surpluses.

But the current account balance says nothing about the foreign exchange budget. For this it is necessary to know how the current account budget matches with the foreign investment decisions which the market makes. This leads to the so-called basic balance.

The Basic Balance

The basic balance shifts long-term capital to the left-hand side of equation (2).

---

[1] $X - M$ in national income accounting is the same as $X + M$ in balance-of-payments accounting, since the former concept uses only absolute amounts, without implicit signs.

$$X + M + LTC = 0 = STC + G . \tag{4}$$

It assumes that long-term capital movements are autonomous, and short-term capital movements transitory. It summarizes the transfer problem. With $X + M + LTC = 0$, transfer is complete. If $X + M$ is positive, then LTC is negative or an outflow. If $M > X$, then LTC must be positive, or an inflow.

If the two sides of equation (4) differ from zero, they must have opposite signs. When the left-hand side is positive, because the export surplus exceeds the capital outflow, the country is accumulating short-term claims or gold from the rest of the world, which are minus or debits. When the two sides of the equation differ from zero, with opposite signs, the economy has not achieved basic balance, capital flows are not being transferred, and the balance of payments is said to be in disequilibrium by those who uphold basic balance as the correct concept of balance-of-payments equilibrium.

Equilibrium is a state of the balance of payments which can be sustained without intervention. It is, of course, unnecessary to have equation (4) hold each hour, day, week, month, season, year or part of cycle so long as over the relevant period, whatever it be, the balance of payments will adjust itself with or without the help of regular seasonal or cyclical policy actions. In the start of the transfer process, long-term capital is balanced by short-term capital and the current account remains unchanged. But if the transfer process has been set in motion, this transitional state is not disequilibrium.

Notice on this definition, a country that is lending at long term more than its export surplus, and borrowing abroad at short term to make up the difference is regarded as in deficit:

$$X + M + LTC = STC + G \neq 0 . \tag{4a}$$

In (4a) assume that the left-hand side is negative and the balancing right side positive, making clear that the long-term capital outflow is matched by a short-term inflow. The country is lending long and borrowing short. On basic balance this is a deficit. Contrariwise, a country that borrows abroad at long term more than it is able to transfer inward through an import surplus, would be said to experience a surplus in its basic balance.

To call equation (4) the "basic" balance does not make it *the* equilibrium concept. It is widely regarded as such. The late Ragnar Nurkse used this concept as his definition of equilibrium (though in prose, not symbols). The U.S. Brookings Report of 1963 also regarded it as the central equilibrium concept and the British authorities tend to discuss their payments problems in terms of basic balance. Others regard it as insufficient. Basic balance may be satisfactory from the point of view of resources (foreign investments are being transferred in real goods and services); or national income (the excess of intended savings over intended domestic investment is equal to intended foreign investment); or the foreign exchange budget (the demand for foreign exchange for foreign investment is equal to the supply created by the export surplus). But it may not account for all the international monetary possibilities.

Suppose, for example, that the right-hand side of the equation $(STC + G)$ is equal to zero, but both STC and G are large and increasing. Foreign deposits in the country are being converted into gold (i.e., a short-term capital outflow, a debit, is offset by gold exports, a credit). It could happen that if foreign claims on the country exceeded its gold stock it could ultimately run out of gold and have to depreciate its exchange rate. The state of the balance of payments may therefore not be capable of being sustained. It is not in equilibrium. Accordingly, the concept of the overall balance or the balance on regular transactions was devised by the Department of Commerce to add a further constraint to the equilibrium position of equation (4).

The Balance on Regular Transactions

The Department of Commerce's definition of balance-of-payments equilibrium is:

$$X + M + LTC + STC_d = 0 = STC_f + G, \tag{5}$$

where short-term capital (STC) is broken down into domestic (STC_d) and foreign (STC_f) components.

This criterion of equilibrium is sometimes called the "liquidity" definition. Its concern is to ensure that foreign claims on the country do not mount to a point where the country will be unable to meet them if they are suddenly presented for payment. Concern is really with the stock position, i.e., the balance of indebtedness discussed below, rather than the balance of payments which is a flow concept. This overall balance goes beyond the basic balance to concern itself with the changes in the country's liquidity position.

Note the sharp asymmetry in the treatment of domestic and foreign short-term capital. This is justified by the Department of Commerce on the ground that the United States cannot be certain of being able to liquidate its claims on foreigners, whereas it must be in a position to make good if foreigners decide to liquidate their claims on the United States. United States short-term claims on the rest of the world are treated as unavailable; foreign claims on the United States are regarded as liable to be presented *in toto* at any instant in time.

This asymmetric treatment is not completely proof against criticism. It separates some items which in fact are joined. If a domestic corporation deposits funds in a Canadian bank in New York which are invested in the call money market which finances the New York Stock Exchange—a balance-of-payments item, since the Canadian bank is treated as a nonresident, but not a foreign exchange transaction—the United States is recorded as in deficit on the overall basis. The short-term liability to the Canadian bank—the call money loan— is regarded as on the right-hand side of the equation—"below the line" in the usual expression,—whereas the U.S. deposit in the Canadian bank is "above the line." Or Japanese deposits in the United States are below the line, whereas U.S. banking loans to Japan—an offsetting amount—are above the line. Or U.S. claims on European financial centers—often in dollars, and proved liquid in the summer of 1966—are regarded as frozen, whereas the counterpart deposit in New York is thought to be a highly volatile and nervous sum.

There is, to be sure, the possibility that funds deposited with Canadian banks or invested in the Euro-dollar market could all be reloaned abroad, and unavailable for recall or repayment when and as needed. But the assumption that this will happen is a strong one, and experience proves it does not hold. This is not to say that STC_d and STC_f belong on the same side of the line. A special committee appointed by the Bureau of the Budget to review balance-of-payments statistics, under the chairmanship of Edward M. Bernstein, proposed a new concept which separated official from private foreign short-term capital.

The Balance Settled by Official Transactions

The balance of payments settled by official transactions puts private foreign short-term capital on the left-hand side of the equation (above the line):

$$X + M + LTC + STC_d + STC_{f_p} = 0 = STC_{f_o} + G \qquad (6)$$

where STC_{f_p} are short-term capital movements attributable to private foreigners and STC_{f_o} are those of foreign monetary authorities or officials. Since U.S. official short-term capital movements are treated along with gold reserves, below the line, it is simpler to transform (6) into:

$$X + M + LTC + STC_p = 0 = STC_o + G \qquad (7)$$

where STC_p is all private short-term capital and belongs above the line, and STC_o is official short-term capital, and goes below the line. Foreign holdings of U.S. securities of more than one-year's maturity—ordinary U.S. governments, and special transactions in Roosa bonds, should go in STC_o not in LTC. So should foreign obligations paid to the U.S. government in advance to hold down the U.S. deficit.

This formulation makes perhaps too sharp a distinction between private and official short-term capital movements. The practice of the Bank of Italy selling off its dollars to commercial banks under a repurchase agreement was mentioned in the last chapter. Swiss and German private banks tend to dump their foreign exchange holdings on the respective central banks each June and December, as they undertake "window-dressing," i.e., prepare for the half-year bank statement of condition in which they presumably like to show large domestic balances and small holdings of foreign exchange—as if they fooled anyone.

Autonomous versus Compensatory Items

Equation (7) which puts all private operations above the line and official transactions plus gold below the line, recalls a distinction made by the International Monetary Fund in its first *Balance of Payments Yearbook,* issued in 1949, between autonomous and private transactions on the one hand, and official or compensatory items on the other. The distinction between autonomous and compensatory movements is valid: when autonomous movements cancel out over some appropriate time period and there is no need for compensatory movements, the balance of payments is in equilibrium. But to identify private movements with the autonomous and official with compensatory may be carrying the analysis farther than it is appropriate to go. Professor Machlup, for example, attacked the IMF when it included the official transfers under the Marshall Plan as compensatory payments. He said it was just as, or even more, accurate to say that official transfers under the Marshall Plan made possible the current account deficits of Europe as it was that the Marshall Plan transfers compensated for the current account deficits.

This is the nub of the difficulty. It is entirely correct to put autonomous movements above the line and compensatory movements below it, but there is no unique and unchanging way to designate which movements are which. Foreign aid may start out as compensatory and subtly evolve as autonomous. When the sea change occurs, it is impossible to say. And any rule of thumb, which argues that such and such kind of transactions is always autonomous, and such and such always compensatory will find itself on occasion in difficulty.

Banker versus Trader

Equations (5), (6), and (7) all put a considerable amount of short-term private capital above the line, or on the left-hand side of the equation. This is because some short-term capital, especially domestic, is regarded as moving in response to deep-seated forces such as trends in the quantity of trade, and hence as in no way responsive to short-term swings in payments. The correlation between short-term outflows of U.S. capital and the volume of trade was noted in Chapter 19. But it is too much to say that all domestic private short-term capital is impervious to short-run stimuli. The proof is available in the short-term capital inflow from abroad in the summer of 1966, which was treated on the balance on regular transactions and the balance settled by official transactions as the equivalent to a long-term capital inflow to the United States.

You will recall from Chapter 19 that short-term capital movements moving in response to changes in interest rates are broadly equivalent in their functioning in the balance of payments, and somewhat in the monetary mechanism, to gold movements. If the gold movement is compensatory, the short-term capital flow which displaces it in two respects and which was stimulated by an official policy action (changing the discount rate, let us say) may also be regarded as compensatory. Hal B. Lary, who was responsible in the Department of Commerce for balance-of-payments estimates, some time before the present official Walther Lederer, argues for including among compensatory movements below the line all short-term capital movements which responded to monetary policy, i.e., to changes in interest rates.

If Lary's reorganization of the balance-of-payments equation is nonoperational, because of the difficulty of separating out short-term capital movements that respond to interest rates from those that do not, his distinction between a trader and a banker is a suggestive one. What it suggests is this: that the rules of thumb appropriate to a trader may not apply to a banker, and that the Department of Commerce's definition of equilibrium may fit a country which is essentially a trader, but leaves something to be desired for the United States, which is in the international banking business.

Take an ordinary business. It likes to have a quick asset or current ratio of 2 to 1; that is, for every dollar of its quick or current liabilities it likes to have two dollars of cash or other quick assets. This provides a safety margin against the sudden presentation of claims against it, and possible difficulties in speedily liquidating inventories or collecting accounts receivable. The current ratio is a liquidity, not a solvency measure. In its calculation, all demand liabilities are regarded as dangerous and not all current assets as cashable.

A bank, on the other hand, operates with a ratio of roughly one to six or eight between its vault cash and reserves with the Federal Reserve System and demand liabilities. It knows from experience that not all its liabilities are going to be presented for conversion into the ultimate reserve. These liabilities are used as money, and pass from hand to hand. The bank must be alive to the possibility of a run, against which it may have to encash its secondary reserves and seek support from rediscounting agencies as the Federal Reserve System and the FDIC. But its solvency depends upon its capacity to match a flow of cash from new deposits and maturing loans and investments against withdrawals of existing deposits. To claim that a bank is in deficit every time its deposits and loans and investments rise, or its quick asset ratio fell below 2, would be to apply the wrong analysis.

The United States is both a firm and a bank, of course, but its liquidity is more akin to that of a bank than of a firm. As all good elementary textbooks explain, bank reserves present paradox. When no one mistrusts the bank, they are not needed (apart from a mismatch in the normal flow of payments and receipts. When no one trusts the bank, 100 percent reserves are hardly sufficient. Moreover while it is true that banks grow, expanding assets and liabilities, without being regarded as in deficit as would be the case if the increase in liabilities were counted against them without the increase in assets counting in their behalf, the assets normally grow proportionately. In the case of the United States, the primary asset, gold, has declined from $23 billion to $12 billion over recent years, while demand liabilities have mounted from $5 billion in 1947 to $29 billion, 20 years later. The 1947 reserve ratio was generously high, but the ratio has declined so steadily that there is a basis for questioning the safety of the bank.

The distinction between official and private deposits implicit in the balance settled by official transactions, assumes that private holders of dollars are willing holders, and official holders are not. There is something to the distinction, as shown by the French action in withdrawing the bulk of its deposits, and the receipt of recent surpluses by other monetary authorities preponderantly in gold. But it is exaggerated. With the dollar the world's medium of exchange and unit of account, even the French authorities keep working balances in dollars, and only precautionary and speculative balances (to borrow the Keynesian terminology) in gold.

A bank is "in deficit" when it is acquiring dubious assets against its undoubted liabilities (which raises the question of solvency, discussed in connection with equation (3)[2] or when its portfolio is unbalanced and includes a shrinking proportion of quick assets. But lending long and borrowing short is not *ipso facto* a deficit, so long as reserve ratios are maintained. Lending long and borrowing short is what financial houses, including banks, do. It can be overdone: portfolios must be balanced among quick, secondary and long-term assets, and deposits must be watched for their nervousness. But rules of thumb which say that this and this asset does not count for, and this and this liability counts against, are too mechanistic.

An old story tells of a man who asked the waitress for two boiled eggs and a kind word. The kind word turned out to be "Don't eat the eggs." Here then are five concepts of balance-of-payments equilibrium. For trading countries, basic balance is sufficient. And for the trader role in the United States, it is equally cogent. When it comes to banking, however, rules of thumb mislead rather than inform. A statistical or stochastic approach could measure the mean of the probability distribution and its variance, that each asset could be turned into cash when it was needed, and that each deposit would be withdrawn. This is the exercise which good bankers perform instinctively rather than with mathematics.

One index of the extent to which the depositors of the United States feel secure in the safety of the bank is afforded by gold withdrawals. Table 24.1 shows the basic balance, balance on regular transactions,

TABLE 24.1

U.S. PAYMENTS IMBALANCE IN RECENT YEARS
UNDER ALTERNATIVE DEFINITIONS
(Billion of Dollars)

	1964	*1965*	*1966*
Basic balance...............................	−0.9	−3.0	−2.1
Balance on regular transactions (liquidity)....	−2.8	−1.3	−1.4
Balance settled by official transactions........	−1.5	−1.3	+0.2
Gold*.......................................	−0.1	−1.7	−0.6

* Sign reversed to indicate deficit financed by gold exports.
SOURCE: U.S. Department of Commerce, *Survey of Current Business*, June, 1967.

[2] If $X + M = 0 = LTC + STC$ where $LTC < 0$, $STC > 0$, it is assumed that the long-term capital assets are worth what they cost. Otherwise $X + M = LTC + STC \neq 0$, with the left-hand side negative, and the right positive, which is a deficit position.

balance settled by official transactions, and the gold losses of the United States in the years 1964, 1965, and 1966. The several measures vary widely in amount, and in year-to-year changes. The fact that the gold loss declined in 1966, after the heavy French withdrawals of 1965, suggests, however, that the bank (the United States) was doing better in 1966 than in 1964 and 1965, despite the contrary evidence of the older measures. It would be ironic if all the sophisticated analysis applied to

TABLE 24.2

MAJOR CHANGES IN U.S. BASIC AND TOTAL NET BALANCES OF PAYMENTS,
AVERAGES FOR 1953–55 AND 1958–60
(Billions of Dollars)

Item	1953–55 Average	1958–60 Average	Change
Goods and services:			
Merchandise exports...........................	13.1	17.3	+4.2
Merchandise imports...........................	−10.9	−14.3	−3.4
Trade balance..............................	2.2	3.0	+.8
Military expenditures.........................	−2.7	−3.2	−.5
Net investment income........................	1.7	2.2	+.5
Other services, net............................	−.2	−.5	−.3
Net goods and services.....................	.9	1.5	+.6
Aid and long-term capital:			
Government aid..............................	−2.1	−2.7	−.7
U.S. private long-term capital..................	−.9	−2.5	−1.6
Foreign long-term capital......................	.3	.4	+.1
Net aid and long-term capital...............	−2.6	−4.9	−2.2
Basic balance....................................	−1.7	−3.4	−1.7
Prepayments of foreign debts......................	...	.1	+.1
Recorded movements of U.S. short-term capital and net errors and omissions........................	.1	−.5	−.6
Total net balance...........................	−1.6	−3.7	−2.1

balances of payments in recent years leads back to the unsophisticated results of the mercantilists who set such store by gold.

The Figures

Table 24.2 gives averages of the balance-of-payments entries for 1953–55 and 1958–60 from the Brookings report. This emphasizes the basic balance and the balance on regular transactions or liquidity balance (here called the total net balance). Table 24.3 presents a condensed summary table from the Bernstein Committee report, reconciling the balance settled by official transactions and the balance on regular transactions. The tables are presented to show the arbitrary relationships between the various concepts, although the official balance is always smaller than the balance on regular transactions.

The tables suggest one point worth great emphasis. It is analytically wrong to connect up two items in the balance of payments unless one has independent evidence of their functional connection, as in the case of the funds deposited in the New York branch of the Canadian bank reinvested in the United States, or the dollar deposits in London

TABLE 24.3

CONDENSED SUMMARY OF U.S. BALANCE OF PAYMENTS, 1958–66, WITH
RECONCILIATION ITEMS
(Billions of Dollars)

	1958	1959	1960	1961	1962	1963	1964	1965	1966
Goods, services and remittances.....	1.5	− 0.7	3.2	4.9	4.3	4.9	7.6	5.8	4.2
Merchandise exports..........	16.3	16.3	19.5	19.9	20.6	22.0	25.3	26.2	29.2
Merchandise imports...........	−13.0	−15.3	−14.7	−14.5	−16.1	−17.0	−18.6	−21.5	−25.5
Services and remittances (net)...	1.4	1.2	1.1	2.0	2.2	2.1	3.0	3.2	3.3
Military payments and receipts..	− 3.1	− 2.8	− 2.7	− 2.6	− 2.3	− 2.2	− 2.1	− 2.1	− 2.8
U.S. government grants and capital (net)*.........................	− 2.6	− 2.4	− 2.8	− 3.5	− 3.7	− 3.9	− 3.7	− 3.6	− 3.9
Long-term private capital (net).....	− 2.6	− 1.4	− 2.1	− 2.2	− 2.7	− 3.3	− 4.3	− 4.6	− 1.5
Short-term claims of foreign banks (net)..........................	0.0	1.1	0.1	0.6	0.1	0.4	1.5	0.1	2.7
Other short-term private capital (net).	− 0.2	− 0.1	− 1.6	− 1.3	− 0.5	− 0.3	− 1.7	1.2	0.1
Foreign official capital, except claims of monetary institutions..........	0.3	0.4	0.6	0.4	0.4	0.3	0.0	0.2	− 1.0
Net errors and omissions..........	0.5	0.4	− 0.8	− 1.0	− 1.1	− 0.3	− 0.9	− 0.4	− 0.4
Balance settled by official transactions.....................	− 3.0	− 2.5	− 3.5	− 2.0	− 3.3	− 2.3	− 1.5	− 1.3	+ 0.2
Less: Selected inflows of foreign capital short-term claims of foreign banks..........................	0.0	1.1	0.1	0.6	0.1	0.4	1.5	0.1	2.7
Other liquid foreign private claims.....................	0.2	− 0.0	− 0.2	0.1	0.1	0.4	0.3	0.3	0.2
Foreign official capital, as above..	0.3	0.4	0.6	0.4	0.4	0.3	0.0	0.2	1.0
Plus: Other adjustments, including rounding......................	0.0	− 0.2	0.1	0.0	0.1	0.1	0.5	0.6	0.3
Balance on regular transactions.....	− 3.5	− 4.2	− 3.9	− 3.1	− 3.6	− 3.3	− 2.8	− 1.3	− 1.4

* Excludes debt prepayments.

which were laid off in New York. We have seen in Chapter 20 the error of comparing interest and dividends with new investments in Latin America. The point is worth making more generally. All the debits determine all the credits in the balance of payments, and vice versa, and it is analytically wrong to say that the imbalance between some collected debits and some credits is the result of a change in any one or more debits and credits. There is a temptation to ascribe the worsening of the basic and overall balance in Table 24.2 to the private capital outflow of the same order of magnitude, but it must be resisted. Or Table 24.3 suggests a villain in U.S. government grants and capital lending. Occasionally we have information that interest and dividends are partly reinvested abroad, so that the items are linked, or foreign aid is tied, so that exports are connected to aid. Lacking such information, we can only say that the system is a general equilibrium one, with all determining all, through links which take them to domestic and foreign prices and incomes, and behind them tastes, resources, technology, domestic and foreign economic policies, and so on. A strong case in fact can be made against comparing merchandise exports with merchandise imports, as in equation (1), despite the long tradition of so doing, since merchandise exports are linked with all other credits to imports and all other debits, and no more to one class of debits than to another (except where we have direct knowledge of barter).

If the merchandise balance is a concept of dubious value, so much more is the tourist balance, the interest and dividend balance, the technology gap, as measured by payments for patents and technology netted out against credits. These are perhaps useful measures of comparative advantage, or specialization, but they seem to imply that zero balance has some validity or that a surplus should be sought. A particularly offensive form of this balancing is the U.S. insistence that Germany should buy as much from the United States in military equipment as it costs the United States to maintain an army (for its own protection) in Germany. That it is futile for the United States to focus on the tourist gap is illustrated by the possibility that foreign countries might in turn seek to narrow the interest and dividend gap. An economist friend of the author attacks the concept sarcastically by bemoaning the U.S. banana gap.

The Balance of Indebtedness

Table 24.4 sets out the balance of indebtedness of the United States for selected years from 1914 to 1966. In the previous editions of this book, the balance of indebtedness was gently derided as a less significant statement than the balance of payments because of the difficulties encountered in valuing various assets, and indeed in obtaining complete coverage. Direct investments abroad are included at book value, i.e., initial investment plus or minus successive annual investment or disinvestment. This is an inaccurate measure of market value or their value as going concerns. Some of the government loans, moreover, have little value as repayment runs in foreign currencies with limited likelihood of collection in hard cash.

Nonetheless, despite its weakness as a statement, the balance of indebtedness has increased in interest, as the concept of the United

TABLE 24.4

INTERNATIONAL INVESTMENT POSITION OF THE UNITED STATES IN SELECTED YEARS,
1914–66
(Billion of Dollars)

	1914	1919	1930	1939	1946	1955	1966
U.S. investments abroad.............	3.5	7.0	17.2	11.4	18.7	44.9	112.0
Private......................	3.5	7.0	17.2	11.4	13.5	29.0	86.2
Long-term...................	3.5	6.5	15.2	10.8	12.3	26.7	75.6
Direct......................	2.6	3.9	8.0	7.0	7.2	19.3	54.6
Portfolio..................	0.9	2.6	7.2	3.8	5.1	7.4	21.0
Short-term..................		0.5	2.0	0.6	1.3	2.4	10.7
U.S. government..................					5.2	15.9	25.6
Long-term.....................					5.0	15.2	21.0
Short-term....................					0.2	0.7	4.4
Foreign investments in the U.S.......	7.2	4.0	8.4	9.6	15.9	29.6	60.4
Long-term.....................	6.7	3.2	5.7	6.3	7.0	12.6	27.0
Direct......................	1.3	0.9	1.4	2.0	2.5	4.3	9.1
Portfolio....................	5.4	2.3	4.3	4.3	4.5	8.3	17.9
Short-term*..................	0.5	0.8	2.7	3.3	8.9	17.0	33.4
U.S. net creditor position............	−3.7	3.0	8.8	1.8	2.8	15.3	51.6
Net long-term..................	−3.2	3.3	9.5	4.5	10.3	29.3	69.8
Net short-term.................	−0.5	−0.3	− 0.7	− 2.7	− 7.4	−13.9	−18.2

* Includes U.S. government securities.

States as a bank has come to the fore. The balance sheet of a bank may
be less than 100 percent communicative because of some assets which
should have been written down and have not been, and of other hidden
assets which do not appear at all. Judging how solvent and liquid the
bank is, is an art for the depositor and bank inspector as for the banker
himself.

Summary

The balance of payments of a country is a systematic record of all
economic transactions between the residents of the reporting country
and residents of all foreign countries. Certain problems must be settled
in determining who is a resident and what is a transaction. But any
consistent scheme of reporting is adequate for the purpose, so long as it
is organized in such a way as to serve the uses to which it is put. The
most important use of the balance of payments of most countries is to
describe in a concise fashion the state of international economic relationships of the country as a guide to monetary, fiscal, exchange, and
other policies. The balance of payments was originally estimated to
reveal the sources and uses of foreign exchange, and then was thought

of in terms of the contribution, positive or negative, of international transactions to domestic income determination. At the current time in the United States, interest is reverting to foreign exchange, and in particular to the international liquidity position of the United States.

While total credits equal total debits in the balance of payments, a number of partial balances have been devised to indicate the degree of approach to equilibrium. The merchandise trade balance and the current account are not highly useful for this purpose. Basic balance or the current account less long-term capital exports (or plus capital imports) indicates whether long-term capital is transferred. The overall balance, or balance on regular transactions, is designed to measure liquidity, rather than solvency, and assumes that demand liabilities will have to be paid, whereas quick assets are not available to meet them. The balance of payments on official transactions assumes that private capital inflows from abroad are voluntary, but official inflows are unwilling, and are undertaken only to compensate the accounts. All these concepts apply more fully to a trader country than to one which acts as a banker.

It is a mistake to match up a debit with a credit item in the balance of payments, or to attribute a deficit or surplus to a single item with opposite sign, unless one has specific information that the items are functionally associated.

The balance of indebtedness is a statement of outstanding claims and liabilities of dubious accuracy, given the difficulties of measurement, but of increasing interest as the liquidity status of a banker country attracts attention.

SUGGESTED READING

TEXTS

See Snider, chaps. xvi, xvii; Yeager, chap. iii; Vanek, part 1; Kemp, chap. xvi, in increasing order of difficulty.

TREATISES, ETC.

See Report of the Review Committee for Balance of Payments Statistics, to the Bureau of the Budget, *The Balance of Payments Statistics of the United States,* A Review and Appraisal (Bernstein Report) (Washington, D.C.: U.S. Government Printing Office, 1965); Walter S. Salant *et al., The United States Balance of Payments in 1968* (Brookings Report) (Washington, D.C.: The Brookings Institution, 1963) (paperback); Hal B. Lary, *Problems of the United States as World Trader and Banker* (Princeton, N.J: Princeton University Press, 1963).

In the periodical literature, see the essay by R. Nurkse in American Economic Association, *Readings in the Theory of International Trade;* Walther

Lederer, *The Balance on Foreign Transactions: Problems of Definition and Measurement,* Special Papers in International Economics, (Princeton, N.J., September, 1963); C. P. Kindleberger, "Balance-of-Payments Deficits and the International Market for Liquidity," *EIF,* May, 1965; and Robert Triffin, "The Balance of Payments and the Foreign Investment Position of the United States," *EIF,* September, 1966.

An older item attacking the Lederer-Department of Commerce position is Walter R. Gardner, "An Exchange-Market Analysis of the United States Balance of Payments," *SP,* May, 1961.

POINTS

Table 24.1 is derived from balance-of-payments statements in the Department of Commerce *Survey of Current Business,* (Washington, D.C.: U.S. Government Printing Office, monthly), which is also the source of Table 24.4. Table 24.2 is from the Brookings Report, p. 15, and Table 24.3 from the Bernstein Committee Report, p. 9, pieced out by subsequent *Surveys of Current Business,* whence also comes, in the August issues, the balances of indebtedness of Table 24.4.

Professor Machlup's attack on the IMF's concept of compensatory finance is presented in "Three Concepts of the Balance of Payments and the So-called Dollar Shortage," *EJ,* March, 1950, reprinted in F. Machlup, *International Payments, Debts and Gold* (New York: Charles Scribner's Sons, 1964).

Chapter 25

DISTURBANCES TO EQUILIBRIUM

Equilibrium

The variety of possible balance-of-payments equilibria discussed in the previous chapter suggests that equilibrium is an elusive concept. For the purposes of this chapter, we use basic balance as the equilibrium from which departures are measured. The current account and the long-term capital flow are adjusted to each other. The movement of long-term capital is appropriate to the levels of intended savings and domestic investment at "full employment." Behind the current account lie tastes, resources, production functions, including technology, and the money supply, which bespeak levels of prices at home and abroad appropriately related to one another through an exchange rate. If prices in one country are too high relative to those abroad, the current account is likely to be adverse, or insufficiently positive, relative to the long-run capital movement, and the exchange rate is said to be overvalued. If, on the other hand, prices are low relative to prices abroad, the current account tends to be insufficiently adverse, or excessively positive, and the exchange rate is said to be undervalued.

The Purchasing Power Parity Doctrine

At the end of World War I, a Swedish economist, Gustav Cassel, devised a means of measuring departures from "equilibrium." During the war, trade had been interrupted, monetary conditions in various countries had gone separate ways, and the problem, when foreign trade was resumed, was to choose a new exchange rate which would balance the accounts. Cassel suggested the purchasing power parity as the appropriate level at which to set the exchange rate. This was calculated by measuring relative departures of price levels from some base period when the balance of payments had been in satisfactory adjustment. Two countries, A and B, whose payments were in reasonable adjustment in period 0, should choose an exchange rate (R) which reflected the changes in their prices between period 0 and a later period 1:

$$R_1 : R_0 = \frac{P_{a1}}{P_{b1}} : \frac{P_{a0}}{P_{b0}}$$

or

$$R_1 : R_0 = \frac{P_{a1}}{P_{a0}} : \frac{P_{b1}}{P_{b0}}.$$

If prices (P) in A doubled relative to prices in B, from period 0 to period 1, the exchange rate (R) should fall in half (or the price of foreign exchange expressed in local currency should double). This is the "relative" version of the purchasing power parity doctrine. Another and "absolute" doctrine rests on the assumption that goods prices should be equalized by trade everywhere in the world. Where goods cost more in A than in B, when A's prices are converted into B's currency at the existing exchange rate, A's currency is overvalued by the percentage of the higher cost.

The absolute version of the purchasing power parity theory cannot, of course, depend on the equalization of goods prices by trade. This is because of transport costs. Transport costs bring it about that not all goods are traded, as we have seen, and that goods are more expensive in the importing country than in the exporting country by the amount of transport costs. Houthakker, who upholds the absolute version of the theory, relied on more complex reasoning. Trade brings about something approaching factor-price equalization. With factor-price equalization and identical production functions for nontraded goods, nontraded goods prices will be the same in countries joined by trade, despite the impossibility of joining such markets through goods movement.

The purchasing power parity doctrine assumes that the balance of payments was in equilibrium in the base period, and further that there have not been "structural" changes in the factors underlying this equilibrium, i.e., changes in technology, resources, and tastes, including the propensity to save. One example of a change which would distort the purchasing power parity, given by Metzler, is a change in capital movements, traceable back, let us say, to a reduced propensity to save. If the country has surplus savings and invests them abroad in period 0, but consumes at a higher and saves at a lower rate in period 1 so that capital exports decline, domestic prices can be higher in period 1 relative to period 0, since there is no need to transfer capital abroad. In an example furnished by Samuelson, with constant costs, and three commodities, where previously country A exported commodity X, and imported commodities Y and Z, a change in tastes now requires A to export X and Y and import Z. No change in costs or prices takes place, but the exchange rate must alter to shift good Y from imports to exports.

These theoretical qualifications to the purchasing power parity are supported by an empirical assault by Balassa, who directs his fire to Houthakker's use of consumer price indices. Houthakker claimed that the U.S. dollar was overvalued by 22.2 percent relative to the Deutschemark in March, 1962, measured by the consumer price indices calculated by the *Statistisches Bundesamt* of the West German government. Many governments calculate the cost of living in various places so that they can adjust the living allowances of their foreign service personnel. The German statistical authorities are particularly careful, and their results are published. Calculated by a Fisher Ideal formula, U.S. prices turned out to be 22.2 percent higher than German prices. The dollar, said Houthakker, was therefore 22.2 percent overvalued in absolute terms.

The choice of what price index to use in calculating purchasing power parities has been a vexed one. If one takes the prices of internationally traded goods for which transport costs are unimportant, the law of one price makes the doctrine a tautology. Such goods are traded in a single market, and in a single market there can be but one price. Consumer price indices contain nontraded goods. They, therefore, get away from the tautological content of the doctrine.

But consumer price indices, Balassa points out, contain a lot of personal services which are not only not traded, but the prices of which diverge with economic growth. The reason is a complex one. With improved efficiency, wages in efficient industries rise. Wages can rise and goods prices remain unchanged in these industries because of technological improvement. But wages have to rise as well in the industries with little or no technological change, in order for them to retain their labor. With constant efficiency and rising wages, their prices have to rise. To the extent that personal services—in barber shops, beauty parlors, lawyers' and doctors' services, teaching, and so on—rise in price, they affect the consumer price index without impinging on the balance of payments. In a world of one-sided technological progress, absolute and relative departures from purchasing power parity cannot be measured by the cost of living.

The point can be made more generally. There are differences in the purchasing power parity, and in the implicit exchange rate, for different types of goods. The OECD undertook to compare real incomes between countries with money incomes converted at the market exchange rate, and found a wide range of differences. Exchange rates of the more productive countries were found to be increasingly overvalued as one moved from commodities to services. It is thoroughly misleading to compare real incomes per capita between countries by converting money incomes at going rates of exchange. Happily for the employment of economists, it is necessary to compare actual outputs for fairly narrow categories of national income. From the resulting estimates, one can compute separate purchasing power parities for different classes of expenditure.

Finally it should be added that the purchasing power parity doctrine applies best only to current account transactions, while exchange markets are influenced by many types of capital flows as well. Metzler's point about savings flows has been mentioned. These may respond to any number of factors other than relative prices among countries. Switzerland traditionally has a current account deficit, indicating that its prices on goods and services may be comparatively high. Yet Switzerland's currrecy is traditionally strong in the exchange market owing to large inflows of liquid capital and, in times of crisis elsewhere, it is often a prime candidate for revaluation upwards. The purchasing power parity doctrine is designed for trader nations and gives little guidance for a country which is both a trader and a banker.

Fundamental Disequilibrium

The Articles of Agreement of the International Monetary Fund, signed at Bretton Woods in 1944, permitted exchange rate adjustment within limitations: 5 percent from the par value agreed to by the Fund at any time; 10 percent upon notification to the Fund, and any amount, with the consent of the Fund's directors, in the case of a fundamental disequilibrium. Nowhere in the Articles of Agreement, however, is fundamental disequilibrium defined, nor have the deliberations of the directors over 20-odd years since the Fund opened its door produced further enlightenment. The previous section has shown the difficulty of measuring disequilibrium through comparing price levels. It is equally difficult to ascribe a fundamental quality to any one particular equilibrium. Fundamental may refer to the size of the disturbance, and to its obduracy. Economic analysis, however, has been unable to single out any one kind of disequilibrium as more fundamental than any other.

Kinds of Disequilibria

A later official body, Working Party No. 3 of the Economic Policy Committee of the OECD found it useful in 1966 to make "a broad distinction between cases where an imbalance is due to an inappropriate level of internal demand in the country concerned, to excessive or deficient competitive strength in world markets, or to excessive capital movements." The report of the Working Party goes on to qualify the analysis by saying that multiple causes of disequilibrium can occur. In some cases, however, the origin of a payments imbalance is comparatively straightforward, as is its cure. An inappropriate level of demand should be corrected by a change in internal demand; excessive or deficient competitive strength by exchange rate adjustment, and excessive capital movements by control of capital movements.

This is too simple. It fails to penetrate to the causes of the inap-

TABLE 25.1

KINDS OF INTERNATIONAL ECONOMIC DISEQUILIBRIUM

	Income	Income and/or Price	Price
Short-term	Cyclical disequilibrium	Inflation; inappropriate exchange rate change	Structural disequilibrium at the goods level
Long-term or deep-seated	Secular disequilibrium	Systematic technological change	Structural disequilibrium at the factor level

propriate level of demand or the change in competitive strength. It makes no allowance for a deficiency of long-term capital movements, leaving the implication that these movements can be too large, but not too small. For present purposes it is desirable to go back to the basic micro- and macroeconomic factors which lie behind the balance of payments.

Let us distinguish between equilibria with and without long-term capital movements or with insufficient capital movements. In the absence of long-term capital, or with insufficient movements, disequilibria can be classified broadly into those stemming from income, those from structural causes, involving relative prices, and those which are a mixture of income and price. Table 25.1 presents a classification scheme of this sort, divided as well into short-term and long-term influences.

Income disequilibria are those in which income changes in relation to national incomes abroad (or vice versa) without significant changes in relative prices; structural changes are those which occur primarily in relative prices, without necessarily significant changes in the level of national income. The intermediate category includes the case of over- and undervaluation of the exchange rate produced by changes in the exchange rate, or by domestic inflation. These are cases of income *and* price. It also covers systematic technological changes which may produce increases in money income, reductions in prices, or both. It must be emphasized again that this breakdown is highly arbitrary. Whatever the convenience of the Keynesian model, in the real world no income change can take place without producing changes in relative prices; the cyclical behavior of the terms of trade between the agricultural and manufacturing sectors of the economy provides one proof of this. Income elasticities for all goods would have to be identical, and supply curves similar, to make possible changes in price level which take place without change in relative prices.

Conversely, there is little chance of change in relative prices without some change in the total level of income. Any change in export or import prices which produces a change in exports or imports, for example, will result in a change in income. Y will be affected by any change in X or in M (Y).

Inflation

There are many economists who regard the great bulk of balance-of-payments difficulties as the result of domestic inflation. It follows as a corollary that most balance-of-payments troubles can be corrected by disinflation (eliminating the inflationary gap and reducing effective demand to the level of full employment), or at least by halting the inflation and adjusting the exchange rate.

There is a large element of truth in this position. In many situations, disinflation can produce substantial improvements in the balance of payments. Partly, the decline in income reduces imports directly and releases goods previously bought in the home market for sale abroad. Partly, a reduction in prices makes the market a better one for foreigners in which to buy and a worse one in which to sell, thus assisting exports and reducing imports. Partly, in these days of administered prices, disinflation results in the cancellation of domestic orders and thus reduces delays in filling orders for export. And, finally, the halting of the inflation and the correction of the exchange rate tend to reverse the destabilizing speculation which added to the loss of foreign exchange reserves produced directly by inflation, and tend to produce, if the operation is well handled, a return flow of domestic capital and a reconstitution of foreign working balances.

Where inflation is demand-led, through excessive consumption, investment, or government expenditure, the disequilibrium is primarily of the income variety, although, as just mentioned, there will be price distortion. Where inflation is the result of a wage-price push—administered wage increases being followed by rises in administered prices—one can point primarily to price relationships. If the country sells in highly competitive markets, export prices are given and the inflationary pressure will squeeze profits of exporters. Where the exporters themselves administer their prices, profit margins may remain intact, but goods will gradually be priced out of world markets.

It will be appreciated that we refer to relative and not to absolute inflation. If all countries inflate at the same rate, and there is no money illusion, so that no one will change his spending habits in the mistaken notion that his real income has increased because his money income has risen, there can be no balance-of-payments disequilibrium. The difficulty arises because the tendency to overspend, or the wage-price push, is faster in one country than another.

Overvaluation after an Interruption in Trade

War and postwar reconstruction bring inflation. During the interruption of trade caused by high domestic demand and shortages, plus in many instances the blockage of trade routes, inflation can proceed at different rates in different countries. With the resumption of trade, exchange rates are out of line. Because of the difficulty in reducing wages and money incomes—wages being asymmetrical in that they rise faster and more easily than they fall—it becomes necessary as a rule to adjust exchange rates to the disparate rates of inflation. This case has already been discussed in connection with the purchasing power-parity doctrine.

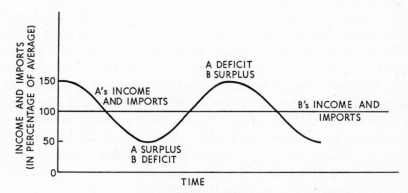

FIG. 25.1 Cyclical Disequilibrium: Different Income Patterns and Identical Income Elasticities for Imports

The Cyclical Path of Income

Cyclical disequilibrium occurs either because the patterns of business cycles in different countries follow different paths or because income elasticities of demand for imports in different countries are different. We may illustrate this with some simple diagrams for two countries. In Figure 25.1, national money income is stable in B and fluctuates cyclically in A. Income elasticities of demand for imports may or may not be the same. The income elasticity of demand for imports in B is not involved, since income is stable. In this situation, A's imports (and B's exports) will decline in depression and rise in prosperity. B's imports (and A's exports) will continue steady. The result is that A will have an export surplus in depression and an import surplus in prosperity. And B will have a deficit when A is depressed, and a surplus when A is prosperous.

If the national incomes of A and B both follow the cyclical path of A and income elasticities of imports in both countries are unity, and hence identical, there will be no disequilibrium. This is illustrated in Figure 25.2. Exports and imports rise and fall with national income,

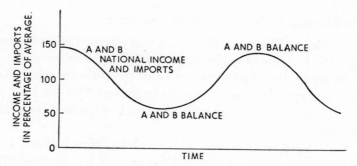

FIG. 25.2.   Cycles without Disequilibrium: Identical Income Patterns and Elasticities

but by the same amount. Cycles are a necessary condition of pure cyclical disequilibrium, but not a sufficient one.

The Role of Income Elasticities

Figure 25.3 suggests the position where national incomes vary in the same cyclical paths but income elasticities for imports differ. In this case, A may have an income elasticity greater than unity; B, an elasticity less than unity. A's imports are luxuries—tourist travel, perfumes, and whisky, let us say. B's imports, on the other hand, are necessities—

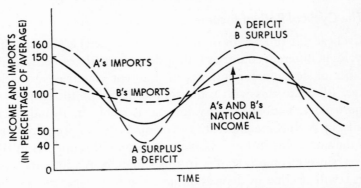

FIG. 25.3. Cyclical Disequilibrium: Identical Income Patterns, Different Income Elasticities for Imports

wheat, coal for space heating, and newsprint. With these assumptions, too, A will have an export surplus in depression, when its imports (B's exports) have sunk lower than its exports (B's imports); and A will have an import surplus in prosperity. B's balance of payments will show the simple obverse.

The Evolving Pattern of Cyclical Fluctuations

In previous editions of this text, it was assumed without question that the U.S. balance of payments turned adverse in prosperity and positive in depression. And the same holds true broadly today. But the shape of the payments cycle is less sharply defined. This has been due to changes in the structure of trade on the one hand, and of expectations on the other.

Imports have become more stable in relation to national income, i.e., the income elasticity of demand for imports has declined. This is partly the consequence of a shift in imports from crude materials and semimanufactures, which tend to fluctuate more widely, to consumers goods, which fluctuate less. This is especially the case when built-in stabilizers in the fiscal system maintain disposable income which is spent on consumers' goods steady within a narrower range of fluctuations than national income. An additional factor seems to have been the change of elastic to inelastic expectations regarding the prices of raw material imports. Before the Korean War, these elastic expectations tended to excite the cyclical movement of raw materials imports; since 1951, recessions and prosperity have proceeded within a narrow price range. The consequence has been that imports move in a reduced amplitude today in the United States as compared with earlier decades.

Moreover, the rapid rate of growth of Western European economies has smoothed out the cycles in that continent since 1950 or so, and exports have been a function more of supply push than demand pull. Result: another familiar cyclical relationship altered. Sir Dennis Robertson once referred to the critical dependence of Europe on cycles originating in the United States, to say that "when the United States sneezed, Europe caught pneumonia." So much has the secular relation altered between the two economies, that the old cyclical description no longer applies. When the United States sneezes today, Europe barely bothers to say "God bless you."

Secular Disequilibrium

In macroeconomic analysis in a closed economy, there may be cycles on the one hand, as a disturbance from stability, and secular waves of stagnation or exhileration. Under secular stagnation, investment opportunities are inadequate to absorb full employment savings; in periods of secular exhileration on the contrary, investment is too high relative to the savings of the economy. The cause of the imbalance in the Keynesian system, of course, is that the forces lying behind savings and investment are different, and both are relatively inelastic with respect to the rate of interest. Savings are a function of income, to some degree of wealth, and of institutional forces such as the practices in life insurance and mortgage amortization. Investment, on the other hand, is responsive to innovation, population change, availability of management, and so on. In particular, countries may tend to have many investment opportunities relative to savings in the early stages of growth, and the opposite at a later stage.

The relations between savings and domestic investment in the growth of a country can be eased in an open economy by long-term capital movements. In the early stages of growth when investment opportunities exceed savings, a country may make up the gap with international borrowing. At a later stage as its income and savings rise beyond its investment requirements, it pays back debt and accumulates foreign investments of its own. Still later, its propensity to save may shift again downward, as consumption rises through demonstration effect but the productive drive flags. At this stage the country may choose to consume some of its accumulated foreign capital. These are the basic factors with widely varying detail, underlying an old classification of balance of payments of various countries, which has existed long before the postwar interest in economic development.

This system of classification was based on the merchandise trade balance. What counts, of course, is the current account and long-term capital. Originally, four stages of development were discerned, based on changes in the balance of indebtedness (Table 25.2).

TABLE 25.2

THE BALANCE OF PAYMENTS BY STAGES
OF DEVELOPMENT, 1

Balance of Indebtedness	*Balance of payments on Current Account*
Young debtor............................	Passive
Mature debtor...........................	Active
Young creditor..........................	Active
Mature creditor........................	Balanced or passive

On this basis, the young debtor is borrowing. The mature debtor is repaying. The young creditor is lending. And the mature creditor has either stopped lending or is consuming capital. The difference between the mature debtor and the young creditor is to be found not in the balance of payments but in the balance of indebtedness. The balance of payments shows a continuous export surplus as the country emerges from the one to the other stage. It is simply that the net excess of liabilities over claims becomes a surplus of claims over liabilities.

While this system is satisfactory for most purposes, the ambiguity about the last stage and the abruptness in the transition between the first and second make it worthwhile to add two more (Table 25.3).

TABLE 25.3

THE BALANCE OF PAYMENTS BY STAGES
OF DEVELOPMENT, 2

Stage	*Balance of Indebtedness*	*Balance of Payments on Current Account*
1.....................	Young debtor	Passive
2.....................	Adult debtor	Balanced
3.....................	Mature debtor	Active
4.....................	Young creditor	Active
5.....................	Adult creditor	Balanced
6.....................	Mature creditor	Passive

Figure 25.4 presents a schematic diagram of the balance of indebtedness and the balance of payments on current account through the various stages of the development of the balance of indebtedness. In the

early stages, debtor position is positive, and the current account in the balance of payments negative. The current account changes to positive in the middle of the second stage (and back to negative in the middle of the fifth stage). When it turns positive the debtor balance of indebtedness starts to diminish, and crosses the zero line (i.e., becomes a creditor position) at the end of the third stage. This change, however, occurs without any change in the credit position in the current account.

In very compressed form this is how the current account should behave in the growth process, and with it long-term capital movements. When long-term capital movements are deficient, however, secular dise-

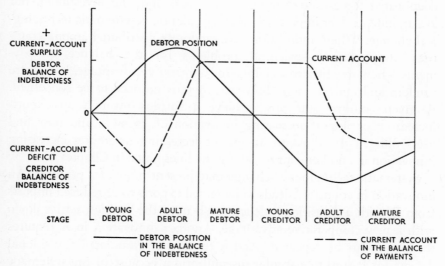

FIG. 25.4.   Schematic Representation of the Balance of Indebtedness and the Current Account in the Balance of Payments, by Stages

quilibrium results. If young and vigorously growing countries have investment opportunities in excess of domestic savings, and land and labor, but foreign loans are not available, they are likely to run deficits on basic balance. The pressure to invest is so strong as to be irresistible, but the capital movements are not forthcoming to fill the gap in the balance of payments. Or in a rich country which has abundant savings relative to its investment opportunities, but lacks the institutions to invest abroad, the basic balance will show a persistent surplus. In a world of countries at different stages of growth and growing at difference paces, long-term capital movements are needed to offset excesses of savings over investment in some countries, and deficiencies in others.

When such long-term capital movements were limited, as was the case in the 1930's and in the early period after the war, the result is secular disequilibrium. The need for long-term capital was recognized at Bretton Woods with the establishment of the International Bank for Reconstruction and Development to fill the need for development lending in the absence of an effective capital market. The foreign capital aid discussed in Chapter 22 serves to fill the same gap.

Technological Change

Another aspect of the development process which is related to the deep-seated forces determining savings and domestic investment, but has an independent impact on the basic balance, is systematic technological change. Where innovations are randomly distributed among countries, they present structural problems for the balance of payments—how to adjust to a change in comparative advantage. If they are random and not too large, however, there is no need to be concerned. A given country will now achieve a surplus through an export-increasing or import-decreasing innovation of its own; and now find itself obliged to adjust to an export-decreasing or import-increasing innovation in another country, along the lines noted in Chapter 4.

Systematic technological change may present more of a problem. An innovation in country A leads to increased exports to or reduced imports from B, with a transitional deficit for B until the position settles down with a new comparative advantage. Another innovation in A requires the process to be repeated. And a third. The cumulated transitional deficits for B sum to a secular disequilibrium because of the systematic character of the innovational process. It is not certain that this cumulative deficit is appropriately financed by long-term capital movements, since the deficit arises partly from consumption which adjusts to the loss in income with a lag; and new investment in new lines of comparative advantage does not so much add to wealth as replaces the investment wiped out by innovation abroad. The consequence is no increased output with which to pay debt service.

During the days of dollar shortage immediately after World War II and extending as late, in the literature at least, to 1957, a number of analysts attributed the U.S. surplus and world deficit to U.S. systematic innovation. Williams, Crowther, Robertson, MacDougall, and Hoffmeyer are among those who set store by this explanation. When the balance of payments of the United States reversed, in 1951 in some views, or in 1958 in others, the cause, according to Samuelson, included Europe's closing of the U.S. technological lead. Prices, income, capital movements, and so on, had become adjusted to the position in which the United States innovated faster than Europe. When Europe learned to produce automobiles, trucks, television sets, refrigerators, and so on for itself, the dollar, appropriately valued for a U.S. technological lead, became overvalued. Whether the so-called technological gap of the United States over Europe in computers, aircraft, space technology, and nuclear energy which a number of European observers discovered in 1966 and 1967 will have a similar impact on the balance of payments in the opposite direction remains to be determined. It may cover too narrow a range of goods to be significant.

Structural Disequilibrium at the Goods Level

Structural disequilibrium at the goods level occurs when a change in demand or supply of exports or imports alters a previously existing equilibrium or when a change occurs in the basic circumstances under which income is earned or spent abroad, in both cases without the requisite parallel changes elsewhere in the economy. The simplest illustration is furnished by a change in demand. Suppose there is a decline in the world demand for Swiss embroidery due to a change in taste. The resources previously engaged in embroidery production must shift into other lines of activity or adjust their expenditures downward. So far as the country as a whole is concerned, the displaced resources or some others must shift into another export line, or the country must restrict imports. If the called-for changes fail to take place or occur in inadequate degree, the country will experience a structural disequilibrium. The resources which continue in embroidery will be earning less than they could earn in another industry, on the assumption that they had been in equilibrium before the decline in demand. Though imports will decline to some extent, owing to the operations of the multiplier and the marginal propensity to imports, imports will exceed exports.

History is full of these changes in demand. The rise of synthetic competition with Japanese silk and Chilean nitrates, the substitution of oil for coal, and of detergents for natural fats and oils, the loss of their world markets by British coal and textiles, the competition of overseas grain production experienced on a large scale for the first time in Europe in the 1870's and 1880's—all furnish examples of more or less significance. Structural disequilibrium may be caused by a nonsystematic change in taste or in technology or in anything which alters the price of an export upward or downward. An increase in the foreign demand for a country's output is structural disequilibrium of a sort, but one with which it is not difficult to deal. The remedy is an increase in output of the product and an increase in consumption and imports by the country.

The cause of the disturbance may be a change in supply. The classical illustration was crop failure, which cut off the supply of a country's exports and produced a short fall of exports below imports. A bumper crop abroad which lowered world prices would have much the same effect. Others are the exhaustion of the soil or of mines.

The domestic demand and the foreign supply of imports can change adversely to cause a structural disequilibrium, as well as the domestic supply and the foreign demand for exports. A crop failure or a strike in a major industry may give rise to an increase in imports, as well as to a decline in exports. The long strike in steel in the United States in 1959 which encouraged European and Japanese exports to the United States provides one among many possible illustrations.

Crop failure is underrated today as a cause of balance-of-payments change. In dry countries, great variability in the harvest is likely to lead to wide changes in the quantity of agricultural products available for export and demanded from abroad as imports. The first five-year plan in India succeeded as well as it did because of a favorable monsoon. In 1947, the bad winter and worse spring together with the summer drought in Europe greatly accentuated the balance-of-payments difficulties of western Europe, while the bumper crops of 1948 exaggerated the efficacy of the Marshall Plan in producing recovery.

More than merchandise trade may be involved. The loss of service income may be a serious blow to the balance of payments on current account. This may arise through bankruptcy of direct investments abroad or their confiscation or nationalization. The Belgian loss of copper income from the Congo is one example, or the Egyptian loss of income from the Suez Canal and tourism after its defeat by Israel in June, 1967. Perhaps the most far-reaching and complex case is that furnished by the impact of the last two world wars on the position of various areas, and particularly on Europe.

War, it has been suggested, speeds up economic change and development at all stages, including the penultimate stage of decline. It might be appropriate, therefore, to regard the effects of war as secular and its disturbances to balance-of-payments equilibrium as long run in character. War produces structural changes which go deeper than goods, down to the level of factor proportions. The European Recovery Program might therefore be regarded as an attempt to correct structural disequilibrium at the factor level. There can be little doubt that the far-reaching effects of war were compounded of every possible kind of disturbance and disequilibrium. For our purposes, however, because the effects were concentrated in such a short space of time and involved so many changes in demand, supply, technology, and institutional arrangements, we may regard the disequilibrium of the postwar period as reflecting in important degree structural disequilibrium at the goods level.

Structural Disequilibrium at the Factor Level

Structural disequilibrium at the factor level results from factor prices which fail to reflect accurately factor endowments. The disequilibrium may not appear directly in the balance of payments. The economy may, for example, adjust to the factor prices as they are, choosing lines of comparative advantage and disadvantage, or exports and imports level of income and exchange rate so that the balance of payments is in equilibrium at those factor prices. The result, however, will be that one or more factors have structural unemployment.

Typically, the price of labor is too high and that of capital too low. The reasons for this may lie in the collective bargaining strength of labor or in the nature of our social interest in economics. The proximate cause, however, may be something like the cessation of emigration from Italy due to World War I and the immigration laws of 1919 and 1921 in the United States, so far as labor is concerned; or the Keynesian doctrine that interest rates are too high and hold back investment, wrongly applied, so far as capital is concerned.

If the price of labor is too high, the country will choose lines of comparative advantage in which labor is used more sparingly than it should be, and will import goods with a higher labor content than is appropriate. The country's comparative advantage in labor intensive commodities and services will be understated, and its comparative disadvantage in these lines will be overstated. Balance in the balance of payments may still be possible, but only at the cost of unemployed labor. If an attempt is made to employ this labor, it will have to be done at factor proportions which differ from those utilized throughout the economy. There is no spare capital, which is already overemployed because it is underpriced; and we may assume that there is no spare land. Accordingly, the generation of additional employment for labor must be, like WPA, on a leaf-raking or domestic construction basis which uses a maximum of labor and a minimum of capital.

In a broader sense, the balance of payments is in disequilibrium when factor prices, out of line with factor endowments, distort the structure of production from the allocation of resources which appropriate factor prices would have indicated. This is true, whatever the relationship of exports to imports. The same can be said for balance-of-payments equilibria in the narrow sense which are below optimum efficient equilibrium owing to the effects of tariffs, subsidies, or other distorting interferences. But the structural disequilibrium resulting from inappropriate factor prices is more nearly disequilibrium in a narrow than would be the case of a tariff; the existence of structural unemployment cries for governmental action, and the action is likely to result in inflation, which gives a narrow static disequilibrium represented by an imbalance between exports and imports.

Excessive Capital Movements

Table 25.1. sets out a scheme of disequilibria on the assumption that the current account was distorted from what it ought to be, given existing resources, technology, tastes, spending propensities, and so on, or that the current account was appropriate to the underlying parameters of the system but that the long-term capital movement fell short of it. We must now consider the case where the capital movement is excessive or in the wrong direction.

Capital flight is one form excessive capital movements can take. A less developed country with high propensities to invest and limited savings needs capital imports but may suffer from capital exports, as its wealthy citizens move their funds to safekeeping abroad as a hedge against war, heavy taxation, or confiscation. This is a familiar pattern of Europe in the 1930's, and of less developed countries today. A few analysts would defend the position that the current account should adjust to the capital movement no matter which direction it was going, or in what amount, but only few. Most economists would argue that capital movements from capital-poor to capital-rich countries—except perhaps for a small gross movement against the main current called for by investment diversification—is uneconomic and should be subject to controls.

Or a crisis of confidence may lead countries which had earlier accumulated foreign exchange reserves in the form of deposits in a particular currency to withdraw them in gold or transfer them to a different financial center. This sort of capital movement is disturbing. We will discuss it later, however, under the topic of the international monetary system, as part of the question of confidence, rather than here with disequilibrium.

The more interesting question is whether private capital movements can be excessive or whether the current account should adjust to such capital movements as the system produces. This is a particularly relevant question for the United States in the mid-1960's, and the imposition of the Interest Equalization Tax (IET), and the Voluntary Credit Restraint Program (VCRP), clearly reveals the governmental position that the capital outflow was excessive. Implicitly it suggests that transfer through deflation of income or relative price deflation in the United States (or income and price inflation in Europe) was not a viable solution. Either Europe would not engineer the expansion which would bring about the transfer through the efforts of the receiving country, or the United States would not produce the contraction through which transfer could have been achieved by the capital exporting country. With transfer excluded, and $X + M < LTC$, in absolute value, the remedy seemed to lie in curtailing LTC.

If one is fully committed to basic balance, the logic of the last sentence is inescapable. And it must be admitted that capital movements can be excessive in economic terms. Investors no less than consumers are subject to demonstration effect, and keeping up with the Joneses. From 1963 to 1966 profits were falling in Europe and rising in the United States but direct investment by U.S. corporations in Europe continued to increase. Nevertheless, interest rates on long-term securities remained higher in Europe than in the United States. It is difficult to claim that capital movements are excessive when they continue to move from areas of lower to areas of higher interest rates.

The answer may lie in the inadequacy of the concept of basic balance when the capital markets of the United States and Europe are as closely joined as they became prior to the IET and as they continued, despite the IET and the VCRP. Basic balance requires short-term capital movements to net to zero and makes no allowance for financial intermediation, under which one capital market may lend long and borrow short from another, with no net movement of capital such as would be called for by a change in $X + M$. Such financial intermediation would be produced by joined capital markets where marked differences in liquidity preference prevailed, or one or more segments of the market were monopolized.

Assume for the sake of argument, that Europe has a marked preference for liquidity compared with the United States, although total savings equals total investment. The basis for the difference in liquidity preference may be the memory of 50 years of wars, inflation and capital levy, which suggests caution with respect to long-term bonds. In these assumed circumstances, long-term rates will be higher in Europe than in the United States and short-term rates lower. If the markets are joined there will be a tendency to produce long-term capital movements from the United States and short-term movements to the United States to and from Europe respectively.

Such gross long- and short-term capital movements with no net would violate the equilibrium conditions under basic balance and the balance on regular transactions. It would not depart from equilibrium under the balance settled by official transactions if the short-term capital movements were undertaken by private Europeans. If, however, European investors have a wider horizon than European savers or European banks, the former will borrow abroad at long term, but the latter will not lend abroad at short term. In this condition, the foreign exchange borrowed will be sold in the market and will find no buyers except for the monetary authorities. This would lead to disequilibrium under the Bernstein definition of balance on official transactions.

The question still remains, however, whether the capital movements are excessive, or the definition of equilibrium inappropriate.

Summary

Balance-of-payments equilibrium requires the appropriate relationship to one another of exports, imports, long- and short-term capital movements, behind which lie prices, incomes, an exchange rate, asset preferences, and behind them, tastes, resources, production functions, technology, and so on. Equilibrium cannot be measured adequately through the purchasing power parity doctrine.

Disequilibria may be divided into those of income, those of price, and those combining income and price. Inflation pure and simple, or the wrong exchange rate, are perhaps the simplest variety. On the income side are the cyclical disequilibria arising from changes in income at home or abroad, affected by income elasticities. Secular disequilibrium is related to the failure of long-term capital to match the gap between domestic savings and domestic investment, or to systematic technological change. Structural disequilibrium at the goods level arises from the lag of adjustment to a change in demand or supply. Structural disequilibrium at the goods level comes from distortions between factor endowments and factor prices.

While for a long time, persistent disequilibrium was the consequence of hesitant capital movements, the problem of excessive capital movements is posed in the 1960's. Capital flight is readily recognized as one such, and also runs on a reserve currency. A question remains whether international financial intermediation should be regarded as involving excessive long-term capital flows, or as pointing up the limitations of the major concepts of international equilibrium.

SUGGESTED READING

TEXTS

Yeager, chap. xxiv, deals with the U.S. balance-of-payments disequilibrium. Clement, Pfister and Rothwell, chap viii, is entitled "Persistent Disequilibrium: Dollar Shortage and Dollar Glut." See also the readings from a variety of sources, including Lary, Balassa, Houthakker, and Triffin in B. Balassa (ed.), *Changing Patterns in Foreign Trade and Payments* (New York: W. W. Norton & Co., Inc., 1964) (paperback).

TREATISES ETC.

See OECD, *The Balance of Payments Adjustment Process,* a report by Working Party No. 3 of the Economic Policy Committee (Paris, August, 1966).

On the purchasing power parity doctrine, see Gustav Cassel, *Money and Foreign Exchange after 1914* (New York: The Macmillan Co., 1923); Lloyd A. Metzler in *International Monetary Policies* (Washington, D.C.: Federal Reserve System, October, 1947); P. A. Samuelson, "Theoretical Notes on Trade Problems," *RE & S,* May, 1964; and B. Balassa, "The Purchasing-Power-Parity Doctrine: A Reappraisal," *JPE,* December, 1964, both of whom criticized H. S. Houthakker's "Exchange Rate Adjustment," in Joint Economic Committee, *Factors Affecting the Balance of Payments of the United States,* 87th Cong., 2nd sess. (Washington, D.C.: U.S. Government Printing Office, 1962).

There is virtually no up-to-date literature on cyclical disequilibrium. On structural disequilibrium, see F. Machlup, "Structure and Structural Change: Weaselwords and Jargon," and "Equilibrium and Disequilibrium: Misplaced Concreteness and Disguised Politics," reprinted in his *Essays on Economic Semantics* (Englewood Cliffs, N.J.: Prentice-Hall, Inc., 1963), who is negative on these concepts.

On secular or persistent disequilibrium, see T. Balogh, *The Dollar Crisis* (London: Basil Blackwell & Mott, Ltd., 1949); C. P. Kindleberger, *The Dollar Shortage* (New York: The Technology Press and John Wiley & Sons, Inc., 1950), S. E. Harris, *Interregional and International Trade* (New York: McGraw-Hill Book Co., Inc., 1957); Sir Donald MacDougall, *The World's Dollar Problem* (London: Macmillan & Co., Ltd., 1957); Sir G. Crowther, *Balances and Imbalances of Payments* (Boston: Harvard University Graduate School of Business Administration, 1957); E. Zupnick, *Britain's Postwar Dollar Problem* (New York: Columbia University Press, 1957); E. Hoffmeyer, *Dollar Shortage* (Copenhagen: Ejner Munksgaards Forlag, 1958); R. Triffin, *Europe and the Money Muddle* (New Haven, Conn.: Yale University Press, 1957). Of all of these, only the last disbelieves in the possibility of long-run imbalance. MacDougall reviewed his findings in the summer of 1960 and was not disposed to alter them fundamentally. See his "The Dollar Problem: A Reappraisal," Princeton University, Department of Economics, *Essays in International Finance,* November, 1960.

The major contributions to the analysis of the reversal of the dollar shortage have been in various congressional hearings and in S. E. Harris (ed.), *The Dollar Crisis,* especially the essays by R. N. Cooper and W. Lederer. See also

P. A. Samuelson, "Stability and Growth in the American Economy," reprinted in *The Collected Works of Paul A. Samuelson* (Cambridge, Mass.: The M.I.T. Press, 1966); and C. P. Kindleberger, "The Cause and Cure of Disequilibrium in the Balance of Payments of the United States, January 1960," in *Europe and the Dollar* (Cambridge, Mass.: The M.I.T. Press, 1966).

For a rigorous expression of the view that the composition of the net capital flow between gross movements in and out, and between private and official accounts is arbitrary and unimportant, see the M.I.T. thesis by Donald G. Heckerman entitled "Models of the Balance of Payments and Standards for Adjustment" (dissertation, M.I.T. 1967).

POINTS

Comparisons of real national income from which purchasing power parities for different classes of expenditure can be derived will be found in Milton Gilbert and Associates, *Comparative National Products and Price Levels: A Study of Western Europe and the United States* (Paris: OECD, 1958).

Chapter 26

NATIONAL AND INTERNATIONAL MEASURES TO CORRECT DISEQUILIBRIUM

Disequilibrium can be repressed, corrected, or financed. If it takes time to recognize and then to repress or correct a disequilibrium, it must in any event be financed to that extent. And financing is needed where automatic forces are at work to produce the desired correction but takes time. Financing then is likely to be inescapable. Financing, repression, and adjustment all have costs.

Quasi-Adjustment Measures

Basic adjustment policies correct disequilibrium; quasi-adjustment represses it. This useful terminological contribution comes from John Williamson. Quasi-adjustment may be called for because deep-seated corrective measures are at work but slowly, and the means of financing the transitional deficit have been stretched. Or they may be applied as a second-best policy because the appropriate corrective measures are politically unacceptable, or the monetary and trade authorities lack an adequate diagnosis of the problem.

Quasi-adjustment takes the form of a number of policies discussed in the preceding pages. Imports may be reduced through temporary surcharges of the sort that the British applied in the fall of 1964; or government may cut back on spending abroad, tie foreign aid, impose restrictions on foreign travel, and cut foreign aid, as the U.S. government has done. Raising interest rates to attract short-term capital to finance a deficit is a quasi-adjustment measure—on the Bernstein definition of a deficit which regards private foreign funds as automonous and above the line rather than as compensatory and below the line. The most extreme form of quasi-adjustment is foreign exchange control, in which demand and supply are matched administratively, rather than through the price system, and in which exchange rate prices, and national incomes at home and abroad are not linked in appropriate relations to one another. This leads not to correction of disequilibrium, but to the "disequilibrium" system under which price, demand, and supply are maintained at nonequilibrium values by administrative action.

Most economists disapprove thoroughly of quasi-adjustments. They prefer to operate with more basic measures, and to finance transitional deficits while they are working out. A defense of these measures can be made under certain circumstances, however. In the major structural recovery from World War II, foreign exchange control limited the size of the transitional deficit to be financed by European liquidation of foreign assets or U.S. aid. Ultimate recovery required abandonment of quota restrictions, and the reallocation of resources into lines of comparative advantage. To attempt to achieve free international markets before the gaps in the productive structure had been repaired, however, would have entailed either a much larger volume of financing, or acceptance of a lower level of income and substantial unemployment as the recovery standard.

Expenditure Switching and Expenditure Changing

In his generalized scheme of balance-of-payments adjustment appropriate to basic therapy, Harry Johnson divides policies into expenditure switching and expenditure changing. The former involve the price adjustments of Chapter 15, which, it will be recalled, involve changing the exchange rate, or, with a fixed exchange rate, altering price levels. The latter, discussed in Chapter 16, involve changing the level of expenditure or income. Switching requires changes between domestic and foreign expenditure. Expenditure changes vary total expenditure, with a constant distribution between foreign and domestic, or a distribution governed only by income elasticities.

Internal and External Balance

The impact of expenditure switching and expenditure changing policies on the balance of payments and the level of employment can be demonstrated with the aid of a diagram worked out by Trevor Swan. On the vertical axis in Figure 26.1 is a cost ratio (R) which represents the ratio of international to domestic prices, or to domestic wages. This is an index of the country's competitive position. The higher one moves up this scale, the larger are exports and the smaller are imports, because the exchange rate is increasingly undervalued, foreign prices are rising relative to domestic prices, or, less likely, domestic prices are falling relative to foreign prices. On the horizontal axis is real domestic expenditure, which increases from left to right.

Two curves are shown in the figure, one for internal balance or full employment, and one for external balance, representing a particular current account balance appropriate to a given autonomous level of long-term capital. There is, of course, a separate external balance curve for each possible level of capital movement. The internal balance curve moves down from left to right, indicating that the lower the cost ratio which limits exports and import-competing production, the higher must be real domestic expenditure to maintain full employment. Positions to the right and above the curve represent inflation, with domestic real expenditure too high relative to exports and import-competing produc-

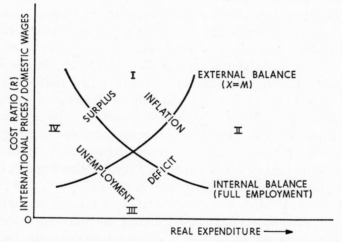

FIG. 26.1.   Internal and External Balance Determined by Real Domestic Expenditure and the Cost Ratio

tion, or the other way round. Below and to the left of the curve there is unemployment because domestic expenditure plus production for exports and import replacements are too low to occupy domestic resources fully.

Let us choose one external balance curve, perhaps where long-term capital movements are zero and $X = M$. This is positively sloped: as one moves north, the balance of payments improves because of the more favorable cost ratio; as one moves east, on the other hand, the balance of payments worsens because of the spillover of expenditure onto imports (and perhaps what were, at lower levels of expenditure, exports). Moving to the northeast, therefore, balances the two forces and gives external balance. Above and to the left of the curve, the balance of payments is in surplus; below and to the right, it is in deficit.

The figure can thus be divided into four quadrants, I with inflation and a balance-of-payments surplus; II with inflation and a deficit; III with surplus; IV with unemployment and a balance-of-payments surplus.

There is, of course, only one point, where the curves intersect, where the country is in complete equilibrium. In zones II and IV, with a deficit and inflation, and a surplus and unemployment, respectively, the country should alter real expenditure, contracting it for zone II and expanding it for zone IV. In zones I and III, on the other hand, the major tool of policy should be to alter the cost ratio, using switching policies, such as, for example, by exchange rate depreciation and appreciation. But these pure policies apply best to positions on the horizontal and vertical lines through the intersection of the two curves (not drawn in Figure 26.1). To each side of the horizontal and vertical lines, the separate policies must be combined with an admixture of the other therapy. To the right of the vertical line through the intersection, in zone I, for example, appreciation to lower international relative to domestic prices should be combined with contraction of spending to help toward internal balance; and below the horizontal line through the intersection, in zone II, contraction of expenditure should be combined with depreciation to move toward external balance. Since each zone in the graph is divided by the horizontal or vertical line through it, there are eight possible combinations of policies.

The internal balance curve assumes only general unemployment because of deficient demand, and makes no allowance for structural unemployment. The curve is displaced to the right by capital formation and additions to the labor force. It is shifted to the left by capital destruction. As mentioned, there is a separate external balance curve for each level of autonomous capital movements, for a given level of productive capacity. Changes in productive capacity will also displace the external balance curve representing a given capital movement. Thus the $X + M$ curve will be displaced leftward and up by capital destruction, and rightward and down by capital formation and additions to the labor force. Additional capacity makes it possible to maintain external balance with increased expenditure, at the same exchange rate, or a higher exchange rate (lower cost ratio) with a given level of expenditure.

We indicate the relations of the curves to productive capacity to illustrate the problem of major structural disequilibrium brought about by war. The destruction of the war, and neglected depreciation, shifted the internal balance curve to the left and down, and the external balance curve to the left and up. Figure 26.2 shows the curves after displacement by war. The postwar position is marked by the dot at *B* which shows a position of inflation and substantial deficit.

A small group of observers thought that sound economic policy after the war called for balancing the budget and depreciating the exchange rate, that is to move from *B* to *C*. But the displaced curves which intersected at *C* reflected a far-reaching structural disequilibrium which would leave structural unemployment and a permanently reduced level of real expenditure. The Marshall Plan, which involved moving from the postwar $X = M$ curve to the postwar $X + M = LTC$ curve, to finance a large capital inflow, gradually restored productivity

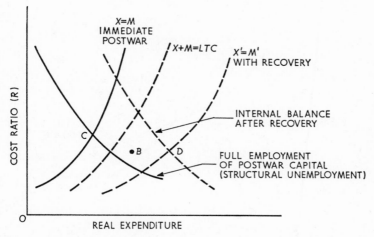

FIG. 26.2.   Internal and External Balance Curves Shifted by Wartime Destruction

and shifted the internal and the external balance ($X = M$) curves out to where they intersected at a point such as *D*.

Monetary and Fiscal Policy

Expenditure-changing policies can be divided further into monetary and fiscal policy. Fiscal policy can be represented by the national budget, whether surplus or deficit, and has effects on both internal and external balance, through changes in spending by government, households, or business, as noted in Figure 26.1. Monetary policy has two effects. In the first place, changes in the interest rate affect business investment, and through the multiplier, consumer spending. Secondly, however, they give rise to short-term capital movements, assuming that the financial sector is willing to undertake exchange risks. External balance in this formulation is $X + M + LTC + STC = 0$, which differs from the equations given in Chapter 25. In Figure 26.3, internal and external balance are plotted against the national budget and the interest rate, representing fiscal and monetary policy, respectively; the steeper slope of the external balance curve indicates that it is more responsive to monetary policy, with internal balance more responsive to fiscal policy. The curves are drawn for a given cost ratio of domestic wages to international prices, as measured along the vertical axis in Figure 26.1. A change in the exchange rate would displace both of them. An increase in domestic costs relative to foreign prices, from currency appreciation, for example, would shift the external balance

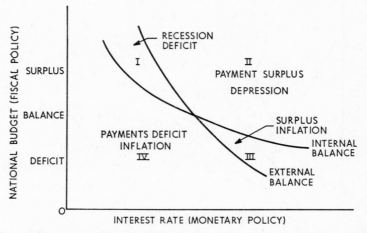

FIG. 26.3. Monetary and Fiscal Policy Used in Pursuit of Internal and External Balance

curve to the right, requiring a higher interest rate to achieve balance at a given government surplus or deficit. At the same time the internal balance curve would be shifted downward and to the left. This follows from the fact that a reduction in spending on exports and import substitutes requires a higher budget deficit at a given interest rate to maintain full employment.

Mundell, who devised this analysis, uses it to address what he calls the assignment problem. In zones II and IV, no assignment problem exists. At a given cost ratio, with stable prices and a fixed exchange rate, monetary and fiscal policy should both be expansionary in zone II and contracting in zone IV. The problems arise in I and III. In the former, with recession and deficit, monetary policy should be assigned to external balance, and tightened, and the fiscal policy to internal balance, and shifted to less surplus or more deficit. To use both in the same direction would be to move in a northeast or southwest direction, parallel to the equilibrium intersection without approaching it, while easier money combined with tighter fiscal policy moves away from equilibrium to the northwest. Since the slope of the external balance curve is steeper than that for internal balance, monetary policy has a comparative advantage in working on external balance, and fiscal policy on internal.

Objection has been raised to Mundell's view of this analysis as adjustment. It is rather, some economists claim, quasi-adjustment. The capital movements produced by capital flows in response to monetary policy are arbitrary, as is the definition of external balance. The capital flows, in particular, may move in the wrong direction from a long-run normative point of view—to the capital-rich country, for example, away from countries needing capital for economic development. This raises a "welfare problem" along with the assignment problem, and detracts from the merits of the analysis except for the short run.

Adjustment in General Equilibrium

The analysis can be made more complex, to include wages, employment, income, money supply, expenditure, the interest rate, and the balance of payments if we move to four quadrants. This is done in Figure 26.4, using the technique of Jaroslav Vanek, modified by Charles Staley. In quadrant I, on its side, are the demand and supply for labor, given in terms of real wages and employment. Employment on the vertical axis is then translated into national income or output in quadrant II, using a production function expressing output in terms of employment which shows diminishing returns to labor inputs, and hence curves upward. In quadrant III, we have the neoclassical income determination synthesis as Samuelson calls it, or a Hansen-Hicks diagram. The LM curve represents a given money supply, and the $IXSM$ the equilibrium level of expenditure where $I + X = S + M$. Under a Keynesian analysis, in the liquidity trap, the LM curve is horizontal and the $IXSM$ curve vertical. In this instance spending determines national income and the money supply affects only the interest rate. Under the classical analysis, on the other hand, the curves would be reversed, the $IXSM$ curve very flat, as expenditure is highly elastic with respect to the rate of interest, and the money curve vertical. In this instance the money supply determines national income (because of constant velocity), and the $IXSM$ curve sets the rate of interest (which is the marginal efficiency of capital). In the neoclassical systhesis, the $IXSM$ curve intersects the LM curve on its upward sloping portion (downward sloping as drawn, because we are upside down in this quadrant). The money supply and equilibrium expenditure together determine both national income and the rate of interest. Note that while exports and imports are involved in the expenditure curve, there is no need for them to balance. The difference between them must equal foreign investment since $X - M = S - I$ (where I is domestic investment).

We reach the balance of payments in the fourth quadrant where the horizontal axis in the first quadrant (real wages or W) is replaced by real output (Y), which is merely measured off the same distance from the origin as in the second and third quadrants. The balance-

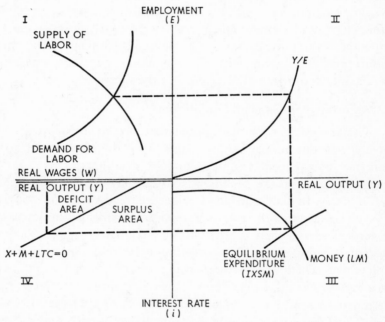

FIG. 26.4. Balance-of-Payment Relationships in General Equilibrium

of-payments schedule here is a function of relative prices at home and abroad (the cost ratio R in Figure 26.1) and of interest rates abroad, as well as of national income and the domestic interest rate. In the purely Keynesian system of Figure 16.8, the balance of payments would be determined exclusively by national income, the interest rate would be fixed in the liquidity trap, and the $X + M + LTC = 0$ curve would be vertical. In a completely classical world, with full employment determining X and M, changes in interest rates alone affect the balance, and the $X + M + LTC = 0$ curve would be horizontal at that level of long-term capital movements which balanced the current account.

The figure is drawn so as to produce balance-of-payments equilibrium in quadrant IV. One can, however, have equilibrium in the labor market, in domestic expenditure, and in the money market, without international payments being balanced. Displace the $X + M + LTC = 0$ downward (from the position drawn), but leave national income and the rate of interest unchanged. This will leave the intersection in quadrant IV at the same place but put it into the deficit area. Such a position could be sustained by spending reserves, as long as they lasted. If it were decided to correct it by basic, rather than quasi-adjustments, a choice would have to be made among:

1. *Exchange depreciation* which would shift the $X + M + LTC = 0$ upward, enlarging the surplus area (it would also shift the *IXSM* curve and possibly the *Y/E*, if the terms of trade changed markedly, but the principal change would occur in the fourth quadrant).

2. *Tight fiscal policy,* which would shift the *IXSM* curve up (as drawn) and to the left, and reduce real output. In the fourth quadrant the reduction of real output would produce a movement to the east, away from deficit, and toward surplus, of the intersection of Y and i despite the lower rate of interest.

3. *A reduced money supply,* which would shift the *LM* curve downward (as drawn), raising interest rates and producing a lower Y and a higher i with a new intersection nearer surplus.

As in all economics, the analysis is relatively simple but there is great difficulty in measuring the slopes of the various curves which determine how the system really works. Under a Keynesian system, expenditure produces equilibrium. Under the quantity theory, it is the money supply, operating on the price level and on the capital flow.

Financing Disequilibrium

"What can't be cured must be endured," and what can't be repressed or corrected must be financed. Financing is required, moreover, when the policies of repression or adjustment take time, or while the automatic forces working for correction produce their results. In the last case, financing may be the best therapy.

The cyclical disequilibria discussed in the last chapter furnish perhaps the most apposite example. To balance international payments in every phase of a business cycle originating at home is to deprive the country of the stabilizing forces of surplus in depression and deficit in prosperity. The payments imbalance will be reduced at the cost of exacerbating domestic imbalance. And to balance international payments in every phase of business cycles originating abroad is to force the country to trace out the foreign cyclical pattern, in greater or lesser degree depending on income elasticities. A system for automatic and immediate payments balance, such as a flexible exchange rate, is thus mistaken to deal with cyclical disequilibrium. It is better to finance the imbalance through the cycle, accumulating foreign exchange reserves through foreign boom, or domestic depression, and spending them in foreign slump or domestic expansion, respectively. When the disequilibria are self-correcting, with or without the aid of built-in stabilizers and regular anticyclical policies, it is better to finance than to suppress or correct, assuming that the financial means are at hand.

Adjustment takes time, and while the adjustment policies are performing their mission, there is need for financing. How much time adjustment takes is likely to be a function of the determination with which the policies are applied, and this may be related to their costs, discussed below. Financing also has a cost. There is a tradeoff between speed of adjustment and readiness to finance the deficit, which is related to the relative costs. But it should also be noted that financing may be undertaken unwisely, as a result of failure to diagnose accurately the nature of the disequilibrium. "If we ignore it, it may go away." The art of government is to know what and what not to ignore in this fashion, and not all administrations have the art.

The Means of Finance

Finance can be provided by national monetary reserves in the form of gold and/or foreign exchange, by short-term capital movements responding automatically to movements of exchange rates, possibly within gold points or similar limits, or by loans from national or international monetary authorities. The use of national reserves presupposes their existence at the start of the trouble. If a primary-producing country, subject to cyclical fluctuations in the price of its exports, adopts a policy of countercyclical financing of the balance of payments at the right moment, at the trough of the cycle, it can accumulate reserves in prosperity and spend them in depression, provided it accurately forecasts the course of prices, incomes, exports and imports, capital movements, and so on, and has the courage not to change its mind as reserves first build up and then dwindle. For the most part, however, it is difficult to start from zero. A country has to have a normal level of reserves as protection against the unexpected, and to seek to operate a cyclical policy from that standard.

International Monetary Fund

Each country can maintain an international reserve provided that there are no persistent deficits (with their accompanying surpluses) which run reserves down for some countries. But this condition was not met in the 1930's, and international monetary reserves became badly skewed. For a fresh postwar start, therefore, the International Monetary Fund was established at Bretton Woods in 1944 to make it possible for countries with limited reserves to finance short-run and transitional deficits. The Fund was established as a pool of central bank reserves and national currencies, available to its members under certain conditions to finance deficits which are likely to be corrected automatically or, in the course of time, with policies already adopted. It could not be used to finance persistent deficits and continue viable, however, so that its operations are undertaken only after a careful examination of a country's conditions and policies.

The Fund differs from an international central bank in that it operates not with its own liabilities but with national moneys. Each member country was originally given a quota, and these quotas have been enlarged from time to time. Twenty-five percent of a country's quota is paid in in gold, and 75 percent in national currency. The gold and national currencies thus accumulated are available for purchase by individual member countries against national currencies, with a limit of 200 percent of the national quota which the Fund can hold in the currency of any country. Since it starts with 75 percent in national currency, this means that a country can purchase foreign exchange up to 125 percent of its quota. The first 25 percent, or "gold tranche," is automatically made available to the country on its request. A further "commodity tranche" is made available quasi-automatically, as noted in Chapter 10, when commodity prices of less developed countries fall. Other 25 percent tranches are dealt in at higher rates of interest, and under more stringent conditions, as the Fund's holding of a national currency increases, in order to ensure that the reserves are used for temporary and not for permanent financing of deficits.

There are limits to the extent of financing of imbalances. The limit of financing by the International Monetary Fund is fixed by Fund policies and a country's quota. How far a surplus country's currency can be used by the Fund depends upon the original quota, 75 percent of which is available in national money. Thereafter the Fund can only acquire the currency with gold. A deficit country using its own gold and foreign exchange reserves is limited by their size. Of course, a country's surplus can be financed much longer; because while there is a finite amount of gold in the world, foreign exchange reserves can be manufactured indefinitely. But the surplus country may be expected to have qualms about exchanging goods with a real cost for claims which may not be convertible in the future into real values. While pressure on the surplus country to bring its financing of balance-of-payments surpluses to a halt is much less than that on the deficit countries, under present institutional arrangements, it nonetheless exists.

Balancing Payments through the Long-Term Capital Account

One special form of financing balance-of-payments disequilibria which has attracted attention in recent years is dealing in long-term securities as if they were short-term, accumulating and running down portfolios of long-term bonds as surplus and deficits succeeded one another. This could be equivalent to financing through short-term capital flows which we have characterized as a quasi-adjustment. The fact that the means of finance is a long-term rather than a demand obligation, seems to make the system more secure.

The question was first raised by Professor Ingram who studied the balance-of-payments adjustment mechanism in Puerto Rico, and observed that Puerto Rican banks accumulated portfolios of U.S. government securities in periods of balance-of-payments surplus and ran them down in deficit. The automatic incomes mechanism was at work, of course, through changes in both spending and in the money supply. But Ingram regarded the change in the security portfolio as complete adjustment through long-term capital, and advocated the spread of the system.

Puerto Rico, however, presents a rather special case. It is part of the U.S. monetary system, and its banks include U.S. bonds among their secondary reserves. The adjustment mechanism is therefore akin to an internal, rather than an external one; that is, one with an integrated long-term capital market, rather than the usual case where only the short-term capital markets are joined. As a rule, banks in one country do not regard the securities of another country as prime investment material. Ingram's adjustment mechanism through the long-term bond market is really equivalent to the interregional adjustment mechanism. Recent interest has been expressed in the adjustment mechanism where national markets are joined by a widely held security common to both, where, that is, the market for financial assets is integrated, as well as the markets for goods and for money (short-term capital). Some interesting theoretical results have been obtained, but it must be stressed that the results are thus far theoretical, rather than practical, since that degree of integration has yet to be achieved.

It may be added, however, that some of the medium-term means of financing the U.S. payments deficit in recent years may have opened the way for medium- and long-term investment of reserves by other countries. The U.S. Treasury has sold large amounts of Roosa bonds to Western European creditor nations. These have included sizable issues of DM-denominated bonds to the German Bundesbank and lira-denominated bonds to the Bank of Italy, the proceeds of which were used to buy back dollars acquired by those banks in exchange operations. The bonds usually have maturities of up to two years and the accumulations of such bonds have risen in periods of surplus for those countries and fallen when Germany and Italy were in deficit. The Swiss authorities have also accumulated large amounts of such special securities from the U.S. Treasury. On the other hand, the British Treasury had a sizable portfolio of U.S. corporate and other securities which had been taken over during the last World War; in recent years that portfolio has been liquidated to bolster official British reserves. Curiously, some of the most recent cosmetic operations by the U.S Treasury—encouraging foreign countries to invest their reserves in time deposits and in government agency securities of more than one-year maturity to improve the "liquidity" balance—work in the direction of establishing medium-term reserves, since many countries have apparently been satisfied to comply, earning higher interest rates in the bargain. Finally, some monetary authorities consider a credit position vis-à-vis the IMF a good medium-term investment. Such loans to the Fund are made by allowing other countries to draw upon the paid-in portion of one's currency under the quota. These claims on the Fund do not earn interest but they carry a tighter guarantee against exchange loss than can be found in foreign currency investments.

The Costs of Adjustment and Financing

There are costs of disequilibria and costs of repressing, correcting or financing them. The costs of disequilibrium have an offsetting benefit. In the deficit country, the benefit is absorption in excess of output; the cost is the loss of reserves, the short-term borrowing, or the unintended foreign aid if the country defaults on its credits, in the last instance a cost borne abroad rather than by the deficit country. There is also likely, however, to be a cost in the loss of credit standing. In the surplus country, the cost is the unintended reduction in absorption below output, whereas the offsetting benefit is the accumulation of claims to future consumption, except where unintended foreign aid offsets the unintended abstinence.

The costs of adjustment have been divided into continuing and transitional. Continuing costs reflect the loss of the benefit from the disequilibrium on the part of the deficit country. But this neglects the offsetting cost of disequilibrium. The real issue is the transitional costs from disequilibrium to equilibrium, and the costs of running the international monetary system so that it is able to function effectively.

Quasi-adjustment have costs in distorting resource allocation, and in operating the system. There is great dispute over the size of these costs. Liberals regard them as high; interventionists as trivial. The latter insist that monopoly, taxation, producer and consumer ignorance are already so great that a little more misallocation through tariffs, quotas, capital restrictions and foreign exchange control fails to hurt. The liberal worries that if a government starts off to intervene by trying to reshape deep-seated forces, it will only make things worse, requiring more and more bureaucrats in time to do a poorer and poorer job. This book is no place to try to resolve these issues, though it is perhaps useful to point both to government success in the area of maintaining employment and its persistent failure successfully to diagnose and cure balance-of-payments disequilibria.

The costs of basic adjustment are on the whole well understood. Adjustment through deflation in the deficit country has a cost of unemployment when wages are sticky, and when world demand is not particularly buoyant. Adjustment through price inflation in the surplus country has a cost in the distortion of debtor-creditor and fixed income/variable income relationships. Adjustment through changing the exchange rate, so frequently that in the limit it approaches the flexible exchange rate system, has the disabilities of possibly encouraging destabilizing speculation, though there is debate on the point, and further of disintegrating the world economy to the extent that traders and investors are risk averters and would choose under these circumstances to abandon foreign trade and investment. The argument is made that the risks of change are as great with fixed exchange rates, and merely take a different form: tariffs, surcharges, exchange controls, and the like. With fixed exchange rates, however, there is a commitment to adjustment and equilibrium about the existing rate which encourages traders and investors to maximize by trading and investing beyond the national borders. With flexible exchange rates, goods and capital markets are less likely to remain integrated. And flexible exchange rates produce some changes in rates, leading to reallocation of resources, e.g., in the business cycle, which later must be reversed.

Financing disequilibria has costs too. A country which balances its foreign exchange over the cycle by running reserves up and down incurs the cost of maintaining an average cyclical level of reserves, a sum which could have been spent for real capital assets had it not been needed to finance disequilibria. The cost of holding gold reserves is the opportunity cost represented by the real productive assets which could have been bought with exports. To the world as a whole, the cost of gold reserves is the labor and capital which went into mining, transporting, and storing it. Holding foreign exchange reserves on which interest can be earned is evidently cheaper than holding gold, but if the return on real assets is higher than that on liquid monetary assets, the cost will be positive.

International reserves can be increased by output in excess of absorption, i.e., by running an export surplus and using it to buy reserves. But reserves can also be borrowed. A credit-worthy country can borrow at long term in an international financial center and hold the proceeds at interest in that center. The cost of holding these reserves is the difference between the long-term rate at which it borrows and the short-term rate at which it lends. When it uses the reserves to finance a deficit, however, it must forego the return on the reserves held, and this is the cost of financing the deficit. If the balance of payments is likely to be restored automatically or with the aid of policies adopted, this cost is not likely to be large. If, on the other hand, the deficit is a persistent one, interest must be paid on the original debt for a long time.

The costs of borrowing are not limited to the payment of interest, and debtor countries often have to pledge drastic policy changes in order to obtain credit. For small countries, the IMF exacts strict promises regarding changes in exchange rates and monetary and fiscal policies before it provides credit-tranche loans. When major industrial countries borrow heavily, even through the IMF, they often have to agree to follow specific policy prescriptions suggested by the creditors. This process among major countries has been formalized into what is called "multilateral surveillance" under which officials of various countries meet monthly to review and often to criticize sharply each others' policies.

Dividing the Costs and the Responsibility for Disequilibria between Deficit and Surplus Countries

In his proposed International Clearing Union circulated before Bretton Woods, Lord Keynes proposed that interest be charged on balances at the clearing union, whether they were positive or negative. The point was to penalize surpluses as well as deficits in international payments, and to provide surplus countries with an incentive to correct their imbalances, parallel to that existing for deficit countries with their cost of deficit. During and after the war, other suggestions were put forward for putting all the burden of adjustment in the surplus country, including some which would have required surplus countries to spend their credit balances within a specified period of time or have them written off. This would have meant that they would give away their export surplus.

The point is well taken that under existing arrangements the cost of disequilibrium falls almost entirely on the deficit country, and that this is not necessarily equitable. It is clearly inequitable where a country permits itself to go into recession and runs a surplus. In this circumstance, the deflating country is responsible for the payments imbalance, and has its internal imbalance (unemployment) moderated by the external imbalance (payments surplus), but the cost falls on the innocent party or parties abroad. On the other hand, when the deficit is owing to inflation at home rather than deflation abroad, the deficit country is responsible for the imbalance, and has its rise of prices dampened by the availability of goods from abroad. In this circumstance it is entirely appropriate that it bear the burden of correcting the imbalance, and of financing it.

The answer as to how the costs of financing and correcting payments disequilibria should be distributed thus depends upon the state of world resource use. In depression, the surplus country is exporting unemployment to the rest of the world and fairly may be asked to take a major share of these costs. This and the memory of the depressed 1930's accounts for the proposals to shift part of the costs to the surplus country. In prosperity, on the other hand, the deficit country is exporting inflation. Responsibility for the imbalance belongs to it, and so should the costs of financing and correcting.

Where the disequilibrium is of the long-run secular type, with secular exhilaration, as we called it above, in developing countries, and an excess of savings over domestic investment in the developed, capital markets must be organized so as to produce capital exports from the surplus country on current account, and capital imports in the countries with capital account deficits. But excess savings in the one need not match excess of investment in the other. The task then is, by successive approximations, to produce capital movements to fit local spending and investing propensities, and then local spending and investing propensities to fit capital movement, until the long-term capital movement matches current account surpluses and deficits which are identical *ex ante*. This requires building capital market institutions in the surplus countries, and credit worthiness in the deficit countries, to the extent that the International Bank and foreign aid do not fill the gap. Under a classical mechanism, of course, the demand for excess savings of the deficit countries is matched by the supply of excess saving of the surplus countries through the interest rate. This mechanism fails to function in depression, but comes into its own more fully in world prosperity.

Summary

Payments disequilibria can be repressed, corrected, or financed. Quasi-adjustments which repress disequilibria distort resource allocation and in the limit, under foreign exchange control, represent the disequilibrium system. Correction involves basic adjustments, typically of either the expenditure-switching or expenditure-changing type. Expenditure switching involves altering the ratio of international prices to domestic prices or wages by exchange rate changes or by relative inflation or deflation with a fixed rate. Expenditure changes may come about through fiscal or monetary policy. Fiscal policy has a comparative advantage on internal balance in the economy, while monetary policy has an advantage in external balance because of its effect on capital movements. To the extent that these are short-term capital movements, or long-term capital movements in the wrong direction, from the point of view of economic development and welfare, the impact of monetary policy on capital flows produces quasi- rather than basic adjustment.

Financing disequilibria is called for when they are self-correcting, or when the basic remedies adopted take time to work out. Repression, correction, and financing all have costs. The burden of these costs typically falls on the deficit country. In depression, however, this is not equitable.

SUGGESTED READING

TEXTS

Yeager, chaps. 6, 7, 8; Clement, Pfister and Rothwell, chap. v.

TREATISES

See essays by Swan, "Longer-run Problems of the Balance of Payments," Johnson, "Toward a General Theory of the Balance of Payments," and Metzler "The Process of International Adjustment under Conditions of Full Employment: A Keynesian View," in American Economic Association, *Readings in International Economics;* Mundell's "The Appropriate Use of Monetary and Fiscal Policy for Internal and External Stability," *SP,* April, 1962, and W. Fellner, F. Machlup, and R. Triffin (eds.), *Maintaining and Restoring Balance in International Payments* (Princeton, N.J.: Princeton University Press, 1966).

POINTS

For the distinction between quasi- and basic adjustments, see John H. Williamson, "The Crawling Peg," *EIF*, 1965. That between continuing and adjustment costs in adjustment is made by Benjamin J. Cohen in *Adjustment Costs and the Distribution of New Reserves*, Princeton Studies in International Finance No. 18 (Princeton, N.J.: Princeton University Press, 1966).

The suggestion of James Ingram for settling balance-of-payments disequilibria through long-term bonds was put forward in "A Proposal for Financial Integration of the Atlantic Community," in Joint Economic Committee, *Factors Affecting the United States Balance of Payments*, 87th Cong., 2nd sess. (Washington, D.C.: U.S. Government Printing Office, 1962). A brilliant theoretical exercise in integrated capital markets is in R. I. McKinnon and W. E. Oates, *The Implications of International Economic Integration for Monetary, Fiscal, and Exchange-Rate Policy*, Princeton Studies in International Finance No. 16 (Princeton, N.J.: Princeton University Press, 1966).

Chapter 27

INTERNATIONAL

MONETARY

ARRANGEMENTS

Adjustment, Liquidity, and Confidence

A group of 32 economists examining the international monetary system broke down the problem into adjustment, liquidity, and confidence. The previous chapter sought to deal with adjustment. In this chapter we take up liquidity and confidence. Liquidity deals with the amount of financing the international monetary system has readily available to meet disequilibria it chooses to finance or must finance during the process of adjustment. Confidence in the system is needed to ensure that individual countries, believing the system to be breaking down, do not bring about the fulfillment of their fears in trying to make money (private destabilizing speculators) or to protect their national interest (the monetary authorities).

Liquidity and confidence cannot be discussed without frequent reference back to adjustment. With persistent disequilibrium, no system can provide enough liquidity, nor can confidence in any system survive. Sooner or later quasi-adjustments are required, and the system develops into a disequilibrium one. If adjustment works well, on the other hand, there will be little need for liquidity in the international monetary system, nor will the maintenance of confidence pose a problem. It is when adjustment works, but slowly and not very well that liquidity and confidence pose real issues.

Foreign Exchange Flexibility

The amount of reserves needed by the international monetary system turns largely on the characteristics of the adjustment mechanism. Under the freely flexible exchange system, with no intervention in the exchange market by monetary authorities, there is no need for international reserves. The foreign exchange market has to clear itself, and that is that. In the opinion of some economists this is a very good system. They regard it likely that monetary and fiscal policy will be operated with a view to maintaining stability in international payments; that speculation in foreign exchange markets will be stabilizing, to adjust the exchange rate to new circumstances smoothly over time; and that the risks which might discourage trade can be met through the development of a forward market. These views do not go uncontested. On the last point, for example, it is argued in Appendix H that forward markets produce no fundamental change in conditions, providing only institutional convenience; it is in any event impossible to use short-term hedging devices as a means of ensuring against long-term risks. Speculation is believed to be destabilizing on occasion, especially under unsettled conditions, causing exaggerated rather than moderated movements of exchange rates. And there is opinion, though the matter is debatable, that fixed exchange rates are a better device for imposing discipline on the authorities than a flexible rate. This implies that monetary and fiscal authorities respond with greater alacrity to a decline in reserves than they do to a decline in the exchange rate—a point on which it is easy to theorize but difficult to have certain knowledge.

The major argument against the freely flexible exchange rate is that it cuts off national economies from one another. Trade, finance, and especially long-term capital movements needed for world integration are almost certain to be reduced by the added risks of exchange fluctuations.

Between the freely flexible exchange rate at one extreme and the permanently fixed rate at the other, four from among a wide number of possibilities may be distinguished: the flexible exchange rate with government intervention; the wide band; the adjustable peg; and the sliding peg. All seek to make use of expenditure-switching policy for adjustment; all require liquidity in the system to finance transitional disequilibria.

The flexible exchange rate with government intervention presupposes that government can recognize transitory influences that should not be allowed to move the exchange rate or set in motion resource reallocation, and those that do. In a business cycle of the sort described in Chapter 25, for example, governmental authorities would spend reserves or draw on the IMF during a deficit period, and restock or repay during a surplus. The authorities would allow the rate to move in response to other influences, such as the structural sort, representing a change in demand or supply. The flexible exchange rate advocate who opposes intervention believes that governments are no better at distinguishing temporary from far-reaching effects than are private speculators. Those who want flexibility with intervention must take the position that they are.

The wide-band proposal, originally put forward by Keynes and revived by George Halm, compromises by having freely fluctuating exchanges within a band wide enough to have effects on resource allocation, but not so wide as to discourage international economic intercourse because of risk. Plus or minus 10 percent of parity is contemplated, in contrast to plus or minus 1 or 2 percent under existing arrangements. It is thought, or hoped, that wider movements in exchange rates will achieve some adjustment through expenditure switching, while containing destabilizing speculation and forestalling exaggerated fluctuations of the exchange rate feared by risk averters. Presumably movements within the band are not so wide as to discourage trade and investment, and not too limited to promote adjustment. The wide-band proposal lies between fixity and flexibility of the exchange. It satisfies the proponents of neither extreme position.

The adjustable peg is a fixed rate which is changed from time to time. This is in fact the position adopted in the Articles of Agreement of the IMF at Bretton Woods in 1944, when it was agreed that small movements in the exchange rate were permitted at any time, and larger movements in the event of fundamental disequilibrium. In practice, however, the international monetary system seems to be evolving toward fixed rates. The adjustable peg is said to stimulate destabilizing speculation by providing speculators a "one-way option": when a currency is in trouble, there is no chance of it going up, and considerable chance of it going down. It is therefore safe to speculate against it. Moreover, when changes in the rate are made they are likely to go too far. An overvalued currency which has been under pressure is set at a new rate where there will be no chance of further adverse speculation, which means that it will be undervalued. Undervaluation of one currency leaves another one or more currencies overvalued, so that bear or short speculation shifts to them. In this fashion, a national crisis of adjustment escalates into "structural" crisis and then possibly into a "systems" crisis in which the monetary mechanism breaks down. But to make only small adjustments leaves open the possibility that more will be needed. When the German mark and the Dutch florin were revalued upward by 5 percent in March, 1961, the market regarded the move as the first step, and shifted heavily into DM and florins out of sterling and dollars. This led to the Basel arrangements for containing crises, under which officials of major central banks meeting at the Bank for International Settlements (BIS) at Basel, Switzerland, undertook to buy and hold the weak currencies in a crisis, thus extending massive short-term credits. When the crisis was over, the dollar position had been reversed, and the *Bundesbank* holdings of sterling were converted into a longer credit at the IMF. While the episode improved the international monetary machinery through the construction of the Basel arrangements, it discouraged further interest in exchange rate adjustment. Exchange rates will be adjusted when the pressure against a currency proves irresistible, as against sterling in 1949 and 1967 and the French franc in 1958. The adjustable peg, however, is not esteemed as a system.

The sliding or crawling peg was devised as a further and more subtle compromise between adjustment through expenditure switching, plus integration through confidence in international values, while limiting destabilizing speculation. Under this scheme, rates are free to move but only in a limited amount each period. Successive movements in the same direction for successive periods will result in a discrete change, but the change in any one period is not sufficient to encourage speculation. One suggestion, for example, is to limit the change in the gold or exchange support point to $\frac{1}{6}$th percent a month, or 2 percent a year if the trend is steadily in one direction. The return to speculation would be relatively uninteresting if the currency under attack had short-term interest rates above those in the "safer" financial center. The sliding peg system has evoked considerable academic interest, but like all proposals for exchange rate flexibility, it has not been taken up by business or governmental circles.

The Canadian Flexible Rate

This last statement is not entirely accurate. Canada adopted a flexible exchange rate with intervention in 1950, but gave it up 11 years later. Short-term capital movements in and out of Canada performed in stabilizing fashion; but long-term capital movements ignored the movement of the exchange rate and continued to drive the exchange rate up because of the high interest rates available in Canada. High interest rates led to deflation not directly through reductions in spending so much as by the attraction of U.S. capital, appreciation of the Canadian dollar, and falling production for exports and of import substitutes. Instead of freeing monetary policy for domestic use, the flexible exchange rate system altered the mechanism.

This may not be a general result, capable of being extended to all countries. The U.S. and Canadian capital markets have long been integrated, and the long-run expectation on both sides of the border is that in the long run, the Canadian dollar and the U.S. dollar will not vary widely from one another. For long-term bonds, any possible premium or discount in the exchange rate divided by the years of maturity of the bond is likely to be less significant than a 1 percent difference in yield year after year. Where there is no benchmark to which the currency is likely to return, or from which it is unlikely to depart widely, it is by no means certain that long-term capital movements would be sustained.

The Canadian experience must therefore be scored as inconclusive. There are those who claim it was a successful test of a flexible exchange rate ruined by ill-conceived Canadian monetary policy. To others, the lesson is that a flexible exchange rate system fails to isolate domestic policy from international effects, rather along the lines of the Laursen-Metzler theorem of Chapter 17. In either case, there is doubt that the lesson has wide applicability.

The Optimum Currency Area

A system of permanently fixed rates is equivalent to the existence of a single world money. A system in which exchange rates can alter on the other hand, divides the world into separate moneys. How finely divided should the world be? Why stop at countries rather than at groups of countries at a higher level, or regions, states, areas at a lower. Would it help Appalachia to have a separate currency and a variable rate of exchange? These questions can be merged in the issue, what is the optimum currency area?

Mundell was the first to pose the question, and he answered it in classical fashion by reference to factor mobility. A region is an area within which factors are mobile, while factors are not mobile between regions. Lacking factor mobility as a means of adjustment, one needs another degree of freedom, such as exchange rate variability provides. The region, in his view, should have a separate currency, a region which would sometimes be larger than a country, as in the European Economic Community, but sometimes smaller than a country, as in the Maritime Provinces of Canada or Appalachia in the United States. Changing money is costly, to be sure, and in terms of convenience one should have as large as possible a currency area. But against this gain is the cost of having to endure unemployment as a means of balancing interregional accounts when the rate is fixed and emigration is limited.

A critic of Mundell, McKinnon, argues that factor mobility is not the essence of the optimum currency area. In his view, the need is for a closed economy, that is an economy which has a large volume of internal transactions and a small volume of external, so that when exchange rate changes occur, the impact of the change in foreign prices on the level of living of the community is not noticed. The need is for what may be called exchange illusion, after the analogy of money illusion which disregards changes in prices and thinks that changes in money incomes are equivalent to changes in real incomes, even when prices have altered. The three goals of economic policy are full employment, balanced external payments, and price stability. In an open economy where exchange rate changes are used to achieve the first two goals, the third goal is missed because exchange depreciation causes foreign prices to rise, or exchange appreciation causes foreign prices to fall. The price changes lead to changes in real income which stimulate changes in spending. In a closed economy, on the other hand, the change in foreign prices goes unnoticed and exchange rate changes do not lead to changes in spending. Closed economies may or may not coincide with regions of external factor immobility suggested by Mundell as the optimum currency area. The criterion is different. The Maritime Provinces and Appalachia would not qualify for a separate currency, quite apart from the transactions cost of money changing. And there may be asymmetries: the United States is a relatively closed economy with exchange illusion; on the other hand; many of the countries with which the United States trades, such as Canada and the countries of Latin America, buy so much from the United States that its prices affect their cost of living. These countries may join the dollar area; the United States is unconcerned whether they do or not.

In a pamphlet put out in Canada, Professor Mundell thought it might be useful to organize the world outside the Soviet bloc into three broad currency areas, tied to the dollar, sterling, and European currencies, with freedom of exchange movements among the three (though with settlement of some imbalances in gold), but fixed exchange rates within the blocs and financing of imbalances in foreign exchange. This is a neat plan—probably too neat. There will be third countries such as Japan or Australia, which straddle the two blocs, as Canada did before the war, and which would want to split the difference if the dollar-sterling rate were changed. Nor should the smaller countries of the sterling area be forced to hold only sterling, or the countries of Europe to evolve a reserve currency to replace their gold and dollars. Economic spheres of influence are not so tidy.

The Fixed Exchange Rate System

The evolution of exchange rates since 1961 suggests that the optimum currency area is the world outside of the Soviet bloc. This system has lost one degree of freedom in producing international adjustment. If deflation is also excluded, adjustment is produced through income changes under the Keynesian system and price inflation in the surplus countries when full employment has been reached. This works slowly. Accordingly it needs a large volume of financing. The cost of the system is the cost of providing the financing, and the costs of inflation in the surplus country. The system should be adopted, nonetheless, if these costs are less than those arising from disintegration of the world economy, in trade or capital markets, under a system in which exchange rates are altered.

Adequacy of Reserves for Liquidity

As early as 1958, a number of observers, notably Lord Franks and Maxwell Stamp in Britain, and Robert Triffin in the United States, came to believe that world reserves were too small to support the system. Professor Triffin pointed to the difficulties of the exchange standard system, which we will postpone for discussion under the section "Confidence," and noted that gold production was expanding at the rate of $1\frac{1}{2}$ percent a year while world trade grew normally at 3 percent a year, with a postwar growth at the phenomenal rates of 8 or 9 percent. Historical comparison with 1938 when world monetary gold equaled more than 90 percent of world imports, was of course misleading, since this was a period when gold had just risen in price (in 1934) and world trade was unduly depressed. But as trade continued to expand after the end of the 1950's, and gold went increasingly into industrial use and monetary hoards outside the United States, the ratio of gold to world trade continued to decline overall. It declined especially in the United States, where it has been very high—over 100 percent of annual imports, and in fact rose outside the United States and Britain.

The rule of thumb put forward by Triffin was that reserves should amount to 40 percent of annual imports. This rule presupposes some constant velocity of circulation of reserves and reflects a quantity theory of international money, perhaps appropriate for trading countries. Countries which function as banks, as noted in Chapter 24, need no reserves if their customers will accept their liabilities, and a very large amount if they have to pay off old liabilities in addition to meeting current deficits. The rule of thumb hardly applies to them. But Triffin assumed that this form of international banking which created reserves against deficits, mainly those under definitions which score international financial intermediation as a balance-of-payments deficit, could not continue. Accordingly he, along with many other observers, saw a need to provide new forms of liquidity for the system.

There are many ways to expand liquidity. Sir Roy Harrod of

Britain and Jacques Rueff of France want to raise the price of gold, thus altering the value of the existing stock and increasing the volume and the value of current gold output. Most economists regard this as a method with arbitrary costs and benefits, which, if seriously contemplated, would set off a speculative rush into gold, and if carried out would make it transparently clear that gold is merely a poker chip of no intrinsic value which can be given arbitrary values from time to time.

If reserves can be held in foreign exchange, countries can undertake mutual swaps at any given time, to add to gross, but not to net reserves; or can choose to settle deficits by increasing the liabilities of the deficit country, rather than reducing its assets.

If balance-of-payments equilibrium were redefined so as to include financial intermediation by principal international financial centers when they lend long and borrow short, reserves in the system could be enlarged when credit-worthy individuals and countries borrow at long term abroad and acquire short-term assets.

What are the criteria for adequacy of reserves for a country, and for the world as a whole? The quantity theory rule of thumb of 40 percent for a trader, and some undecided ratio for a banker country have been mentioned. More sophisticated analysis suggests a variety of possibilities. There may be some optimum level of reserves for a country, where the costs of holding reserves balance the benefits they produce. These benefits must be expressed in terms of probabilities, calculated on the basis of the likelihood of running out of reserves and the penalty for doing so. Or in some formulations, what counts is not the absolute level of reserves but the change, which is satisfactory so long as it is positive. Professor Machlup has immortalized his wife's wardrobe by suggesting that reserves may be like ladies' dresses with no finite level sufficient and the optimal position one of steady accretions.

For the world as a whole, there is again the quantity theory, based on trade, and criteria which emphasize the behavior of the system. Many analysts say that reserves are adequate if world prices are steady, or creep upward at a sufficiently modest rate. World price deflation would then bespeak inadequacy of reserves, and rapid inflation excess abundance. Or the matter may be put in terms of pressures on the deficit and surplus countries: when the burden of adjustment falls primarily on the deficit countries, Mundell has suggested, world reserves are inadequate; when it falls primarily on the surplus countries, they are excessive. This formulation has the advantage of pointing to the distribution of world reserves, but lacks operational significance. There is no way to measure and compare the pressures to adjust balances of payments.

Confidence

If reserves are measured in terms of gold and foreign exchange, instead of merely gold, it turns out that the total is highly variable. Total reserves can be expanded when gold in *B* is sold for foreign exchange on *A*. There are now both gold and foreign exchange when there was only gold before. Or foreign exchange can be converted into gold and shrink the reserves of the system. Triffin observed that the gold exchange standard was highly unstable. A given currency is strong. Various countries try to accumulate foreign exchange reserves on that country. They succeed, with the result that it now has a large volume of liabilities to the rest of the world and looks weak. The consequence is that foreign countries convert their exchange reserves to gold or to other stronger currencies and total reserves in the system are reduced. If the reserve center acted as a bank in lending out the reserves deposited with it, and could not cash in its assets or rediscount them, the country might not be able to meet its liabilities, and would be forced to depreciate its currency.

This criticism of the gold exchange standard is a valid one. Unless it is stabilized in some way, the gold exchange standard is unstable. The phenomenon is an ancient one embodied in the principle discovered by Sir Thomas Gresham, who was the Chancellor of the Exchequer under Queen Elizabeth I, that bad money drives out good. Two moneys function badly side by side unless their price is firmly established, as firmly, for example, as that between demand deposits and paper money in the United States. Bimetalism, or coins with a high metal value functioning alongside paper, or gold and a national currency tend to constitute unstable monetary systems.

A number of suggestions have been put forward to cope with the confidence problem. One class of such plans tries to fix the price between gold and foreign exchange, by giving gold guarantees to holders of foreign exchange. Such guarantees pose such serious administrative problems that they have not been adopted. Professor Posthuma of the Netherlands has suggested that central banks should all hold a standard proportion of foreign exchange and gold. This is felt to be unworkable since the maximum that certain banks would accept is well above present levels of many central banks and would become their minimum, with increased rather than reduced immediate conversion of exchange into gold.

Another class of proposals is to reduce international reserve media from two categories, gold and foreign exchange, to one. Under French plans, propounded principally by Professor Rueff, foreign exchange holdings would be abolished. As already noted, this would require an increase in the gold price to prevent a substantial reduction in the volume of world reserves. The alternative is to move out of gold into foreign exchange. Machlup and Despres have each suggested that the United States should lower the gold price, or undertake to sell gold but not to buy it back, as a means of discouraging gold hoarders and stimulating them to disgorge. At the extreme, the purpose would be to demonetize gold as an international money and move to a single foreign exchange standard.

The Triffin Plan

Triffin's remedy for the weakness of the gold exchange standard, and to correct for the inadequacy of world reserves, current or prospective (it is not entirely clear which), has been to internationalize foreign exchange holdings. A new international organization, or an expanded International Monetary Fund (XIMF), would have existing dollar and sterling balances transferred to it as liabilities, with a corresponding claim against the United States and Britain, which would be liquidated slowly at a rate appropriate to world balance-of-payments stability. The liabilities would be expressed in terms of a new currency, *bancor,* which would become an international reserve asset, along with gold. New bancor could be created by the XIMF, through open-market operations which exchanged new bancor liabilities for national securities. Or the XIMF could buy the bonds of the International Bank for Reconstruction and Development with bancor which the IBRD would lend to the less developed countries (LDC's). In this way the XIMF could kill three birds with one stone: stabilize the gold exchange standard, expand world reserves, and provide real resources to the LDC's. The last item was also the central feature of the Stamp plan which would increase world reserves by issuing new international money to the LDC's to be spent by them on exports of the developed countries.

Questions have been raised on the first and third features of the Triffin plan. Conversion of foreign exchange reserves to bancor still leaves two international reserve assets, gold and bancor, with the possibility of instability between them. So long as national central banks could switch back and forth between gold and bancor, the instability problem had been altered, but not inevitably cured. The creation of reserves by lending to the LDC's for spending in the developed countries, moreover, suggests persistent deficits and persistent credits, which are an unsatisfactory basis for a clearing system. As the liabilities of the

LDC's to the IBRD mount, and the claims of the developed countries on the XIMF, it will be increasingly difficult to sustain the essential myth that bancor has value. The value of an international money is what it will buy. Behind the dollar and sterling stands the productivity of the U.S. and British economies. Claims on the LDC's with their indifferent productivity, however, are hardly a better basis for an international money than the counterpart funds which the United States does not include in its foreign exchange reserves.

Reserve Units

The Triffin analysis on the volume of liquidity was accepted more widely than that on the instability of the gold exchange standard with two reserve assets. Proposals for expanding liquidity were put forward on all sides. Most of these took the form of adding a third international reserve asset in the form of paper gold, reserve units, or international units. Most prominent among them were the proposals of Robert V. Roosa, as he resigned from the Undersecretaryship of the U.S. Treasury; of E. M. Bernstein, formerly of the IMF staff; and of Giscard d'Estaing, the then French Minister of Finance. For a while the air was blue with plans for international monetary reform.

In 1963, the U.S. Treasury itself accepted the position that the world needed more liquidity. United States balance-of-payments deficits, it was hoped, would be halted by the IET and the VCRP; when that happened, it was clear that new gold production would be insufficient to expand international reserves at 3 percent a year by itself. There was doubt whether European central banks would be willing to accept more dollars. Accordingly the Secretary of the Treasury proposed the U.S. plan for monetary reform, based largely on the ideas of Roosa and Bernstein. When it became clear that no plan could be negotiated so long as the U.S. balance-of-payments deficit persisted, the United States shifted to a "contingency plan," to be ready when the deficit did come to a halt and left annual additions to world liquidity inadequate. The task of negotiating a plan was taken up by the Group of Ten, representing the 10 leading financial countries of the world, other than Switzerland, which had extended extra borrowing powers to the IMF in September, 1961, after the Basel arrangement of the previous March, called General Arrangements to Borrow (GAB). Various bodies of the Group of Ten (sometimes called the G-10) prepared reports on the development of a new reserve unit, reports issued in August, 1964, May, 1965, and July, 1966. But the G-10 could not for a time agree on a single plan.

The proposed new international asset was to be created primarily by pledging national currencies. Various countries would put up their own money and be issued international reserve units, RU's, which they would agree to accept along with gold as an ultimate means of international settlement. A series of questions immediately arises:

Who decides about RU's, and especially, does any one country or group of countries have a veto?

Who receives the original issues of RU's, and in particular, are RU's to be kept within the narrow circle of financially responsible countries, which are in a position to pledge a valuable national currency, or should LDC's be accorded added reserves?

Should RU's be created according to the needs of trade, or of finance as well? How many should be created? Should the amount be fixed several years at a time, or varied to meet current conditions?

How can RU's be kept in circulation? Will they be as good as gold, but no better than dollars and sterling? Is it desirable to set limits to holdings, a minimum which a country must hold, a maximum beyond which it can convert RU's to gold?

Are the RU's issued outright, or are they borrowed and subject to repayment like IMF drawing rights?

On these questions, the deficit and the surplus countries naturally disagreed. The United States reluctantly admitted that no plan was needed so long as its balance-of-payments deficit continued, and that no plan would work while major deficits persisted. It nonetheless wanted larger amounts issued, on a regular basis, and in outright form, while the surplus countries, led by France, leaned to smaller amounts, on a repayment basis. The French once even proposed issuing RU's on the basis of world gold holdings, which would have touched off a scramble for gold and run world reserves sharply down. Such a plan would have been equivalent to an increase in price of existing gold stocks, and could have been extended to new production. One proposal was to require gold settlements to be accompanied by a fixed proportion of RU's, which would have raised the gold price for current transactions, but without the destabilizing initial scramble. But the fourth in the list of questions above indicates that the Group of Ten had a difficult if not impossible task on its hands in creating a new international unit along with gold and existing supplies of foreign exchange, and solving the Gresham or Triffin problem of confidence. If there is difficulty in maintaining equality between gold and dollars, it is squaring the circle to create a new international asset which is as good as gold but no better than the dollar.

In the summer of 1967, agreement was reached by the G-10 on

lines largely favoring the position of the creditor countries. Rather than RU's or paper gold which would be issued by on an irredeemable basis, the IMF would issue Special Drawing Rights (SDR's), in addition to its regular quotas and the General Arrangements to Borrow. These SDR's would have to be partly repaid in that each country which used them would be obligated to reconstitute at least 30 percent of its original allotment at specified times, through exchanging gold or foreign exchange reserves for SDR's. SDR's would be issued in proportion to national quotas in the IMF, which would provide the LDC's with a limited increase in reserves when issues took place. Once the Articles of the IMF had been amended to make the issue of SDR's possible, actual issues required an 85 percent majority vote, which gave the EEC the possibility of vetoing a new issue.

As these lines are written, the new program has a long way to go—approval by the Board of Governors of the IMF, approval by the legislatures of the various countries, and particularly by the Congress of the United States, and finally the achievement of an 85 percent majority in the IMF and the actual issuance of SDR's. It is premature to comment on how the plan will work in operation, and futile to criticize the negotiators who got the best agreement they could from a world of disagreement. But the total international monetary machine begins to acquire a Rube Goldberg look: gold, dollars and sterling, IMF drawing rights, special arrangements to borrow, swaps, Roosa bonds, and now a new hybrid drawing right. The international liquidity problem may be solved, in a mechanical quantity-theory way, but to keep the various reserve assets equivalent to one another, as the confidence problem requires, does not look so easy. And is the machinery complicated!

Owned versus Borrowed Reserves and Crises

The volume of owned reserves necessary to finance an outflow of capital in a crisis is likely to be unduly large for periods of calm, so large in fact that the cost of holding such reserves—the opportunity cost of not spending them for real assets—would weigh heavily on the country concerned. An international banking system needs owned reserves for normal periods, but rediscount facilities for conditions of upset, just as a domestic banking system does. Walter Bagehot, the first economist to rationalize the system of central banking, asserted that the task of a central bank in a crisis was to discount and discount freely. Most of the discussion of liquidity has run in terms of owned reserves, appropriate for trading firms and settled conditions. Missing from the bulk of the discussion, however, has been the provision of rediscount facilities, needed especially by the financial centers when they are subject to the strain of destabilizing speculation.

The Basel agreement provided such a mechanism, and the original rediscounting of dollars and sterling in March, 1961, has been followed by similar operations in the Canadian dollar, the Italian lira, and on three further occasions, the pound. The arrangements are informal. The country under attack has no rights to require other central banks to extend it credit as a commercial bank has vis-à-vis its domestic central bank; it has merely a right to ask. But the system has worked well. An international central bank would doubtless be better if there were sufficient consensus on the needs of the system to enable the statutes of such an institution to be drawn up. The Bretton Woods experience is not encouraging: the IMF operates in national currencies and with strict limits, in contravention to the Bagehot rule that there should be no limit. And the G-10 discussions reveal the current basic rift among countries. (It is ironic that the United States was the power that held back the grandiose schemes of Lord Keynes in 1944, when the United States was the major creditor country of the world, but shifted sides when its payments moved to deficit.) An informal arrangement which works is better than a more elaborate organization with a constitution which represents a lower common denominator of agreement at a level which fails to meet the problem.

Liquidity and International Financial Intermediation

The distinction between owned and borrowed reserves has significance beyond financial crises. The literature on the international monetary system largely assumes that reserves must be owned, earned by payments surpluses taken in foreign exchange, with the latter matched by payments deficits on the part of the financial centers. But these surpluses and deficits by no means necessarily represent saving and dissaving respectively. Given present widely used definitions of balance-of-payments equilibrium, they may consist in financial intermediation, lending long and borrowing short by the deficit country, and borrowing long and lending short by the surplus. This creates liquidity for the system and for the surplus country through borrowing foreign exchange. Liquidity furnished in this way is provided when and as needed. In this respect it differs from that injected into the international monetary system by gold mining, or pumped in by an XIMF, both of which are rather arbitrary.

A well-functioning international capital market can furnish liquidity to countries of good credit standing, and to firms and governmental entities within such countries. The process requires a redefinition of balance-of-payments disequilibrium, to ensure that not all international financial intermediation is regarded as a deficit. A country can overdo lending long and borrowing short, just as a bank can. But just as a bank is not necessarily in deficit and headed for bankruptcy when it lends long and borrows short, neither is a country. Provided the loans are good, and the acceptance of foreign deposits does not go so far as to raise questions as to the capacity of the country to meet its obligations, financial intermediation performs a useful function, and constitutes a desirable method of providing liquidity for the system.

The international monetary system finds itself today in a paradoxical position. Most economists, and most government officials, think the system is unsatisfactory and want to change it drastically by a major reform. The difficulty is that while the diagnoses of the system agree—not enough adjustment, liquidity, or confidence—the remedies do not. As a result, the unsatisfactory system cannot be altered and must limp along, with many observers predicting crises, as they have done for 10 years. Meanwhile, however, the system seems to work very well indeed. World trade grows from year to year. A French attempt to alter the system by converting dollars into gold produced no perceptible effect. Adjustment in the balance of payments of the United States is slow, but the current account moved from less than $1 billion of surplus to more than $7 billions from 1959 to 1964. Despite the Interest Equalization Tax and the Voluntary Credit Restraint Program, dollars move abroad, and the Euro-dollar market performs a highly useful function in providing liquidity to countries in need of it, Italy to the extent of $1.5 billions in 1963 and 1964, and the United States for $2.5 billions in the summer of 1966. There seems to be almost nothing wrong with the system except that economists and government officials fail to understand it, and therefore dislike it. It is ironic that the United States should undertake to destroy the links between the New York and the international capital market, running a flexible and effective means of providing liquidity for the international monetary system, while prepared to substitute a cumbersome and contrived device to take its place.

Summary

It is agreed that the major problems of an international monetary system are adjustment, the provision of liquidity, and the maintenance of confidence, three issues which are intimately related. Under a flexible exchange rate system with no intervention, there can be no adjustment problem, and no need for liquidity or confidence. But it is likely to encourage destabilizing speculation and to isolate rather than integrate national economies. As a means of speeding adjustment, four compromise solutions have been proposed between the freely flexible exchange rate and the fixed rate: the floating rate with government intervention, the wide band, the adjustable peg, and the sliding peg. In each of them liquid reserves are needed. The optimum currency area which should use one money, or have fixed exchange rates, may be determined by the immobility of resources (Mundell) or the closed character of the economy (McKinnon).

Under the fixed exchange rate system, liquid reserves are needed. These have been provided by gold and foreign exchange. New gold production is added to the total stock more slowly than world trade is growing, and in recent years has gone into hoarding. World reserves could be increased by raising the gold price. Foreign exchange reserves can be produced readily by earned surpluses and deficits, by swaps and by international lending. They suffer the disability that their sustained creation gives rise to a problem of confidence.

The confidence problem is not readily handled by guarantees, fixed transfer ratios, internationalizing reserves, or creating a new reserve asset. Reducing the number of reserve assets to one would do it. World monetary reform is hung up on a wide range of disputes how to go about it, disputes in which the deficit and the surplus countries are lined up on different sides.

Most reform plans call for owned reserves. But sufficient owned reserves to meet a crisis would be redundant in periods of calm. More useful is an elastic reserve with the amount of owned reserves appropriate to the calms, but extendable through rediscounting in crisis. The Basel agreement is one mechanism for rediscounting. An international central bank would be another. Some elasticity in liquid reserves is provided through international financial intermediation in a world capital market.

SUGGESTED READING

TEXTS

See Delbert A. Snider, *International Monetary Relations* (New York: Random House, Inc., 1966) (paperback); and W. M. Scammell, *International Monetary Policy* (2nd ed.; London: Macmillan & Co., Ltd., 1961) (paperback).

TREATISES

For a general overview, see Fritz Machlup and Burton G. Malkiel (eds.), *International Monetary Arrangements: The Problem of Choice*. Report on the

Deliberations of an International Study Group of 32 Economists (Princeton, N.J.: Princeton University Press, August, 1964); and Robert Triffin, *Gold and the Dollar Crisis* (New Haven, Conn.: Yale University Press, 1960) (paperback).

On particular issues, see Milton Friedman, "The Case for Flexible Exchange Rates" in American Economic Association, *Readings in International Economics;* Egon Sohmen, *Flexible Exchange Rates* (2d ed.; Chicago: The University of Chicago Press, 1968); and C. P. Kindleberger, "Flexible Exchange Rates," in *Europe and the Dollar;* George N. Halm, *The "Band" Proposal: The Limits of Permissible Exchange Rate Variations,* Special Papers in International Economics, No. 6 (Princeton, N.J.: Princeton University Press, February, 1965); John H. Williamson, "The Crawling Peg" *EIF,* No. 50, December, 1965; Miroslav A. Kriz, "Gold: Barbarous Relic or Useful Instrument?" *EIF,* No. 60, June, 1967; Robert A. Mundell, "A Theory of Optimum Currency Areas," *AER,* September, 1961; and R. I. McKinnon, "Optimum Currency Areas," *AER,* September, 1963.

The G-10 documents on international monetary reform are:

Ministerial Statement of the Group of Ten and Annex Prepared by the Deputies, 10th August, 1964.

Group of Ten, Report of the Study Group on the Creation of Reserve Assets, 31st May, 1965.

Group of Ten, Communique of Ministers and Governors and Report of Deputies, July, 1966.

One among many valuable Joint Economic Committee papers is *Contingency Planning for U.S. International Monetary Policy,* statements by Private Economists, 89th Cong., 2nd sess. (Washington, D.C.: U.S. Government Printing Office, 1966).

POINTS

The Mundell proposal for flexible rates among the three major currency areas and fixed rates within them is in his *The International Monetary System: Conflict and Reform* (Montreal: The Private Planning Association of Canada, July, 1965).

The Roosa plan is set out in R. V. Roosa, *Monetary Reform for the World Economy* (New York: Harper and Row, 1965). A valuable collection of Mr. Roosa's official papers on the subject, along with other documents and comment, is provided in his *The Dollar and World Liquidity* (New York: Random House, 1967).

The Basel operations in dollars are discussed from time to time by Charles Coombs, vice president of the Federal Reserve Bank of New York in charge of foreign exchange, in various issues of that bank's *Monthly Review.*

For a useful discussion of the plan for Special Drawing Rights, see "New Plan for International Monetary Reserve," Hearing before the Subcommittee on International Exchange and Payments of the Joint Economic Committee, September 14, 1967. Included as an appendix to this brief hearing is a U.S. Treasury memorandum on "The Need for International Reserve," with up-to-date tables.

Chapter	THE INTERNATIONAL
28	ECONOMIC SYSTEM

The Classical System

The classical international economic system comprises three institutions: free trade, the annually balanced budget, and the gold standard. With the assistance of pure competition, free trade produced efficient allocation of resources in each country. The annually balanced budget was not an explicit prescription, but full employment, maintained by the inelasticity of factor supply and Say's law of markets, left no need to vary expenditure. The gold standard brought about adjustment through varying the volume of money in separate countries, raising prices in surplus, and reducing prices in deficit countries.

Free trade and the benevolent rule of Say's law left no work for a government to do. Government was called upon to play the "rules of the gold standard game," never thoroughly expounded. It is partly for this reason that ultraclassicists today want to shift from the fixed exchange rate to the more "liberal" market mechanism of freely flexible exchange rates without government intervention. If the gold standard is replaced by the flexible exchange rate, it is thought, government can lock up the international economic system and throw the key away.

Very few people would be prepared to adopt laissez-faire to this extent today. National governments are committed to maintain full employment through the use of monetary and fiscal policies. Membership in the world economic community means that countries are unwilling on the whole to adopt a system of flexible exchange rates which reduces international economic intercourse through increasing their risks. The gold standard must be modified for full employment, and free trade may have to be diluted when altered foreign conditions call for sudden and far-reaching changes in domestic resource allocation which would effect domestic hardship. But to replace laissez-faire government with a decision-making maximizer requires government to decide what to maximize.

Maximizing National Income

A government, engaged in maximizing income in the short run, presumably adopts policies for optimum tariffs and optimum capital movements, provided the benefits exceed the probability of retaliation times its cost. In the macroeconomic field, it will stay clear of the flexible exchange rate which would deprive it of the dampening effect of foreign trade on business cycles, of both domestic and foreign origin. Changes in the exchange rate may be used from time to time to produce domestic income effects and to redistribute domestic income between the domestic and foreign-trade sectors. The monetary authorities will shift back and forth between gold and interest-bearing foreign exchange, depending upon the outlook for changes in the gold price, exercising the one-way option which speculation in gold offers.

There is some doubt, however, whether a world of countries with short-run market power, all determined to exercise it, would in fact be viable. If most countries, and particularly the powerful countries, take a long-run view of the international economic machinery, one or two governments can exercise their short-run market power and get away with it. Optimum tariffs will improve their terms of trade because there will not be retaliation. Destabilizing speculation between gold and foreign exchange will be offset by the stabilizing counteraction of other governments. The system is weakened by these short-run maximizing actions, but if they are limited, it can survive them.

When all governments apply optimum tariffs and optimum capital movements, all use the foreign market actively for national income stabilization and speculate to protect the national position, however, the system may not work. The larger governments, unlike the average firm, have market power. One country applies an optimum tariff, and others will retaliate, since this will frequently make them better off. In time, the object of the exercise may change from maximizing national income to preventing other stronger countries from gaining from their attempts at the expense of the rest of the world. Police action may be undertaken regardless of cost. When no country or countries is willing to hold foreign exchange, and all rush for gold, the price of gold rises, exchange rates bounce around chaotically, and risk averters withdraw from foreign trade and lending, turning inward to domestic transactions. Similarly, when the international monetary system breaks down, as it did in the 1930's, countries must operate, as did Germany under Dr. Hjalmar Schacht, with a disequilibrium system of foreign exchange control, permitting limited barter and clearing transactions with the outside world, and the major economic thrust of policy concentrated on the home front.

Building the International Economic System

All firms, and all the smaller and less developed countries have a duty to maximize in the short run. But the larger and more powerful countries, or most of them, must be careful not to follow that lead. The fallacy of composition operates here. The world of Adam Smith does not obtain. The question is how to run the system.

One possibility is for every country to operate in the general rather than the national interest. The categorical imperative of Emmanuel Kant calls for individuals acting only in ways which can be generalized. Actions which are possible if only one person or country tries them are to be abhorred. Like the central bank which is not supposed to make money as do commercial or savings banks, but to act only in the interest of the banking system, highly enlightened governments might be enjoined to operate in the interest of the international economic system. This means avoiding optimum tariffs and optimum rates of lending, and supporting the system against destabilizing speculation. In a world of sovereign national governments, this is a hard line to follow. When the short-run is the enemy of the long, it may be hard to justify or explain why a government passed up an opportunity to advance the country in the concrete short run in the interest of the nebulous long.

International agreement is a useful device. Countries may bind themselves against short-run gains at the expense of the system if other countries are equally bound. Agreements to lower tariffs, as in the Kennedy Round, or to improve the international monetary system make possible action by one because of favorable action of others. Multilateral surveillance in Working Party No. 2 of the OECD, subjects the monetary and fiscal policy of each country to the scrutiny of the group, and limits the possibility that any one country can for long benefit at the expense of others.

The U.S. Department of State frequently complains that it has no constituents, no body of voters who will raise their voices in the Congress and apply pressure to get measures of general interest passed. Unlike the Departments of Commerce, Labor, Interior, Treasury, and so on, it represents the country as a whole, rather than an intensely concerned portion of it. Commitments to foreign countries and benefits from their commitments to this country moderate, but do not entirely dispel, the force of this argument. Foreign trade is between us and them. The Departments of Commerce, Labor, Interior, and Treasury, are concerned with us. The Department of State unpatriotically worries about them.

Coordinating National Action

The problem becomes exacerbated when we go beyond merely refraining from taking action which would benefit one country at the expense of others, to those where it is necessary for two or more countries to coordinate positive steps. In the foregoing pages we have mentioned a number of such occasions:

If it be decided by the developed countries that the less developed countries might appropriately have income redistributed toward them, better than the optimum tariff is a lesser tariff by the less developed countries plus a subsidy to correct the resource misallocation on the part of the developed countries (page 209).

When the incomes of countries are joined in a foreign-trade multiplier with foreign repercussion, and spending policies are adopted in both countries for internal and external equilibrium, there are three equations and four unknowns until the countries decide how to divide the burden of the spending policies between the two countries (page 587).

International economic integration calls for more than free trade and an absence of barriers to factor movement. It requires harmonization of tax, wage, foreign exchange, monetary and fiscal policies (page 193).

The rise of the international corporation, too, may require harmonization of policies in various fields, notably corporate taxation and antitrust, to forestall international corporations from undertaking action affecting one country, which is not permitted, in another. At the same time the international corporations should not be put in the impossible position of being ordered by two or more governments to take antithetical actions. This is the equivalent of double taxation. Again it calls for harmonization (page 404).

On a flexible exchange rate system with government intervention, the governments on both sides of a given exchange rate must collaborate to ensure that they do not each try to push the rate in different directions: the monetary authorities in A trying to depress their rate, offering A currency for B, while those in B try to depress their rate, offering B currency for A. The result would be mutual acquisitions of the currency of the other but with no change in the exchange rate.

If short-term capital markets are closely linked through such an institution as the Euro-dollar market, monetary authorities tend to lose control of national monetary policy. Pumping money into the money market tends to push it abroad, as the lower interest rate makes funds seek higher rates abroad; taking money out of the system attracts new funds from abroad. To make monetary policy effective, it must be coordinated among the joined money markets, with the monetary authorities operating simultaneously in the same direction. There is something of an asymmetry between New York as the largest financial center and the others: when New York changes its interest rate, it tends to move the whole structure up and down. When other financial centers try to change an interest rate, there is a short period of differential before the mass of foreign funds in, or domestic funds out, restores the old level. This statement exaggerates the position, but the asymmetry is real. There is more need, therefore, for British, French, German, Italian, and so on, representation on the Federal Open Market Committee, perhaps renamed an Atlantic Open-Market Committee, than the other way round.

When a currency is under attack, others must rescue it in the short run, and the rescued currency's country must ensure the rescuers against loss from their aid. In 1931, the Bank of Belgium and the Netherlands Bank both lost substantial sums when sterling was devalued while they maintained large balances in pounds. This proved a costly affair in increasing suspicion and reducing cooperation for the international monetary system. The world's currencies are in the same boat. They can afford one boat rocker, if the others stabilize by leaning against the pushes, but three or four rockers would make the life of the stabilizers difficult. As soon as possible after a Basel-like operation which is successful, the purchases of the currency under attack should be paid off through the International Monetary Fund. Should a support operation fail, which is unlikely, the currency on behalf of which the effort had been made must, in the interest of the system, make good any losses of the supporters. If it does not, the system breaks down.

Constitution Writing versus Evolution

The system of international economic collaboration built up in this way is mostly an unwritten one. After the war, the United States took the lead in signing up countries to a host of institutions with elaborate articles of agreement: the United Nations, the IMF, the IBRD, the Havana Charter of the International Trade Organization, Food and Agriculture Organizations, and so forth. The IMF had little to do for 10 years. The Havana Charter of the ITO was stillborn, never signed by its sponsor the United States. The IBRD found it could not tackle reconstruction, and was obliged to develop unforeseen techniques in lending for development. The most interesting postwar economic institution in international economics is the Euro-dollar market which evolved from market forces, more or less by accident, without an origin in economic analysis or in international agreement.

The propensity of lawyers is to dot each "i" and cross each "t," providing for every contingency before it occurs. In the international monetary system, this is a bootless and even dangerous inclination. The task of negotiating a precise agreement as to what will happen under a series of imagined catastrophes, who will do what, and how the accounts will be settled, is a disturbing experience. United States political processes, moreover, make enacting such an agreement into legislation a long drawn-out affair, with much unsettling discussion of hypothetical disasters. In the end, it is likely that the economists and lawyers would have failed to foresee exactly the character of the conditions with which the crisis had to cope. Accordingly it is preferable to have what the sociologists call a "diffuse" understanding of the sort that obtains among persons or peoples joined in a community, that in the event of trouble people will help as they can, and that no one will be penalized unfairly for so doing. Lend-Lease was the first of these diffuse international economic understandings. It was a success as the loan contracts of World War I were not. Formal attempts at negotiating major changes in the international economic system seem to emphasize the differences between national points of view. Piecemeal changes in response to felt needs, or evolutionary responses to problems, may fail to provide the assurance needed in advance of difficulty, but produce collaboration at a wider and more effective level than would such agreement as could be negotiated in advance.

International Economic Integration

In the last chapter it was suggested that the optimum currency area may well be the world, outside the Soviet bloc. This refers, to be sure, to the developed countries, and not to the less developed countries in so many of which devaluation and inflation follow one another in dreary succession. The Kennedy Round has reduced tariffs to levels of approximately 10 percent. Capital markets are joined, and likewise the labor market for highly skilled scientific personnel. International corporations begin slowly to operate by producing in the cheapest market for sale in the dearest, as opposed to the nationalistic system of producing in each market in which they sell. If governmental policies were coordinated and harmonized more fully, the position, with fixed exchange rates, would begin to approach that within a large federal state such as the United States.

Admittedly, the action of the federal government in taxing according to ability to pay, and spending without regard to regional lines (for the most part), makes a significant difference. There are thus far few international redistributive activities—the United Nations budget, the budgets of specialized agencies, peacekeeping operations in the Congo and, prior to June, 1967, in the Gaza strip, and, most important, foreign aid. Even these, however, fall short of the standard applicable inside countries. The French and Soviet governments chose not to pay a share of the peacekeeping expenses of the Congo or the Gaza strip, and economic aid was partly divided into spheres of influence, and partly competitive. The concern of some regions of the United States that they are paying more in taxes than they are receiving in benefits reflects the residual sovereignty of countries that refuse to contribute to world undertakings, and is subversive of the national unity.

Apart from the budgetary point, however, with its implication for automatic regional redistribution of income, which probably helps balance the interregional accounts of the less developed and hence poorer regions of the country, the analogy between the spatial economy of the United States and the international system as it appears to be evolving is a striking one. There are no tariffs. Domestic resistance to incursions of national firms—such as the antichain store legislation—is gone. The local firm knows it must compete with firms from outside the region by product differentiation, or superior service. National corporations contemplating expansion are bound to no traditional locality. The less developed areas seek to attract them not with tariffs, but with tax subsidies. There is a brain drain from the center of the country to the two coasts. Financial centers are organized in a hierarchy with San Francisco, Philadelphia, Boston, Chicago, and New York at the apex. New York performs financial intermediation services for the country as a whole. There is little or no regulation of this function, save for the Securities and Exchange Commission's interest in preventing fraud, state regulation of insurance, and a rather archaic regulation of banking. The local central bank authorities in the 12 districts perform mainly housekeeping functions. Their contribution to policy is presented in Washington, D.C., with the major responsibility for policy being assumed by New York and Washington.

It is unnecessary to spell out the international parallel to this picture of a national economic system: the weakening influence of tariffs, the rise of the international firm; the efforts of the developed (not the less developed) countries to attract such firms; the movement of skilled personnel; the hierarchical organization of financial centers; the importance of New York (read the Euro-dollar market) in international financial intermediation; and the preponderance of the Federal Reserve System in determining international monetary policy.

National versus International Policy

The policy dilemma remains. In the comfortable classical world, each country, as each person, advances the general interest when it advances its own interest. He governs best who governs least. Free trade, balanced budgets, and the gold standard, or more classically still, the freely flexible exchange rate, put government out of business. Or with world government, a single coherent set of policies would be imposed on the separate countries, now components of a larger entity. With no world government, however, and little prospect of one, countries may achieve the same result by harmonizing policies and coordinating actions. But they have the sovereign right to withhold compliance, or even to take advantage of the opportunities for short-run income maximization and risk minimization which independence gives in a world committed to operate the system.

But suppose the question is not one of taking advantage of the international system, but of minding one's own national business. Assume that Europe insists on high-interest rates because of its analytical conclusions or prejudices about the relative merits for domestic stabilization of fiscal and monetary policy. Suppose further that this means high-interest rates in the United States, to prevent capital outflows, and reduced capital formation and growth. Short-run stability of high-level employment can be achieved with the aid of fiscal policy, but this tends to promote consumption at the expense of capital formation (lower taxes and higher interest rates). If one cares about the rate of growth and the monetary fiscal mix, the insistence of Europe on high-interest rates is difficult to support. American domestic economists call for flexible exchange rates, or restrictions on capital outflows to isolate the U.S. money market from the world market and to recapture independence of monetary policy. The international trade economist who puts a high value on the maintenance of international markets for goods and factors urges the coordination of international policies, but knows well the beliefs or prejudices of the European authorities and is not sanguine that they will alter their position in the interest of an opposing theory in the United States.

Or take administrative convenience. One reason that American economists interested in domestic stability want monetary policy freed of integration into international capital markets is because they are aware that the Federal Reserve System has discretionary power to alter monetary policy, while changes in fiscal policy must be submitted for legislative approval, a time-consuming and even a chancy process. In countries with cabinet responsibility, as the United Kingdom, fiscal policy can be altered as speedily as monetary, and such countries are not always sympathetic with economic policies adopted for the sake of a particular (and inefficient?) political system. Harmonization and coordination of policies are difficult with different traditions, institutions, and pressures.

It is normal for the domestic and the international economist to differ on these issues, normal and on the whole salutary. Benevolent despotism is the best form of government, provided that the despot not only remains benevolent which thus far has been impossible, but also omniscient. In problems with many variables, however, today called system problems, it is difficult and often impossible for the benevolent despot to have in mind all the possible main and side effects coming from a particular policy. It is important to have specialists concerned with various parts of the problem, who can look at it from the vantage point of a particular perspective or interest. The clash between the perspectives or interests will illuminate the policy choices to be made and make for more intelligent decisions. But the international trade economist sometimes feels like the Department of State, that the broader interests of the system tend to be subordinated to the interests of the parts, with these being resolved for reasons of convenience and tradition, in ways which do not always fit the general weal. Like the Department of State, the international trade economist is probably indulging in the pathetic fallacy when he thinks this way. There is a chemical trace of truth in the contention.

A classical world of competitive markets, including the market for foreign exchange, and no government, or a world government somehow constructed along the lines of a benevolent, omniscient despot, makes an international economic system a reality. One wonders whether governments with power to act, and the need to act in the national interest, in ways dictated by national traditions and within the logic of national institutions, can in fact be sufficiently integrated and coordinated as to constitute an international economic system. Most of the work is still left to be done by the price system. Part of the governments' task is not to interfere, rather than to seek to interfere optimally. Even when it comes time to interfere, more often than not, the interests of the unit and those of the system coincide.

In the limited number of cases when they do not, it is not the task of the international trade economist to uphold the interests of the system against those of the unit. The job is to specify the range of alternatives and their consequences for both.

Summary

The classical economic system with limited government presupposes no conflicts between the interests of the parts and the whole, nor need to make decisions on the part of a government. On the whole, it is an illusion. With national governments playing roles, the question arises whether they maximize the short-run interest of the country, at the expense of other countries, or adopt longer range policies to uphold the international system, perhaps leaving room for less altruistic governments to take advantage of their restraint. Governments may bind each other to altruistic conduct by agreement. But there will be times when separate parallel action is insufficient, and action must be coordinated. Not all the possibilities can be foreseen and provided for in agreements. Nor can countries be expected to behave in identical fashion, given their different traditions, institutions, and possibly purposes.

The international economic system with governmental intervention is a close analogue to the operations of a national governmental system, save for the redistribution of income, with its effects on payments disequilibria which go through central budget, and the fact that the decisions are made in many lesser bodies, rather than in a single central one. Making separate national decisions, in the international economic system, calls for harmonizied policies and coordinated actions, difficult to achieve.

The role of the economist is not to make choices, especially when the interests of the country and the international economic system clash, but to indicate the alternatives and their implications for the national and system interests.

Appendix A to Chapter 2

FACTOR SUPPLY, TECHNOLOGY, AND PRODUCTION POSSIBILITIES

Derivation of the Transformation Curve from the Production Function and Factor Supplies

A production function is a statement of the relationships between physical quantities of inputs of factors and the physical output of a given commodity. Geometrically it can be shown by plotting the various combinations of two factors needed to produce given amounts of the commodity in question. In Figure A.1a, T–T is an *isoquant* representing a given quantity of a single commodity, cloth. T'–T' is a higher isoquant, i.e., a greater amount of cloth such as 200 yards, in comparison with the 100 yards represented by T–T. At a given point such as W, production is in equilibrium if the ratio of marginal physical products of labor and land is equal to the ratio of the prices of the two factors. A line tangent to an isoquant represents the relative price of land and labor. Given the production point W one can deduce the relative price of the factors, equal to the slope S–S, or given the quantity to be produced, T–T and the price of the factors, S–S, one can find the least-cost combination, W. OR is an expansion path for the relative price S–S (to which S'–S' is parallel). By adding inputs of land and capital, with the relative prices equal to the slope of S–S, one proceeds to higher isoquants by the path OR. If there are constant returns to scale, the expansion path at constant factor price will be a straight line. This simplest form of production function is called *linear homogeneous*. The isoquant T–T in Figure A.1a shows that labor can fairly easily be substituted physically for land, in the production of cloth, and vice versa.

The foregoing is by way of review. In Figure A.1b we show two production functions, for wheat and cloth, in which factor proportions are rigidly fixed but different in each commodity. The expansion paths, OX for cloth and OY for wheat, are straight lines for any positive set of factor prices. Any different set of factor proportions, such as OR instead

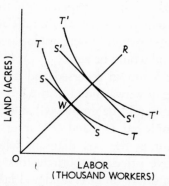

FIG. A.1*a*. Production Function for Cloth

FIG. A.1*b*. Production Functions with Fixed Factor Proportions

of *OW* on the isoquant *T–T* will reduce the marginal physical product of one factor (in this case land) to zero. Its price will also fall to zero.

In Figure A.1*b* cloth is unambiguously labor intensive and wheat unambiguously land-intensive. At any positive relative price of land and labor, cloth will use more labor relative to land than wheat.

In Figure A.2 we construct a so-called Edgeworth-Bowley box diagram, in which the dimensions of the box represent the amounts of land and labor in a country, which we shall call Britain. These factor supplies are assumed to be homogeneous in character and fixed in amount. The production function for cloth is drawn with its origin in the lower left-hand corner of the box at *O,* and with its isoquants, *T–T,*

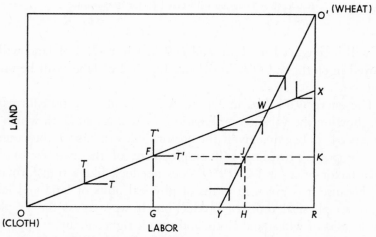

FIG. A.2. Edgeworth-Bowley Box Diagram with Fixed Factor Proportions

T'–T', and so on, moving out and up to the right. Its expansion path is *OX*. If all the labor in Britain (*OR*) were used to make cloth, only *RX* of land would be required, and *O'X* of land would be left unemployed. At *X*, the marginal physical product of land would be zero.

The production function for wheat is drawn reversed and upside down, with its origin at *O'* and extending downward and to the left. Its expansion path is *OY*. At *Y*, all the land would be employed, and *YR* of labor, but *OY* of labor would be unemployed. *OX* and *O'Y* intersect at *W* which is the only production point in the box diagram where there can be full employment and positive prices for both factors. At any other point on either expansion path, say *F*, on *OX*, land and labor will be able to produce at *J* on the expansion path for wheat; *OG* of

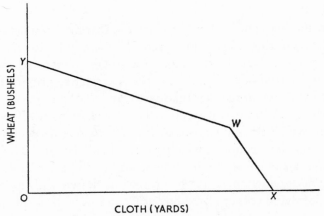

FIG. A.3. Transformation Curve Derived from Edgeworth-Bowley Box Diagram with Fixed Factor Proportions

labor will be engaged in cloth, and *HR* in wheat. *RK* of land will be employed in cloth, and *O'K'* in wheat. But *GH* of labor will be unemployed.

The curve *OWO'* as in Figure A.2 is in effect a transformation curve, showing the various combinations of wheat and cloth which can be produced in Britain, given the factor endowments of the country. The only point providing full employment of the two factors and positive factor prices is *W*. *OWO'* does not look like a transformation curve, because it is given in terms of physical units of land and labor, rather than physical units of production. If we express the graph in terms of units of wheat and cloth, and turn it right side up, it appears to be a normal production-possibilities curve, though kinked at *W*, as in Figure A.3.

If cloth and wheat were produced with fixed factor coefficients, and these were identical, the two expansion paths would coincide, as in A.4*a,* and the transformation curve becomes a straight line as in A.4*b.* But this means that land and labor are always used in the same combination so that they might well be regarded as a single factor. This is equivalent to the labor theory of value and its resultant straight-line transformation curve. A similar straight-line transformation curve would be produced by constant costs and identical production functions in the two commodities. But note the difference between constant costs and constant opportunity costs. The straight-line transformation curve represents constant opportunity costs. If the production functions for the two commodities differ, the transformation curve will exhibit curvature even though there be constant returns to scale in each commodity taken separately.

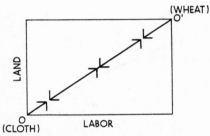

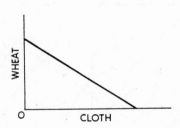

FIG. A.4*a.* Constant Opportunity Costs: Identical Fixed Factor Proportions

FIG. A.4*b.* Transformation Curve Derived from Figure B.4*a*

Where there is the possibility of substitution between factors in the production of a commodity, there is no unique expansion path. Instead, a separate expansion path can be drawn for any given set of factor prices, or we can draw in the isoquants for both commodities, and trace out a locus of points of tangency between them. This locus represents the efficiency path, or the maximum combinations of production of the two goods which can be produced with the existing factor supply. It is shown in Figure A.5*a.* Suppose that production were to take place at *W,* away from the efficiency locus. *W* is on cloth isoquant 7, and on wheat isoquant 5. But there is a point *T,* also on cloth isoquant 7, which is on a higher isoquant (6) of wheat. It would therefore be possible to produce more wheat without giving up any cloth. Or there is a point *T'* on wheat isoquant 5 which is on cloth isoquant 8. It would equally be possible to produce more cloth and the same amount of wheat. Any point off the locus of tangencies of isoquants of the two production functions is therefore inefficient, insofar as it would be possible to get more output of one commodity without losing any of the other, by moving to the locus.

The efficiency locus is the exact analogue of the "contract curve" in exchange theory. Here the dimensions of the box are given by fixed supplies of commodities, a point off the contract curve represents initial endowments of two individuals, with utility maps measured from origins in the two corners, and the two individuals can improve their utility by moving from the initial endowment point to the contract curve.

When the Edgeworth-Bowley box is used for production, it shows not only the efficient combinations of outputs, but also factor combinations and factor prices. Unlike the transformation curve (A.5*b*), however, it cannot show the relative price of wheat and cloth. If we assume that production is at *T,* however, the factor proportions in cloth are

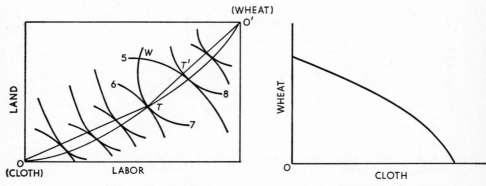

Fig. A.5*a.* Maximum Efficiency Locus under Variable Factor Proportions   Fig. A.5*b.* Transformation Curve Derived from Figure A.5*a*

represented by the slope of *OT,* and the factor proportions in wheat by *O'T.* It will be obvious that the indicated allocation employs all the land and all the labor. The relative price of land and labor with these outputs is represented by the slope of the tangency to the maximum efficiency locus at *T.*

Opportunity Costs versus Real Costs

The original theorists who developed the law of comparative costs using the labor theory of value thought of labor as disutility and of the cost of goods as a real cost. With the substitution of the law of variable proportions for the labor theory of value, there was seen to be a difficulty. Land and capital may not involve real costs. One can think not of real costs, but only of the opportunity cost, i.e., the cost of giving up something else.

Real cost theorists, however, have not been willing to abandon their position. In particular, Professor Viner has continued to adhere to a real cost position, claiming that in many respects one can regard labor as the main cost, or capital as past labor, and adhere to something very close to the labor theory of value. Less time is spent in defense, however, than in attack. The opportunity cost doctrine is strongly criticized for its assumption that men are indifferent among occupations and willing to work no matter what the price of labor. This assumption of inelastic supplies of factors is evidently unrealistic. If the transformation schedule is built up out of production functions which are statements of physical possibilities, there is no necessary reason, in Viner's view, why a country should be on the frontier of its transformation curve rather than somewhere inside it. The implicit assumption of the transformation curve that the supply of factors is completely inelastic vitiates its validity. The opportunity cost doctrine has no room for the possibility that trade enables a country to work less for the same real income rather than work the same amount and earn a higher return in commodities.

But difficulties are not absent from the real cost side. It is impermissible to gloss over the question of the absence of real costs in land, and the sunk character of real costs in capital. More, the doctrine fails to take account of the possibility that different people have different responses to different kinds of work, so that a given volume of output will represent a different real cost depending upon who is engaged in it.

J. Vanek has demonstrated that it is possible to distinguish between two kinds of production possibilities curves, one showing the technical transformation schedules between two goods, which does not allow for reactions of the factors to changes in factor prices, and an economic one, which takes such reactions into account. The economically possible curve lies within technically feasible curve, except at one or more points where they coincide, since the technical possibilities frontier is an envelope curve of various feasible curves.

SUGGESTED READING

The literature on comparative advantage and factor supply is enormous, and the student is referred to R. E. Caves, *Trade and Economic Structures,* chaps. iii, iv, and v, for a review and bibliography. Two of the oustanding articles: Romney Robinson, "Factor Proportions and Comparative Advantage," *QJE,* May, 1956, and T. M. Rybczynski, "Factor Endowment and Relative Commodity Prices," *Econ,* November, 1955; are gathered in the 1967 American Economics Association, *Readings in International Economics,* Part I.

On the controversy between real and opportunity costs, see Viner, pp.

489–93, Haberler, pp. 126, 175, and J. Vanek, "An Afterthought on the 'Real Cost-Opportunity Cost Dispute' and Some Aspects of General Equilibrium under Conditions of Variable Factor Supplies," *RES,* June, 1959. See also Haberler, "Real Costs and Opportunity Costs," in *International Social Science Bulletin,* Spring, 1951.

FACTOR-PRICE

EQUALIZATION

Factor-Price Equalization

There are at least three ways to demonstrate the factor-price-equalization theorem. The first, taking off from the Edgeworth-Bowley box which was explained in Appendix A, is illustrated in Figure B.1. There we construct Edgeworth-Bowley boxes for each of two countries, the United States and Britain, with widely different factor proportions, but identical production functions, which differ as between the two commodities, wheat and cloth. The two boxes have a common origin in cloth at O. The different factor proportions result in two separate origins for wheat, Y in the United States and Y' for Britain. Before trade, the two countries are assumed to be producing and consuming at S and T, respectively, determined separately with the help of demand conditions. The land/labor ratio is higher in wheat and cloth, respectively, in the United States than in Britain. (The diagonals are not drawn in, to simplify the diagram, but OS is steeper than OT in cloth, and SY than TY' in wheat.) With more land employed in both commodities in the United States than in Britain, land will be relatively less expensive, compared to labor. Conversely, with a higher labor/land ratio in both commodities, Britain will have a lower return to labor than the United States.

When trade becomes possible, it is assumed that prices are fully equalized in the two countries because of the absence of transport costs and other barriers to trade. With identical production functions showing constant returns, and equal prices of goods produced, the returns to factors must be identical if the factor proportions in the production of each commodity are identical between countries—if, that is, trade results in production at such points as R and U. At R and U, the equality of factor proportions is demonstrated by the fact that R lies on the straight line OU (there are identical factor proportions in the production of cloth in both countries) and YR and $Y'U$ are parallel.

There are a variety of reasons why two such points as R and U may not exist. After trade, one or both countries may be completely specialized, Britain producing cloth at Y' or the U.S. wheat at O. Demand conditions may be so sharply different in the two countries that trade results in shifting production in the United States from S toward Y, rather than toward O so that it would export the labor-intensive good despite its abundance of land. Or land and labor may so substitute for one another in the production of either cloth or wheat that wheat is

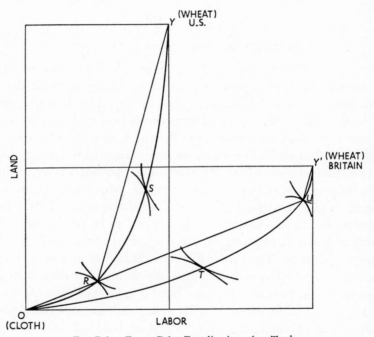

FIG. B.1.   Factor-Price Equalization after Trade

labor intensive in Britain and land intensive in the United States. This possibility can be illustrated on this diagram, but is more conveniently set out in the other two methods.

The second method of illustrating factor-price equalization is one worked out by A. P. Lerner, and is shown with the aid of single isoquants representing the production functions of the two commodities, as shown in Figure B.2. The trick is to pick isoquants for the two commodities which represent their relative prices, or the quantities in which they are exchanged, after trade is established. Thus the isoquants may represent, say, 3 yards of cloth and 2 bushels of wheat, or 30 yards

of cloth and 20 bushels, or 300 and 200. Since the production functions
are linear homogeneous, the shape of successive isoquants representing
larger quantities is always the same (and the expansion path along
which is represented by larger and larger outputs at given factor prices
is a straight line). Since the units chosen reflect goods prices which are
the same in the two countries after trade (assuming no transport costs
and perfect competition), Figure B.2 applies to the United States and
Britain alike. And as the figure is drawn, there can be only one factor-
price ratio, the line of tangency to the two isoquants, *A–B*. This then is
factor-price equalization.

But notice what happens if the isoquants cross more than once, as
in Figure B.3. This situation implies that there is a wide range of factor

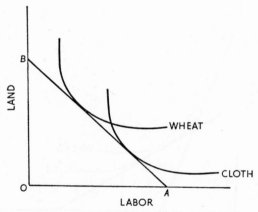

FIG. B.2.   Factor-Price Equalization Illustrated with Production Functions

substitution possible in at least one of the commodities, which permits
the same goods prices to prevail in two countries, but differing factor
prices. In Figure B.3, the production function for wheat is the same as in
Figure B.2, but there is much more room for factor substitution in
cloth. In these circumstances, Britain, with a high labor/land ratio, may
produce cloth with the factor proportions represented by the ray from
the origin (not drawn) *O–T,* and wheat with the proportions *O–S,*
yielding a factor price *A–B.* In this country cloth is relatively labor intensive. But in the United States, land is substituted for labor in producing cloth, and with production at *S'* and *T',* cloth is land intensive,
wheat labor intensive. Factor prices will differ, and one cannot tell from
factor endowments which country will export which commodity.

The third method of illustrating factor-price equalization is at the same time the most complex and the most helpful, since it puts factor proportions, goods prices, and factor prices all on the same diagram. Figure B.4 shows the relations between land/labor ratios and wage rates in the upper half of the diagram, and the relationship between wages and goods prices in the lower half. The central horizontal line is the wage/rent ratio, or the wage rate, which rises as it moves to the right. In the upper half of the diagram, land/labor ratios for cloth and wheat are shown rising as wages increase: the higher the wage, the more incentive there is for firms to substitute land for labor. Note that cloth is unambiguously more labor intensive, i.e., less land intensive, at

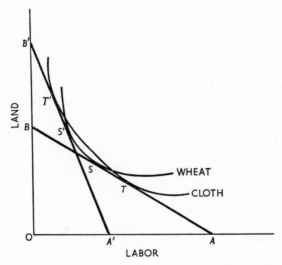

FIG. B.3.   Failure of Factor Prices to Equalize because of Factor Intensity Reversal

every wage rate, since the X–X schedule for cloth lies everywhere below the Y–Y schedule for wheat.

The relation between goods prices and factor prices is shown in the bottom part of the diagram. Here relative goods prices are measured in reverse order, i.e., downwards. The higher the wage, the higher the relative price of cloth, i.e., the higher the P–P line, measured negatively from O. This relationship is obvious enough after the student has become used to handling rising prices upside down: as wages rise, the price of the labor intensive commodity rises, and cloth is labor intensive at every land/labor ratio portrayed in the diagram.

British and U.S. factor proportions are given by horizontal lines in the upper half of the diagram which show that the United States is relatively land intensive, and Britain labor intensive. Before trade, production in the separate countries is determined by demand conditions, but as portrayed, the vertical lines for Britain and the United States before trade show that the price of cloth is lower in Britain than in the United States, and the wage rate lower. Conversely, of course, the price of wheat is higher and the rental rate for land higher. When trade is opened up, goods prices have to move together, and under the conditions drawn, the relative wage becomes identical which means factor-price equalization.

The separate conditions necessary for factor price equalization can

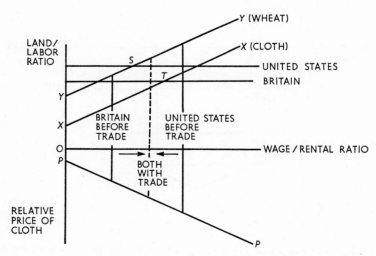

FIG. B.4. Factor Price Equalization with Factor Proportions, Goods Prices and Factor Prices

be illustrated by varying this diagram, but we shall content ourselves with word pictures except for factor intensity reversals. Linear homogeneity of production functions are required to have the land/labor ratios for the separate commodities straight lines, as shown, or at least not crossing. Perfect competition and the absence of transport costs are required to have identical goods prices after trade on the *P–P* line. Lack of complete specialization is a little more difficult to make clear, but if the price line after trade moves to the left of *S*, where the United States is fully specialized in wheat, or to the right of *T* where Britain is fully specialized in cloth, goods-price change no longer implies factor-proportion change and factor proportions are no longer uniquely related to factor prices.

The condition that demands must not be too skewed is to make sure that after trade is opened up the price of cloth in Britain rises, rather than have the country so addicted to cloth that it tries to buy more cloth from the United States, and so that trade makes the price of the goods produced intensively by the abundant factor fall.

The condition about factor reversals is illustrated in Figure B.5. In Britain wheat is land intensive relative to cloth, but in the United States, with a much higher land/labor ratio, land is so plentiful that it is copiously substituted for labor in making cloth. This is not very realis-

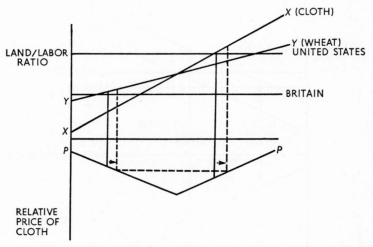

FIG. B.5. Failure of Factor Prices to Equalize because of Factor-Intensity Reversal

tic, perhaps, but it might be more confusing to shift the commodities. Notice that as the wage rate rises, the price of cloth rises relative to wheat until the land/labor curves cross. When cloth is more land intensive than wheat, the relative price of cloth declines as wages rise. In these circumstances, it is possible to get goods-price equalization without factor-price equalization. After trade, each country exports the labor intensive good, and trade raises wages in both countries.

Empirical Testing of the Factor-Price-Equalization Theorem

There is no doubt that in the world factor prices have not been equalized by trade, which must equalize goods prices because of the assumptions of perfect competition and no transport costs. This means that some of the assumptions of the theorem have not been met. The question, still unanswered, is which. It is obvious that transport costs prevent full equalization of goods prices for many bulky commodities, that tariffs prevent it for others, that perfect competition exists in neither goods nor factor markets, that there is complete specialization or would be without tariffs, in many manufactured goods and primary products alike. The conditions of the theorem come closest to being met in, say, the Common Market in Europe, where the various economies are roughly similar, adjacent to one another and incompletely specialized in manufactures. Here the tendency to factor-price equalization through trade is strong. Elsewhere, however, there is much greater doubt of the relevance of the theorem.

The Leontief paradox, mentioned in the text, was developed from input-output analysis of the U.S. economy, and showed that contrary to general expectation, U.S. imports were less labor intensive than U.S. exports. A wide variety of explanations for the paradox have been advanced. Many commentators thought that the statistical basis for the demonstration was inadequate. Leontief held that U.S. labor was three times as productive as other labor—and not because of more capital—which made this country really labor intensive. Vanek blames a third factor, natural resources. Travis asserts that the Leontief paradox is a reflection of tariff interferences in trade which means that production and trade do not accurately reflect factor proportions. Minhas and Diab, and to some extent the writer, are of the opinion that factor reversals occur in the real world, but some current research of the National Bureau of Economic Research throws doubt on this explanation for manufactures, even though such reversals occur in agriculture. The question then is still open.

SUGGESTED READING

Again the literature is enormous. The classic articles, by Samuelson, "International Trade and the Equalization of Factor Prices," were published in the *EJ* for June, 1948, and June, 1949. The second of these is reproduced in American Economic Association, *Readings in International Economics.* The original Leontief article "Domestic Production and Foreign Trade: The American Position Re-examined" is available either in *Economia Internazionale,* February, 1954, or in the American Economic Association, *Readings* just cited, in the part on empirical testing. If a student goes no further, these are the articles to read. This appendix is based on A. P. Lerner, "Factor Prices and International Trade," *Econ,* February, 1952, and H. G. Johnson, "Factor Endowments, International Trade and Factor Prices," in *Manchester School,* September, 1957, reprinted in American Economic Association, *Readings in International Economics,* Part I.

For the rest, on factor-price equalization, see Caves, chap. iii, Meade, *Trade and Welfare,* pp. 331–92, and for a useful summary of the literature, Bela Balassa, "The Factor-Price Equalization Controversy," *Weltwirtschaftliches Archiv,* 1, 1961. On the Leontief paradox, see especially B. S. Minhas, *An International Comparison of Factor Costs and Factor Use* (Amsterdam, North-Holland Publishing Co., 1963); W. P. Travis, *The Theory of Trade and Protection* (Cambridge, Mass.: Harvard University Press, 1964); and J. Vanek, *The Natural Resource Content of United States Foreign Trade, 1870–1955* (Cambridge, Mass.: The M.I.T. Press, 1963).

Appendix C to Chapter 3	# THE RELATION OF THE OFFER CURVE TO THE PRODUCTION POSSIBILITIES CURVE AND THE CONSUMPTION INDIFFERENCE MAP

John Stuart Mill thought of the offer curve as developed from fixed supplies of commodities to be exchanged. This is the concept to which Frank Graham objected, as he drew attention to the possibility of producing goods, at constant costs, as he thought, for export. But there is no need to limit the offer curve to the case of fixed goods supply. Professor Meade has set out a neat geometric device, building the offer curve out of the production possibilities curve and the consumption indifference map. The beauty of the technique rests partly in its bridging this gap, but also in that it enables one to demonstrate neatly and simply, the impact of trade on production, consumption, the gains from trade, and so on. While many students may remain terrified at the prospect of learning still another geometric technique, the braver among you are encouraged to plunge ahead and acquire a highly useful analytical tool.

The first step is to draw the production block and consumption indifference curve for country A without trade, in the usual way, except for the fact that they are in the northwest rather than the usual northeast quadrant of the system of coordinates. This is done in Figure C.1. Following Meade's notation, the horizontal axis measures A's exportables, which are B's importables; the vertical axis, B's exportables.

Now, holding it level and upright, slide the A production block up and down the no trade consumption indifference curve, keeping it tangent to the same consumption indifference curve, *I*. The origin of the block, *O*, will trace out a trade indifference curve *i*. At every point on this curve. A will be indifferent whether it trades or not. It can remain at *O* and produce and consume at *F*. Or it can move along the curve to the point where the origin of its production possibilities block is at *T*. It will then produce at *G*, and trade *HT* of A-exportables for *HO* of B-exportables. The reason that it is indifferent between *O* and *T* is that it can produce at either *F* or *G* along its production possibilities schedule (transformation along the schedule is assumed to be costless); and *G* is on the same consumption indifference curve as *F*. At *G*, of course, it consumes *GS* + *HO* of B-exportables, and only *SH* of A-exportables.

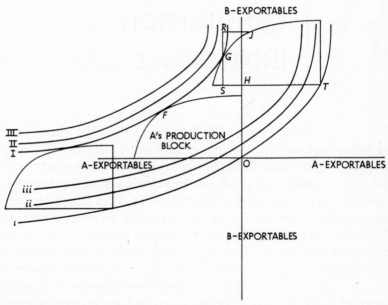

FIG. C.1. The Derivation of the Trade Indifference Map from the Consumption Indifference Map

Note that the trade indifference curve has a different shape than the consumption indifference curve. This is because production has shifted as well as the proportions of goods consumed. If *J* in the upper right-hand position of the A-block corresponds to *F* in the no trade position, it is clear that in shifting from *O* to *T*, production of A-exportables has increased by *RJ*, and production of B-exportables decreased by *RG*. A trade indifference curve is flatter to take account of these production changes. When production is fixed and no movement of resources is possible, the trade indifference curve will parallel the consumption one.

There is a trade indifference curve corresponding to every consumption indifference curve, and hence a trade indifference map. A country is better off, the higher the trade indifference curve it is able to reach. Along any single curve, it is indifferent between one position and another. But in Figure C.1 country A is better off the higher the trade indifference curve it can reach (moving from southeast to northwest).

A's offer curve will now be constructed. It represents the locus of a series of tangencies of various price lines to the trade indifference map of successively higher indifference curves. This is shown in Figure C.2. The initial slope of the offer curve through the origin represents the

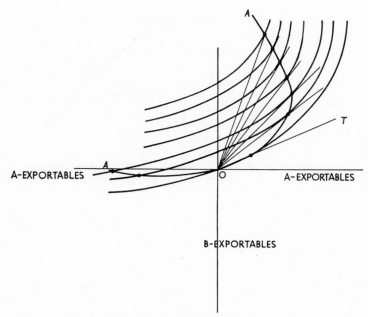

FIG. C.2.   The Derivation of the Offer Curve for Country A from Its Trade Indifference Map

price which would prevail without trade. As higher and higher prices for A-exportables are offered in terms of B-exportables, A will be enabled to move to higher and higher trade indifference curves, and will be disposed to offer, as the figure is drawn, first more and more A-goods for larger quantities of B-exportables, and then less. Note that if the price for B-goods gets higher than *OT,* A will export B-exportables in exchange for A-goods. The offer curve moves into the southwest quadrant, but only for very high prices for B-exportables, which have their name belied by being imported by B.

Country B's offer curve can similarly be traced out from a series of trade indifference curves imposed on the same set of coordinates, but developed from sliding B's production possibilities block along its consumption indifference curves in the southeast quadrant. Figure C.3 shows the A and B offer curves intersecting at the balanced trade position where the terms of trade line, *OT,* is tangent to trade indifference curves of A and B and go to the origin. There are other tangencies of trade indifference curves, and a contract curve, *K–K,* may be drawn along them. This contract curve, like that of the Edgeworth-Bowley box in Figure A.5*a* when it is used in exchange, and not as an efficiency locus

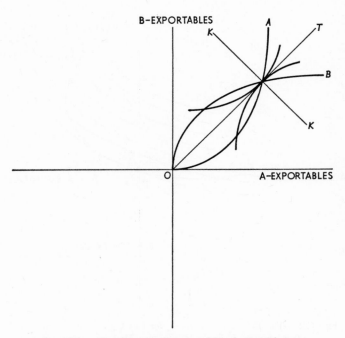

FIG. C.3.   The Contract Curve and Trade Equilibrium

in production, represents different distributions of welfare between A and B. A is better off the further the point of trade is toward the northwest; and B the nearer it is to the southwest. Only at the intersection of *OA* and *OB,* however, do the terms of trade balance A's exports and B's imports under free trade.

These three figures neatly show the relationship of the offer curve to consumption indifference curves and to production. The technique can be used in its simple manifestation, however, to show the gains from trade. This is done by leaving the A and B production possibilities blocks at the trading position, as in Figure C.4. Trade and consumption indifference curves and the offer curves are omitted to eliminate clutter.

In Figure C.4, production is measured from the intersection of the origins, *T*, of the production blocks. In A, production consists of *QG* of B-exportables and *GM* of A-exportables. B produces *NH* of B-exportables and *FH* of A-exportables. These outputs can readily be added to give production of *GJ* of A-exportables in the two countries and *JH* of B-exportables.

Consumption is measured from the original coordinates, intersecting at *O*. A consumes only *GR* of A-exportables, but *GL* of B-exportables; in its turn, B consumes only *SH* of its B-good, and *KH* of

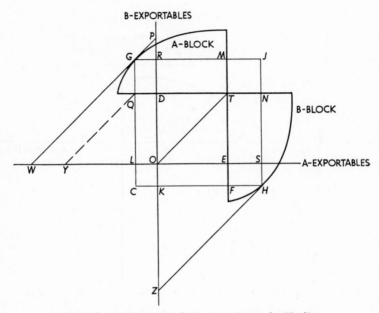

Fig. C.4.　Production and Consumption under Trading

the A-exportable. This is made possible by trade, in which A exchanges *DT* of the A-good against *TE* of the B-good, at the terms of trade *OT*.

This is a free trade position, without transport costs. Thus the terms of trade are equal to the internal prices (*WG* and *ZH* are parallel to *OT* and to each other). National income in A is *WO* expressed in A-exportables, or *PO* expressed in B's good, whether we take income produced, or income consumed. These are the same because trade is balanced. Income produced directly in A-goods is *YO*, which is the same as *GM* or *QT* (*YQ* is drawn parallel to *OT*). That part of income produced which originally consisted of B-goods, *GQ*, is the equivalent, at the price *WG*, of *WY*.

For income consumed, *GR* of A-exportables is equal to *LO*, and *GL* of B-exportables, at the price *WG* is the equivalent in A-exportables of *WL*. *WL + LO = WO*. Similar exercises can be carried through for national income in A measured in B-goods and for income produced and consumed in B in either good.

The gains from trade are more elusive and present an index number problem. We can measure A's gain in terms of either prices

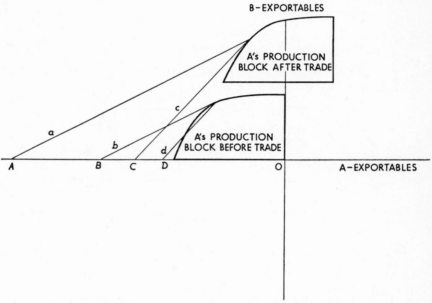

FIG. C.5. The Gains from Trade Measured in Terms of A-Exportables

before trade, or prices after trade. In Figure C.5, *a* and *b* are the before-trade terms of trade drawn to the A production block after and before trade, respectively. On the other hand, *c* and *d* represent the post-trade prices drawn to the same block positions; *a*, *b*, *c*, and *d* intersect the horizontal axis at *A,B,C*, and *D*. The gains from trade in *A*, expressed in A-exportables, may then be regarded *AB*, using the terms of trade before trade, or *CD*, representing it in after-trade prices. But one should not make the mistake of regarding the gains from trade as measured from the national income in the no trade position at no trade prices (*BO*) to national income with trade at the with-trade price (*CO*). In that event, the gain from trade would be negative, or a loss (*BC*).

It is true that the gains from trade will be larger, the larger the change in prices before trade and after. The larger the price change, the higher the consumption indifference curve and the higher the trade indifference curve the country can reach. But measurement of the distance between indifference curves requires a scale, and this can be one commodity or the other, but only at a consistent set of prices.

SUGGESTED READING

This appendix is based on J. E. Meade, *A Geometry of International Trade,* chap. i–iv.

THE OPTIMUM

TARIFF

A tariff improves the terms of trade if the offer curve facing the imposing country is less than infinitely elastic. But a country must be careful not to raise the tariff too high, or the loss in the quantity of trade will outweigh the improvement in the terms of trade. What is the tariff which will maximize a country's gain, improving the terms of trade more than the volume is reduced?

In Figure D.1, A's and B's offer curves are drawn in the usual way, and at the original free trade intersection *A* has reached its trade indifference curve, as described in Appendix C, which we can designate no. 5. The question is can it do better? And the answer is that it can. It needs to distort its offer curve by a tariff so as to reach the point where B's offer curve is tangent to its highest trade indifference curve, here numbered 10. Note that a tariff which displaces A's offer curve to the left anywhere short of *F* will leave it better off, but the optimum tariff, as drawn, takes it to its highest possible trade indifference curve touching B's offer curve. Only points on B's offer curve are feasible, of course, since it takes two to trade.

It should be pointed out that the trade-distorted offer curve in this diagram, which follows the Meade analysis, is different from that in the text of Chapter 7. In the text, the tariff was measured by the distance between the two offer curves and the proceeds of the tariff were removed from trading by governments and swept under the rug. With the tariff collected as $P'-V$ of cloth in Figure 7.4, the new terms of trade are $O-P'$. This is the Lerner diagram. In the Meade analysis, however, the government takes the revenue and gives it back to consumers as subsidies; they spend it on the two goods in their normal fashion. As a consequence of the subsidy, they are in a position to spend more than they earn. The new terms of trade are drawn not to the origin which is the case only when there is free trade, but to the horizontal axis elsewhere. The terms of trade line is drawn tangent to the tariff-imposing country's trade indifference curve. Where it intersects the horizontal axis is a measure of the tariff (*SO* in Figure D.1.) and of the gain through the imposition of the tariff.

The rate of the optimum tariff can be calculated in terms of the elasticity of the foreign offer curve. In Figure D.2, *T* is the point where A's tariff distorted offer curve cuts B's offer curve. At *T*, B is willing to trade *TQ* of wheat for *OQ* of cloth. But the price line *OT* (not drawn) is not tangent to A's trade indifference curve, and A will not be in equilibrium trading *OQ* of cloth. A will trade at *T* only at a

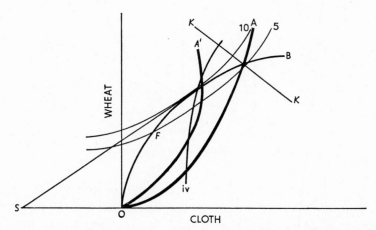

FIG. D.1.   The Tariff-Distorted Offer Curve and the Optimum Tariff

price tangent to its trade indifference curve at *T* (also tangent to the offer curve, since this is the optimum tariff). Draw such a line of tangency and extend it through the vertical axis at *R* to the horizontal axis at *S*. This is the equilibrium price in A. A will trade along the slope *ST* and B along *OT* if exports of cloth are subject to an export tax of $\frac{SO}{OQ}$ in A, or imports of wheat *UR* are subject to a tax of $\frac{RO}{UR}$.

What is the import elasticity of the B offer curve at *T?* To measure this elasticity, which represents the change in imports relative to the change in price of imports, we use the tangent drawn to the relevant axis—in this case B's, and at the same time drop a perpendicular to it. The elasticity of the offer curve at the given point is represented by the distance from the point of intersection of the perpendicular on the vertical axis to the origin (*UO*) divided by the distance from the intercept of the tangent to the origin (RO). If R lies halfway between U and O, the elasticity of the B offer curve at T is 2. If the offer curve is a straight line from O to L, the elasticity at L is infinity, since the vertical distance to L divided by O (where the tangent to the trade

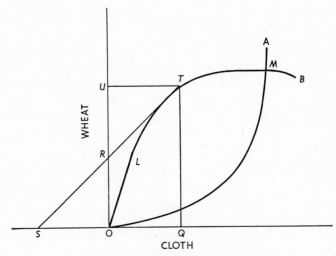

FIG. D.2. Calculating the Optimum Tariff

indifference line intersects the vertical axis) is infinity. The import elasticity of the offer curve at M, where the tangent and the perpendicular line are assumed identical, is 1. If the B offer curve slopes downward after M, its elasticity is less than 1 since the tangent intersects the vertical axis further from the origin than the straight line to the axis.

We are now in a position to derive the formula for the optimum tariff. If T is a point on B's offer curve which touches the highest possible trade indifference curve of A, the optimum tariff at point T is $\dfrac{SO}{OQ}$.

$OQ = UT$. By similar triangles,

$$\frac{SO}{UT} = \frac{RO}{UR} = \frac{1}{\dfrac{UR}{RO}} = \frac{1}{\dfrac{UO - RO}{RO}} = \frac{1}{\dfrac{UO}{RO} - 1}.$$

Since $\dfrac{UO}{RO}$ is the elasticity of the offer curve at point T, the optimum tariff

$$\left(\frac{SO}{OQ}\right) = \frac{1}{\dfrac{UO}{RO} - 1} = \frac{1}{e - 1}.$$

If at point L the elasticity of the offer curve is infinity, the optimum tariff is evidently zero $\left(\dfrac{1}{\infty - 1} = 0 \right)$. Where the offer curve is a straight line, no tariff can improve the terms of trade. At M, where the elasticity of the foreign offer curve is one, the optimum tariff is infinity $\left(\dfrac{1}{1 - 1} = \infty \right)$, which is to say that the optimum tariff has to be at a point where the elasticity of the opposing offer curve is greater than 1 but less than infinite. At any lower elasticity it is evident that a higher indifference curve can be reached by a tariff.

SUGGESTED READING

Meade, *A Geometry of International Trade*, pp. 76, 87–90; Marsh, chap. xxi, and esp, pp. 316–21. See also a series of articles in *RES* by J. de Graaf (1949–50); H. G. Johnson (1950–51 and 1953–54); J. J. Polak (1950–51); T. Scitovsky, "A Reconsideration of the Theory of Tariffs" in American Economic Association, *Readings in the Theory of International Trade*.

THE MONOPOLY EFFECT

OF A QUOTA

A significant difference between a tariff and a quota is that the conversion of a tariff into a quota which admits exactly the same volume of imports may convert a potential into an actual monopoly. Figures E.1 and E.2 provide a demonstration.

In Figure E.1, AR is the average revenue or demand curve for a commodity in the domestic market. In the absence of international trade, MR is the marginal revenue curve facing the domestic industry. AC and MC are the relevant average and marginal cost curves of the domestic import-competing industry. The world price, assumed to be unchanged by anything which might transpire in the importing country, is OP. A tariff $P–P'$ raises the price at which imports can be sold to OP'.

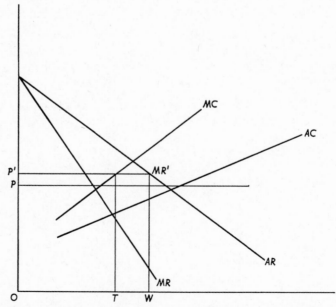

FIG. E.1.   Potential Monopoly in Partial Equilibrium with Tariff

With international trade, and the tariff *P–P'*, *O–P'* is not only the domestic price at which foreigners will supply goods. It also becomes the marginal revenue curve facing the domestic industry (*MR'*). No consumer will be willing to pay more than *O–P'* for a domestic product when he can get the same thing from abroad for that price. The domestic industry will produce where marginal cost equals marginal revenue, i.e., the amount *OT*. The remaining demand at this price will be supplied by imports, *TW*.

Let us now suppose that the tariff is converted to a quota, and that the licenses are auctioned off. The revenue, terms of trade, and the initial balance-of-payments effects are the same as under the tariff. But the protective, consumption, redistribution, and ultimate balance-of-payments effects are altered because the potential domestic monopoly has been converted to an actual one.

In Figure E.2, the *AR* curve is displaced to the left by the amount of the quota, *TW*, and a new marginal revenue curve, *MR'*, drawn to the displaced curve, *AR'*. Both *AR'* and *MR'* have an independent existence until the former gets to the world price plus tariff (*OP'*). This then becomes the average revenue curve and the marginal revenue curve until the old average revenue curve is reached, where the marginal revenue curve returns to its original course. This volume of domestic production plus the import quota, *TW*, will produce a price of *OP''*, which is well above the old world price plus tariff, *OP'*.

Conversely, to be sure, the conversion of quota restrictions into

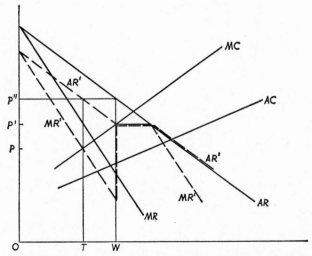

FIG. E.2. Potential Monopoly Converted to Actual Monopoly under Quota

tariffs which admit an equal volume of imports will eliminate domestic monopolies by threatening them with potential competition from increased imports. This is a strong argument for customs unions, and for trade liberalization, i.e., removal of QR's and their conversion to tariffs.

SUGGESTED READING

See H. Heuser, *The Control of International Trade* (London: George Routledge & Sons, Ltd., 1939), chap. xi, and especially diagrams 8 and 9.

J. Bhagwati generalizes the possibilities of monopoly among domestic producers, quota holders and foreign exporters in "On the Equivalence of Tariffs and Quotas," in R. E. Baldwin *et al., Trade, Growth and the Balance of Payments,* Essays in Honor of Gottfried Haberler (Chicago: Rand McNally & Co., 1965).

THE MARSHALL-LERNER CONDITION[1]

In this appendix we examine the model underlying the discussion of Chapter 15 in a formal and rather exhaustive fashion. Let us assume two countries A and B. We shall establish the conditions under which devaluation of A's currency improves its balance of trade expressed in either foreign exchange or domestic currency. The following notation will be employed throughout.

X_A = A's physical quantity of exports.
M_A = A's physical quantity of imports.
X_B = B's physical quantity of exports.
M_B = B's physical quantity of imports.
p_x = Price of A's exports expressed in terms of A's currency.
p_m = Price of A's imports expressed in terms of A's currency.
r = Exchange rate expressed as units of A's currency paid per unit of B's currency.
$e_x{}^A$ = A's elasticity of supply for exports.
$e_m{}^A$ = A's elasticity of demand for imports.
$e_x{}^B$ = B's elasticity of supply for exports.
$e_m{}^B$ = B's elasticity of demand for imports.
V_m = Value of A's imports expressed in terms of A's currency.
V_x = Value of A's exports expressed in terms of A's currency.
B_d = A's balance of trade expressed in terms of A's currency.
B_f = A's balance of trade expressed in terms of foreign exchange (i.e., B's currency).
T = A's terms of trade, i.e., $\dfrac{p_x}{p_m}$.

Asterisks on p_x and p_m will imply that they are expressed in terms of B's currency.

Before embarking upon the formal analysis the reader is reminded of the following definitions, identities, functional relationships, and assumptions.

[1] By Miltiades Chacholiades.

Definitions

$$e_x{}^A \equiv \frac{dX_A}{dp_x} \cdot \frac{p_x}{X_A} \equiv X'_A \frac{p_x}{X_A}$$

$$e_m{}^A \equiv \frac{dM_A}{dp_m} \cdot \frac{p_m}{M_A} \equiv M'_A \frac{p_m}{M_A}$$

$$e_x{}^B \equiv \frac{dX_B}{d(p_{m/r})} \cdot \frac{p_m/r}{X_B} \equiv X'_B \frac{p_m}{rX_B}$$

$$e_m{}^B \equiv \frac{dM_B}{d(p_{x/r})} \cdot \frac{p_x/r}{M_B} \equiv M'_B \frac{p_x}{rM_B}$$

$$V_m \equiv p_m M_A \equiv p_m X_B$$
$$V_x \equiv p_x X_A \equiv p_x M_B$$

Identities[2]

$$M_A = X_B \qquad p_x{}^* = \frac{p_x}{r}$$

$$X_A = M_B \qquad p_m{}^* = \frac{p_m}{r}$$

Functional Relationships

$$X_A = X_A(p_x)$$
$$M_A = M_A(p_m)$$
$$X_B = X_B(p_m/r)$$
$$M_B = M_B(p_x/r)$$

The independent variables in parentheses which appear in the above relationships will be omitted in what follows in order to simplify the notation. The reader is advised, however, to keep them in mind.

Assumptions

$$\frac{dX_A}{dp_x} \equiv X'_A \geq 0, \quad \frac{dM_A}{dp_m} \equiv M'_A \leq 0,$$

$$\frac{dX_B}{d(p_m/r)} \equiv X'_B \geq 0, \quad \frac{dM_B}{d(p_x/r)} \equiv M'_B \leq 0.$$

Effects of Devaluation on A's Balance of Trade Expressed in Terms of B's Currency

A simplifying assumption usually made to render the arithmetic more easily manageable is that the supply elasticities in both countries

---

[2] The reader is reminded that these identities hold for the *ex post* (or realized) quantities traded. They should not be confused with the willingness to export or import. However, when the export and import markets are in equilibrium, the two coincide.

are infinite. Thus the domestic prices of each country's exports expressed in terms of its own currency (i.e., p_x and $p_m^* = p_m/r$) are constants. This assumption, of course, does some violation to the facts. For this reason it is considered desirable to indicate briefly in the final section of this appendix how the general case can be handled.

A's export revenue expressed in terms of B's currency is equal to $(p_x/r)X_A$. However, since e_x^A is assumed infinite, this product does not have much meaning except in relation to B's demand for imports. In other words, under the assumption of infinite supply elasticities, the foreign demand is the limiting factor of the export revenue. Thus, A's export revenue should be written as: $(p_x/r)M_B$. In the same way, A's expenditure on imports expressed in terms of B's currency is equal to: $(p_m/r)M_A \equiv p_m^*M_A$. Finally, A's balance of trade expressed in terms of B's currency is defined as follows:

$$B_f = \left(\frac{p_x}{r}\right) M_B - p_m^*M_A \qquad (1)$$

Our problem is to find out what happens to B_f when r increases (i.e., when A's currency is devalued). In other words, we are interested in the value of the derivative $\dfrac{dB_f}{dr}$. More specifically, we are interested to know whether A's balance of trade improves (i.e., $\dfrac{dB_f}{dr} > 0$), deteriorates (i.e., $\dfrac{dB_f}{dr} < 0$), or, remains the same (i.e., $\dfrac{dB_f}{dr} = 0$). Of course, the precise numerical value of $\dfrac{dB_f}{dr}$ is of great importance too. Thus, assuming the $\dfrac{dB_f}{dr} > 0$, the higher the derivative $\dfrac{dB_f}{dr}$ the smaller the degree of devaluation necessary to eliminate a certain deficit. In this appendix, however, we are interested only in knowing the conditions under which devaluation is successful, irrespective of the degree of success.[3]

Differentiating[4] B_f with respect to r, we get

---

[3] The student whose calculus is rusty will find in a very brief mathematical note at the end of this appendix all the rules used below. Besides these few rules, only high school algebra is necessary.

[4] We shall adopt the convention of using primes to indicate derivatives, i.e.,

$$\frac{dM_A}{dp_m} = M_A', \quad \frac{dM_B}{dp_x^*} = M_B'.$$

$$\frac{dB_f}{dr} = -\frac{p_x}{r^2} M_B - \frac{p_x}{r} M_B' \frac{p_x}{r^2} - p_m^* M_A' p_m^*$$

$$= \frac{V_x}{r^2} \left(-1 - \frac{M_B'}{M_B} \cdot \frac{p_x}{r} - \frac{V_m}{V_x} \frac{M_A'}{M_A} p_m \right).$$

Using now the definitions of elasticities given previously, we get

$$\frac{dB_f}{dr} = \frac{V_x}{r^2} \left(-1 - e_m{}^B - \frac{V_m}{V_x} e_m{}^A \right). \tag{2}$$

Devaluation (i.e., an increase in r) improves the balance of trade (i.e., it increases B_f in algebraic terms) when $\frac{dB_f}{dr} > 0$. This occurs when the expression in parenthesis on the right-hand side of equation (2) is greater than zero. In other words, devaluation improves the balance of trade when:

$$-1 - e_m{}^B - \frac{V_m}{V_x} e_m{}^A > 0$$

or

$$-e_m{}^B - \frac{V_m}{V_x} e_m{}^A > 1. \tag{3}$$

If B's demand for imports is elastic (i.e., $e_m{}^B < -1$), then A's balance of trade always improves with devaluation, as can be verified by inequality (3). If B's demand for imports is inelastic, the outcome can be anything. It will all depend upon the condition of the balance of trade before devaluation (or, more precisely, on the ratio V_m/V_x) and A's elasticity of demand for imports. The larger the ratio V_m/V_x and the higher A's demand elasticity (in absolute terms), the bigger the chance for balance-of-trade improvement.

A country will never consider devaluation, unless it suffers from a balance-of-trade deficit. Thus according to the previous paragraph, the least favorable situation for successful devaluation as far as the balance of trade is concerned, is when we start with a balanced trade, i.e., $V_m = V_x$. In this case, inequality (3) becomes:

$$-e_m{}^A - e_m{}^B > 1. \tag{4}$$

Inequality (4) is what is known in the literature as the Marshall-Lerner condition. In words, devaluation always improves the balance of trade expressed in terms of foreign exchange when the sum of the two demand elasticities (taken in absolute terms) is greater than unity. If we start with a balance-of-trade deficit, the Marshall-Lerner condition becomes sufficient. This is because

$$-e_m{}^B - \frac{V_m}{V_x} e_m{}^A \geq -e_m{}^A - e_m{}^B$$

where the equality sign holds when $e_m{}^A = 0$. Thus, when $-e_m{}^A - e_m{}^B > 1$, we must also have $-e_m{}^B - (V_m/V_x)e_m{}^A > 1$. The reverse is not true, however. Hence, the balance of trade might improve even when the Marshall-Lerner condition is not satisfied.

Effects of Devaluation on A's Balance of Trade Expressed in Terms of A's Currency

By definition, $B_d = rB_f$, hence,

$$\frac{dB_d}{dr} = B_f + r\frac{dB_f}{dr}. \tag{5}$$

If the balance of trade is in equilibrium to begin with, equation (5) takes the form: $\dfrac{dB_d}{dr} = r\dfrac{dB_f}{dr}$. Therefore, when $B_d = B_f = 0$, $\dfrac{dB_d}{dr}$ is positive if and only if $\dfrac{dB_f}{dr}$ is positive. Thus the previously derived conclusions for improving B_f guarantee also improvement in B_d. However, when the balance of trade is out of equilibrium before devaluation, there emerges a divergence between these conditions. In particular, if we start with a deficit, an improvement in B_d necessarily implies a corresponding improvement in B_f. But the reverse is not generally true. The real possibility of having an improvement in B_f and a deteriorating in B_d exists and cannot be eliminated by any deductive reasoning.

Substituting the values of B_f and $\dfrac{dB_f}{dr}$, as given by equations (1) and (2) respectively, into equation (5) and rearranging, we get:

$$\frac{dB_d}{dr} = \frac{V_x}{r} - \frac{V_m}{r} + \frac{V_x}{r}\left(-1 - e_m{}^B - \frac{V_m}{V_x}e_m{}^A\right)$$

$$= \frac{V_m}{r}\left(-1 - e_m{}^A - \frac{V_x}{V_m}e_m{}^B\right).$$

Thus, B_d improves with devaluation only when:

$$-(V_x/V_m)e_m{}^B - e_m{}^A > 1. \tag{6}$$

If A's demand for imports is elastic, B_d always improves with devaluation. It should be pointed out, however, that the Marshall-Lerner condition is not sufficient for improving B_d. On the other hand, condition (6) does imply the Marshall-Lerner condition. This is illustrated in the following diagram. Any point in the shaded area satisfies inequalities (3) and (6) as well as the Marshall-Lerner condition. Hence, any combination of demand elasticities lying in this region is sufficient for improving both B_f and B_d. However, any point in the triangle *LMN*

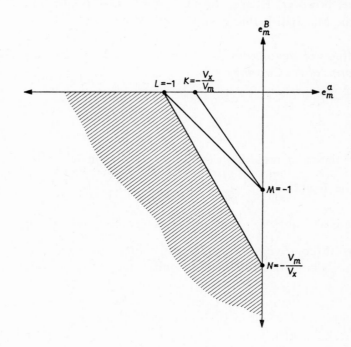

satisfies inequality (3) and the Marshall-Lerner condition (and thus B_f improves) but it does not satisfy condition (6) (and thus B_d deteriorates). Finally, any point in the triangle *KLM* satisfies only inequality (3). Thus, B_f improves—though the Marshall-Lerner condition is not satisfied—and B_d deteriorates. The areas of these triangles obviously depend on the ratio V_m/V_x. As V_m/V_x increases points *K* and *N* move away from points *L* and *M* respectively and the two triangles become bigger and bigger. On the other hand, as V_m/V_x decreases both triangles shrink. When $V_m/V_x = 1$, points *K* and *N* coincide with points *L* and *M*, respectively, and both triangles vanish together with the paradoxes they give rise to. Finally, it should be pointed out that when B's demand elasticity is zero, the Marshall-Lerner condition is sufficient for improving B_d. This is a general proposition which holds irrespective of the values of the supply elasticities.

Effects of Devaluation with Supply Elasticities Less than Infinite

In this general case, the derivative of B_f with respect to r is equal to:[5]

$$\frac{dB_f}{dr} = \frac{V_x}{r^2}\left[\frac{V_m}{V_x}\frac{e_m^A(1+e_x^B)}{(e_m^A-e_x^B)} - \frac{e_x^A(1+e_m^B)}{(e_x^A-e_m^B)}\right] \tag{7}$$

or

$$\frac{dB_f}{dr} = \frac{e_x^A e_x^B V_x}{r^2(e_x^B - e_m^A)(e_x^A - e_m^B)}\left[\frac{e_m^A e_m^B}{e_x^A e_x^B}\left(\frac{V_m}{V_x} + \frac{V_m}{V_x}e_x^B + e_x^A\right)\right.$$

$$\left. + \frac{e_m^A}{e_x^B}\left(1 - \frac{V_m}{V_x}\right) + e_m^A\frac{V_x - V_m}{V_x} - (1 + e_m^A + e_m^B)\right]. \tag{8}$$

Further, substituting the values of B_f and $\dfrac{dB_f}{dr}$, as given by equations (1) and (7) respectively, into equation (5), we also get:

$$\frac{dB_d}{dr} = \frac{V_x}{r}\left[\frac{V_m}{V_x}\frac{e_x^B(1+e_m^A)}{e_m^A - e_x^B} - \frac{e_m^B(1+e_x^A)}{e_x^A - e_m^B}\right]. \tag{9}$$

B_f does not change with devaluation (i.e., $\dfrac{dB_f}{dr} = 0$) in the following two cases: (*a*) when A's elasticities are zero (i.e., $e_x^A = e_m^A = 0$), and (*b*) when the balance of trade is in equilibrium before devaluation and B's elasticities are zero (i.e., $B_f = e_x^B = e_m^B = 0$). On the other hand, B_d does not change with devaluation in the following two cases: (*c*) when B's supply elasticities are zero (i.e., $e_x^B = e_m^B = 0$), and (*d*) when the balance of trade is in equilibrium before devaluation and A's elasticities are zero (i.e., $B_d = e_x^A = e_m^A = 0$). These statements can be verified through direct substitution in equations (7) and (9).

When both supply elasticities are zero (i.e., $e_x^A = e_x^B = 0$), equations (7) and (9) become: $\dfrac{dB_f}{dr} = \dfrac{V_m}{r^2} > 0$, $\dfrac{dB_d}{dr} = \dfrac{V_x}{r} > 0$, respectively. In other words, when both supply elasticities are zero, both B_d and B_f improve with devaluation—excluding, of course, the singular cases (*a*)–(*d*) referred to in the previous paragraph.[6]

The right-hand side of equation (8) is the product of a ratio which

[5] See J. Robinson in *American Economic Association, Readings in the Theory of International Trade*, p. 90, n. 8, and J. Vanek, chap. v.

[6] The cases (i) $e^A = e_m^B = 0$, and (ii) $e_m^A = e_x^B = 0$ should be excluded because the balance of trade cannot be meaningfully defined.

is generally positive and a long bracketed expression. For $\dfrac{dB_f}{dr} > 0$, the bracketed expression must be positive. Now, this expression consists of four terms. The first three are always nonnegative provided the balance of trade is not in surplus to begin with. Hence, if the fourth term is strictly positive, we know that $\dfrac{dB_f}{dr} > 0$, and therefore the balance of trade improves with devaluation—except in the two cases (a) and (b) referred to above. But the condition that this fourth term be positive is simply the Marshall-Lerner condition. In other words, excluding the two singular cases referred to above, the Marshall-Lerner condition is generally sufficient but not necessary for successful devaluation. It should be observed that when the first three terms of the bracketed expression of equation (8) drop to zero, the Marshall-Lerner condition becomes both necessary and sufficient. This happens in the following three cases: (i) when A's demand elasticity is equal to zero (i.e., $e_m{}^A = 0$), (ii) when the balance of trade is in equilibrium to begin with and B's demand elasticity is equal to zero (i.e., $B_f = e_m{}^B = 0$), and (iii) when the balance of trade is in equilibrium to begin with and both supply elasticities are infinite.

If A's demand for imports is elastic, B_f improves with devaluation except when $B_f = e_x{}^B = e_m{}^B = 0$. Also, if B's demand for imports is elastic, B_f improves with devaluation except when $e_x{}^A = e_m{}^A = 0$. Further, when A's demand for imports is elastic, B_d improves except in the singular case $e_x{}^B = e_m{}^B = 0$. Also, if $e_x{}^B = 0$, B_d always improves except in the two singular cases (c) and (d). It should be pointed out, finally, that the condition $e_m{}^B < -1$ is neither sufficient nor necessary for improving B_d.

Mathematical Note

Assume that u and v are continuous, differentiable functions of x. The following are the only rules of differentiation used in this appendix.

a) Differentiation of a Sum. The derivative of the sum $(u + v)$ with respect to x is given by the formula:

$$\frac{d}{dx}(u + v) = u' + v'.$$

b) Differentiation of a Product. The derivative of the product uv with respect to x is given by the formula:

$$\frac{d}{dx}(uv) = vu' + uv'.$$

c) *Differentiation of a Quotient.*　The derivative of the quotient u/v with respect to x is given by the formula:

$$\frac{d}{dx}\left(\frac{u}{v}\right) = \frac{vu' - uv'}{v^2}.$$

d) *Differentiation of a Function of a Function.*　The derivative of the compound function $f(u)$ with respect to x is given by the formula:

$$\frac{df(u)}{dx} = f'(u)u'.$$

<table>
<tr><td>Appendix
G
to Chapter 16</td><td>FOREIGN-TRADE
MULTIPLIERS[1]</td></tr>
</table>

In this appendix we examine more rigorously the Keynesian macroeconomic model underlying the discussion of Chapter 16. Although the discussion in this appendix will not depart from the Keynesian assumptions of the text in any major way, it is formulated in such a general way as to leave the door open for the analysis of more complicated cases. It should be pointed out, however, that in the final section of this appendix some policy problems are briefly considered. These problems do not require any additional mathematical tools than those required for the rest of this appendix. Nevertheless, they lead to more complicated algebraic expressions. If the student is not particularly interested in these problems, he is advised to skip that section.

The following notation will be used throughout this appendix.

Y_A = National income in country A.
C_A = Total consumption in country A.
I_A = Total investment in country A.
G_A = Total government expenditure in country A.
X_A = Total exports of country A.
M_A = Total imports of country A.
S_A = Total savings in Country A.
Z_A = Total absorption in country A.
C_{Ad} = The part of A's total consumption produced by domestic resources.
I_{Ad} = The part of A's total investment produced by domestic resources.
G_{Ad} = The part of A's total government expenditure on domestic resources.
X_{Ad} = The part of A's total exports produced by domestic resources.
Z_{Ad} = The part of A's total absorption of domestic resources.
C_{Af} = The part of A's total consumption produced by foreign resources.
I_{Af} = The part of A's total investment produced by foreign resources.
G_{Af} = The part of A's total government expenditure on foreign resources.
X_{Af} = The part of A's total exports produced by foreign resources.
Z_{Af} = The part of A's total absorption of foreign resources.
α = Shift parameter.

[1] By Miltiades Chacholiades.

578

p_A = Policy parameter in country A.
λ, μ = Arbitrary constants.
T = A's balance of trade.

A similar notation with subscript B applies to country B.

Functional Relationships and Identities

C_A, C_{Ad}, C_{Af}, I_A, I_{Ad}, I_{Af}, G_A, G_{Ad}, G_{Af}, and S_A are assumed to be continuous differentiable functions of Y_A; and similarly for country B.[2] M_A is assumed to be a continuous differentiable function of Y_A, a, and P_A, whereas M_B is assumed to be a continuous differentiable function of Y_B, a, and p_B.

We shall adopt the convention of writing "primes" for first partial derivatives of the above variables with respect to Y. In other words,

$$C_A' = \frac{\partial C_A}{\partial Y_A}, \quad I_A' = \frac{\partial I_A}{\partial Y_A}; \text{ etc.}$$

Before embarking upon our main problem, the following identities are worth noting:

$$C_A = C_{Ad} + C_{Af} \tag{1}$$
$$I_A = I_{Ad} + I_{Af} \tag{2}$$
$$G_A = G_{Ad} + G_{Af} \tag{3}$$
$$X_A = X_{Ad} + X_{Af} \tag{4}$$
$$M_A = C_{Af} + I_{Af} + G_{Af} + X_{Af} \tag{5}$$
$$Z_A = C_A + I_A + G_A \tag{6}$$
$$Z_{Ad} = C_{Ad} + I_{Ad} + G_{Ad} \tag{7}$$
$$Z_{Af} = C_{Af} + I_{Af} + G_{Af} = M_A - X_{Af} \tag{8}$$
$$Z_A = Z_{Ad} + Z_{Af} \tag{9}$$
$$M_A = X_B \tag{10}$$
$$M_B = X_A \tag{11}$$
$$T = X_A - M_A = M_B - M_A \tag{12}$$
$$C_A' = C_{Ad}' + C_{Af}' \tag{13}$$
$$I_A' = I_{Ad}' + I_{Af}' \tag{14}$$
$$G_A' = G_{Ad}' + G_{Af}' \tag{15}$$
$$Z_A' = Z_{Ad}' + Z_{Af}' \tag{16}$$
$$Y_A = C_A + I_A + G_A + X_A - M_A \tag{17}$$
$$Y_A = C_{Ad} + I_{Ad} + G_{Ad} + X_{Ad} \tag{18}$$
$$Y_A = Z_A + T = Z_{Ad} + X_{Ad} \tag{19}$$
$$S_A = Y_A - C_A \tag{20}$$
$$S_A + M_A = I_A + G_A + X_A \tag{21}$$
$$S_A + C_{Af} = I_{Ad} + G_{Ad} + X_{Ad} \tag{22}$$
$$C_A' + S_A' = 1 \tag{23}$$
$$C_{Ad}' + C_{Af}' + S_A' = 1 \tag{24}$$

[2] It should be pointed out that C is rather a function of disposable income, $Y_d = Y - t$, where t stands for taxes. However, since t is a function of Y, we can consider C as a function of Y directly. This facilitates the algebra. The student should bear in mind, however, that S stands for the sum: private saving (i.e., $Y_d - C$) plus taxes.

If $I_{Af}' = G_{Af}' = 0$, then $M_A' = C_{Af}'$, and identity (24) takes the form:

$$C_{Ad}' + M_A' + S_A' = 1 . \tag{25}$$

The same identities hold for country B as well.

In view of the fact that the above identities are elementary in nature, no explanation will be offered.

The Basic Model

The most general form of the basic income identities of the two countries A and B for our purposes is identity (17). Some writers prefer identity (18) over identity (17). This does not give rise to inconsistent results, provided the assumptions of the two groups of writers are identical. Despite the obvious simplicity of identity (18), identity (17) is much richer and permits the formulation of several problems—in particular policy problems—with less effort and complexity. In this appendix we shall work with (17). We thus start with the following system:

$$Y_A = Z_A + M_B - M_A + \mu\alpha \tag{26}$$
$$Y_B = Z_B + M_A - M_B + \lambda\alpha . \tag{27}$$

In the initial equilibrium the parameter α is assumed to be equal to zero. Our problem is what happens to national income when a change occurs, i.e., when α shifts for one reason or another, and how to derive the foreign-trade multiplier $\dfrac{dY}{d\alpha}$, which will differ for different types of shift in α. We must also explain the constants λ and μ.

The best way to clarify the meaning and function of these parameters is to consider various concrete cases. In so doing, we shall be able to clarify several other points as well.

1. An autonomous increase (decrease) in Z_{Ad} (i.e., an autonomous change in the absorption of domestically produced goods) can be treated as an autonomous increase (decrease) in the parameter α, with the constants μ and λ taking the values 1 and 0, respectively. Further,

$$\frac{\partial M_A}{\partial\alpha} = \frac{\partial M_B}{\partial\alpha} = 0 .$$

2. An autonomous increase (decrease) in Z_{Af} (i.e., an autonomous change in A's absorption of B's goods—which has to be distinguished from a shift in the composition of A's expenditure in favor of its imports referred to below—can be treated as an autonomous increase (decrease) in the parameter α, with the constants μ and λ taking the values 1 and 0,

respectively. Also $\dfrac{\partial M_A}{\partial a} = 1$. However, as far as $\dfrac{\partial M_B}{\partial a}$ is concerned, we have to distinguish between the following two cases: (*a*) when the autonomous increase in B's exports does not give rise to a simultaneous increase in B's imports, i.e., when only X_{Bd} changes, and (*b*) when the autonomous increase in B's exports does give rise to a simultaneous increase in B's imports, i.e., when both X_{Bf} and X_{Bd} change. In the first case, we have $\dfrac{\partial M_B}{\partial a} = 0$. In the second, $\dfrac{\partial M_B}{\partial a} > 0$.

3. An autonomous increase (decrease) in Z_A may be due to an increase (decrease) in Z_{Ad}, or, Z_{Af}, or both. The first two alternatives have been treated in cases (1) and (2), respectively. In the present case, the third alternative (i.e., a change in both Z_{Ad} and Z_{Af}) will be considered. This again can be treated as an autonomous change in a, with the constants μ and λ taking the values 1 and 0, respectively. Further, $\dfrac{\partial M_B}{\partial a} = 0$, and $0 < \dfrac{\partial M_A}{\partial a} < 1$.

At this stage it is necessary to point out that the partial derivative $\dfrac{\partial M_A}{\partial a}$ is not in general equal to A's marginal propensity to import, i.e., M'_A. In the first place, since we are talking about an *autonomous* change, the partial derivative (i.e., the number of cents out of every dollar of the autonomous change in A's expenditure spent on B's products) may take any value whatsoever between 0 and 1. But besides this important reason, there is another more fundamental reason why $\dfrac{\partial M_A}{\partial a} \neq M'_A$. The marginal propensity to import (M'_A) shows how much out of each extra dollar increase in A's *national income* is spent on imports. On the other hand, the partial derivative $\dfrac{\partial M_A}{\partial a}$ shows how much out of each extra dollar increase in A's *expenditure* is spent on imports. But when A's national income increases by ΔY_A, A's expenditure does not increase by ΔY_A; it rather increases by $\Delta Y_A(1 - S'_A)$. Further, an increase in expenditure by $\Delta Y_A(1 - S'_A)$ gives rise to an increase in imports equal to:

$$\Delta M_A = \Delta Y_A(1 - S'_A)\frac{\partial M_A}{\partial a}.$$

Hence,
$$\frac{\Delta M_A}{\Delta Y_A} = (1 - S'_A)\frac{\partial M_A}{\partial a}. \tag{28}$$

Thus, if the autonomous change in A's expenditure is divided between expenditure on domestic and expenditure on foreign goods according to the existing marginal propensities, the partial derivative $\dfrac{\partial M_A}{\partial a}$ is not equal to M'_A.

4. An autonomous shift in the *composition* of A's expenditure can be treated as an autonomous change in the parameter a with the constants λ and μ being zero. For a shift from domestic goods to foreign, the partial derivative $\dfrac{\partial M_A}{\partial a}$ takes the value of 1. On the other hand, for a shift from foreign to domestic goods, the partial derivative $\dfrac{\partial M_A}{\partial a}$ takes the value of -1. The value of $\dfrac{\partial M_B}{\partial a}$ is determined as in case (2) above.

5. An autonomous increase in X_{Ad} may be due to either an autonomous increase in B's expenditure on A's products, or, a shift in the composition of B's expenditure in favor of A's products. If the increase in X_{Ad} is due to a net increase in B's expenditure on A's products, then we have the following: $\mu = 0$, $\lambda = 1$, $\dfrac{\partial M_A}{\partial a} = 0$, $\dfrac{\partial M_B}{\partial a} = 1$. If, on the other hand, the increase in X_{Ad} is due to a shift in B's expenditure in favor of A's products, we have: $\mu = 0$, $\lambda = 0$, $\dfrac{\partial M_B}{\partial a} = 1$, $\dfrac{\partial M_A}{\partial a} = 0$.

For a decrease in X_{Ad}, we must have $\dfrac{\partial M_B}{\partial a} = -1$ in the above two cases. All other parameters retain the same values.

6. An autonomous increase Z_{Ad} matched exactly by an autonomous decrease in Z_{Bd} can be treated as a change in a with the constants λ and μ taking the values -1 and 1, respectively. Further, $\dfrac{\partial M_A}{\partial a} = \dfrac{\partial M_B}{\partial a} = 0$. Other examples of this nature are left to the reader.

The Foreign-Trade Multiplier without Foreign Repercussion

Since the foreign repercussion is absent in this section, we dispense with the subscripts A and B. Thus, the basic income identity takes the form:

$$Y = Z + X - M + \lambda a \qquad (29)$$

where the parameter α has zero value in the initial equilibrium. Differentiating equation (29) totally with respect to α, we get:

$$\frac{dY}{d\alpha} = \frac{\lambda - \dfrac{\partial M}{\partial \alpha}}{1 - Z' + M'}. \tag{30}$$

We are now ready to study the following specific cases:

a) An autonomous increase in Z_d or X_d, which implies $\lambda = 1, \dfrac{\partial M}{\partial \alpha} = 0$.

b) An autonomous increase in Z or X, which implies $\lambda = 1, \dfrac{\partial M}{\partial \alpha} > 0$, or

more specifically, $\dfrac{\partial M}{\partial \alpha} = \dfrac{M'}{1 - S'}$

c) An autonomous shift in the composition of expenditure in favor of domestic goods, which implies $\lambda = 0. \dfrac{\partial M}{\partial \alpha} = < -1$.

The results are tabulated in the following table.

TABLE I

Case (*a*)	Case (*b*)	Case (*c*)
$\lambda = 1, \dfrac{\partial M}{\partial \alpha} = 0$	$\lambda = 1, \dfrac{\partial M}{\partial \alpha} = \dfrac{M'}{1 - S'}$	$\lambda = 0, \dfrac{\partial M}{\partial \alpha} = -1$
$\dfrac{dY}{d\alpha} = \dfrac{1}{1 - Z' + M'}$	$\dfrac{dY}{d\alpha} = \dfrac{1 - S' - M'}{(1 - Z' + M')(1 - S')}$	$\dfrac{dY}{d\alpha} = \dfrac{1}{1 - Z' + M'}$

Foreign-Trade Multipliers with Foreign Repercussion

Differentiating equations (26), (27), and (12) totally with respect to α, we get:

$$\frac{dY_A}{d\alpha} = Z'_A \frac{dY_A}{d\alpha} + \left(\frac{\partial M_B}{\partial \alpha} + \frac{\partial M_B}{\partial Y_B} \frac{dY_B}{d\alpha} \right) - \left(\frac{\partial M_A}{\partial \alpha} + \frac{\partial M_A}{\partial Y_A} \frac{dY_A}{d\alpha} \right) + \mu \tag{31}$$

$$\frac{dY_B}{d\alpha} = Z'_B \frac{dY_B}{d\alpha} + \left(\frac{\partial M_A}{\partial \alpha} + \frac{\partial M_A}{\partial Y_A} \frac{dY_A}{d\alpha} \right) - \left(\frac{\partial M_B}{\partial \alpha} + \frac{\partial M_B}{\partial Y_B} \frac{dY_B}{d\alpha} \right) + \lambda \tag{32}$$

$$\frac{dT}{d\alpha} = \left(\frac{\partial M_B}{\partial \alpha} + \frac{\partial M_B}{\partial Y_B} \frac{dY_B}{d\alpha} \right) - \left(\frac{\partial M_A}{\partial \alpha} + \frac{\partial M_A}{\partial Y_A} \frac{dY_A}{d\alpha} \right). \tag{33}$$

Solving equations (31) and (32) simultaneously, we get:

$$\frac{dY_A}{d\alpha} = \frac{1}{\Delta} \left[(1 - Z'_B) \left(\frac{\partial M_B}{\partial \alpha} - \frac{\partial M_A}{\partial \alpha} + \mu \right) + (\mu + \lambda) M'_B \right] \tag{34}$$

$$\frac{dY_B}{d\alpha} = \frac{1}{\Delta}\left[(1 - Z'_A)\left(\frac{\partial M_A}{\partial \alpha} - \frac{\partial M_B}{\partial \alpha} + \lambda\right) + (\mu + \lambda)\, M'_A\right] \quad (35)$$

where,

$$\Delta = (1 - Z'_A + M'_A)(1 - Z'_B + M'_B) - M'_A M'_B . \quad (36)$$

Substituting these results into (33), we also get

$$\frac{dT}{d\alpha} = \left(\frac{\partial M_B}{\partial \alpha} - \frac{\partial M_A}{\partial \alpha}\right) + \frac{1}{\Delta}\left[M'_B(1 - Z'_A)\left(\frac{\partial M_A}{\partial \alpha} - \frac{\partial M_B}{\partial \alpha} + \lambda\right)\right.$$
$$\left. - M'_A(1 - Z'_B)\left(\frac{\partial M_B}{\partial \alpha} - \frac{\partial M_A}{\partial \alpha} + \mu\right)\right]. \quad (37)$$

Equations (34) and (35) are the most general forms of the foreign-trade multipliers. We do not plan to apply these multiplier formulae to all cases considered previously. This is left as an exercise for the student. We shall, however, consider one case referred to in the text. Thus, for an autonomous increase in expenditure on A's goods which may come about either through an increase in Z_{Ad} (in which case we have $\lambda = 0$, $\frac{\partial M_B}{\partial a} = 0$, $\frac{\partial M_A}{\partial a} = 0$, $\mu = 1$), or, an increase in X_{Ad} due to a net increase in B's expenditure on A's products (in which case we must have $\mu = 0$, $\lambda = 1$, $\frac{\partial M_A}{\partial a} = 0$, $\frac{\partial M_B}{\partial a} = 1$), the multiplier formulae (34) and (35) take respectively the following specific forms:

$$\frac{dY_A}{d\alpha} = \frac{1 - Z'_B + M'_B}{(1 - Z'_A + M'_A)(1 - Z'_B + M'_B) - M'_A M'_B} \quad (38)$$

$$\frac{dY_B}{d\alpha} = \frac{M'_A}{(1 - Z'_A + M'_A)(1 - Z'_B + M'_B) - M'_A M'_B} . \quad (39)$$

Further, if $I'_A = G'_A = I'_B = G'_B = 0$, then $Z'_A = C'_A$ and $Z'_B = C'_B$ and equations (38) and (39) become:

$$\frac{dY_A}{d\alpha} = \frac{1 + \dfrac{M'_B}{S'_B}}{S'_A + M'_A + M'_B \dfrac{S'_A}{S'_B}} \quad (40)$$

$$\frac{dY_B}{d\alpha} = \frac{M'_A}{S'_A S'_B + S'_A M'_B + S'_B M'_A} . \quad (41)$$

Policy Considerations

The previous analysis is now extended to cover the case where one, or, the other, or, both countries adopt certain policy measures to nullify the effects of an *autonomous* change on a target variable, such as the national income (internal balance), or, the balance of trade (external balance). For this purpose, equations (26) and (27) are modified as follows:

$$Y_A = Z_A + M_B - M_A + \mu\alpha + p_A \tag{42}$$

$$Y_B = Z_B + M_A - M_B + \lambda\alpha + p_B \tag{43}$$

In the initial equilibrium position, all parameters (i.e., p_A, p_B and a) are equal to zero. When an autonomous change takes place, it can be treated again as a change in the parameter a, with the constants λ and μ taking the appropriate values as before. But now we have to consider the policy parameters as well. Whenever one country does not pursue any policy whatsoever, its policy parameter does not change when a changes, i.e., $\dfrac{dp}{da} = 0$. Thus, when both countries do not pursue any policy, all previous conclusions can also be derived from this general formulation when we put $\dfrac{dp_A}{da} = \dfrac{dp_B}{da} = 0$. However, when a country does pursue a policy for either internal or external balance, we must have $\dfrac{dp}{da} \neq 0$, in general. Further, $\dfrac{dp}{da}$ is not a datum but it has to be determined in such a way as to satisfy the policy objective pursued. The technique of determining the right value for $\dfrac{dp}{da}$ will become clear in what follows.

Let us first consider this problem in the simple case where foreign repercussion is absent. We again dispense temporarily with the subscripts A and B. Thus, the basic income identity takes the form:

$$Y = Z + X - M + \lambda\alpha + p \tag{44}$$

where the parameters a and p have zero values in the initial equilibrium position. Differentiating equation (44) totally with respect to a and rearranging, we get

$$\frac{dY}{d\alpha} = \frac{\lambda - \dfrac{\partial M}{\partial \alpha} - \dfrac{\partial M}{\partial p}\dfrac{dp}{d\alpha} + \dfrac{dp}{d\alpha}}{1 - Z' + M'}. \tag{45}$$

If a policy for internal balance is pursued, we must also have: $dY/da = 0$. Substituting this into (45), we end up with:

$$\frac{dp}{a\alpha} = \frac{\dfrac{\partial M}{\partial \alpha} - \lambda}{1 - \dfrac{\partial M}{\partial p}} .$$ (46)

Equation (46) gives us the required rate of change of the policy parameter per unit change of α, which guarantees internal balance.

If a policy for external balance is pursued, we must have:

$$\frac{dT}{d\alpha} = - \left(\frac{\partial M}{\partial \alpha} + M' \frac{dY}{d\alpha} + \frac{\partial M}{\partial p} \frac{dp}{d\alpha} \right) = 0 .$$ (47)

Equations (45) and (47) can now be solved simultaneously for $\dfrac{dY}{d\alpha}$ and $\dfrac{dp}{d\alpha}$.

In order to allow for foreign repercussion, we differentiate equations (42), (43), and (12) totally with respect to α.

$$\frac{dY_A}{d\alpha} = Z'_A \frac{dY_A}{d\alpha} + \left(\frac{\partial M_B}{\partial \alpha} + \frac{\partial M_B}{\partial p_B} \frac{dp_B}{d\alpha} + \frac{\partial M_B}{\partial Y_B} \frac{dY_B}{d\alpha} \right)$$
$$- \left(\frac{\partial M_A}{\partial \alpha} + \frac{\partial M_A}{\partial p_A} \frac{dp_A}{d\alpha} + \frac{\partial M_A}{\partial Y_A} \frac{dY_A}{d\alpha} \right) + \mu + \frac{dp_A}{d\alpha}$$ (48)

$$\frac{dY_B}{d\alpha} = Z'_B \frac{dY_B}{d\alpha} + \left(\frac{\partial M_A}{\partial \alpha} + \frac{\partial M_A}{\partial p_A} \frac{dp_A}{d\alpha} + M'_A \frac{dY_A}{d\alpha} \right)$$
$$- \left(\frac{\partial M_B}{\partial \alpha} + \frac{\partial M_B}{\partial p_B} \frac{dp_B}{d\alpha} + M'_B \frac{dY_B}{d\alpha} \right) + \lambda + \frac{dp_B}{d\alpha}$$ (49)

$$\frac{dT}{d\alpha} = \left(\frac{\partial M_B}{\partial \alpha} + \frac{\partial M_B}{\partial p_B} \frac{dp_B}{d\alpha} + M'_B \frac{dY_B}{d\alpha} \right) -$$
$$- \left(\frac{\partial M_A}{\partial \alpha} + \frac{\partial M_A}{\partial p_A} \frac{dp_A}{d\alpha} + \frac{\partial M_A}{\partial Y_A} \frac{dY_A}{d\alpha} \right) .$$ (50)

The above three equations contain five unknowns, i.e., $\dfrac{dY_A}{d\alpha}, \dfrac{dY_B}{d\alpha}$, $\dfrac{dp_A}{d\alpha}, \dfrac{dp_B}{d\alpha}$ and $\dfrac{dT}{d\alpha}$. Thus, in order to be able to solve this system uniquely, two additional equations must be specified. This is done as soon as we know what policy is pursued by each country. All possible policy combinations are tabulated in Table II.

TABLE II

A's Policy / B's Policy	No Policy	Internal Balance	External Balance
No policy	$\frac{dp_B}{d\alpha} = \frac{dp_A}{d\alpha} = 0$	$\frac{dp_B}{d\alpha} = 0 \quad \frac{dY_A}{d\alpha} = 0$	$\frac{dp_B}{d\alpha} = 0 \quad \frac{dT}{d\alpha} = 0$
Internal balance	$\frac{dY_B}{d\alpha} = 0 \quad \frac{dp_A}{d\alpha} = 0$	$\frac{dY_B}{d\alpha} = 0 \quad \frac{dY_A}{d\alpha} = 0$	$\frac{dY_B}{d\alpha} = 0 \quad \frac{dT}{d\alpha} = 0$
External balance	$\frac{dT}{d\alpha} = 0 \quad \frac{dp_A}{d\alpha} = 0$	$\frac{dT}{d\alpha} = 0, \frac{dY_A}{d\alpha} = 0$	$\frac{dT}{d\alpha} = 0$

Thus, except for the case where both countries are pursuing a policy for external balance, we have two additional equations which together with equations (48–50) form a system of five equations in five unknowns, and, in general, can be solved uniquely for the five unknowns. The student should not be frightened by the fact that we are talking about a system of five equations because this is a very simplified system and can be easily solved.

If both countries were pursuing a policy for external balance, we would face a problem of indeterminacy simply because there is only one balance of trade and two policy parameters for achieving balance-of-trade equilibrium. If we know the relative burden of each country in achieving external balance (thus supplying the missing equation), the indeterminacy is removed.

Appendix

H

to Chapter 23

THE FORWARD

EXCHANGE MARKET

The Forward Exchange Market

The forward market for exchange is not normally a separate market, and it is inaccurate to speak of it as such. It is more properly regarded as a segment of the foreign exchange market as a whole. The link between the forward and the spot rates of exchange is the rate of interest in the two markets involved, and what is known as "interest arbitrage." In the absence of anticipated movements of the foreign exchange rate, the future rate will be the same as the spot rate if rates of interest are the same in the two money markets concerned. If the three months' interest rate is 6 percent per annum in London and 4 percent in New York, however, three months' sterling should sell at a discount equivalent to 2 percent per annum. This rate, by the way, is $2.388, given a spot rate of $2.40 and a discount of $0.012 (2 percent $\times$ $2.40 $\div$ 4 = $0.012). But a usual way to express the discount or premium is in terms of percent per year.

If forward sterling sold at any higher figure, it would be profitable for banks in New York to put more spot funds in London and sell these forward, because they could earn more than 4 percent. If the discount on the pound were greater or the premium on the dollar more, it would pay London banks to put more money in New York, where it could earn 4 percent per annum plus a premium on forward dollars of more than 2 percent. This would be better than the 6 percent obtainable at home. Interest arbitrage, i.e., the lending of funds at interest in a foreign money market covered by forward sales of the foreign exchange, is the link between the spot and the forward market. In actual practice the discount or premium in the forward market will depart from the interest differential, despite arbitrage, by as much as $\frac{1}{2}$ percent per annum, which represents the minimum that the banks require as a return to undertake arbitrage. When the differential exceeds $\frac{1}{2}$ percent per annum, it is a sign that interest arbitrage is restricted in some fashion.

588

Interest rates may differ between national markets for a number of reasons. The monetary and banking authorities may be trying to expand or contract lending by the banks, and the rate, therefore, will be low or high, respectively. The rate may be dominated by considerations affecting the government bond market. Or, as we shall see presently, the rate may be changed upward or downward in order to attract or repel foreign funds.

When interest arbitrage is prohibited by the exchange authorities in charge of a currency, in order to limit the outflow of capital, the forward market and the spot market become separate. Discounts or premiums on a currency can now rise to as high as 30, 40, or 50 percent per annum. Rates of this magnitude will mean that the forward market is thin; those people anxious to sell the currency forward must offer a large discount to entice buyers. Any forward sale consummated must find a forward purchaser, since swaps of spot for forward exchange are not permitted. When the forward market is cut adrift from the spot market in this way, it fails to perform its hedging function and provides only a limited outlet for a balanced number of speculative buyers and sellers.

When it is functioning as an integral portion of the foreign exchange market as a whole, through swaps which carry out interest arbitrage, the forward market performs a credit as well as a hedging function. Suppose that a prospective importer in the United States anticipates a need for sterling. Assume that the forward dollar is at a discount and sterling at a premium, because the interest rate is higher in New York than in London. If the importer buys forward sterling, he drives the premium on forward sterling still higher. This encourages a New York bank, let us say, to buy spot sterling and sell it forward at a premium (to the importer). The spot funds transferred to London and held by a New York bank against its forward contract with the U.S. importer may be regarded as those which the importer will ultimately use to make his purchase. Exactly the same result would have been achieved if he had borrowed the amount from a bank in New York, bought spot sterling, and invested it at 4 percent per annum in London until he ultimately needed it in three months. The net cost of covering the exchange risk in this case is the cost of funds in New York less the possible return in London. This is the same as the premium on sterling in the forward market. For the New York banks and for the importer it makes little difference which way the transaction is carried through, except that the importer is less well equipped than the New York banks to handle the London transaction. On this account, the forward market provides him with an alternative way to eliminate the exchange risk to that achievable through borrowing, and the hedging facility has an element of credit connected to it. By the same token, the forward market is either a device which translates the net position taken by nonbank speculators into a short-term capital movement in the spot market, or, if it is cut off from the spot market by fiat and forced to clear itself, a limited device for hedging.

Covered Working Balances

The question may be asked how the New York banks can have a covered position—i.e., assets in foreign currency equal to liabilities—and still have supplies of foreign currency on hand to sell to customers who need it. A covered position means no excess of claims or liabilities; and yet there must be a working balance of sterling to cover the requirements of customers who want to buy telegraphic transfers. The banks cannot expect to be offered each day in telegraphic transfers the foreign currency they sell each day in the same way. Like any business, they must have some inventory.

The answer lies in the forward market and in the fact that the foreign exchange market embraces London as well as New York. All the banks in New York have a minimum need for working balances of, say, £50,000,000. It would be possible to hedge these in the forward market in New York if the banks' customers were willing to buy forward £50,000,000 more than they sold forward. But there is no reason to expect these customers to go long in the forward market by this amount. They, too, may be expected, as a rule, to have a balanced position, with spot and forward claims balanced by net spot and forward liabilities. Under these circumstances, they will not be able to buy £50,000,000 forward from the banks, except in the unlikely situation in which they have in prospect an import surplus of £50,000,000 for which importers require more sterling than exporters are able to provide.

The solution for the banks is found by selling £50,000,000 forward in London. In order to buy this much forward sterling (sell this many dollars forward), the London banks must buy the equivalent number of dollars ($120,000,000 at $2.40) in the spot market. In this fashion, the London and New York foreign exchange markets can be provided with working balances in each other's currencies without undertaking an exchange position, each market contracting to sell the spot exchange forward in the other. New York will then hold £50,000,000 spot and sell the same amount forward in London. London will hold

$140,000,000 in New York, which it has sold forward to New York banks. Neither country has an open exchange position. Each has an inventory of exchange for sale to customers desiring it.[1]

If New York banks on balance want to open an exchange position, let us say £2,000,000 short, they can now sell this amount spot or forward. The spot sale will simply eliminate £2,000,000 of their £50,000,000 of working balances (a capital inflow into the United States, it may be observed). If they choose to make a forward sale, however, this must be done in London unless the nonbanking public in the United States fortuitously undertakes an equal exchange position of opposite sign, i.e., is willing to go £2,000,000 long. The forward sale of sterling in London by New York banks will require London banks to sell dollars and buy sterling forward. In order to keep their position covered, the latter will be obliged to buy more dollars spot. In this way the sale of forward sterling by New York banks would result in an increase in London deposits in New York (a capital inflow into the United States) in the amount of $4,800,000.

A debated point is whether the addition of facilities for forward trading to an exchange market alters the character of the exchange market. The general view is that it does. The theoretical possibility exists, however, that it does not. Whether it does or not in the real world, of course, is an empirical question. But the analysis can be shown in terms of elasticities of demand and supply for forward and spot exchange.

There are two types of arbitrage, trader and professional. Trader arbitrage arises from exporters and importers shifting back and forth between the spot and forward markets in response to differences between the forward premium, or discount, and the interest differential. They are hedged by buying and selling foreign exchange against their trade needs, but indifferent as between the spot and forward market except as a discrepancy between the forward discount or premium and the interest differential opens up an incentive to change. Professional arbitrage, on the other hand, operates in the two markets simultaneously.

---

[1] It should perhaps be pointed out that the forward contract does not count as a current asset or liability in calculating capital movements. New York owns £50,000,000 and owes $120,000,000 spot. It is therefore on balance neither a borrower nor a lender. Conversely, London has a balance of assets and liabilities. So far as the capital movement is concerned, the currencies in which claims and debts are denominated make no difference. The forward contract is neither an asset nor a liability except in a contingent sense, in which it is both, so that it does not count in reckoning the balance of indebtedness.

Figure H.1*a* shows the spot market and Figure H.1*b* the forward market with the demand for sterling against dollars coming from U.S. importers (British exporters) and the supply from U.S. exporters (British importers). The position is shown by the solid lines, *D–D,* and *S–S,* with short-term interest rates identical in London and New York (an interest differential of zero) and the spot and forward rates identical. Now assume that the discount rate is raised in London. This will induce certain demanders of sterling to shift from the forward to the spot market to take advantage of the higher return on funds in London, increasing the demand for spot and reducing the demand for forward as

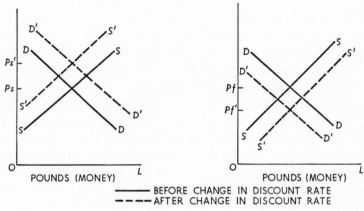

BEFORE CHANGE IN DISCOUNT RATE
AFTER CHANGE IN DISCOUNT RATE

Fig. H.1*a*.   Spot Market   Fig. H.1*b*.   Forward Market

indicated by the dotted lines, *D'–D'*. It will also shift some suppliers of sterling from the spot to the forward market, again to take advantage of the higher rates, so that the spot supply curve shifts to the left and the forward curve to the right. These shifts of demand and supply in the two markets will raise the spot rate and lower the forward rate, sending forward sterling to a discount. If the spread between the spot and forward rate (*Ps'–Pf'*) converted to percent per annum equals the interest differential, there will be no capital movement undertaken by professional arbitrage. As Figures H.1*a* and H.1*b* are drawn, moreover, there is no capital movement carried through by trader arbitrage, the same amount of spot exchange being traded as before. This is because in addition to the shift of the spot demand curve, to take one example, there is also a shift along the displaced curve. The traders who shift from the forward to the spot market are matched by traders and speculators who withdraw from the market at the new higher price.

If the trader arbitrage falls short of or exceeds the amount needed to produce a forward discount equal to the interest differential, professional arbitrage would be called into operation. This would move funds to London (buying spot and selling forward), and producing new $D''-D''$ curves, not drawn, to the right in Figure H.1*a* and a new $S''-S''$ curve to the right in Figure H.1*b*. This would produce a capital movement to London. If trader arbitrage had gone too far, and produced an excessive discount on sterling, professional arbitrage would sell spot and buy forward, partway closing the gaps between the $S'-S'$ and $S-S$ curves in the spot market and between $D'-D'$ and $D-D$ curves in the forward market.

With an abundance of trader and professional arbitrage funds, there is, as indicated, no significant change produced by the addition of a forward market, unless it should increase the volume of stabilizing speculation. The question at issue, and an empirical one, is whether the forward market adds new traders and speculators, or merely redivides the existing body of speculators and traders between the two markets. If it redivides, it produces no change; if it increases the volume of speculation and the elasticity of the demand and supply curves, it does stabilize the behavior of rates between the gold points or the support limits on the fixed change standard, and in general on the flexible exchange standard, provided always, that the speculation is stabilizing.

When a currency under the fixed standard is under heavy attack, raising the interest rate will not help. In some analyses, this is said to be because interest arbitrage dries up. A more realistic way to put it is that the movement of interest arbitrage funds to a market requires stabilizing speculation. When a currency is known to be stable, the forward rate cannot fall below the lower support limit because the speculation demand for the forward currency becomes infinitely elastic at that limit. A higher interest rate leads to purchases of spot and sales of forward at the limit, until the spot rate is bid up to the interest differential. But if the prospect of devaluation within the three-months' period of most forward contracts is real, speculative support is not forthcoming at this price, and the forward rate can sink without limit. The result is that it is no longer possible for the interest arbitrager to cover his spot purchases with forward sales at the small discount which enables him to make money. It is on such occasions when there is a real point to supporting the forward rate provided the monetary authorities are certain that the devaluation will not take place.

On occasion there may be a real drying up of interest arbitrage funds, if what is feared is not a change in rate but foreign exchange control which would block foreign balances.

SUGGESTED READING

The major work on the subject of forward exchange is Paul Einzig's *A Dynamic Theory of Forward Exchange* (London: Macmillan & Co., Ltd., 1961). Mr. Einzig is highly critical of the view expressed here that the addition of a forward market does not greatly alter the way the foreign exchange market performs. See also Herbert G. Grubel, *Forward Exchange, Speculation and the International Flow of Capital* (Stanford, Calif.: Stanford University Press, 1966) who holds that three-way arbitrage makes a significant difference; J. L. Stein, "The Nature and Efficiency of the Foreign Exchange Market," *EIF*, No. 40, June, 1962; Peter B. Kenen, "Trade Speculation and the Forward Exchange Rate," in R. E. Baldwin *et al.*, *Trade, Growth, and the Balance of Payments* (Chicago: Rand McNally & Co., 1965); and Fred R. Glahe, *An Empirical Study of the Foreign Exchange Market: Test of a Theory*, Princeton Studies in International Finance (Princeton, N.J.: Princeton University Press, 1967).

Indexes

INDEX OF NAMES AND AUTHORS

INDEX OF SUBJECTS

601

D

This book has been set in 12 and 10 point Garamond No. 3, leaded 1 point. Part titles and numbers and chapter titles and numbers are in 18 point Spartan Medium. The size of the type page is 27 by 46 picas.